Mixed Use, Manhattan

Photography and Related Practices, 1970s to the Present

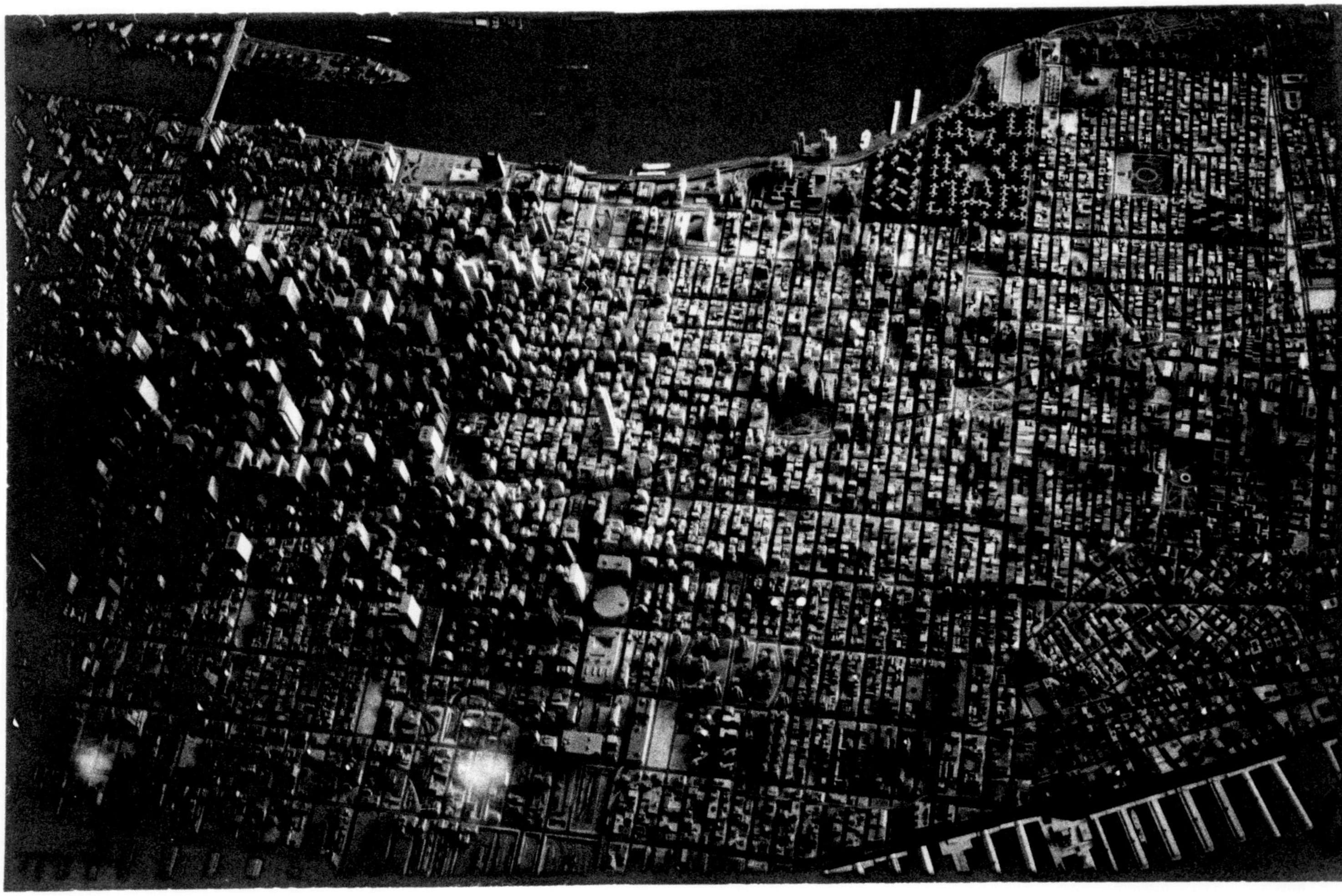

Mixed Use, Manhattan

Photography and Related Practices, 1970s to the Present

Edited by Lynne Cooke and Douglas Crimp,
with Kristin Poor

Museo Nacional Centro de Arte Reina Sofía Madrid
The MIT Press Cambridge, Massachusetts London, England

Frontispiece Zoe Leonard, *Model of New York no. 1*, 1989/1990

Contents

Foreword

From the 1920s onward cities saw their new optimism and vitality reflected in the symphonic vision offered by the cinema with its carefully constructed, harmonious productions of the day; the period covered by the current exhibition at the Reina Sofía Museum, beginning in the 1970s and continuing to the present day, reveals another, more contemporary form of creation: that of improvisation.

The conversion of former industrial spaces into venues for artistic creation and the transformation of entire run-down, abandoned districts into forests of signs that reveal their human and creative potential at every step encourage us—once again—to realize that without the spontaneous, unhindered participation of civil society, real life will disappear from cities. The chance encounter in the city that Baudelaire defended in the nineteenth century would become an entire social phenomenon when Manhattan was poised on the threshold of postmodernity. It produced an intermingling of artistic manifestations as crucial as the evolution of the performative arts and an exploration of the relationship between work and exhibition space. In addition, it problematized issues of major social importance such as sexual identity, ways of socializing public space, and an awareness of the need to recycle—in broad intellectual and material terms—in times of crisis.

Starting in the 1970s with the onset of the recession that shook the very foundations of Western society, this exhibition takes an approach that is not simply a historical one. Rather, it continues up to the present day in order to reveal to us a city that functioned as an experimental workshop and as a space whose narrow physical limits did not constrict the imagination. The fact that the island of Manhattan has remained an icon for the art world is due to its ability to reinvent itself over the decades, rising once more from the ashes of the utopias, fashions, and chance events of history. It is to be hoped that with this new exhibition, visitors to the Reina Sofía will discover and learn more about forms of dialogue with the urban environment, and as a consequence consider themselves to be more active participants in their own surroundings.

Ministry of Culture

Introduction

When New York—the quintessential modern city, symbolic of the great utopian projects associated with a confident, rational, and progressive modernity—began to show signs of cracks due to the early 1970s recession, new types of occupation of industrial spaces started to appear, together with innovative forms of social life. Arising within the very fabric of the city, this permanently altered urban experience. From a unitary, functional city with clearly separated elements, like the different parts of a living organism, the downtown urban environment became a dysfunctional, half-ruined space, which offered alternative modes of coexistence and unexpected meanings.

The exhibition *Mixed Use, Manhattan* offers a case study of the shift from modernity's grandiloquent and visionary spaces with its architectural and urbanistic deliriums to the city's conversion into zones of mixed use, brought about by the creative will of its inhabitants. In the 1970s, the process of gentrification in Manhattan, later extended to numerous other cities in the developed world, ran parallel to new forms of social life: sexuality in the public realm, creative activity, interaction, leisure, intermingling; and growth. The result was to permanently break down the frontiers imposed by public and financial authorities so that public and private spaces could be read as symbols of dissent open to appropriation.

The identity of the city's spaces thus became blurred, ceasing to operate according to their designated functions. As Lynne Cooke has described, Lower Manhattan moved from being a site to a non-site, in artist Robert Smithson's terms. This space, defined by *Mixed Use, Manhattan*, could be related to that posthistorical one that simultaneously fascinated and terrified Pier Paolo Pasolini: a late, transatlantic echo of European images of urban ruin in the aftermath of the Second World War.

By means of new artistic practices, as Douglas Crimp describes, Lower Manhattan was transformed. As small artists' communities evolved, they in turn generated new facilities: restaurants, discotheques, and galleries. The result was to offer a counter-response to the homogenization and surveillance of urban space that had arisen through long-established urban policies first promulgated by Haussmann in Paris in the 1860s and later reprised with the construction of the World Trade Center.

It is not by chance that photography, video, and film are this exhibition's chosen formats, given that the vision of the city as a fragmented space in a semi-ruined state and undergoing a continuing identity crisis and material crisis demands the immediacy of documentation. Difficult to grasp, the city's vital "flux" was expressed in performative practices and the arts "of the moment." The artists included in *Mixed Use, Manhattan* range from Gordon Matta-Clark to Matthew Buckingham, from David

Wojnarowicz to Gabriel Orozco, and from Dara Birnbaum to Emily Roysdon. The interplay of their works generates subtexts in the exhibition: the rise of queer practices, the debates on the public realm as a space for individual protest and non-institutional social conflict, the emergence of a hybrid type of creativity that combined the tangible and the performative, and the exploration of the medium of video and its affiliates.

Mixed Use, Manhattan invites us to consider the site in which we view and interpret works of art. In addition, the show underlines our vision of the museum as a space of dialogue, in which we are obligated to reconsider our own urban environment and its social and cultural potential.

Manuel J. Borja-Villel
Director, Museo Nacional Centro de Arte Reina Sofía

Alvin Baltrop
Bernd and Hilla Becher
Dara Birnbaum
Jennifer Bolande
Stefan Brecht
Matthew Buckingham
Tom Burr
Roy Colmer
Moyra Davey
Terry Fox
William Gedney
Bernard Guillot
David Hammons
Sharon Hayes
Peter Hujar
Joan Jonas
Louise Lawler
Zoe Leonard
Sol LeWitt
Glenn Ligon
Robert Longo
Vera Lutter
Danny Lyon
Babette Mangolte
Gordon Matta-Clark
Steve McQueen
John Miller
Donald Moffett
James Nares
Max Neuhaus
Catherine Opie
Gabriel Orozco
Barbara Probst
Emily Roysdon
Cindy Sherman
Shunk-Kender
Charles Simonds
Thomas Struth
James Welling
David Wojnarowicz
Christopher Wool

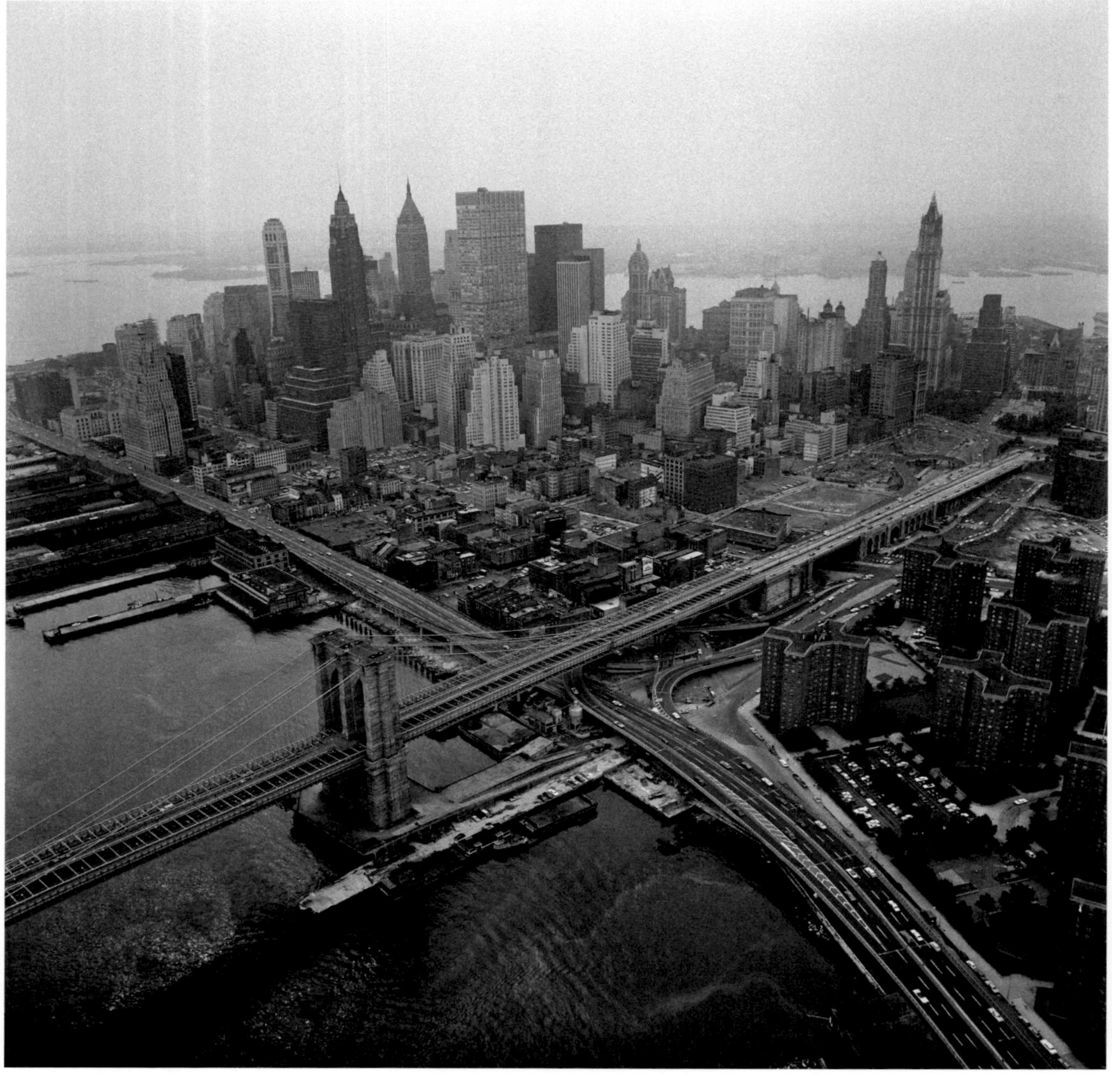

Plate 1 Danny Lyon, *Lower Manhattan and the Brooklyn Bridge from above the East River*, 1967

The Destruction of Lower Manhattan

Danny Lyon

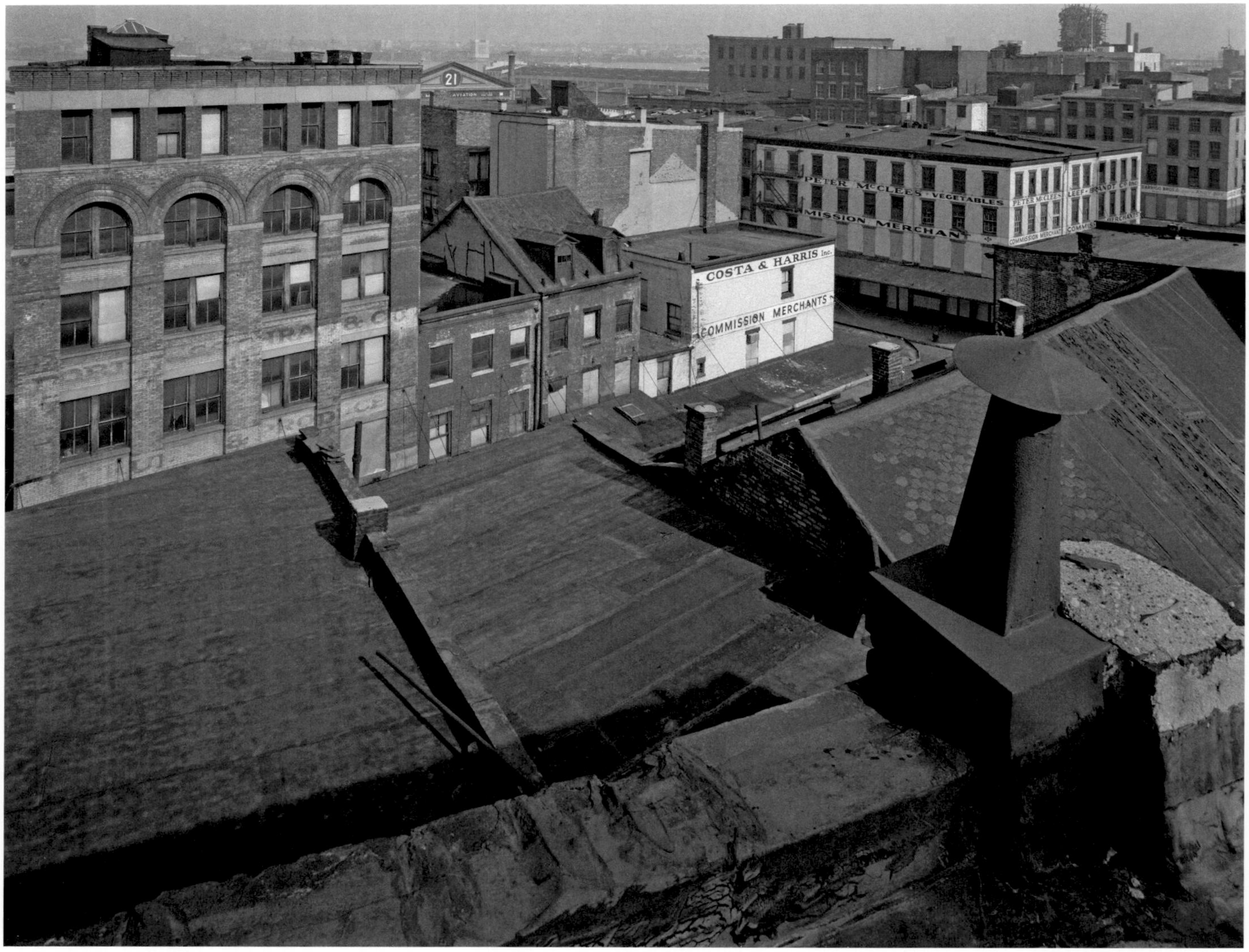

Plate 2 Danny Lyon, *View west from a Washington Street rooftop*, 1967

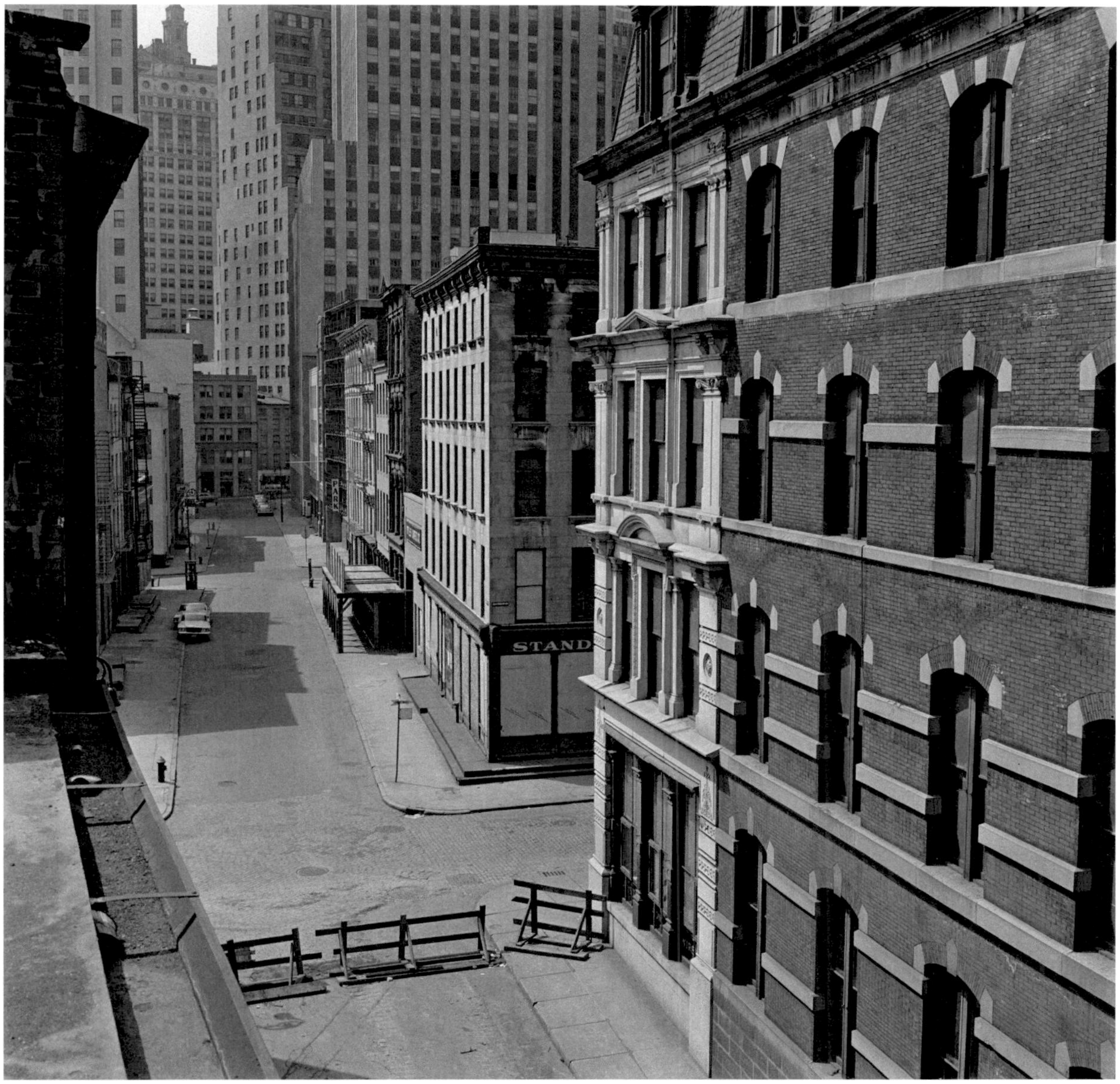

Plate 3 Danny Lyon, *View south on Cliff Street at its intersection with Beekman*, 1967

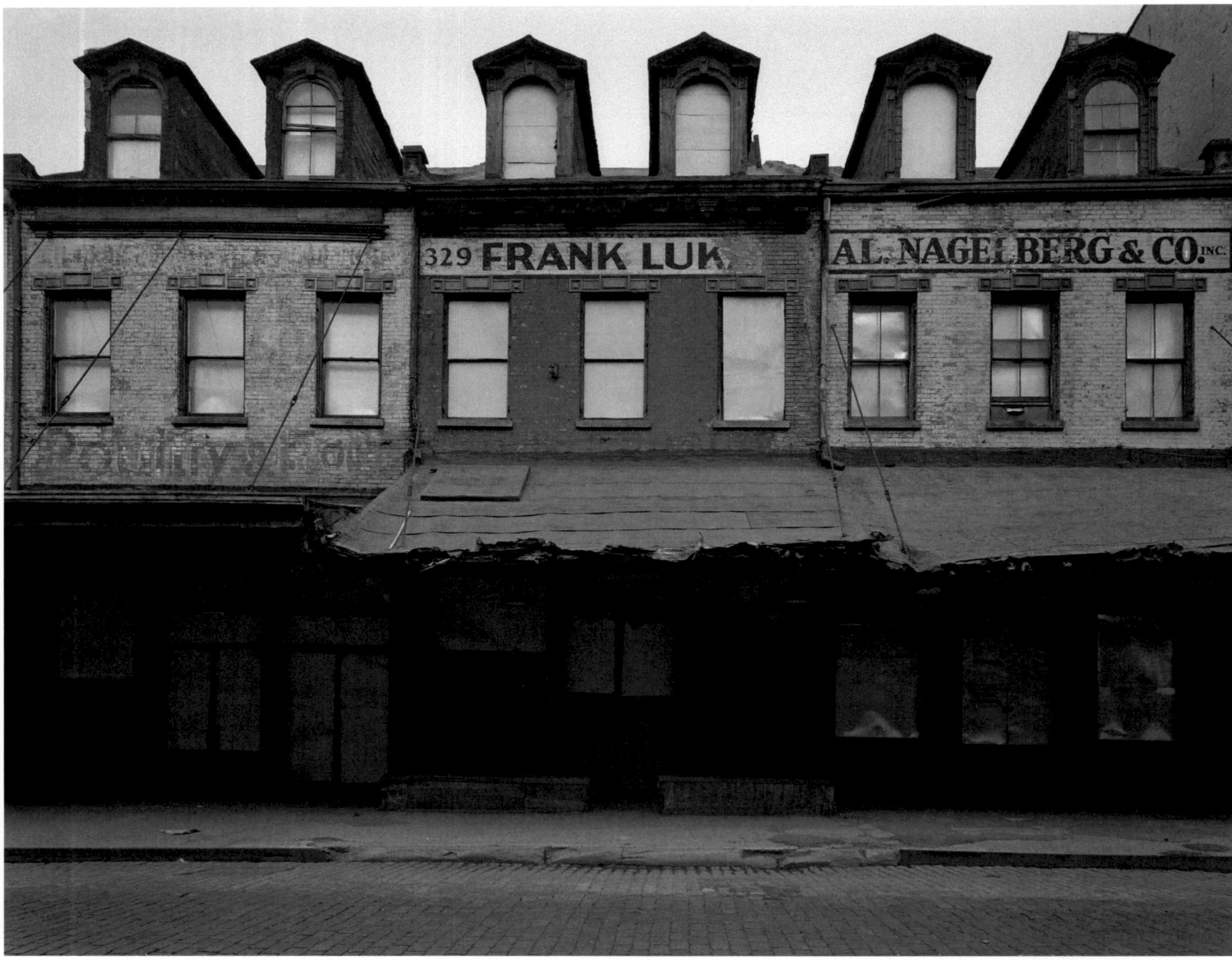

Plate 4 Danny Lyon, *327, 329, and 331 Washington Street, between Jay and Harrison streets*, 1967

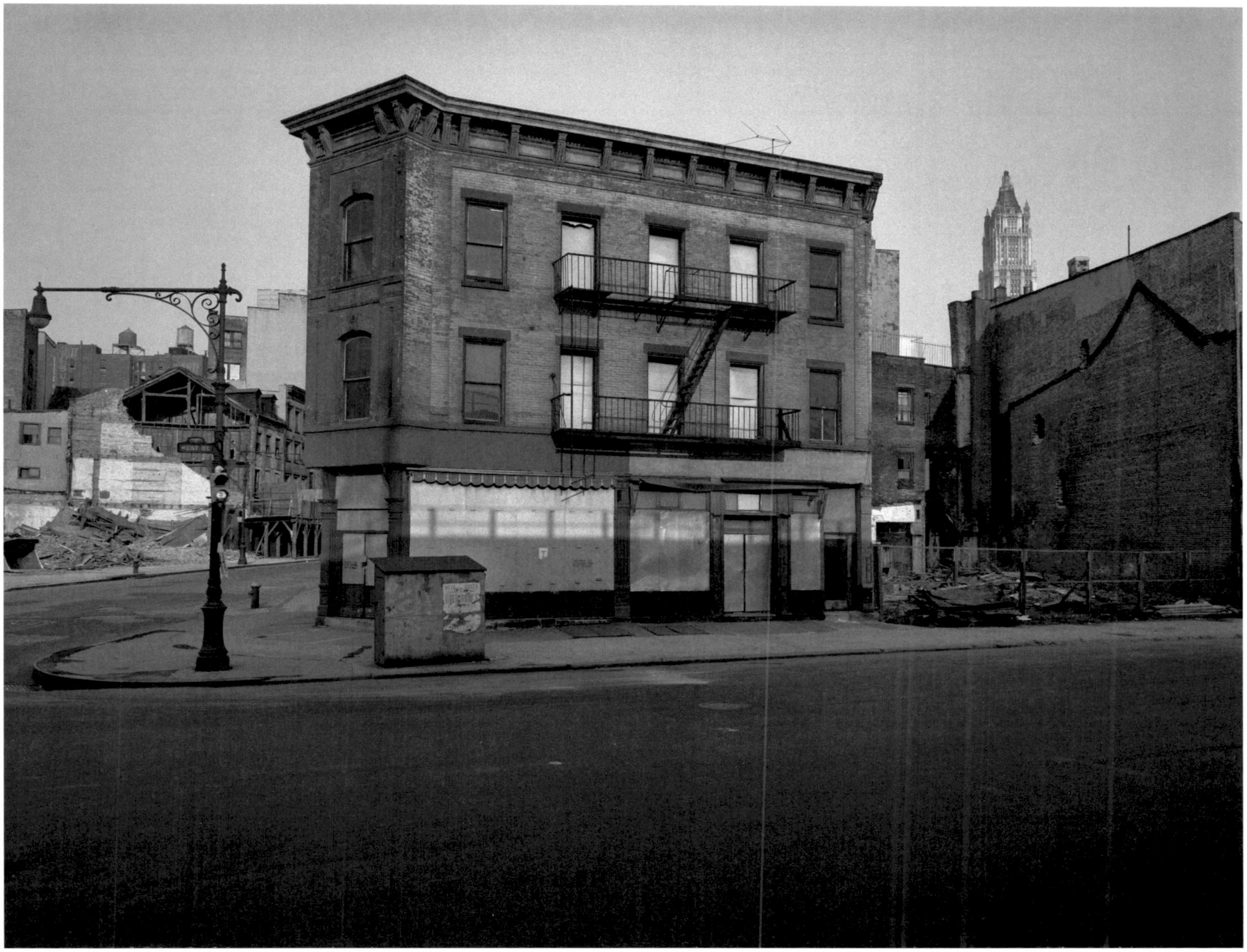

Plate 5 Danny Lyon, *185 West Street at Chambers*, 1967

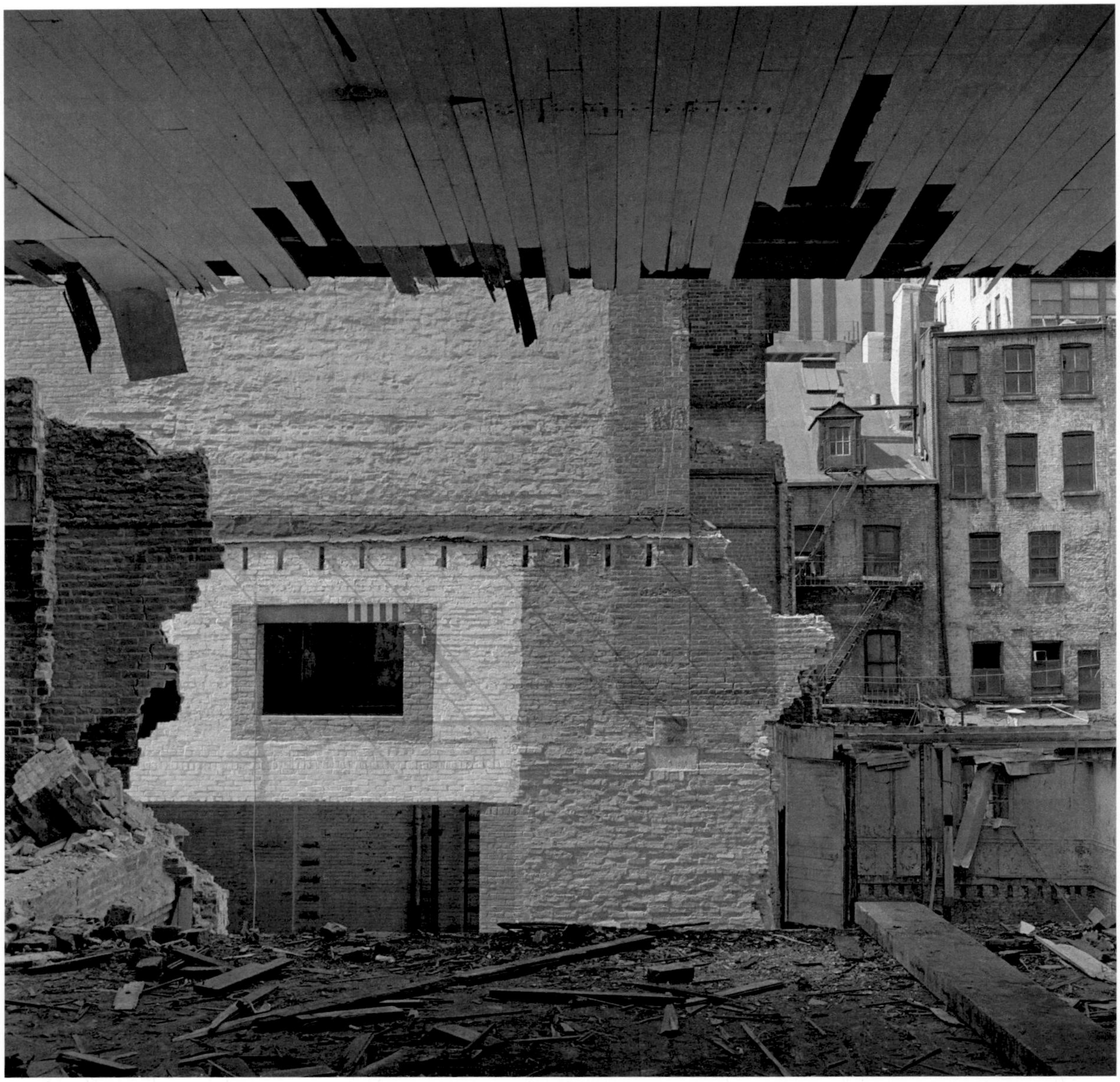

Plate 6 Danny Lyon, *View through the rear wall, 89 Beekman Street*, 1967

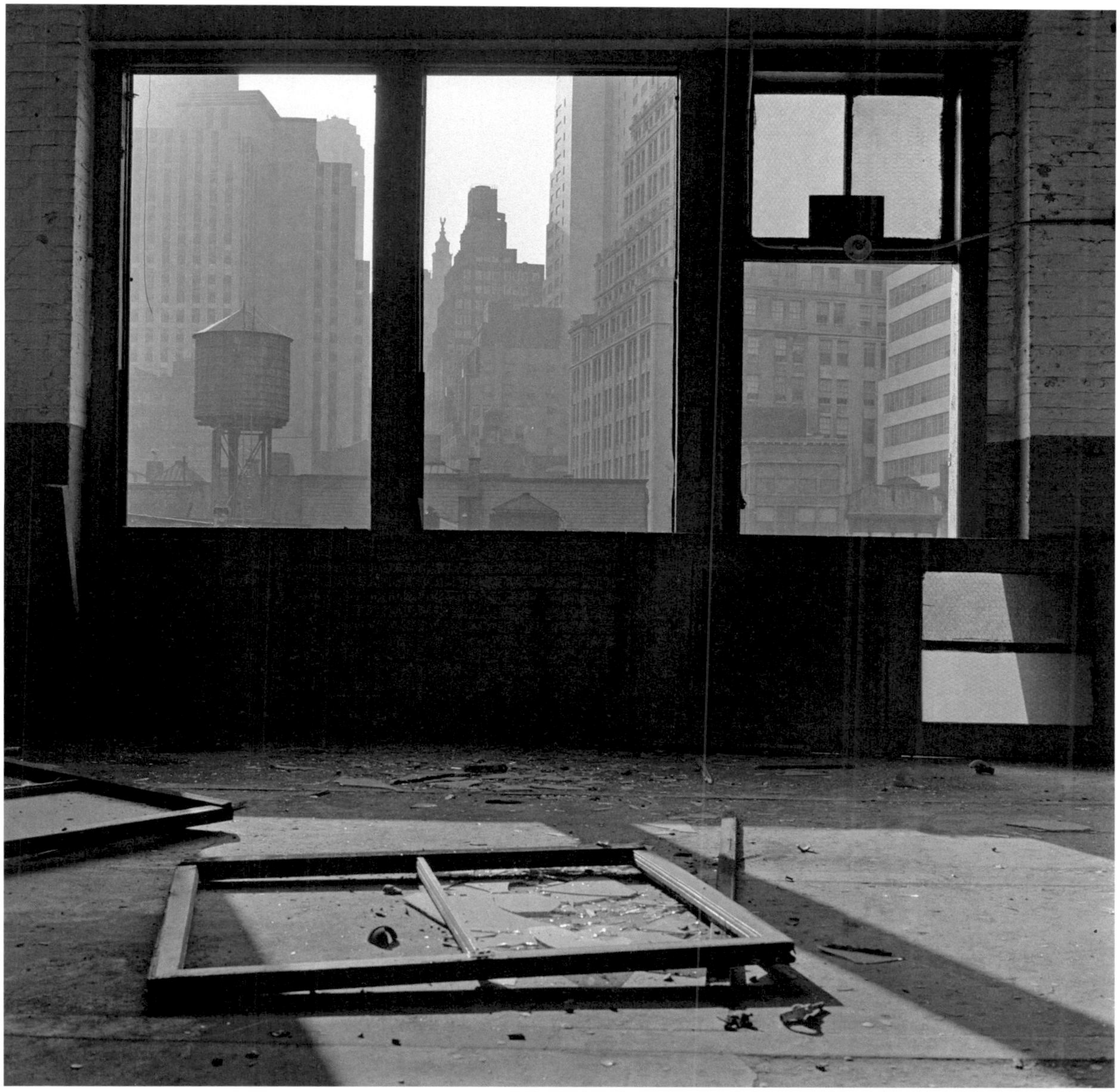

Plate 7 Danny Lyon, *View south from 88 Gold Street*, 1967

From Site to Non-Site: An Introduction to *Mixed Use, Manhattan*

Lynne Cooke

Mixed Use, Manhattan: Photography and Related Practices, 1970s to the Present, the exhibition that generated this book, started out as a project focusing on the great corpus of still-underrated work Peter Hujar shot in New York City in the 1970s and 80s. Consideration particularly of photographs he took on the West Side and the piers, areas that he explored daily in his life and work, quickly led Douglas Crimp and me to two other major photographic projects by younger artists, David Wojnarowicz and Zoe Leonard. Both had known Hujar personally, as a close friend and/or as an artistic mentor. Wojnarowicz's seminal *Arthur Rimbaud in New York* series was produced in the neighborhoods he and Hujar frequented. While this proved to be one of Wojnarowicz's few forays into photography, he chronicled his own life through short stories, essays, diaries, and a memoir, up to his premature death from AIDS in 1992. In the 1990s, Leonard began photographing urban minutiae—everyday and unexceptional details and events in streetscapes usually characterized as run-down in the Lower East Side—where she had lived and worked for some years. When her neighborhood, long the first home to waves of immigrant groups from Europe and elsewhere, began to undergo the kind of belated makeover that had transformed SoHo and Tribeca in the 1980s, Leonard embarked on what would turn into a decade-long project charting the gentrification of, first, her immediate environs and, later, a broader hinterland.[1]

pp. 165–70

Of course, these three bodies of exceptional work were far from isolated responses to the deindustrialization and decline that had begun in New York City in the late 60s. As the Lower Manhattan cityscape and waterfront suffered increasing devastation, artists were drawn to its abandoned and decrepit sites as inexpensive places to live, to rent studio space, and to present their work.

Our initial focus on the trio of Hujar, Wojnarowicz, and Leonard soon widened to take in a range of works, part of the extraordinary efflorescence of artistic activity in this downtown milieu. As we tracked the shift, over the course of less than twenty years, from an alternative art scene to what became, albeit briefly, *the* contemporary-art-world mecca, the exhibition's chronological parameters became clear. The terminus would be the present. For even though the economic booms that had transformed SoHo, the Lower East Side, and Tribeca by the end of the century had made studio and living space there unaffordable for an emerging generation, who consequently moved to Williamsburg, Red Hook, Fort Greene, and other areas farther

afield (which in turn stimulated nascent scenes in those neighborhoods), younger artists continue to be drawn to Lower Manhattan as a vital site to contest and reclaim. In recent years, Matthew Buckingham, Andrea Geyer, Sharon Hayes, and Emily Roysdon, among others, have not only generated works in public spaces downtown but also, in different ways, referenced the multifaceted legacy of the 1970s generation. The exhibition's starting point became the late 1960s, when a government-backed program of demolition that would cover some sixty acres downtown was initiated. Perhaps the most powerful record of that planned devastation is a series of photographs, shot in 1967 by the twenty-five-year-old Danny Lyon, who had recently returned to New York City (where he was born) after a seven-year absence. Seeking solitude, Lyon moved to an isolated neighborhood that he regarded as deserted but where one of his friends lived. (Tellingly, that friend was an artist, the sculptor Mark di Suvero, who would continue to reside some five blocks away, near the Fulton Fish Market, for decades.) "No one really lived there then," Lyon later recalled. "As I gazed out of my fourth-floor window...I decided that there was no story in Lower Manhattan. Not about people anyway."[2] After realizing that, in fact, "the story was the destruction," he applied for support from the New York State Council on the Arts for a project that would record a growing wasteland, as great swaths of buildings, including some of the oldest in the city, were razed.[3] "I came to see the buildings as fossils of a time past," Lyon wrote in the opening sentence to his text for *The Destruction of Lower Manhattan*,
p. 12 the book that resulted.[4] Its frontispiece shows an aerial view—an immaculate panoramic vista—from a point over the East River just north of the Brooklyn Bridge. From this distanced perspective, no signs are visible of the ruins and dereliction that already surrounded Lyon's untimely relics. Thereafter he worked at close range, at street level, within the crumbling structures, or on the rooftops as the buildings succumbed to the wreckers. The seventy-five black-and-white images he selected for the book range from sober shots of historic facades surrounded by vacant lots to portraits of the demolition crews and the tawdry abandoned interiors, together with macabre views that resulted from chance overlappings of partially and wholly demolished structures
p. 18 (see, for example, *View through the rear wall, 89 Beekman Street*). Classically composed and crisply detailed, Lyons's images infuse these fossils with an affecting dignity and pathos. The final picture, *The Ruins of 100 Gold Street*, references a ruined temple from antiquity. Yet given their finely graduated tonal range and limpid light, his photographs, in toto, are too cool to be nostalgic.[5]

The self-consciously documentary style of this now-legendary project sets his work apart from much else that followed, with two notable exceptions: both are series of black-and-white images made by artists highly attuned to the history of
pp. 23–25 architectural photography as a genre. While on a fellowship to the United States in 1978, Thomas Struth shot deserted street scenes in locations across the city's inner boroughs. An old-world stylistic idiom and a formal compositional structure that he

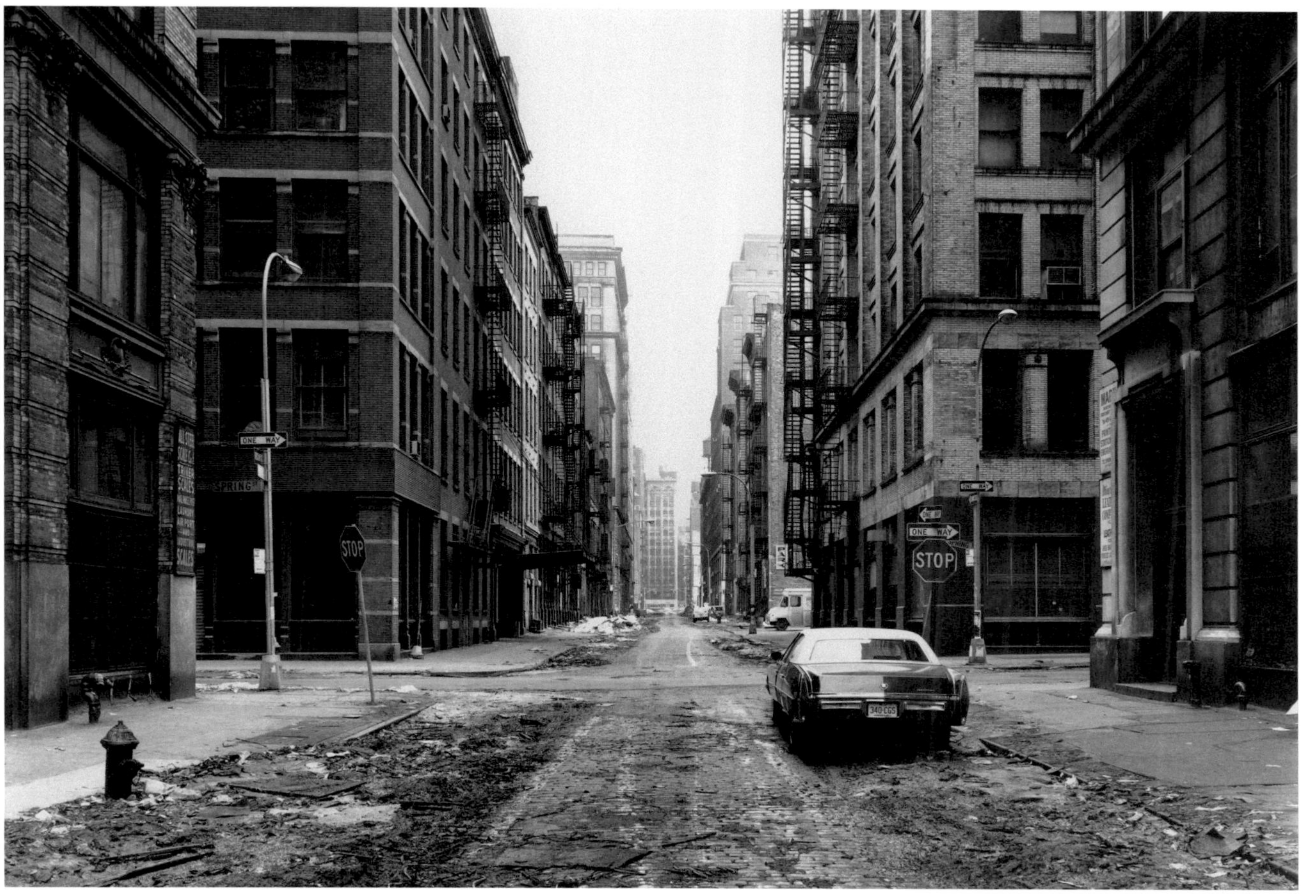

Plate 8 Thomas Struth, *Crosby Street, New York/SoHo*, 1978

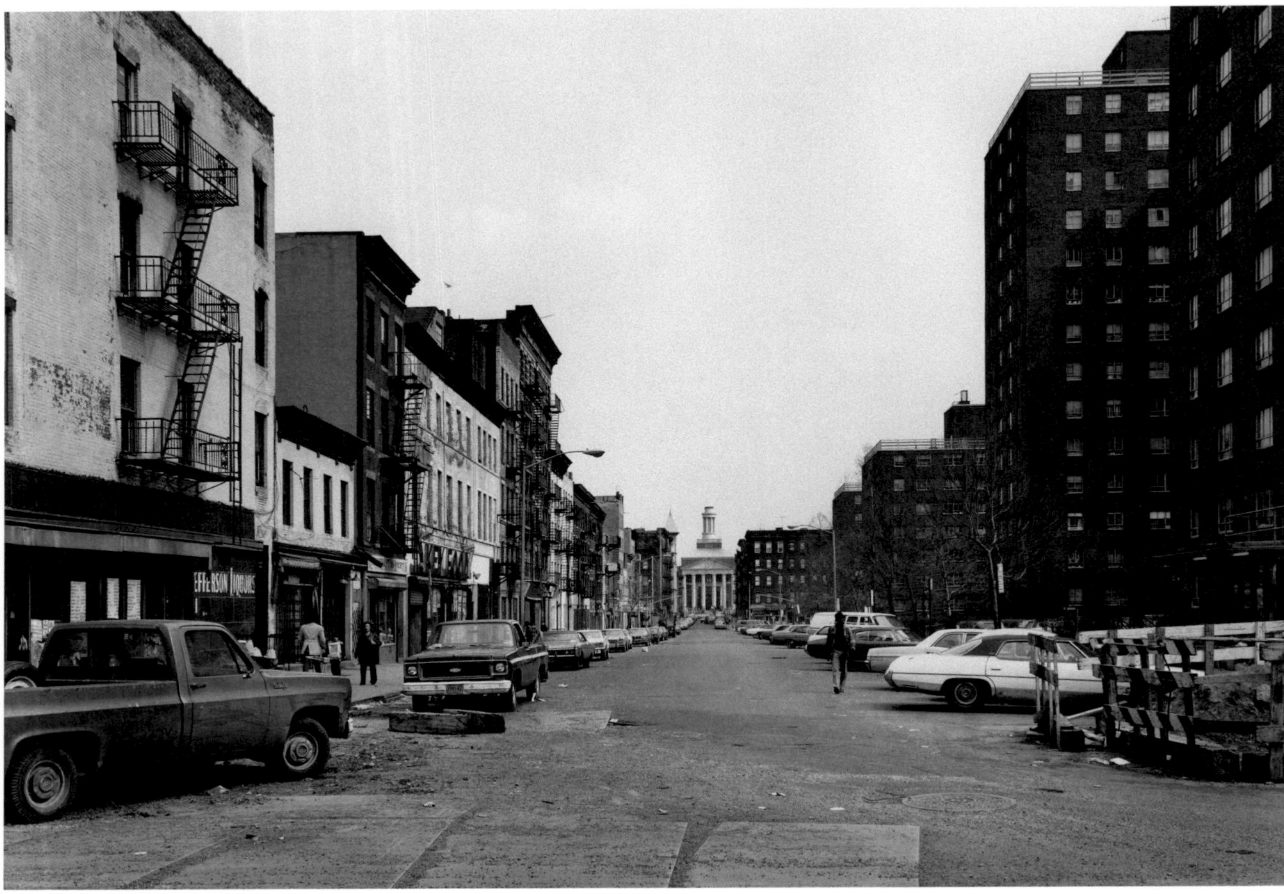

Plate 9 Thomas Struth, *115th Street at 2nd Avenue, New York/Harlem*, 1978

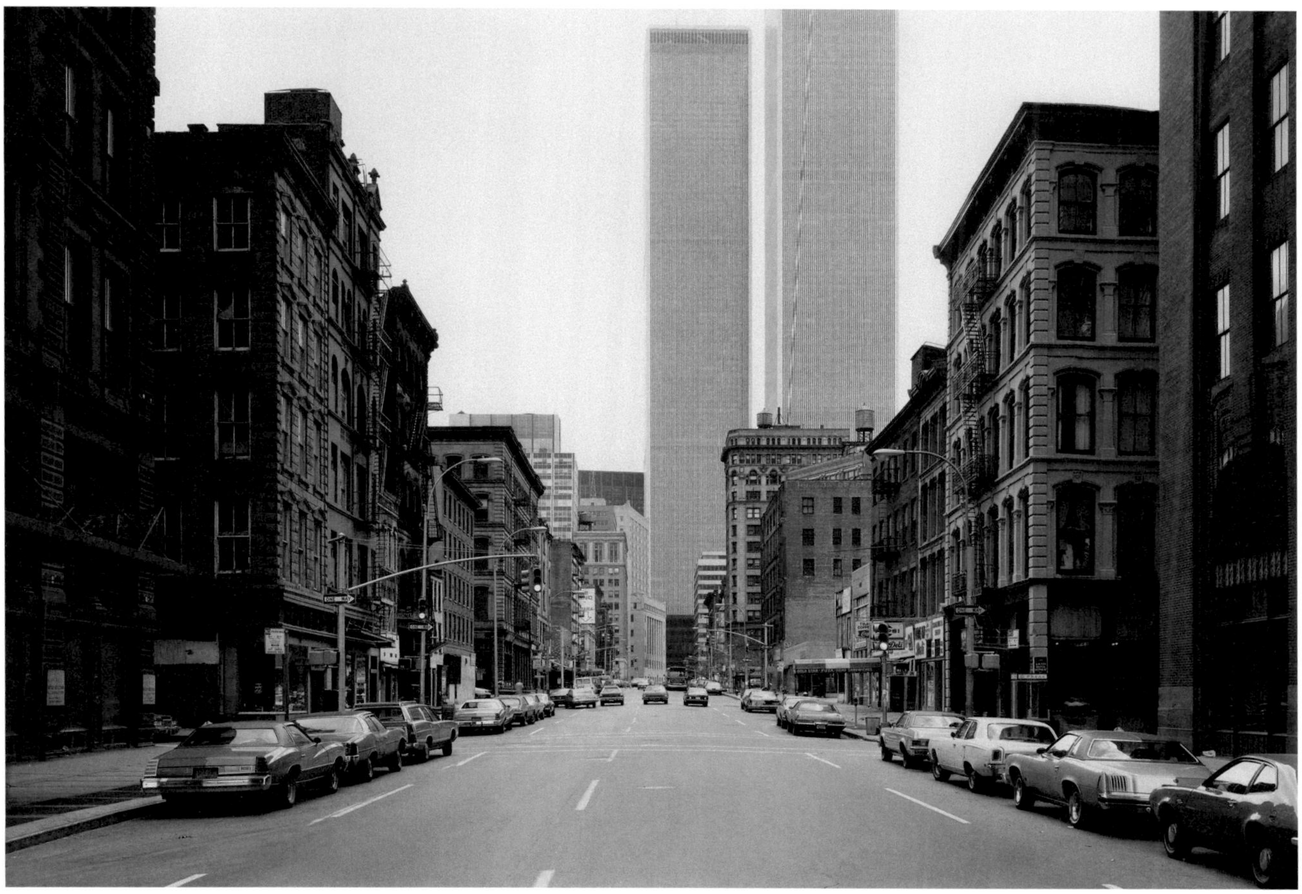

Plate 10 Thomas Struth, *West Broadway, New York/Tribeca*, 1978

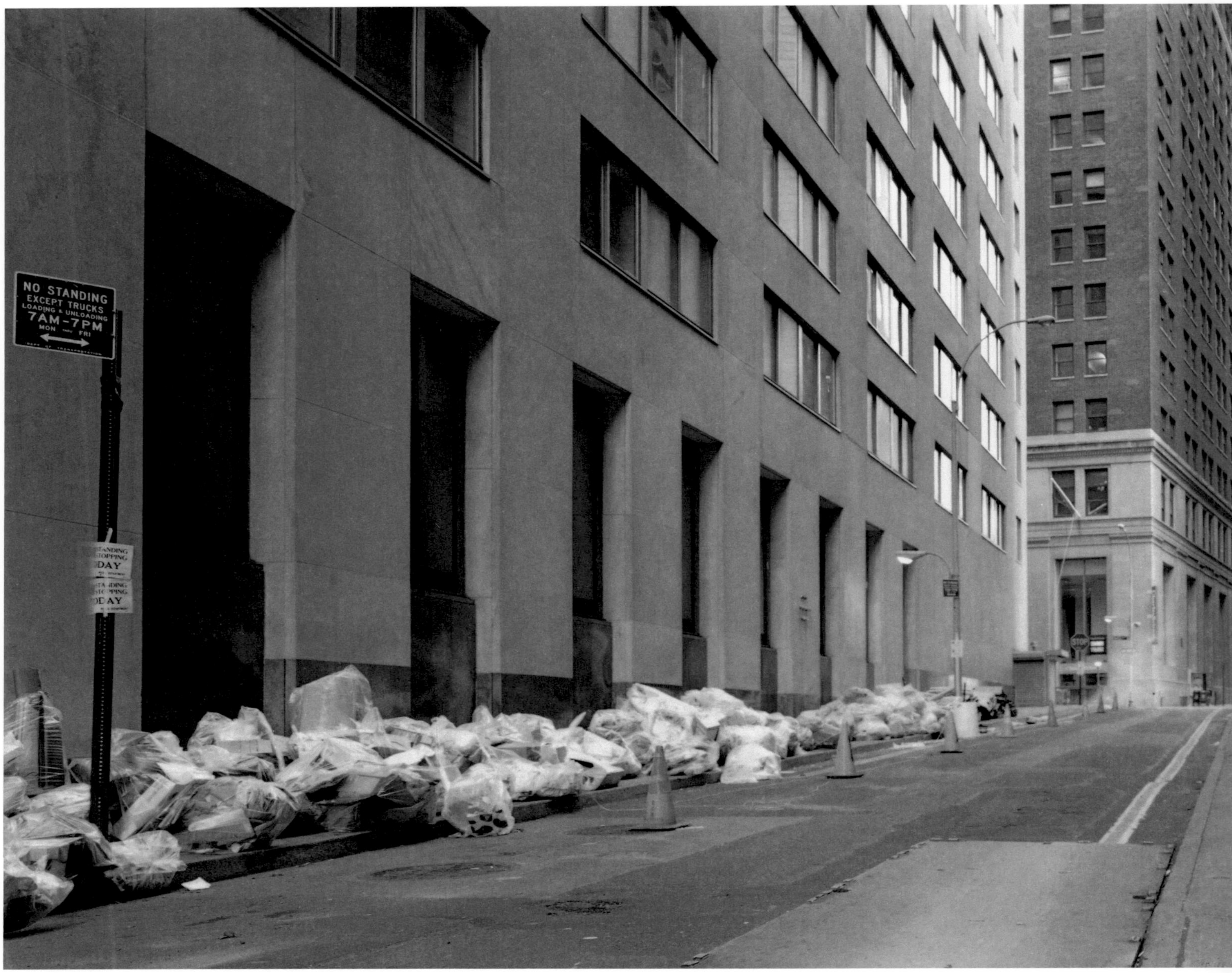

Plate 11 Catherine Opie, *Untitled #2 (Wall Street)*, 2001

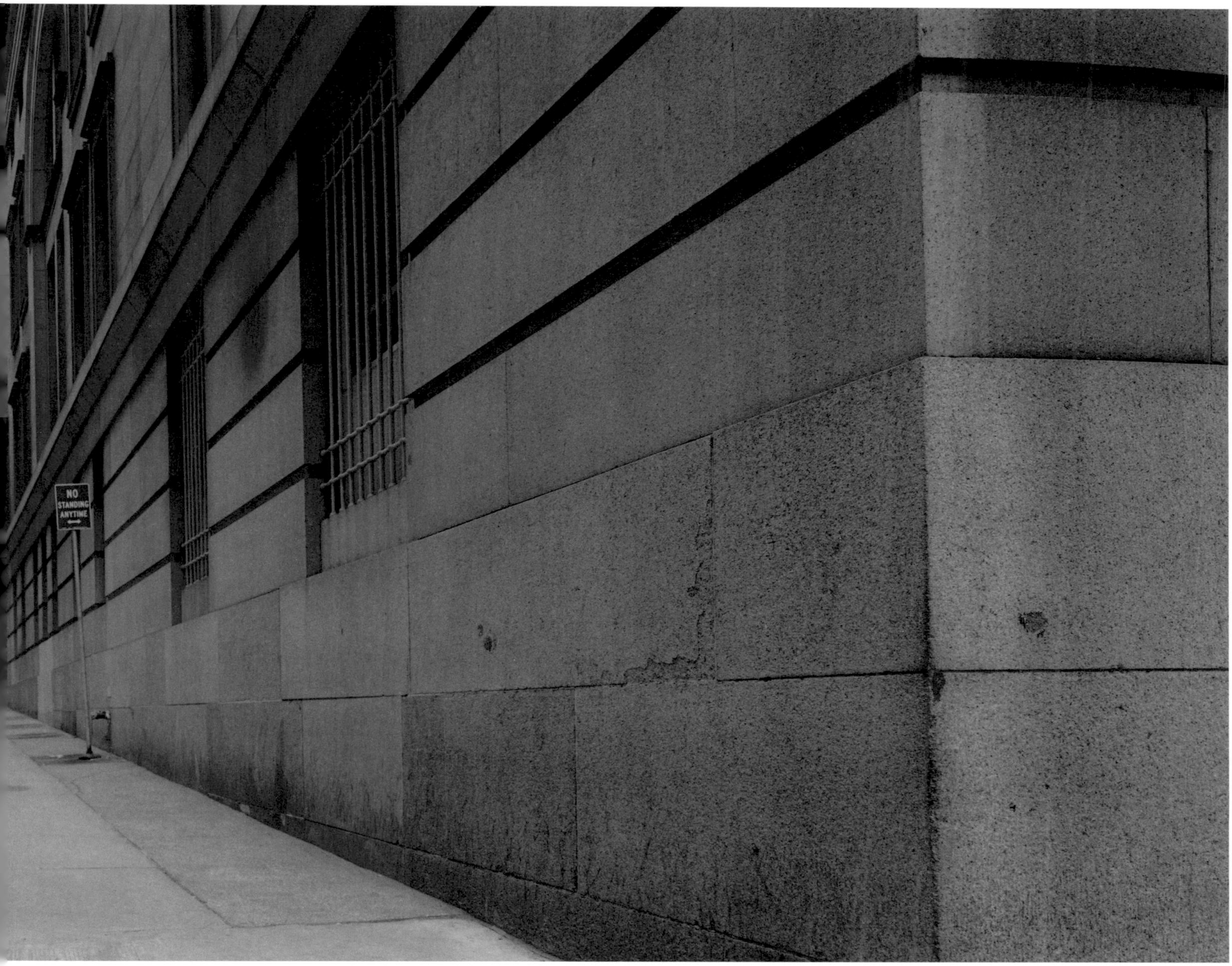
NO
STANDING
ANYTIME

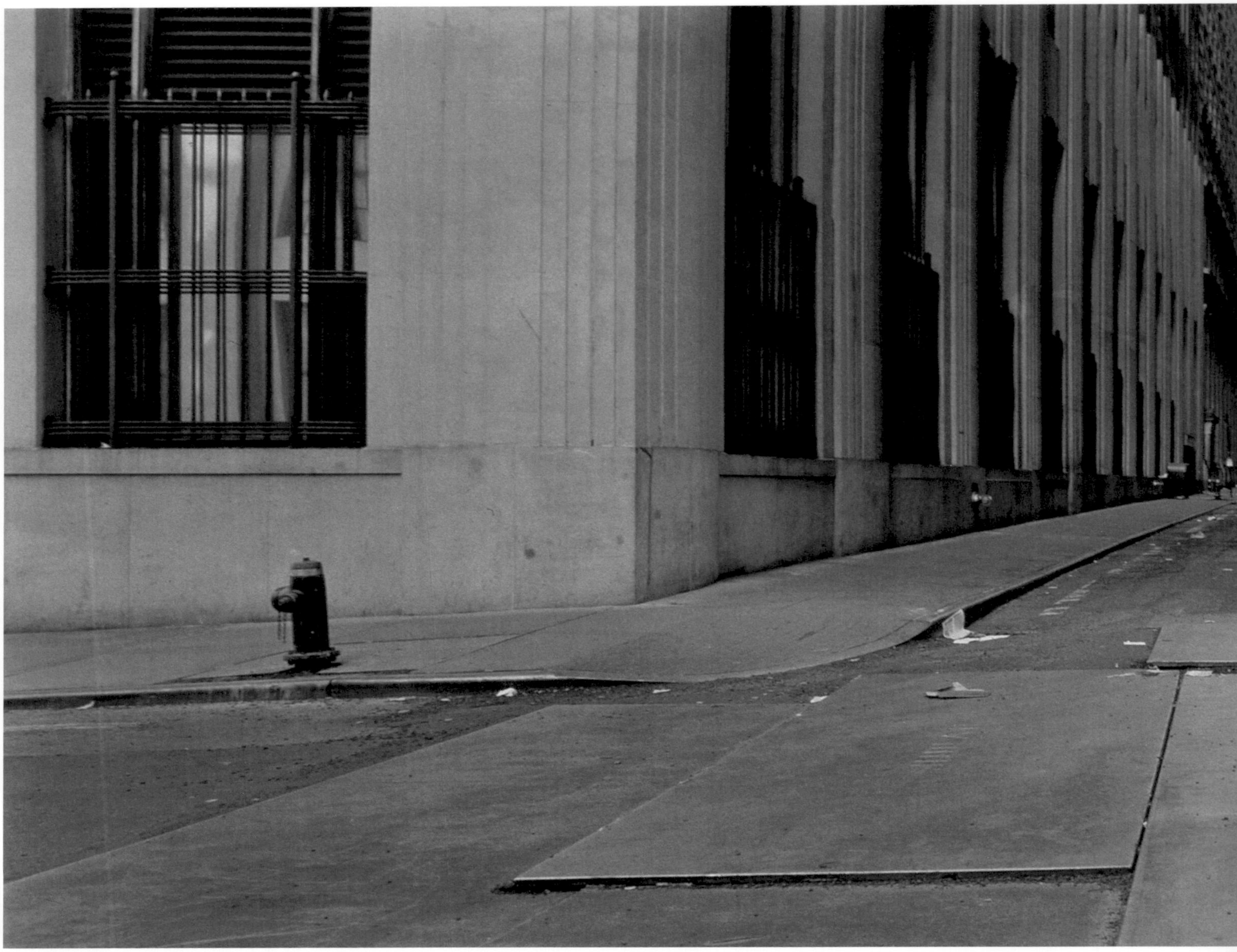

Plate 12 Catherine Opie, *Untitled #14 (Wall Street)*, 2001

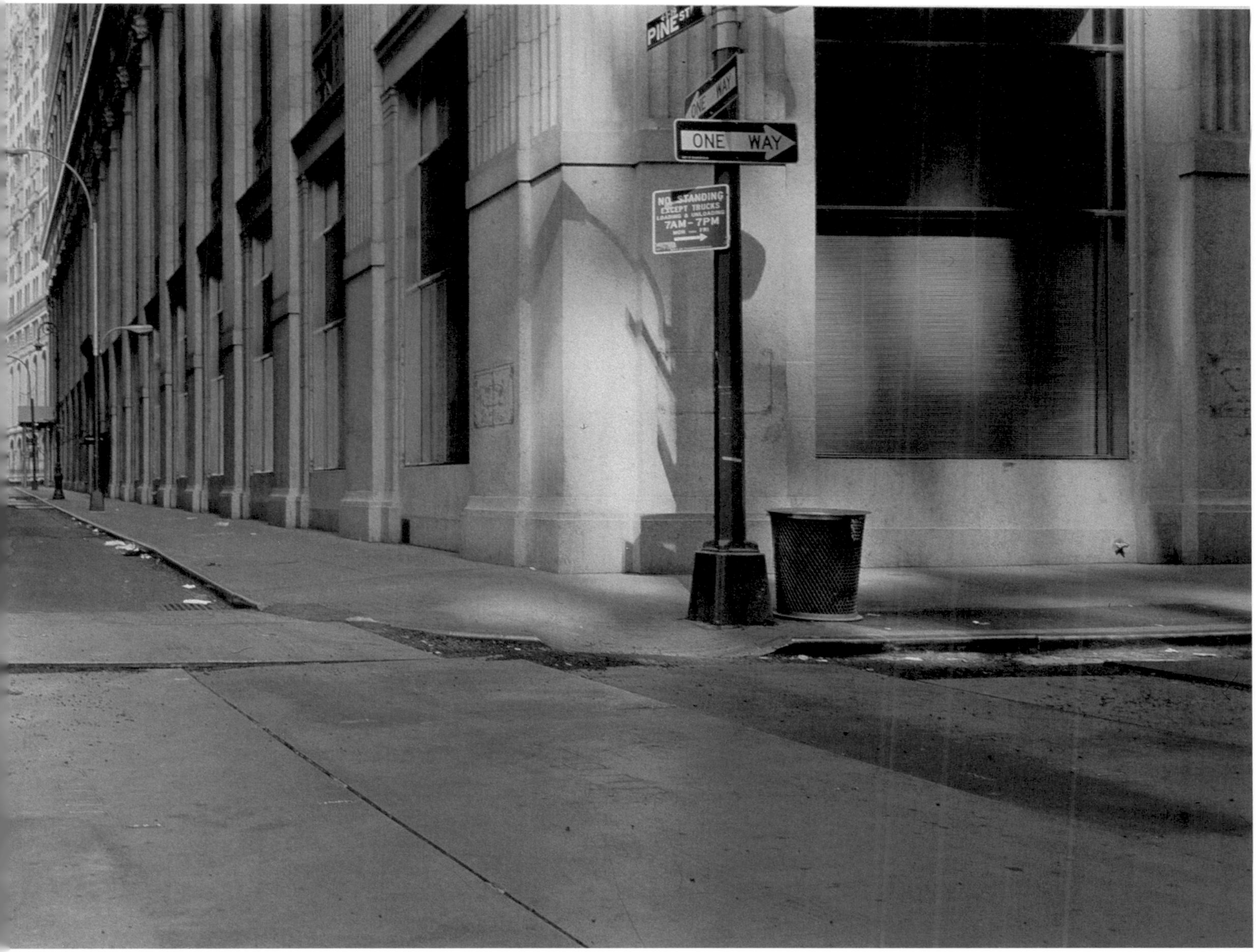
PINE ST
ONE WAY
ONE WAY
NO STANDING
EXCEPT TRUCKS
LOADING & UNLOADING
7AM - 7PM
MON - FRI

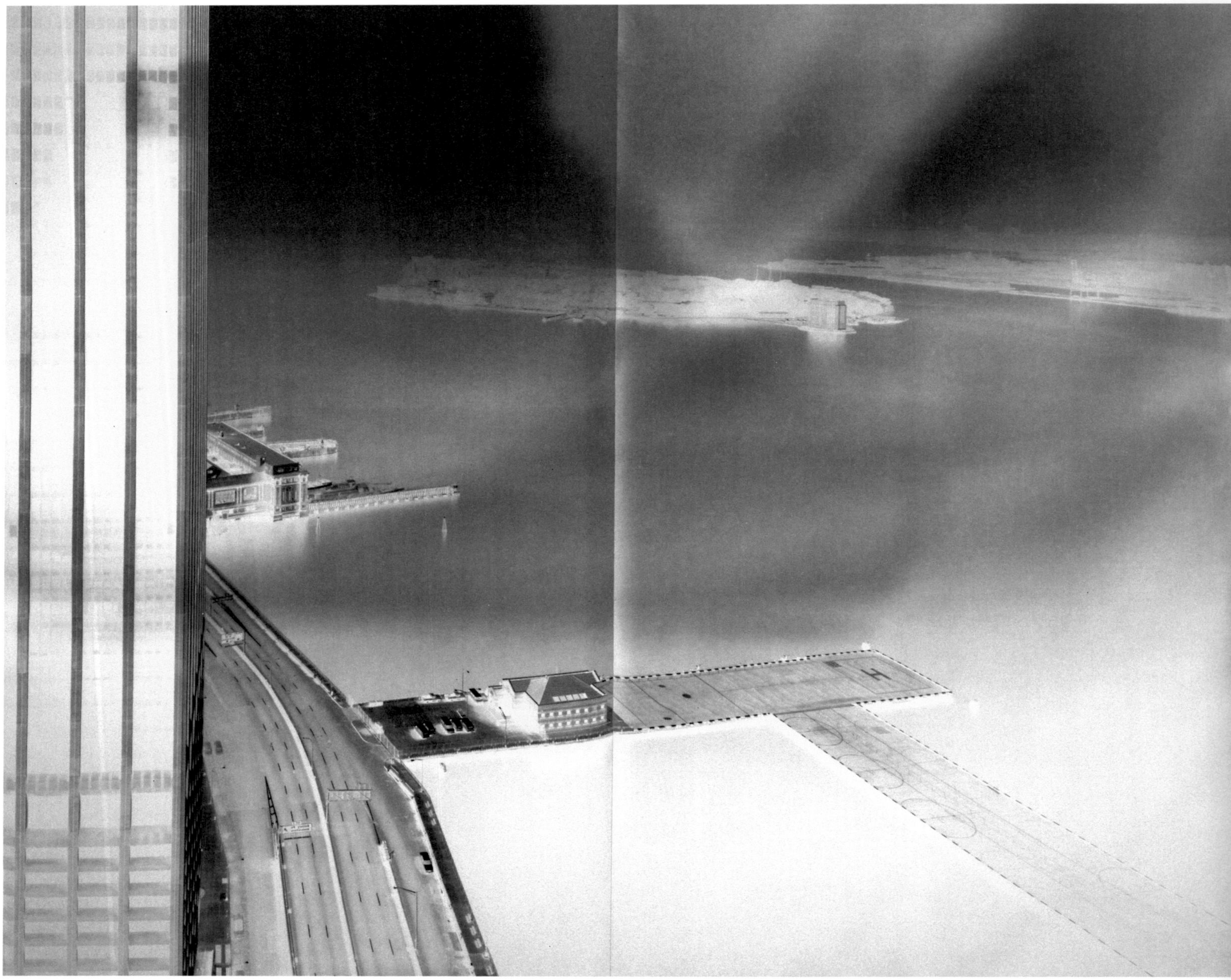

Plate 13 Vera Lutter, *South View, Old Slip, New York: October 8, 1994*, 1994

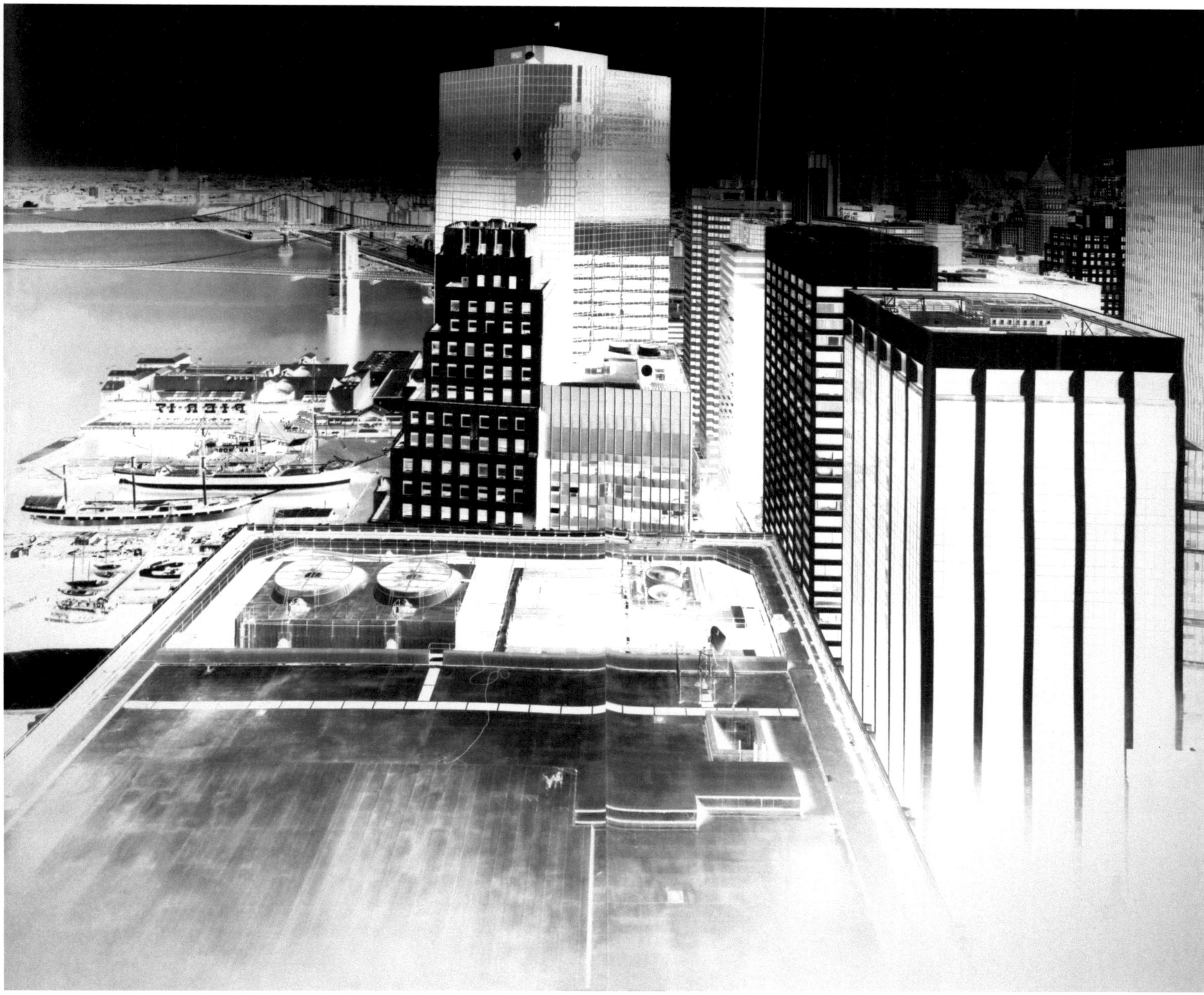

Plate 14 Vera Lutter, *North View, Old Slip, New York: October 10, 1994*, 1994

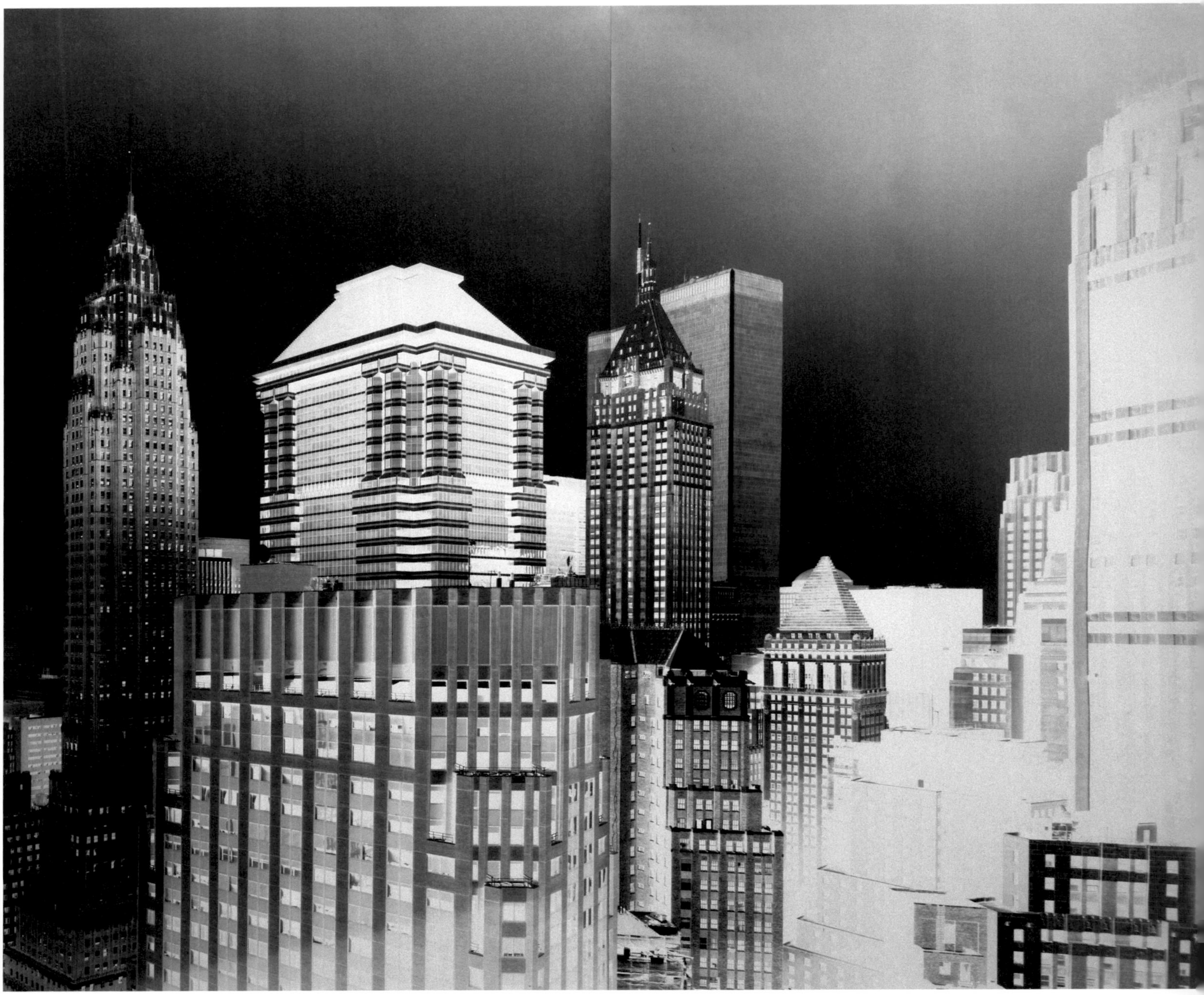

Plate 15 Vera Lutter, *West View, Old Slip, New York: November 11, 1994*, 1994 **Plate 16** Vera Lutter, *East View, Old Slip, New York: April 29, 1995*, 1995

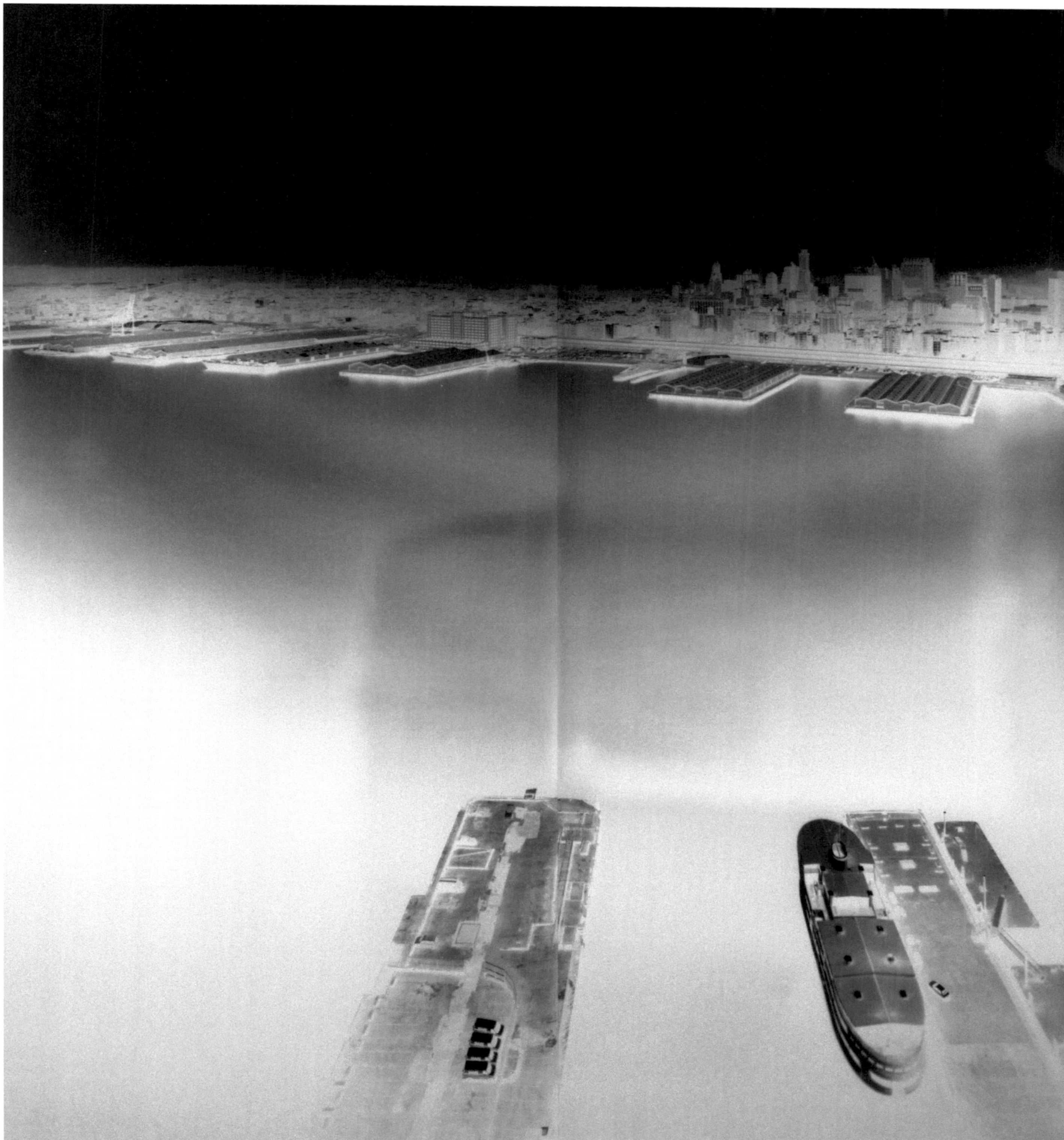

had learned from his teachers Bernd and Hilla Becher at the Düsseldorf Academy of Art served him well when confronted with unknown terrain. In contrast to Struth, whose work in New York formed part of an ongoing engagement with urban landscapes, pp. 26–29 Catherine Opie deliberately circumscribed *Wall Street*, her project of 2001. Within what has proved a wide range of photographic modes, Opie's *Wall Street* photographs constitute a distinct if unexpected reprise on a location freighted with pictorial traditions. Both these younger artists achieved a sense of solitude and silence comparable to that found in Lyon's work. But whereas Lyon could have photographed at any time of day, so abandoned was his neighborhood, both Struth and Opie had to work in the early-morning hours. Viewed from the beginning of the twenty-first century, the stillness and emptiness that pervade their works seem eerie, as if the island's streets had once again been divested of life.

Three little-known and seldom-exhibited groups of work from the late 1950s and 60s by William Gedney provide a second point of departure for this exhibition. All three groups were made while Gedney lived in Brooklyn but nightly trained his camera on subjects in the city, beginning with the Brooklyn Bridge, his point p. 231 of transit into Lower Manhattan. Another favorite subject was the Washington Street Market before it was demolished in 1967–68 to make way for the World Trade Center. Gedney also made an extensive series of images based on the streetscape visible from pp. 232–33 his apartment window on Myrtle Avenue; from there, he could survey the elevated railway, soon to be torn down. Indeed, so intense was his preoccupation with this street, whose historic identity he also explored in notebooks filled with literary quotations and newspaper clippings, and so concerned was he by the imminent demise of the El, that he left precise instructions on at least one occasion for his landlord to continue the series in his absence. Gedney's concentration on this familiar location manifests a guiding tenet in his aesthetic, evidenced in a quote from Eudora Welty he copied into a notebook on May 27, 1973: "Place has the most delicate control over character, location pertains to feeling."[6] If Gedney's nocturnal forays into Manhattan's streets prefigure Hujar's nighttime ramblings, his finely nuanced, open-ended Myrtle Avenue series has p. 235 echoes in much else in this exhibition, not least the views James Welling shot between 1997 and 2000 from his loft window on Greene Street. Gedney's legacy extends, too, to a project that poet Stefan Brecht began in 1985 when he took up photography specifically to record the pavements he traversed on his daily walk from his house in the West Village to the room in the Chelsea Hotel on West 23rd Street where he wrote. Though pp. 238–39 the book in which Brecht planned to juxtapose xeroxed images of these close-ups with a selection of poems never got beyond the stage of handmade versions distributed to a few close friends, the photographs were published separately, as were the poems.[7]

Living in Chinatown but painting in a studio on East 9th Street, Christopher Wool too shot his daily route for some years, eventually collecting the pp. 210–14 grainy images of this nightly journey into a publication, *East Broadway Breakdown* (2003), and still later printing them digitally for exhibition.[8] More obliquely, a number of Sol LeWitt's sporadic forays into photography in the later 1970s have affinities with several of Gedney's unrealized Manhattan projects: *Brick Wall* (1977), a taxonomy of some thirty images of this subject ranging from light to dark, never advanced beyond the stage of a maquette for a publication, in contrast to the grandest of his photographically based, conceptually driven ventures in his neighborhood, *On the Walls of the Lower East Side* (1981). Shot in full color, LeWitt's compendium comprises hundreds of examples of signage, ranging from the printed, painted, handwritten, scribbled, and graffitied to the diagrammatic. This compelling taxonomy resonates, in turn, with several subsequent projects included here, notably those of Wool and Leonard, as well as with another by one of LeWitt's peers, the pioneering Conceptualist Henry Flynt. For his still-unpublished project, Flynt tracked Jean-Michel Basquiat, in the guise SAMO©, tagging buildings throughout the downtown area in 1979. Conversely, for Roy Colmer, dedication to taxonomy could be put in service of the miniature, as seen in his studies of all the doors on a single side of the street on a particular block, and of a range of trucks viewed head-on, in close-up. From such disarmingly deadpan shots, Colmer self-published modestly scaled, xeroxed books, each dedicated to a single subject: *Doors N.Y.C.: Two Intersections* (1975–76), *Trucks N.Y.C.* (1977–88), *Movie Houses N.Y.C.* (1977–87), and *W.T.C.* (1993).

pp. 244–45

pp. 236–37

★

On July 25, 1971, in her regular weekly column for the *New York Times*, Art Notes, critic Grace Glueck commented on an amendment recently passed in the state legislature to the Multiple Dwelling Law. The amendment had been designed to make that law more flexible for artists in SoHo who wished to convert their lofts into joint studio-living spaces.[9] With this legislation in place, a long period of illegal occupancy in the former industrial area ended, and the neighborhood began to diversify in order to accommodate the needs of its resident art community. New restaurants like Food (opened by Gordon Matta-Clark and friends) soon appeared, as did artist-run galleries such as 112 Greene Street and their only slightly more commercial counterparts, beginning with the Paula Cooper Gallery as early as 1968 and solidified by the opening in 1972 of 420 West Broadway, which housed the Leo Castelli, Sonnabend, and John Weber galleries. At this same moment, the heterogeneous but nonetheless fairly cohesive community of artists began to commandeer an array of outdoor sites—streets, rooftops, piers, vacant lots, community parks, and transit systems—in SoHo and farther afield, as desirable places to present their works.[10]

Also part of Glueck's column that day was a review of the exhibition *Projects: Pier 18* at the Museum of Modern Art. Legendary but seldom seen since, the group of some 350 photographs that composed this show joins works by Lyon and

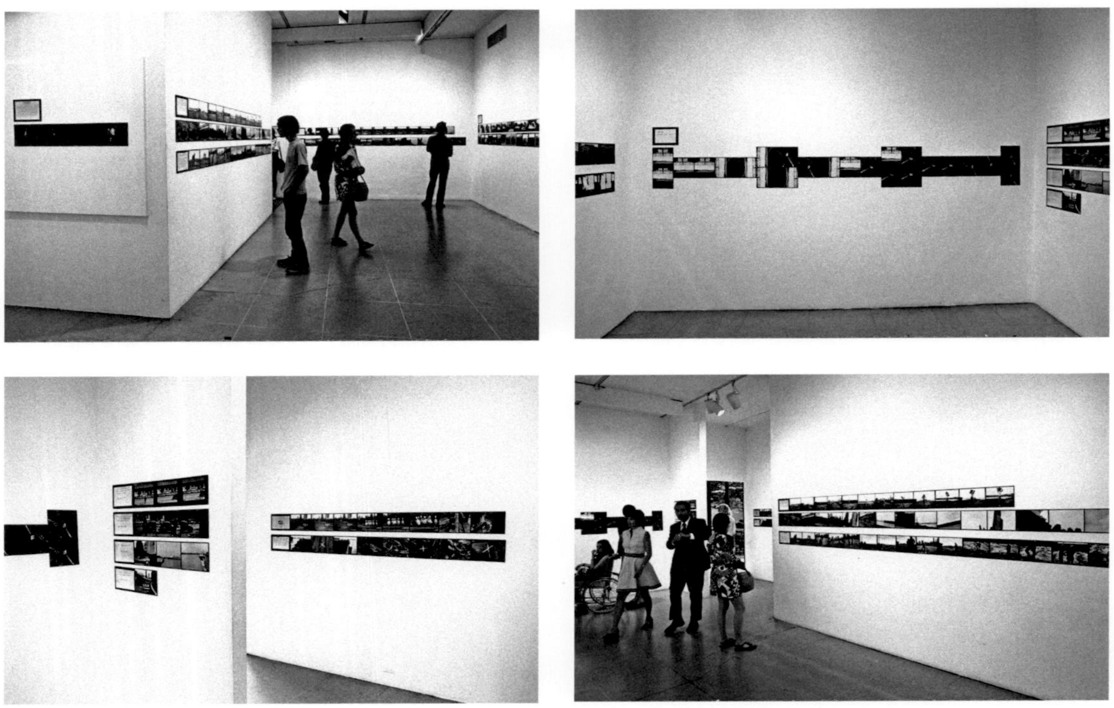

Installation views, *Projects: Pier 18*, Museum of Modern Art, New York, June 18–August 2, 1971

Gedney in becoming a key point of departure for *Mixed Use, Manhattan.* At MoMA, *Projects: Pier 18* took the form of a display of small black-and-white prints of mostly p. 36 ephemeral works that had been commissioned by the impresario—curator, publisher, editor, artist, and critic—Willoughby Sharp over the winter of 1970.[11] Sharp invited twenty-seven (male) artists—many local, several from the West Coast, and a few from abroad—to create works on a derelict pier just north of the site where the twin towers were then being completed. For Sharp, this rotting hulk was "a perfect place, totally disassociated from art-making and open to a large variety of work."[12] Yet the project was something of a guerrilla action, given that Sharp, predicting official refusal due to the wharf's derelict condition, had not sought permission to work there. Assuming that the wharf could not safely accommodate an audience, he conceived the project from its inception for a museum presentation. It consequently would depend heavily on Shunk-Kender, a professional photographic duo he invited to participate in the venture.[13] As Shunk-Kender responded to the artists' disparate proposals, their anticipated role changed significantly. On the most basic level, they documented works that took the form of performances. For example, ten images record Allen Ruppersberg's pp. 72–73 project, which involved the West Coast Conceptualist placing a brick he had brought from Houdini's house in the Hollywood Hills into a suitcase, securing the suitcase with chains, and throwing it into the river. The performance had an appropriately magic denouement: unaccountably, the case did not sink but floated slowly away. George Trakas launched his kayak from the side of the rotting wharf in order to paddle across to Pier 17 and draw its facade. In the section of *Projects: Piers 18* devoted to his work, six pictures taken by Shunk-Kender of the artist midstream are paired with prints of Trakas's sketchbook pages.

The photographers also executed works according to instructions sent by participants who could not be present. Thus, for the Dutch artist Jan Dibbets they produced a series of twelve over- and underexposed images, from white to black, taken during the daytime from a single vantage point with a predetermined set of f-stops, together with a second series of a dozen shots, once again taken from a single vantage point, and once again spanning the light-dark spectrum, but this time recorded at sunset. By contrast, Mario Merz required Shunk and Kender to select and record twenty different images of their own choosing that would nonetheless fully document the location. Douglas Huebler challenged their aesthetic sense somewhat differently, requiring two images each of the "most pictorially aesthetic" near and far vistas; those pp. 74–75 vantage points were then marked with "X"s and photographed. If Merz and Huebler provoked the photographers to go beyond simply recording and reveal their taste, other projects drew specifically on the properties of the medium to interrogate the protocols and precepts that underpinned the professionals' practice. Thus, Richard pp. 77–79 Serra's piece, which entailed the creation of a trapezoidal frame through which Serra produced images of the city skyline with a square format, relied, for its intelligibility,

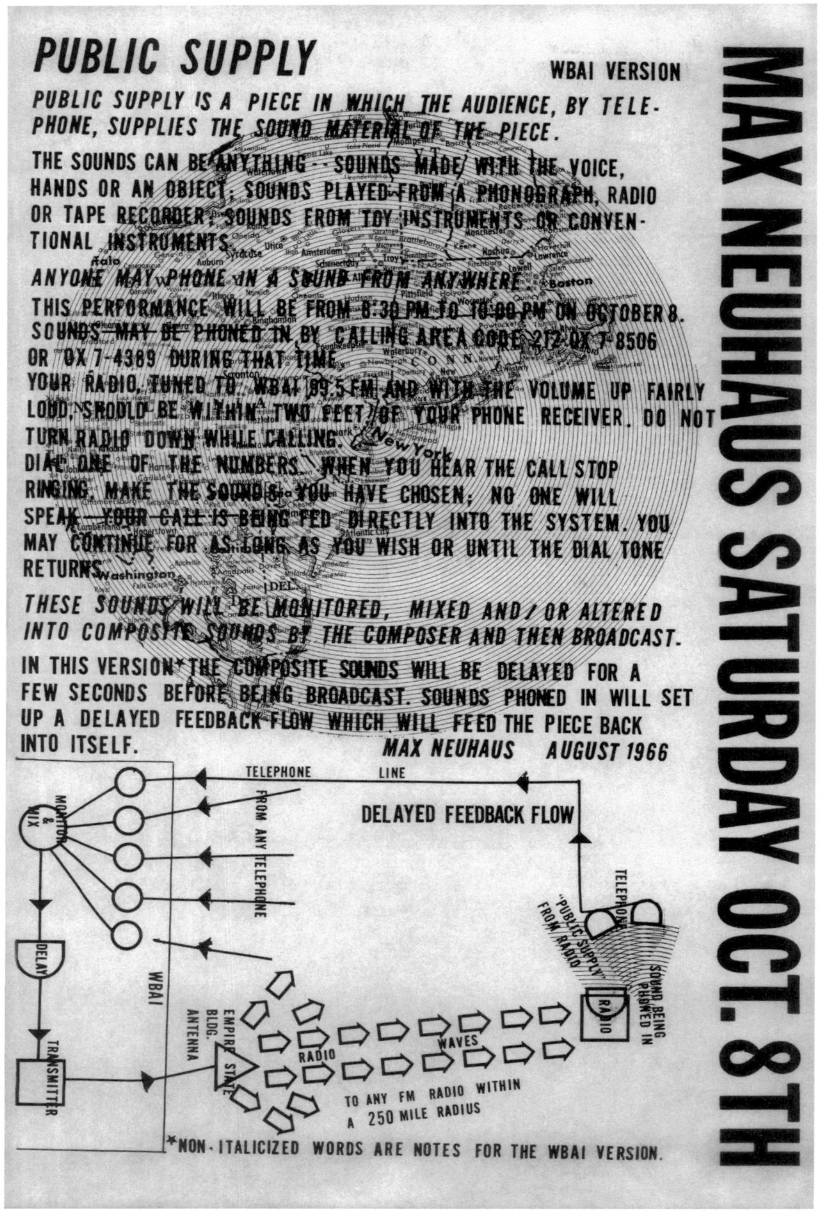

Plate 17 Max Neuhaus, poster for *Public Supply I*, 1966

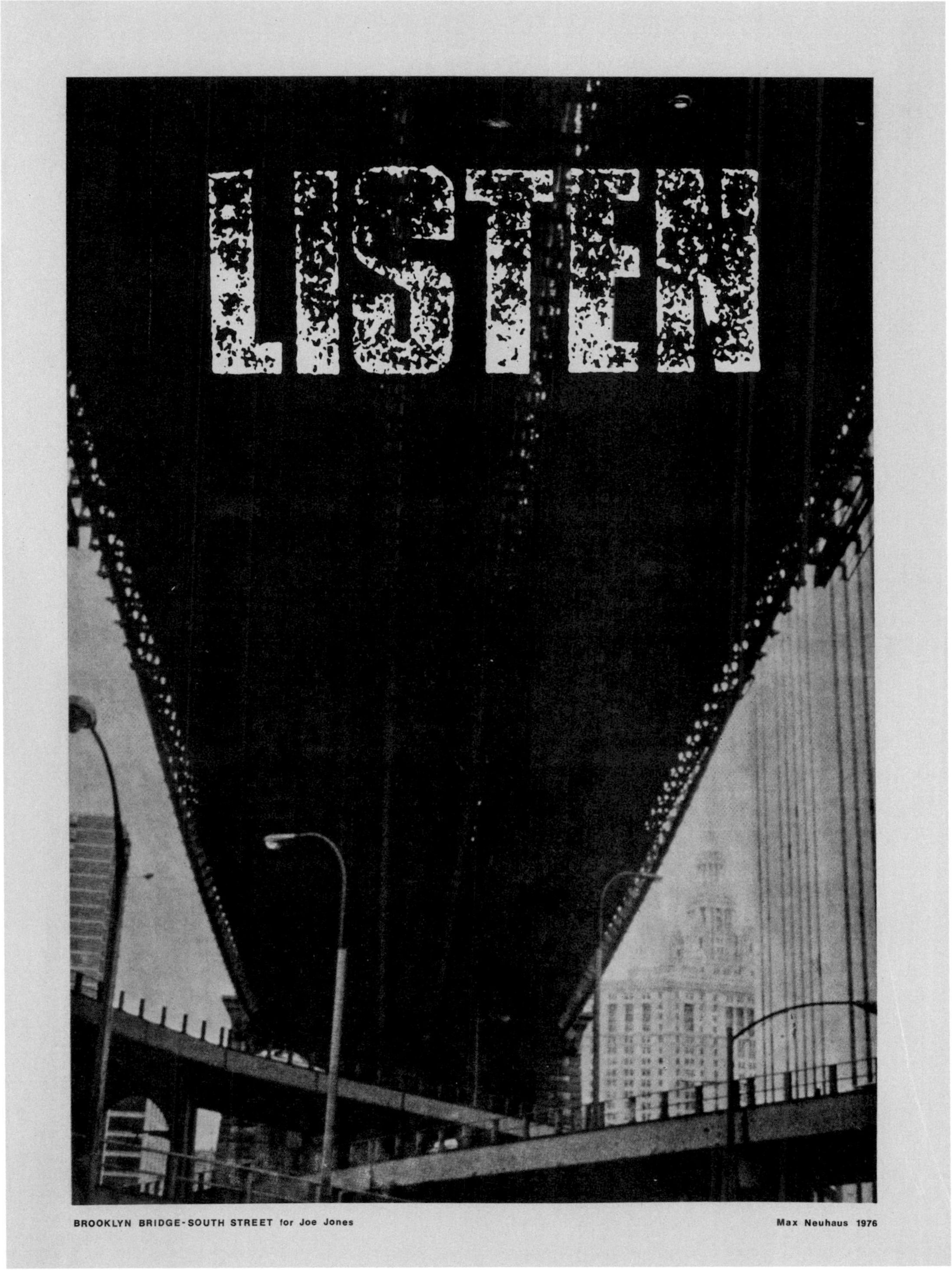

Plate 18 Max Neuhaus, poster for *Listen* with photograph of Brooklyn Bridge from South Street, New York, 1976

on a juxtaposition of Shunk-Kender's documentary images with those made by the pp. 68–71 artist. In a related work, Dan Graham played with the notion of an embodied viewpoint—that is, with the corporeal basis of any typical vantage point—by balancing the apparatus on various parts of his frame so that his body literally served as a tripod. This resulted in a counterpointing of Graham's wildly random vistas with the coolly focused sequence of shots recording the position of the camera at each moment he pressed the shutter. Yet other proposals played dialectically with the role and identity of this p. 67 medium, as seen in John Baldessari's gesture of framing a nearby ship with his fingers, leading to a print in which the lens collapsed near and far space. In contrast to the pp. 80–81 straightforwardly performative works by, say, Ruppersberg, Lee Jaffe, and Bill Beckley, the relationship between the photographers and the artist here verged on the collaborative. Put simply, a significant number of proposals required the making, as distinct from the taking, of photographs—a shift in emphasis that would be felt in much of the work made subsequently that forms part of this exhibition.

Taken together, the diversity of the twenty-seven projects meant not only that different types and levels of participation were required from the photographers but also that very different numbers of images were needed to accurately portray or realize each endeavor: nothing beyond the instruction card (which reads "DONE p. 76 WITHOUT") in the case of New York-based Lawrence Weiner (who was traveling at the time), compared with some twenty-four frames in the case of Michael Snow, who, exceptionally, declined to disclose the system underpinning his complex proposition.

Even though he saw the project as an extension of his attempt to work outside the museum and gallery structure, Sharp had accepted Helene Winer's invitation to curate the pier project for the Pomona College Museum of Art. That proposal eventually fell through; in the meantime, and independent of Sharp's negotiations with Winer, MoMA curators Kynaston McShine and Jennifer Licht had seen the material at Shunk-Kender's Westbeth studio and arranged to bring it to the museum that summer without Sharp's input. The impromptu presentation, titled *Projects: Pier 18,* opened to an enthusiastic press and public on June 18. Glueck, who praised the project, not only singled out the "brilliant documentary photographs" of Shunk-Kender for special attention but claimed these were "works of art—art objects—in their own right." For her, a clear distinction existed between what she characterized as Sharp's show (staged the previous winter on the pier) and the documentation—in which "the show lives on"—then on display at MoMA.[14] By contrast, Alfred Frankenstein, writing for the *San Francisco Chronicle*, also enthused but in significantly different terms. Leading with the claim that though "small in the space it occupie[d]," the show was "very big in its implications," Frankenstein acknowledged its origins in the combined forces of Sharp and Shunk-Kender before concluding that it was "the richest, most clearly defined and most meaningful show of conceptual art I have ever had the pleasure of seeing."[15] He consequently focused on what he considered the most successful seventeen among the contributions. That is, he treated *Pier 18* as a group exhibition of the work of a coterie of Conceptualists; it was not documentation of a show that had occurred some months earlier, as Glueck had portrayed it; for him, there was nothing exceptional in the role played by either its curator or the photographers who shot the pieces. So began what has proved a problematic characterization of this complex project and of its curiously indeterminate authorship.[16]

Clearly, the role played by photography in *Projects: Pier 18* was not simply one of documentation, even if that may have been the initial presumption on the parts of Sharp and Shunk-Kender. When conceiving their proposals, the artists had reflexively "detourned" the assignment to address, among other things, the ways in which pictorial knowledge is produced, the relation of this marginal venue to the city beyond, and the terms in which site could be defined visually and materially. Given that the project was crucially shaped and honed by contributions that engaged critically with the language of the medium in which it was to be manifest, the properties and potential of the medium became a prime subtext; representation of the site and its place within the urban sociocultural infrastructure became another. Just as *Projects: Pier 18*'s authorship was plural, so were its modes of inquiry.

Non-site is the term Robert Smithson coined for the production (via various forms of documentation ranging from film and text, through maps, drawings, diagrams, and photographs, to material samples—geologic specimens) of an artifact that could be used for presentation in a gallery or museum to conjure a site that was elsewhere—in both space *and* time. In the interview published in *Avalanche* the year before *Projects: Pier 18*, Smithson responded to Sharp's request that he elaborate on the term: "There's a central focus point which is the non-site; the site is the unfocused fringe where your mind loses its boundaries and a sense of the oceanic pervades, as it were.... One might even say that the place has absconded or been lost. [The non-site] is a map that will take you somewhere, but when you get there you won't really know where you are. In some sense the non-site is the centre of the system, and the site itself is the fringe or edge."[17] For Sharp, the location (the pier) was valuable primarily for its convenience (its openness and extensive space) and its lack of associations with art-making. For many of the artists, by contrast, it was something quite else: its identity and place within the urban milieu could not be ignored, nor could art associations or, better, aesthetic considerations, given that, for some of them, whatever they created necessarily required reference to the means and protocols of its making. When realized, the project became a composite artifact, a synthesis of documentary, conceptual, and process-based actions by multiple authors relayed through the medium of the camera. In its relation to its point of origin, the abandoned rotting wharf on the Hudson, *Projects: Pier 18* might be read, pace Smithson, as a non-site in relation to a site. Melding the curatorial, documentary, and artistic impulses in a novel, compound

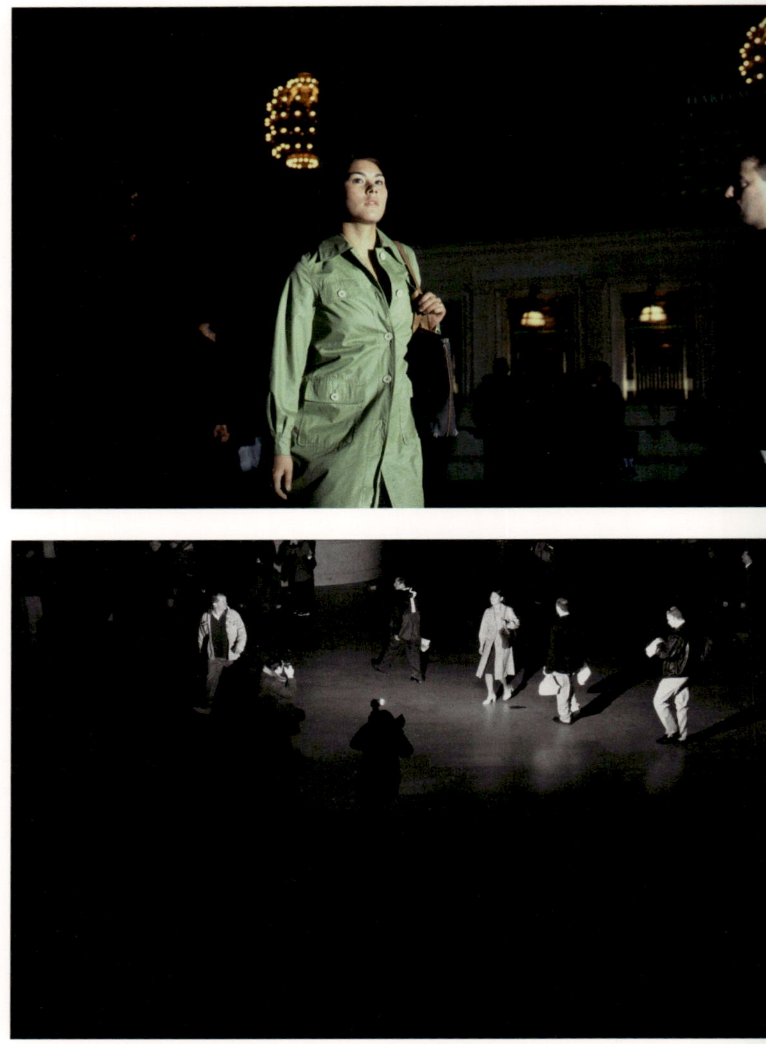

Plate 19 Barbara Probst, *Exposure #9: N.Y.C., Grand Central Station, 12.18.01, 1:21 p.m.*, 2001

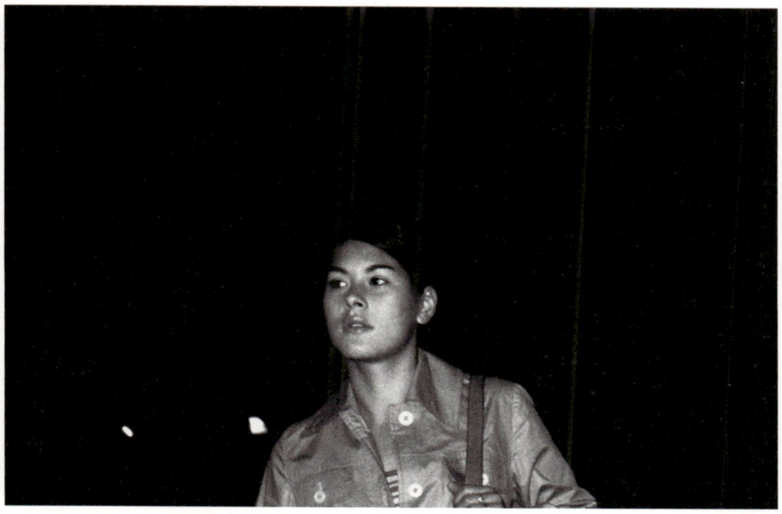

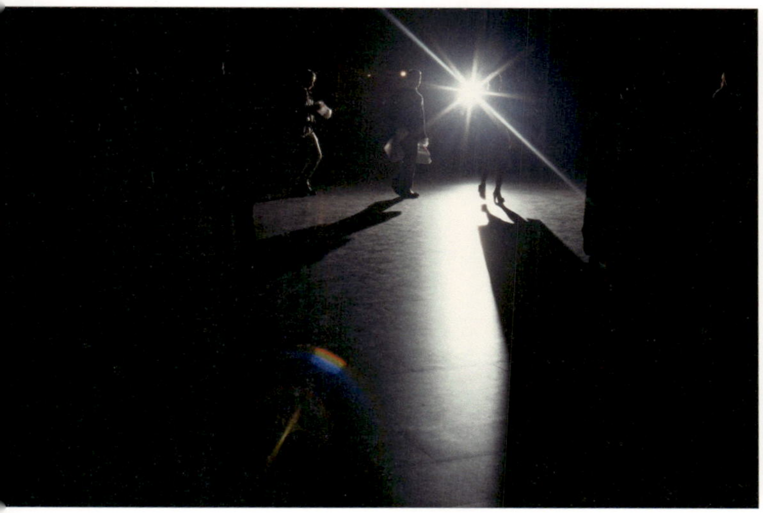

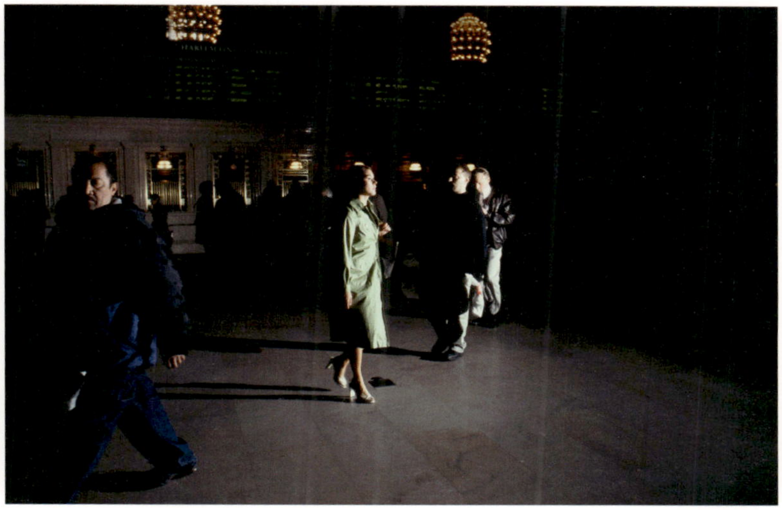

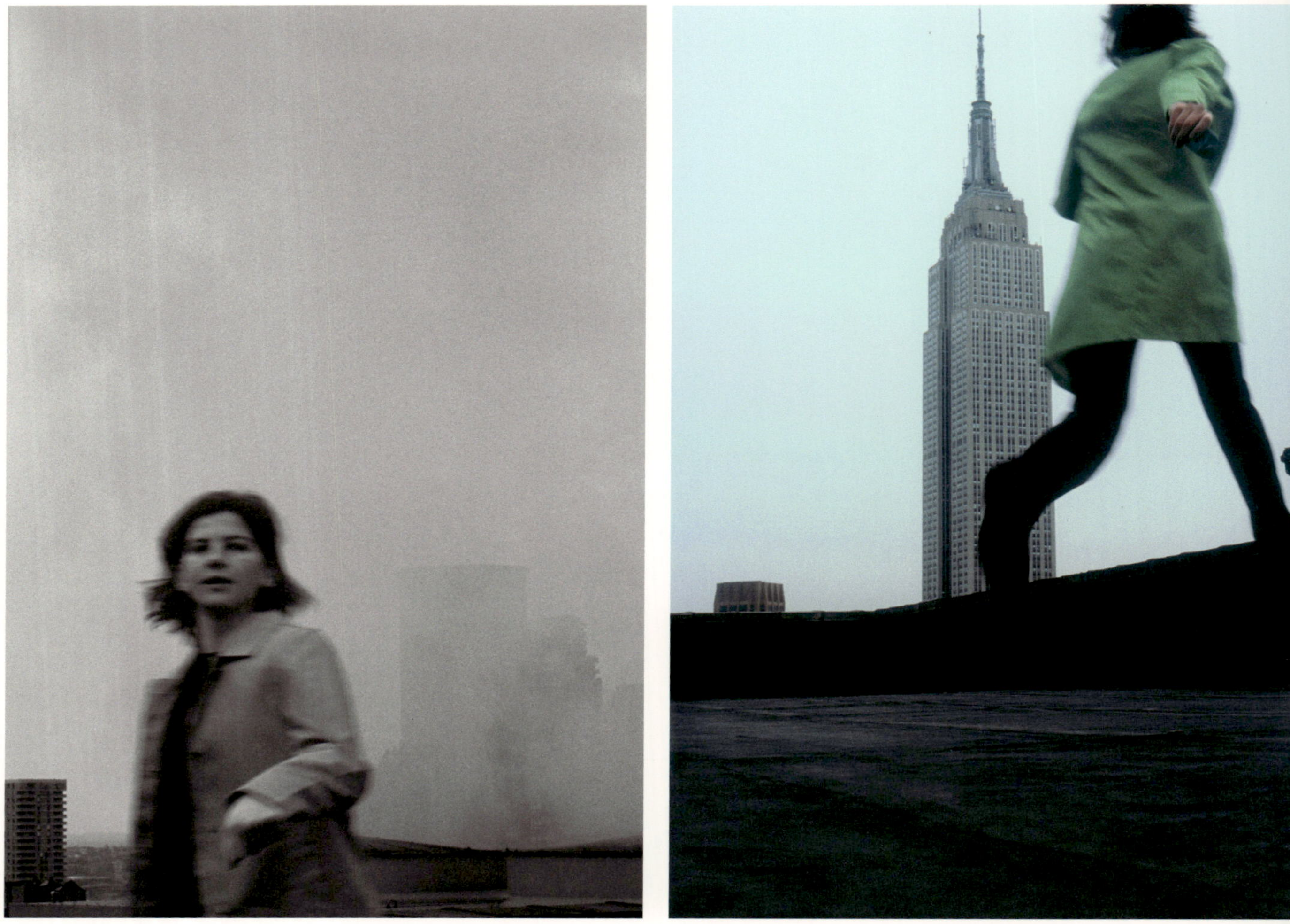

Plate 20 Barbara Probst, *Exposure #18: N.Y.C., 498 Seventh Avenue, 02.26.03, 1:29 p.m.*, 2003

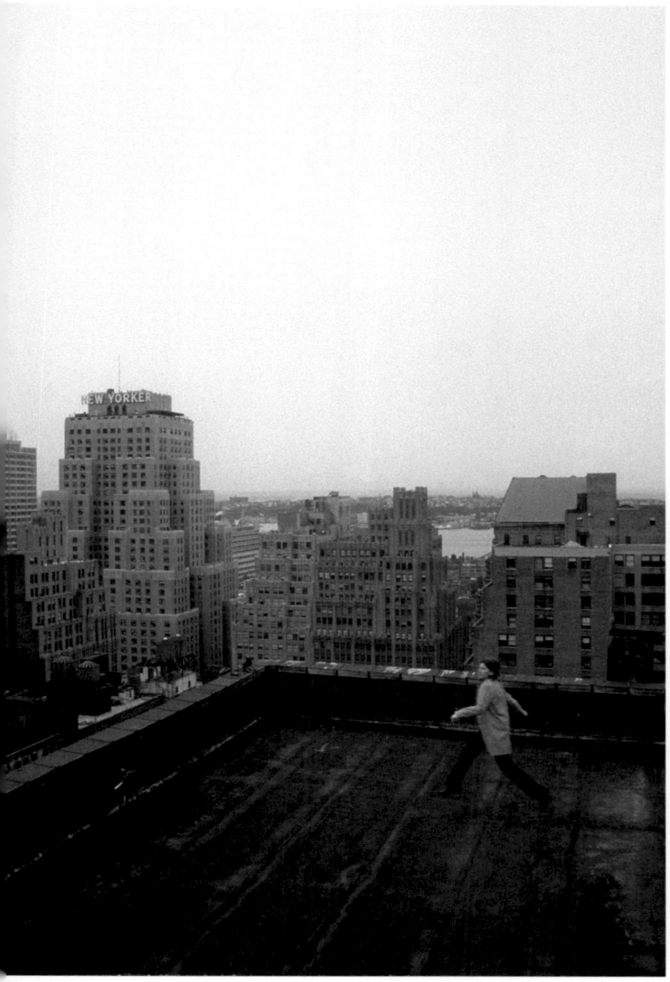
NEW YORKER

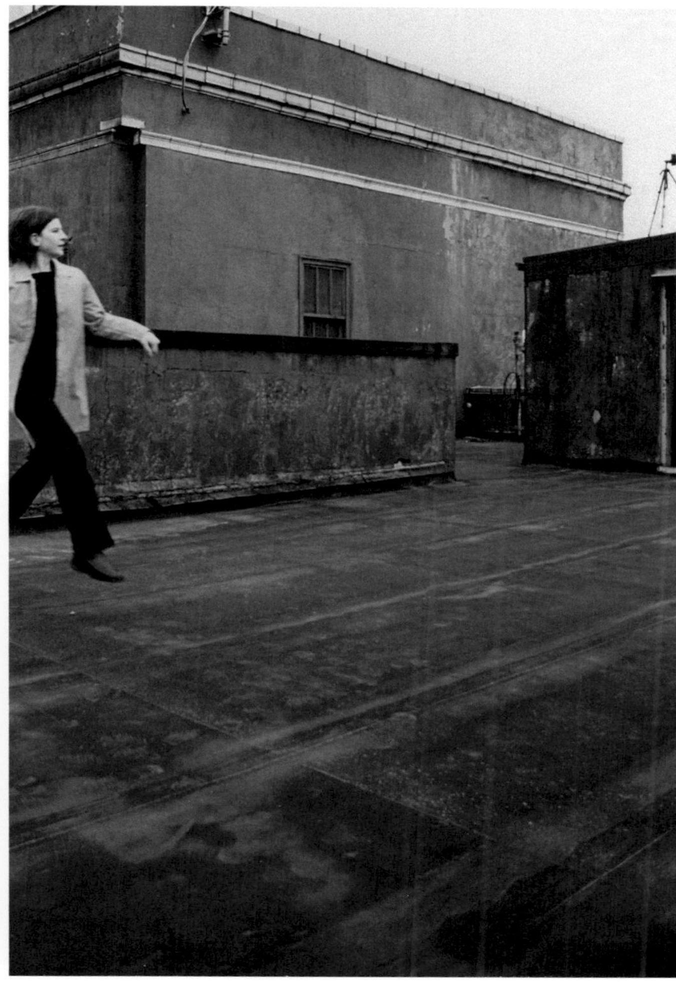

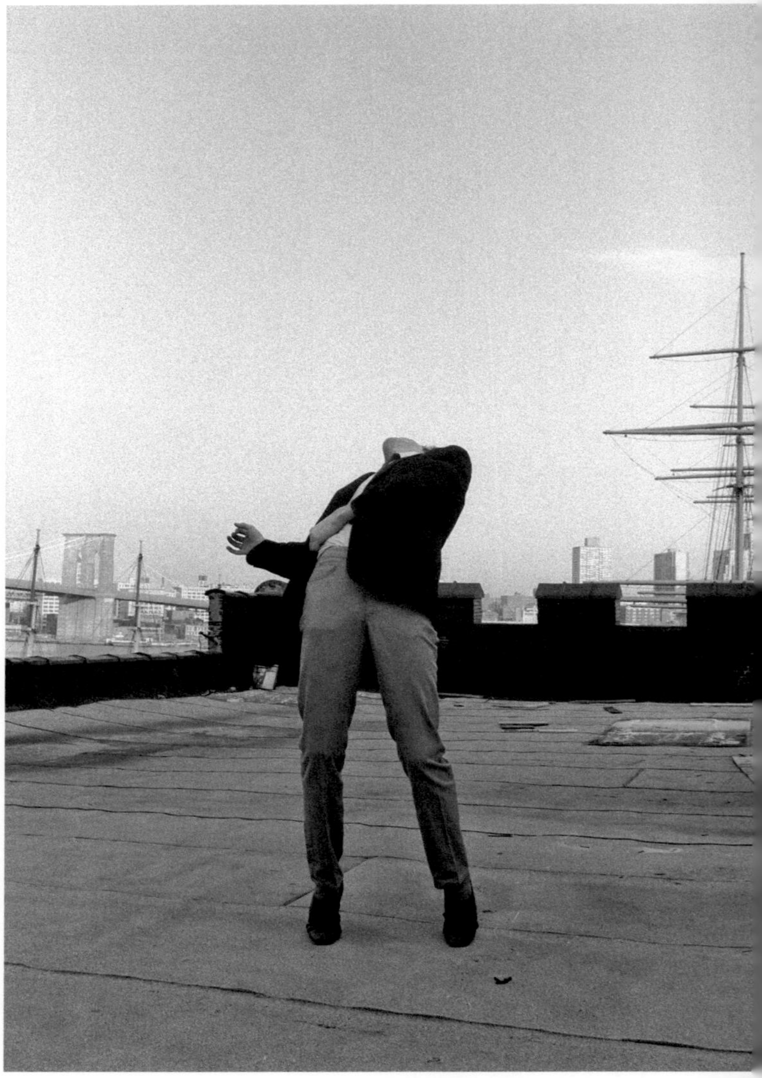

Plate 21 Robert Longo, *Untitled (Men in the Cities)*, 1979/2009

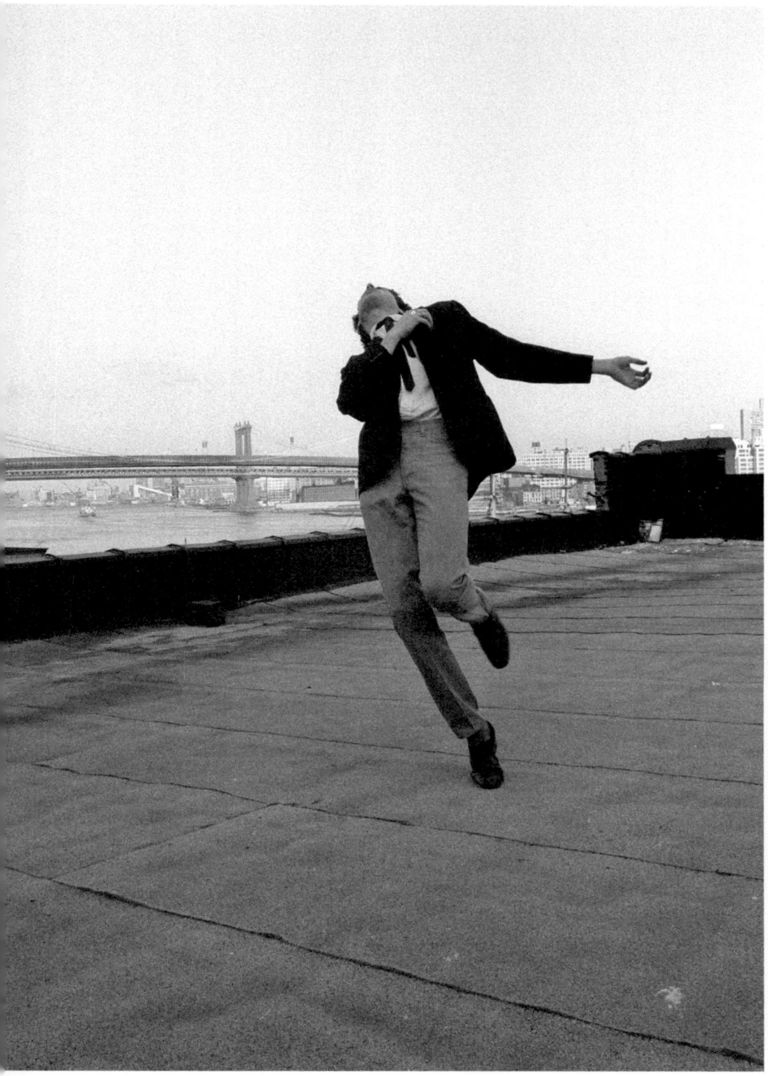

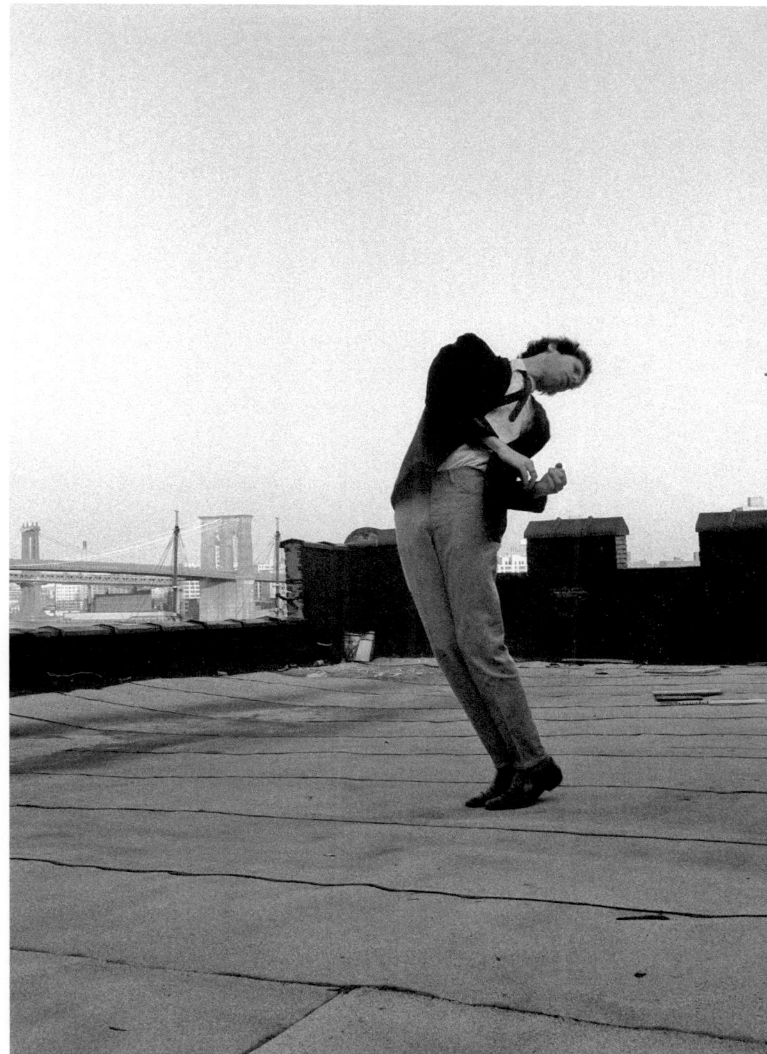

form, this singular project prefigures later conceptually generated works by a number of younger artists also included in this exhibition.

In yoking together professional photographers and artists, *Projects: Pier 18* proved immediately prophetic. In the early 70s, visual artists turned to the camera, sometimes making photographic, film, or video pieces an integral, if intermittent, part of their practices (as seen in the case of LeWitt) and sometimes simply recording ephemeral events, such as performances, dances, and acoustic projects. For example, percussionist-turned–visual artist Max Neuhaus designed flyers as invitations to his p. 39 *Listen* pieces, acoustic concerts composed of "worldly" sounds that he generated by means of tours he led through carefully selected downtown neighborhoods. Occasionally, these relationships took the form of "work-for-hire," as evidenced in p. 141 the series of *Lunar Rambles* screenings Terry Fox staged over five nights at the Kitchen in 1976. For these events, video footage (shot by an unacknowledged professional) of the acoustic pieces that Fox had performed that same day at various sites in Lower Manhattan, including the Brooklyn Bridge, was presented in conjunction with a sound installation. Other artists preferred neither to rely solely on their own often-limited skills with what were unfamiliar technologies nor to depend on professionals to document their actions. Instead, they preferred collaborative endeavors that went beyond the strictly documentary to become artworks in their own right.[18] Babette p. 103 Mangolte's photographs of Trisha Brown's *Roof Piece*, performed on SoHo rooftops in 1973, are exemplary of this kind of interaction, as is the film shot by Betsy Sussler and p. 149 Gordon Matta-Clark of *Day's End*, the installation Matta-Clark made on another derelict pier over the summer of 1975. Joan Jonas and vanguard cinematographer Robert Fiore (who had advised and worked with Robert Smithson on his *Spiral Jetty* pp. 100–101 film of 1970) collaborated on the landmark *Songdelay* (1973), based on Jonas's 1972 p. 124 performance of *Delay Delay* on an area of vacant lots where the Washington Market had once stood. And Rudy Burckhardt and Charles Simonds worked together to produce p. 263 *Dwellings Winter* (1974), a film of the sculptor creating miniature structures in another blighted locale, this time located on the Lower East Side.

Alfred Frankenstein concluded his review with a rousing paean to the devastated site that had generated *Projects: Pier 18* and to the artistic lineage into which it positioned these artists: "It seems to me that the choice of setting is important," he argued. "The deserted, tumble-down pier is the place for art, not the World Trade Center beyond. The artists are out of that world—at least these artists are—and into a world of the ramshackle, the derelict, and the discarded. This contrast is, of course," he conceded, "one of the hardy perennials of American art. In that sense, the conceptualists reaffirm a great tradition, and they are themselves among its most convincing practitioners."[19] With hindsight, Frankenstein seems to have been deeply wrong on two counts. It was not the "ramshackle, the derelict, and the discarded" that would continue to preoccupy artists but the opportunities offered by lens-based media that would

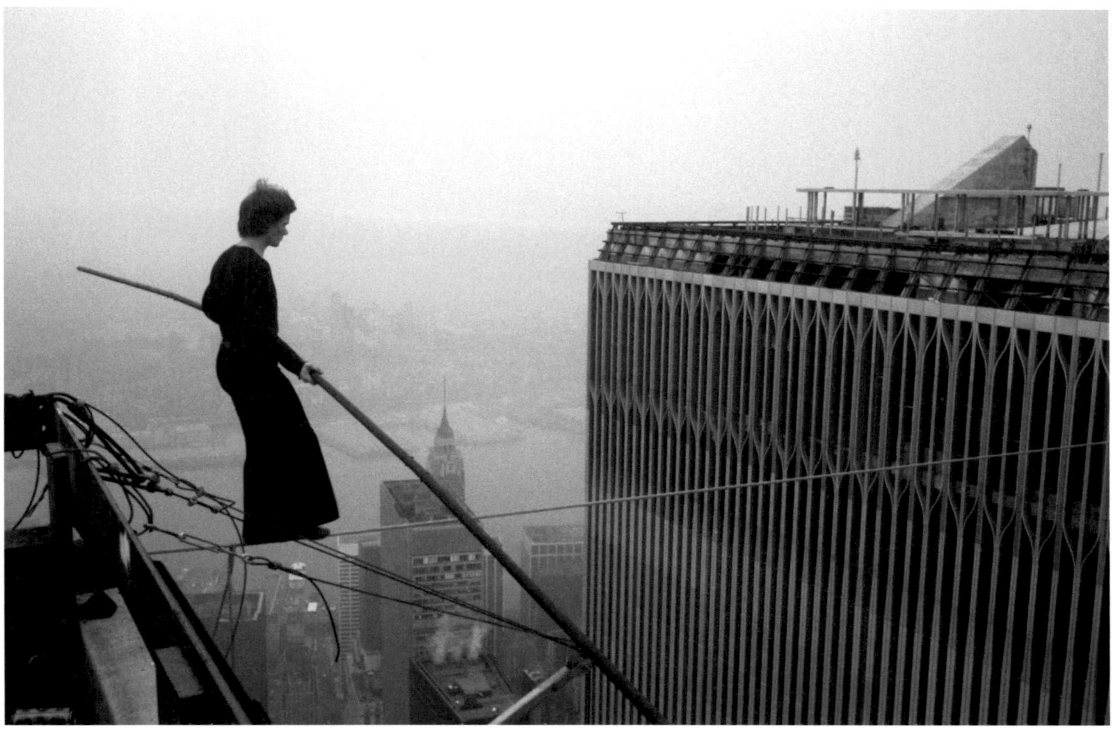

Philippe Petit on tightrope between the World Trade Center towers, August 7, 1974.
Photograph by Jean-Louis Blondeau

prove so fertile. Even Gabriel Orozco, who constructed a studiedly artless cityscape, dominated by the twin towers' iconic profile, from bits of timber scavenged from the riverbank, preserved his fragile scenario by means of the camera. Much reproduced,
p. 265
Island within an Island (*Isla en la Isla*) (1993) is but one of a small group of poetic images he captured at this time based mostly on observations of Manhattan's minutiae. Nor were the piers and similarly derelict sites to dominate artists' exclusive attention for long, as Frankenstein had prophesied. It took just three years for the World Trade Center to be commandeered as a prime art site. On the morning of August 7, 1974,
p. 49
twenty-four-year-old funambulist Philippe Petit strung a cable between the two buildings, which, as Lytle Shaw states, functioned as "a blatant embodiment of the transition from goods to services, from production and distribution to financial management."[20] According to the sergeant in the New York Police Department who arrested Petit for illegal trespass and disorderly conduct, his behavior during the forty-five minutes he performed on the wire suspended some 1,350 feet aboveground could more aptly have been described as dancing than as walking.[21] As news of this extraordinary feat flashed around the globe, Petit's "aesthetic assault"[22] on the building assumed iconic proportions: "Petit's act was that of an artist who, with supreme technical skill, took a public space and turned it into a place of personal expression," one critic opined recently when reviewing James Marsh's account of the episode, the 2008 film *Man on Wire*.[23] The original act was widely acclaimed as an extraordinary artistic gesture. Petit's feat, however, has now become inextricably interwoven with the tragic history of the twin towers. Even in Marsh's documentary, which makes no direct reference to the terrorist attacks of September 11, 2001, they underpin its every moment. For Ann Hornaday, of the *Washington Post*, his film did more than tell a "gripping, affecting story"; it was "deeply cathartic," she argued: "a place of loss and grief [was] transformed, briefly, into a place of transcendence and lyricism."[24] Cosmo Landesman, writing for London's *Sunday Times*, had a similar view: "It's been said that, with *Man on Wire*, we have, at last, the great 9/11 film.... One of the best things about this film is that it has taken the twin towers away from the terrorists, the killers and the destroyers, and given it [*sic*] back to the poets, the goofballs and the eccentrics—people who see a place to dance, not a chance to destroy."[25]

pp. 54–57
In Steve McQueen's *Static* (2009), as in Marsh's film, that history is referenced only elliptically.[26] At once mesmerizingly beautiful and deeply unsettling, *Static* takes as its ostensible subject the Statue of Liberty. Shooting from a helicopter that relentlessly circles the monument, McQueen moves in close to isolate details: the burning torch held aloft, the statue's idealized classical head, the book grasped in her left hand. As the immersive throbbing sound generated by the machine rises and falls, and the camera bounces and shakes, *Static* seems to cause the monument itself to grow unsteady. This destabilizing of the image suggests that were the statue to be pressed too directly, this icon of democracy would fracture into myriad meaningless shards.

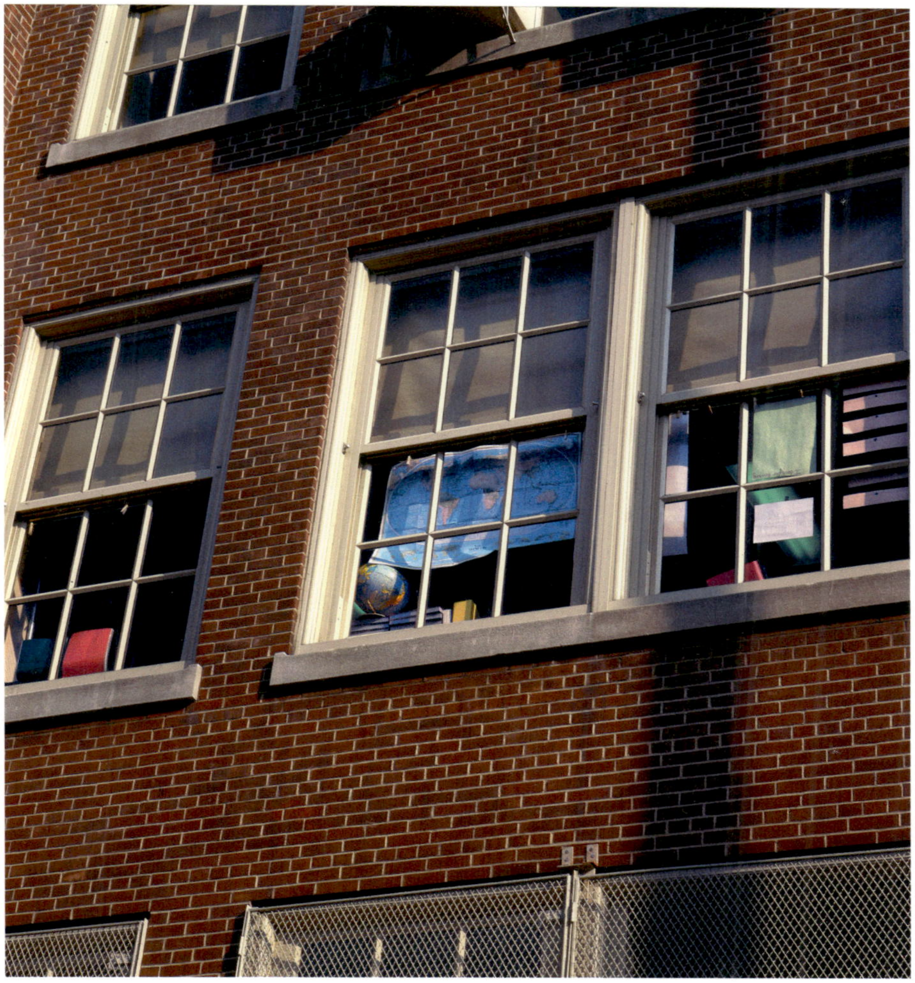

Plate 22 Jennifer Bolande, *Globe Sightings: Avenue B, Day, NYC*, 2000–2001

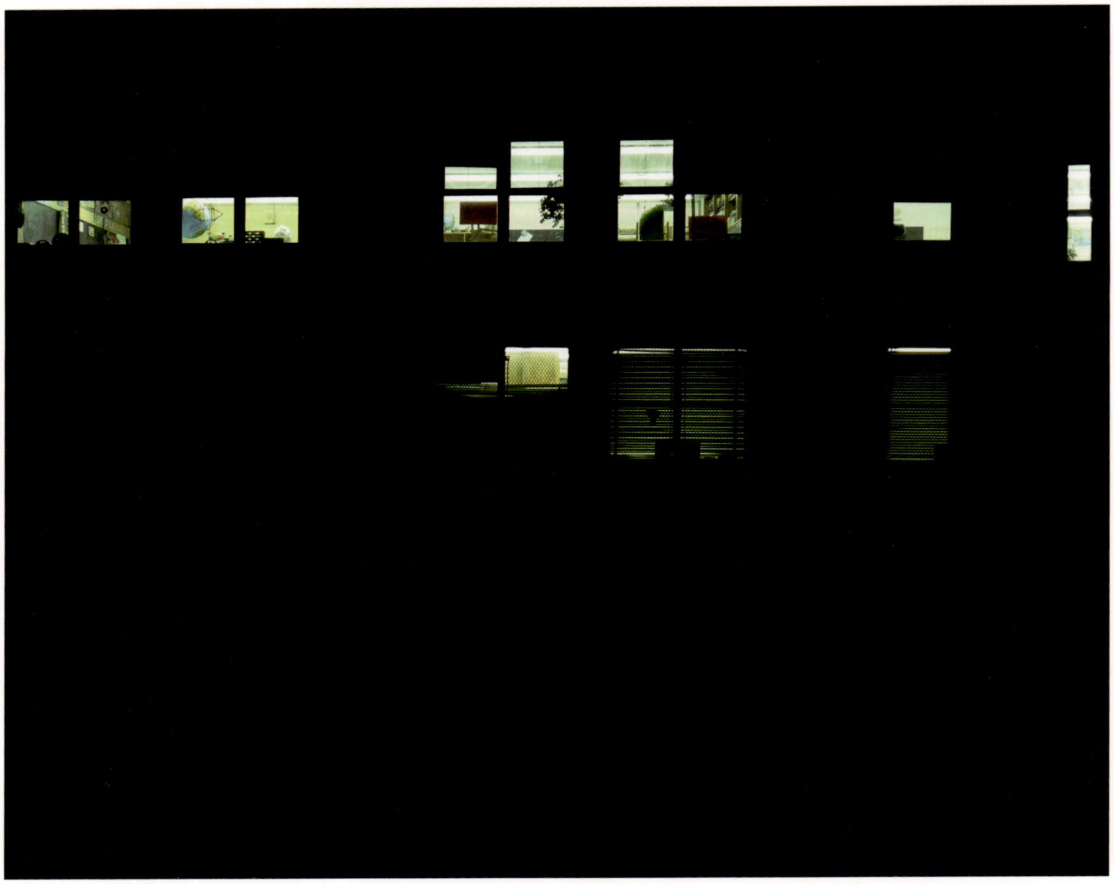

Plate 23 Jennifer Bolande, *Globe Sightings: Rutherford Place, NYC*, 2000–2001

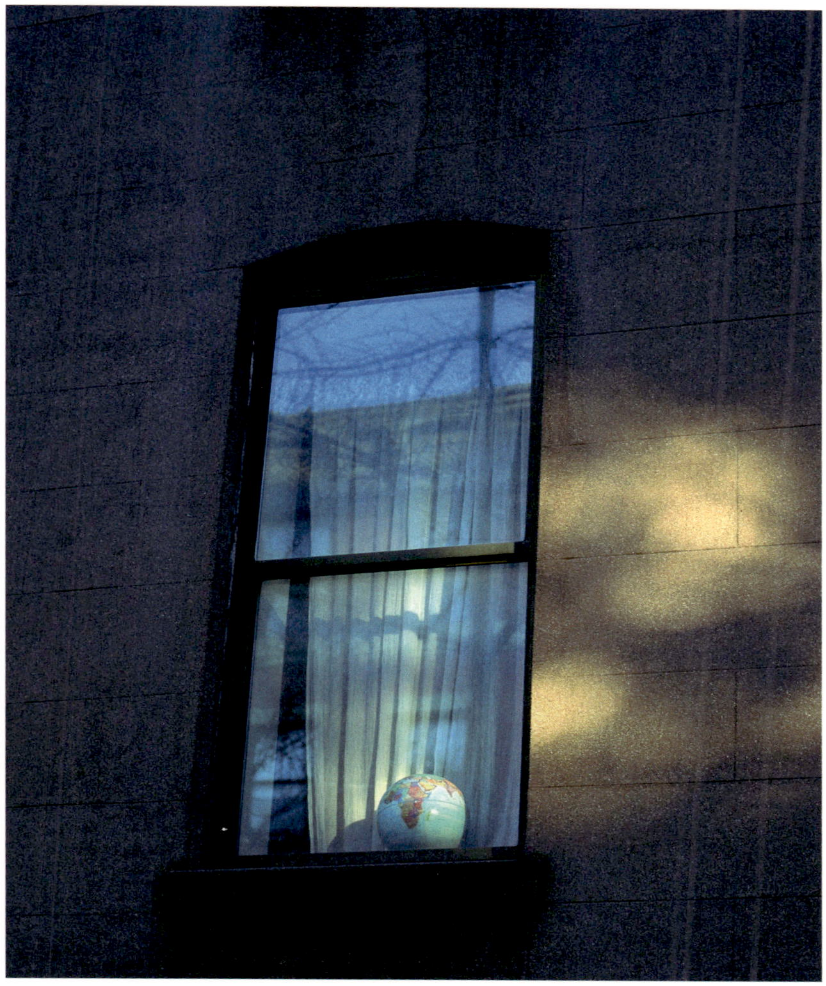

Plate 24 Jennifer Bolande, *Globe Sightings: St. Marks Place, NYC*, 2000–2001

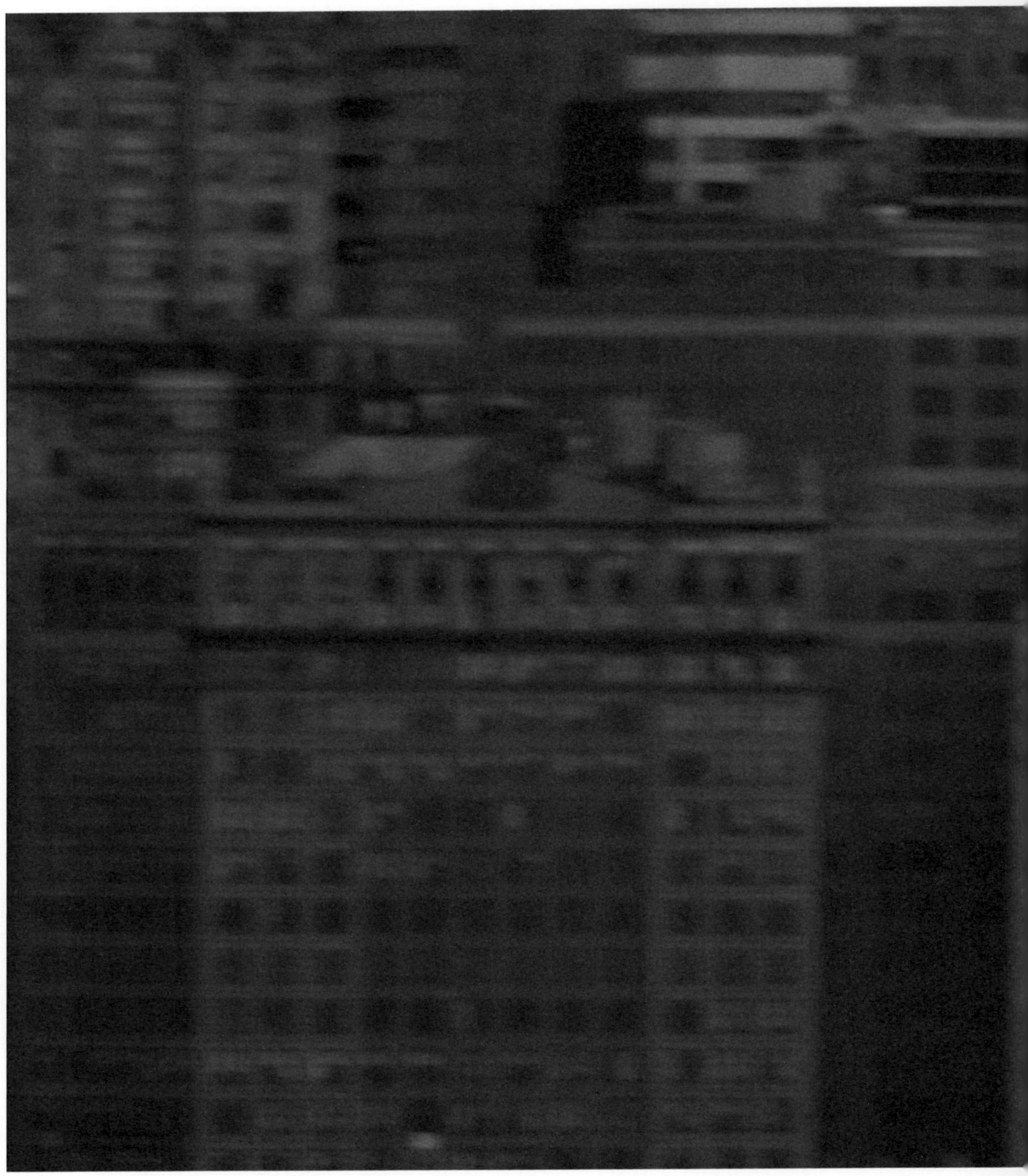

Plate 25 Steve McQueen, still from *Static*, 2009

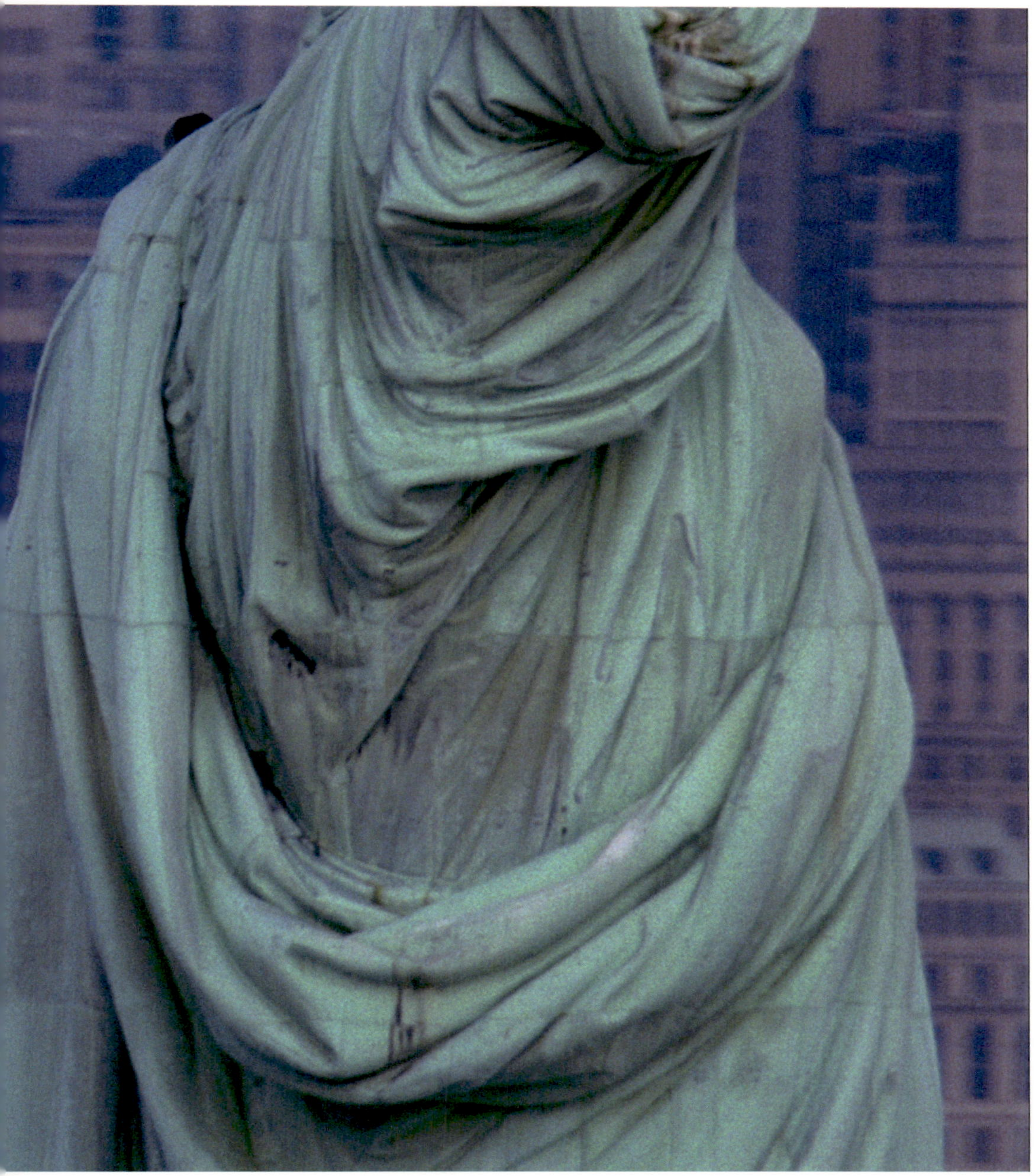

Plate 26 Steve McQueen, still from *Static*, 2009

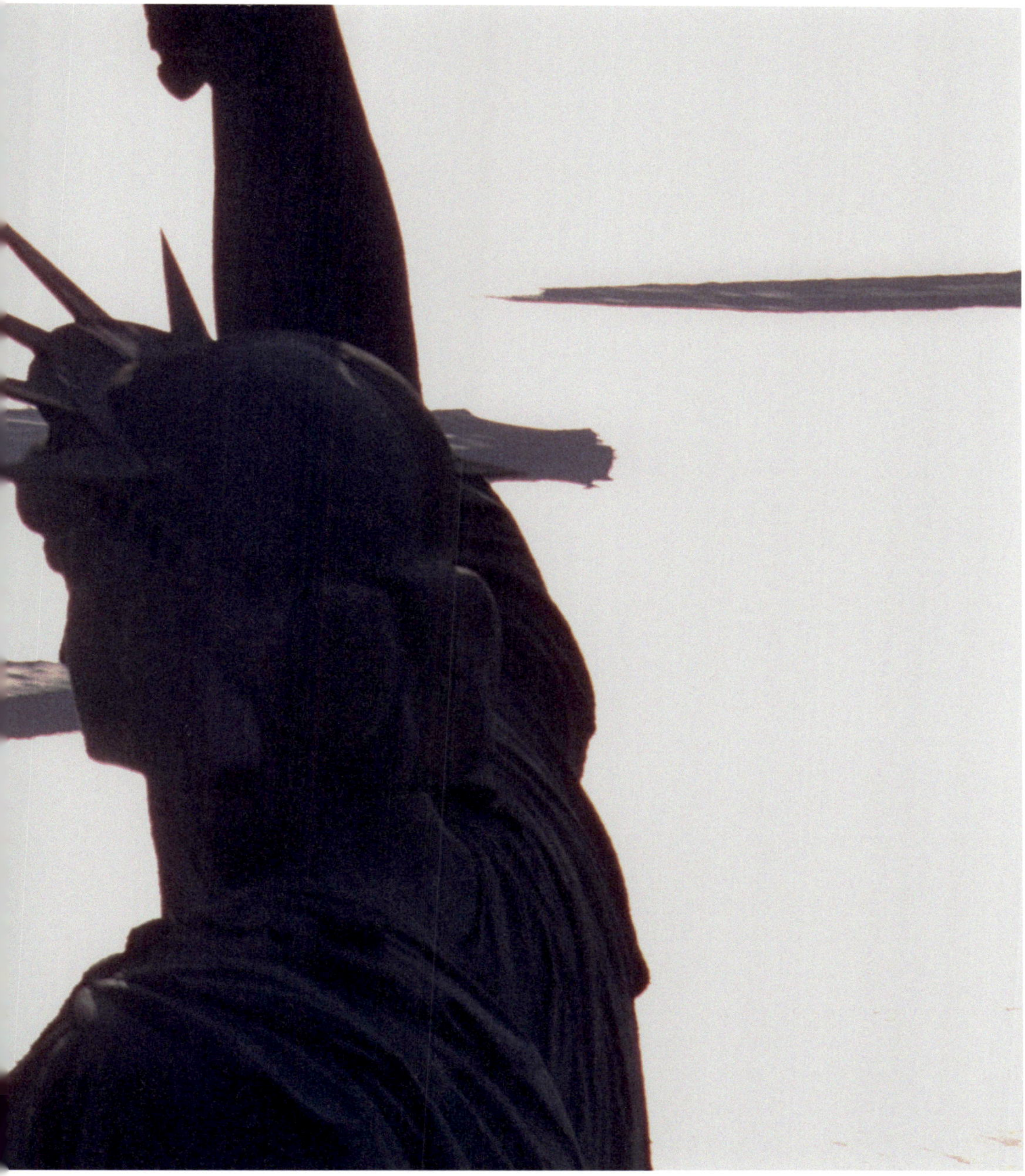

Static's charge derives in large part from its marked level of abstraction. Since the site's specifics constantly dissolve, and neither plotline nor anecdote disrupts the seamless loop, its point of address comes to stand outside historical time and geographic space.

Though it picks up directly from Petit's appreciation of the resonance of an iconic site, *Static* stands apart from most else produced recently and included here in its elision of overt references to history and context. For many younger artists referencing Manhattan today, the city can no longer be approached without a discursive filter—whether that be by reference to the past or via its ubiquitous mediatization. pp. 256–57 Matthew Buckingham's *One Side of Broadway* (2005) exists in two guises: a sixteen-minute slide piece with audio, and an artist's book. Each version is based (as the voice-over states at the beginning of the slide piece, and the text in the book's opening pages confirms) on Rudolph De Leeuw's publication from 1910, *Both Sides of Broadway.* The partiality of Buckingham's focus, like the doubling of the work's form, concedes that not only can the past not be remade but any endeavor to engage it must be partial in both senses of the term—incomplete and biased. Toward the end of the slide piece, the speaker becomes introspective: "Are these the words and images to use?" she asks herself and us, her audience. Further questions—"Am I speaking too loud, looking from too far away, or too close?"—are followed by yet others. In the book, the reader may discover a short note at the end of the text: "The text appearing on the last sixteen pages is excerpted from the voice-over narration of Jean-Luc Godard's motion picture, *Two or Three Things I Know About Her* (1967)."[27] Information that the voice-over contains a quotation from a Godard film is not vouchsafed to the audience of the slide piece. Does knowledge that the text (like the visual structure) was partly prefigured strengthen and ground its inquiry, underpinning its reflexivity, its sense that history is a process of constantly rewriting preexisting representations? What kind of efficacy, if any, does command of this piece of information represent? Does it serve to substantially differentiate the two projects, so that they no longer can be seen as equivalents or counterparts, and, in so doing, reinforce recognition of the limitations inherent in all acts of transmission and translation?

Like Buckingham, Vera Lutter engages a historical frame determined, on the one hand, by associations particular to her medium and, on the other, by her choice of subject. In 1994 and 1995, she temporarily transformed four offices in the pp. 30–33 headquarters of the German financial company HypoBank into camera obscuras. Four images made with this age-old pinhole technique reveal Manhattan's sky- and shoreline from four different directions in negative. In these spectral prints, New York's past, as a center of international commerce, and its present, as a financial capital, join forces. For Lutter's reference to outmoded photographic technologies, coupled with the ethereality of the resulting images—which seem to lack not only detail but substance—evokes an industrial waterfront now largely defunct: the decline that set in with the introduction of containerization, which moved the port of New York to New Jersey's harbor, was soon reinforced by a broader-based replacement of goods with services. Encapsulated in the view from on high, at a distancing remove, so to speak, is the immateriality and abstraction characteristic of the corporate sector that dominates this part of the city.

Barbara Probst, a Munich-based artist who has lived intermittently in Manhattan, stages photographs that highlight the sense of spectacularization and mediatization that has come to infuse almost any location in Manhattan. Appending the precise address and time of day as titles to her works, she deploys this register in counterpoint to generic and stereotypical formulations, scenes that could come out of any lifestyle magazine or fashion spread. Camerapersons are often revealed in the multiple shots that capture their quarry from different angles, with different lenses, and on different film stocks. The voyeurism that has become so much a part of everyday Manhattan life, subject as it is now to a barrage of television series, movies, advertisements, and the like, is Probst's key subtext. Whether or not we live there on its endlessly reproduced shores, it has become an unavoidable point of almost daily reference. pp. 42–45

Although Jennifer Bolande, like Probst, also reveals the address of the site where she found her motif in her titles, Bolande's *Globe Sightings* series eschews the evident finesse and high-tech resources the German artist requires to stage her work. Bolande's images seem disarmingly modest, deceptively mundane. Their vantage points were wherever the artist could best position herself, sidling up close to the building when possible, trespassing when necessary, and making do with whatever light was available. Meditating on the fascination the globe holds for others as well as for herself, Bolande writes: "The famous first photograph of earth from space is cited by many as having triggered a consciousness raising, which led to the Green movement among other things. Although [that image was shot] not so long ago, it seems hard to imagine today that a photograph could have such power."[28] Although her project began by chance in 1977 when she was living in New York, after relocating to Los Angeles in 2002 she continued the series there, as well as in other cities whenever she happened upon the motif. The actual sites are therefore largely incidental in that they have little significance beyond the fact that they range widely geographically and encompass a variety of locations: domestic interiors, schools, stores. Bolande characterizes her role as "part anthropologist...part flaneur, voyeur, witness...discoverer...audience." Tucked and squeezed onto sills, the fragile spheres reveal that the early belief in photography as a "window onto the world" has been redefined. "Today, the word 'global' is ubiquitous and applied to all manner of things," she argues. "I try to reconcile what the word conjures with the wistful entities peering back at me through countless windows. It seems to me that the idea of the earth is shrinking daily in our imagination. These photographs catch and perhaps stall the earth in its transit through our collective imaginations."[29] In this reading, Manhattan has become an everyplace. Images like these could be shot in countless places around the world, while the commonality of pp. 51–53 an impulse so widely shared is attested through the medium's traditional evidentiary properties. Once again, photography is not merely used to reflect the world but to shape a discourse about both that world and the medium's place within it.

★

"Could this city be ours?" was a title that co-curator Douglas Crimp proposed at an early point during the planning of this exhibition. As his essay details, Douglas is a longtime resident of Manhattan and activist in the downtown scene. His question was couched in the present tense. While it was presumably asked often, and expectantly, in that earlier, openly activist era, what is perhaps surprising is how strongly it still resonates for certain artists working now: Moyra Davey, Zoe Leonard, Glenn Ligon, and Sharon Hayes, among others. As Douglas and I pondered it, the difficulty with choosing it as the title came to seem less a question of whether it might be possible to answer it affirmatively—and, if so, in what terms—than the problem of who the "we" it implied might be. In retrospect, now that the show has taken shape and the list of participants has been finalized, this seems less of an issue. "We" are all those who choose to be part of the audience for this exhibition. Manhattan is a non-site—it exists for all of us virtually, imaginatively, through the lens of media (noir films, television series, postcards, and souvenirs)—as well as a site, a sociocultural and historical place. While for some artists, and viewers, the point of address may begin here, in the local and specific, for many others, Gotham City will serve primarily as a touchstone, a point of departure for questions aimed elsewhere.[30]

As we debated the title, so we also mulled over whether to include
p. 12 Lyon's frontispiece to *The Destruction of Lower Manhattan* among the group of his images
we planned to show. Its role as a prologue in that book is clear. Literally set apart from all that follows, its vision of an encompassing, pristine wholeness is in many ways contradicted and undermined by what follows. As we speculated on what might serve as a frontispiece to our show, we realized we already had it in hand. It would be one or the other of two pictures Zoe Leonard took in 1989 of the Panorama of the City of New York built in 1964 for the New York World's Fair by order of Robert Moses and housed in the Queens Museum of Art since its opening in 1972. Grainy, fragmentary,
p. 4 unevenly lit, one shot crops the panorama so that the West Side piers slide out of the
bottom right-hand edge of the frame, and midtown dissolves in darkness. Leonard's
p. 276 second shot is rendered similarly contingent and partial by the intrusion of the gallery's
fluorescent lighting system. What makes Leonard's and Lyon's pictures so radically different is not merely their subjects but their aesthetics and the values they encode. "Our" frontispiece depicts a model—a construction, a fabrication, a hypothesis...

Endnotes

1
Titled *Analogue* (1998–2007), this work exists in three forms: a monumental environmental piece comprising nearly four hundred images; a series of forty photographs culled from the larger corpus, produced as dye transfer prints; and a book, *Analogue* (Columbus, OH: Wexner Center for the Arts; Cambridge, MA: MIT Press, 2007).

2
Danny Lyon, "Epilogue," in *The Destruction of Lower Manhattan* (New York: Powerhouse Books, 2005), unpaginated.

3
Ibid.

4
Danny Lyon, "Introduction," in *The Destruction of Lower Manhattan* (New York: Macmillan, 1969), unpaginated. When it was reprinted in 2005, the book contained seventy-three images. That the resulting photographs were first presented in the form of a book rather than an exhibition was typical for this period. The first exhibition featuring these prints was held in 2005 at the Museum of the City of New York.

5
Perhaps it is no surprise to learn that Lyon, eager to move on to his next self-defined project, had left the city even before he signed the contract on a book that would eventually come to be viewed as anomalous among his better-known publications. These typically focused on people—bikers, prison inmates, and other denizens of subcultural communities—located in the farther reaches of the United States.

6
What Was True: The Photographs and Notebooks of William Gedney, ed. Margaret Sartor with Geoff Dyer (New York: Center for Documentary Studies, 2000), p. 47. I am deeply indebted to this sole publication on Gedney. A loner, by all accounts, Gedney never seems to have pushed his projects for his Manhattan-based works to a final form. Gedney's work and archive are now housed in the Rare Book, Manuscript, and Special Collections Library at Duke University, Durham, North Carolina.

7
Stefan Brecht, *8th Avenue* (Paris: Onestar Press, 2006) and *8th Avenue Poems* (New York: Spuyten Duyvil, 2006).

8
Christopher Wool, *East Broadway Breakdown* (Berlin: Holzwarth Publications, 2003).

9
This law applied only to SoHo; it was only in 1982, when the New York state legislature passed the Loft Law, that loft living in other parts of Manhattan became legal. See the timeline in this volume, pp. 277–82.

10
For many artists, working in such locations was not considered a rejection of the museum or gallery scene but complementary to it, something that went on in parallel—opportunities of another kind.

11
By the beginning of the 1970s, Sharp, a denizen of Lower Manhattan, was renowned for a number of innovative projects. In 1969, he curated a show devoted to Earth Art for Cornell University in Ithaca, New York, that included both works in the galleries and in situ pieces outdoors from key exponents of this emerging practice, including Dennis Oppenheim and Robert Morris. Not only was it the first exhibition devoted to the subject, it also broke ground by including only new commissions, that is, works specifically created for the exhibition. In 1970, the first issue of what was to prove a highly regarded magazine during this period, *Avalanche*, continued the focus on the subject of Earth Art by devoting the greater part of its debut volume to the new phenomenon. See Willoughby Sharp, *Earth Art* (Ithaca, NY: Andrew Dickson White Museum of Art, Cornell University, 1970) and "Discussions with Heizer, Oppenheim, Smithson," *Avalanche* 1 (Fall 1970), pp. 48–71. Founded by Sharp and Liza Bear, *Avalanche* prioritized the voices of artists over those of critics and art historians. Typically, its pages were devoted to extensively illustrated projects by individual artists, coupled with a long interview. In place of exhibition reviews, it had two columns, "Rumbles" and "Messages," which commented in a colloquial manner to its inner circle of readers on artists' doings and related art-world activities. Produced from its headquarters on Grand Street in SoHo, which also hosted occasional performances, screenings, and other events, *Avalanche* was seen as the voice of the downtown art world, as opposed to *Artforum*, the other influential publication of the day, then noted for its theoretical and critical coverage. Gwen Allen argues that Smithson's site/non-site dialectic offers a compelling model for the relationship between *Avalanche* and the art it documented in Lower Manhattan ("Against Criticism: The Artist Interview in *Avalanche* Magazine, 1970–76," *Art Journal* 64, no. 3 [Fall 2005], p. 52). Dennis Oppenheim, who, like Smithson, met Sharp for the first time when working on the Cornell project, described him as "an artist curator" and not "an artists' curator," though he was that, too.

12
Quoted in Grace Glueck, "Art Notes: Surprise Catch from Pier 18," *New York Times*, July 25, 1971, Section D, p. 22.

13
Harry Shunk and János Kender were already well known for their images of vanguard *Nouveau Réaliste* works, including the picture of Yves Klein's (fabricated) fabled leap into the void. For Sharp and many of the artists he featured in the pages of *Avalanche*, photography was an essential part of their practice. Illustrations were to become as important to *Avalanche*'s style as its texts, most of which would incorporate the words of artists. Whether in the guise of cutting-edge celebrity shots designed for the magazine's cover, or the extensive record of the process of making an artwork by a featured artist, photography was a central feature of Sharp's publications, as well as of his curatorial projects. For Sharp, as for certain of these featured artists, notably Robert Smithson, the pages of a magazine could function as an exhibition space.

14
Glueck, "Art Notes," p. 22.

15
Alfred Frankenstein, "Pier 18 Conceptual Projects of Artists," *San Francisco Sunday Examiner & Chronicle*, July 4, 1971, p. 30. The illustrations in the copy of this article in Sharp's archive have been neatly decorated by stamps that say "BULLSHIT" in bold blue capitals or that show a fist giving the finger. In addition, there is a handwritten addendum: the word "Art" is followed by "(or the emperor's new clothes)"; and the word "Conceptual," ringed in blue, gives rise to "in this case the 'concept' is synonomous [*sic*] with a huge put on."

16
MoMA's press release, dated July 1971, stated: "The exhibition consists of series of photographs by Shunk-Kender documenting the work of twenty-seven artists.... The artists were invited to use the pier by Willoughby Sharp." Years later, after Shunk bought out the ailing Kender from a partnership that had grown increasingly sour, Shunk endeavored to remove Kender's name from all their work, including this complex project. The version that was presented at the Musée d'Art Moderne et d'Art Contemporain in Nice, in 1992, is titled simply *Harry Shunk, Projects: Pier 18*. In the interview in the catalogue, Shunk recounts that it was because of a visit to "mon studio" by MoMA curators Jennifer Licht and Kynaston McShine that the show was presented there. Loïc Malle and Harry Shunk, "Entretien," *Harry Shunk, Projects: Pier 18* (Nice: Musée d'Art Moderne et d'Art Contemporain, 1992), p. 13.

17
"Discussions with Heizer, Oppenheim, Smithson," p. 67. In the interview devoted to a discussion of the Earth Art show at Cornell that had been featured in the first issue of *Avalanche*, Smithson's cinematic masterpiece, the *Spiral Jetty* film (not a documentary but a 35mm non-site), offered another brilliant lesson to the quick-thinking Sharp, an expansion of the non-site into a gallery installation. (Smithson at first re/presented the *Spiral Jetty* in a sequence of photographs in Kynaston McShine's *Information* show at MoMA in summer 1970; by autumn, he had created the *Spiral Jetty* film as the gallery-based counterpart to the sculpture on the shores of the Great Salt Lake.) Shunk-Kender's role as professional photographers in *Projects: Pier 18* might be likened to that played

by the cinematographer Robert Fiore in generating Smithson's filmic non-site of the *Spiral Jetty*.

18

This distinction forms one of the central premises determining the selection of this show: all the works on view may be considered artworks in their own right; everything that could be deemed simply documentation of performances or installations has been excluded.

19

Frankenstein, "Pier 18," p. 31.

20

See Lytle Shaw, "The Powers of Removal: Interventions in the Name of the City," p. 230 in this volume.

21

A. O. Scott, "Walking on Air between the Towers," *New York Times*, July 25, 2008, Section E, p. 1.

22

Ibid.

23

Ann Hornaday, "A Walk across Space and Time," *Washington Post*, August 8, 2008, Weekend section, p. 24.

24

Ibid.

25

Cosmo Landesman, "When Art Went over the Edge," *Sunday Times* (London), August 3, 2008, Features section, p. 14. Similar remarks have been made about Colum McCann's book *Let the Great World Spin* (New York: Random House, 2009), called "the first great 9/11 novel" in that it too focuses on Petit's feat and not the events of 2001, though they are ever-present in the reader's mind.

26

In its intermittent silhouetting of the monument against the boundless sky, *Static* also brings to mind Petit's aerial escapade, though there is no known footage of the Frenchman's walk between the towers. One striking difference in the staging of the two works is that Petit's was an extraordinary coup carried out clandestinely and illegally (and, in that respect, of its time with many of the art projects referenced here, including *Projects: Pier 18* and Matta-Clark's *Day's End*). By contrast, McQueen readily secured permission to approach and film a landmark that for several years after 9/11 was wholly, or partially, off-limits to the general public. (On August 3, 2004, the pedestal level was reopened for visitation, but only on July 4, 2009, was the statue's crown restored to public access.) The full title of Frederic-Auguste Bartholdi's monument, often described as the most famous statue known today, is *Liberty Enlightening the World* (1886).

27

Matthew Buckingham, *One Side of Broadway* (Münster: Wesfälischer Kunstverein; St. Gallen: Kunstverein St. Gallen; Frankfurt: Revolver, 2005), unpaginated.

28

Jennifer Bolande, unpublished text, 2002.

29

Ibid.

30

Bolande, McQueen, and Probst no longer live in New York City, although each has spent varying periods there. Residence was never a requirement for the artists included in this exhibition, just as community was arguably always more a question of commonality than of a self-defining cohesive unity. Unsigned, unmarked, Max Neuhaus's acoustic work *Times Square* (1977–) has been installed in a subway grating on Broadway between 45th and 46th streets for more than three decades. Resistant to audio recording and visual documentation, it is available only to those who actually experience it and who thereby perceive how space is shaped and formed, and hence how place is determined through the introduction of an almost imperceptible electronically generated sound within a given acoustic, social, and material environment. Whatever sense of community is galvanized by this work is a function of serendipity, coexistence, and contiguity. It automatically encompasses those who recognize and engage with the work, but as Branden Joseph argues, referencing Giorgio Agamben's 1990 text *The Coming Community*, this fugitive collectivity implies and entails nothing beyond itself at that moment: for it is built on "adjacency rather than identification with whatever exclusionary ideal." Branden Joseph, "An Implication of an Implication," in *Max Neuhaus: Times Square/Time Piece Beacon* (New York: Dia Art Foundation, 2009), p. 76. Neuhaus's work, unlike most works in this exhibition, depends on being there: it cannot be known through representation, and no non-site could be imagined for it.

Projects: Pier 18 Shunk-Kender

Photographs by Harry Shunk and János Kender

Curated by Willoughby Sharp

Participating artists

Vito Acconci
David Askevold
John Baldessari
Robert Barry
Bill Beckley
Mel Bochner
Daniel Buren
Jan Dibbets
Terry Fox
Dan Graham
Douglas Huebler
Lee Jaffe
Richard Jarden
Gordon Matta-Clark
Mario Merz
Robert Morris
Dennis Oppenheim
Allen Ruppersberg
John van Saun
Italo Scanga
Richard Serra
Michael Snow
Keith Sonnier
Wolfgang Stoerchle
George Trakas
William Wegman
Lawrence Weiner

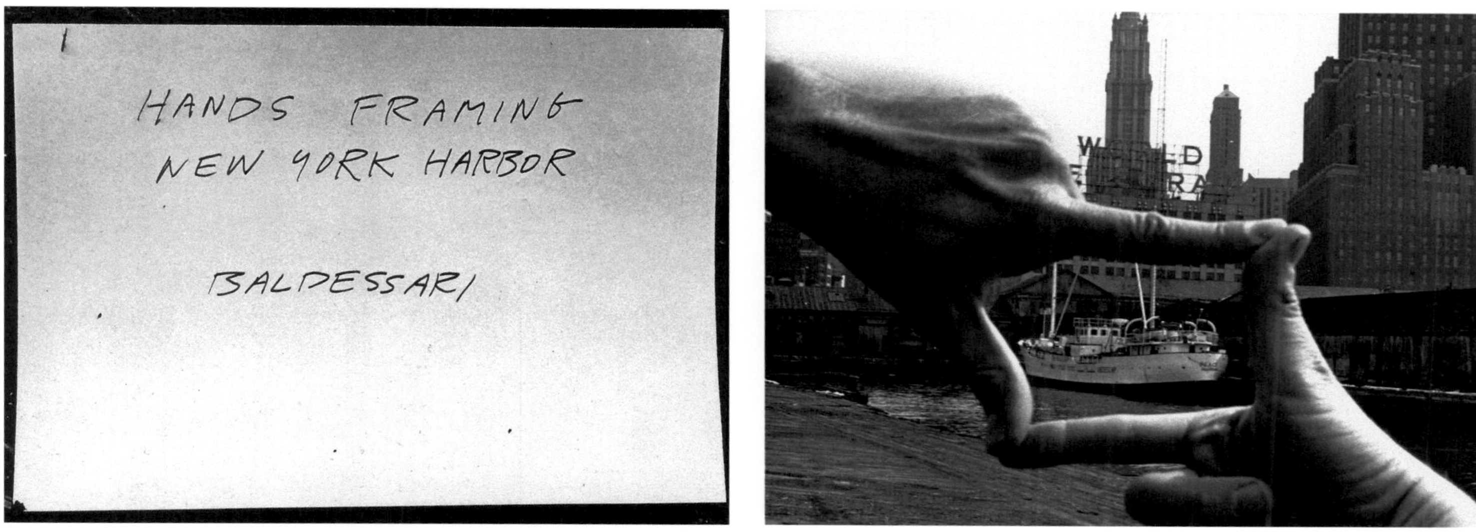

Plate 27 John Baldessari, *Hands Framing New York Harbor* (from *Projects: Pier 18*), 1971

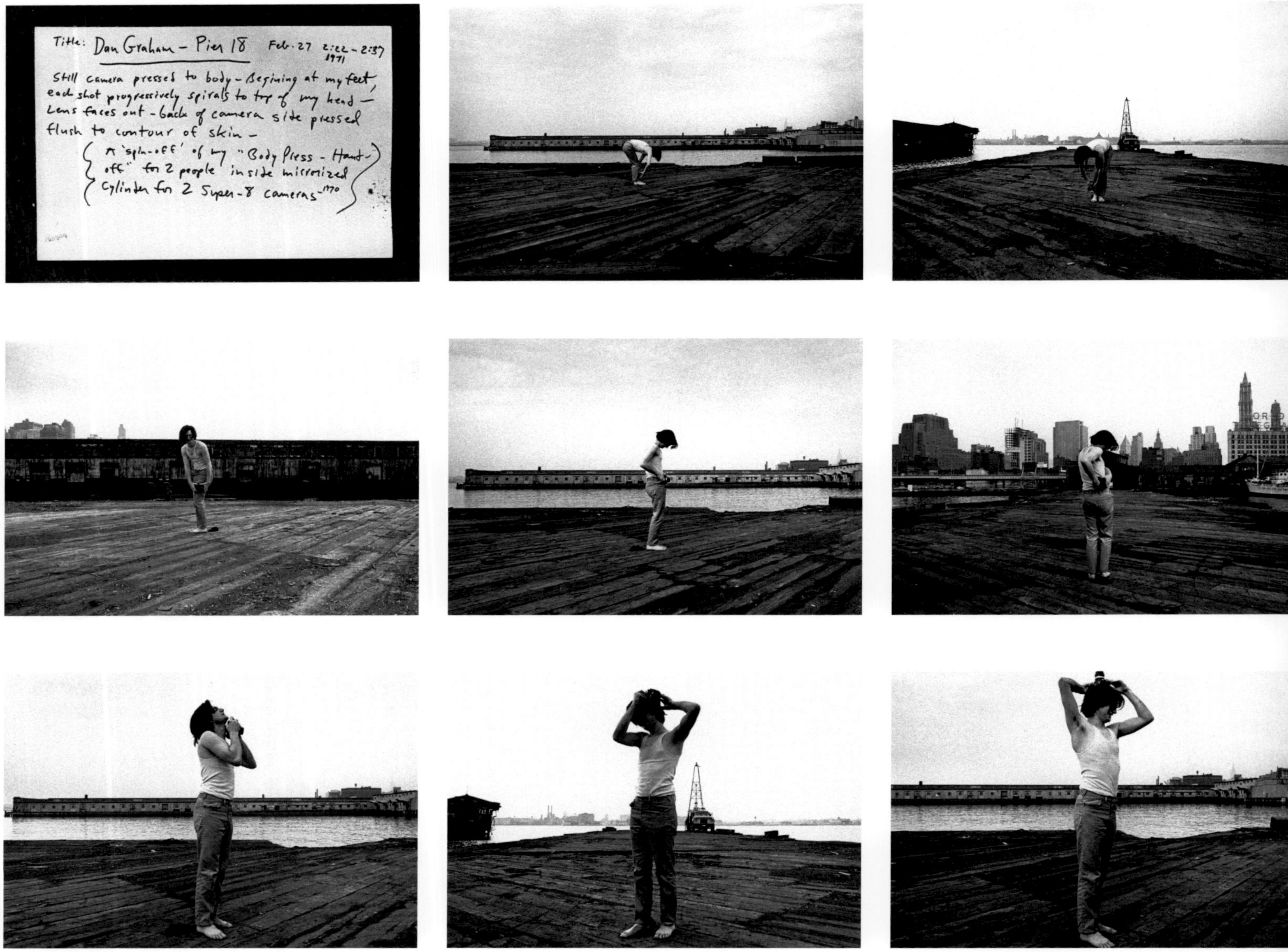

Plates 28–29 Dan Graham, *Dan Graham—Pier 18* (from *Projects: Pier 18*), 1971

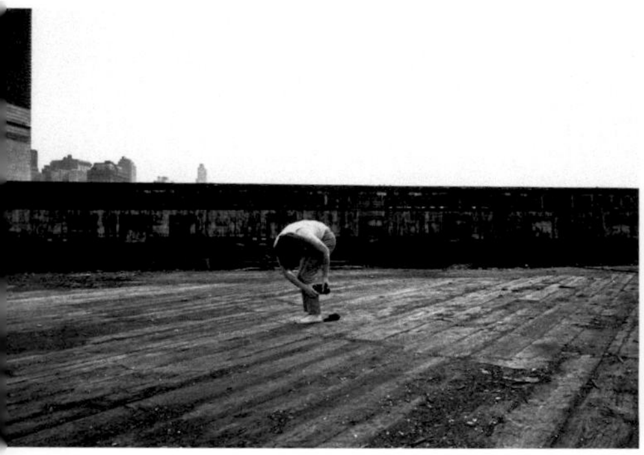

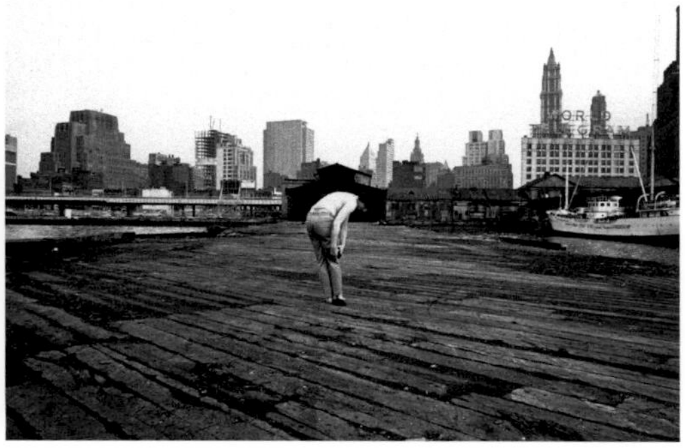

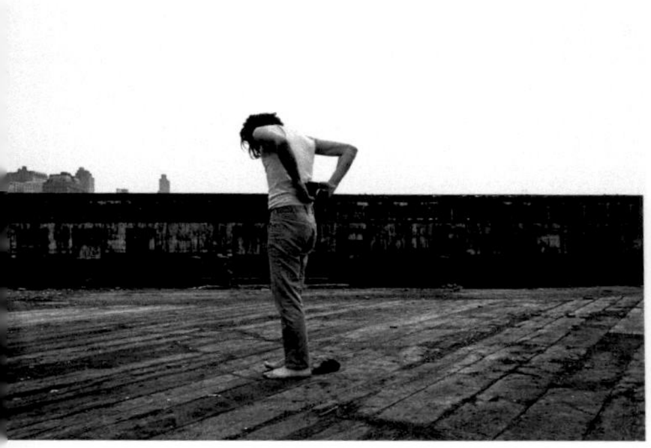

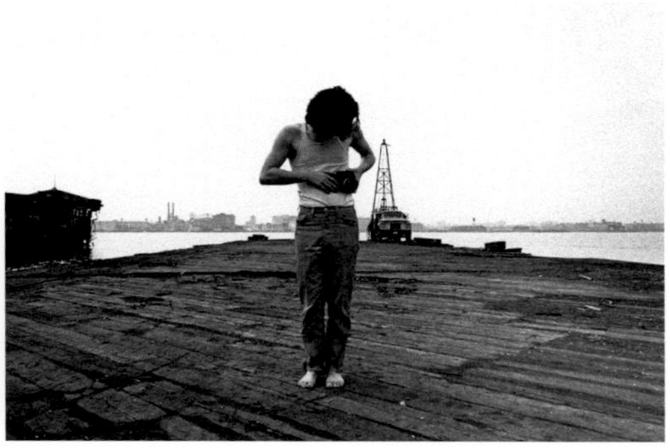

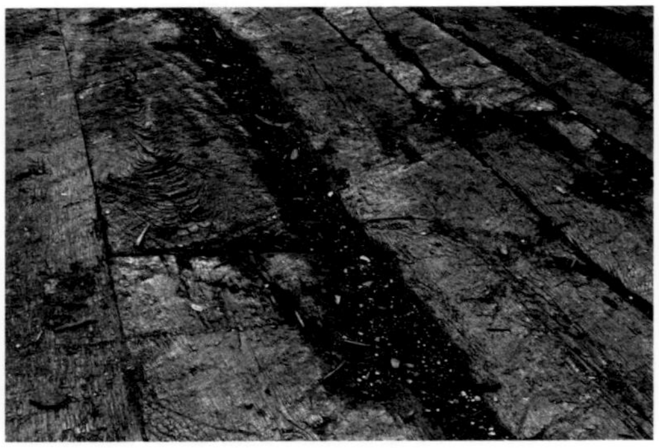

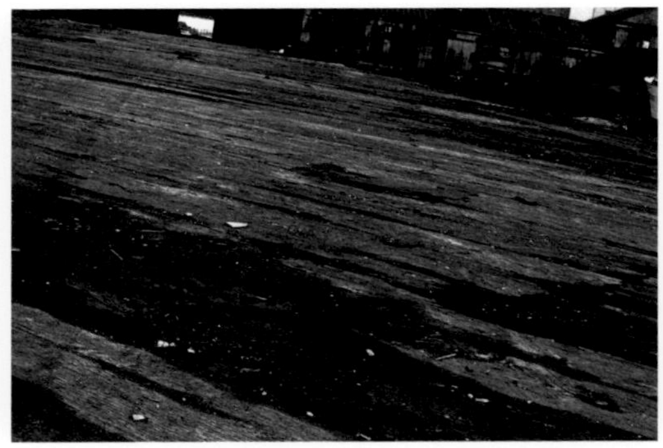

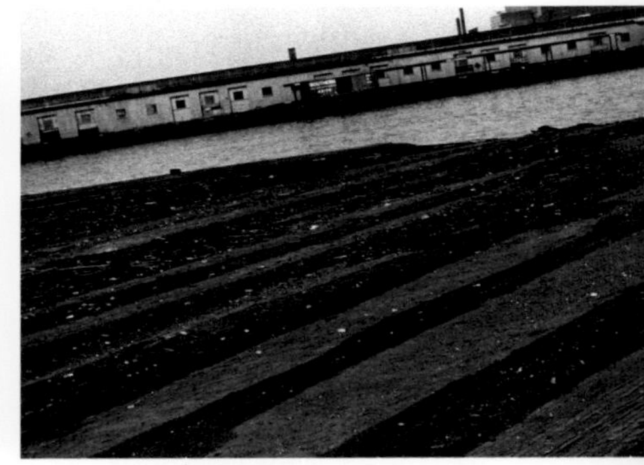

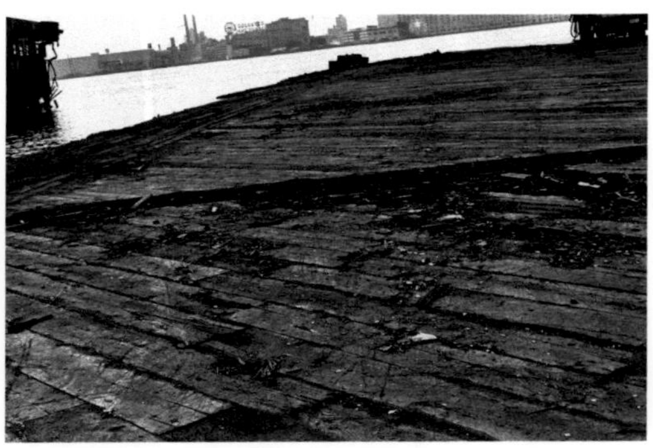

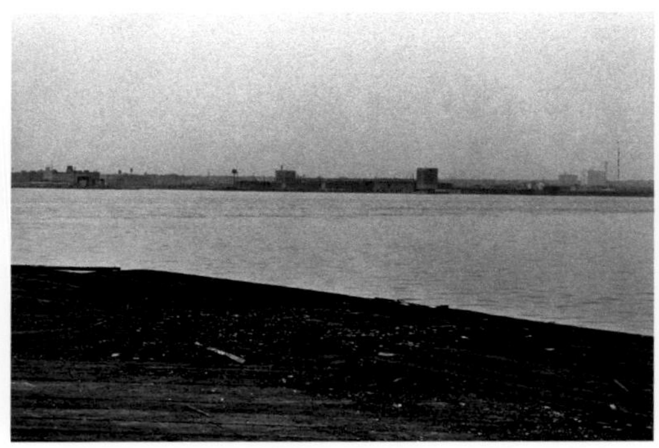

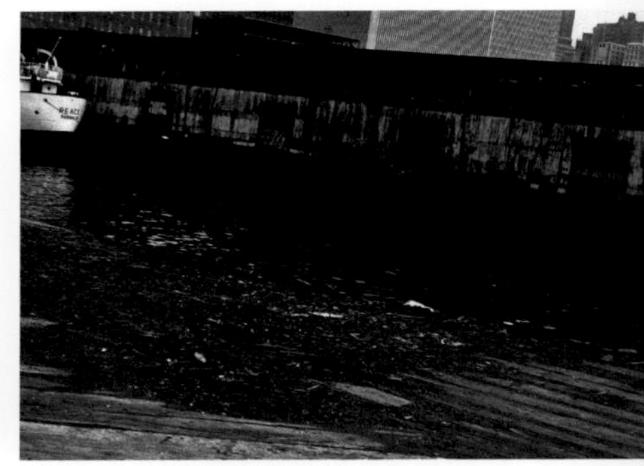

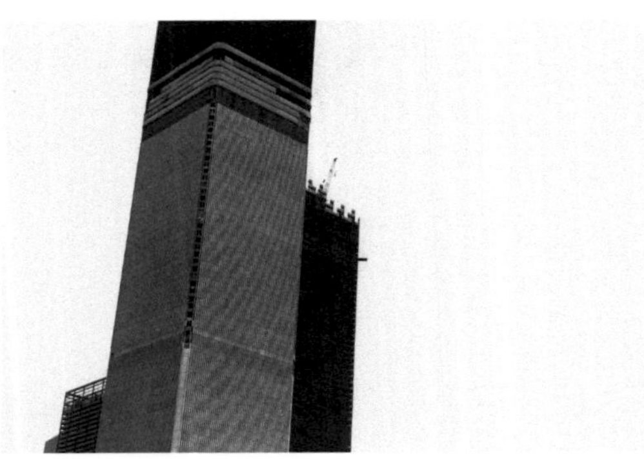

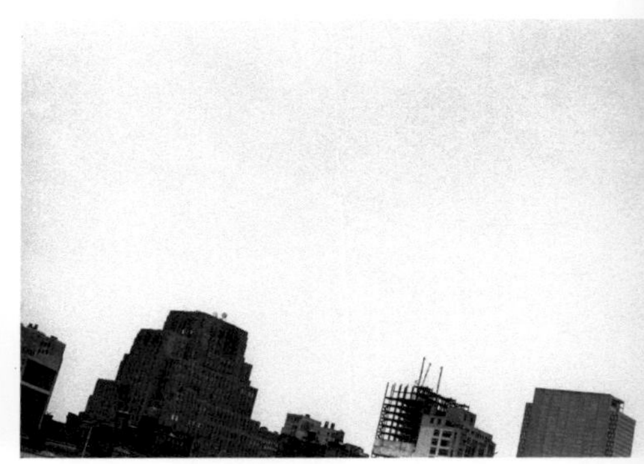

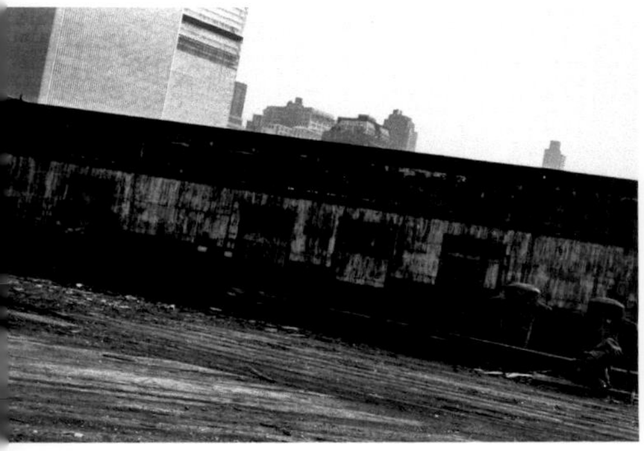

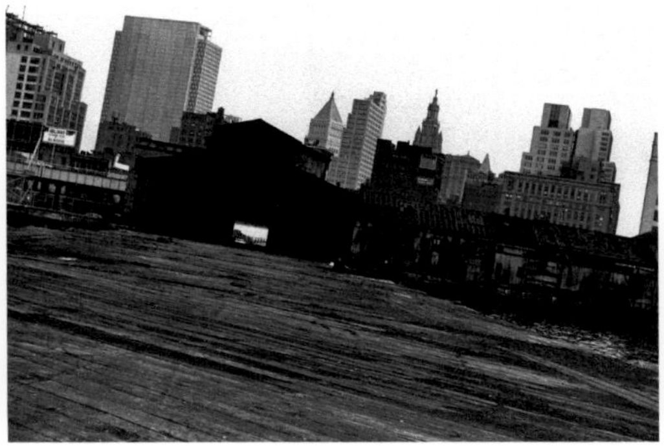

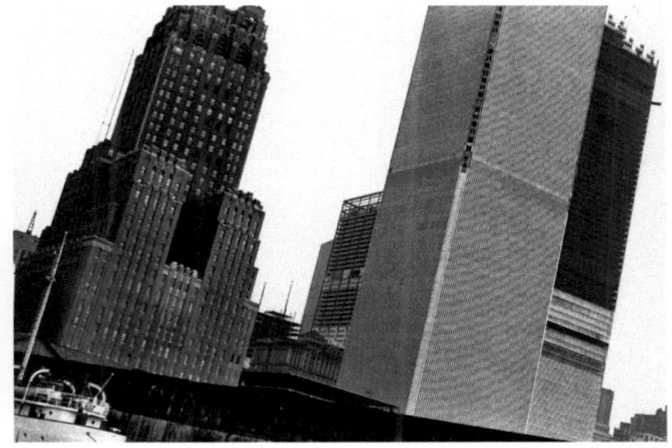

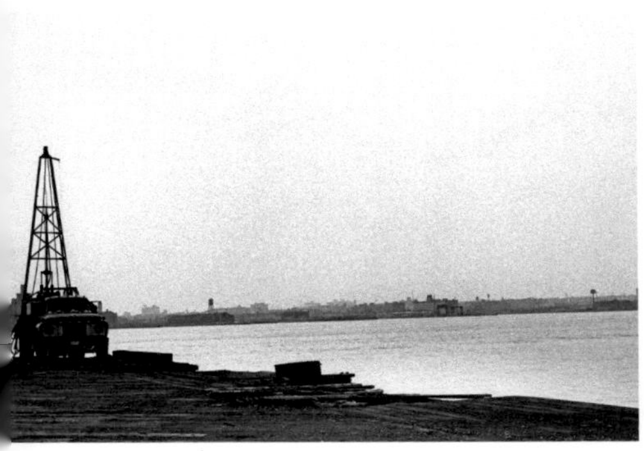

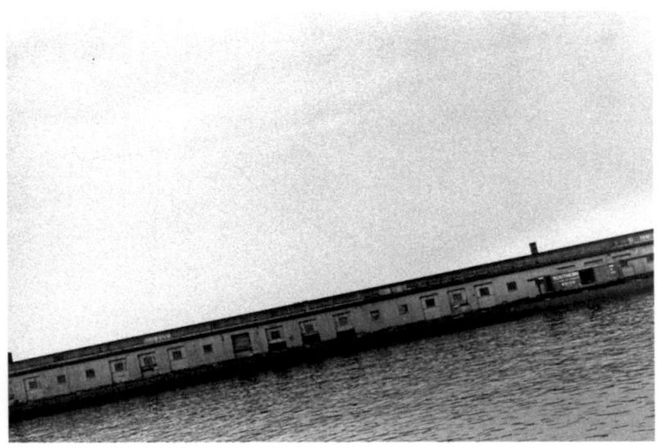

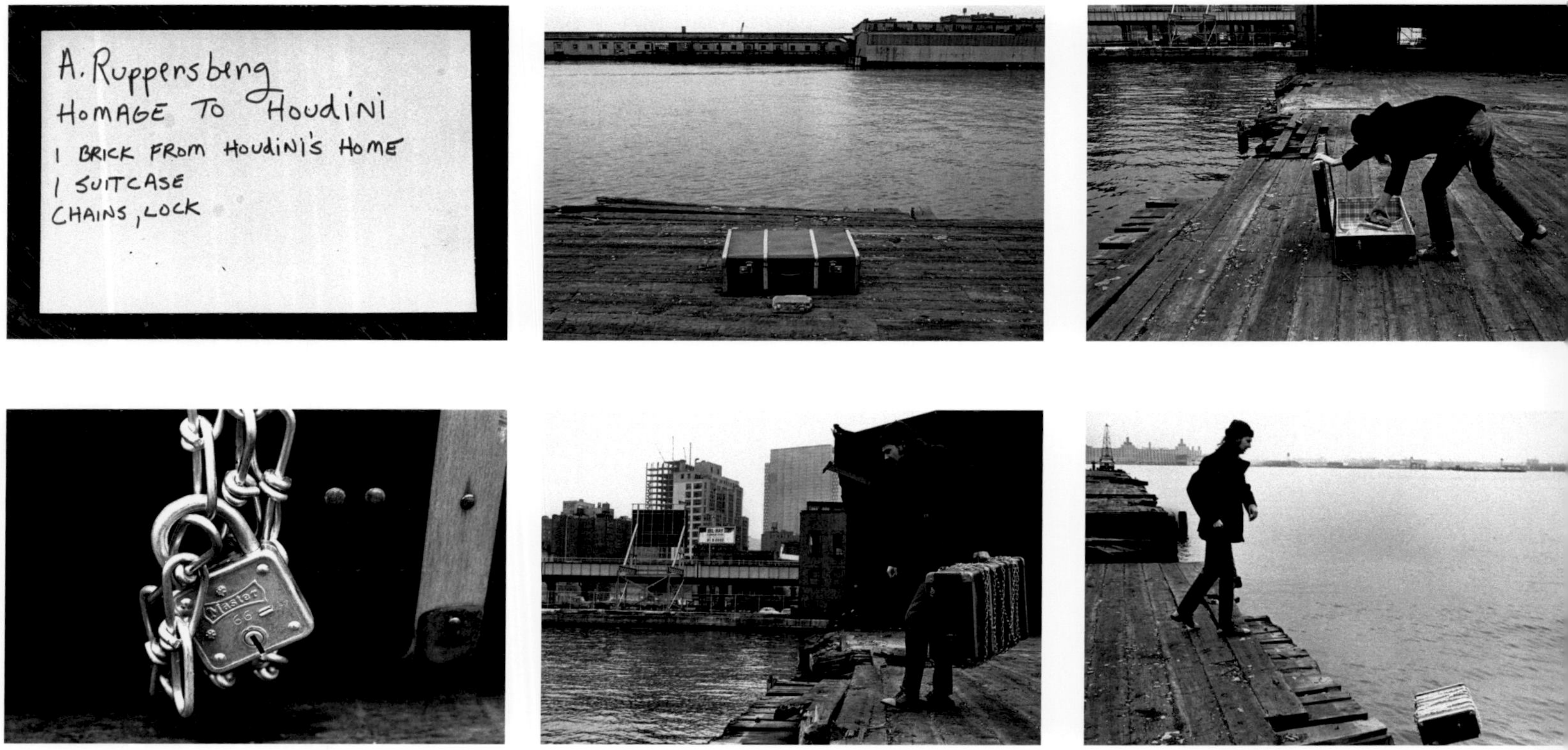

Plate 30 Allen Ruppersberg, *Homage to Houdini* (from *Projects: Pier 18*), 1971

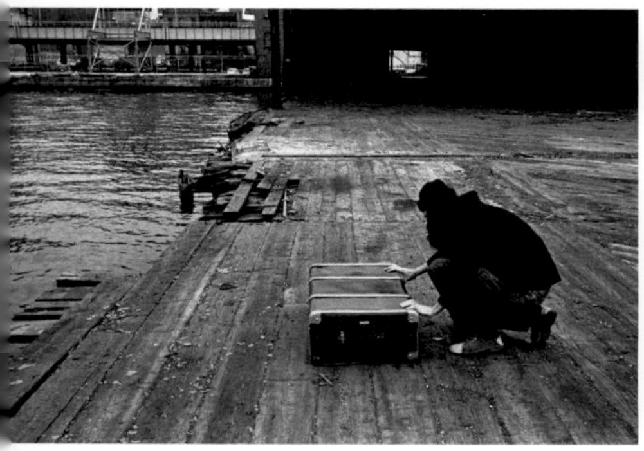

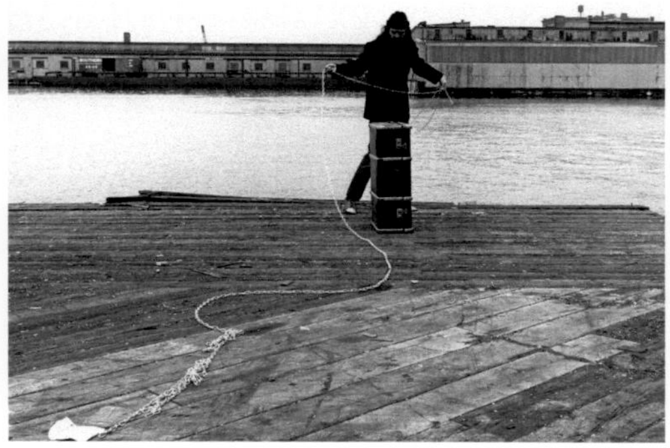

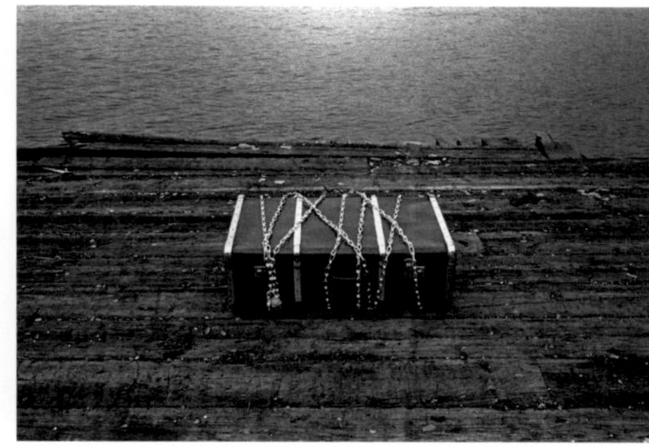

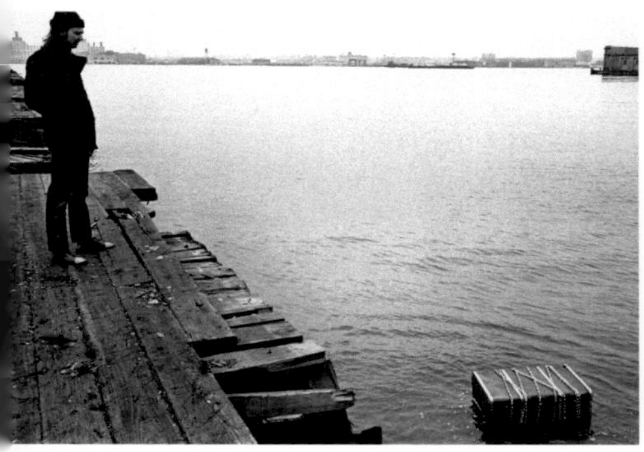

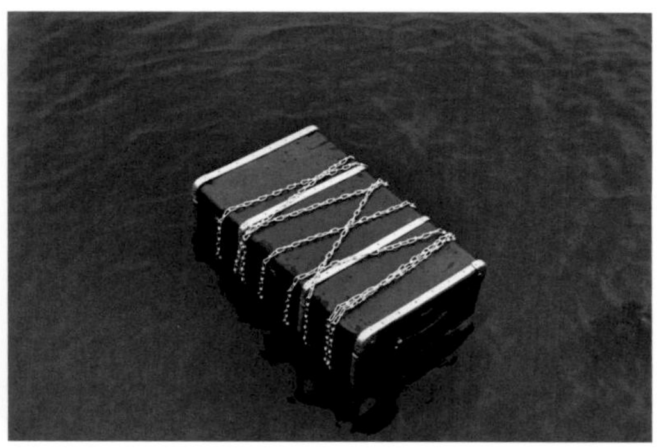

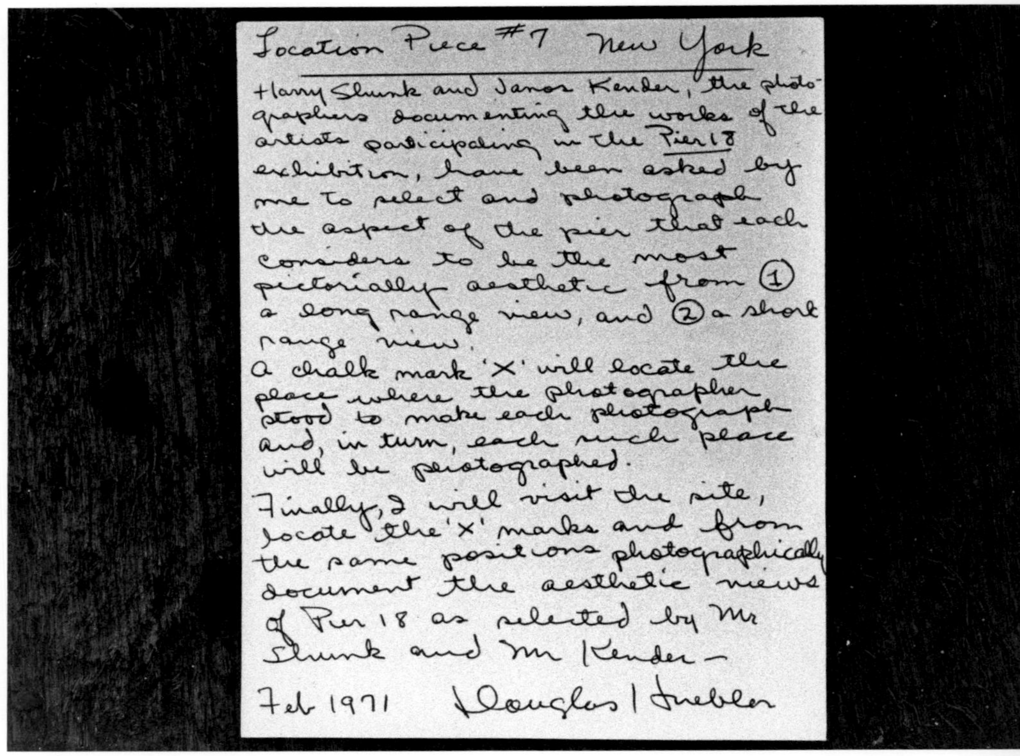

Location Piece #7 New York

Harry Shunk and Janos Kender, the photographers documenting the works of the artists participating in the Pier 18 exhibition, have been asked by me to select and photograph the aspect of the pier that each considers to be the most pictorially aesthetic from (1) a long range view, and (2) a short range view.

A chalk mark 'X' will locate the place where the photographer stood to make each photograph and, in turn, each such place will be photographed.

Finally, I will visit the site, locate the 'X' marks and from the same positions photographically document the aesthetic views of Pier 18 as selected by Mr Shunk and Mr Kender—

Feb 1971 Douglas Huebler

Plate 31 Douglas Huebler, *Location Piece #7* (from *Projects: Pier 18*), 1971

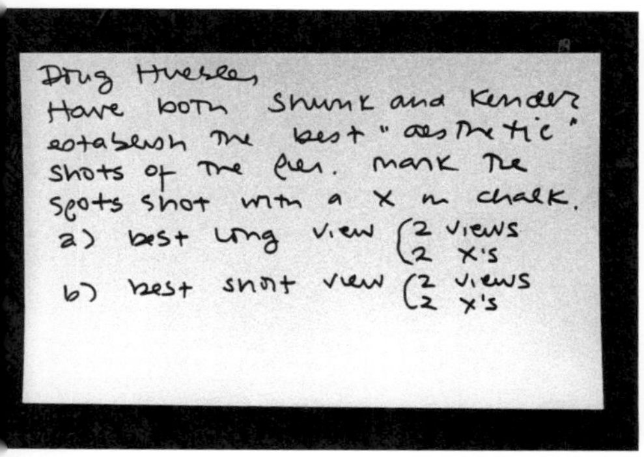
Doug Huebler,
Have both Shunk and Kender
establish the best "aesthetic"
shots of the pier. Mark the
spots shot with a X in chalk.
a) best long view (2 views 2 X's
b) best short view (2 views 2 X's

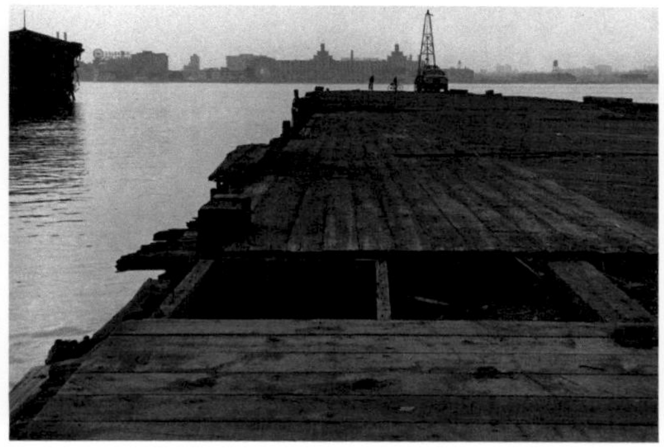

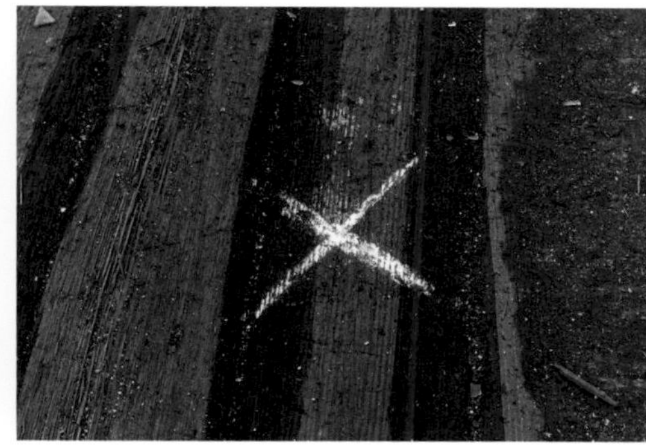

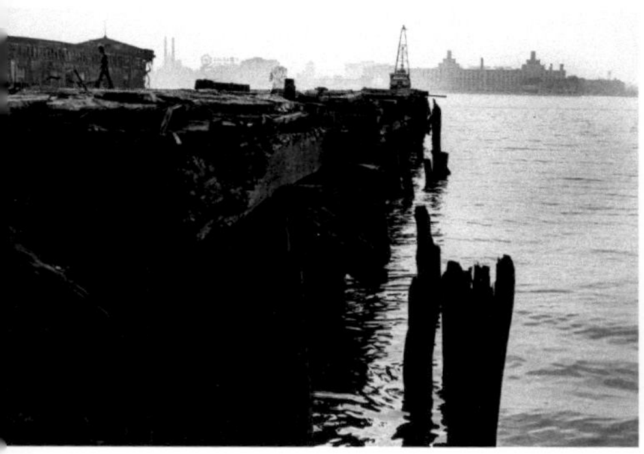

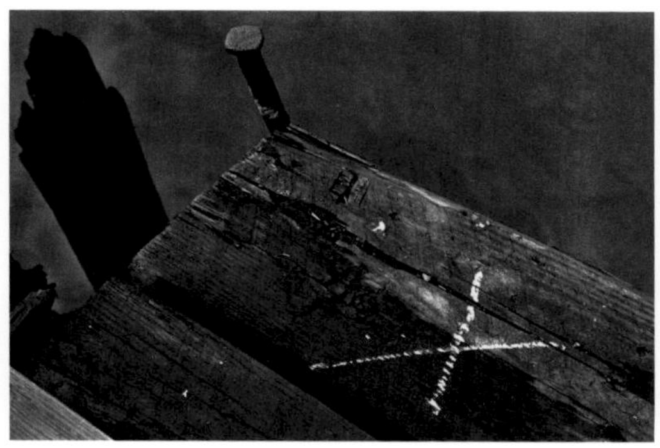

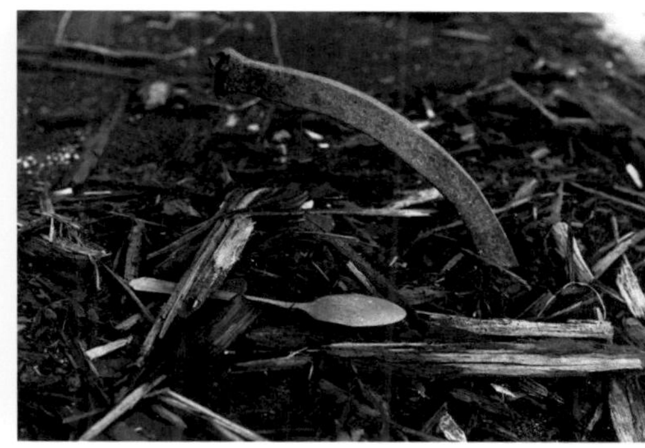

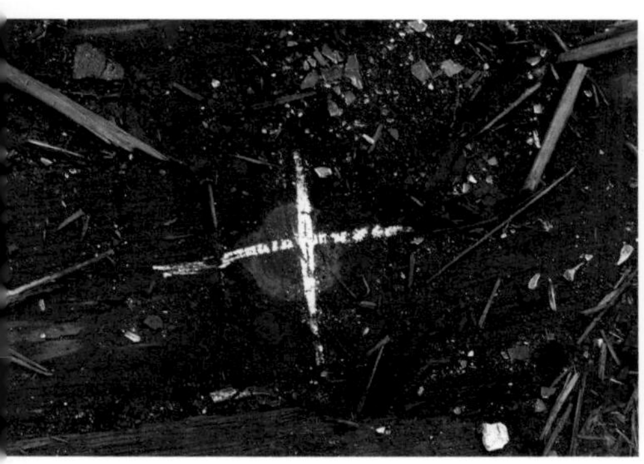

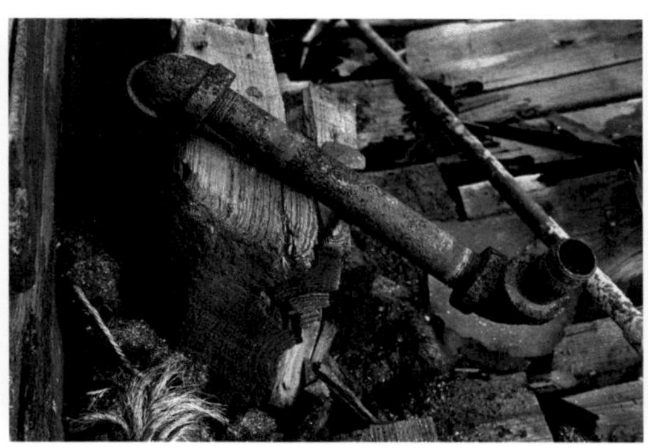

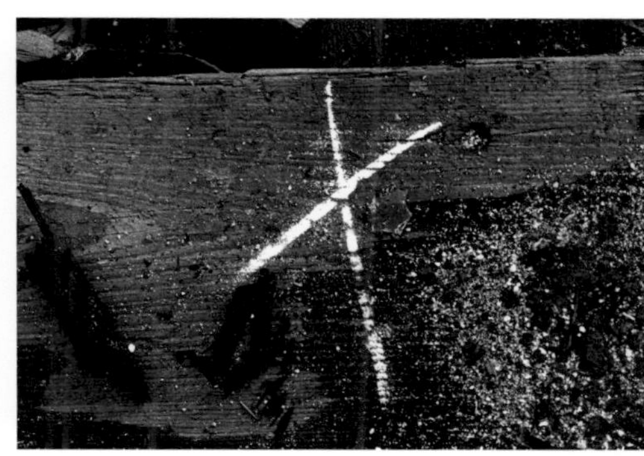

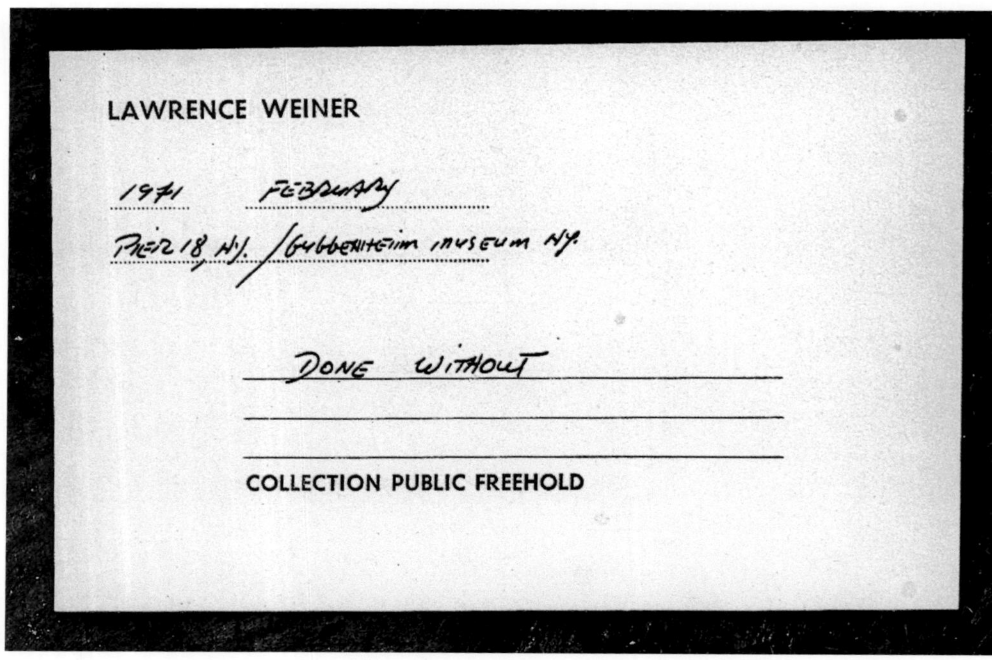

Plate 32 Laurence Weiner, *Done Without* (from *Projects: Pier 18*), 1971

Plates 33–34 Richard Serra, *Shooting a Square thru a Trapezoid, Camera Angle Measured* (from *Projects: Pier 18*), 1971

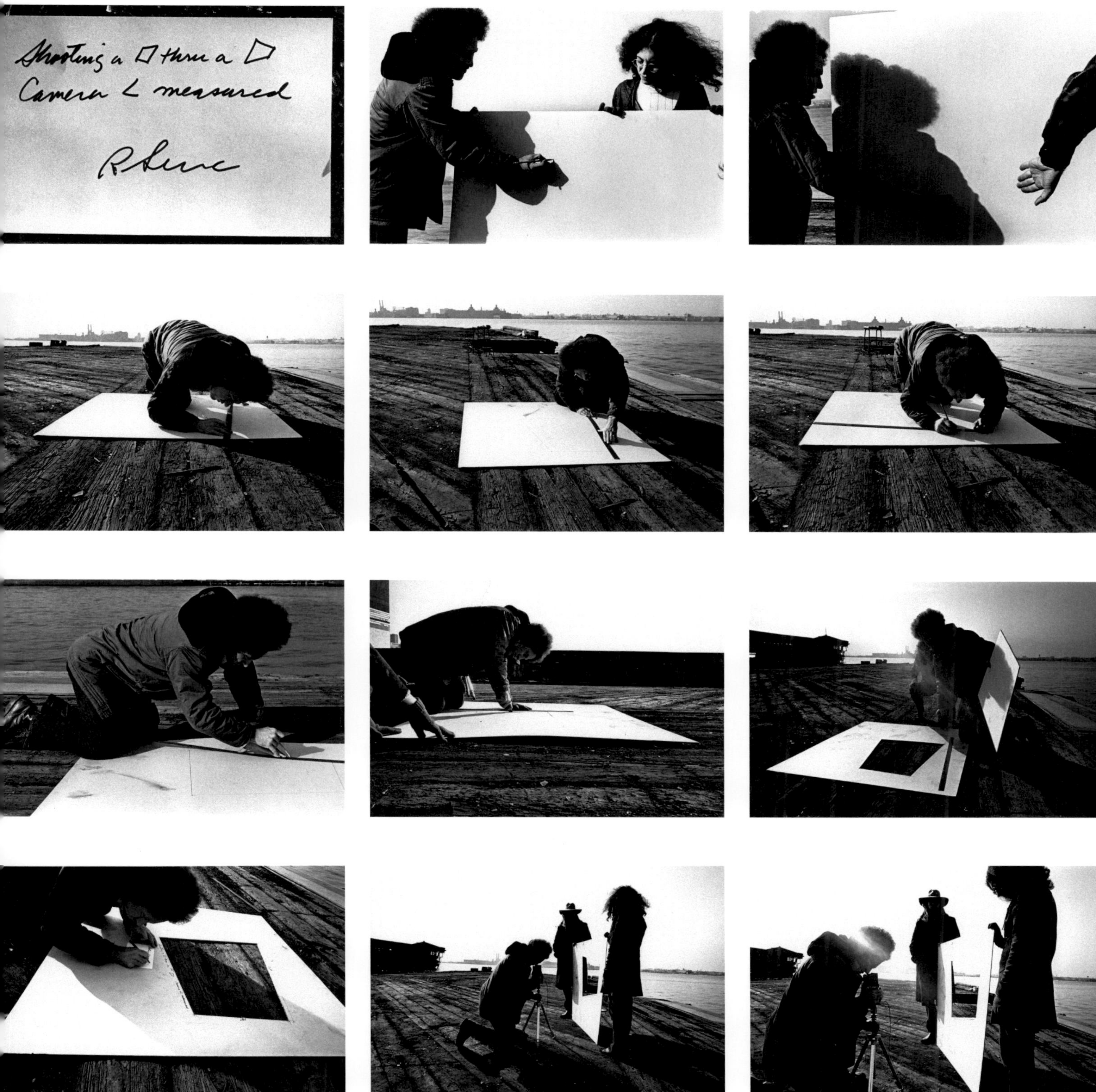
Shooting a □ thru a ◇
Camera ∠ measured

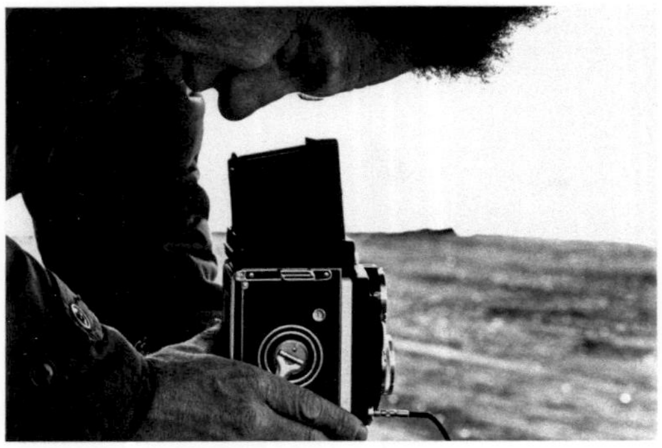

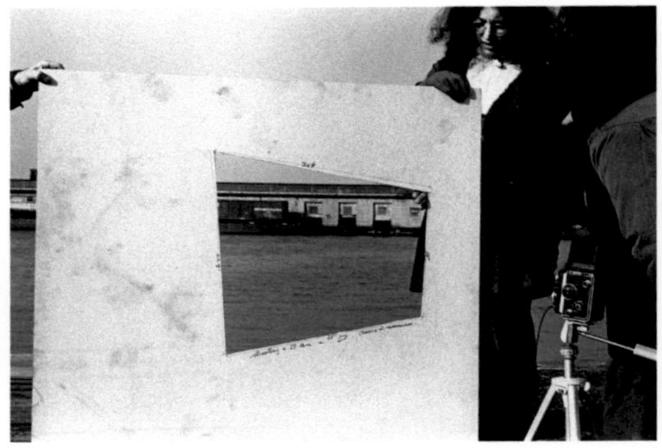

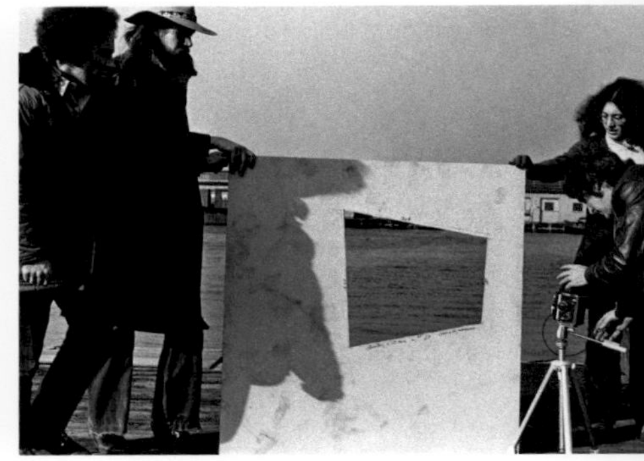

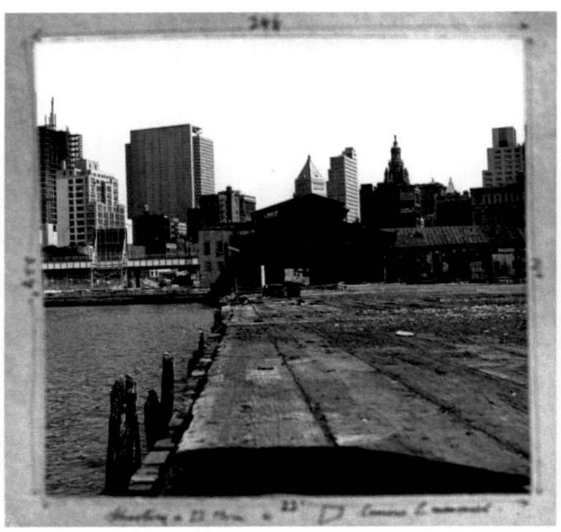

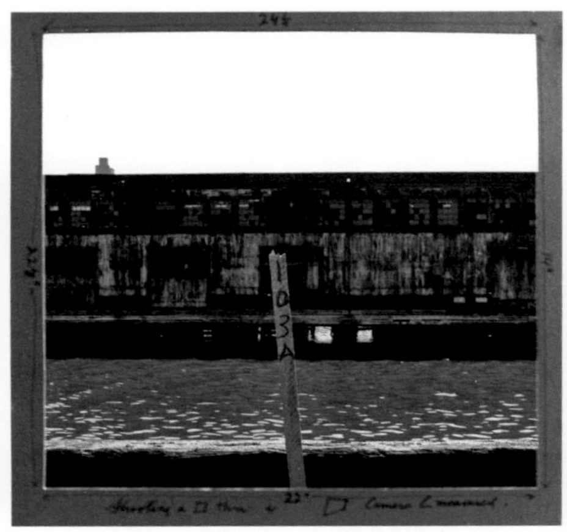
103A

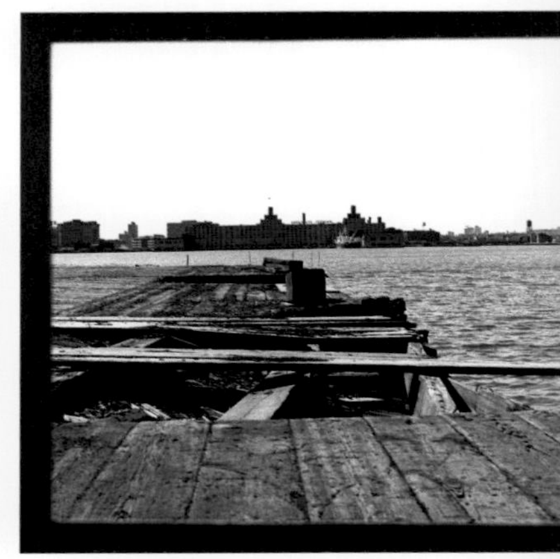

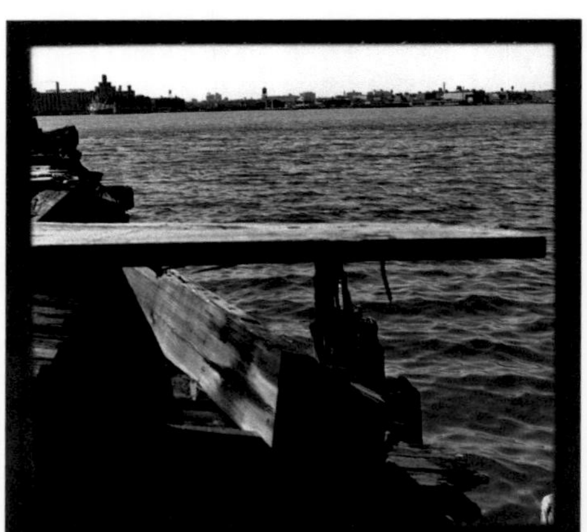

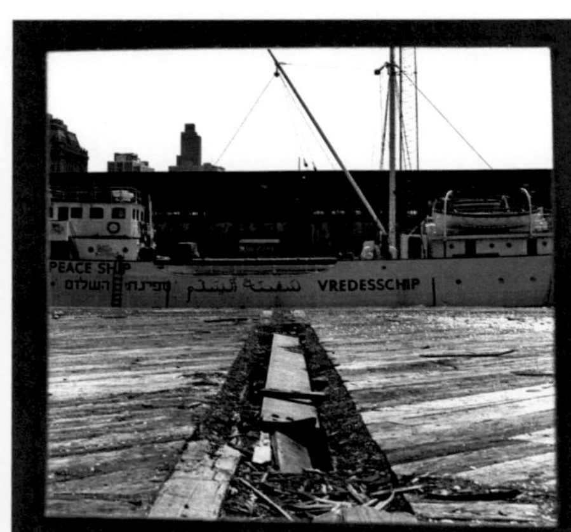
PEACE SHIP
VREDESSCHIP

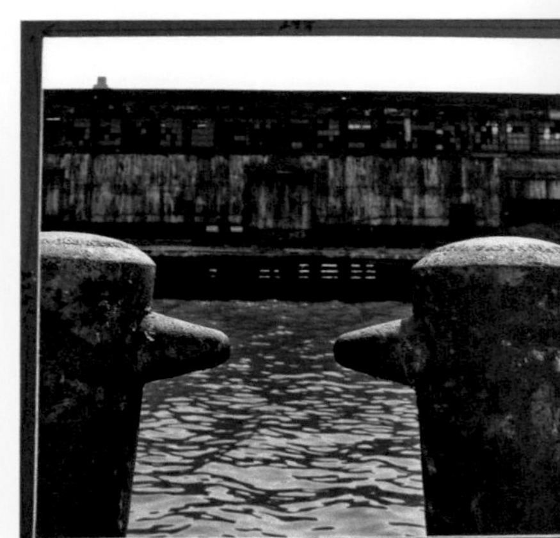

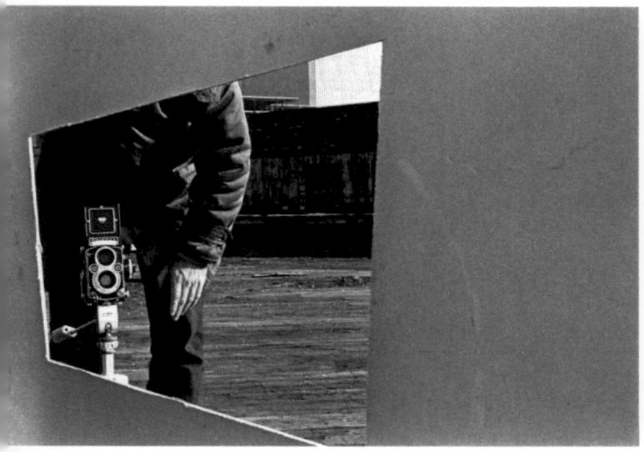

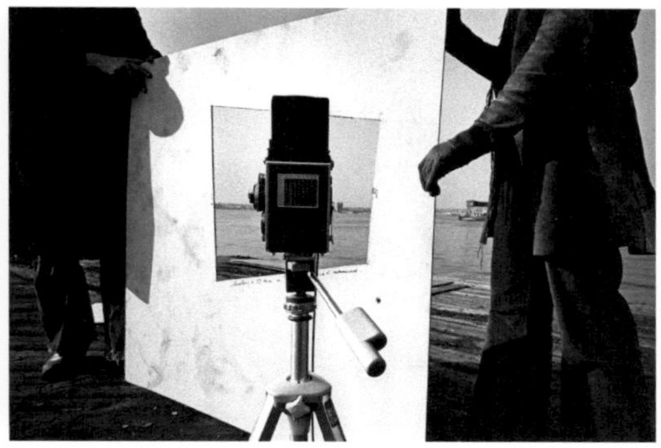

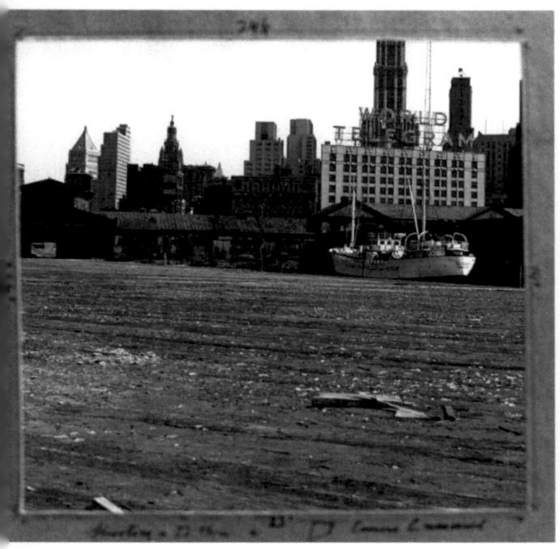

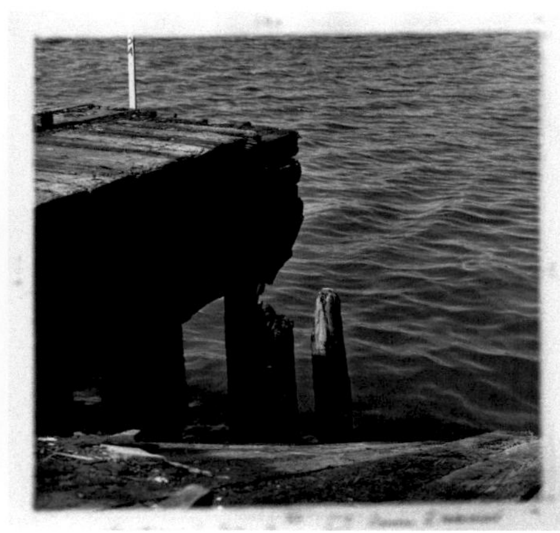

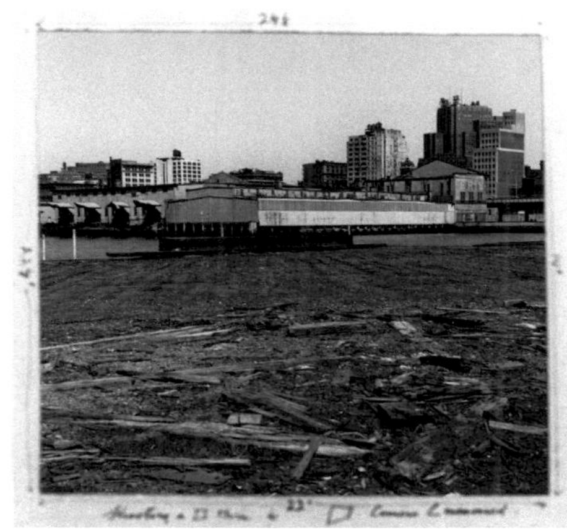

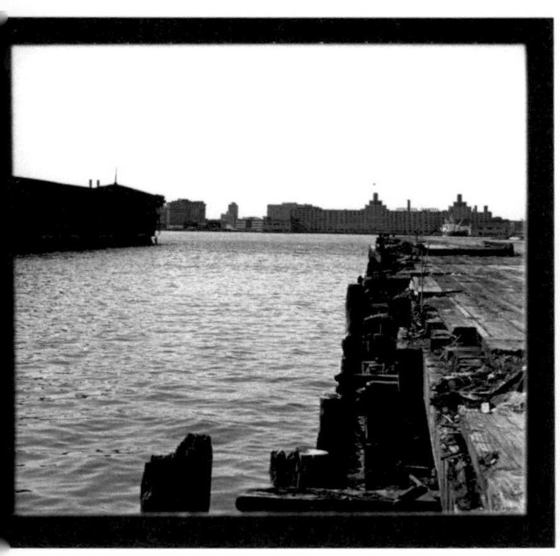

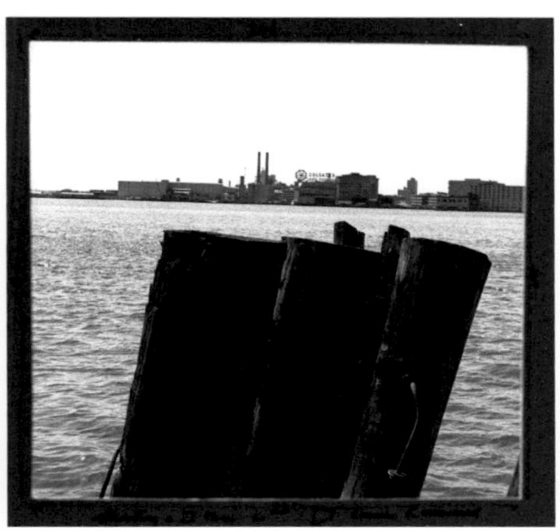

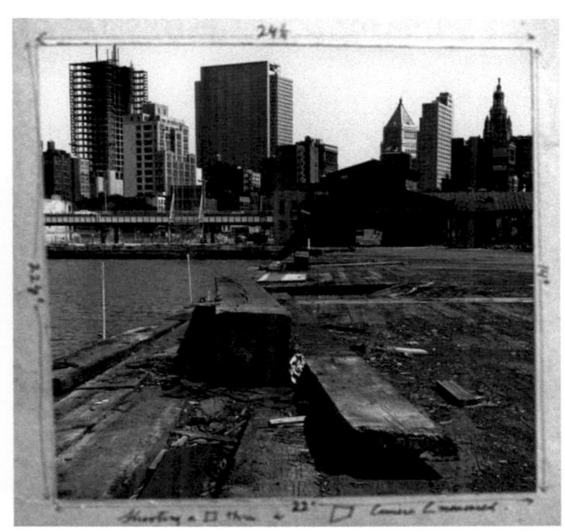

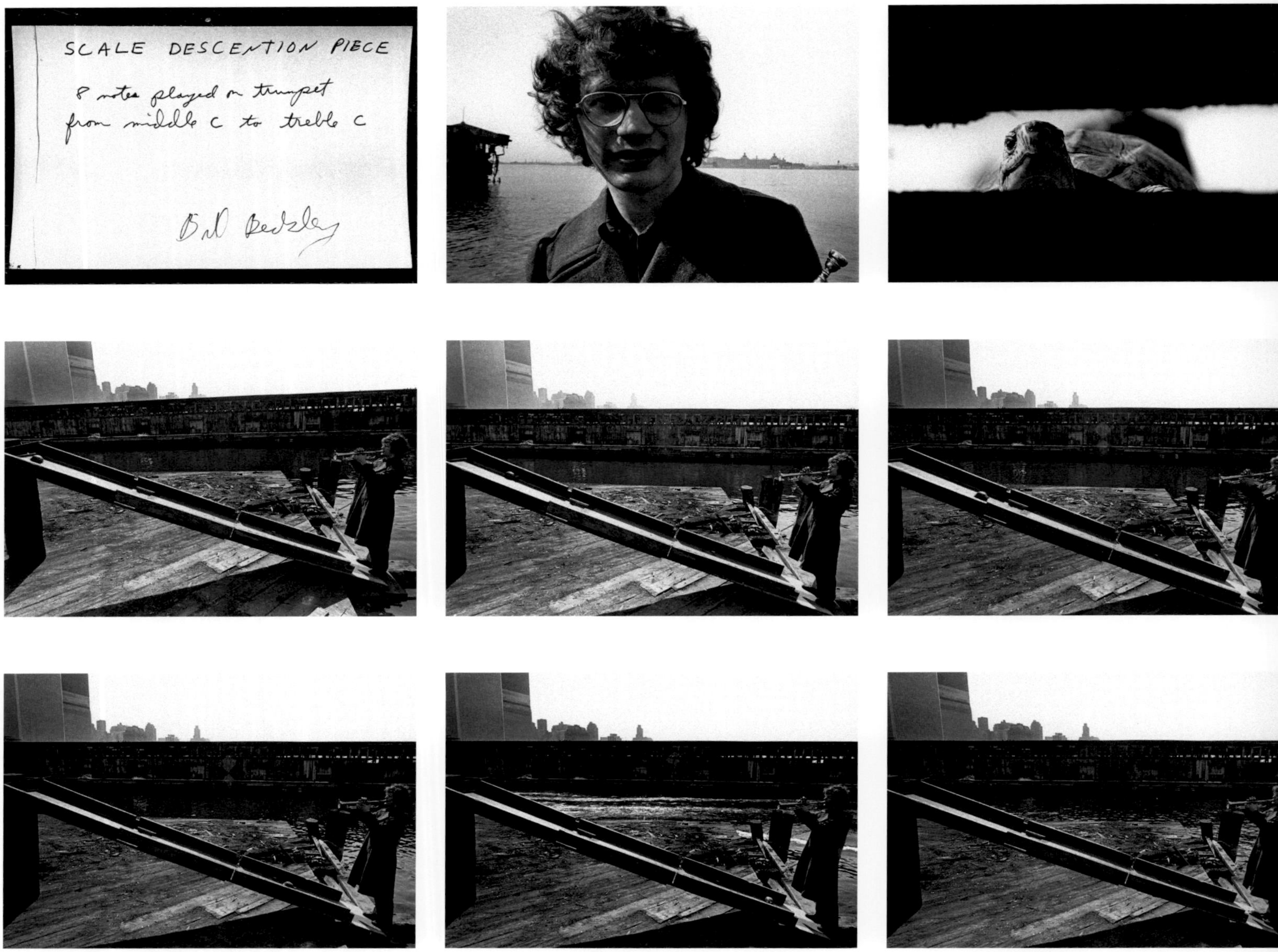

Plate 35 Bill Beckley, *Scale Descention Piece* (from *Projects: Pier 18*), 1971

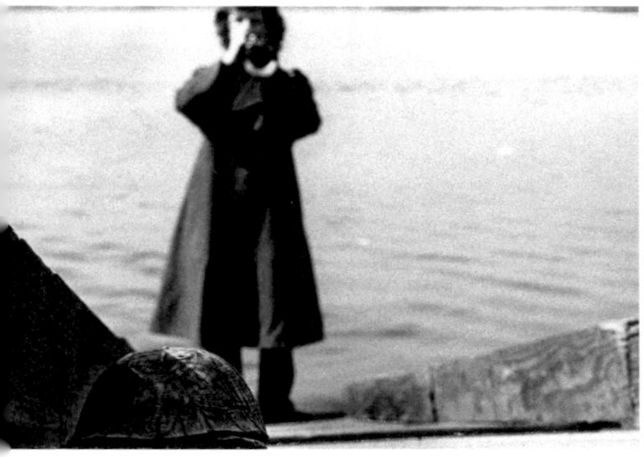

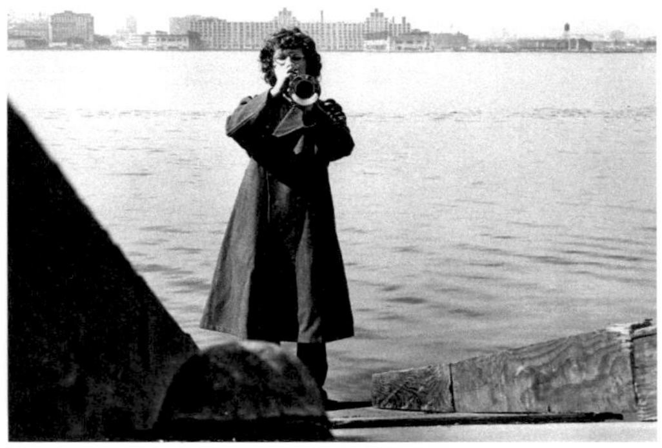

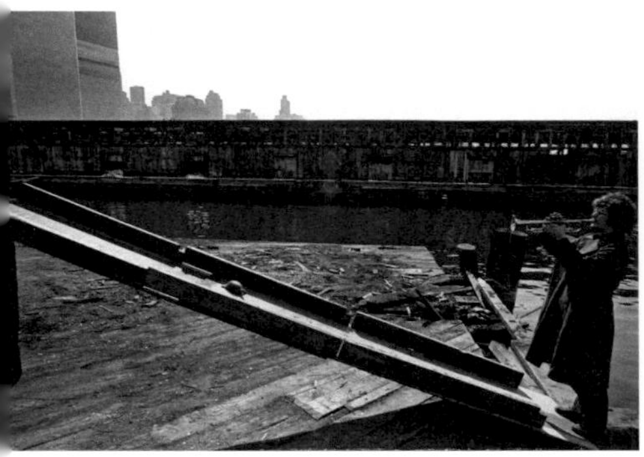

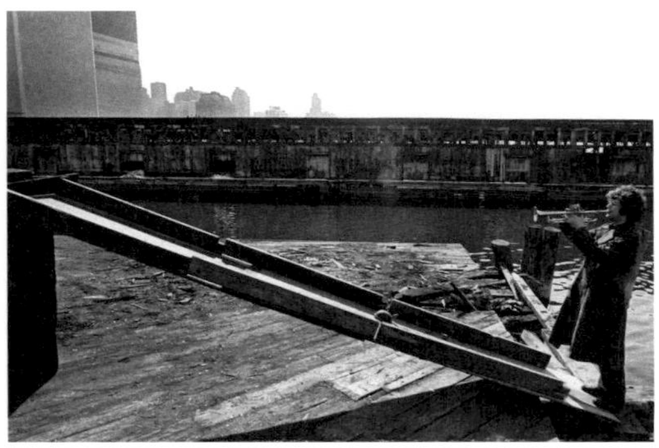

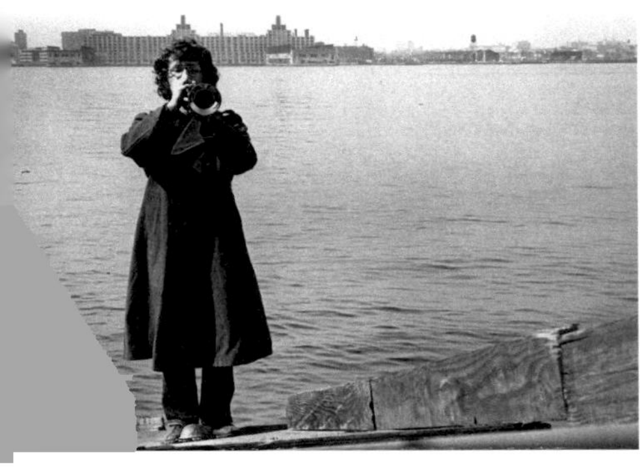

Action around the Edges Douglas Crimp

I should start with how it happened. I mean, what it's like to wander for months around New York trying to find a space to do a piece of work, and especially something to the scale that I have been able to do in other places but not in New York City.... Originally what I had sighted on were the facades because as you go down the Pier, driving down the pier along that empty highway in front, the facades are an incredible, animated grouping of different eras and different personalities. And I wanted to deal with one of the earlier ones, which this is—a turn of the century facade. There's the classic sort of tin classicism. And to cut at the facade. So the ones that I found originally were all completely overrun by the gays. And S&M, you know that whole S&M shadows of waterfront...

—Gordon Matta-Clark to Liza Bear, March 11, 1976

The day in August I'd chosen to move from Greenwich Village to Tribeca was one of the hottest of the summer of 1974. I rented a van and got my on-again, off-again boyfriend, Richard, to help out. My apartment on 10th Street just west of Hudson Street was a fourth-floor railroad flat; my new place was a spacious skylighted loft on Chambers Street, also west of Hudson. I'd arranged to use the loft building's freight elevator for the day, a rickety old contraption operated by pulling down hard on the hoist cable on a pulley system and stopped by yanking the other cable. It was a challenge to get the elevator to stop level with the floor. After piling all of my belongings onto the elevator's platform, Richard and I and the artist next door, from whom I was subletting the loft, managed to get the overloaded elevator to start its ascent, but by the time we'd reached the third floor it came to a grinding halt and began sliding back downward. We all grabbed the cable in an effort to slow the elevator's plunge and did manage to prevent a free fall, but it crashed onto the basement floor nevertheless. After recovering our wits and luckily finding ourselves unharmed, we had to lug my belongings through the old industrial building's dank basement and up the back stairs, make our way with them through a jam-packed hardware store on the ground floor, and then haul them up four more flights of stairs.

My new loft had a few other amenities besides its skylight, one of which had a classy provenance. The space had previously been rented to the set designer Robert Israel, who sold me the fixtures he'd installed when converting it from a commercial loft to a residence (plumbing and appliances for the kitchen and bathroom, space heaters, and so forth). Among these was a stagelike platform about ten feet square that stood two feet above the floor; Robert must have used it for mock-up designs.

I positioned it underneath the skylight and put a mattress on it, so that it became my bedroom. I didn't pay undue attention to the symbolism of bedroom-as-brightly-lit-stage, but I guess it was apt for that moment of my life. The fixture with the important provenance was a large refrigerator-freezer that had been given to Jasper Johns by Marion Javits, the art collector and socialite wife of New York's famous liberal Republican senator Jacob Javits. Johns had given it to Robert, and Robert sold it to me. It stopped working the following summer, so I found a thirty-five-dollar replacement at a used-appliance store on Kenmare Street, just east of SoHo. This one was a Raymond Loewy–designed General Electric model from the 1940s with a freezer compartment just big enough for a couple of ice-cube trays. I kept it for the next twenty years, and it was still working well when I finally replaced it.

My move from the Village to Tribeca came about as a result of my decision to get serious about being an art critic, to replace the gay scene with the art scene. I suppose it was a moment of my latent Calvinism taking hold. I'd come to feel myself adrift, not accomplishing enough, not spending enough time with the crowd to which I "rightly" belonged. My exchange of one scene for another was destined to fail, but my attempt to achieve it with an essentially spatial implementation interests me now. The immediate impulse is not easy for me to reconstruct, but it had something to do with the boyfriend who'd helped me move and crashed with me in the elevator. A friend had told me that Richard was "inappropriate" for me, something that has been said more than once about the objects of my sexual interest. In this case, I took the opinion more or less to heart, because Richard had become my tormentor. The on-again, off-again character of the affair was in fact quite brutal: as soon as I'd become really hooked on him, he'd abruptly ditch me, and then just as I'd be getting over being jilted, he'd come back pleading that he couldn't live without me, and I'd get hooked once again. This emotional S&M had its physical side, too, which is no doubt what enthralled me in the first place. But beyond these commonplace facts of what's called "a relationship," Richard was indeed very different from me, intellectually, politically. I came most fully to realize this when he informed me one day in the summer of 1975 that he was going to work for the Jimmy Carter election campaign. I was horrified: a born-again Christian from the South? The man who'd famously proclaimed he had sinned in his heart because he'd had impure sexual thoughts? But I'm getting ahead of my story, because by the time Jimmy Carter's campaign was under way, I was about to move out of the Chambers Street loft, farther downtown to Fulton Street; this time, I had the good sense to hire professional movers.

The emotional turmoil of my affair with Richard had come to symbolize for me my participation in the gay scene more generally—unjustly, of course. And my sense that I'd be better off living farther downtown, in Tribeca, was determined, in my memory of it now, by an event that represented a substitute love object. Sometime in the spring of 1974, I saw the Grand Union perform. The Grand Union

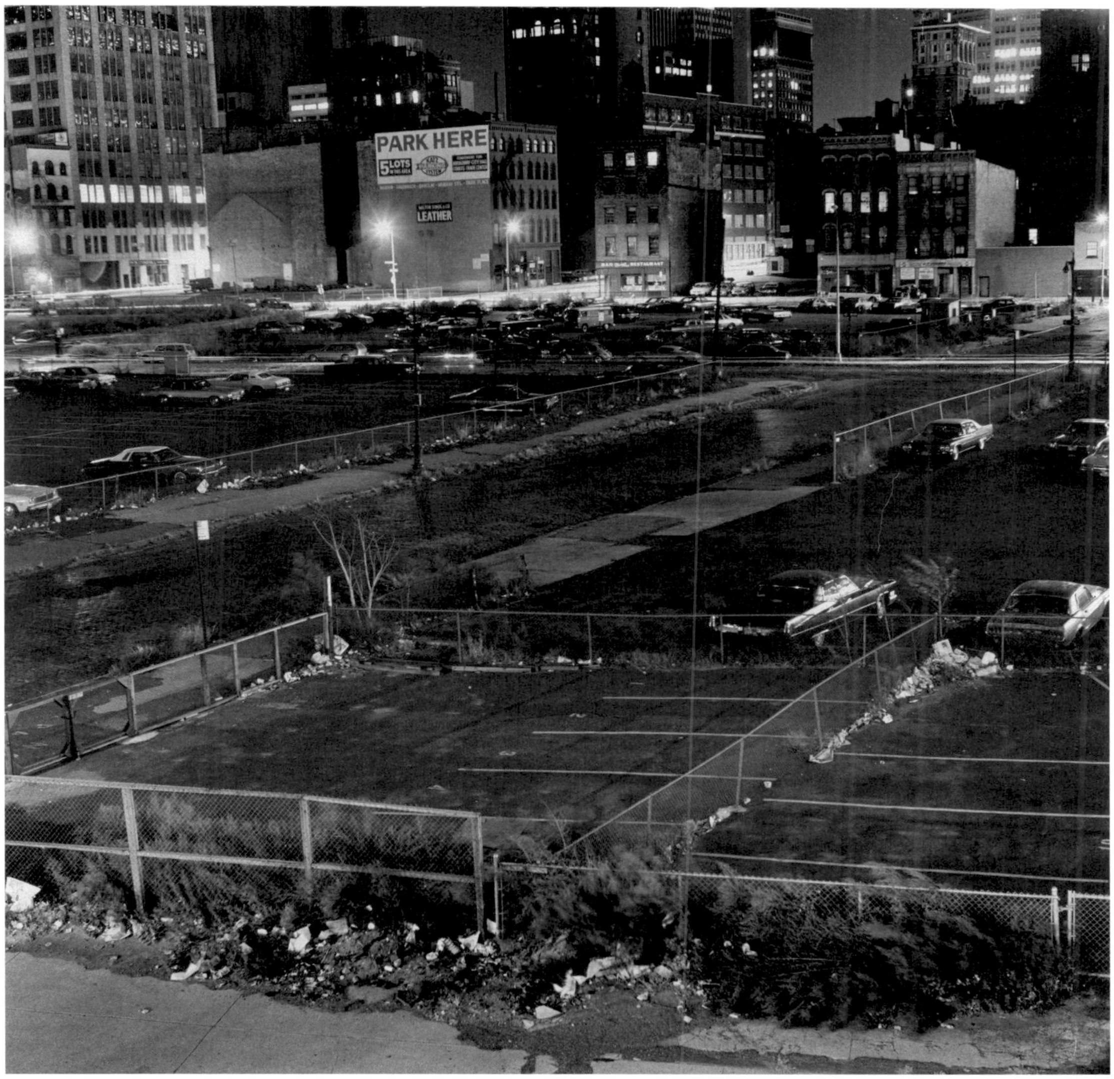

Plate 36 Peter Hujar, *West Side Parking Lots*, 1976

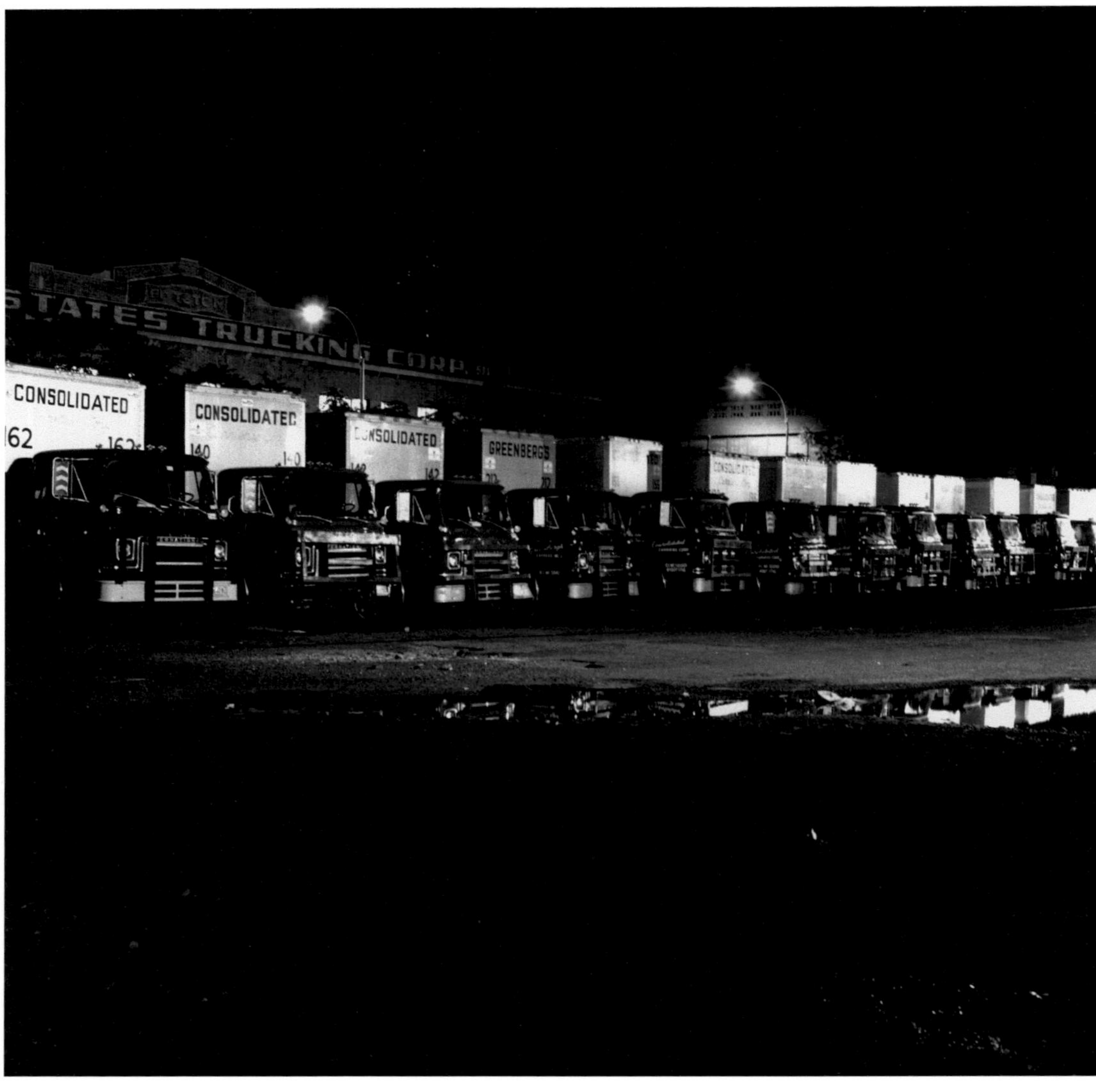

Plate 37 Peter Hujar, *Trucks, Night*, 1976

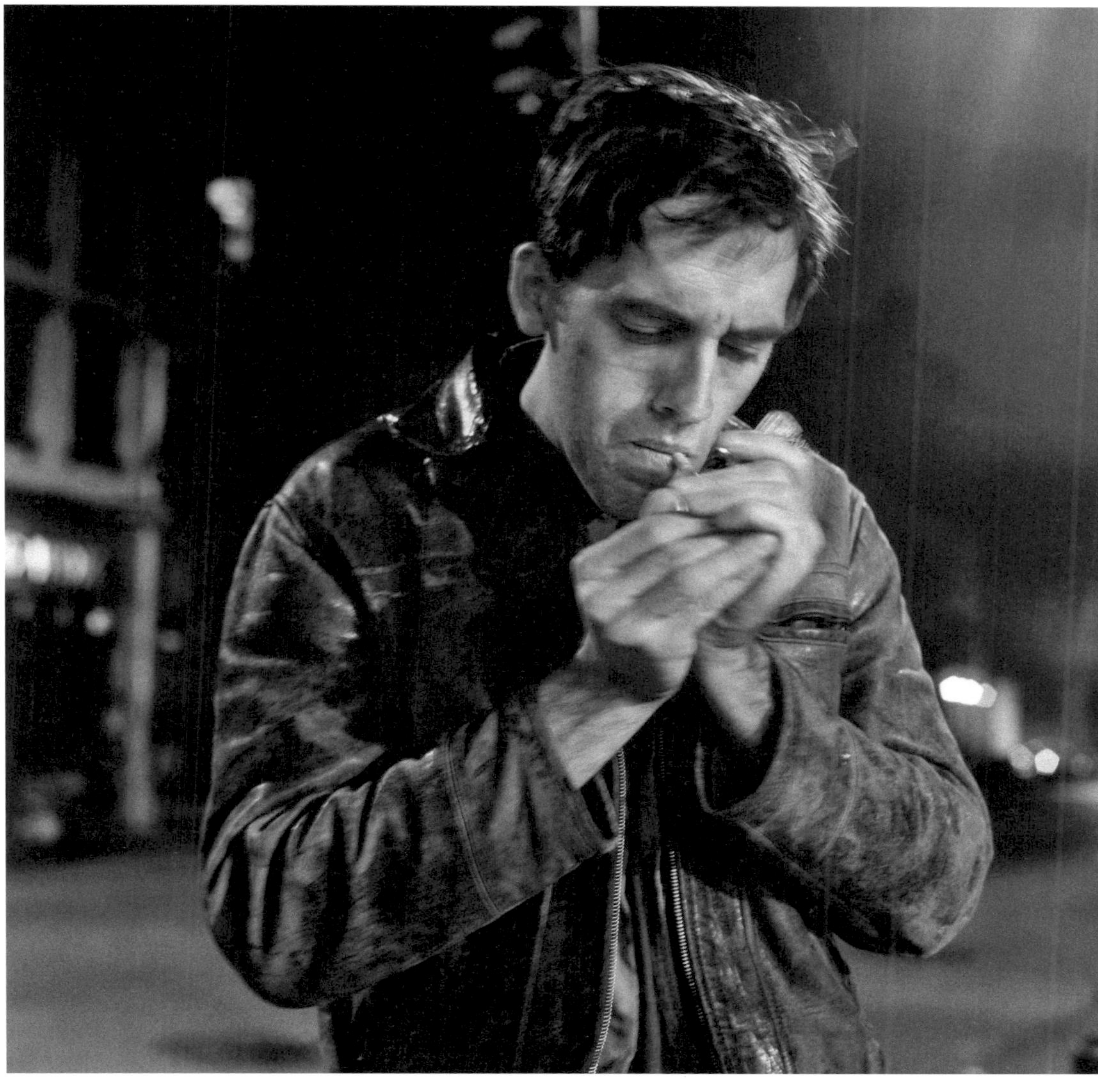

Plate 38 Peter Hujar, *David Lighting Up, Manhattan—Night (I)*, 1985

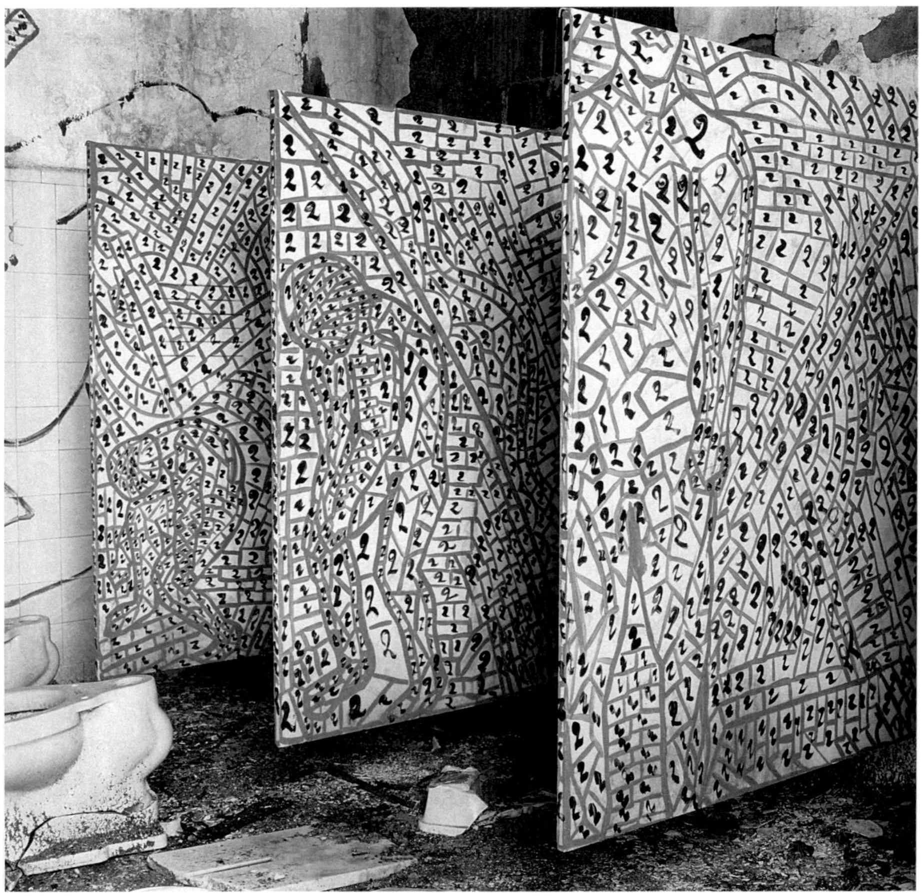

Plate 39 Peter Hujar, *Canal Street Piers: #2 Mural*, 1983

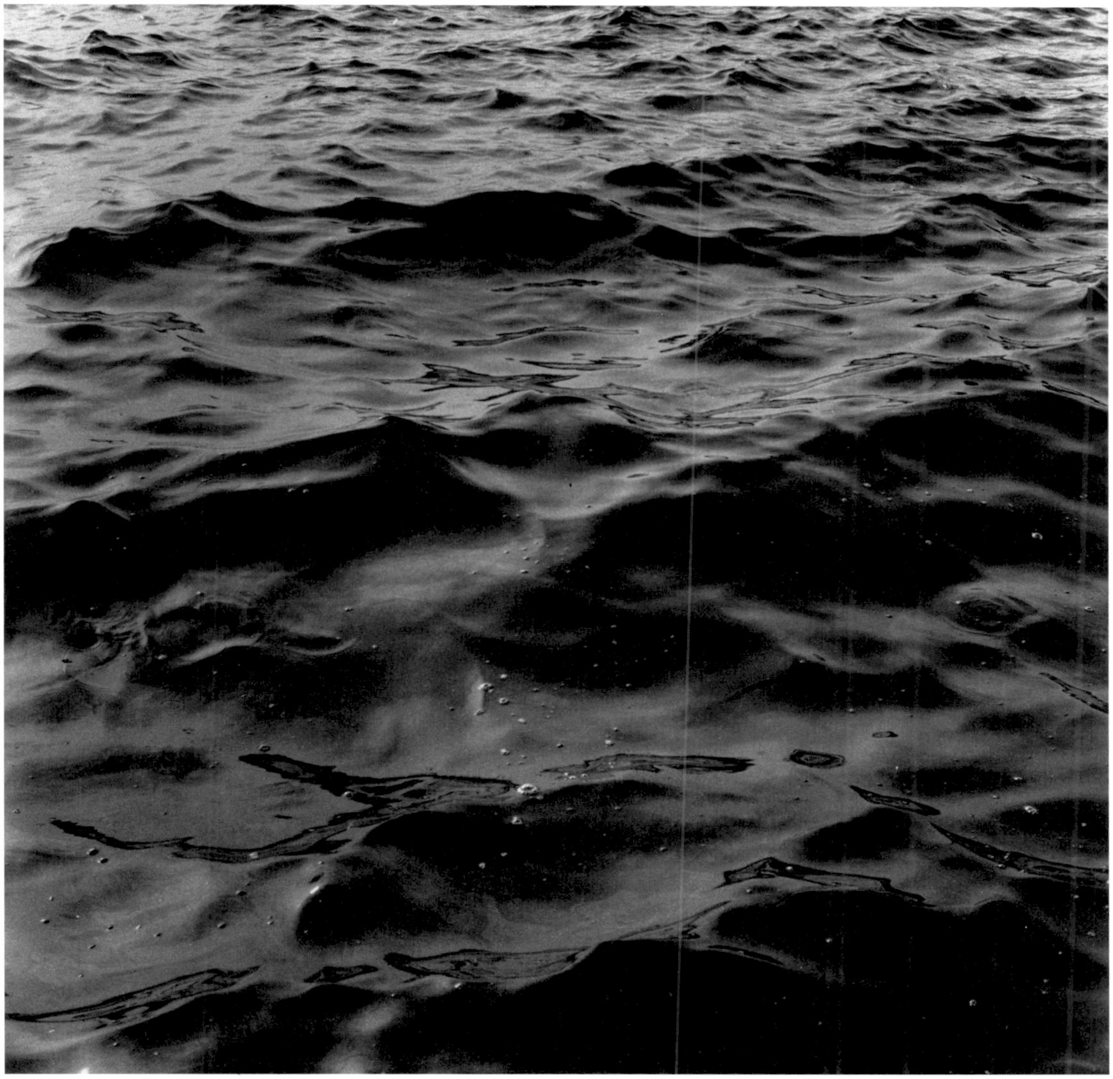

Plate 40 Peter Hujar, *Hudson River (IV)*, 1975

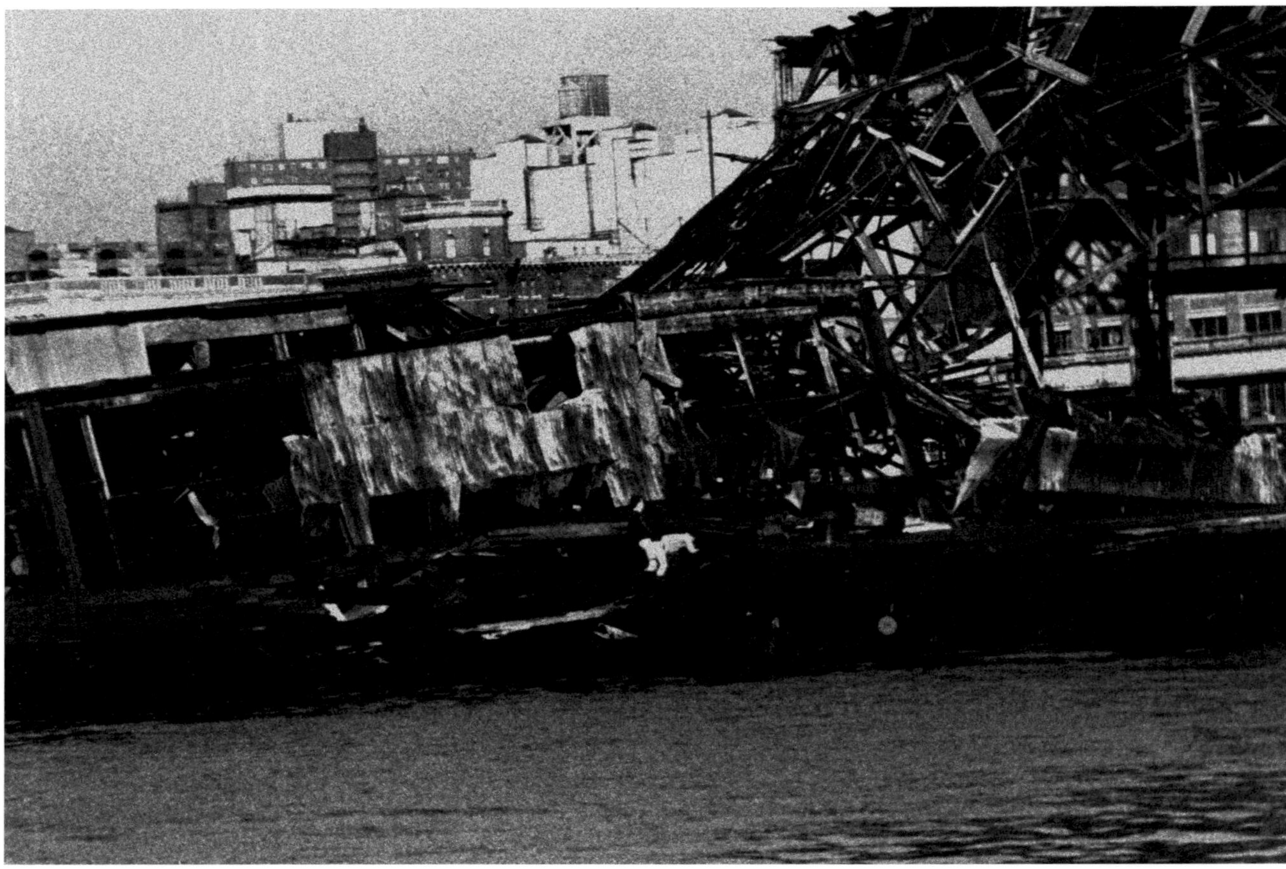

Plate 41 Alvin Baltrop, *Untitled* (from the series Pier Photographs), 1975–86

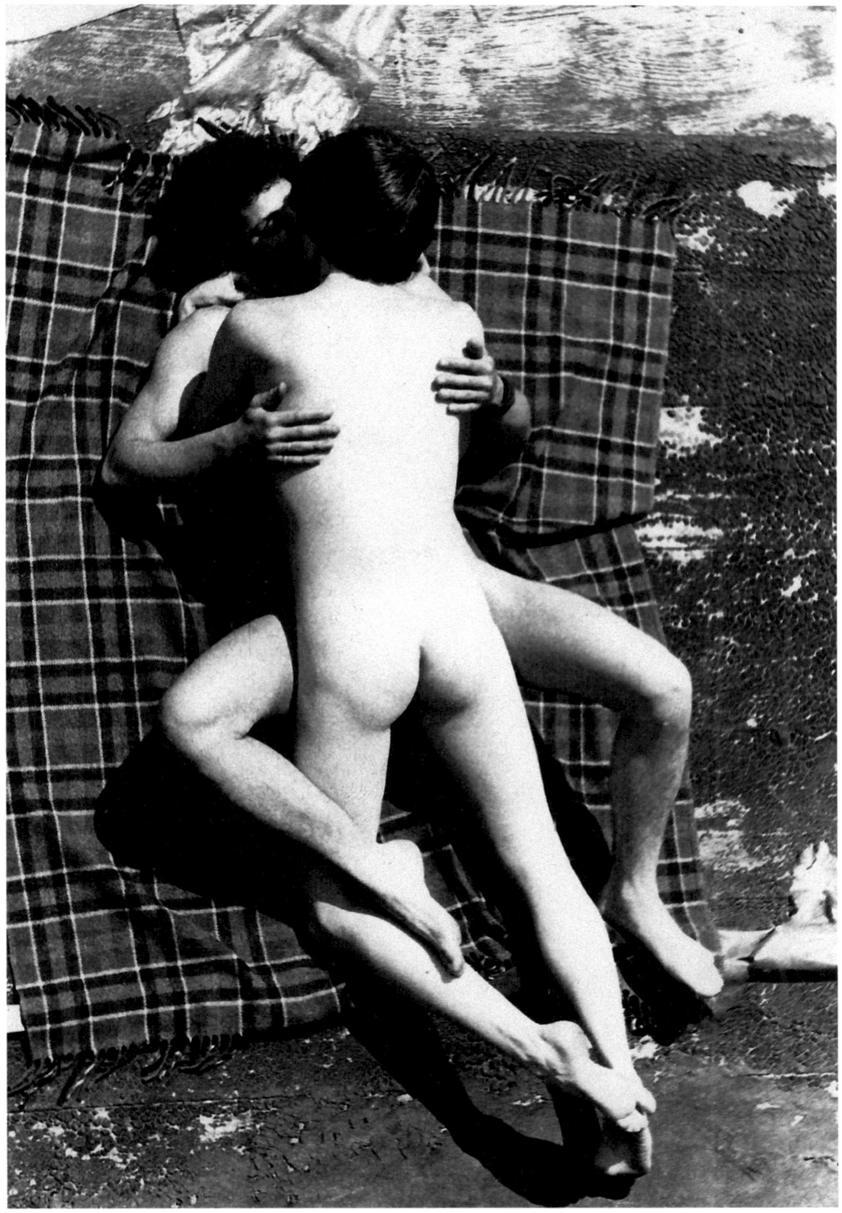

Plate 42 Alvin Baltrop, *Untitled* (from the series Pier Photographs), 1975–86

Plate 43 Alvin Baltrop, *Untitled* (from the series Pier Photographs), 1975–86

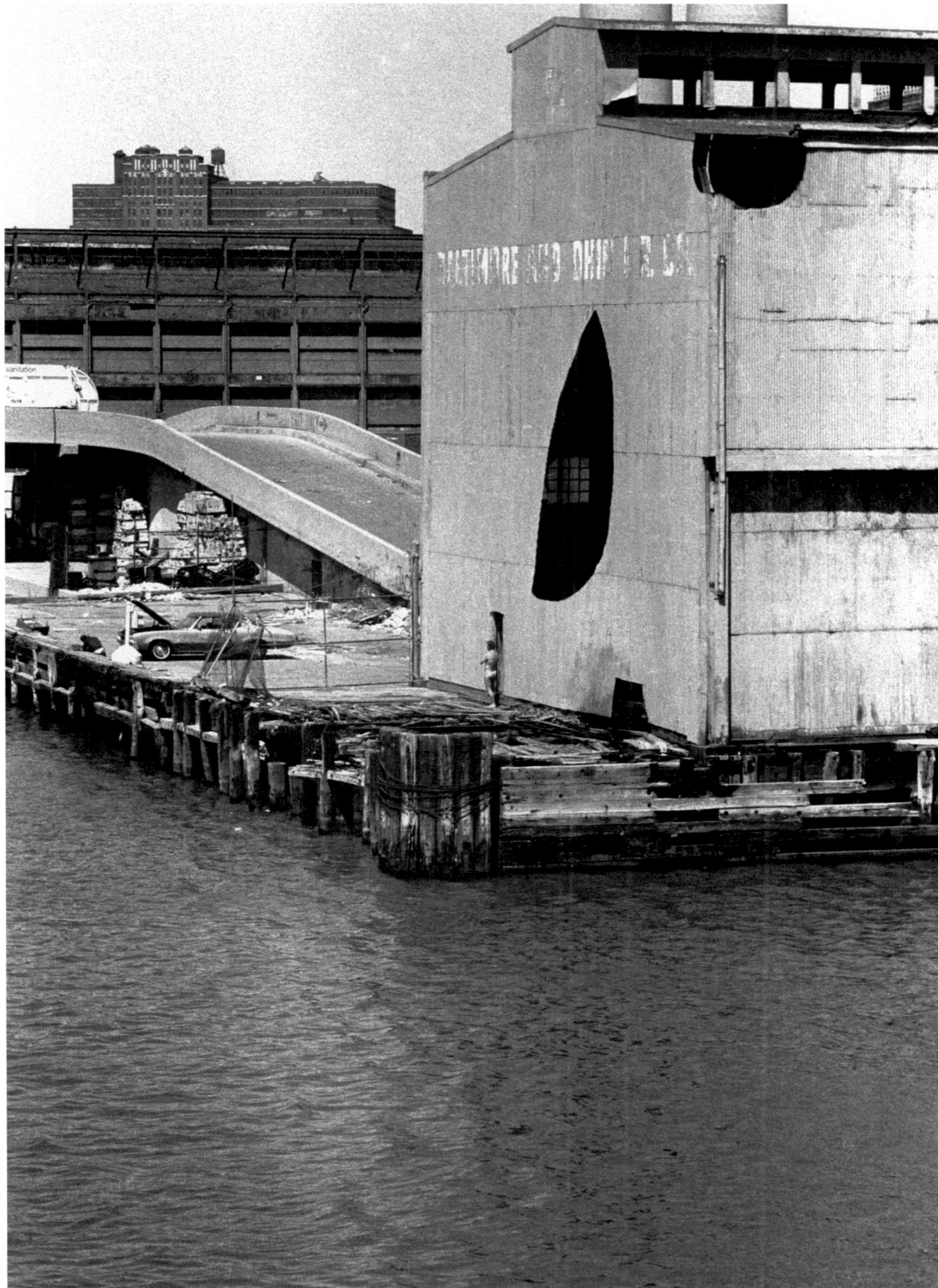

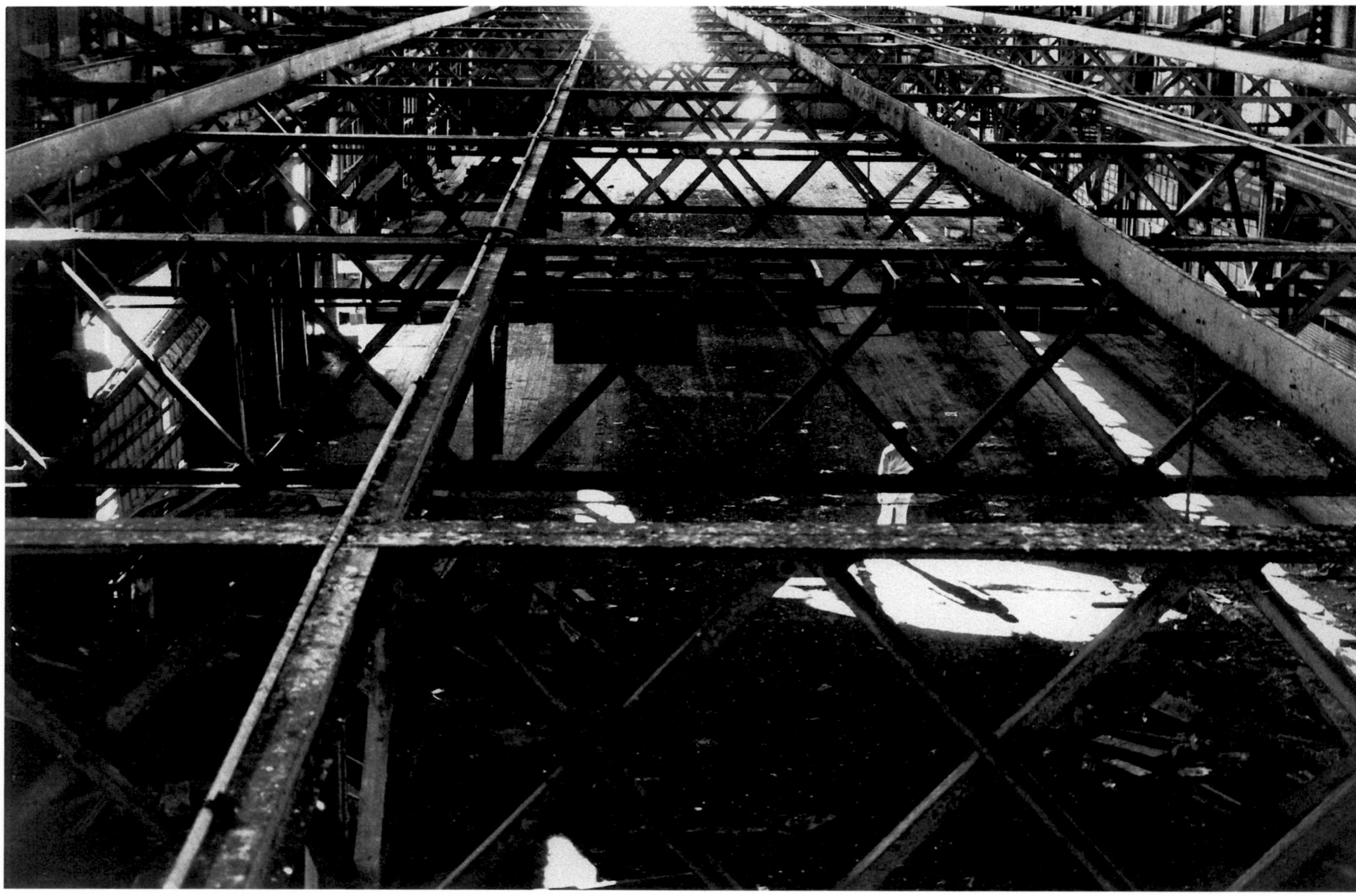

Plate 44 Alvin Baltrop, *Untitled* (from the series Pier Photographs), 1975–86

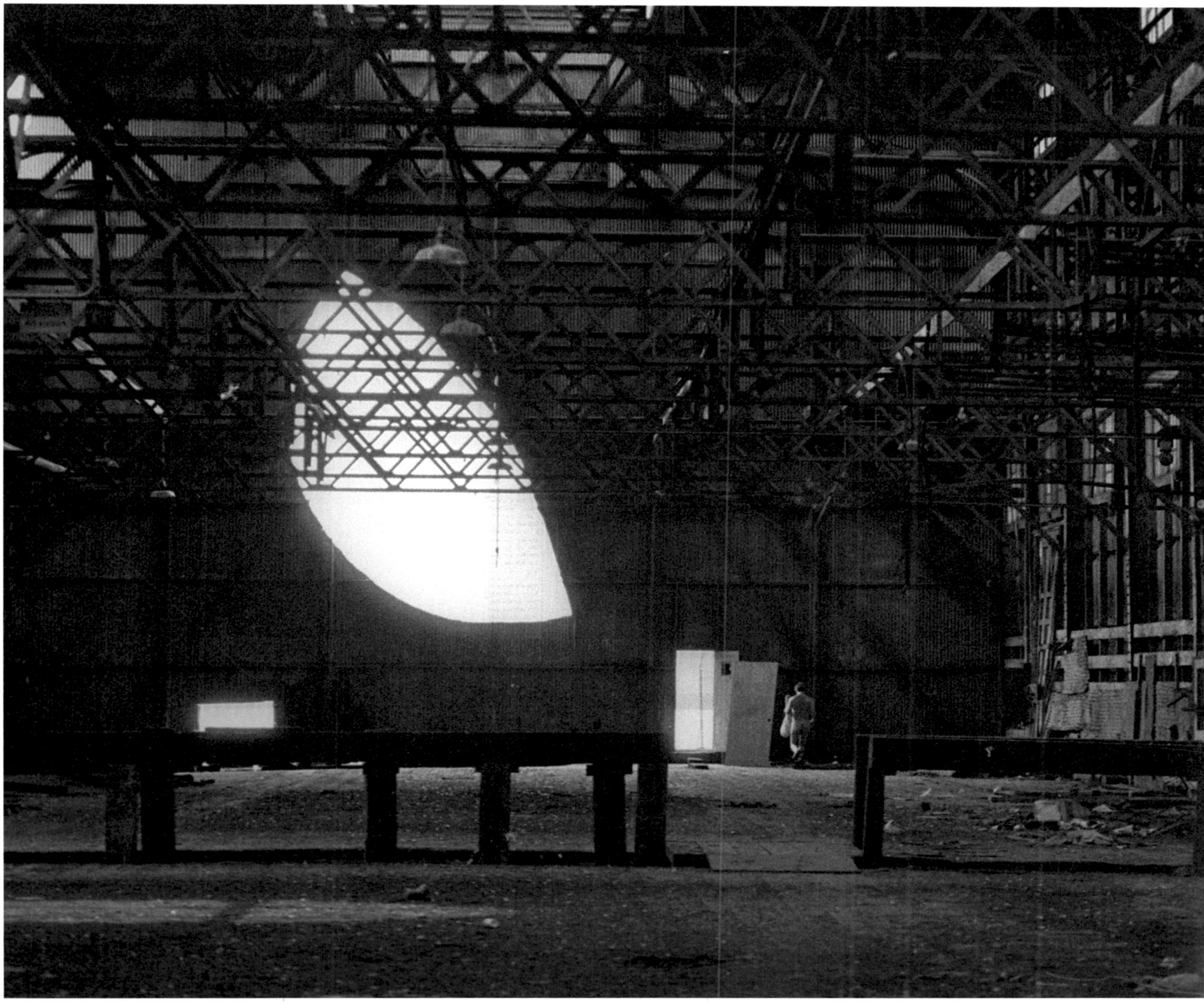

Plate 45 Alvin Baltrop, *Untitled* (from the series Pier Photographs), 1975–86

was an improvisational dance group that grew out of Yvonne Rainer's late 1960s Performance Demonstrations, especially *Continuous Project—Altered Daily* (1970). Its members were mostly dancers who had played a role in the Judson Dance Theater, including, in addition to Rainer, Trisha Brown, Barbara Dilley, Douglas Dunn, David p. 97 Gordon, Nancy Green, and Steve Paxton—though by the time I saw the Grand Union perform, Rainer had already left the group. I'd seen very little dance after my first ecstatic exposure to it in Merce Cunningham's Brooklyn Academy of Music engagement in the winter of 1970, where I saw, most memorably, *Rainforest* (1968), with Andy Warhol's helium-filled silver Mylar clouds as the set and music by David Tudor; *Walkaround Time* (1968), with Jasper Johns's clear plastic rectangular elements printed with images from Marcel Duchamp's *Large Glass* (1915–21), to the music of David Behrman; *Tread* (1970), with a set by Bruce Nauman of evenly spaced industrial pedestal fans across the front of the proscenium blowing toward the audience, music by Christian Wolff; and *Canfield* (1970), whose set by Robert Morris was a gray columnar light box that moved back and forth on a track, also at the front of the proscenium, illuminating the stage as it moved, music by Pauline Oliveros.

I saw Martha Graham dance *Clytemnestra* (1958) that same season, but I wasn't nearly as moved by Graham's expressionism as by Cunningham's repudiation of it, and Graham herself had by then become a self-parody. But Cunningham was something else entirely, something that thrilled me as much as anything I'd ever seen. I date my love of dance to that moment, so I can't understand now why I didn't continue to pursue it. By the time I first saw Rainer's work, she had already turned to filmmaking. p. 97 I did see *This is the story of a woman who…*, presented at the Theater for the New City in the West Village in 1973. In it Rainer performed *Three Satie Spoons* (1961), *Trio A* (1966), and *Walk, She Said* (1971), but otherwise the closest she came to dancing was when she performed the task of vacuuming the stage while wearing a green eyeshade.

It was, in fact, more performance art than dance that I was drawn to in the improvisational antics of the Grand Union dancers. And indeed, it was performance art that seemed to beckon as a substitute object for my libido. By this time, I had seen early works by Joan Jonas, who acknowledges a debt to Judson. In 1971, I sat with other audience members on the floor of Jonas's loft on Grand Street in SoHo to watch p. 97 her *Choreomania*, performed on a swinging mirrored wall constructed by Richard Serra. Here is a description of the performance space that Jonas and I wrote together ten years later for her Berkeley Art Museum exhibition catalogue:

> A twelve-by-eight-foot wall of wood hangs by chains from the ceiling two-and-a-half feet from the ground. Ropes and handles are attached to the back so that the five performers can climb the wall unseen by the spectators. The right-hand third of the front of the wall is mirrored. The wall can be swung back and forth and sideways by the performers, and their movements are

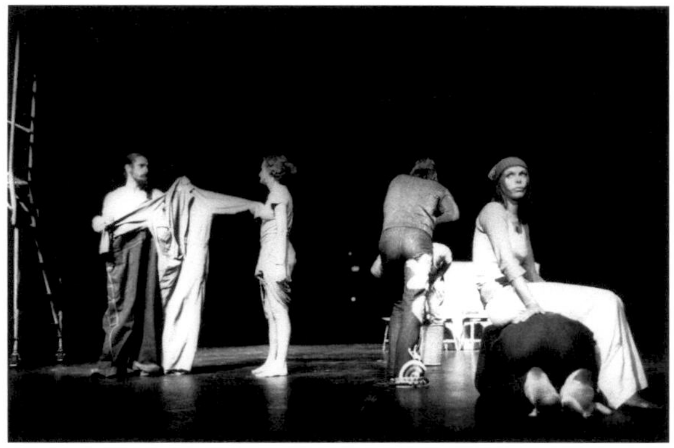

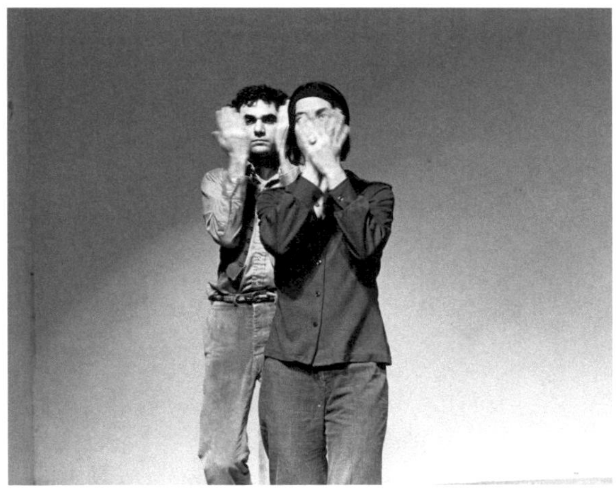

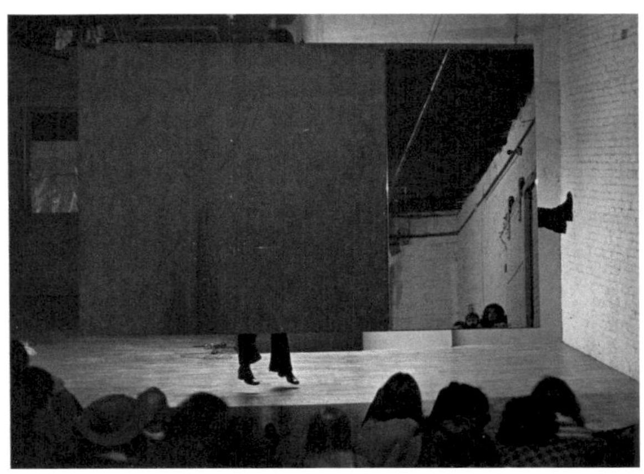

The Grand Union, *"There were some good moments…"*, 1973. Performance at Buffalo State College, Buffalo, NY, September 1973. Left to right: Steve Paxton, Trisha Brown, David Gordon, and Nancy Green. Photograph by Gwenn Thomas

Yvonne Rainer, *This is the story of a woman who…*, 1973. Performance at the Theater for the New City, New York, March 1973. Left to right: John Erdman and Yvonne Rainer, performing *Walk, She Said* (1971). Photograph by Babette Mangolte

Joan Jonas, *Choreomania*, 1971. Performance at Jonas's Grand Street loft, New York. Photograph by Carol Mersereau

> choreographed in relation to the wall's motion. The swinging of the wall on its chains, hung from the ceiling beams, creates the sound of the piece, a rhythmic creaking like that of a ship moving through the ocean's wake.
>
> The wall is hung so that it bisects the long narrow space of the loft. The spectators sit in the front half of the loft, facing the prop. The spectators' space and the spectators themselves are reflected in the mirrored portion of the wall as it swings from side to side. Because this wall is also the fourth wall of the spectators' space, the illusion is created that their space is swaying.
>
> The main function of the wall is to fragment the performance in such a way that much of the performance action is seen only around the wall's four edges. The appearing/disappearing actions recall a magic show.[1]

The few existing photographs that document *Choreomania* provide a good sense of what downtown New York performance spaces were like at the moment of performance art's birth. Often they were artists' private living and work spaces, large compared with the typical New Yorker's apartments, but small compared with public performance venues, even essentially makeshift ones like the Judson Church sanctuary. Seating was strictly on the floor, usually in an uncomfortable jumble of fellow audience members.

Artists' resourceful uses of the forsaken spaces of Manhattan's light industry in this era are now legendary. The deindustrialization of New York City in the postwar period had reached its most wrenching moment by the early 1970s, but some of us were unintended, temporary beneficiaries of the crisis even as others lost their jobs and homes at the same moment that social services were slashed. Some of the refashioned industrial spaces are now well known, such as 112 Greene Street, the alternative exhibition venue founded by Jeffrey Lew,[2] and the Kitchen, a performance space founded by Woody and Steina Vasulka, both of which predate by a year or so the relocation of many commercial galleries from uptown to SoHo. Less well documented is the fact that artists with large and relatively accessible lofts would open their spaces to guests for performances and concerts. I remember, for example, hearing Philip Glass's *Music in Twelve Parts* (1971–74) at an informal artist-loft gathering on a Sunday afternoon in SoHo. To enhance the experience, joints were freely passed around among the listeners.

Equally legendary, but rarely considered within this context, is the significance of these loft spaces to the birth of a very different kind of music and performance scene.[3] In 1970, David Mancuso started throwing rent parties in his SoHo loft that represented the pinnacle of disco for a generation and spawned a dance-club scene that persists today. A group of such clubs was at the center of New York nightlife throughout the decade. In 1974, just down the street from the Loft at the corner of Broadway and Houston Street, Michael Fesco opened a private gay disco called Flamingo on the second floor of a building that extended all the way through to Mercer

Street. A year later, 12 West opened in an old plant nursery at 12th and West streets on the northwestern edge of Greenwich Village. Toward the end of the decade, what some consider the greatest of all discos opened in a former truck garage on King Street west of 7th Avenue. It was called, appropriately enough, the Paradise Garage.[4]

But before these discos that followed the Loft came into being, there was another place for post-Stonewall liberated gay men and women to dance, an unused firehouse on Wooster Street in SoHo that had been taken over in the spring of 1971 by the Gay Activists Alliance. On Saturday nights, the old fire-engine garage became a dance hall, while up on the second floor, where firefighters once whiled away their time, dancers rested, drank beer, and cruised one another. In 1974, the firehouse was burned down, probably by neighborhood kids angry that fags and dykes were invading their territory every Saturday night. One of the perils of going to the Firehouse dances was the possibility of running into gangs of baseball-bat-wielding Italian-American kids. Most everyone knows that SoHo was an industrial area before it became a gallery/residential district. But what is now called SoHo had in fact already been a mixed-use neighborhood. The South of Houston Industrial District overlapped with an Italian residential neighborhood known as the South Village. The Feast of Saint Anthony, an Italian street fair, is still held every summer in front of the Shrine Church of Saint Anthony of Padua on Sullivan Street just below Houston Street. When I was searching for my first New York apartment in the early fall of 1967, I looked at a railroad flat on this very street but was frightened away by how rough the area seemed. I rented a place uptown in Spanish Harlem instead. Later, around the time I started going to the Firehouse dances, I spent one summer house-sitting for my friend Pat Steir, who lived in a loft on Mulberry Street in Little Italy, on the other side of SoHo, and again I remember feeling distinctly like an outsider and fearing that the neighborhood toughs would figure out that I was gay. I loved buying prosciutto and fresh mozzarella at the local markets, but the framed photographs of Mussolini in many of the shopwindows certainly gave me pause. Paradoxically—or maybe not—an interior designer I met at the Firehouse dances who became a sometime sex buddy and a lifelong friend was one of those very working-class New York Italians. He grew up in the projects on the Lower East Side, but when I met him in 1971 he lived a block north and east of Saint Anthony of Padua and then later, for years, a block south and west of the church in a garret apartment rented from family friends who owned a house in the old Italian neighborhood.

The one place to get a bite to eat in SoHo in the earliest years of artists living in the area was Fanelli Cafe, also a remnant of the area's Italian-American heritage. It got some competition from a very different kind of eatery in the fall of 1971, when dancer-choreographer Caroline Goodden, artist Gordon Matta-Clark, and a group of their friends opened a restaurant called Food, just up the street from the GAA Firehouse. Although Food survived into the early 1980s, it is now remembered

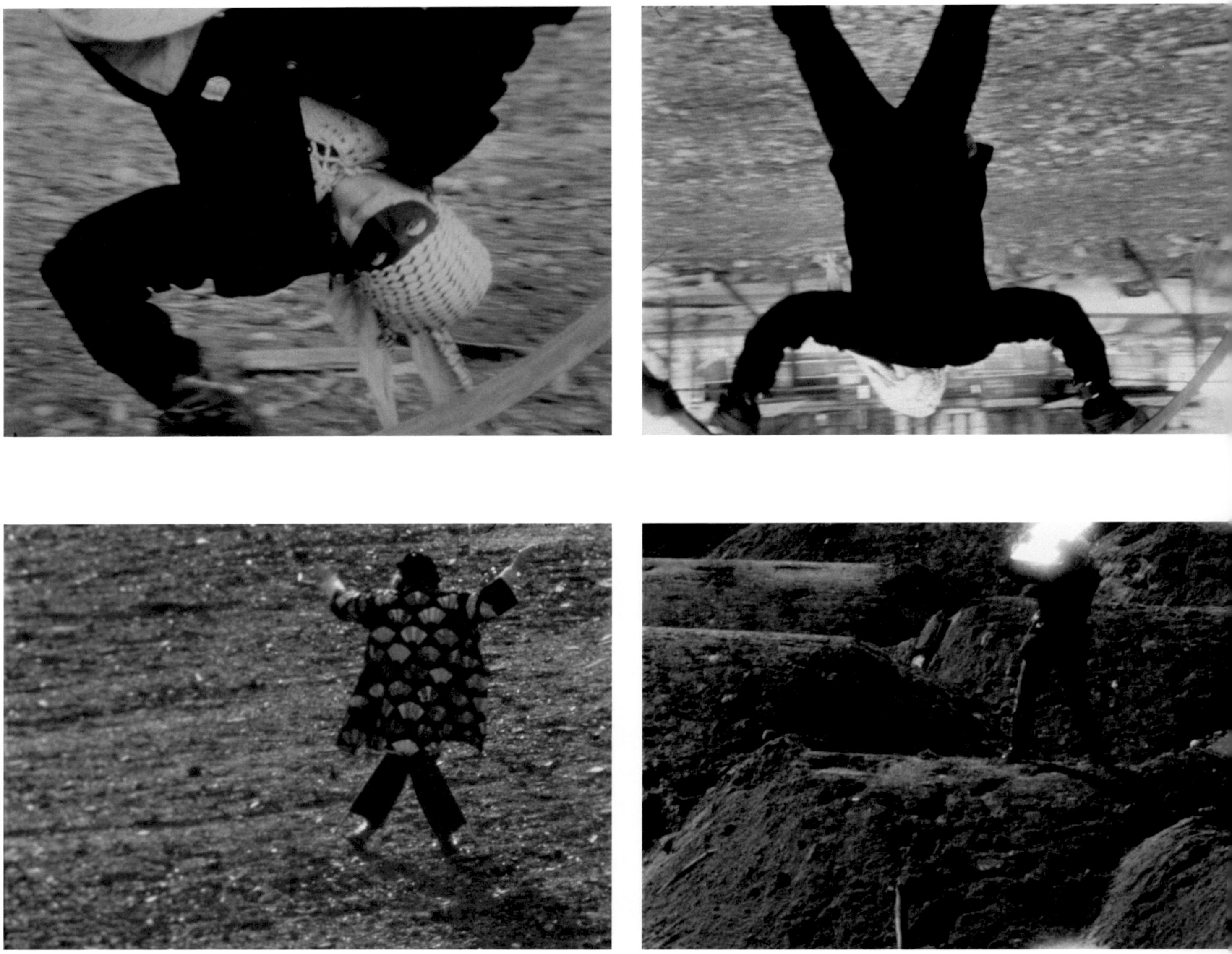

Plate 46 Joan Jonas, stills from *Songdelay*, 1973

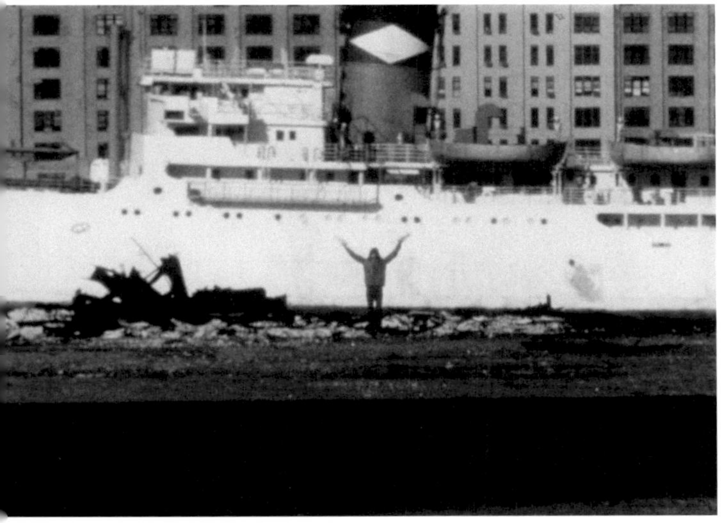

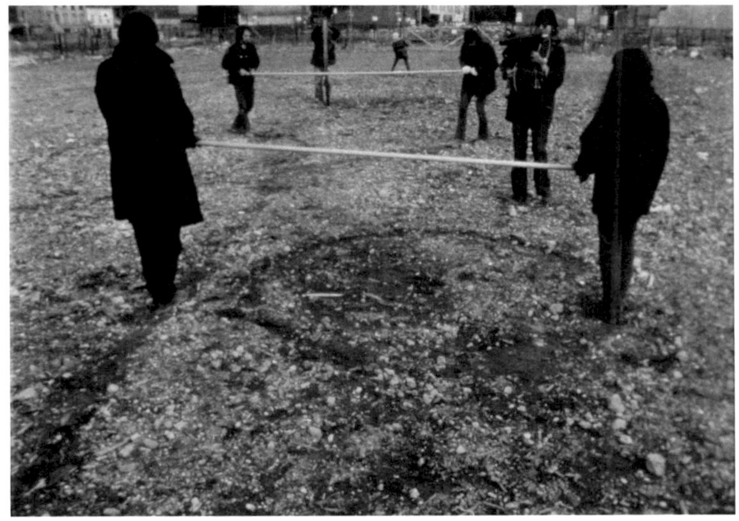

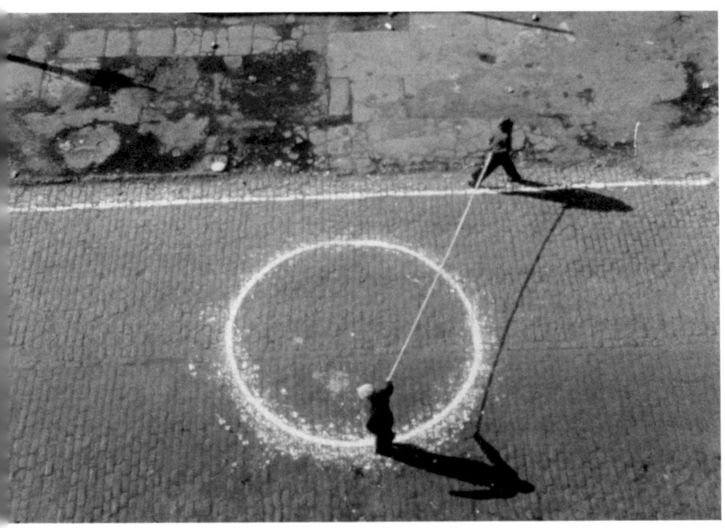

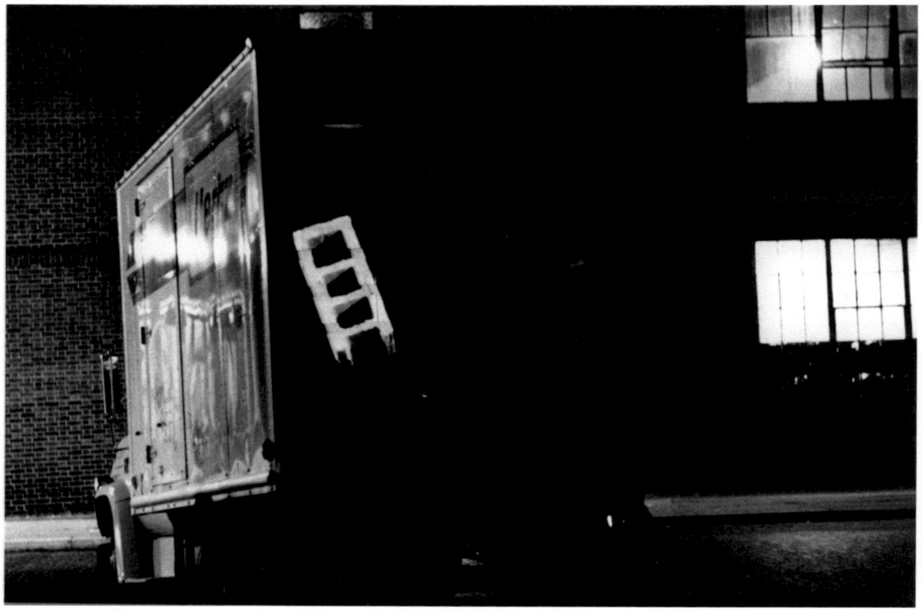

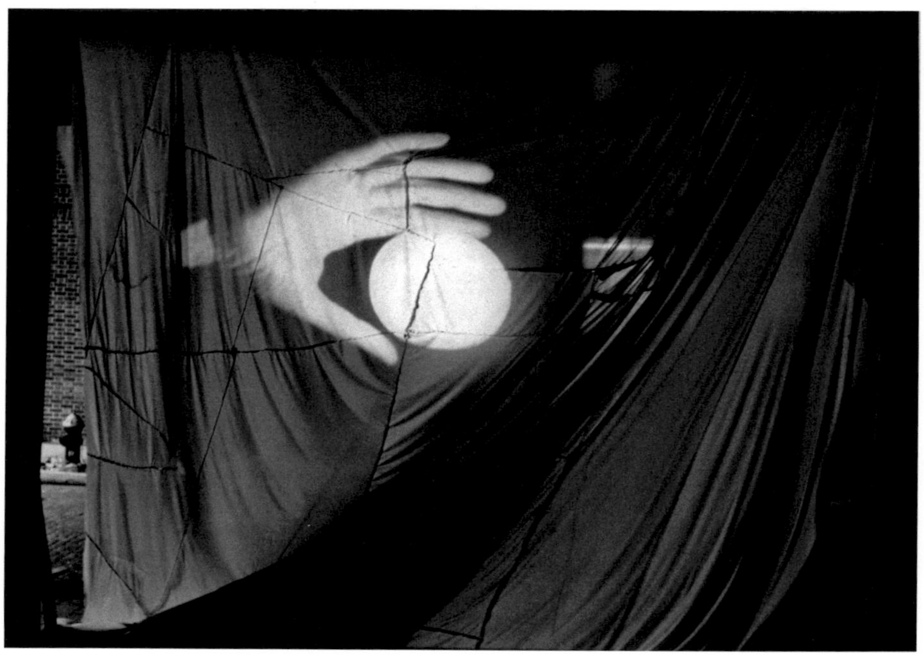

Plate 47 Babette Mangolte, *Light Touch (Robert Whitman)*, 1976.
Photographs of Robert Whitman's theater piece *Light Touch* (1976), performed at 393 Washington Street, New York, May 13–15, 1976

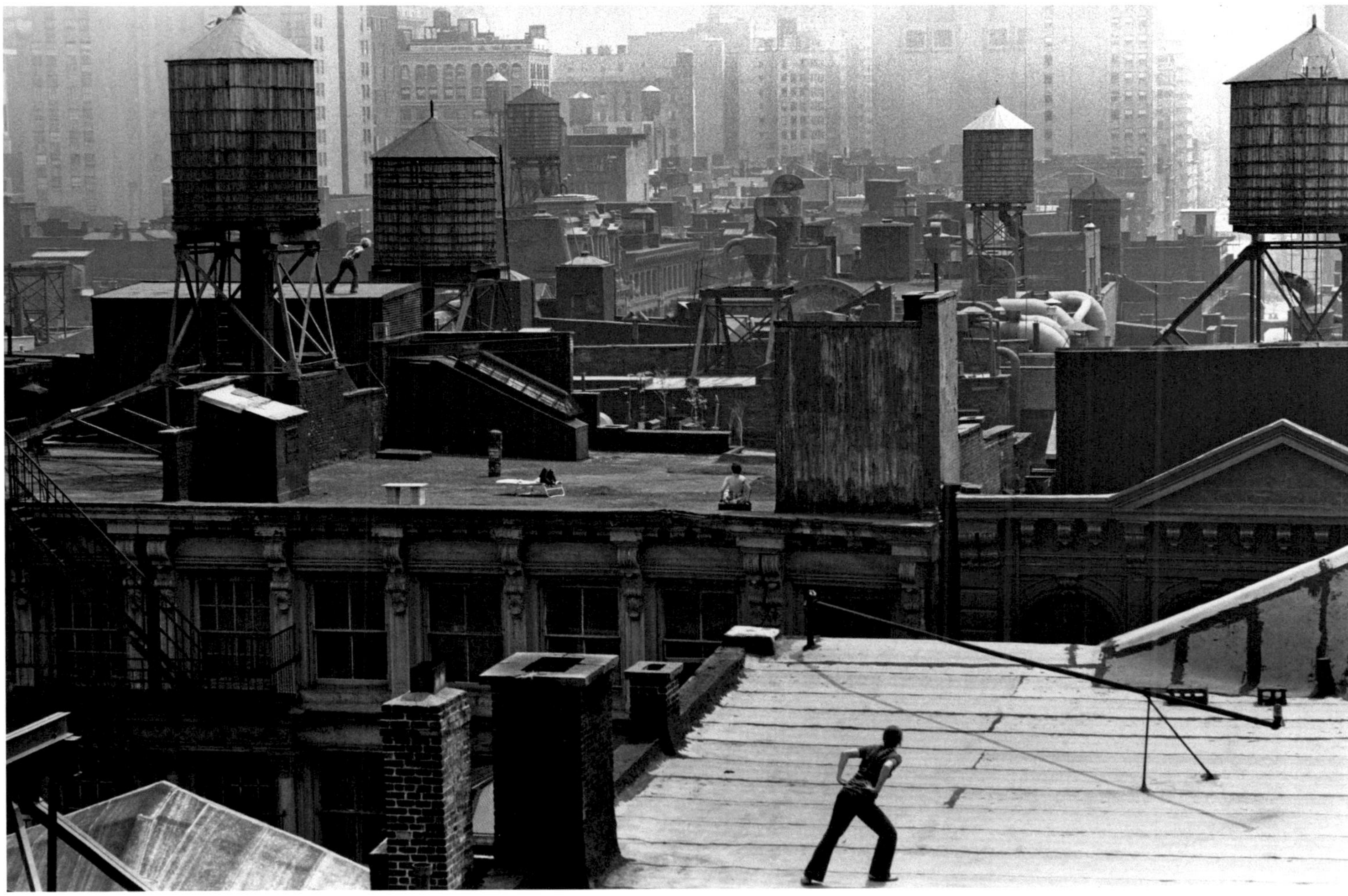

Plate 48 Babette Mangolte, *Roof Piece (Trisha Brown)*, 1973. Photograph of Trisha Brown's dance *Roof Piece* performed from 420 West Broadway to 36 White Street, New York, June 24 and July 1, 1973

best for its first two years of operation and is regarded as a long-running Matta-Clark performance piece. The documentary film that Matta-Clark made with Robert Frank and others in Food's first year reveals something of the place's communal feel, but it doesn't suggest performance art nearly as much as it does the daily labor of operating a restaurant. The film begins with before-dawn shopping at the Fulton Fish Market and ends after the restaurant has closed for the night, the chairs have been stacked on the tabletops, and a great many loaves of bread are being baked for the next day by a solitary baker, presumably, like most of Food's staff, an artist.

Matta-Clark is currently the figure most identified with the spirit of downtown Manhattan as a utopian artists' community and site of artistic experimentation in the 1970s, a status that no doubt derives in part from the fact that he died so young; his youth is all we know of him, and his short career coincided with a moment of particularly intense artistic ferment. But the identification also certainly has to do with the fact that the subject and the site of Matta-Clark's art were the city itself, the city experienced simultaneously as neglected and usable, as dilapidated and beautiful, as loss and possibility. Matta-Clark wrote,

> Work with abandoned structures began with my concern for the life of the city of which a major side effect is the metabolization of old buildings. Here as in many urban centers the availability of empty and neglected structures was a prime textural reminder of the ongoing fallacy of renewal through modernization. The omnipresence of emptiness, of abandoned housing and imminent demolition gave me the freedom to experiment with the multiple alternatives to one's life in a box as well as popular attitudes about the need for enclosure....
>
> The earliest works were also a foray into a city that was still evolving for me. It was an exploration of New York's least remembered parts of the space between the walls of views inside out. I would drive around in my pick-up hunting for emptiness, for a quiet abandoned spot on which to concentrate my piercing attention.[5]

"Hunting for emptiness" in a dense urban fabric like Manhattan might seem incongruous, and indeed today it would be well-nigh futile. But New York was a very different city three decades ago. I offer as evidence several series of photographs taken in the pp. 109–13 mid- to late 1970s, among them Bernard Guillot's *12th Avenue (dedicated to Orpheus and Eurydice)* (1977). Guillot, a French artist who lived for several years in New York during this period, was an indefatigable explorer of the city's overlooked neighborhoods, which resulted in, among other things, his living clandestinely in a ninth-floor loft at the corner of Broadway and Canal Street. Since the loft was in a still-working industrial building, its elevator was available to Bernard and his guests only from 9:00 am

to 5:00 pm, and Bernard was not a nine-to-five kind of guy. You had to be a determined friend to visit him at home. Guillot's exploratory bent resulted, more importantly, in *12th Avenue*, a series of 184 photographs of Manhattan's farthest western periphery shot along a route from Greenwich Village northward to 42nd Street. The photographs were taken on two outings in 1977 and record—systematically, but not rigorously so, at intervals of several paces—views of the city looking north and east along the streets bordering the Hudson River (12th Avenue exists only north of 22nd Street). In them, we recognize a few landmarks of their time, most memorably the gay sex club the Anvil at the foot of 11th Avenue at 14th Street; and familiar landmarks of today in their p. 111
1970s guise, such as the Gansevoort Market, the High Line, and the Starrett-Lehigh p. 109
Building in Chelsea. What is difficult for us to comprehend now is the bright-daylight emptiness these photographs show. Together with a few signs of still-existing industry—tractor trailers backed into loading docks, the parked cars of factory workers, lots full of delivery trucks and moving vans, luncheonettes—there are empty lots overgrown with weeds, heaps of rubble, barricaded streets, abandoned cars, and railroad tracks no longer in use. Almost entirely absent from the images are people.

Similarly showing urban emptiness is a group of photographs by pp. 85–86
Peter Hujar dating from 1976, taken not during the day but at night and on a route that goes in the opposite direction from Guillot's, down the Far West Side of Manhattan, southward from the Meatpacking District to the Battery Park City landfill and around the Financial District and Civic Center. These photographs are of two kinds, one showing desolate, fading industrial areas, and the other, downtown Manhattan emptied out after business hours. Mediating the two are photographs of parking lots. All of them, to my mind, are cruising pictures—cruising pictures with no people in them: this, too, might seem incongruous. But the point of cruising—or at least *one* point of cruising—is feeling yourself alone and anonymous in the city, feeling that the city belongs to you, to you and maybe a chanced-on someone else like you—like you at least in an exploration of the empty city. Is there by chance someone else wandering these deserted streets? Might that someone else be on the prowl? Could the two of us find a dark corner where we could get together? Can the city become just *ours* for this moment?

Not everyone experiences urban emptiness this way. A year after Hujar made these pictures, Cindy Sherman began shooting her famous series of *Untitled* pp. 120–23
Film Stills (1977–80), also on the deserted streets of Lower Manhattan. Hers are very different kinds of pictures, not least because most of them are taken, like Guillot's, during the daytime (Lower Manhattan, too, was deserted back then, even during the day on weekends). But they are also different because they always include a lone female character played by Sherman herself and are staged in such a way as to suggest an incident in that character's story. The few of them that were shot on the streets at night are noirish images of threatened femininity, showing an apprehensive woman walking

down a dark and forlorn street. But this woman is not Cindy Sherman and the city is not New York; the city in these pictures is a generic city, like a film location. This is a woman in a city, and the city is not a good place for her to be right now. (Of course, the notion that a city street at night is no place for a woman is also belied by Sherman's use of this very street to make her photograph.)

Another work that suggests—and simultaneously pokes fun at—the dangers facing women on desolate Manhattan streets was made in response to artists' using the abandoned city in the early 1970s. The work is Louise Lawler's sound piece p. 119 *Birdcalls* (1972/1981), in which Lawler "squeals, squawks, chirps, twitters, croaks, squeaks, and occasionally warbles the names—primarily the surnames—of twenty-eight contemporary male artists, from Vito Acconci to Lawrence Weiner" (I borrow Rosalyn Deutsche's concise description).[6] Lawler explains that the work

> originated in the early 1970s when my friend Martha Kite and I were helping some artists on one of the Hudson River pier projects. The women involved were doing tons of work, but the work being shown was only by male artists. Walking home at night in New York, one way to feel safe is to pretend you're crazy or at least be really loud. Martha and I called ourselves the *dewey chantoosies*, and we'd sing off-key and make other noises. Willoughby Sharp was the impresario of this project, so we'd make a "Willoughby Willoughby" sound, trying to sound like birds. This developed into a series of bird calls based on artists' names.[7]

The show in question was *Projects: Pier 18*, a sequence of projects by twenty-seven artists, all male, commissioned by Sharp and photographed by the art-world photographic team Shunk-Kender. The resulting photographic series were subsequently exhibited at the Museum of Modern Art.[8] While the works were situated on the pier and often took it as their subject, many also provide intriguing views of a greater p. 67 expanse of the city in 1971. For example, John Baldessari's *Hands Framing New York Harbor* is a single photograph of a freighter moored at the pier, framed by a rectangle in the foreground made by the artist's thumbs and index fingers pressed together. Above and to the right of the hands we see the downtown skyline, including the Woolworth Building on Broadway, the top of the U.S. Courthouse in Foley Square, and the New York Telephone Company building on West Street. Looming up in front of the Woolworth Building is the huge sign for the *New York World-Telegram*, a newspaper that had been defunct for several years by 1971.

p. 68 Dan Graham's description of his work for *Projects: Pier 18* reads: "Still camera pressed to body—Beginning at my feet, each shot progressively spirals to top of my head—Lens faces out—back of camera side pressed flush to contour of skin."[9] pp. 70–71 The photographs Graham took as he moved the camera in a spiral around his body capture oblique views of the pier, the river, and the skyline. In some, we see fragments of the twin towers of the World Trade Center, their summits not yet completed.

Most of the old industrial piers along the West Side of Manhattan on the Hudson River, including Pier 18, stood abandoned and in partial or nearly total ruin at that time; when you walked on them you were in constant danger of falling through the floor or falling off the rotting timbered edges into the river six or eight feet below. On those piers that retained their superstructures, the upper rooms could also be hazardous. Vito Acconci's work for *Projects: Pier 18*, titled *Security Zone*, made at least oblique reference to the sense of remoteness and danger of Manhattan's Lower West Side piers. Acconci—with hands bound behind his back, blindfolded, and wearing earplugs—entrusted his safety to fellow artist Lee Jaffe as he walked around the far end of the pier. The piece was, Acconci wrote, "designed to affect, improve, an everyday relationship" by forcing himself to develop trust in someone about whom he had "ambiguous" feelings.[10] Looking at the photographs, you sometimes can't tell whether Jaffe is about to push Acconci off the edge of the pier or is saving him from falling off.

Acconci made even more explicit the sense of danger in the piers in an untitled project for Pier 17 a month later. He posted a notice at the John Gibson Gallery during his exhibition there, announcing that from March 27 to April 24 he would wait at the end of the pier for one hour every night, beginning at 1:00 am, and that anyone who came there to meet him would be rewarded by being told a secret he had never before divulged, something about which he felt ashamed and that could be used against him. In addition to having to make himself vulnerable by revealing to whoever showed up a dirty secret, Acconci had to confront the dangers of the deserted pier itself: on the "first night," he writes, "I'm waiting outside, afraid to go in (inside I'll be on unfamiliar ground—I could be taken unawares—from outside I can get a view of the whole—if anyone comes, I'll have to go in after him, overtake him before he stakes out a position)."[11] Acconci recalls what ensued one night when a visitor showed up: "Someone shouts my name at the entrance. I don't answer him: he has to be willing to throw himself into it, he has to come and get me (I'm in the position of prey—I have to be stalked)."[12]

Gordon Matta-Clark, too, made a project for *Pier 18*, but his reference to endangerment was, as in so much of his work, one of bravura, of physical derring-do rather than psychological vulnerability. At Pier 18, he planted an evergreen tree in what he called "a parked island barge" and suspended himself by rope upside down above it. But this stunt was only a harmless rehearsal for what would be Matta-Clark's most audacious act and certainly one of his most magnificent works, *Day's End* (1975), his summer-long transformation of the dilapidated Pier 52, which stood at the end of Gansevoort Street in New York's Meatpacking District.

Like most people, I know *Day's End* only from photographs, written descriptions, and the film that documents its making. Regrettably, I didn't see the actual work. Matta-Clark talked about it in a number of interviews; the one he gave in Antwerp at the time he made *Office Baroque* (1977), a few years after he completed *Day's End*, is for me the most evocative:

> Pier 52 is an intact nineteenth-century industrial relic of steel and corrugated tin looking like an enormous Christian basilica whose dim interior was barely lit by the clerestory windows fifty feet overhead.
>
> The initial cuts were made through the pier floor across the center forming a tidal channel nine feet wide by seventy feet long. A similar shape through the roof directly above this channel allows a patch of light to enter which arches over the floor until it's captured at noon within the watery slot. During the afternoon the sun shines through a cat's-eye-like "rose window" in the west wall. At first a sliver and then a strongly defined shape of light continues to wander into the wharf until the whole pier is fully illuminated at dusk. Below the rear "wall-hole" is another large quarter circle cut opening the floor of the south-west corner to a turbulent view of the Hudson water. The water and sun move constantly in the pier throughout the day in what I saw as an indoor park.[13]

Matta-Clark referred to the three months of work on *Day's End* as his "summer
p. 149 vacation...by the water."[14] Judging from the film that Betsy Sussler shot of it, it wasn't a restful vacation. Working with his friend Gerry Hovagimyan, Matta-Clark used such heavy-duty tools as a chain saw and a blowtorch to cut through the timbers of the pier's floor and corrugated tin roof and facade. The most dramatic moments of the film show Matta-Clark wielding the blowtorch as he dangles on a small platform strung up by rope pulley about twenty feet above the pier's floor. Often shirtless but wearing protective goggles as sparks fly about, Matta-Clark cuts the west-end oculus through the tin siding in a performance that is equal parts Harold Lloyd and Douglas Fairbanks. Matta-Clark speaks of the "element of absurdity in the whole activity,"[15] even as his references to the basilica-like structure and "rose window" that he added to it sacralize the setting. Some who had the good fortune to see *Day's End* relate a sense of awe enhanced by fear. Sculptor Joel Shapiro recalls that "the piece was dangerous," that Matta-Clark "was creating some kind of edge—flirting with some sort of abyss."[16] But Matta-Clark intended the opposite kind of experience:

> The one thing that I wanted was to make it possible for people to see it...in a peaceful enclosure totally enclosed in an un-menacing kind of way. That when they went in there, they wouldn't feel like every squeak or every shadow was

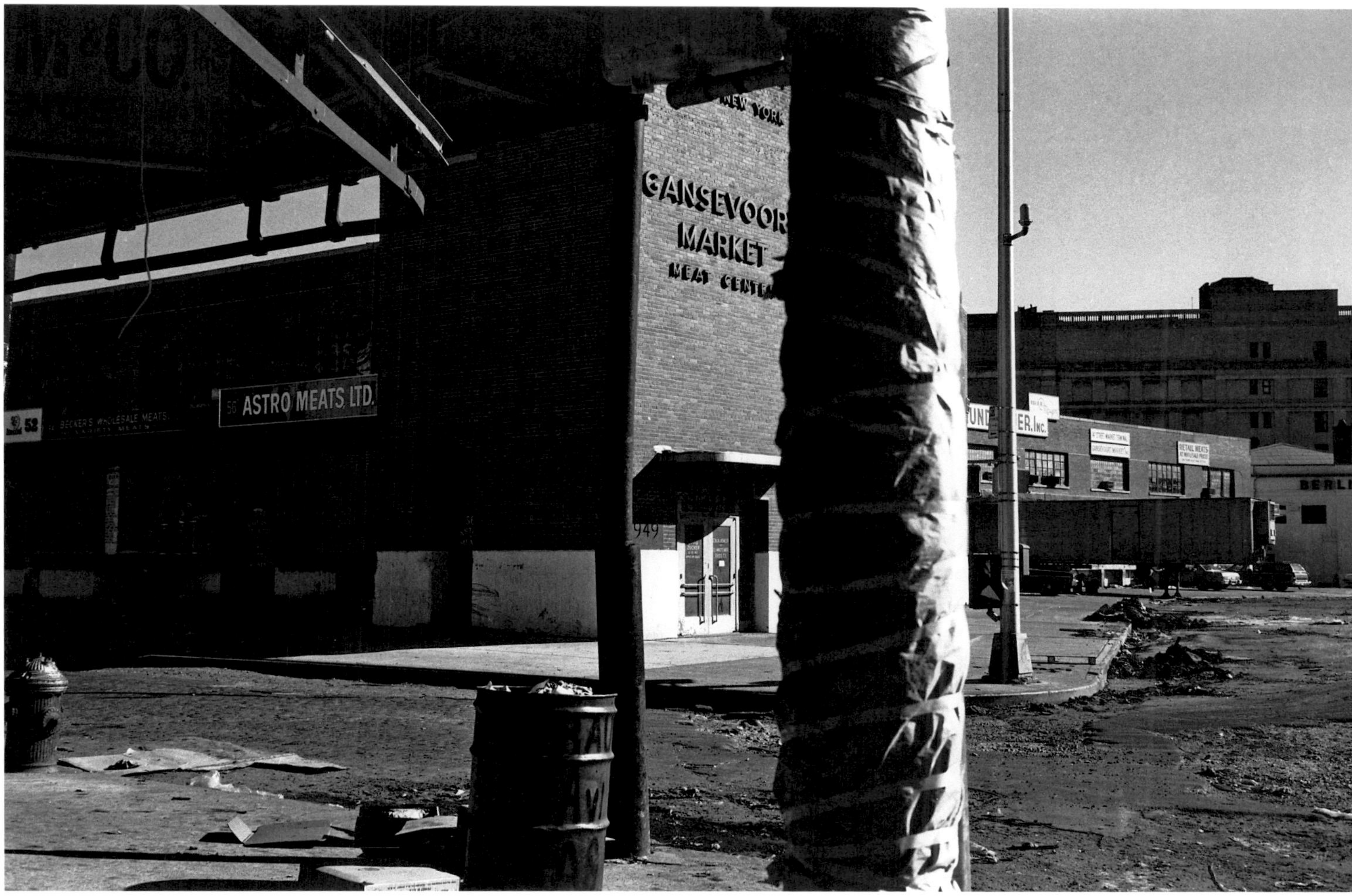

Plate 49 Bernard Guillot, *12th Avenue (dedicated to Orpheus and Eurydice)*, 1977

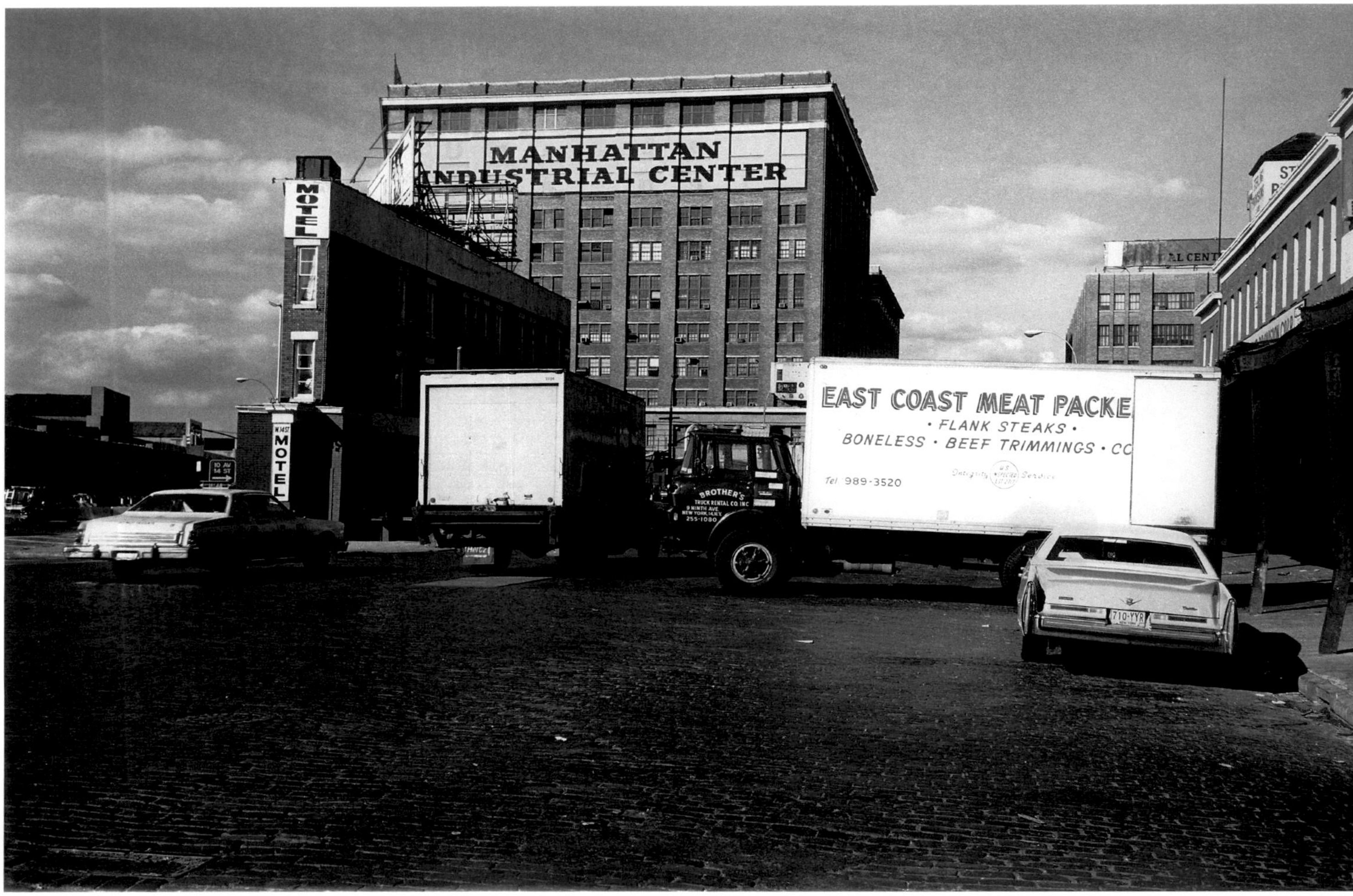

Plate 50 Bernard Guillot, *12th Avenue (dedicated to Orpheus and Eurydice)*, 1977

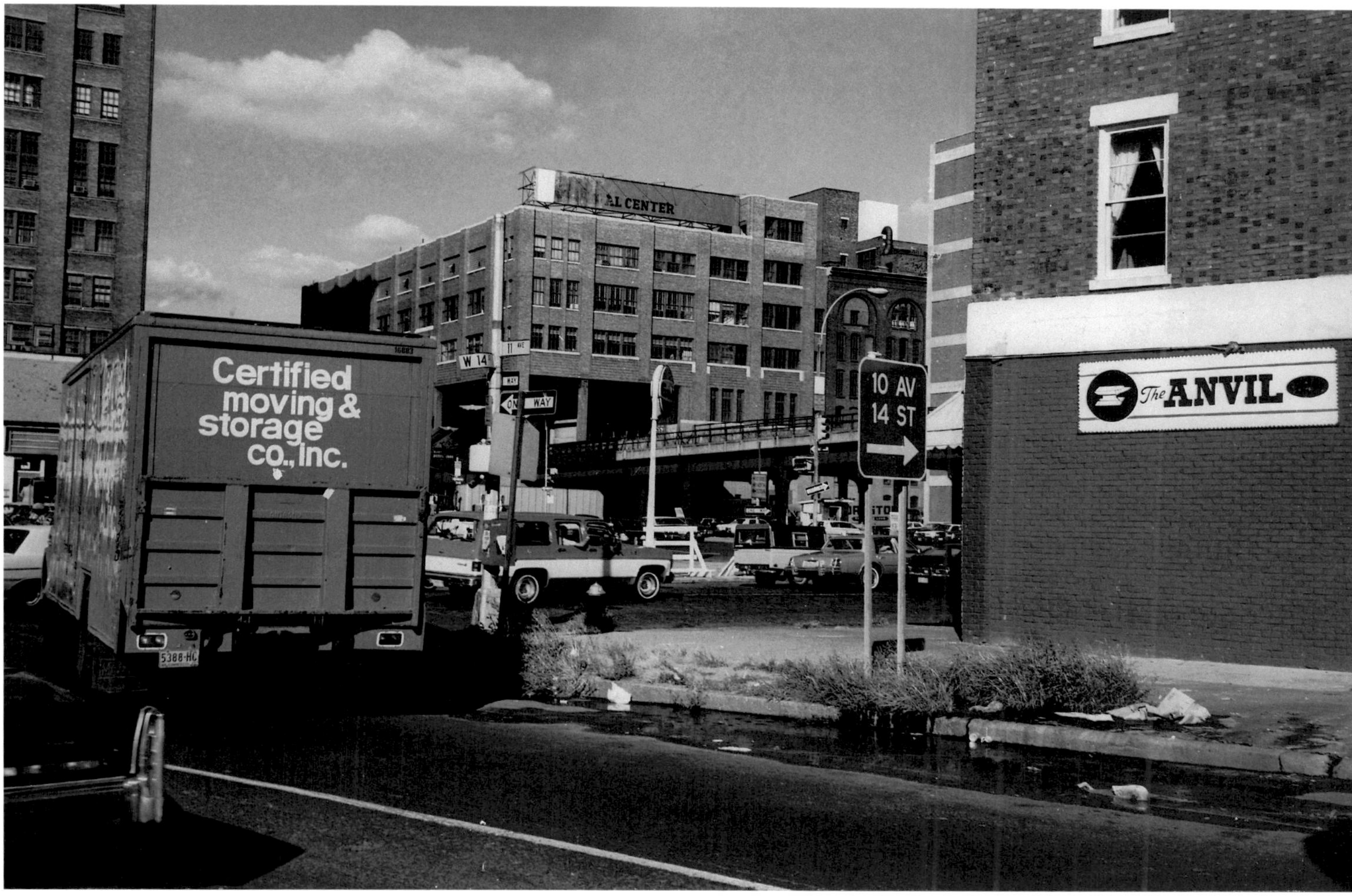

Plate 51 Bernard Guillot, *12th Avenue (dedicated to Orpheus and Eurydice)*, 1977

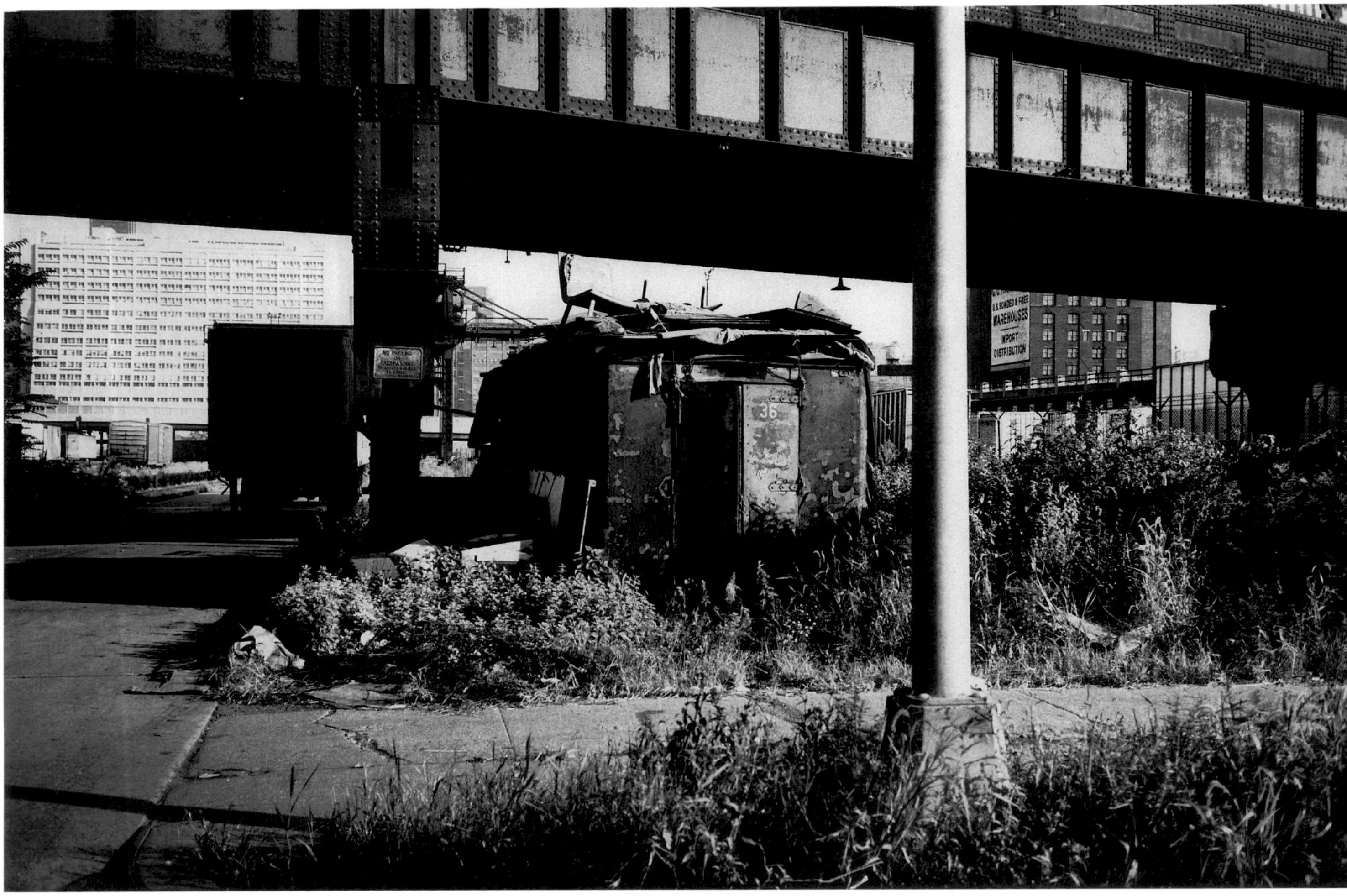

Plate 52 Bernard Guillot, *12th Avenue (dedicated to Orpheus and Eurydice)*, 1977

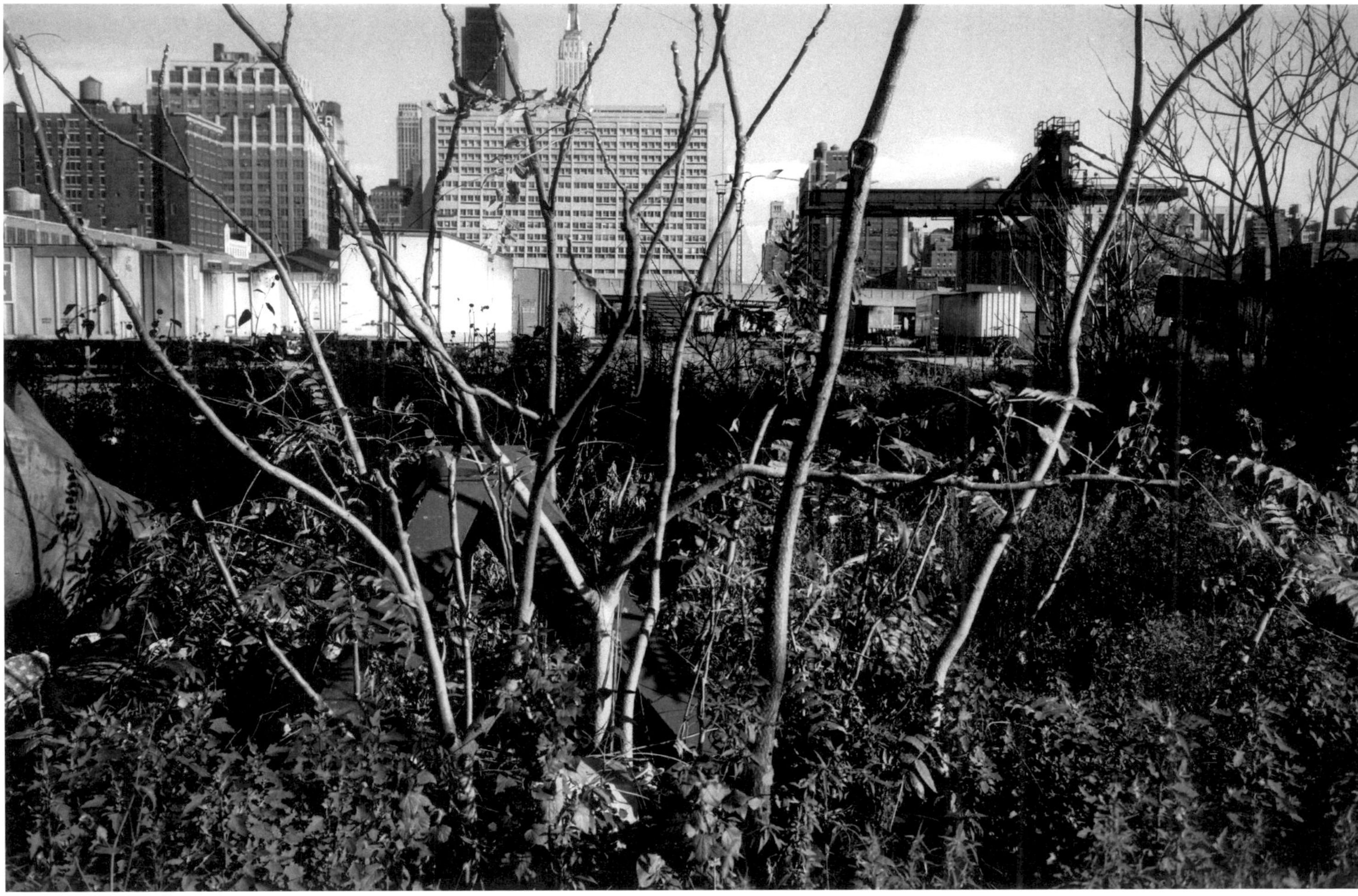

Plate 53 Bernard Guillot, *12th Avenue (dedicated to Orpheus and Eurydice)*, 1977

> a potential threat. I know in lots of the earlier works that I did, the kind of paranoia of being in a space where you didn't know who was there, what was happening or whether there were menacing people lurking about, was just distracting. And I just wanted it to be a more joyous situation.[17]

"An indoor park," "joyous," "dangerous," "absurd," "flirting with the abyss": descriptions of *Day's End* by Matta-Clark and others make it impossible for me not to think of the experiences of those other pier occupants, the ones from whom Matta-Clark seems in nearly all his statements about the work to want to differentiate himself—"you know, that whole S&M," as he put it.[18] Although in many instances Matta-Clark aligned his work with others who took over or otherwise made their mark on abandoned parts of cities, particularly workers, homeless people, and disenfranchised youth, in the case of Pier 52, Matta-Clark not only disavowed any bond with the gay men who were using the piers as cruising grounds but went so far as to lock them out:

> After looking up and down the waterfront for a pier, I just happened on this one. And of all of them, it was the one that was least trafficked. It had been broken into and was continuing to be broken into when I was there. But it remained a kind of side step from their general haunt. So I went in and realized without very much effort I could secure it. And it then occurred to me that while I was closing up holes and barb-wiring various parts, I would also change the lock and have my own lock. It would make it so much easier.[19]

It may be that Matta-Clark had no particular animus toward the gay men who were using the pier but that he simply wanted to be able to go about his work undisturbed, to protect himself from intruders of any kind. He might even have worried about liability should someone get hurt as a result of his cutting away sections of the pier's floor. But it's difficult to say, because Matta-Clark wasn't especially careful to differentiate among the various dangers that journalists writing at the time about the sexual activity at the piers often conflated: hazardous, disintegrating structures; threatening, perverse sexuality; and criminals who preyed on, robbed, and sometimes even murdered the piers' clandestine users:

> Besides my personal feelings of base mismanagement of the dying harbor and its ghost-like terminals, is the inextricable evidence of a new criminal situation of alarming proportions. The waterfront was probably never anything but tough and dangerous but now with this long slow transition period, it has become a veritable muggers' playground, both for people who go only to enjoy walking there and for a recently popularized sado-masochistic fringe.[20]

Gay men were acutely aware of the piers' dangers, and they painted, together with vernacular artwork and graffiti, signs warning fellow cruisers to watch their wallets. Moreover, Matta-Clark wasn't the only one who took to the piers for a summer vacation by the water. Shielded from public view by the warehouse structure, gay men used the pier's end that jutted far out into the river as a place to sunbathe. It doesn't, I think, diminish the accomplishment of *Day's End* to say that a romantic grandeur was perceptible in the ruined piers before Matta-Clark ever wrought a single change on Pier 52 and that much of the pleasure that gay men took in being at the piers was what drew artists to them as well. It's not just that the piers were there and available; they were also vast and hauntingly beautiful. Nor was the sex play on the piers only of the rough and kinky variety, unless you think that any kind of sex outside a domestic setting is kinky.

The entire range of pleasures and dangers of the piers was captured by a too-little-known African-American photographer, Alvin Baltrop, who documented the goings-on there during the 1970s and 80s, up to and including the piers' demolition in the mid- to late 1980s. A number of Baltrop's photographs show gay men at Pier 52, taking in the beauty of Matta-Clark's *Day's End* along with whatever other beauties they might be pursuing. Indeed, these photographs wonderfully portray the "peaceful enclosure" and "joyous situation" that Matta-Clark said he wanted to achieve.[21] Like Matta-Clark, Baltrop also hoisted himself on a harness high in the air to make his work. In the preface for a book that he worked unsuccessfully to complete before dying of cancer in 2004, Baltrop wrote: pp. 93–95

> Although initially terrified of the Piers, I began to take these photos as a voyeur, but soon grew determined to preserve the frightening, mad, unbelievable, violent, and beautiful things that were going on at that time. To get certain shots, I hung from the ceilings of several warehouses utilizing a makeshift harness, watching and waiting for hours to record the lives that these people led (friends, acquaintances, and strangers), and the unfortunate ends that they sometimes met. The casual sex and nonchalant narcotizing, the creation of artwork and music, sunbathing, dancing, merrymaking and the like habitually gave way to muggings, callous yet detached violence, rape, suicide, and in some instances, murder. The rapid emergence and expansion of AIDS in the 1980s further reduced the number of people going to and living at the Piers, and the sporadic joys that could be found there.[22]

Baltrop photographed obsessively: men engaged in sex shot from the distance of a neighboring pier or clandestinely through a doorway, and men happy to become exhibitionists for the camera at close-up range; portraits of men and women Baltrop came to know at the piers, including some who had no place else to live; guys cruising for sex, sometimes as naked as the nearby sunbathers; people just strolling about, transfixed by the rays of sunlight streaming through disintegrating roof structures; graffiti, some of it the skillful handiwork of an artist known as Tava, who painted in a style that amalgamates Greek vase painting with Tom of Finland; gruesome corpses dredged up from the river and surrounded by the police and onlookers. Most of all, Baltrop photographed the piers themselves. The phantoms of New York's bustling industrial past appear in his pictures as vast heaps of trusses, buckled tin siding, rotting wooden pilings and floors, rickety staircases, and broken windows, sometimes with a ragged curtain still flapping in the river breezes. Baltrop's camera often zeros in on a just-discernable scene of butt fucking or cock sucking amid the rubble, but even when the sex is absent, we recognize the piers as the sexual playground they were.

Unlike Baltrop, I didn't feel consciously afraid of the piers. They were part of my neighborhood cityscape and one of many nearby places to play outdoors. Located a short walk from my apartment on 10th Street, Pier 42, which no longer had a structure on it, was a local place to hang out and be cooled by the Hudson River's breezes on hot summer days and watch the sun set over New Jersey in the evening. Even closer was Pier 45, the main gay-cruising pier, where the upper-floor warren of rooms along the West Street end functioned day and night like a sex club with no cover charge. Pier 45 was only one of many nearby places for outdoor sex play. Another Greenwich Village haunt of men seeking other men was known simply as "the trucks," a designation for the empty lots along Washington Street north of Christopher Street where delivery trucks were parked at night. After the bars closed at 4:00 am, gay men gathered in the spaces behind the trucks and often up inside the back of them for group sex. If you lived in the Village, this was an efficient way to bring your night at the bars to a satisfying end without having to repair to a bathhouse in another neighborhood. I remember a short period around 1973, before I first discovered the scene at the piers, when, late at night and into the morning, gay men also took over the half-completed structures of the West Village Houses, going up along Washington Street across from the trucks. The West Village Houses were a long-debated, underfinanced, and therefore architecturally diminished project of 420 units of low-rise, middle-income housing that indirectly resulted from Jane Jacobs's 1961 classic critique of modern urbanism, *The Death and Life of Great American Cities*.[23] Although Jacobs's ideas about what made cities great—short blocks, dense concentrations of people, mixed uses, and aged buildings—grew out of her love of her own neighborhood, Greenwich Village, I don't think they included men meeting for sex in construction sites, parking lots, and waterfront warehouses, but this was part of the Village life I knew at the time.

Come to think of it, maybe I *was* afraid of the piers—afraid not only of their very real dangers, of which I tended to be overtly and stupidly dismissive, but also of their easy proximity and constant promise. I was struggling to write about art professionally as a freelancer then, which took more discipline than I could usually muster, since the frustrations of being unable to find a good subject, devise a sound argument, even compose a sentence I was happy with or choose a word that rang true, could be easily if only momentarily alleviated by just walking out my door and into the playground that was my immediate neighborhood. This must be why seeing the Grand Union perform sticks in my mind as being such a momentous event for me, why it propelled me to another part of the city and another world. Apart from monthly reviewing for *Art News* and *Art International*, the most ambitious writing I managed during the several years I lived in the Village was a short monographic essay on Agnes Martin called "Number, Measure, Ratio" and a commissioned essay, which I titled "Opaque Surfaces," for the catalogue of an exhibition held in Milan of American Minimalist painters from Martin and Ad Reinhardt to Brice Marden and Richard Tuttle.[24] In both essays, I struggled to think beyond the Greenbergian formalism that still held sway in so much American art criticism at that time. What would finally free me from its grip was not painting but performance art.

The loft in Tribeca to which I moved in 1974 was just a block or so from the site of what had been perhaps the most ambitious and imaginative use of the deindustrializing city as the stage for an artwork, Joan Jonas's 1972 performance *Delay* p. 124 *Delay*.[25] A year later, the performance was translated into the language of film in *Songdelay*, as compelling an aesthetic document of New York City of its era as Paul pp. 100–101 Strand and Charles Sheeler's 1921 city-symphony film *Manhatta* is of the city half a century earlier. Once again, Jonas and I describe the performance space of *Delay Delay* in our 1983 book:

> The spectators view the performance from the roof of a five-story loft building facing west, located at 319 Greenwich Street in lower Manhattan. The performing area is a ten-block grid of city streets bounding vacant lots and leveled buildings. Beyond these lots are the elevated West Side Highway, the docks and piers along the Hudson River, and the factories of the New Jersey skyline across the river. Directly in front of the spectators at the back of the performance area is the Erie Lackawanna Pier building painted with large numbers 20 and 21. These indicate the old pier numbers.[26]

By the time I moved to Tribeca, these downtown piers had been torn down to make way for Battery Park City, which was then put on hold during the city's fiscal crisis. New York was going bankrupt, and its infrastructure was badly deteriorating, visibly symbolized in late 1973 by the collapse of a section of the elevated West Side Highway under the weight of an asphalt-laden repair truck. Just half a block down the street from the loft I moved into, the city trailed off into vacant lots. Beyond the razed blocks that had once been the Washington Market was the elevated highway, now empty, too, and beyond that, where the piers had been, a barren landfill that Lower Manhattan residents

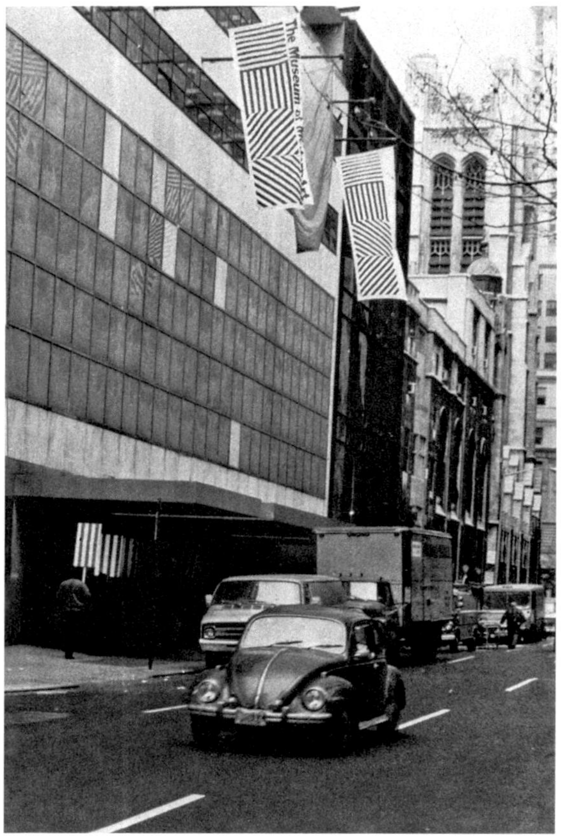

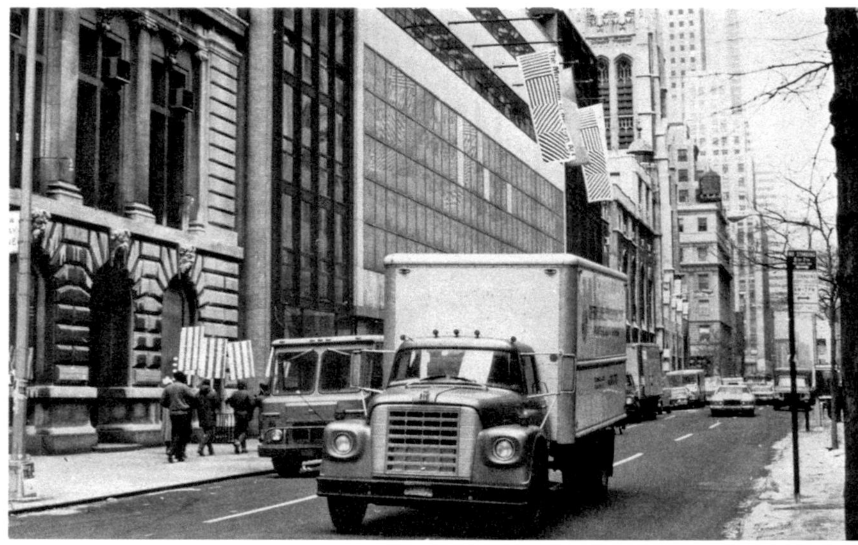

Plate 54 Louise Lawler, *Volkswagen*, 1978. Postcard with photograph of Daniel Buren's performance *Seven Ballets in Manhattan: Ballet no. 6 "Central Park"* (1975) in front of the Museum of Modern Art, New York, June 1, 1975

Plate 55 Louise Lawler, *Truck,* 1978. Postcard with photograph of Daniel Buren's performance *Seven Ballets in Manhattan: Ballet no. 6 "Central Park"* (1975) in front of the Museum of Modern Art, New York, June 1, 1975

VITO ACCONCI
CARL ANDRE
RICHARD ARTSCHWAGER
JOHN BALDESSARI
ROBERT BARRY
JOSEPH BEUYS
DANIEL BUREN
SANDRO CHIA
FRANCESCO CLEMENTE
ENZO CUCCHI
GILBERT and GEORGE
DAN GRAHAM
HANS HAACKE
NEIL JENNEY
DONALD JUDD
ANSELM KIEFER
JOSEPH KOSUTH
SOL LEWITT
RICHARD LONG
GORDON MATTA-CLARK
MARIO MERZ
SIGMAR POLKE
GERHARD RICHTER
ED RUSCHA
JULIAN SCHNABEL
CY TWOMBLY
ANDY WARHOL
LAWRENCE WEINER

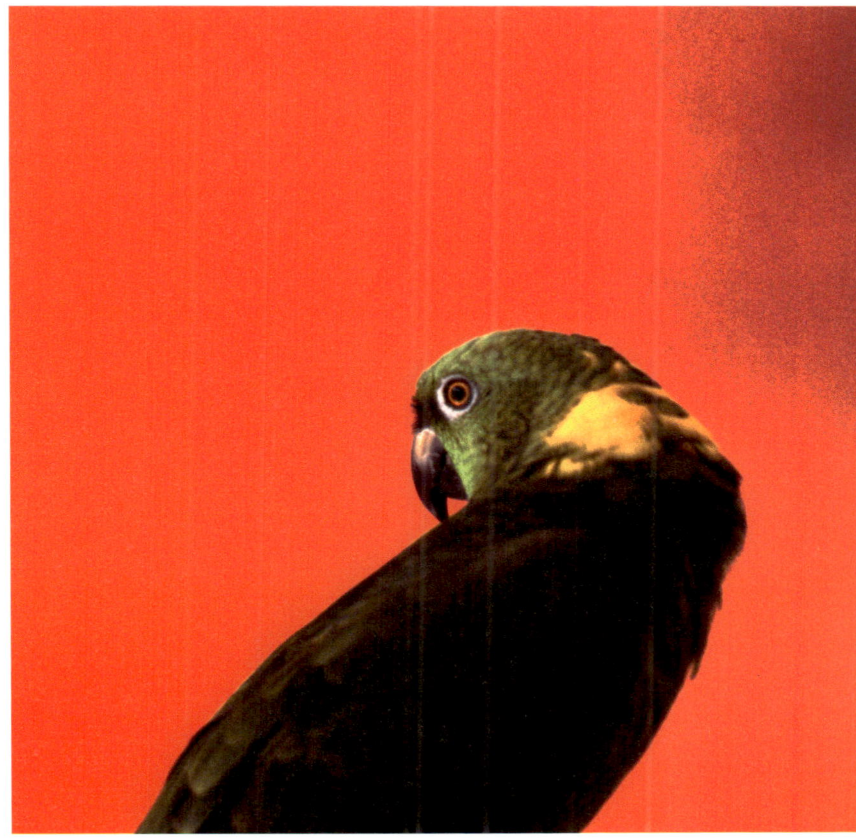

Plate 56 Louise Lawler, *Birdcalls*, 1972/1981

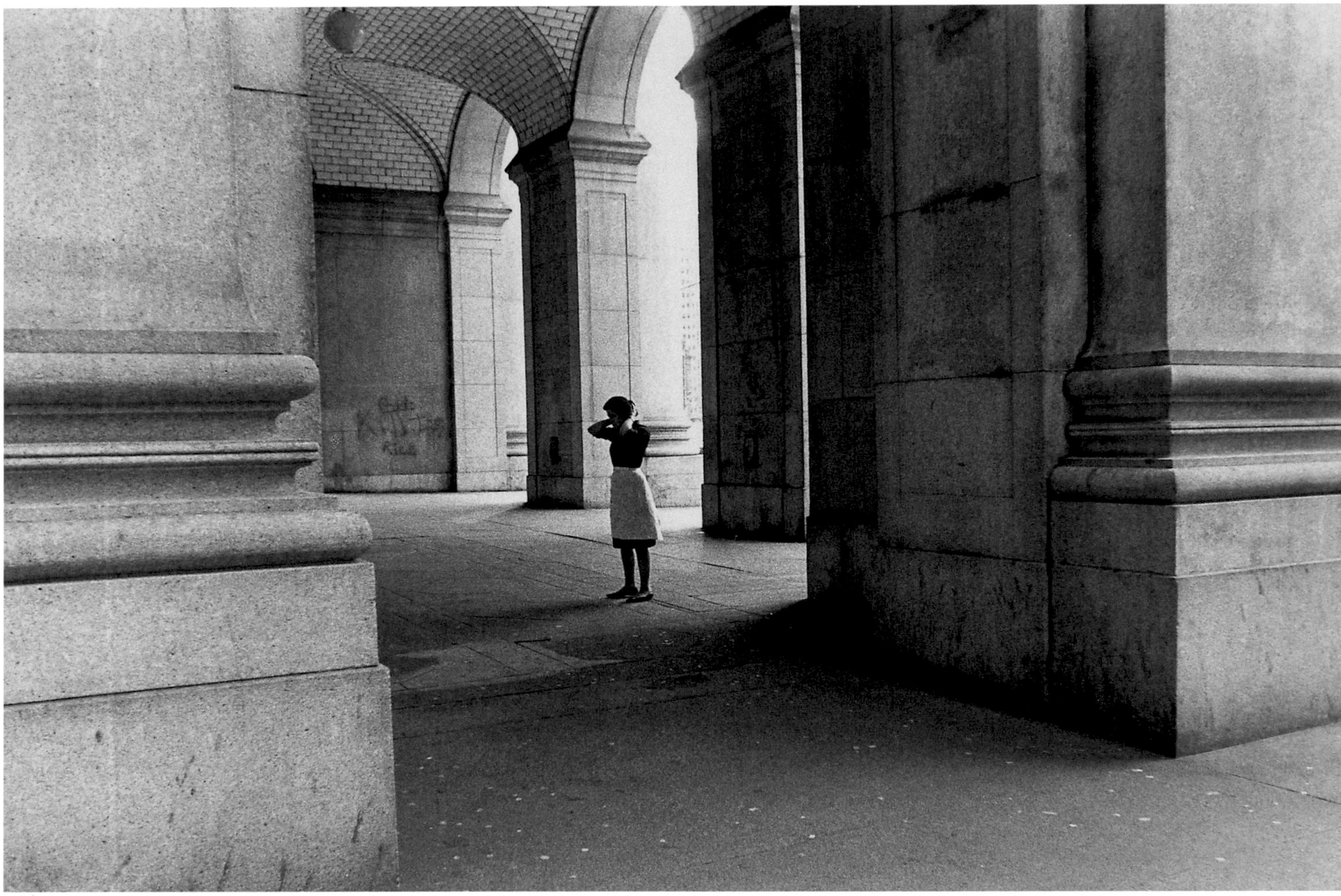

Plate 57 Cindy Sherman, *Untitled Film Still #64*, 1980

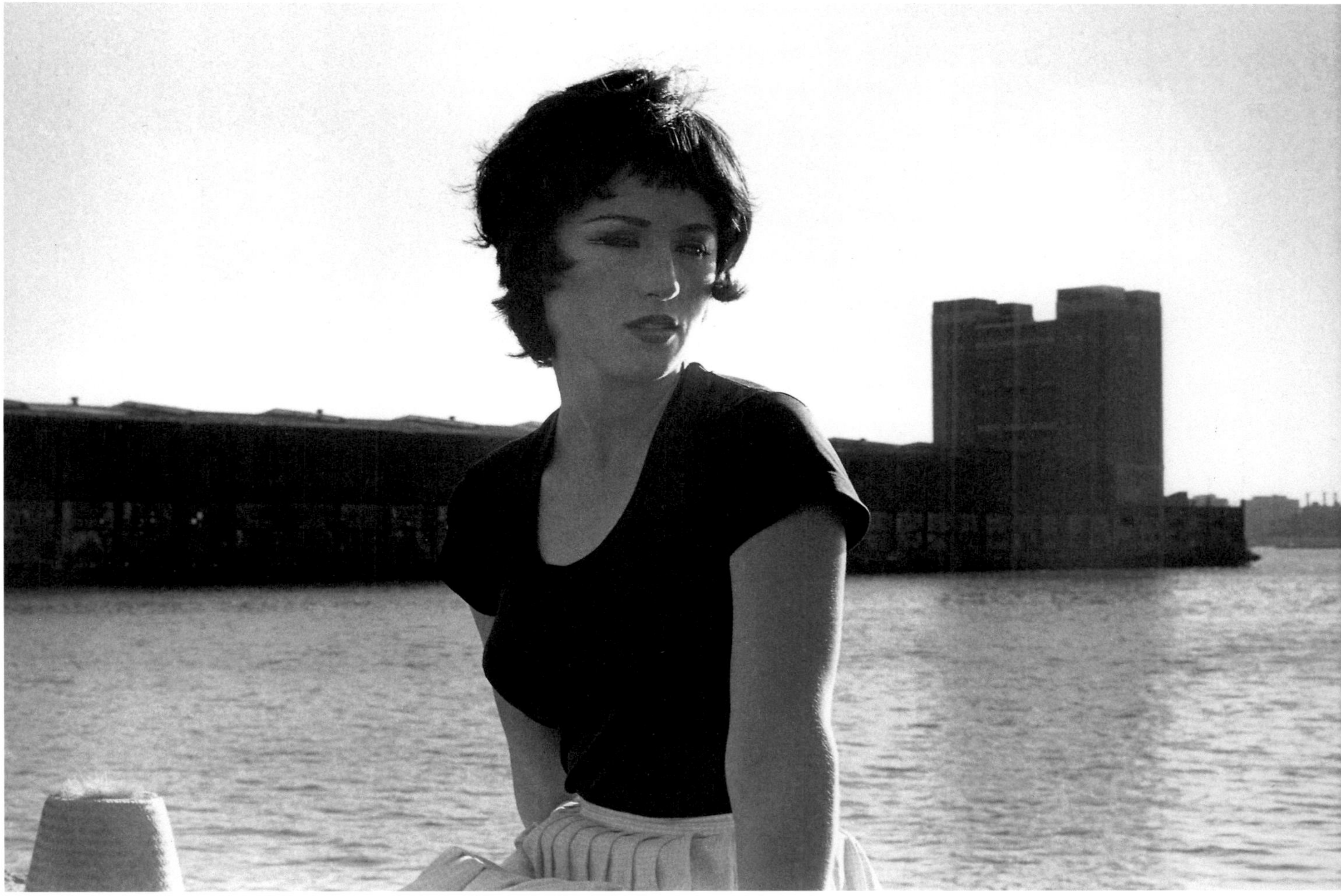

Plate 58 Cindy Sherman, *Untitled Film Still #24*, 1978

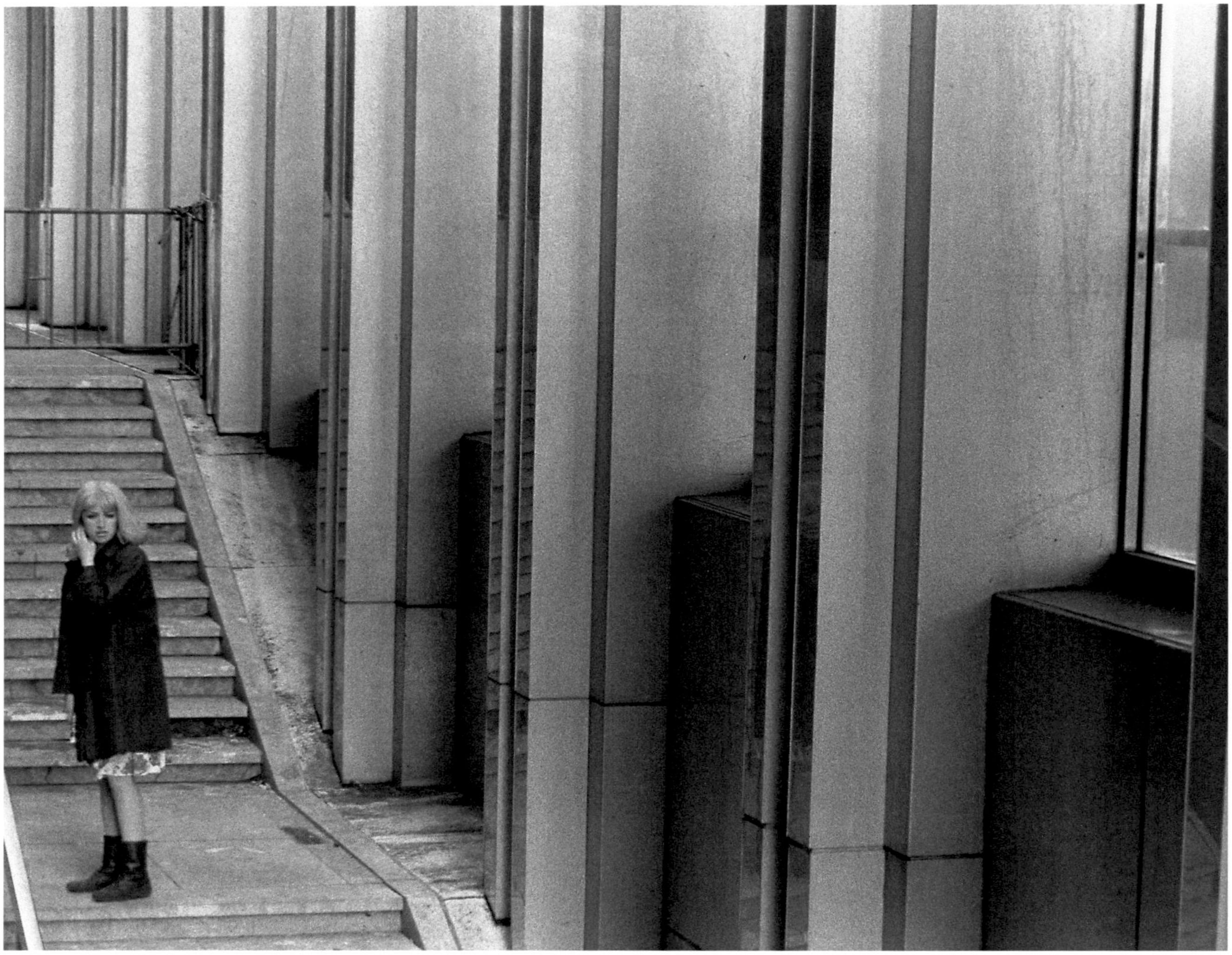

Plate 59 Cindy Sherman, *Untitled Film Still #63*, 1980

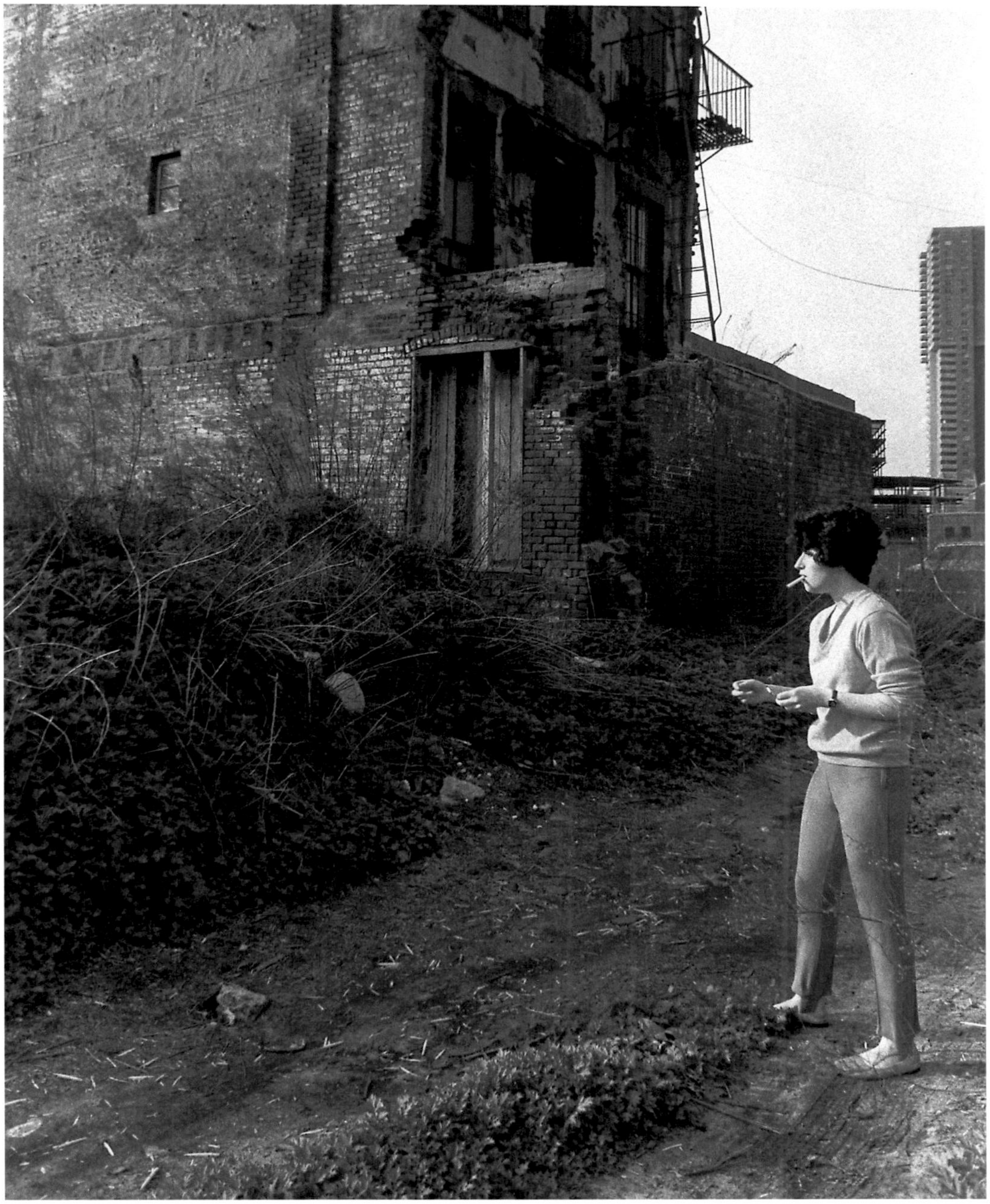

Plate 60 Cindy Sherman, *Untitled Film Still #60*, 1980

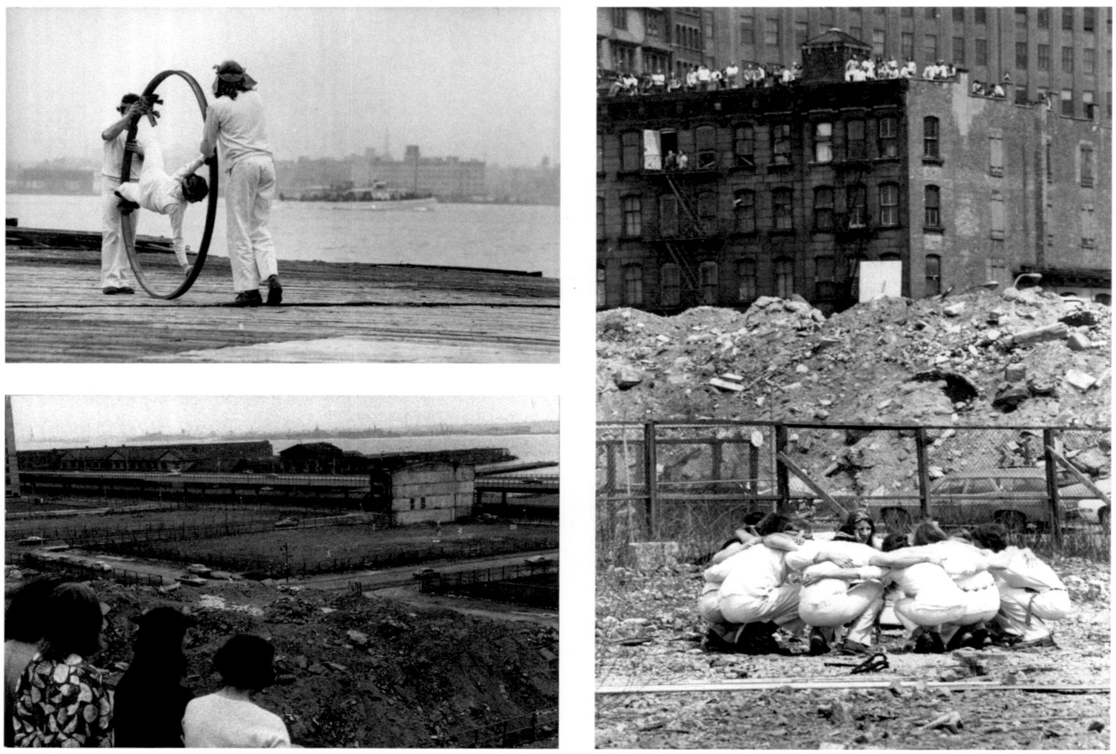

Joan Jonas, *Delay Delay*, 1972. Performance near 319 Greenwich Street, New York. Photographs by Gianfranco Gorgoni (top left; right) and Gwenn Thomas (bottom left)

christened "the beach." A few years later, the newly founded arts organization Creative Time would begin a series of outdoor exhibitions there called *Art on the Beach*.[27] An era of officially sponsored public art was underway, with its commissioning entities, panels of experts, permits, contracts, and eventually controversies and court cases.

I didn't manage to change worlds by moving to Tribeca. I still spent nearly every evening in the Village, but now most of them ended with a long walk down the West Side to my new neighborhood, through the empty streets that Peter Hujar was photographing at just this time. It was a time when I could cherish the illusion that these Manhattan streets belonged to me—to me and others who were discovering them and using them for our own purposes. But I did nevertheless manage to become an art critic. The first article I wrote after moving downtown was "Joan Jonas's Performance Works," published in a special issue of *Studio International* devoted to performance art. Jonas was more clear-sighted than I was at the time about the possibility of appropriating city spaces. I quote her in my essay as saying: "My own thinking and production has focused on issues of space—ways of dislocating it, attenuating it, flattening it, turning it inside out, always attempting to explore it without ever giving to myself or to others the permission to penetrate it."[28]

I was still preoccupied enough with painting in the mid-1970s that I misinterpreted Jonas's explorations of spatial illusionism as reflecting her continuing involvement with the history of painting.[29] I overlooked in her statement what it foretold about the actual spaces Jonas was performing in: just how provisional was their availability for experimental uses. This is what her film *Songdelay* captures so well pp. 100–101
about the New York of its moment. Jonas's use of a telephoto lens in *Songdelay* shows the performance area and cityscape beyond, unlike the vista that opened out in front of the spectators beyond the rooftop from which they watched *Delay Delay*, collapsed into a single plane. A performer who appears to be in the near middleground claps blocks of wood together; a sound delay tells us that in fact he stands a great distance from us. A warehouse in Jersey City appears to be right behind him, but the sudden, uncanny appearance of a huge freighter between him and the building tells us otherwise—that in between lies the great expanse of the Hudson River.[30] A cut to a slow-motion, tight close-up shot of Jonas, limbs outstretched while rotating in a large hoop, makes clear how limited and fragmented is our perspective on the overall location, for beyond Jonas's torso we see only the street's cobblestones, a curb, a bit of sidewalk, and some rubble. Behind another figure, whose movements are rendered puppetlike by bamboo poles held in her outstretched arms and thrust into the opposite trouser leg, we glimpse a chain-link fence and rear-ground automobile traffic. Only one sequence grants us sufficient distance to make the location comprehensible: at the top right of a scene that shows several performers moving back and forth through a vacant lot, the back of the Federal Office Building on Church and Barclay streets is visible, and just below it, at the frame's right edge, we can make out the sole survivor of the wrecking balls of the

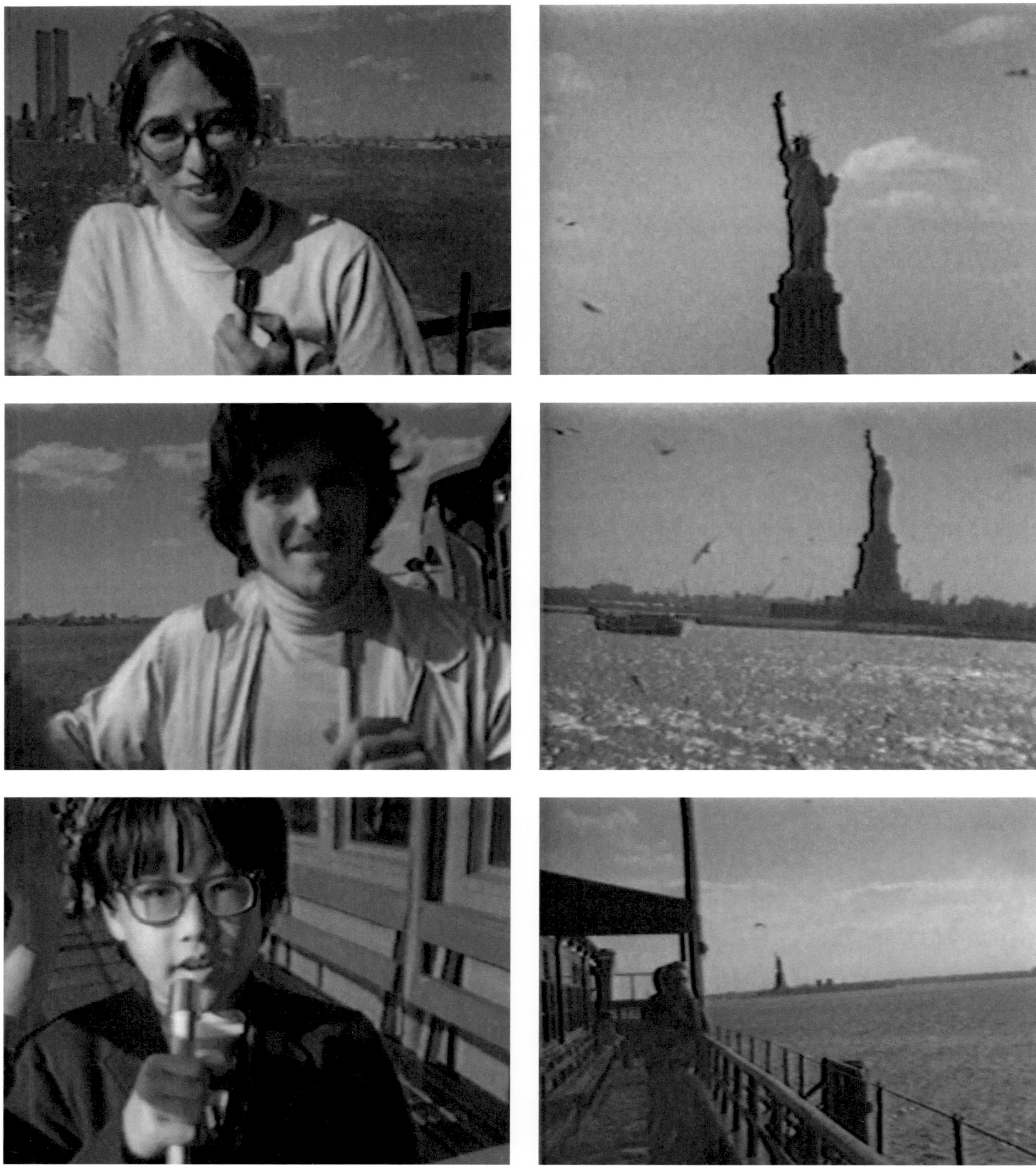

Plate 61 Dara Birnbaum, stills from *Liberty: A Dozen or So Views*, 1976

prior decade, a nineteenth-century building that stood alone and forlorn at the corner of West and Warren streets until 2003.[31] This means that the streets we see bordering the vacant lot's south and west sides must be Warren and Greenwich streets—right around the corner from where I lived between 1974 and 1976.[32] But just as we begin to be able to orient ourselves, Jonas cuts to another close-up of herself rotating in the hoop, and this time not only is she upside down but the film frame is also. Throughout *Songdelay*, sequences of action are interrupted by quick inserts—so quick they are nearly subliminal—of Jonas in the hoop, the puppetlike figure, flashes of light from a mirror that Jonas holds up to reflect the sun into the lens, and a pair of wooden blocks whose clacking together has provided much of the film's sound. Together with the shots through the telephoto lens, extreme close-ups of individual performers' bodies, and bird's-eye views of two people playing at being a slider-crank mechanism as they walk along a line and circle painted on the cobblestone pavement, these elements make us fully aware of the filmic mediation of the performance events. But that is far from the sole meaning of *Songdelay*'s varied techniques. The film also uses these techniques to thwart our desire to know or possess the city beyond our immediate experience of it in the moment of use. We see the city in fragments, not unlike those that Gordon Matta-Clark—one of *Songdelay*'s performers—gave us a few years later in his film *City* p. 148
Slivers (1976), in which New York appears as a series of vertical striations made by masking the camera's lens. We glimpse the city in pieces, in the background, in our peripheral vision—and in recollection.

Endnotes

1
Joan Jonas: Scripts and Descriptions 1968–1982, ed. Douglas Crimp (Berkeley: University Art Museum, University of California, Berkeley; Eindhoven: Stedelijk van Abbemuseum, 1983), p. 22. Jonas's exhibition at the University Art Museum took place in 1980.
2
See *112 Workshop, 112 Greene Street: History, Artists & Artworks*, ed. Robyn Brentano with Mark Savitt (New York: New York University Press, 1981).
3
An exception to this statement is the inclusion in *New York—Downtown Manhattan: SoHo* (Berlin: Akademie der Künste, 1976) of a 1976 flyer headlined "STOP DISCOS IN SOHO!," protesting the plans for a fourth disco in SoHo after the Loft, Flamingo, and Frankenstein; see p. 25. A more significant exception is Tim Lawrence, *Hold On to Your Dreams: Arthur Russell and the Downtown Music Scene, 1973–92* (Durham, NC: Duke University Press, 2009). Arthur Russell, music director of the Kitchen Center for Video and Music in 1974–75, straddled the experimental-music and gay-disco scenes.
4
For an account of my own experience at these discos, see my "*Disss*-co (A Fragment)," *Criticism: A Quarterly for Literature and the Arts* 50, no. 1 (Winter 2008), pp. 1–18.
5
Gordon Matta-Clark, "Work with abandoned structures," typewritten statement circa 1975, in *Gordon Matta-Clark: Works and Collected Writings,* ed. Gloria Moure (Barcelona: Ediciones Polígrafa, 2006), p. 141.
6
Rosalyn Deutsche, "Louise Lawler's Rude Museum," in *Twice Untitled and Other Pictures (Looking Back)*, ed. Helen Molesworth (Columbus, OH: Wexner Center for the Arts, 2006), p. 130.
7
Louise Lawler, "Prominence Given, Authority Taken: An Interview with Louise Lawler by Douglas Crimp," *Grey Room* 4 (Summer 2001), p. 80. Lawler recorded the *Birdcalls* in 1981 with a somewhat altered and updated roster of male artists' names. Lawler and Kite's pretense of craziness as self-protection has a venerable New York history. From the introduction to Edwin G. Burrows and Mike Wallace's *Gotham*, we learn that the designation of Manhattan as "Gotham" originates in Washington Irving's 1807 *Salmagundi* papers, mocking the foolish people of Manhattan. But the notion of Manhattan as an island of fools has a redeeming side taken from a story about the village of Gotham in Nottinghamshire: "In the early 1200s…King John traveled regularly throughout England with a retinue of knights and ladies, and wherever the royal foot touched earth became forever after a public highway (i.e., the King's). One day John was heading to Nottingham by way of Gotham, and he dispatched a herald to announce his arrival. The herald reported back that the townspeople had refused the king entry, fearing the loss of their best lands. The enraged monarch sent an armed party to wreak vengeance, but the townsfolk had prepared a scheme to turn aside John's wrath. When the knights arrived, they found the inhabitants engaged in various forms of idiotic behavior: pouring water into a bottomless tub; painting green apples red; tying to drown an eel in a pool of water; dragging carts atop barns to shade the wood from the sun; and fencing in a cuckoo. The chortling knights reported back to the monarch that the townsfolk were clearly mad, and John accordingly spared them" (Edwin G. Burrows and Mike Wallace, *Gotham: A History of New York City to 1898* [New York: Oxford University Press, 1999], pp. xiii–xiv).
8
See *Harry Shunk, Projects: Pier 18* (Nice: Musée d'Art Moderne et d'Art Contemporain, 1992). For this incarnation of *Projects: Pier 18*, János (Jean) Kender's name was erased from the collaboration. Between 1957 and 1973, Harry Shunk and János Kender worked collaboratively, and all of their photographs taken during this period were credited as Shunk-Kender. This was the case when *Projects: Pier 18* was shown at the Museum of Modern Art in 1971. The collaboration was dissolved in 1973, with Shunk retaining the photographic archive (see "Roy Lichtenstein Foundation Acquires Harry Shunk Archive," http://www.lichtensteinfoundation.org/shunk01.htm [accessed December 24, 2009]).
9
The artists' handwritten instructions for the projects were also photographed by Shunk-Kender and shown as part of the exhibition. See plates 27–35.
10
Vito Acconci, Sarina Basta, and Garrett Ricciardi, *Vito Acconci: Diary of a Body 1969–1973* (Milan: Charta, 2006), p. 248.
11
Ibid., p. 258
12
Ibid., p. 259.
13
"Interview with Gordon Matta-Clark, Antwerp, September 1977," in Moure, *Gordon Matta-Clark*, pp. 252–53.
14
"Gordon Matta-Clark: The Making of Pier 52, an Interview with Liza Bear, March 11, 1976," in Moure, *Gordon Matta-Clark*, p. 217.
15
Ibid., p. 220.
16
Quoted in Pamela M. Lee, *Object to Be Destroyed: The Work of Gordon Matta-Clark* (Cambridge, MA: MIT Press, 2000), p. 130. Lee argues for a combination of phenomenology and the sublime to capture the experience of Matta-Clark's work.
17
"Gordon Matta-Clark: The Making of Pier 52," p. 220.
18
Ibid., p. 215.
19
Ibid., p. 218.
20
Gordon Matta-Clark, "My understanding of art," typewritten statement circa 1975, in Moure, *Gordon Matta-Clark*, p. 204. On the journalistic conflation of the dangers *to* gay men using the piers with the supposed dangers *of* gay men's sexuality, see Lee, *Object to Be Destroyed*, pp. 119–20.
21
Many others photographed the piers; none to my knowledge as extensively or beautifully as Baltrop. Included among those who took photographs of the piers were Peter Hujar and Leonard Fink. The latter's vast trove of photographs of the gay scene are held in the National Archive of Lesbian, Gay, Bisexual, and Transgender History in New York. In addition to photographic documentation, the piers are the setting of a gay-porn feature film called *Pier Groups*, made by Arch Brown in 1979.
22
Alvin Baltrop, *Ashes from a Flame: Photographs by Alvin Baltrop*, ed. Randal Wilcox, http://baltrop.org/ashesintro.htm (accessed February 1, 2008).
23
Jane Jacobs, *The Death and Life of Great American Cities* (New York: Random House, 1961).
24
Douglas Crimp, "Agnes Martin: numero, misura, rapporto," *Data* 3, no. 10 (Winter 1973), pp. 83–85; "Opaque Surfaces," in *Arte Come Arte* (Milan: Centro Communitario di Brera, 1973), reprinted in James Meyer, *Minimalism* (London: Phaidon, 2000).
25
See Janelle Reiring, "Joan Jonas' *Delay Delay*," *The Drama Review: TDR* 16, no. 3 (September 1972), pp. 142–50; and Katie Stone, *Joan Jonas: Beyond the Frame* (master's thesis, Courtauld Institute of Art, 2003).
26
Joan Jonas: Scripts and Descriptions, p. 34.
27
The *Art on the Beach* events at the Battery Park City landfill extended from 1978 to 1985. For a thorough analysis of the uses of a different version of "public art" in the interests of real estate development at Battery Park City, see Rosalyn Deutsche, "Uneven Development: Public Art in New York City," in *Evictions: Art and Spatial Politics* (Cambridge, MA: MIT Press, 1996), pp. 49–107.
28
Joan Jonas with Rosalind Krauss [misspelled "Krause"], "Seven Years," *The Drama Review: TDR* 19, no. 1 (March 1975), p. 13.

29
I wrote: "By presenting real space as an impenetrable illusion in her performances, Jonas has made the experience of performance equivalent not only to film and videotape—the other two mediums she works with—but also to painting. At issue in her work, then, is an ambitious relationship to the history of painting and a reversal of the priorities of most contemporary art" ("Joan Jonas's Performance Works," *Studio International* 192, no. 982 [July/August 1976], p. 10).
30
The warehouse in question is visible in the distance, across the Hudson River, in a number of the photographs in *Projects: Pier 18*.
31
The building, at 179 West Street just north of Warren, survived until 2003 because a court ruling in favor of the tenant, sculptor Mardig Kachian, prevented his eviction until the renewal projects for the site had been fully approved by all necessary government agencies. The building also appears in Cindy Sherman's *Untitled Film Still #60* (1980).
32
In one shot of the puppetlike figure, it is possible to make out a street sign that says "Greenwich Street."

Styles of Occupation: Manhattan in Experimental Film and Video from the 1970s to the Present

Juan A. Suárez

Around 1960, there was a perceptible change in the way experimental film portrayed the metropolis. A symptom of this shift was the waning of the so-called city film, an important subgenre of experimental cinema in the first half of the twentieth century, and the ascension of works that, while keeping the city on the horizon, were less concerned with observing it than with recording how its spaces were used. Concomitant with this shift, there was a transformation in the investments that filmmakers brought to the cityscape—from the production of knowledge through optical exploration to the activation of space through performance and occupation.

In the early decades of the twentieth century, city films such as *Manhatta* (1921), *Berlin: Symphony of a Great City* (1927), and *Man with a Movie Camera* (1929), to name just a few, were among the best-known experimental titles, popular in the programs of film societies and "little cinemas."[1] They documented particulars of city life, from the static forms of buildings to the transitory configurations of traffic and pedestrian flow. Their attitude toward their subject ranged from the celebration of the technology-saturated metropolis to nostalgia for disappearing sites, and their varied affects included fascination with the multiplicity of urban existence, indignation at its inequalities (*Rien que les heures* [1926] and *Footnote to Fact* [1933]), and bemusement at its absurd juxtapositions (*À propos de Nice* [1930]). Regardless of how embodied or subjective their perspectives, these titles portrayed the city as essentially knowable. They showcased textures, cycles, and rhythms, uncovered visual parallels and rhymes, and captured subliminal stories glimpsed in passing. The gaze of the camera mimed that of the flaneur, the distracted navigator of the crowd, but was also akin to the focused eye of the policeman or the ethnographer. In these films to look is, to a great extent, to know. As an epistemological tool, the cinema was particularly apposite to the eminent visuality of city life—a quality amply commented on by urban sociologists, from Georg Simmel and Robert Park to Louis Wirth and Richard Sennett.

The contingencies of modernity prompted these films and made them popular. Like the urban panoramas and "city confidential" literature of the nineteenth century, and like the actualities and panorama films of the 1900s, of which they are direct descendants, city films harnessed the perceptual barrage of urban life, transmuting disorientation and shock into knowledge and aesthetic form.

Yet in or around the early 1960s, such attitudes toward the city begin to erode. If *Manhatta*, *Berlin*, and *Man with a Movie Camera*, with their taxonomic ambition and epistemological self-assurance, were typical of an early modernist moment, films like Chris Marker's *Le joli mai* (1963), Edgar Morin and Jean Rouch's *Chronique d'un été* (1960), Alfred Leslie and Frank O'Hara's *The Last Clean Shirt* (1964), and
p. 138
Chantal Akerman's *News from Home* (1976) are more characteristic of a time when city life seemed less amenable to totalizing filmic inspection. Depictions of life in Paris, *Le joli mai* and *Chronique d'un été* are fragmentary and subjective and mix documentary footage, statistics, interviews, and poetic reflections spoken off-screen. Rather than providing a stable picture of the city, these films offer a conglomerate of colliding perspectives that at times cancel one another out. For their part, Leslie, O'Hara, and Akerman explore New York from deliberately limited standpoints, abstaining from any attempt at completeness or explanation. *The Last Clean Shirt* is almost entirely shot in one take, from the back of a convertible in which a black man and a white woman drive from downtown to midtown, where they park and leave the car. (Near the end, the long take is briefly interrupted by a shot of the car turning a corner and by a reverse angle.) The city swishes by, partly blocked by the frame of the windshield, and recedes in the tiny rectangle of the rearview mirror. Urban space seems incidental to the unequal interaction between the characters; while the man remains supremely taciturn, focused solely on his driving, the woman sings and talks torrentially in Finnish. Akerman's *News from Home* consists of long takes of New York. Most are static shots of empty or sparsely peopled corners, streets, and subway stations. On the soundtrack, a woman reads from her letters to her daughter, a filmmaker temporarily in New York. In *News from Home* and *The Last Clean Shirt* city space is actualized through particular itineraries, and each brings into being a different city out of infinite possibilities. Like the Paris portrayed by Marker, Morin, and Rouch, New York appears in these titles as a porous territory, multiply inhabited and decodable, whose variety thwarts straightforward capture and demands tentative, at times self-canceling approaches.

In the United States, the transition between the two modes of portraying the city is marked by the postwar films of Rudy Burckhardt (*Under the Brooklyn Bridge* [1953]), by Burckhardt and Joseph Cornell's collaborations (*The Aviary* [1955], *Nymphlight* [1957], *A Legend for Fountains* [1954–57]), by Helen Levitt's *In the*
pp. 136, 135
Street (1952), by Jack Smith's *Scotch Tape* (1959–62), and by Ken Jacobs's *The Whirled* (1956–63), among many others. They are, in many ways, paradigmatic of the way city space at large, and Manhattan in particular, was portrayed in experimental film in the second half of the twentieth century.

Rather than picturing "the city," these titles depict uses of its spaces as they register the spontaneous theatricals of everyday life. Filmed in East Harlem, the Bronx, and the Lower East Side, *In the Street* shows old ladies conversing on stoops, young couples flirting, and children at play in a manner that modulates from jocular to slightly sinister, as a Halloween street party becomes an all-out fight, and the initial cuteness turns out to hide a layer of violence in youngsters and adults. Cornell and Burckhardt's films are often populated by children as well. In *The Aviary*, they are reminiscent of the pigeons with which they share a run-down, empty Union Square. In *Nymphlight*, a teenage girl in vaguely Victorian attire and carrying a tattered parasol grants Bryant Park a dreamy quality. And in *Under the Brooklyn Bridge* and *A Legend for Fountains*, the kids animate their respective environments with their acrobatic playfulness, as they bathe in the East River or, with their impish and enigmatic presence, play in the streets of Little Italy, where *Legend* was filmed. In Jack Smith's *Scotch Tape*, the defamiliarization of urban space does not emanate from "found" events but from staged activity. *Scotch Tape* was shot in the ruins of San Juan Hill, a largely black and Latino neighborhood razed in the late 1950s to make way for Lincoln Center. It shows three figures dancing, jumping, and climbing among the broken concrete and twisted girders to the rhythm of Peter Duchin's "Carinhoso," a pastiche of Brazilian music dubbed by Tony Conrad for the film's premiere.[2] *Scotch Tape* derives from the films that Smith and his then friend Ken Jacobs—one of the performers in *Scotch Tape*—had been making in Lower Manhattan since 1956. These were collected in *The Whirled* and, in a more expansive form, in *Star-Spangled to Death* (1957–59/2003–2004). Jacobs's films often show Smith, in drag or otherwise extravagantly costumed, dancing in courtyards, stately walking down the street followed by a solemn entourage and a gaggle of neighborhood kids, performing an undefinable dance covered in plastic in a busy street, or affecting despondency against a caryatid in an old building.

None of these films evokes the city as a totality to be inferred from a more or less elliptical visual mosaic. They are devoid of landmarks or intelligible perspectives and dwell instead on fragmentary locations, fragmentarily portrayed and seemingly disconnected from the rest of the urban fabric. They are filmed in degraded or ruinous settings inhabited by marginal social groups—dropouts like Smith and his cohorts, working-class immigrants, ethnic minorities, children, and the old. Though they are significant as filmic texts—they are all beautifully shot and cleverly edited—perhaps their main source of interest lies in their performative aspects: in the bodily expressiveness of their subjects—Smith's gambols, the children's unself-conscious gestures—and in the creative manner in which these urban dwellers occupy public space, appropriating it to uses that go against habit and social sanction.

⋆

Occupying space has been the dominant motif in a number of films and videos from the early 1970s onward by artists such as Joan Jonas, Terry Fox, James Nares, Gordon Matta-Clark, Peter Hutton, Nelson Sullivan, and Matthew Buckingham, among others. Many of these artists worked—and still work—across various disciplines and media.

The strategies of occupation in their films are more consciously staged than found, and in this regard they are closer to Smith and Jacobs than to Burckhardt, Cornell, or Levitt. At the risk of simplifying a complex, overlapping field, it might be said that the films of the 1970s are produced in a Minimalist or Postminimalist vocabulary. They are fundamentally concerned with duration, process, and the materiality of film and of the milieus they portray. The films made during the 1980s and after are more concerned with the projection of dissident subcultural identities onto city space. And more recently, there has been renewed interest in the artistic idioms of the 70s without entirely abandoning the situated perspectives of the 1980s. In all cases, it seems that after midcentury, filmed urban space is no longer perspectival or geometric but fully social;[3] it is no longer an expanse to be observed but a location already filled in and taken over—or in the process of being taken over—and therefore is to be experienced in haptic, not merely optical, terms. What matters about the city at this point is no longer its outline, surface, or enclosing quality, but the vectors that traverse it, the distribution of resistances, the areas for transit and rest, the kinds of action that become possible in it.[4]

The interest in occupation responded to a variety of factors. One of them was the sheer amount of space that, after the late 1950s, was freed from residential and industrial use and became available for other, often deviant, purposes. Between 1950 and 1986, around 650,000 manufacturing jobs were lost in New York City as light industries moved out of the metropolitan area.[5] Several thousand more were lost owing to the decline of the port of New York, as ocean-borne passenger travel became rare and freight operations were moved to the Elizabeth Marine Terminal on the New Jersey coast across the bay.[6] As a result of these displacements, industrial and warehouse districts such as SoHo, Tribeca, and the once-bustling waterfront became underutilized or abandoned.

In addition, large areas of Lower Manhattan suffered from disinvestment, warehousing, and demolition after the passage of the Housing Act of 1949, part of Truman's Fair Deal. Title I of the act granted federal subsidies for slum clearance and urban renewal and made it more profitable for landlords and city governments to liquidate aging housing stock and failing infrastructures than to maintain them. During the 1950s and 60s, the city's Slum Clearance Committee, chaired by Robert Moses, embarked on "revitalization" programs that condemned run-down but lively and perfectly viable neighborhoods with the purpose of rebuilding them. Renewal was uneven, stalled by resistant tenants who refused to vacate. But even when tenants did move and buildings were torn down and the land cleared and improved, new projects often failed to materialize for years. In the 1970s and much of the 80s, areas like Alphabet City and the Lower East Side, south of Houston Street, were pockmarked by boarded-up structures and empty lots awaiting redevelopment, a condition that continued until the full-scale gentrification that started in the mid-1980s. A spectacular example of vacancy was "the beach." The bare, dunelike landfill created with the

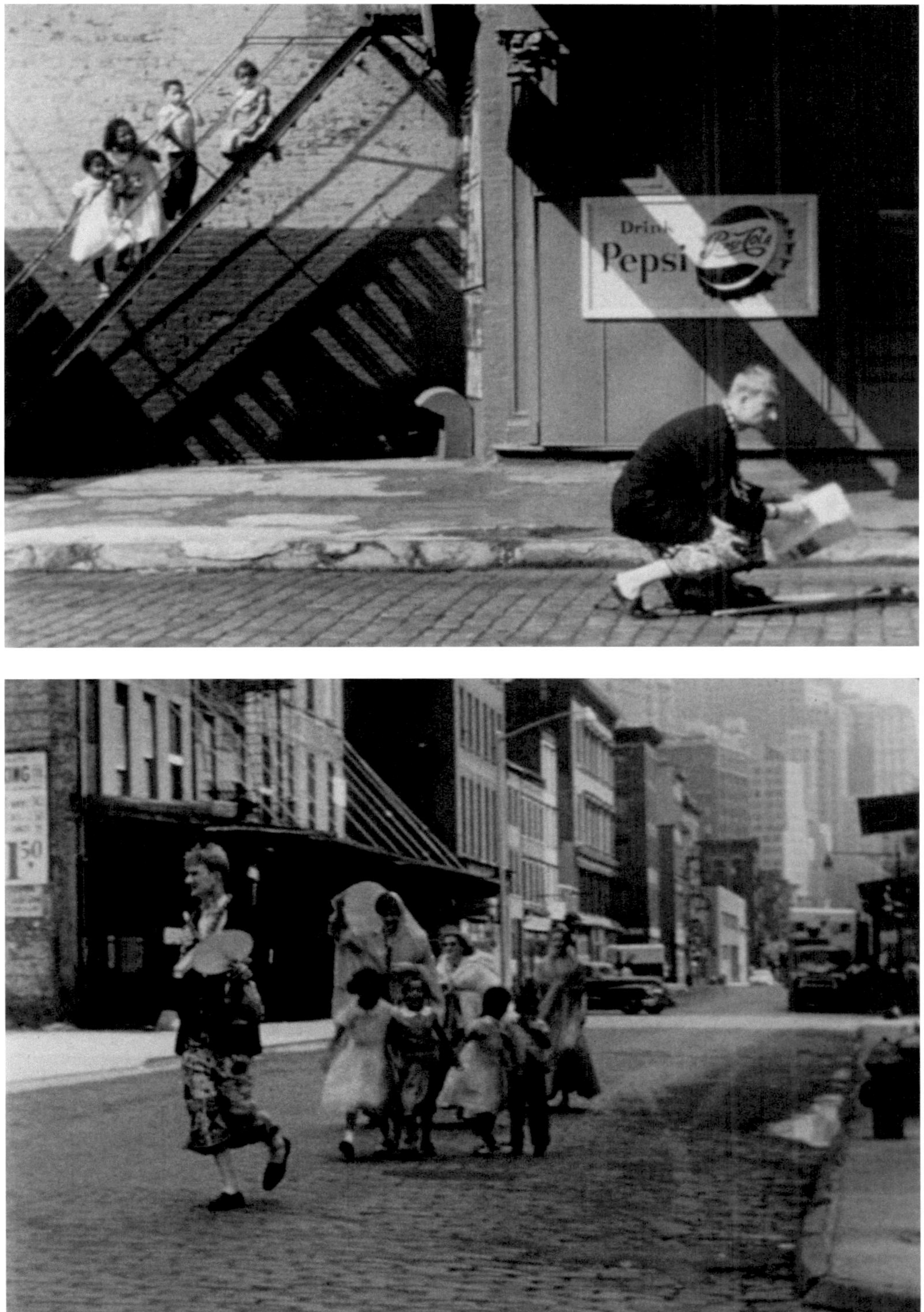

Plate 62 Ken Jacobs, stills from *The Whirled*, 1956–63

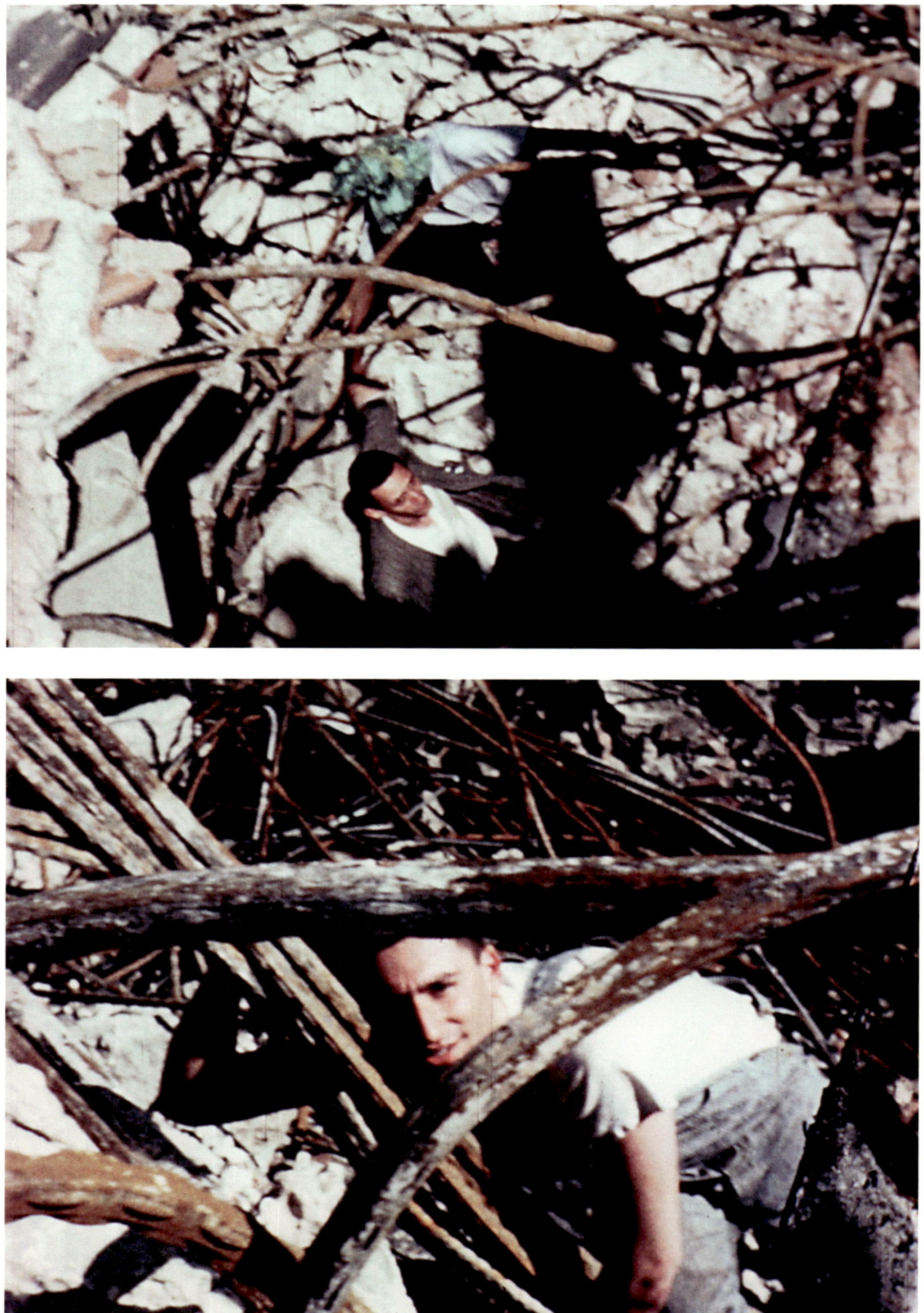

Plate 63 Jack Smith, stills from *Scotch Tape*, 1959–62

rubble from demolitions and the earth excavated to build the foundations of the World Trade Center complex remained empty from the early 1970s to the early 80s, when construction of Battery Park City began. At times fenced off and guarded, it was intermittently appropriated by filmmakers and artists—Jack Smith and Hélio Oiticica, to name just two, staged photo shoots there—and was the location of the periodic *Art on the Beach* shows curated by Creative Time between 1978 and 1985.

During the late 1960s and early 1970s, many vacant locations downtown were recycled as exhibition spaces, studios, artists' residences, art centers, or even artistic material.[7] The city as medium and material was featured at 112 Greene Street, an artist-run space opened in 1970 by Jeffrey Lew, where the building itself became an integral part of the work exhibited there.[8] Likewise, *Rooms,* the opening show at P.S. 1 in Long Island City, in 1976, consisted of site-specific installations that incorporated the traits of the dilapidated former school. The artist who most consistently used the vacated city as his medium was Gordon Matta-Clark, active at 112 Greene Street and a participant in *Rooms*. In his intervention *Day's End* (1975), Matta-Clark transformed Pier 52, a disused hangarlike structure of corrugated metal on the Hudson River, into "a temple of sun and light" by removing sections of the ceiling, floor, and walls. Similar projects were *Bronx Floors* (1972–73), *Splitting* (1974), *Bingo/Ninths* (1974), and *Conical Intersect* (1975). They were performed on tenements, family homes, and apartment buildings that had been condemned by "renewal" (the quotation marks are Matta-Clark's) and were eventually demolished, on some occasions only a few hours after the artist had finished his transformations.

Works such as these, and the films that documented them, partake of the indexical character that Rosalind Krauss attributed to much 1970s art.[9] She described the indexical as being open to the contingency of the world, which is not so much encoded in the work as captured and impressed on its surface, just as a photograph registers an image. Spatial occupation was, in this respect, indexical; it was a way of framing and capturing sites that were contiguous with art-making at the time: former locations of production and profit now available for play.

Space was available not only materially but also conceptually. Since the late 1950s and early 60s, with the emergence of Happenings, environments, Earthworks, body art, and site-specific installations, art expanded its range of activity and its media. It opened up from the flat canvas and the self-contained sculptural object to the three-dimensionality of architecture and landscape and to the theatricality of action in space. For New York–based artists especially, "space" was less an abstract Cartesian plane than the vacated downtown. As these artistic developments were taking place, theorists such as Henri Lefebvre and the Situationists in France and Jane Jacobs and Christopher Alexander in the United States were rethinking the city. They rejected extreme modernist functionalism and specialized land use and defended the traditional city, characterized by density, informal contact, shared public areas such as squares and

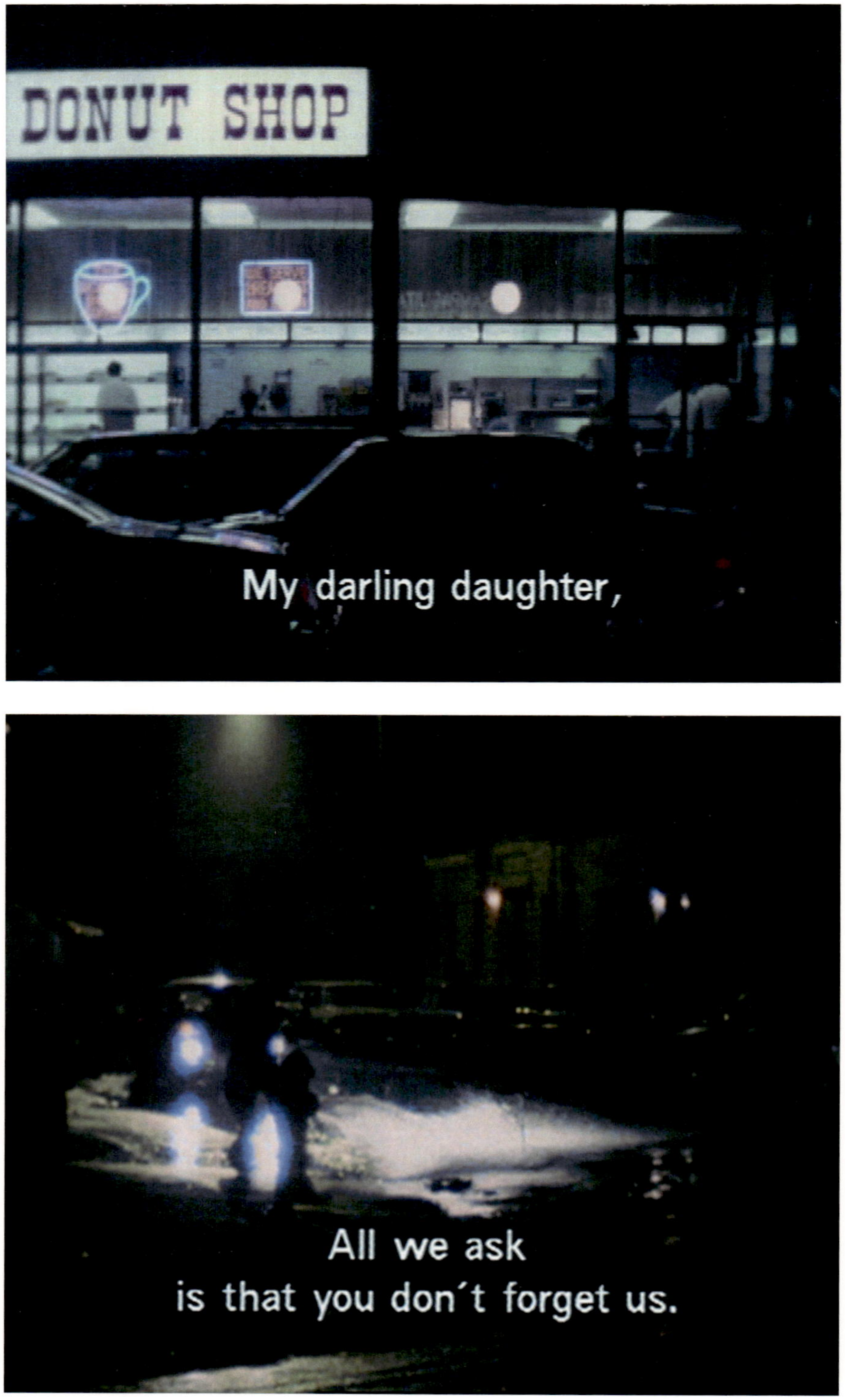

Plate 64 Chantal Akerman, stills from *News from Home*, 1976

parks, and the coexistence of multiple functions and uses. In the process, they redefined urban space: far from a neutral container for action, they saw it as a crucial catalyst for communal life. Countercultural groups such as the Diggers in San Francisco's Height-Ashbury, the People's Park coalition in Berkeley, and the Columbia University students, who took over the campus to protest the construction of a university gymnasium in Morningside Park in 1968, instinctively confirmed the centrality of public space in social struggles and communal affirmation.[10] This was corroborated as well by the manner in which downtown New York was taken up, later on, by a number of what sociologists at the time would have called deviant groups. During the 1970s, a racially mixed, polysexual, underground dance culture developed in disused workshops, warehouses, and garages turned into party venues like the Loft, on lower Broadway and later on Prince Street, or discos like the Gallery, on Mercer and Houston, and Paradise Garage, on King Street east of Hudson Street.[11] Concurrently, as Douglas Crimp notes in "Action around the Edges," in this volume, the West Side Piers in Chelsea, the Village, and SoHo were appropriated by the post-Stonewall gay community as places for sex and sociability. The subcultural activation of the city, however, did not become significant in experimental film and video until the 1980s. Filmic appropriations in the 1970s had a different character altogether.

*

Joan Jonas's *Songdelay* (1973) is exemplary among the 1970s films. It is a cinematic version of the performance *Delay Delay*, first staged in 1972 as one of Jonas's "open landscape pieces."[12] They were early works inspired by the Judson Dance Theater and by process art, as well as by folk rituals that Jonas had witnessed in her travels in North Africa and the American Southwest. In these landscape pieces, simple, repeated actions (running and walking in various patterns, turning inside a metal wheel, or reflecting light with mirrors) were performed across vast surfaces. Distance was a central component of these events. In *Jones Beach Piece* (1970), performers and audience were a quarter of a mile apart; in *Nova Scotia Beach Dance* (1971), the action took place at sea level while the audience watched from the top of a cliff; and in the first version of *Delay Delay*, the performers were in an empty lot by the waterfront on New York's Lower West Side while the audience watched from the top of a building a block away. Jonas has pointed out that the stark separation between performers and audience made these early works largely about perception: the interpretation of patterns flattened out by distance or the delay/relay of signals (screams and the knocking of wooden blocks) from performers to audience.[13] But the combination of distance and signaling also makes these works about space: about separation and its canceling by means of signals. Space asserts its prerogatives but is also questioned and relativized by communication, even if imperfectly relayed.

pp. 100–101
p. 124

Songdelay recreates these motifs through cinematic means. Telephoto shots reproduce the flattening effect of distance on spatial depth and make performers appear closer to the camera and to one another than they really are. Meanwhile, the time lapse between the production of sound signals and their perception by the spectator reveals the vastness of the space they occupy. Distance is bridged by patterns of sound and movement, but nearness reveals emotional and psychological detachment. A wide-angle shot shows two couples in conversation: two women far apart shout at each other, while two men huddled together in the foreground mumble away, barely audible over the background roar of the city. The actions of the performance are cut up and scattered throughout the film in arbitrary permutations, while the setting appears disjointed and confusing. *Songdelay* was filmed in the empty lots near the recently demolished Piers 20 and 21 of the Erie-Lackawanna Railroad Company, at the intersection of Greenwich and Warren streets. The mounds of rubble, the empty stretches, and the river (massive freight ships traverse the background of the frame on several occasions) mark it as a transitional location, urban yet evocative of natural landscapes. It is an urban version of the mud flats at Jones Beach or the Nova Scotia strand, or of the desert, which inspired Jonas's first performance, *Oud Lau* (1968). This leveled-down plateau, the result of destruction, dedifferentiation, and sedimentation, evokes a clean slate on which community and connectivity might be reinvented through stripped-down motion and sound.

p. 141 Terry Fox's 1976 video recordings of his sound piece *Lunar Rambles* show a similar rapport with the city. Fox was videotaped performing his work unannounced on five consecutive days in a different location each day—the Brooklyn Bridge, a construction site on Canal Street, the Fulton Fish Market, the underground pedestrian tunnel on 42nd Street, "and a Lower Westside Street (probably Greenwich Street)."[14] At the end of each day, the resulting tape was screened in the Kitchen next to a sound installation by Fox also called *Lunar Rambles*, consisting of piano wires of different lengths and thicknesses strung on wooden bridges across the floor, which acted as a resonator for the wires. In the videos, Fox crouches on the ground bowing a metal bowl and a steel plow disk simultaneously—they were also part of the installation—producing two symmetrical, cyclical tones several ranges apart. The camera records his playing in long static takes but also pans and tilts away from the artist to catch minute particulars of each setting—the patterns formed by the wooden boards and the shadows of the cables on Brooklyn Bridge, dirt and debris in a construction site on Canal Street, ruined buildings and casual passersby on ("probably") Greenwich Street.

Fox is less concerned than Jonas with humanizing space. He takes for granted a certain opacity in his music and locations. These last are not pliable conduits for performance or communication but resistant environments where his sounds often drown in ambient noise. Much of Fox's work at the time sought to turn sound, body, and space into matter devoid of allegorical content. For the show *Sound*

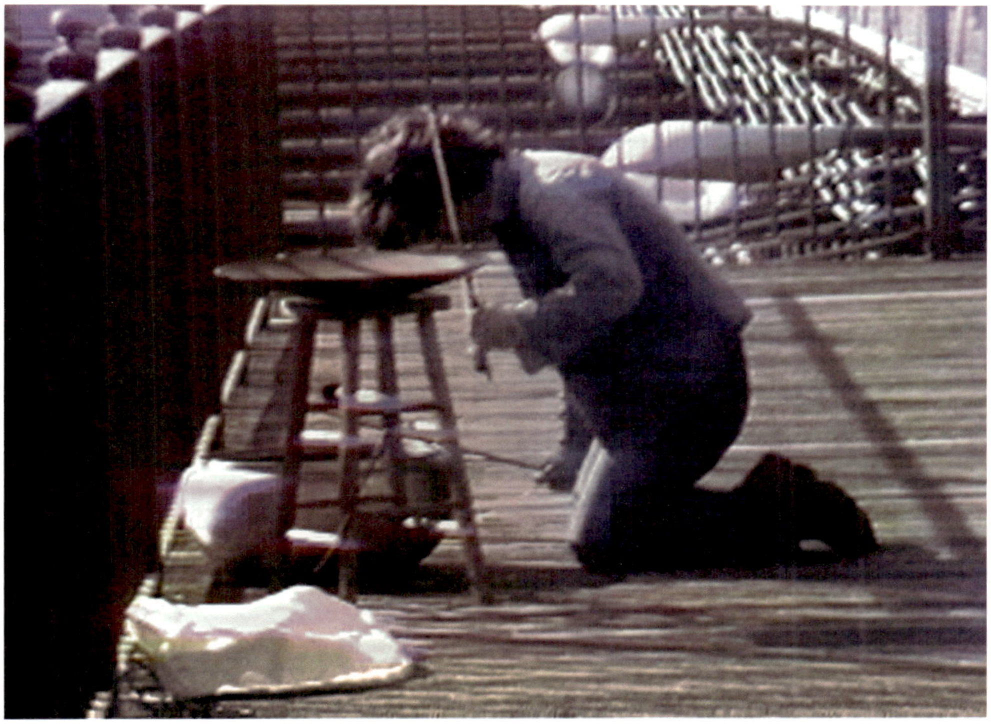

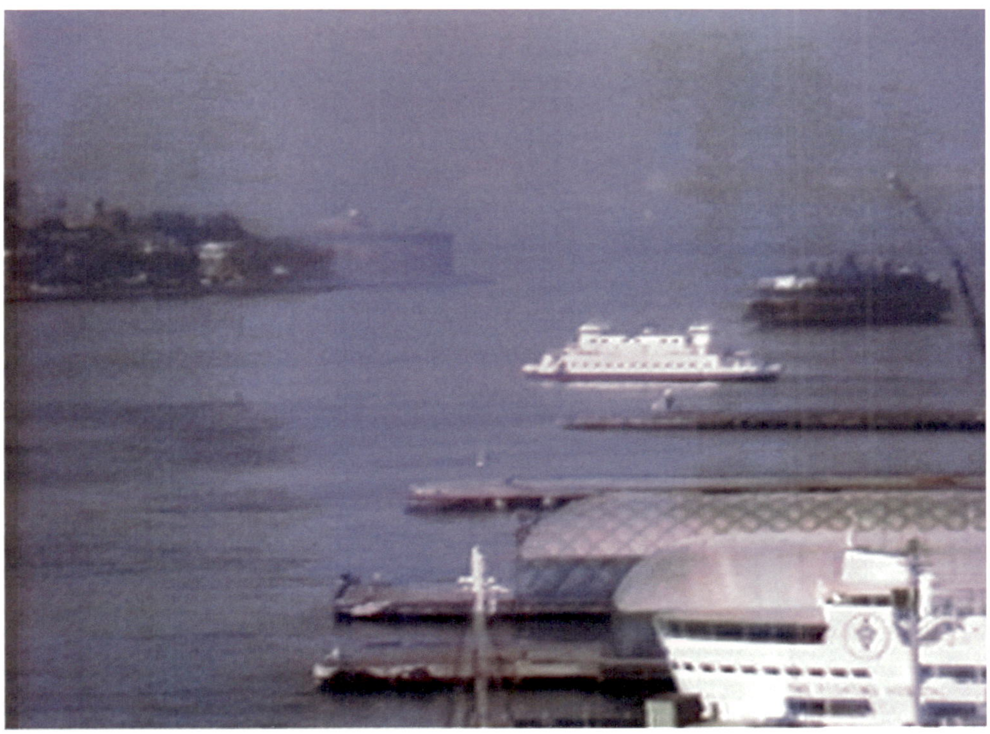

Plate 65 Terry Fox, stills from *Lunar Rambles: Brooklyn Bridge*, 1976

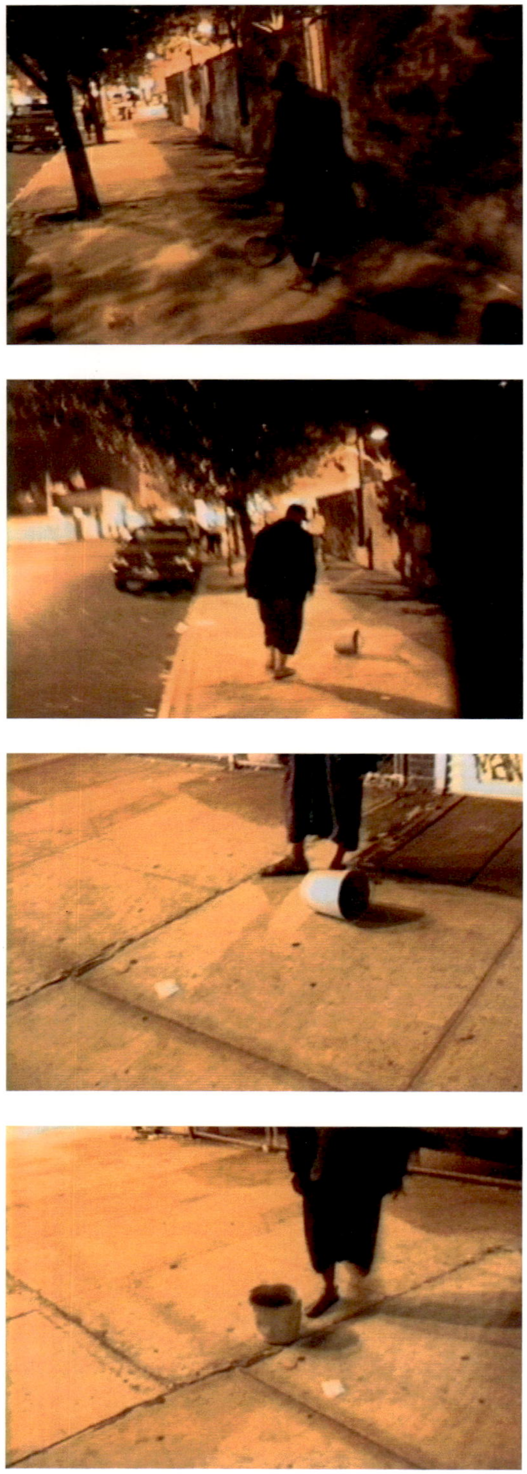

Plate 66 David Hammons, stills from *Phat Free*, 1995

Sculpture As, held at the San Francisco Museum of Conceptual Art in 1970, Fox scraped a shovel across the linoleum floor and vibrated a Plexiglas sheet. At the Reese Palley gallery in New York early the next year, he placed a microphone in a drain and used the amplified dripping and gurgling as sonic background for a performance. And his sound piece *Berlin Wall Scored for Sound* (1982) translated the outline of the wall to six tones that played simultaneously in an endless loop. In an interview published in *Avalanche* in 1970, he claimed that in his work he treated his body as material, "an element in its own right rather than as an initiator of some act," and that in his interactions with space (in pieces such as *Push Wall* and *Pushing into a Corner* [both 1970]) he sought to establish communication and equivalence between his body and architectural elements.[15]

Fox appears fascinated with urban tectonics. His *Lunar Rambles* videos evidence a pull downward toward the base layer of dirt, stone, and asphalt that covers the city; they render the city as an unformalizable material aggregate, the result of stratified sedimentation, overlapping construction, and alluvial ruin—all especially prominent in *Lunar Rambles: Greenwich Street*. For their geologic vocation, these videos bear some similarities to work by Robert Smithson and Michael Heizer, even though the subject matter of these artists was not city space. They also recall Marie Menken's film *Sidewalks* (1966), consisting of vertical tracking shots that register the cracks, stains, assorted refuse, and textural variation on the concrete surface; and Stefan Brecht's photographic series *8th Avenue* (1985), which showcases accidents at ground level, pp. 238–39 random deposits of dirt, shadows, litter. In all cases, urban space remains fragmentarily rendered, but the concentration on detail forces an intimacy with its molecular aspects, which were frequently omitted in the aerial perspectives of the early city film.

Gordon Matta-Clark and painter and performer James Nares also made films that explored in a sustained way the city as material. As a filmmaker, Nares is best known for *Rome '78* (1978), a Factory-style toga epic filmed in Super 8. He is often referred to as an exponent of No Wave cinema, a trend associated with punk, with venues such as Club 57 and the Mudd Club, and with the New Cinema, on St. Mark's Place, a screening room he ran with filmmakers Eric Mitchell and Becky Johnston, among others, in the late 1970s.[16] (At the time, they were all members of the Colab collective.) However, he was also linked to the 1970s performance scene, and his early films, made in Super 8, show a Minimalist sensibility. He performed his piece *Desirum Probe* at Joan Jonas's loft on Mercer Street in 1978.[17] His films *Studio Pendulum* (1976) and *Arm and Hammer* (1976) have similarities to Richard Serra's *Hand Catching Lead* (1968) for their repetitiveness, frontality, and exploration of endurance, mass, and weight. In the first one, a pendulum swings repeatedly, in still frames, and in fast and slow motion, in a bare, ill-lit interior; the filmmaker occasionally walks into the frame with a rudimentary title card indicating the number of the take (which abruptly jumps from "5" to "13"). *Arm and Hammer* looks like a kinetic re-creation of the brand name's shield: limb and tool rise and fall repeatedly, dropping out of camera range and reappearing again; when they go down, the hand twirls the hammer but holds it tight again when it rocks back into view.

Other works reprise this interest in weight and gravity while referencing the materiality of the city. *Steel Rod* (1976) presents a repeated, gamelike action: a young man filmed in long shot on the top of a loft building—Nares's living and working space on Jay Street—repeatedly catches and throws a rod with an unseen p. 294 partner. *Ramp* (1976) shows a concrete ball rolling down the off-ramp of the old West Side Highway—out of use since 1973—until it crashes against a wall; each roll-down is filmed in one frantic take, with the filmmaker breaking into a run to keep up with the growing speed of the ball. *Block* (1976) consists of a three-minute take of a hand that rubs its fingers along the outer wall of what looks like an institutional building. (It was actually the southern side of the post-office building on Vesey Street between West Broadway and Church Street.)[18] "A tribute to the city block," wrote Nares.[19] In p. 294 *Twister* (1976), plastics, papers, and pulverized garbage swirl hypnotically, caught in a pp. 259–61 draft. And *Pendulum* (1976), the most arresting of his films, follows the motion of a ball swinging from a metal footbridge that joined two New York Hospital buildings on Staple Street, in Tribeca. The ball is first shot sideways, as it sways into view in an empty intersection, and is later filmed frontally, showing the entire arc of its trajectory—at its nearest point, the ball comes perilously close to the camera—and from the footbridge above. Subsequently, the camera was attached to the pendulum, and the pavement, buildings, and street crossing loom into and out of view with each swing of the sphere. Nares himself is visible in a few frames, running alongside his contraption. The steady motion of the ball and the gradual, cautious approach suggest the enormous power of the pendulum, which was actually a hollow copper sphere filled with water and, in Nares's words, "would have cracked open like an egg if it had hit something hard."[20] Framed through the metal slats of the footbridge, it looks like a caged mechanical monster. Yet perhaps more than a sense of threat, the film conveys a dreamlike unreality through the slightly slowed-down motion, the silence, broken by the rhythmic groan of the rigging amplified through a microphone, and the deserted streets, nearly devoid of human presence. In addition to its figurative content, the film contains numerous abstract takes: white-outs, blurred masses, and illegible granularities caused by the high-contrast black-and-white stock, the constant movement, and the abrupt changes in lighting, from the bleached summer sky to the shady bottom of the narrow street. *Pendulum*, like most of Nares's films, indexes the city in an extremely elliptical manner as a series of inclines, blocks, vacant spaces, and solid walls—an eminently material domain inhabited by potentially dangerous masses that fall, swing, and roll, barely averting disaster.

Matta-Clark's films insist on the materiality of the city while exploring, like his anarchitectural projects, the interplay between matter and visibility. p. 145 Perhaps the most obtrusively material of his films is *Substrait: Underground Dailies* (1976),

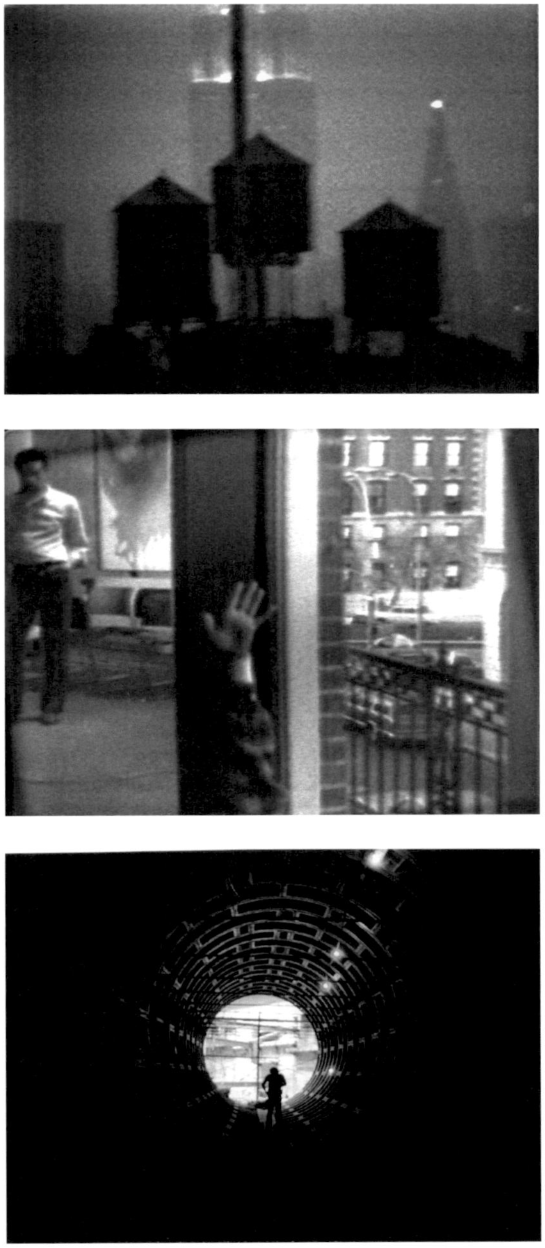

Gordon Matta-Clark, stills from *Chinatown Voyeur*, 1971. black-and-white; sound; 60 min. (top), *Automation House*, 1971. 16mm film; black-and-white; sound; 32 min. (middle), and *Substrait: Underground Dailies*, 1976. 16mm film; black-and-white and color; sound; 30 min. (bottom)

made to be shown as daily rushes at Holly and Horace Solomon's 98 Greene Street gallery during an exhibition of his work.[21] It records several excursions to subterranean aqueducts, sewage-pumping stations, utility conductors, church vaults, and subway tunnels under construction. These locations are an unmapped maze that adds a layer of unknowability to the city. They are vaguely unnerving—"Dracula came that way," joke the children who escort Matta-Clark and his friends to the entrance of the Croton Reservoir tunnel—but also immensely evocative, with their unpredictable turns and impossible design. In this found environment, flashlights and lamps cut swaths of visibility. *Substrait* acknowledges the forbidding mass of the masonry and live rock underground but also works toward overcoming it by means of light. The procedure is close to Matta-Clark's architectural interventions, in which, by means of incisions and removals, he connected formerly separate areas of buildings and opened up the structures to the street, creating unusual perspectives. Beatriz Colomina has proposed that modern architecture created machines not only for living but also for looking; not only enclosures but places for movement and transient perception.[22] It seems as if Matta-Clark sought to radicalize this idea, applying it to old and new buildings alike, producing ruins that expressed exorbitantly one of the driving motivations of architectural modernity.

p. 145 p. 148 Transient perception and movement are in part what *Chinatown Voyeur* (1971) and *City Slivers* (1976) are about. They create moving architectures by means of the video and film frames alone. *Chinatown Voyeur* was Matta-Clark's first video. Recorded overnight from an apartment in Chatham Square, it surveys the skyline and surrounding buildings and pries into neighboring apartments, catching glimpses of domestic life—people cooking, washing, or watching television. These views are always partial. Of a man busy at a sink, we catch only his lower trunk, waist, and legs; other people face away, their expressions invisible and the meaning of their actions opaque, a quality accented by the thick pixelation of the black-and-white image. Buildings and windows create secondary frames inside the video frame. They are cuts through which new perspectives emerge, not opened by the artist this time but haphazardly purveyed by the urban layout. *City Slivers* obeys a similar conception. It was shot with an anamorphic lens, which yields an elongated image and eliminates spatial depth. The lens was masked in order to allow only thin vertical sections of the negative to become exposed.[23] In most of the film, these vertical, sliverlike views are combined by means of multiple exposures. The result is a precarious and strangely haunting depiction of the city, conspicuously blocked in a sort of peep-show effect or incongruously matted. The contrast between the blacked-out and the exposed sections of the image is comparable to the difference between opaque buildings and transparent windows in *Chinatown Voyeur* and to the complementariness of walls and gaps in Matta-Clark's architectural interventions. But while *Chinatown Voyeur* is fairly static, *City Slivers* orchestrates movement across the simultaneous strips: traffic and pedestrians in motion, often mirrored in reflecting surfaces, and the panning of the camera up and down high-rises.

Automation House (1971) extends *City Slivers*'s exploration of movement and split perspective. It is named after the headquarters of Theodore W. Kheel's American Foundation on Automation and Employment, located on East 68th Street and conceived as a "a multi-purpose place that would demonstrate the ability of the new technology to help individuals and to solve problems."[24] It was a conference center for labor-management and community-city disputes that featured an exhibition space and sponsored art projects. Matta-Clark's film, commissioned for a collective show there, is a visual study of the building in long, static takes that consistently juxtapose in the same frame interior and exterior space; the sedate activity inside the building and the fast pace of the city street, where cars and people flit by. The vertical splitting of the shots rhymes with the mattes in *City Slivers*, only in *Automation* this structure is created through camera placement, using walls, mirrors, and balconies to fragment the visual field. p. 145

Peter Hutton's New York films have been discussed as purely optical artifacts that extend Alfred Stieglitz's and Paul Strand's classic photography and replay the aesthetics of the earlier city symphonies.[25] However, they are as fragmentary and tentative as those of his contemporaries and are similarly invested in exploring the materiality of the city. Hutton was trained as a painter and sculptor at the San Francisco Art Institute, where he attended Robert Nelson's film classes, and started making films in the late 1960s as an offshoot of his sculptural projects. He moved to New York in 1971, where he first worked as Red and Mimi Grooms's assistant and participated in their installation-performance *Hippodrome Hardware*, later made into a film.[26] In New York, he became primarily a filmmaker, producing, among other titles, *New York near Sleep for Saskia* (1972) and the series *New York Portrait, Chapter I* (1978–79), *Chapter II* (1980–81), and *Chapter III* (1990). Hutton's works isolate minute occurrences and fleeting views from the flow of city life—curtains stirring in the breeze, clothes hanging to dry on the roof of a tenement, a man traversing a deserted park covered in snow, shot from a high angle. These are extremely contemplative images—silent, roughly equal in length, occasionally slowed down, and rhythmically separated by blackouts. pp. 152–53

Like Nares's and Matta-Clark's, Hutton's New York is a material assemblage that provides unusual visual textures and frames. At the end of *New York Portrait, Chapter II*, a ghostly man in a white raincoat wades knee-deep in water through a flooded intersection in the middle of a storm, apparently trying to unclog a drain. Subsequent shots show the intricate patterns that form on the surface of the water as it flows into the sewer. Many sections of the *New York Portraits* emphasize the way in which buildings, windows, sidewalks, and street crossings create spontaneous frames; into them drift slight events, ephemeral formations that would immediately disappear without trace were it not for their cinematic registration. A dirigible slides majestically

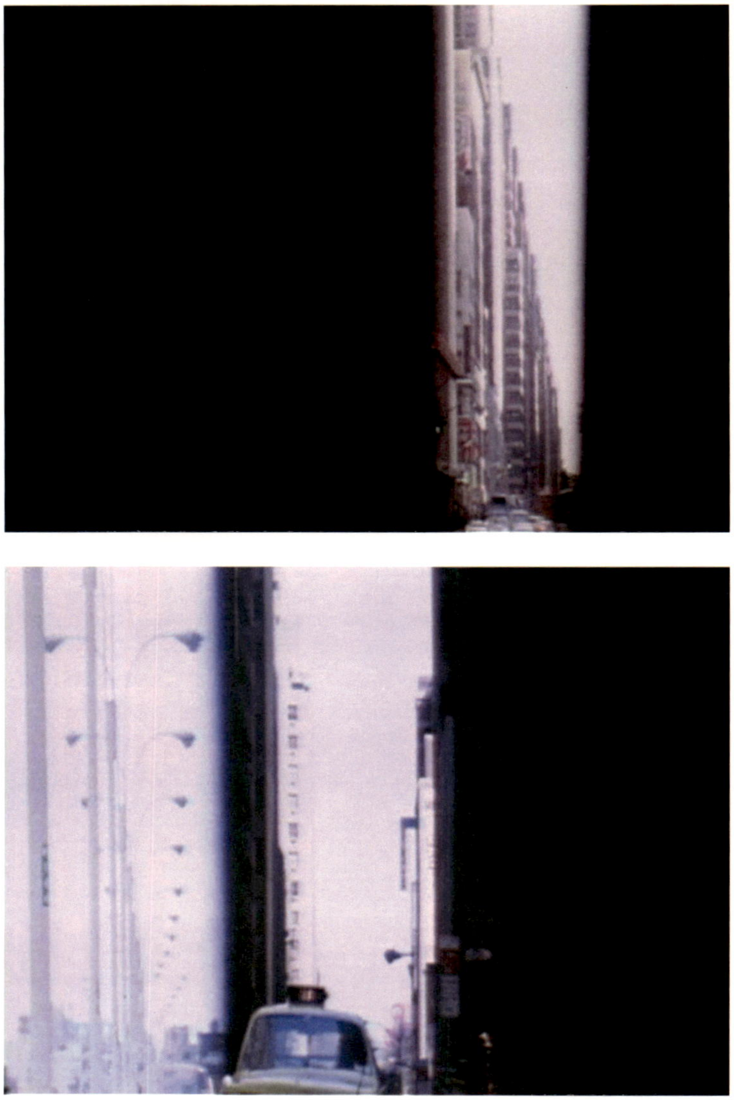

Plate 67 Gordon Matta-Clark, stills from *City Slivers*, 1976

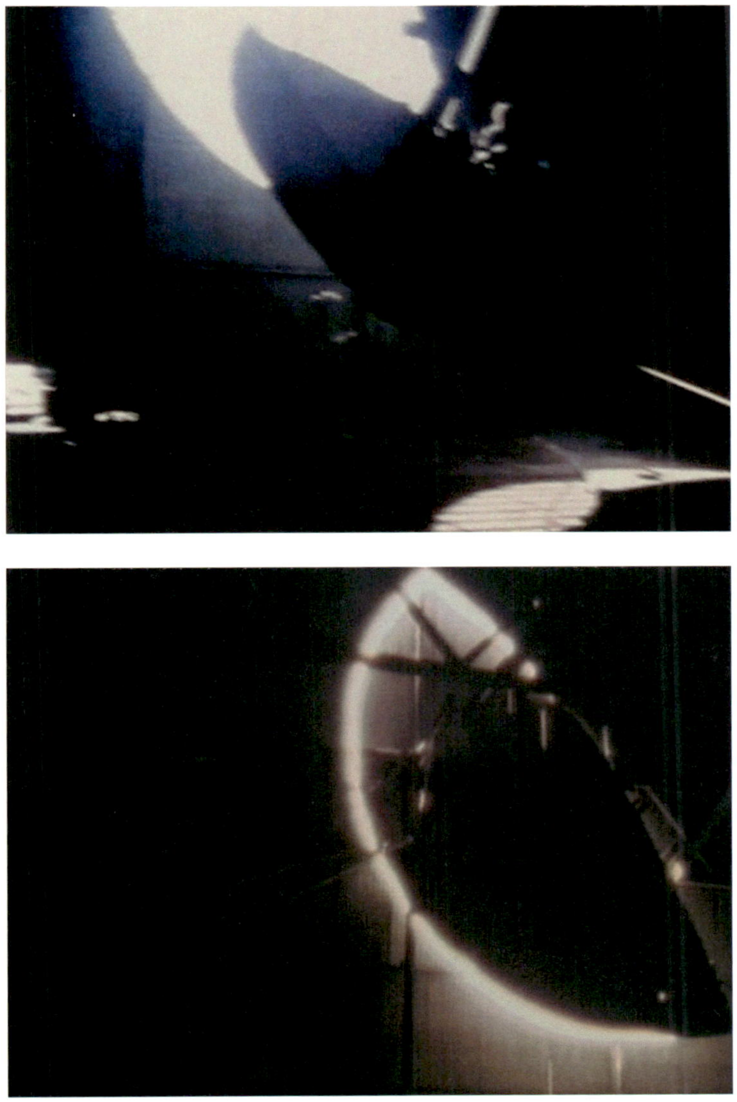

Plate 68 Gordon Matta-Clark, stills from *Day's End*, 1975

into the opening between two glass towers; an abandoned chair sits on a sidewalk; a cardboard model of the Mercury capsule goes by on the street below, followed by a person holding an open umbrella, the absurd remains of a tawdry, rained-out parade. At the end of *Chapter III*, there is a rare narrative moment, spread across various takes whose framing varies slightly as the camera seems to come closer to its subject. A man collapses on the sidewalk, attracting the attention of several pedestrians and a policeman. Eventually, an ambulance arrives and the man is lifted into the vehicle and driven off. The vertical perspective gives the scene an abstract quality; framed by the edge of the curb and a fire escape, it looks like a canvas gradually filled with dots and masses that converge around a dark splotch—the sprawling victim. Abstraction is not uncommon in Hutton's films. Mixed with clear figurative images, there are patterns of light and shadow, surface and mass. The manner in which the city generates such views imparts ambiguity to the title of the series. These could be portraits *of* the city or *by* the city—the city itself an endless image generator, and the filmmaker a mere shutterlike device that preserves their memory.

Aware of the city as material, Hutton still privileges the imagistic aspects of urban life that rise from its hardware and float above it like ectoplasm. The shots of dust particles suspended in a light beam (in *New York near Sleep*), of mist and steam, and of clouds above the skyline emblematize this relationship between the city and its images. Hutton's films, more than those of any other artist of his generation, make visible a dialectic between urban materiality and immateriality, solidity and image, that was wittily formulated by Nam June Paik in "The Selling of New York," a section of the collaborative video work *Suite 212* (1975/1977). Over a dense collage of images lifted from American and Japanese television and from classic film noir, an off-screen voice states that New York has become the world capital of the knowledge industries—broadcasting, advertisement, data processing and storage. It is dominated by information technologies and trades in immaterial images that move at the speed of light. It was this shift in the economy of the city—from the manufacture of tangible goods to the dissemination of immaterial data—that depopulated downtown and brought about, as a paradoxical side effect, a thickening of its material configuration: spaces without function, ruins, and incongruous accidents like "the beach" or the flats and embankments in *Songdelay*. This overwhelming environment was at once the setting and the subject matter of much art of the 1970s and after. It prompted peculiar uses and deliberately fragmentary depictions. Both—uses and depictions—were forms of occupation, at once immaterial and material, imagistic and tactile. They took the form of ephemeral actions captured as traces of light on celluloid or videotape, but, at the same time, they indexed the stubborn solidity of a milieu that they sought to explore, inhabit, and subvert.

★

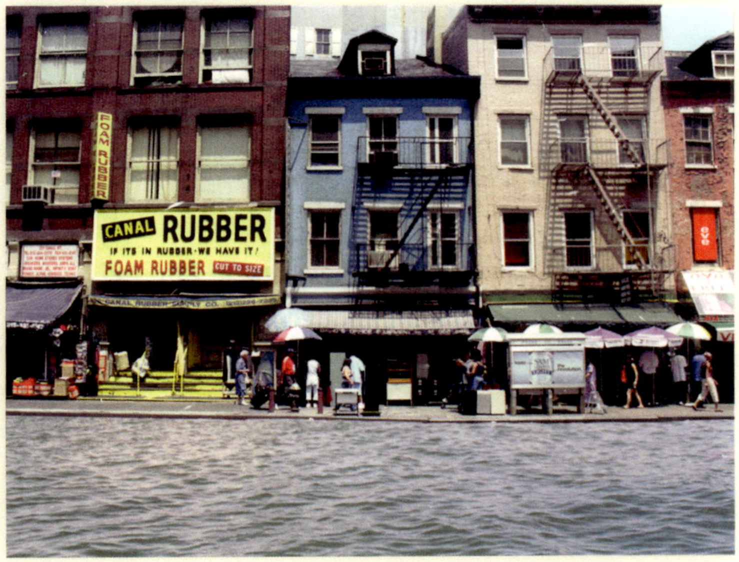

ABOVE: a section of Canal Street as it might look today if a 1791 proposal to build a "Venetian-style" canal connecting the Hudson and East Rivers across lower Manhattan had been realized. The canal and an accompanying commercial harbor were meant to replace both a small stream which ran along present-day Canal Street, and the so-called Fresh Water or Collect Pond, a befouled 70-acre swamp that one New York newspaper of the day called a "shocking hole." Instead, real-estate interests prevailed, and the stream was widened only enough to drain the pond so it could be filled in and developed. Many basements of new buildings on the landfill soon flooded, so the stream was further enlarged to increase drainage—making it, in effect, an open sewer. After much complaint about odor, and despite efforts to beautify the waterway with a tree-lined promenade, it was covered over in 1819. Flaws in this redesign kept Canal Street smelling foul for years. It is rumored that the natural spring which once fed the Fresh Water Pond still flows deep below Canal Street today.*

*Luc Sante defines nostalgia as a state of inarticulate contempt for the present combined with a fear of the future.

Matthew Buckingham, *Canal Street Canal*, 2002. Postcard

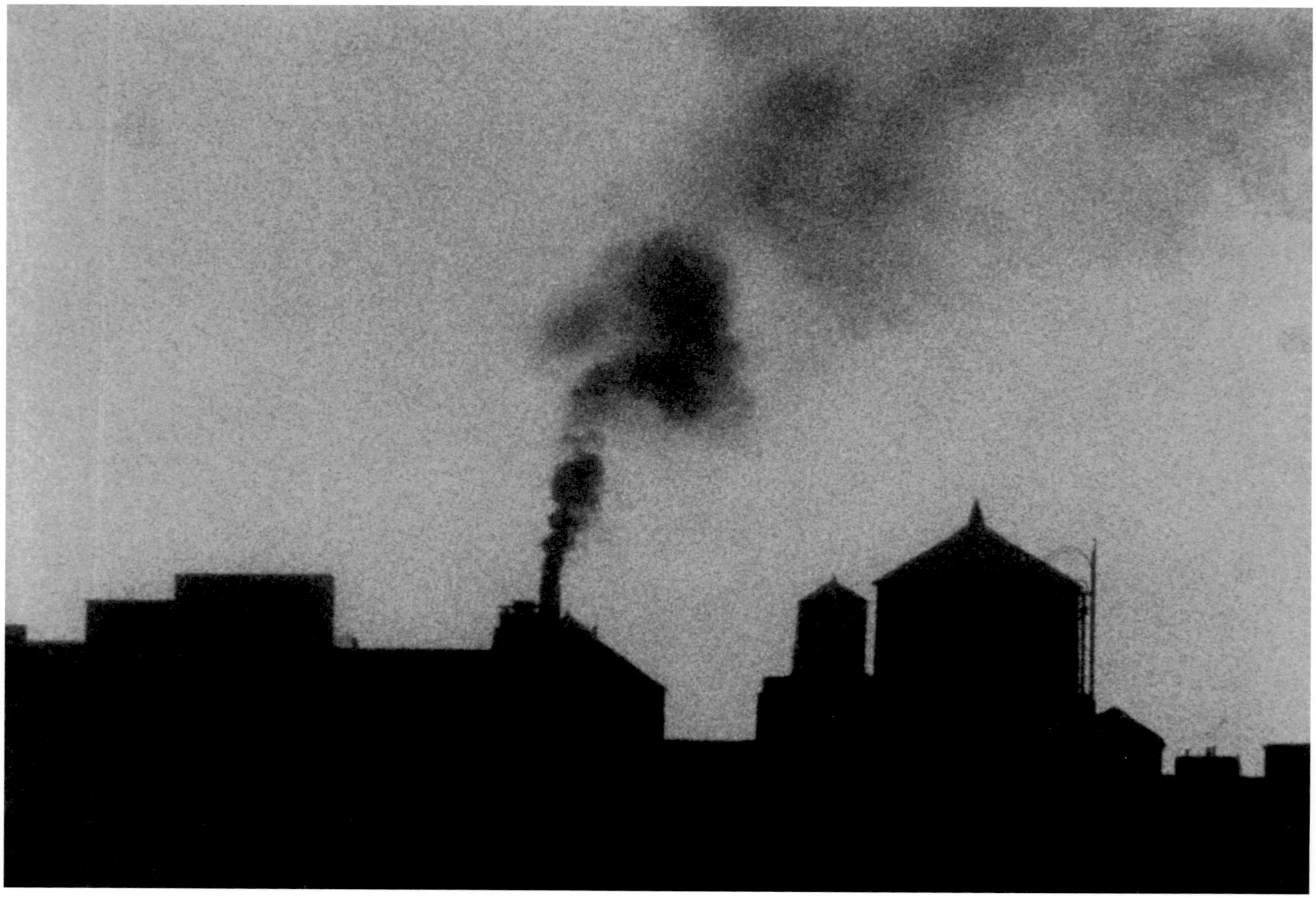

Plate 69 Peter Hutton, still from *New York Portrait, Chapter I*, 1978–79

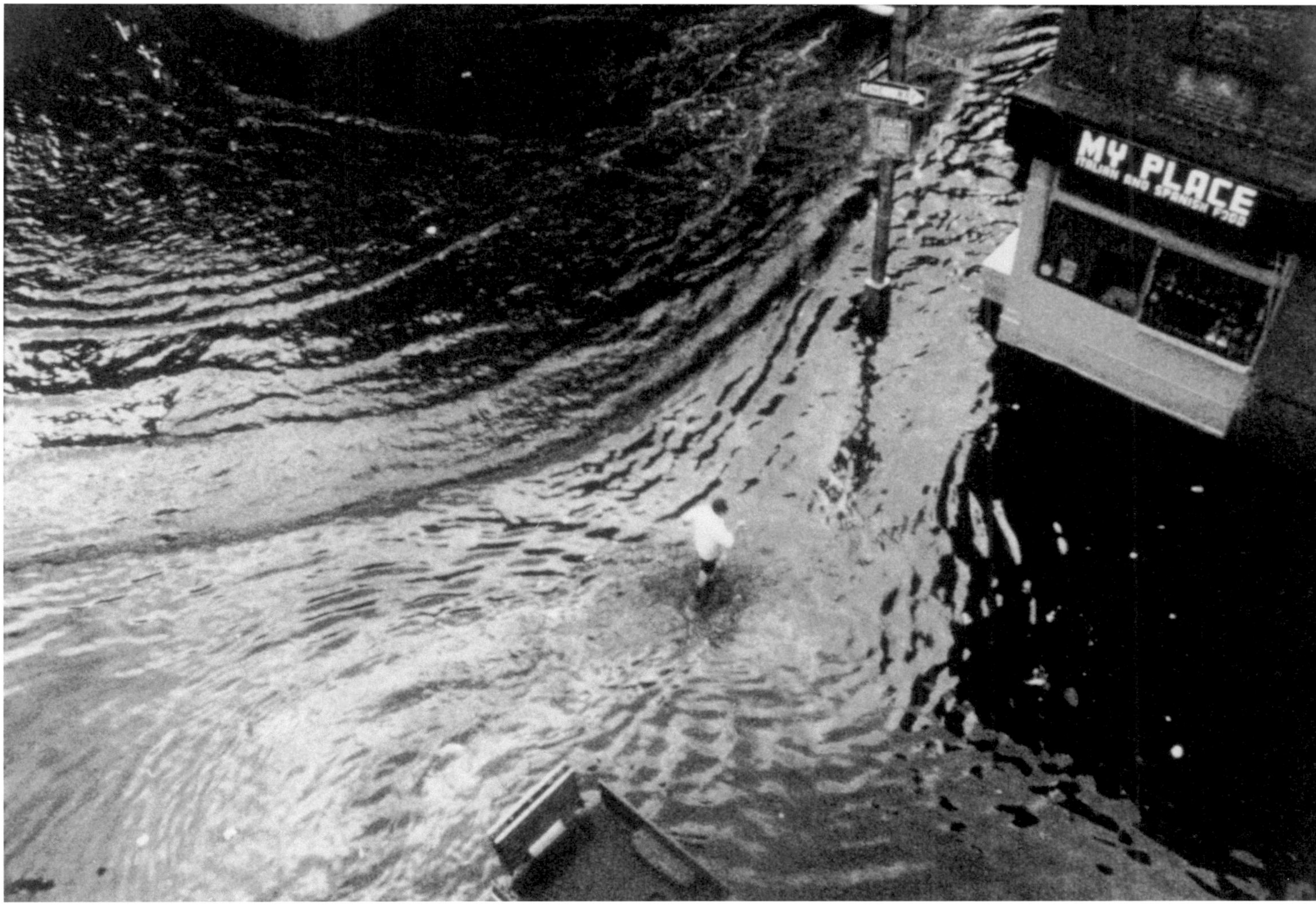

Plate 70 Peter Hutton, still from *New York Portrait, Chapter II*, 1980–81

Gilles Deleuze has influentially proposed that cinema experienced a crisis shortly after World War II. At that point, what he calls the classical cinema, based on transitive perception and action (the "linkages of situation-action, action-reaction, excitation-response, in short, the sensory-motor links which produced the action-image"), gave way to a "modern" cinema of "pure optical and sound situations."[27] The classical models did not disappear—they remain operative in mainstream commercial film, Deleuze noted—but the "the soul of the cinema" was no longer in them. The new cinema required "more thought" and, therefore, different forms—looser action, more ambiguous characters and situations. Filmed spaces shed their former cohesiveness, resisted holistic portrayal, and could be traversed and assembled, through editing, in a multiplicity of ways. They became disjointed and incomplete (as in Bresson) or deserted (as in Pasolini or Antonioni), or gained an extraordinary material density (as in Straub-Huillet and Resnais). They forced themselves onto the action, which reached down to the earth while, simultaneously, the ground rose to the surface and the image turned "archeological, stratigraphic, tectonic."[28] (A few years earlier, Robert Smithson had written, "Everything about movies and moviemaking is archaic and crude. One is transported by this Archeozoic medium into the earliest known geological eras.")[29] For Deleuze, the factors that contributed to the decline of the classical cinema and its tidy spatiality were the exhaustion of the old genres, the influence of modernist literature and art, waning faith in the possibility of significant human action, "the new consciousness of minorities," and the war and its consequences.[30] Among these last, Deleuze gave particular prominence to the shattered cities, improvised shantytowns, and desolate sprawls that pitted Europe after the armistice—impossible spaces that could not be articulated with meaningful action. One might say that this is also what happened in the Manhattan of the 1960s and 70s. In the transition toward a postindustrial socioeconomic regime, the city lost the perceptual/motor axis of industry. Ruins and dysfunctional spaces spread, prompting different styles of occupation, which included a cinema of fragmentary views, process, tectonics, and duration.

The other crucial characteristic of the modern cinema is the floating speech act—the autonomous "sound situation." Language, music, and sound, similarly to space, exceeded their expressive and narrative functions and gained autonomy and density. Image and sound became tangential to each other; they connected without constituting an integrated, organic whole, as is the case in *The Last Clean Shirt*, the *Lunar Rambles* tapes, and *News from Home*. Rather than corroborate the image track, the aural plane entertained an "irrational" relationship with the image and invoked the inexpressible.[31]

One of the inexpressible contents invoked by the disjunctive sounds and images of modern film is the impossibility of depicting a community—for Deleuze, an immediately political problem. The postwar cinema is political, he claims, insofar as it engages with "the absence of a people." This is the subject for the greatest political filmmakers of the time: the fact that "there have never been people here."[32] In the West, they were evacuated by prewar totalitarianisms and by the "dissolution" of the American public; in much of the rest of the world, by imperialist domination. Spatial eviction might be both cause and symptom of this disappearance. Although Deleuze does not say as much, following Lefebvre and the Situationists, one might venture that "the people are not there" largely because there is no "there" anymore. After World War II, traditional urban spaces, with their miseries and squalor, certainly, but also with their vitality, unpredictability, and commonality, were replaced by soulless suburbs, degraded inner cities, and dehumanizing housing projects—habitats that effected various forms of spatial and class segregation. In response, the cinema and other arts enlisted the shards that were left—archaeological remains, disjointed and deserted spaces, autonomous aural situations—in the attempt, however doomed, to "[invent] a people."[33]

In a way, all depictions of the city seek to invent a people—to produce its images and clear out its spaces, to articulate its life on the substratum of the built environment. During the 1970s, this was done by integrating the materiality of the city—its "geology" and mass—into a number of artistic projects that, quite often, were communal projects as well. During the 1980s and 90s, tectonic-material-geologic concerns gave way to the subcultural activation of space, based on the presence of deviant bodies in public locations and on the concomitant mobilization of sound, fashion, and style. If 1970s artists and filmmakers delved into the materiality of the milieu, those from later decades showcased the materiality of bodies in space, along with their sexuality, ethnicity, gestures, and noise. They gravitated toward break-dancers and rappers, punk music, downtown club performance, actions of queer visibility (see Nelson Sullivan's video *Drag Queens in Times Square* [1986]), ACT UP demonstrations, p. 156 and the homeless. By focusing on these actions and collectives, the art world rose against the enormous violence of a double eviction: gentrification, which advanced fast through downtown Manhattan from the 1980s onward, and the evacuation of minority concerns from official politics during the Reagan-Bush years, evident in the slighting of AIDS, the dismantling of federal antipoverty programs, and the culture wars around National Endowment for the Arts funding of art projects.[34]

In their depictions of subcultural life, filmmakers of the 1980s and 90s resorted to story- and character-centered formats, and they humanized space: they swerved away from the impersonal assemblages characteristic of the 1970s and focused instead on personal vicissitude and social interaction. Characteristic of these decades were documentaries such as Jennie Livingstone's *Paris Is Burning* (1991), on voguing, and Marcia Reaven and Beni Matias's *The Heart of Loisaida* (1979), on the homesteading initiatives of mostly Latino tenants in Alphabet City. Also typical were feature-length works halfway between documentary and fiction, such as Charlie Ahearn's *Wild Style* (1982), and fictional titles such as Charles Lane's *Sidewalk Stories* and Spike Lee's *Do the Right Thing* (both 1989).[35] Markedly more experimental are the diary films indefatigably

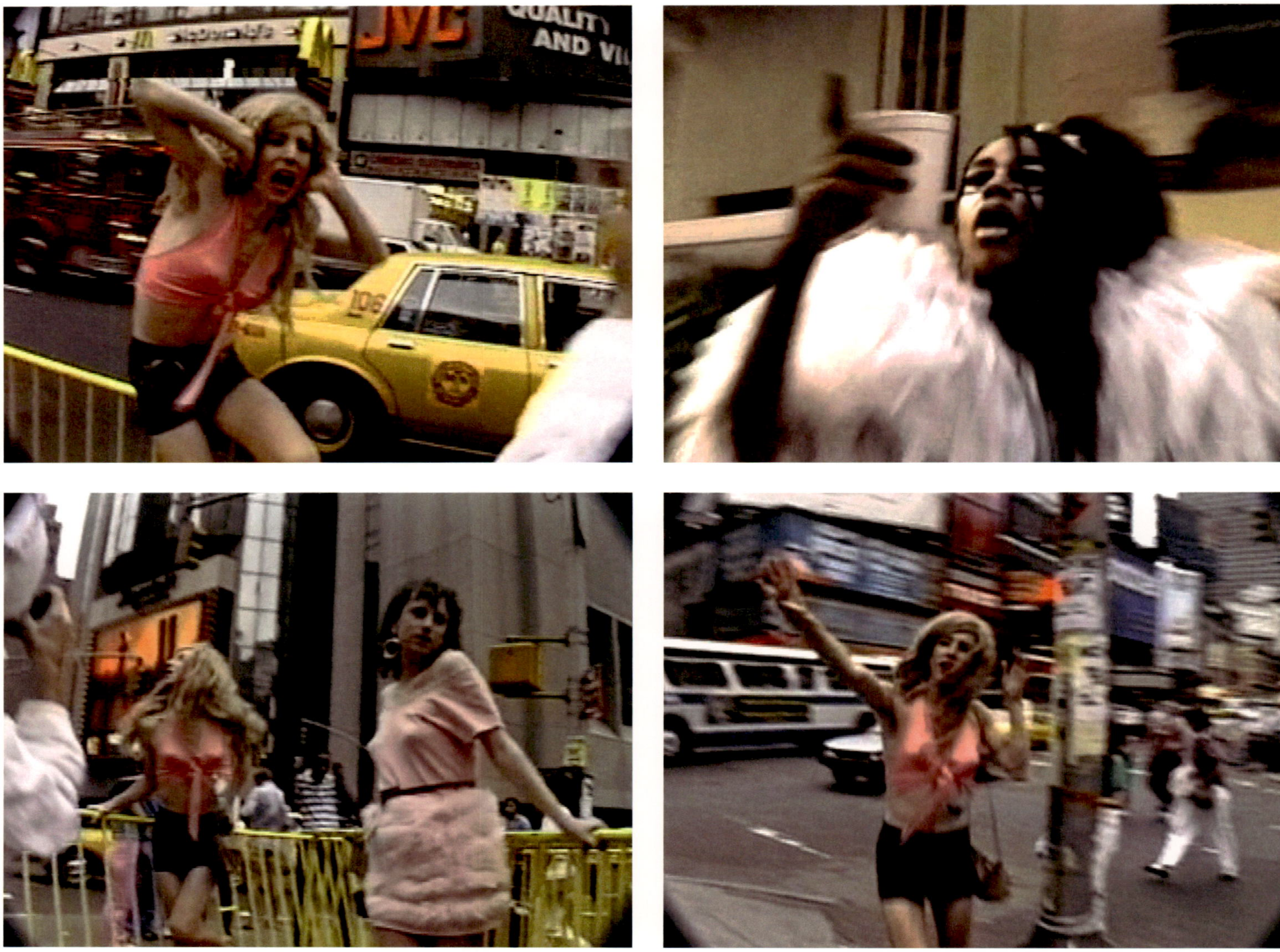

Plate 71 Nelson Sullivan, stills from *Drag Queens in Times Square*, 1986

produced by Nelson Sullivan during the 1980s—a personal record of parties, gay-pride demonstrations, club performances, and street action shot with an 8mm camcorder.

And yet the exploration of the city as material did not disappear after the early 1980s. It has recently become generative for visual artists such as Cyprien Gaillard, Patricia Esquivias, Pedro Ortuño, and Matthew Buckingham, among others. They combine the material interests of the 1970s with the situated critiques of the 1980s and 1990s and produce works that are at once geologic-stratigraphic *and* based on bodily and sonic occupation. Personal testimonies, music, and, in Buckingham's case, historical and historiographical reflection, rise from the foundations of the image, haunt it, and make it resonate with an alternative history of missed possibilities and repressed conflict.

Buckingham's works explore concrete visual evidence through "speech acts"—in Deleuze's formulation—that take the form of historical reconstructions and critical ruminations about the relation of the past to the present. For Buckingham, the sediments of the past evoke alternatives to the way things are. They relativize the present by recalling a time when things were different and by underlining the contingency of the current state of affairs: the product of unpredictable concatenations, contemporary reality might have turned out otherwise. His various works about New York, for example, recall forgotten accidents, submerged histories, and transformations of public space and of the way in which it has been represented over time.

Canal Street Canal (2002) is a photographic re-creation of contempo- p. 151 rary Canal Street as a picturesque waterfront with a running stream instead of asphalt between the sidewalks, accompanied with a printed text recalling late eighteenth-century plans to turn the street into a Venetian-style canal. It was produced as an unlimited-edition postcard and sold by street vendors alongside other tourist souvenirs in the downtown area. A forgotten project, now an obscure footnote to Manhattan's history, might have become one of the city's characteristic sights, destined to be trivialized and disseminated as a cheap memento. *Muhheakantuck—Everything Has a Name* (2003) p. 250 consists of two aerial views of the Hudson River from a helicopter—one taken while flying north, the other while flying south. The images are matched to Buckingham's spoken reflections on the interactions between the early Dutch settlers and the Lenape Native Americans in the Lower Hudson Valley in the mid-seventeenth century, on cartography and place naming as exercises of power, and on the potential of hidden histories to dislocate established identities. It has been shown as a 16mm film loop in gallery spaces and was also screened by Creative Time on board a water taxi traveling from Christopher Street to near the Statue of Liberty at twilight, when the river was still visible through the windows of the boat and the image on the screen could be contrasted with its referent outside. And *One Side of Broadway* (2005) is a slide projection pp. 256–57 of photographs of the east side of Broadway in the wintertime taken by Buckingham himself. Over the images, a recorded voice describes photographs, never shown, from the book *Both Sides of Broadway, from Bowling Green to Central Park, New York City*, published in 1910 by the De Leeuw Riehl Publishing Company. The photographs, Buckingham recalls, were taken on plates manufactured by the Lumière brothers; ironically, some show a number of Broadway movie theaters at a time when the actuality film of the kind pioneered by the Lumières had been replaced in popular taste by the fiction film. The ambition of the book to provide a thorough picture of the street—"important buildings, street corners and scenes along Broadway, from the earliest times to the present," reads the *New York Times* description of the volume[36]—contrasts with the deliberately limited perspective of Buckingham's re-creation, and photographic representation contrasts with the abstract, linguistically mediated description, which both references and resists the former.

The distance between the 1910 book and Buckingham's re-creation is analogous to that between the early twentieth-century city symphonies and the depiction of the city in post-1960s film and video. The city symphony, nearly contemporary with *Both Sides of Broadway*, was an attempt to render the spectacle of urban life—and urban life as spectacle—in a totalizing manner. Its post-1960s progeny was much more tentative and fragmentary—two qualities that describe as well Buckingham's activation of the city's memory. Tentativeness is imposed by the very character of history and of urban space. Neither may be definitely settled and mastered, only partially inhabited for limited times and for particular purposes. But far from a damaging limitation, this condition warrants that there will always be room—and need—for further invention, occupation, and play.

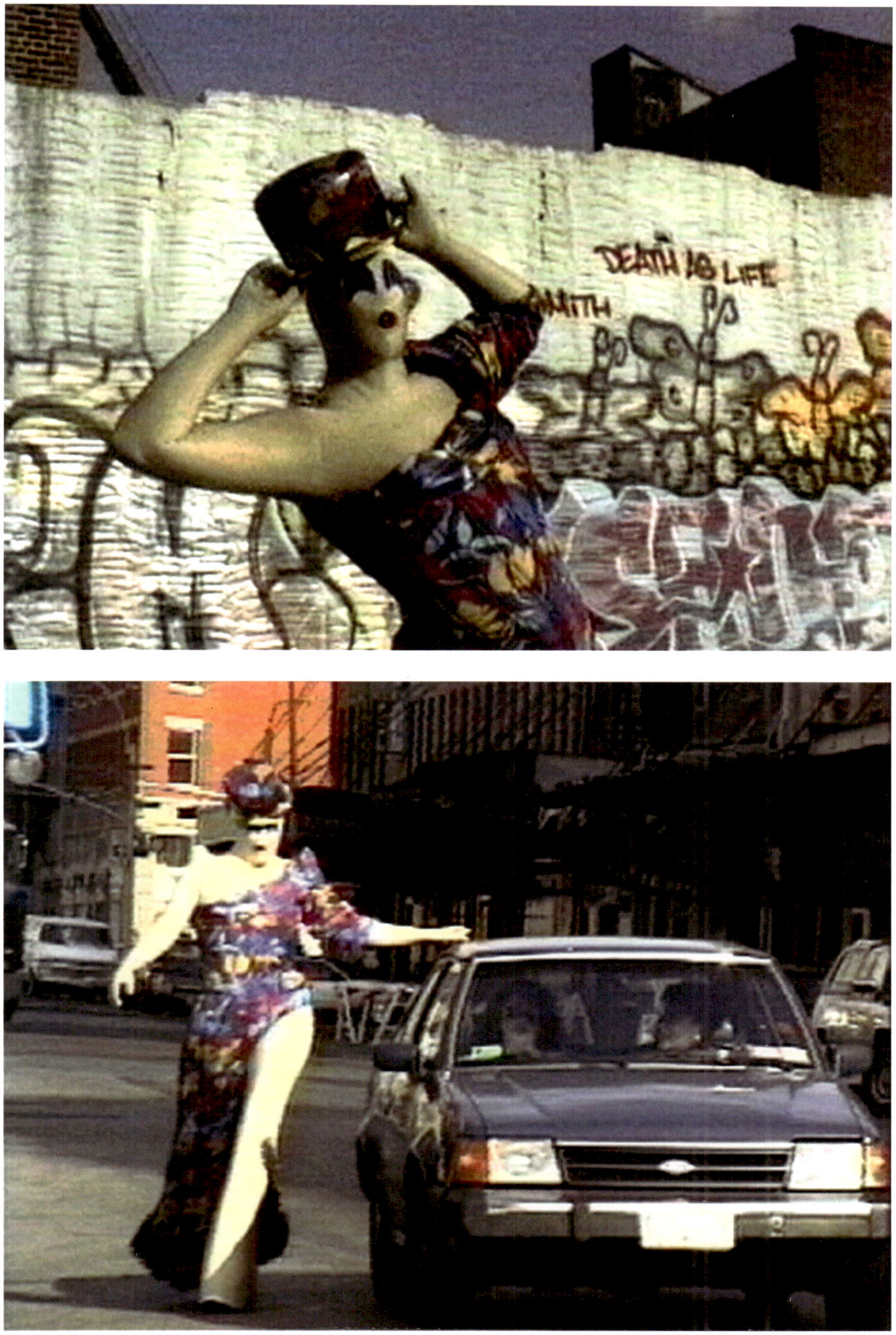

Plate 72 Charles Atlas, stills from *Mrs. Peanut Visits New York*, 1999

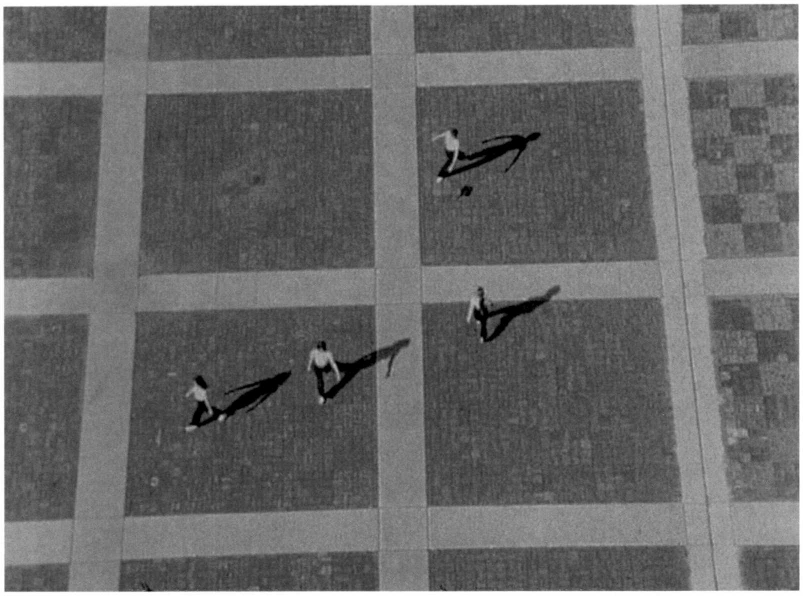

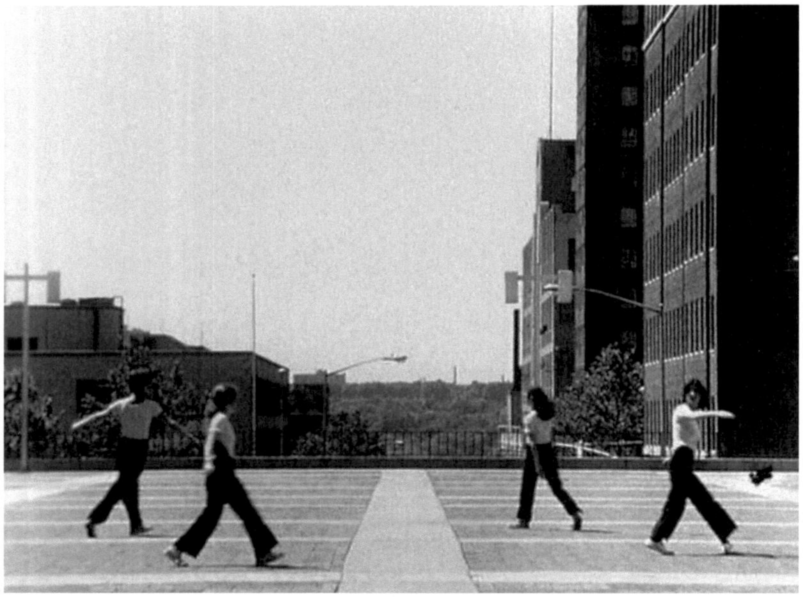

Plate 73 Babette Mangolte and Lucinda Childs, stills from *Calico Mingling*, 1973

Endnotes

1
On the concept and the history of the "little cinema," see Jan-Christopher Horak, "The First American Film Avant-Garde, 1919–1945," in *Lovers of the Cinema: The First American Film Avant-Garde, 1919–1945*, ed. Jan-Christopher Horak (Madison: University of Wisconsin Press, 1995), pp. 13–66, esp. 20–29.

2
J. Hoberman, *On Jack Smith's Flaming Creatures (and Other Secret-Flix of Cinemaroc)* (New York: Granary Books/Hips Road, 2001), p. 81.

3
On the rise and implications of the production of social space, see Rosalyn Deutsche, "Krzysztof Wodiczko's Homeless Projections and the Site of Urban 'Revitalization,'" in *Evictions: Art and Spatial Politics* (Cambridge, MA: MIT Press, 1996), pp. 3–48.

4
This should not be understood in absolute terms. Some films from this period are still aesthetically and ideologically indebted to the early city films, as Hilary Harris's *Organism* (1975) and Godfrey Reggio's popular diptych *Koyaanisqatsi* (1982) and *Powaqqatsi* (1988) attest. However, they are far from the ethos and aesthetics of the contemporary avant-garde.

5
Robert Ross and Kent Trachte, *Global Capitalism: The New Leviathan* (Albany, NY: State University of New York Press, 1990), pp. 156–57.

6
On the port of New York in the postwar years, see Eric Darton, *Divided We Stand: A Biography of New York's World Trade Center* (New York: Basic Books, 1999).

7
My view of New York in the 1970s is totally indebted to Douglas Crimp's essay "Action around the Edges," printed in this volume, which I had access to—thanks to Douglas—when it still was in manuscript form.

8
See Martin Beck, "Alternative: Space," in *Alternative Art New York, 1965–1985*, ed. Julie Ault (Minneapolis: University of Minnesota Press, 2002), esp. pp. 249–54; on 112 Greene Street generally, see *112 Workshop, 112 Greene Street: History, Artists & Artworks*, ed. Robyn Brentano with Mark Savitt (New York: New York University Press, 1981).

9
Rosalind Krauss, "Notes on the Index, Parts 1 and 2," in *The Originality of the Avant-Garde and Other Modernist Myths* (Cambridge, MA: MIT Press, 1986), pp. 196–219.

10
On street protest in the 1960s, see Bradford D. Martin, *The Theater Is in the Street: Politics and Performance in 1960s America* (Amherst: University of Massachusetts Press, 2004).

11
See Tim Lawrence, *Love Saves the Day: A History of American Dance Music Culture, 1970–1979* (Durham, NC: Duke University Press, 2003).

12
Songdelay's cinematographer is Robert Fiore, who earlier helped Robert Smithson edit *Spiral Jetty* (1970) and went on to codirect the successful bodybuilding documentary *Pumping Iron* (1977).

13
See, for example, Joan Jonas, "Interview with Joan Simon" and "*Jones Beach Piece* (1970)," in *Joan Jonas. Performance, Video, Installation 1968–2000*, ed. Johan Karl Schmidt (Ostfildern-Ruit: Hatje-Cantz, 2002), pp. 27–28, 73. The best review of Jonas's early work remains *Joan Jonas, Scripts and Descriptions 1968–1982*, ed. Douglas Crimp (Berkeley: University Art Museum, University of California, Berkeley; Eindhoven: Stedelijk van Abbemuseum, 1983).

14
E-mail from Terry Fox to Stephen Vitiello, at the Kitchen, February 2002. In this communication, Fox uncertainly attributes the camera work of *Lunar Rambles* to Michael Shamberg: "These performances were done each day over a five day period and video-taped by (I think) Michael Shamberg." Shamberg, author, with the Raindance Corporation, of the influential *Guerrilla Television* (New York: Holt, Rinehart and Winston, 1971), was involved by then with the video collective TVTV, started in 1972 to produce alternative coverage of the Democratic and Republican conventions in Miami. See Deirdre Boyle, *Subject to Change: Guerrilla Television Revisited* (New York: Oxford University Press, 1996), esp. pp. 55–65 and passim. Many thanks to Leah Churner, of Electronic Arts Intermix (EAI), for sharing with me a copy of Fox's e-mail, and to Josh Kline, also at EAI, for alerting me to Fox's tapes.

15
Terry Fox, "I Wanted to Have My Mood Affect Their Looks," *Avalanche* no. 2 (Winter 1970), p. 70 and ff.

16
Matthew Yokobosky, "Not a Part of Any Wave: No Wave Cinema," in *The Downtown Book: The New York Art Scene, 1974–1984*, ed. Marvin J. Taylor (Princeton, NJ: Princeton University Press; New York: Grey Art Gallery, New York University, 2006), p. 120.

17
Amy Taubin, "Repetition Compulsion: The Films of James Nares," *Artforum* 46 (May 2008), p. 83.

18
Personal communication from James Nares, January 26, 2010. My gratitude to Nares for his generous replies to my queries.

19
James Nares, program notes for the retrospective "James Nares: Motion Pictures," Anthology Film Archives, May 13–22, 2008.

20
Nares, January 26, 2010.

21
For information about the production of Matta-Clark's films I am relying on Jane Crawford, "Twenty Adventures," in *City Slivers and Fresh Kills: The Films of Gordon Matta-Clark*, ed. Steven Jenkins (San Francisco: San Francisco Cinematheque, 2004), unpaginated.

22
Beatriz Colomina, *Privacy and Publicity: Modern Architecture as Mass Media* (Cambridge, MA: MIT Press, 1996), pp. 7–9, 50–52.

23
Crawford, "Twenty Adventures."

24
Theodore W. Kheel as quoted by Calvin Tomkins in "The Talk of the Town: Automation House," *The New Yorker* (March 14, 1970), p. 30.

25
See Scott MacDonald, "Peter Hutton," in *A Critical Cinema 3: Interviews with Independent Filmmakers* (Berkeley: University of California Press, 1998), pp. 241–52.

26
For biographical information on Hutton, I am relying on *Screening Room: Peter Hutton*. WCVB-TV, broad-cast March 1977. DVD (Cambridge, MA: Studio 7 Arts/Documentary Educational Resources, 2005). For a contemporary account of *Hippodrome Hardware*, see Ronald Argelander, "Red Grooms' Homemade Theatre: *Hippodrome Hardware*," *The Drama Review: TDR* 17, no. 2, Visual Performance Issue (June 1973), pp. 92–100.

27
Gilles Deleuze, *Cinema 1: The Movement-Image*, trans. Hugo Tomlinson and Barbara Habberjam (Minneapolis: University of Minnesota Press, 1986), p. 206; Gilles Deleuze, *Cinema 2: The Time-Image*, trans. Hugh Tomlinson and Robert Galeta (Minneapolis: University of Minnesota Press, 1989), p. 12.

28
Deleuze, *Cinema 2*, p. 243.

29
Robert Smithson, "The Spiral Jetty" in Smithson, *The Collected Writings*, ed. Jack Flam (Berkeley: University of California Press, 1996), p. 150.

30
Deleuze, *Cinema 1*, p. 206 and ff.

31
Deleuze, *Cinema 2*, pp. 225–31.

32
Ibid., p. 217.

33
Ibid.

34
On eviction as a critical trope to examine the politics of this period, see Deutsche, *Evictions*, especially "Agoraphobia," pp. 269–327.

35
On Lee's *Do the Right Thing* as a modern-day version of the city symphony, see Scott MacDonald, *The Garden in the Machine: A Field Guide to Independent Films about Place* (Berkeley: University of California Press, 2001), pp. 170–82.

36
"Both Sides of Broadway," *The New York Times Saturday Review of Books*, July 9, 1910, BR6. http://query.nytimes.com/mem/archive (accessed January 26, 2010).

Arthur Rimbaud in New York

David Wojnarowicz

Untitled (David Wojnarowicz Project)

Emily Roysdon

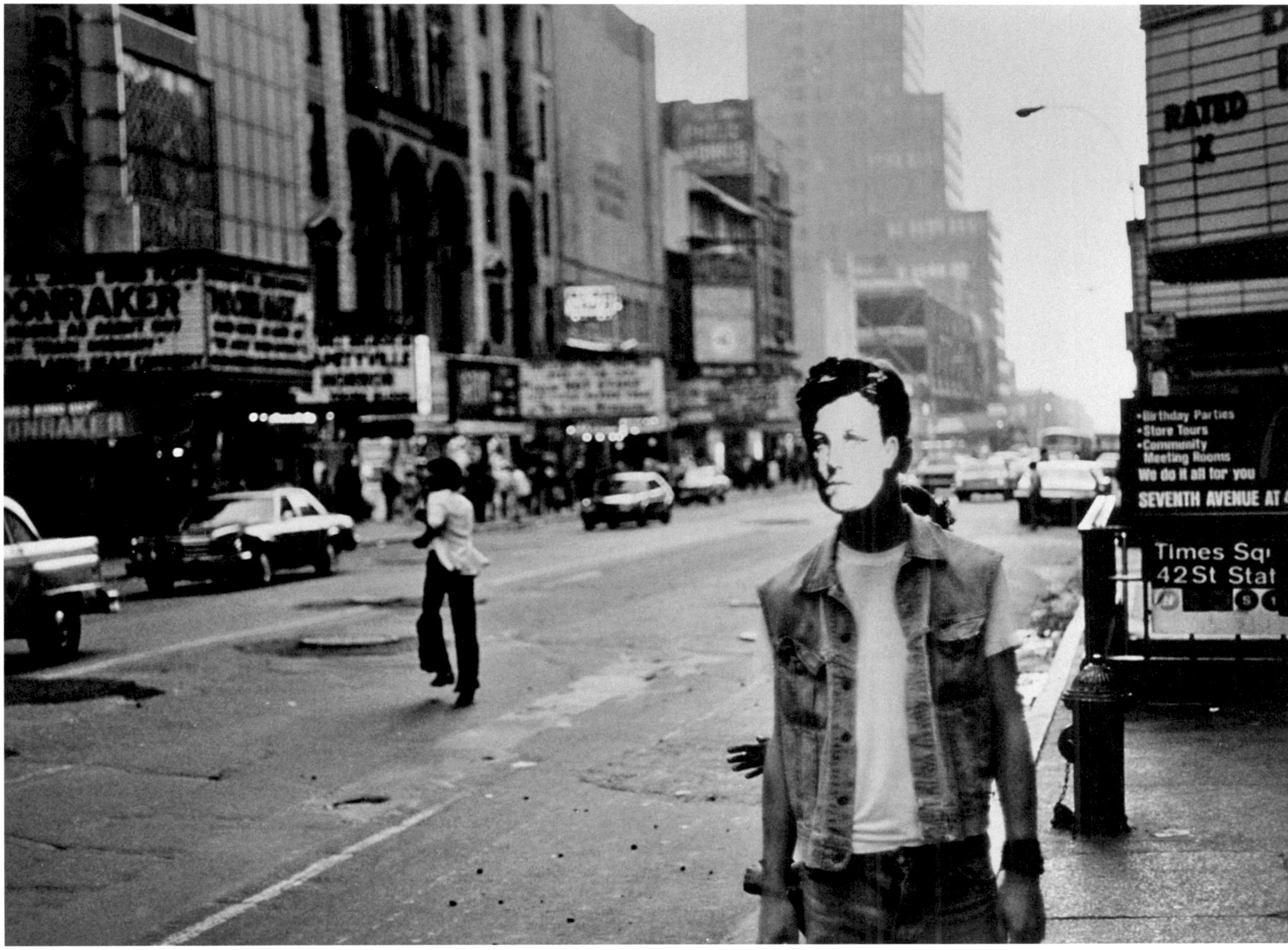

Plate 74 David Wojnarowicz, *Arthur Rimbaud in New York*, 1978–79

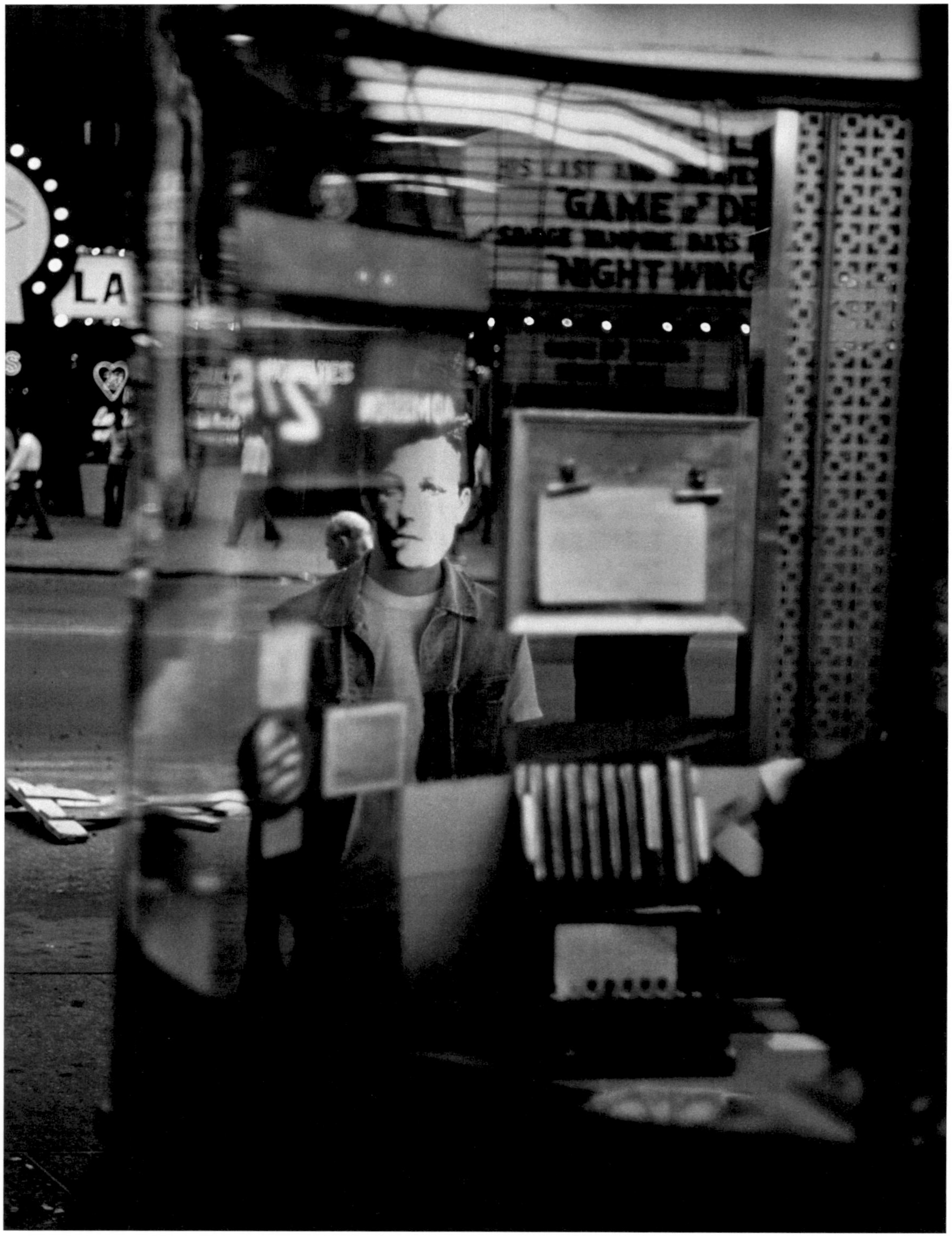

Plate 75 David Wojnarowicz, *Arthur Rimbaud in New York*, 1978–79

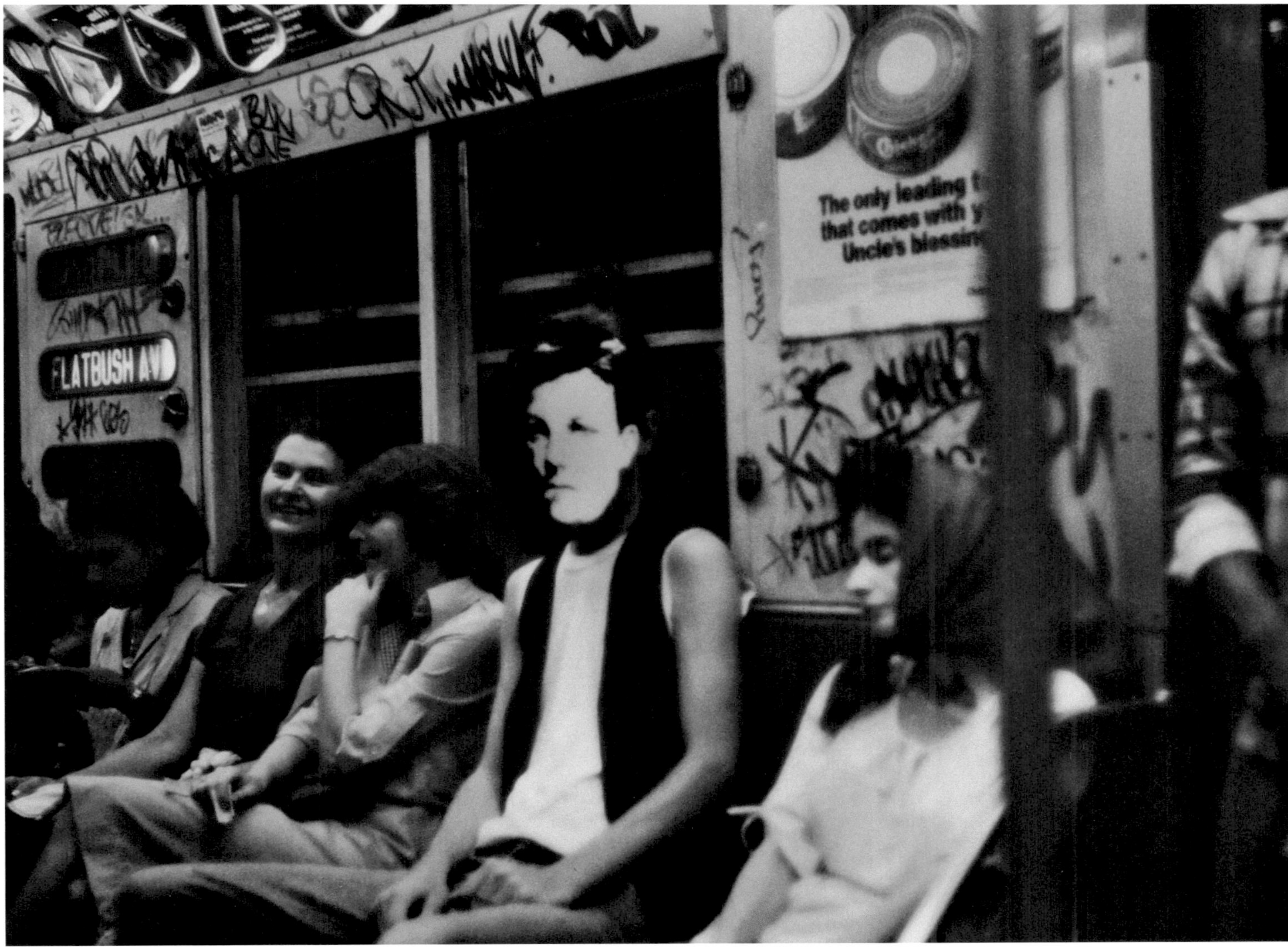

Plate 76 David Wojnarowicz, *Arthur Rimbaud in New York*, 1978–79

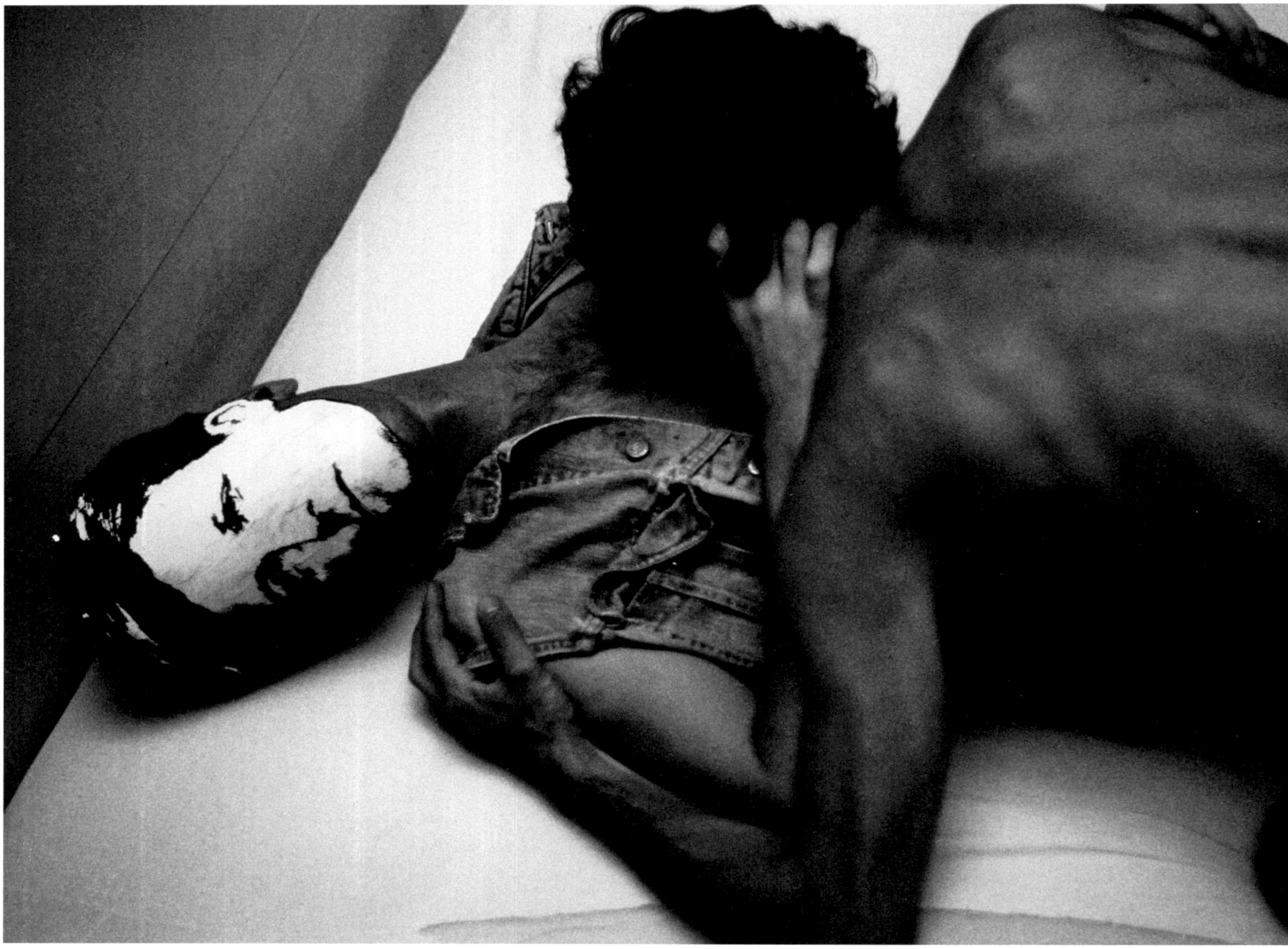

Plate 77 David Wojnarowicz, *Arthur Rimbaud in New York*, 1978–79

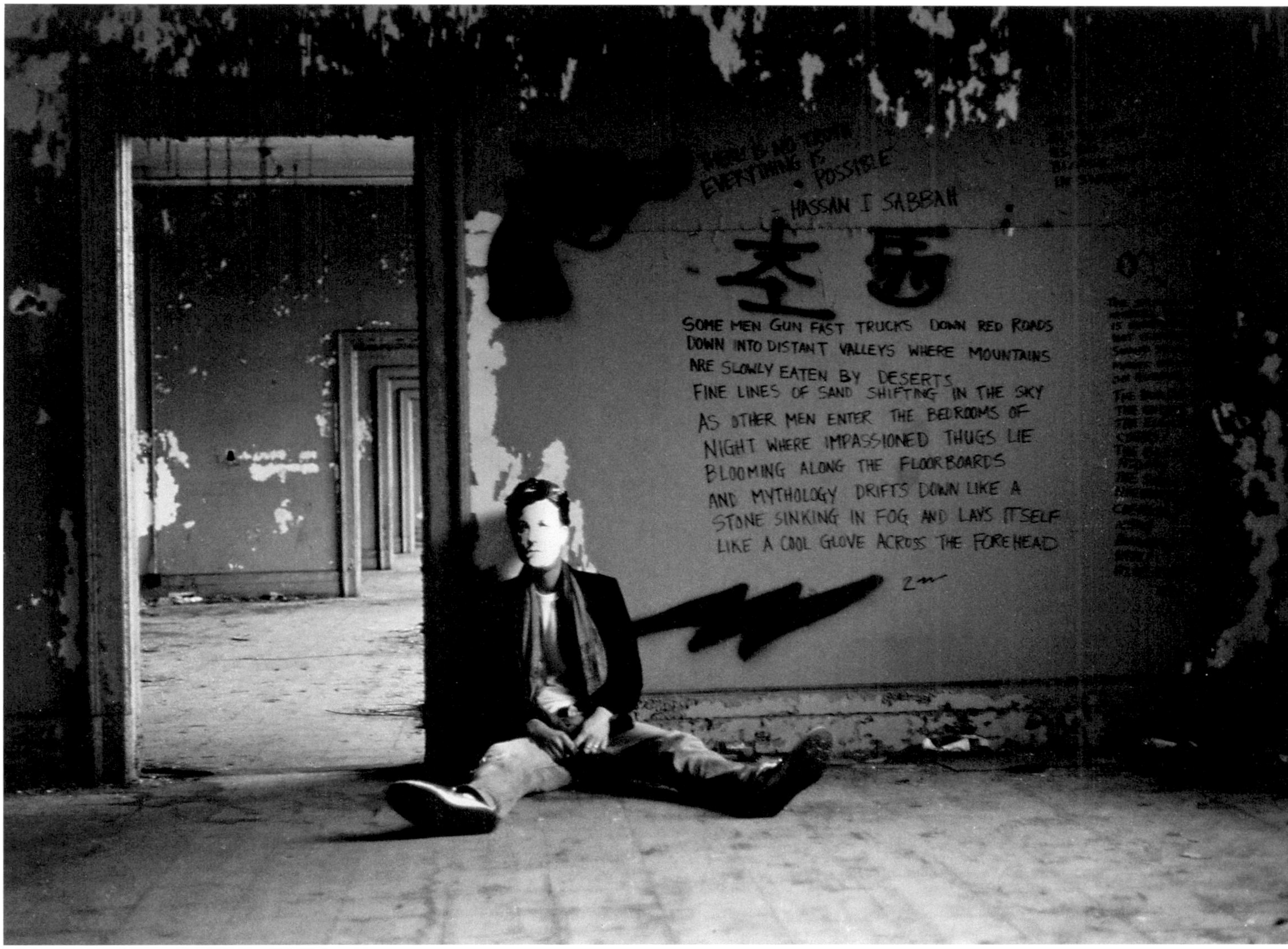

Plate 78 David Wojnarowicz, *Arthur Rimbaud in New York*, 1978–79

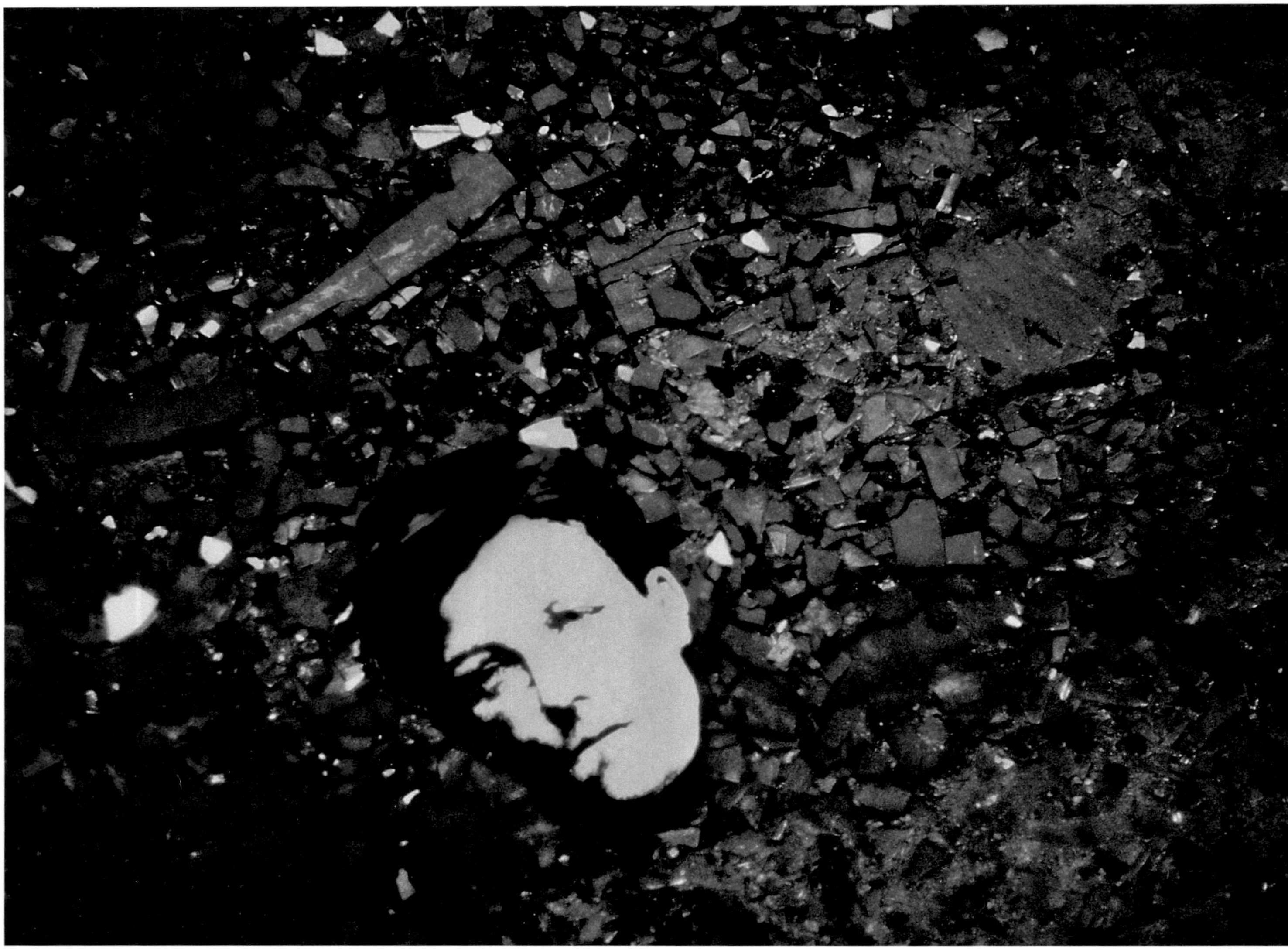

Plate 79 David Wojnarowicz, *Arthur Rimbaud in New York*, 1978–79

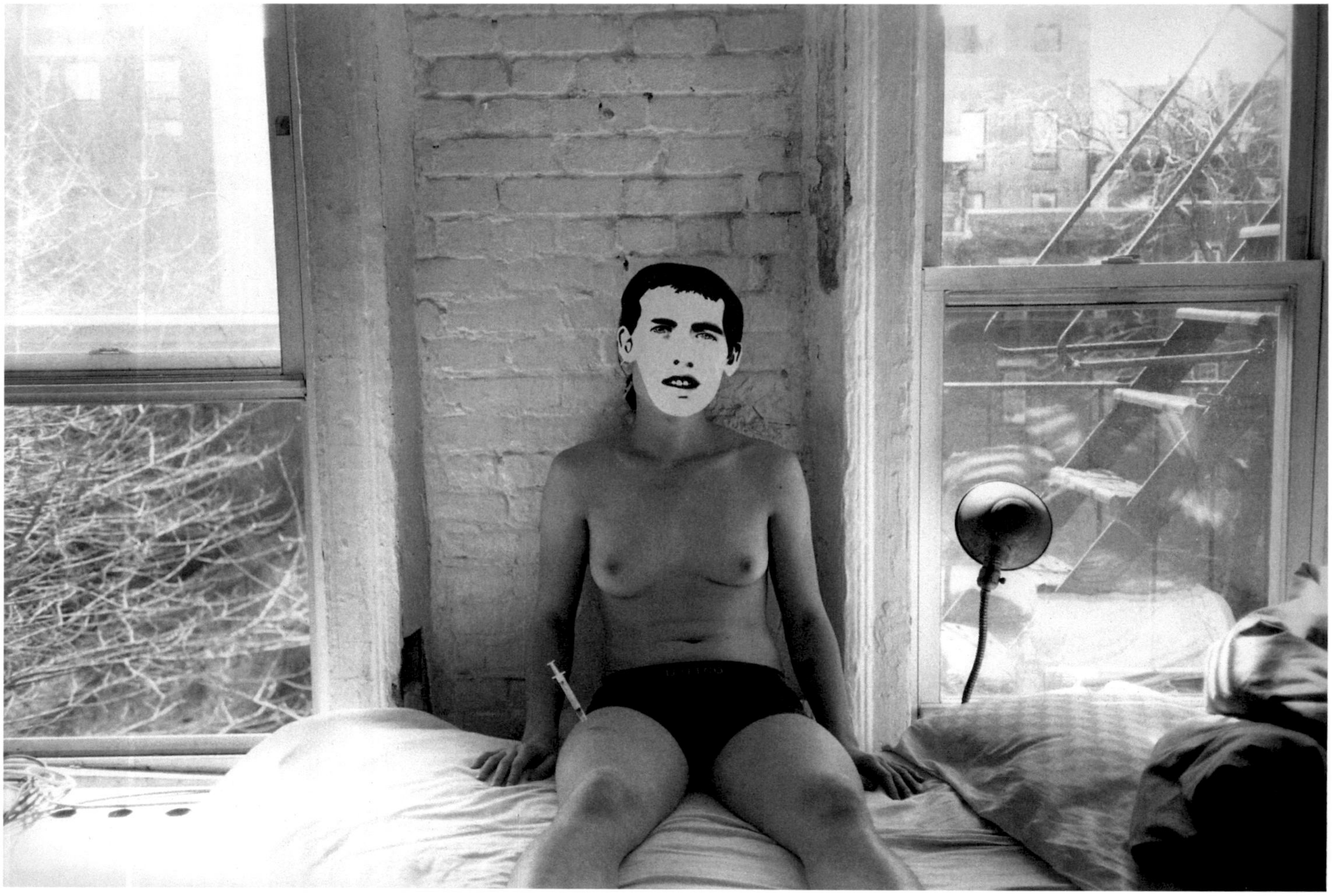

Plate 80 Emily Roysdon, *Untitled (David Wojnarowicz Project)*, 2001–2007

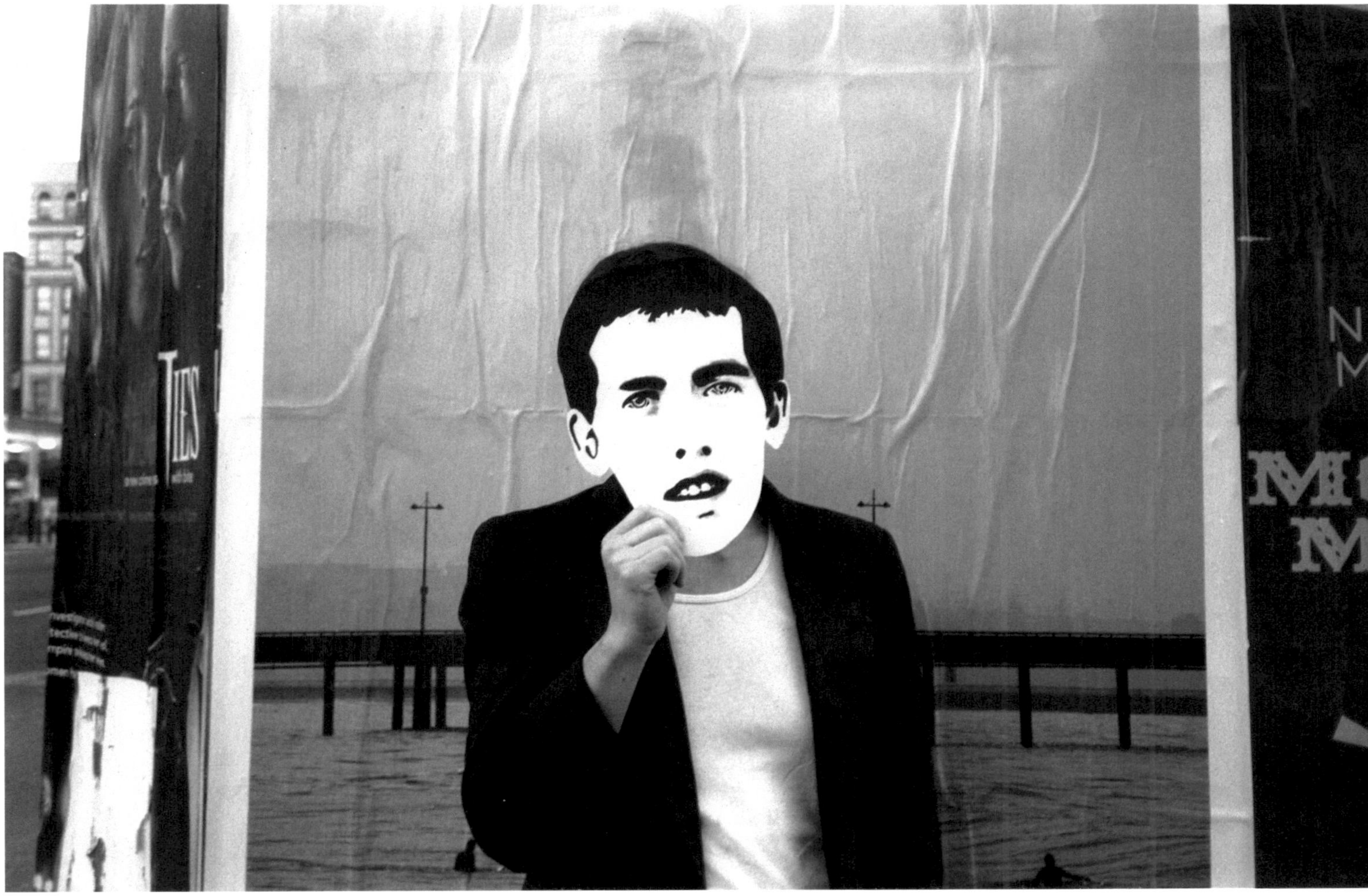

Plate 81 Emily Roysdon, *Untitled (David Wojnarowicz Project)*, 2001–2007

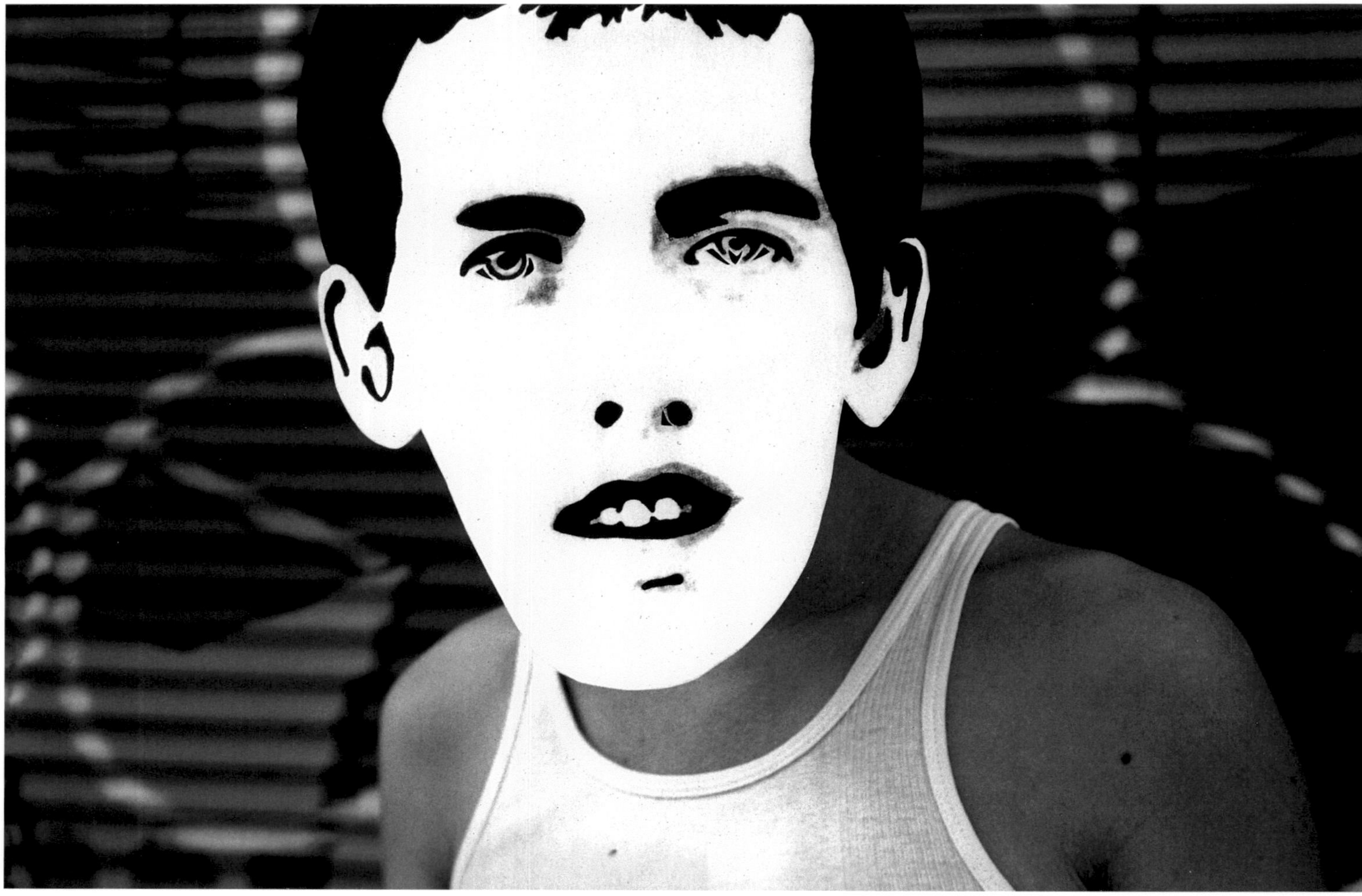

Plate 82 Emily Roysdon, *Untitled (David Wojnarowicz Project)*, 2001–2007

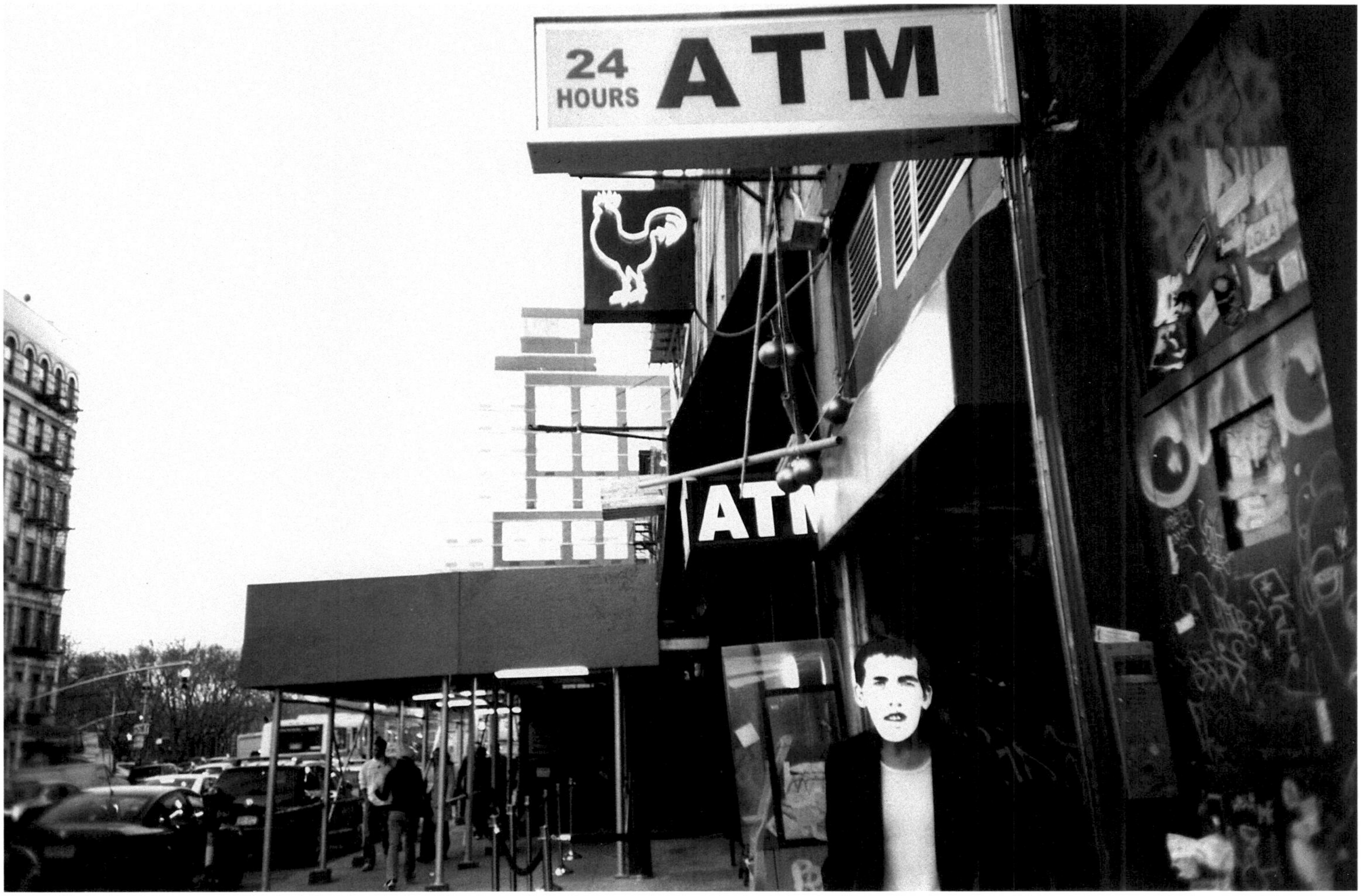

Plate 83 Emily Roysdon, *Untitled (David Wojnarowicz Project)*, 2001–2007

Losing the Form in Darkness

David Wojnarowicz

It's so simple: the man without the eye against a receding wall, the subtle deterioration of weather, of shading, of images engraved in the flaking walls. See the quiet outline of a dog's head in plaster, simple as the splash of a fish in dreaming, and then the hole in the wall farther along, framing a jagged sky swarming with glints of silver and light. So simple, the appearance of night in a room full of strangers, the maze of hallways wandered as in films, the fracturing of bodies from darkness into light, sounds of plane engines easing into the distance.

It is the appearance of a portrait, not the immediate vision I love so much: that of the drag queen in the dive waterfront coffee shop turning toward a stranger and giving a coy seductive smile that reveals a mouth of rotted teeth, but the childlike rogue slipped out from the white-sheeted bed of Pasolini; the image of Jean Genet cut loose from the fine lines of fiction, uprooted from age and time and continent, and hung up slowly behind my back against a tin wall. It's the simple sense of turning slowly, feeling the breath of another body in a quiet room, the stillness shattered by the scraping of a fingernail against a collar line. Turning is the motion that disrupts the vision of fine red and blue lines weaving through the western skies. It is the motion that sets into trembling the subtle water movements of shadows, like lines following the disappearance of a man beneath the surface of an abandoned lake.

He was moving in with the gradual withdrawal of light, a passenger on the shadows, heat cording his forehead and arms, passion lining the folds of his shirt. A handsome guy with unruly black hair, one eye like the oceans in fading light, the other a great vacant yawn shadowed black as the image of his leather jacket, all of it moved with mirage shivers over his heavy shoulders. There is a slight red color like a bruise or a blush to his cheeks, the muscles of his face smoothing into angles: hard jaw and a nose that might have once been broken. I was losing myself in the language of his movements, the slow rise and fall of a cigarette as he lifted it to his lips and brought it back down again, each drag leaving a small spherical haze to dissipate against his face.

Outside the windows the river light turned from blues to grays to flashes of rain. A serious dark veil ran the length of the horizon; there's a texture to it, a seediness like dream darkness you can breathe in or be consumed by. It swept down bringing with it strong waves and water, sending tiny people running for cars or shelter among the warehouse walls. Headlights began appearing, rain swinging through the holes in the roofs, through the windows emptied of glass. Sounds of dull puddles spreading along the floorboards. The stranger turned on his heel in the gray light and passed into other rooms, passing through layers of evening, like a dim memory, faceless for moments, just the movements of his body across the floor, the light of doorway after doorway casting itself across the length of his legs.

The river was dirty and coming toward me in the wind. A sixteen-wheel rig parked idling near the corner of the warehouse. Through the dark windows I could see this cowboy all the way from Wyoming sitting high up in the front seat, a woman with a blond bouffant seated next to him raising a bottle of whiskey to her lips. The refrigeration motor hummed while big gauze-covered bodies of cattle swung from hooks in the interior of the truck. Out along the waterfront asphalt-strip cars were turning and circling around. Headlights like lighthouse beacons drifted over the surface of the river, brief and unobtrusive, then swinging around and illuminating the outlines of men, of strangers, people I might or might not have known because their faces were invisible, just black silhouettes, outlined suddenly as each car passes one after the other, pale interior faces turned toward the windows, then fading into distance.

Sitting in the Silver Dollar restaurant earlier in the afternoon, straddling a shining stool and ordering a small cola, I dropped a black beauty and let the capsule ride the edge of my tongue for a moment, as usual, and then swallowed it. Then the sense of regret washes over me like whenever I drop something, a sudden regret at what might be the disappearance of regular perceptions: the flat drift of sensations gathered from walking and seeing and smelling and all the associations; and that strange tremor like a ticklishness that never quite reaches the point of being unbearable. There's a slow sensation of that type coming into the body, from the temples to the abdomen to the calves, and riding with it in waves, spurred on by containers of coffee, into the marvelousness of light and motion and figures coasting along the streets. Yet somehow that feeling of beauty that comes riding off each surface and movement around me always has a slight trace of falseness about it, a slight sense of regret, felt at the occurring knowledge that it's a substance flowing in my veins that cancels out the lines of thought brought along with time and aging and serious understanding of the self.

So there was that feeling of regret, a sudden impulse to bring the pill back up, a surge of weariness with the self, then the settling back and the wait for the sensations to begin. I smoked a fast cigarette and the door opened bringing with it sunlight and wind.

Restless walks filled with coasting images of sight and sound: cars bucking over cobblestones down the quiet side streets, trucks waiting at corners with swarthy drivers leaning back in the cool shadowy seats and the windows of buildings opening and closing, figures passing within rooms, faraway sounds of voices and cries and horns roll up and funnel in like some secret earphone connecting me with the creaking movements of the living city. Old images race back and forth and I'm gathering a heat in the depths of my belly from them: flashes of a curve of arm, back, the lines of a neck glimpsed among the crowds in the train stations, one that you could write whole poems to. I'm being buoyed by these discrete pleasures, walking the familiar streets and river. The streets were familiar more because of the faraway past than the recent past—streets that I walked in those odd times while living among them in my early teens when in the company of deaf mutes and times square pederasts. These streets are seen through the same eyes but each time with periods of time separating it: each time belonging to yet an older boy until the body smoothes out and lines are etched until it is a young man recalling the movements of a complicated past. I can barely remember the senses I had when viewing these streets for the first time. There's a whole change in psyche and yet there are slight traces that cut me with the wounding nature of déjà vu, filled with old senses of desire. Each desire, each memory so small a thing, becomes a small river tracing the outlines and the drift of your arms and bare legs, dark mouth and the spoken words of strangers. All things falling from the earth and sky: small movements of the body on the docks, the moaning down among the boards and the night, car lights slanting across the distance, aeroplanes falling as if in a deep surrender to the rogue embraces. Various smiles spark from the darkening rooms, from behind car windows, and the sounds of the wind-plays along the coast sustained by distance and leveled landscapes, drifting around the bare legs and through doorways and into barrooms. Something silent that is recalled, the sense of age in a familiar place, the emptied heart and light of the eyes, the white bones of street lamps and moving autos, the press of memory turning over and over. Later, sitting over coffee and remembering the cinematic motions as if witnessed from a discreet distance, I lay the senses down one by one, writing in the winds of a red dusk, turning over slowly in sleep.

*

The tattooed man came through the sheets of rain, and swinging headlights from cars entering the riverside parking lot caught him among the fine slanting lines of wind and water. Late this evening, I was sitting by the dock's edge, sitting in the rain remembering old jersey showers as a kid and the quiet deliciousness of walking through coal-gray streets where trees leaned over and by the fields where nuns in the cool green summers would hitch up their long black skirts and toss a large white medicine ball to each other in a kind of memory slow motion.

Over the jersey coast, seen through the veils of rain, the old Maxwell House coffee cup, a five-story neon cup of white, tipped over on its magical side with two red neon drops falling from its rim and disappearing into the darkness of the brush-covered cliffs. The tattooed man came up suddenly and sat down beside me in the rain like a ceramic figurine glazed with water running down the smooth colors of his shirtless chest. Huge fish fins were riding his shoulders and tattooed scales of komodo dragons, returned from the wilds of jungular africa, twisting outlines and colors of clawed feet and tails smoothing over his aged biceps and the cool white of his head, shaved to permit tattoos of mythological beasts to lift around his neck like frescoes of faded photographs of samurai warriors: a sudden flash of Mishima's private army standing still as pillars along the sides of the river.

*

He had a tough face. It was square-jawed and barely shaven. Close-cropped hair wiry and black, handsome like some face in old boxer photographs, a cross between an aging boxer and Mayakovsky. He had a nose that might have once been broken in some dark avenue barroom in a distant city invented by some horny young kid. There was a wealth of images in that jawline, slight tension to it and curving down toward a hungry-looking mouth.

Sitting in a parked car by the river's edge, he leaned over and placed the palm of his hand along the curve of my neck and I was surprised how perfectly it fit, stroking me slowly, his arms brown as the skin of his face, like a slight tan quietly receding into a blush. He seemed shy for a moment, maybe because of what he saw in my eyes, but the heat was pumping inside the car and the waves, turned over and over by the coasting winds, barreled across the surface of the river beneath darkening clouds. Some transvestites circled down from the highway, going from car to car, leaning in the driver's windows checking for business.

He eases his hands down toward my legs and slides it back up beneath my shirt, saying, "Take it off." I reached down and lifted the sweater and the t-shirt up together and pull them over my head, dropping them to the floor where my pants are straddling my ankles. He pulls off his green naval sweater revealing a t-shirt the color of ice blue, reaches down and peels that off too. We are looking at each other from opposite sides of the car. He's got a gleaming torso, thick chest with a smooth downy covering of black hair, brick-red nipples buried inside the down. He leans and bends before me licking my body softly down my sides, one hand massaging slowly between my legs, his other hand wetted briefly against his mouth and working his cock up until it is dark and red and hard.

When he lifted away from my chest I saw his eyes, the irises the color of dark chips of stone, something like the sky at dusk after a clear hot summer day, when the ships are folding down into the distance and jet exhaust trails are uttered from the lips of strangers. The transvestites were back and leaning in the window refusing to go away. We pulled our clothes back on and closed up the car, heading toward one of the abandoned structures.

Inside one of the back ground-floor rooms there are a couple of small offices built into the garagelike space. Paper from old shipping lines scattered all around like bomb blasts among wrecked pieces of furniture; three-legged desks, a naugahyde couch of mint-green turned upside down, and small rectangles of light and wind and river over on the far wall.

I lean toward him, pushing him against the wall, lifting my pale hands up beneath his sweater, finding the edge of his tight t-shirt and peeling it upward. I placed my palms against the hard curve of his abdomen, his chest rolling slightly in pleasure. Moving back and forth within the tin-covered office cubicle, old soggy couch useless on the side, the carpet beneath our shifting feet reveals our steps with slight pools of water. We're moving around, changing positions that allow us to bend and sway and lean forward into each other's arms so that our tongues can meet with nothing more than a shy hesitation. He is sucking and chewing on my neck, pulling my body into his, and over the curve of his shoulder, sunlight is burning through a window emptied of glass. The frame still contains a rusted screen that reduces shapes and colors into tiny dots like a film directed by Seurat. Pushing and smoothing against the tides, this great dark ship with hundreds of portholes entered the film. His head was below my waist, opening his mouth and showing brilliant white teeth; he's unhooking the button at the top of my trousers. I lean down and find the neckline of his sweater and draw it back and away from the nape of his neck which I gently probe with my tongue. In loving him, I saw a cigarette between the fingers of a hand, smoke blowing backwards into the room, and sputtering planes diving low through the clouds. In loving him, I saw men encouraging each other to lay down their arms. In loving him, I saw small-town laborers creating excavations that other men spend their lives trying to fill. In loving him, I saw moving films of stone buildings; I saw a hand in prison dragging snow in from the sill. In loving him, I saw great houses being erected that would soon slide into the waiting and stirring seas. I saw him freeing me from the silences of the interior life.

*

Stopped in the Silver Dollar just as dusk was rolling in, paid for some takeout coffee, there's a group of ten drag queens standing outside leaning on shining car fenders, applying lipstick and powders out of tiny mirrored compacts. One young man in a tight white t-shirt, hard white arms, no more dreams, heavy beer belly, had fallen on his face moments before. A couple of his teeth having popped out, there were two vermillion streaks running down the sides of his mouth and some cops were standing over him as he lay on his back, his cheekbones glistening and arms flailing like in some stream, backstroking his way out of this world, out of this life, away from this sea of blue uniforms and white boneless faces, away from this sea of city heat and faraway motion of his eyes fluttering behind dark sunglasses. Walked onto the pier and stood with my back to the river and way over the movements of the city was what looked like a falling star, a photographic negative of one in the night: a jet streak short and vertical falling from the sky, like a falling jet with a single illuminated flame tracing the domed curve of the heavens, a scratch in the sky, a blinding light caught in the scratch from the unseen sun, and slowly changing direction and connecting the rooftops of the buildings one after the other.

In the warehouse just before dark, passed along the hallways and photographed the various graffiti on the walls, some of hermaphrodites and others of sharp-faced thugs smoking cigarettes; in passing through a series of rooms, saw this short fat man with a seedy mustache standing in a broken closet filled with old wet newspapers and excrement and piss, standing with his hands locked behind his head and with a hard-on poking out through his trousers from beneath a grimy heavy overcoat: he was doing this strange dance, undulating his hips, sweat rolling down the sides of his face, beneath dark glasses, grimacing and stabbing the air with his cock and saying in a loud whisper: "...come in here...I'll make ya feel so *goood...so good...*"

Later, about 3:00 am, a terrific storm swept down on the city, the waves rolling like humpbacked whales just beneath the water's surface: whole schools of them riding first toward and then away from the piers. With another coffee I stepped along the walls of the warehouse and ducked beneath the low doorway to get out of the rain. Somewhere in the darkness men stood around. I thought I could hear the shuffle of their feet, the sense of their hearts palpitating in the coolness. Dark cars outside the windows slowly covered in rain, headlights clicking on suddenly, waves slashing at the pier and huge pieces of unhooked tin, torn down by the wind, clanging and crashing against the upper walls. I thought I saw a person in a white jacket disappearing as I reached the upper hallways. Walked around sloshing hot coffee over the rim of the open cup with every few steps. Looked out the side windows into the squall, tiny motions of the wet city. Inside, for as far as the eye could see, there was darkness and waving walls of iron, rusting sounds painful and rampant, crashing sounds of glass from remaining windows, and no sign of people: I realized I was completely alone. The sense of it slightly unnerving in the cavernous space. Street lamps from the west-side highway burn in the windows, throwing shadows behind staircases and burying doors and halls. Walked out on the catwalk and watched the terrific gale and tossing waves of the river from one of the side doors. Huge panoramas of factories and water tanks were silhouetted by green roof lights and cars moving down the highway seen only by the red wink of their taillights.

Walking back into the main section of the warehouse I stopped in one of the rooms facing the elevated highway. The rain had slowed down and the streets were burning with a brassai light and texture. I suddenly felt a hand on my crotch in the darkness and turned toward the dark void where the face should be, stepping back as I did so. The hand belonged to a small, dwarfish man, someone out of an old Tod Browning image. I put my hand to his shoulder and said, "Sorry...just walking around..." And as I passed through a series of rooms, he followed from a distance, sliding along the walls and appearing unexpectedly in the doorways ahead of me, the rise and fall of his cigarette describing a clear arc, like a meteorite, then disappearing into the shadows of his face. As I left by the back stairs, he drifted out of a room over to the top of the staircase and stood silently watching me descend from view.

★

Standing in a waterfront bar, having stopped in for a beer in mid-afternoon: smoky sunlight riding in through the large plate-glass windows and a thumping roll of music beating invisibly in the air. Over by one window and side wall, a group of guys are hanging out playing pool—one of them is this chicano boy, muscular and smooth with a thin cotton shirt of olive green, black cowboy hat pushed down over his head, strong collarbones pressing out, a graceful curve of muscles in his back and a solid chest, his stomach pressed like a slightly curved washboard against the front of his shirt, muscles in the arms rising and falling effortlessly as he gesticulates with one hand, talking with some guy who's leaning into the sunlight of the window; in his other hand the pool-stick is balanced against his palm, a cigarette between his fingers. He leans back and takes a drag and blows lazy smoke rings one after the other that pierce the rafts of light and dissolve within the shadows. The guy that he was talking to looked like some faraway character straight from the fields of old skittering wheat and someone I once traveled with by pickup truck with beer cans in the dusty backseat and buzz in the head from summer: dark eyes and a rosy complexion, roughly formed face made of sharp lines and his hair cut short around the sides and back of his neck. Standing there sipping from a green bottle, I could see myself taking the nape of his neck in my teeth as he turned and stared out the window at the rolling lines of traffic for a moment. Light curved around his face and the back of his head, the shaved hair produced sensations that I could feel across the palm of my hand, my sweating hand, all the way from where I stood on the other side of the room. He looked around after turning away from the windows and set his eyes on me for a moment, studying me for indiscernible reasons, and I felt myself blush: felt the movement of the bass tapping against some chord where the emotions or passions lie, tilted my head back and took another swig from the beer, a humming gathering from my stomach and rising up past my ears.

He turns away and the chicano guy leans over the pool table for a shot, his back curved and taut like a bow, arm drawing back to softly clack the balls on the table: a couple dropping into the side pocket, and for a moment the two of them were lost in the drift of men entering the bar. I move over a few feet to bring them back into view and some sort of joke developed between them. The country boy reaches into the bottom slot of the table and withdraws a shiny black eight-ball and advances toward the chicano, who drew back until his buttocks hit the low sill of the window. He giggles and leans his head back at an angle and lets a hardness come from his eyes. The country boy's face turned a slight shade of red in the light and he reached out with his hands: one hand pulling the top of the chicano's shirt out and the other deftly dropping the eight-ball into the neckline. The ball rolled down and lodged near his belly and the two of them laughed as he reached in, hand sliding down the chest and stomach retrieving the ball. I took a last swig from my beer, overcome with the sensations of touch, of my fingers and palms smoothing along some untouched body in some imagined and silent sun-filled room, overcome with the heat that had been gathering in my belly and now threatened to overpower me with a sense of dizziness. I barely managed to place the bottle upright on the nearby cigarette machine and push open the doors, into the warm avenue winds, push open the doors and release myself from the embrace of the room and the silent pockets of darkness and the illuminating lines of light thinking it was Jacques Prévert who said "why work when you have a pack of cigarettes and sunlight to play with?," and listened to the horns of ships along the river, far behind the fields of buildings and traffic, turned a corner and headed across town.

⋆

Passing down a long hallway there were glimpses of frescoes, vagrant frescoes painted with rough hands on the peeling walls, huge murals of nude men painted with beige and brown colors coupling several feet above the floorboards. Some of them with half-animal bodies leaning into the room's darkness with large outlined erections poised for penetration. Other walls contain crayoned buddhas and shining gems floating above their heads in green wax. One wall where a series of black wire-strewn holes pull apart the surface, where crowbars and hammers searched out copper pipes and wires, but still filled with floating faces almost japanese with pink high-boned cheeks and multicolored eyelids, a stream of hair touched by loving or by winds, small crudely drawn lanterns serving no discernible purpose but to genie these faces from the vague surface of the plaster.

Passing doorways in slow motion, passing through shadowed walls and along hallways, seeing briefly framed in the recesses of a room a series of men in various stages of leaning. Seeing the pale flesh of the frescoes come to life: the smooth turn of hands over bodies, the taut lines of limbs and mouths, the intensity of the energy bringing others down the halls where guided by little or no sounds they pass silently over the charred floors. They appear out of nowhere and line the walls like figurines before firing squads or figures in a breadline in old times pressed into history. Stopping for a moment, I thought of the eternal sleep of statues, of marble eyes and lips and the stone wind-blown hair of the rider's horse, of illuminated arms corded with soft unbreathing veins, of the wounding curve of ancient backs stooped for frozen battles, of the ocean and the eyes in fading light, of the white stone warthog in the forest of crowfoot trees, and of the face beneath the sands of the desert still breathing.

New York, Beside Itself Johanna Burton

> *But have we a right to assume the survival of something that was originally there, alongside of what was later derived from it? Undoubtedly.*
> —Sigmund Freud, *Civilization and Its Discontents*

Eve Kosofsky Sedgwick begins the first chapter of her 2003 book, *Touching Feeling: Affect, Pedagogy, Performativity*, by narrating an experience she had on the streets of New York City. "In the couple of weeks after the World Trade Center was destroyed in September 2001," she writes,

> I had a daily repetition of an odd experience, one that was probably shared by many walkers in the same midsouthern latitudes of Manhattan. Turning from a street onto Fifth Avenue, even if I was heading north, I would feel compelled first to look south in the direction of the World Trade Center, now gone. This inexplicably furtive glance was associated with a conscious wish: that my southward vista would again be blocked by the familiar sight of the pre-September 11 twin towers, somehow come back to loom over us in all their complacent ugliness. But, of course, the towers were always still gone. Turning away, shame was what I would feel.[1]

On first reading this passage, I stopped short. Recognizing that I had often engaged in the behavior described by Sedgwick, I was nonetheless vexed by her conclusion. *Why shame?* I wondered, before noticing that Sedgwick's very next line anticipated this question—an explicit acknowledgment that her claim was somehow odd, or at the very least not to be taken for granted. "Why shame?" she asks, before answering:

> I think this was, in effect, one of those situations in which, as Silvan Tomkins puts it, "one is suddenly looked at by one who is strange, or...one wishes to look at or commune with another person but suddenly cannot because he is strange, or one expected him to be familiar but he suddenly appears unfamiliar, or one started to smile but found one was smiling at a stranger." Not that an urban vista is quite the same as a loved face, but it isn't quite different, either: the despoiled view was a suddenly toothless face, say, or suddenly preoccupied, or suddenly dead—to say nothing, even, of the historical implications surrounding that particular change of landscape.[2]

I turn to Sedgwick at the beginning of this essay—a brief survey of some contemporary artists' engagements with the urban landscape of New York—not to suggest that every work made about the city after 9/11 need directly engage the impact of that event; nor, exactly, to mime Sedgwick's invocation of "shame" (though this is perhaps closer to my present interests, given her provocative explanation that such an affective response may underscore a nexus of the personal and the collective).[3] Rather, I turn to Sedgwick for her unabashed leap into pathetic fallacy, her deft, anthropomorphic conflation of spatial and historical shifts whereby the city is not "quite the same as a loved face, but it isn't quite different, either." That face, as Sedgwick has it, is capable of unexpected physical and emotional expressions ("toothless" and "preoccupied") in addition to states of existential being ("suddenly dead")—of behaving, in other words, with psychic capacities, including memory and feeling.

Cities, of course, have long been theorized as "living" things—organic, responsive, transitional, both tied to and constitutive of their various strata of occupants. They have also long served as metaphors for all types of structures, not least that of the human mind. Sigmund Freud himself, in *Civilization and Its Discontents*, famously attempts to describe memory's accretion by painting an impossible picture of Rome. In order to grasp the fact that nothing "in mental life…which has once been formed can perish"[4] (while, of course, granting that past events are often repressed or transformed), Freud asks his readers to imagine that ancient city's buildings all standing exactly as they once stood, without any of them having been altered, destroyed, or ruined. In such a place, he says, "all the earlier phases of development continue to exist alongside the latest one"[5]—as does the mind in all of its activities. Yet despite Freud's enthusiasm for mapping psychic operations onto the Eternal City, he eventually concluded that it was a deeply flawed comparison, deeming the terms incompatible and calling his exercise to a halt:

> There is clearly no point in spinning our phantasy any further, for it leads to things that are unimaginable and even absurd. If we want to represent historical sequence in spatial terms we can only do it by juxtaposition in space: the same space cannot have two different contents. Our attempt seems to be an idle game. It has only one justification. It shows us how far we are from mastering the characteristics of mental life by representing them in pictorial terms.[6]

But when it comes to modes of representation and discursive strategies in some art being made today (and while bearing in mind the experiences described by Sedgwick), we might ask whether Freud's precise conclusion—the site of things "unimaginable and even absurd"—allows for productive speculation. Indeed, the *inverse* of Freud's statement that "the same space cannot have two different contents" might well encapsulate a shared terrain, both literally and figuratively. There are more than a few contemporary artists whose practices have made New York an aesthetic-mnemonic palimpsest, who have laid claim to various iterations of this place's histories. And it is significant to note that these artists have not always had "proper" access to these histories, which is to say that they were not always experienced firsthand.

Such an abridged description risks creating the impression of a group of artists who share a restorative aim, or whose goals are aligned in recovering and preserving delicate, ephemeral narratives otherwise lost to time—artists, in other words, with purely altruistic or archival aims. Such a portrayal doesn't account enough for the ways in which history can also be compellingly *used*, abused, digested, desired, retooled, re-regarded, or even disregarded.[7] There is, in fact, a ravenousness, an uncouthness, an unruly *drive* (in the Freudian sense), among these contemporary figures. Indeed, it is precisely an infidelity to history, which is not the same as a lack of respect. Or, perhaps better, there is a faithlessness to the presumption of history as singular, solid, sealed, or fully relegated to the past that makes their practices something other than mournful or nostalgic. Even more to the point, this inconstancy allows for different kinds of "content" to occupy space both "impossibly" *and* with real stakes and effects. That New York can be seen as so many iterations of itself only underscores its potential to function as a site both actually *and* perpetually pictured; its terra firma, one might argue, is less the ground underfoot than myriad terms of engagement, held in trust.

To gain, then, a better sense of this ground—that arena where different recollections, personal and public alike, can weave through the same urban fabric—consider the model Jonathan Flatley proposes in his book *Affective Mapping: Melancholia and the Politics of Modernism*, which grants potential agency and purpose to otherwise unwieldy psychic mechanisms. Positing that Fredric Jameson's important 1988 essay "Cognitive Mapping" offered a way of thinking the self in relation to various vectors of social space, Flatley insists that another, related mode of mapping be acknowledged as well. His "affective mapping" redirects our consideration toward the dense network of both compulsory and divergent social relations in which we partake. Giving us "a view of terrain shared with others in the present," the affective map "also traces the paths, resting places, dead ends, and detours we might share with those who came before us."[8] Thus, for Flatley, as for so many theorists who came before him, a subject can never really consider him- or herself independent or autonomous. Every affective map, then, can be seen to shift and become entangled with so many others, forming, out of necessity, a messy, unsettled topography.

But Flatley goes further, stressing that the metaphorically cartographic extensions he describes include relationships or affiliations not only with things, people, events, and knowledge close at hand but also, importantly, with those that have been lost or that have never been found. And it is, counterintuitively, often in this unexpected site of *absence* that one can imagine and create real social and political

Plate 84 Tom Burr, *Unearthing the Public Restroom*, 1994

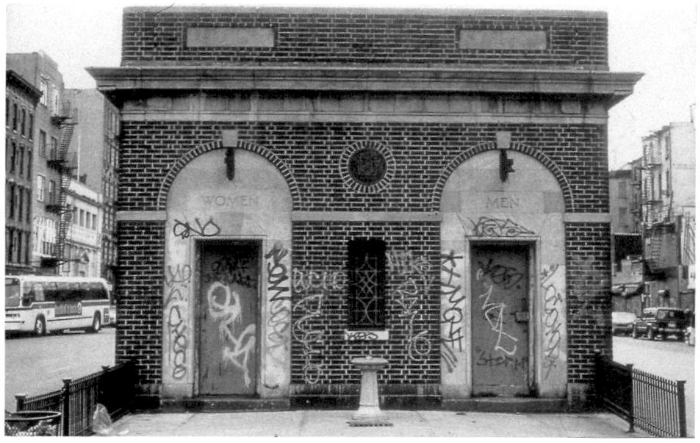
WOMEN
MEN

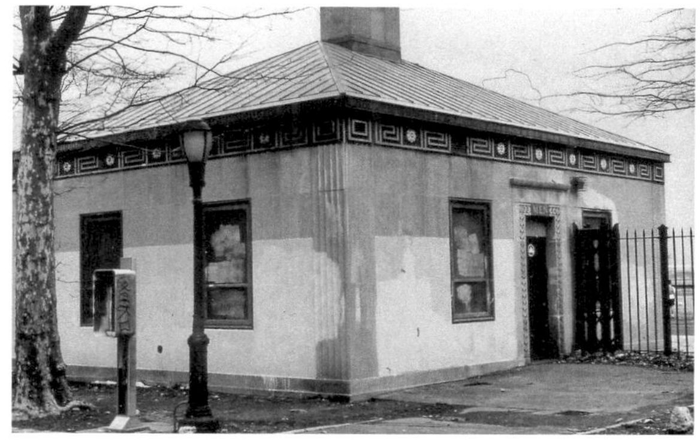

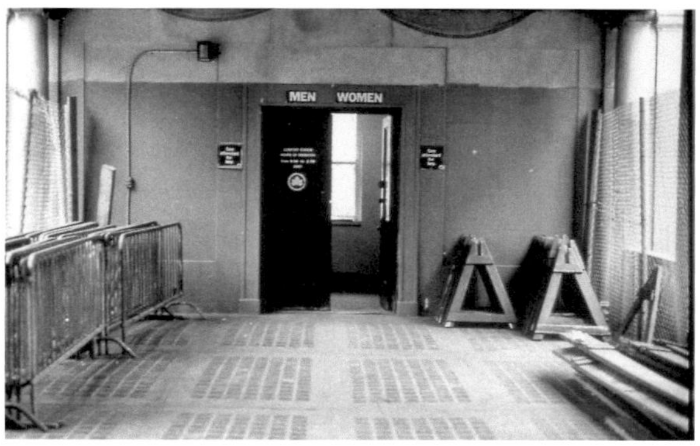
MEN WOMEN

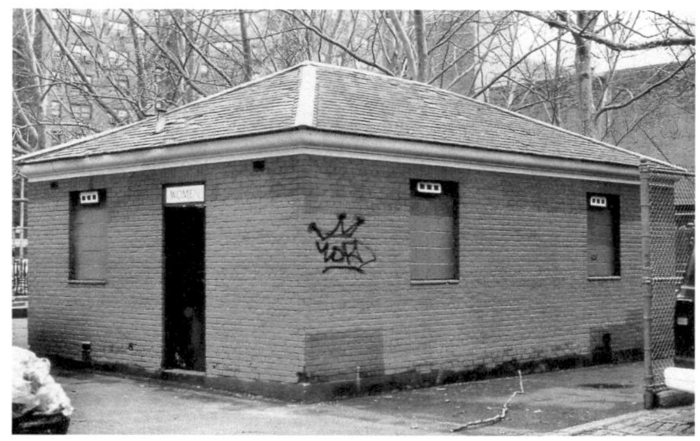

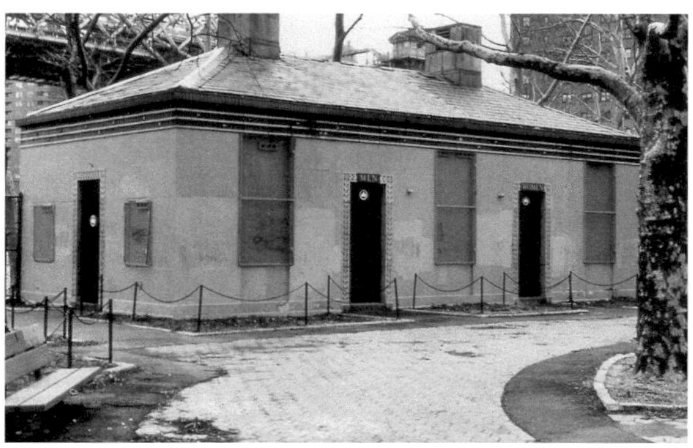

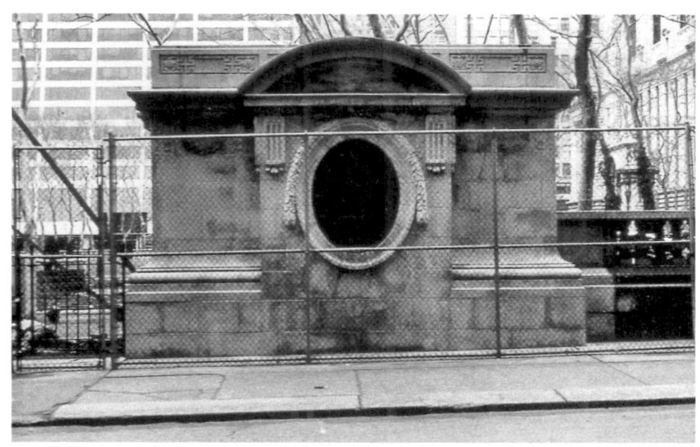

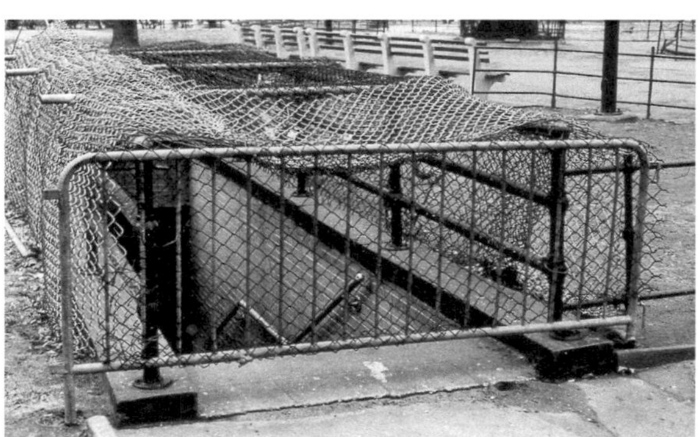

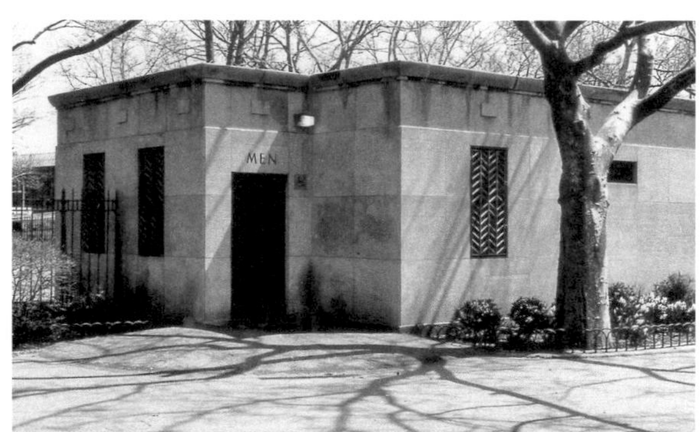
MEN

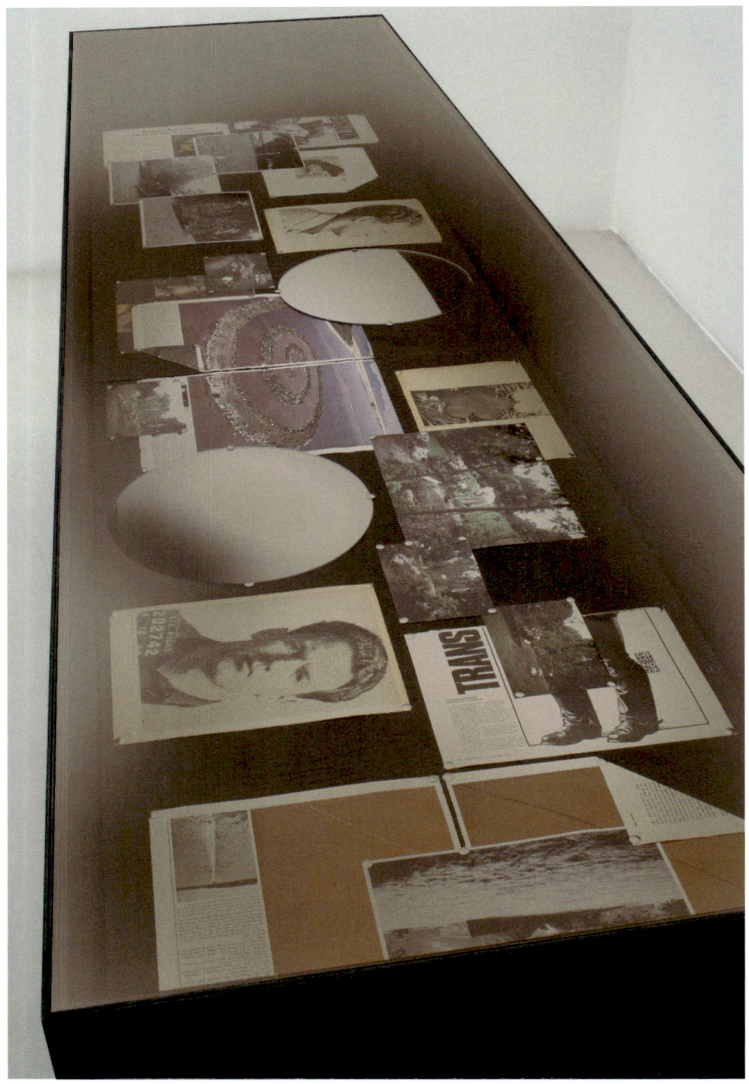

Plate 85 Tom Burr, *In Loving Memory of: An American Garden (for Frank O'Hara, "meet me in the park if you love me")*, 1993/2007 (detail)

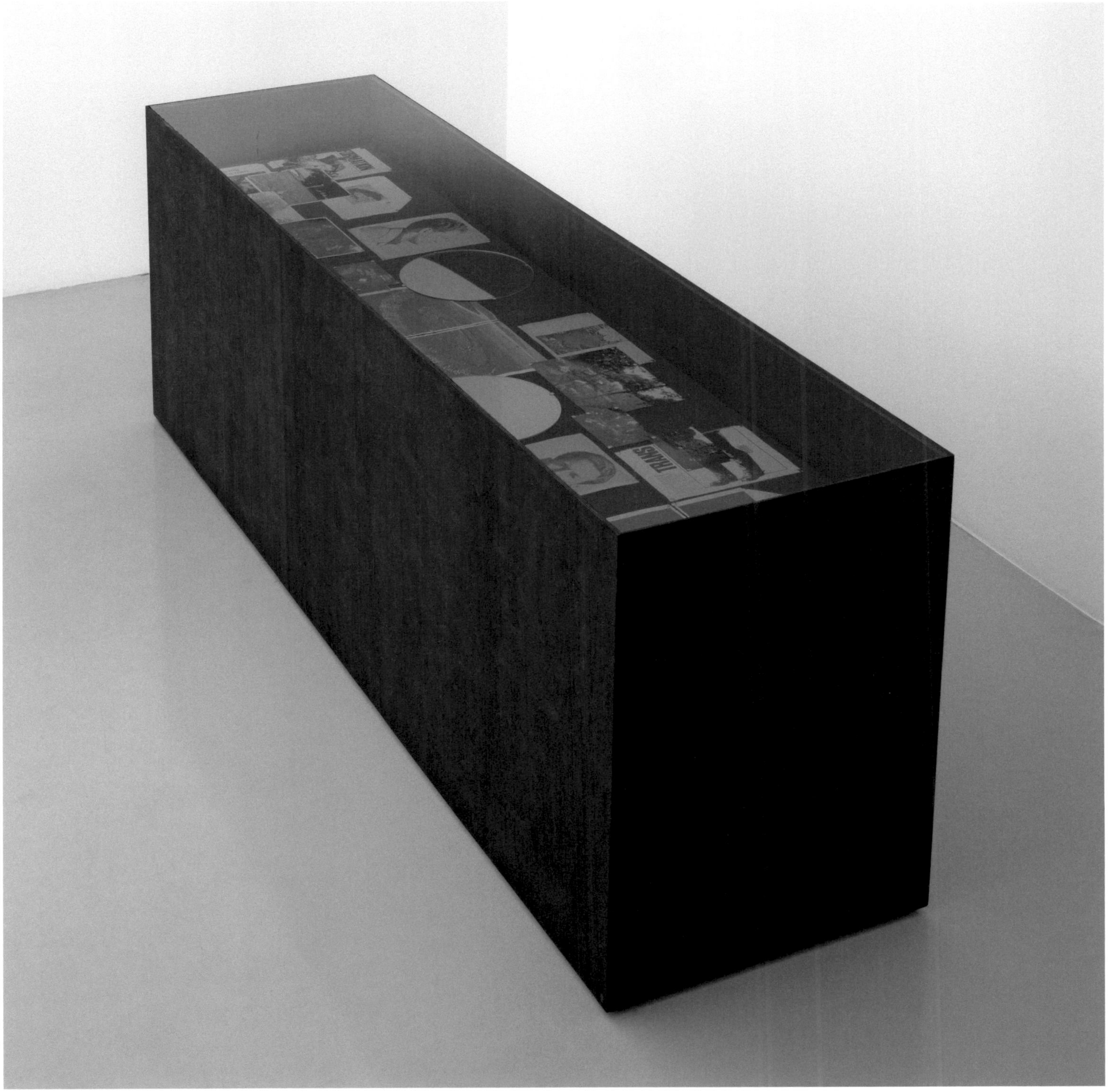

Plate 86 Tom Burr, *In Loving Memory of: An American Garden (for Frank O'Hara, "meet me in the park if you love me")*, 1993/2007

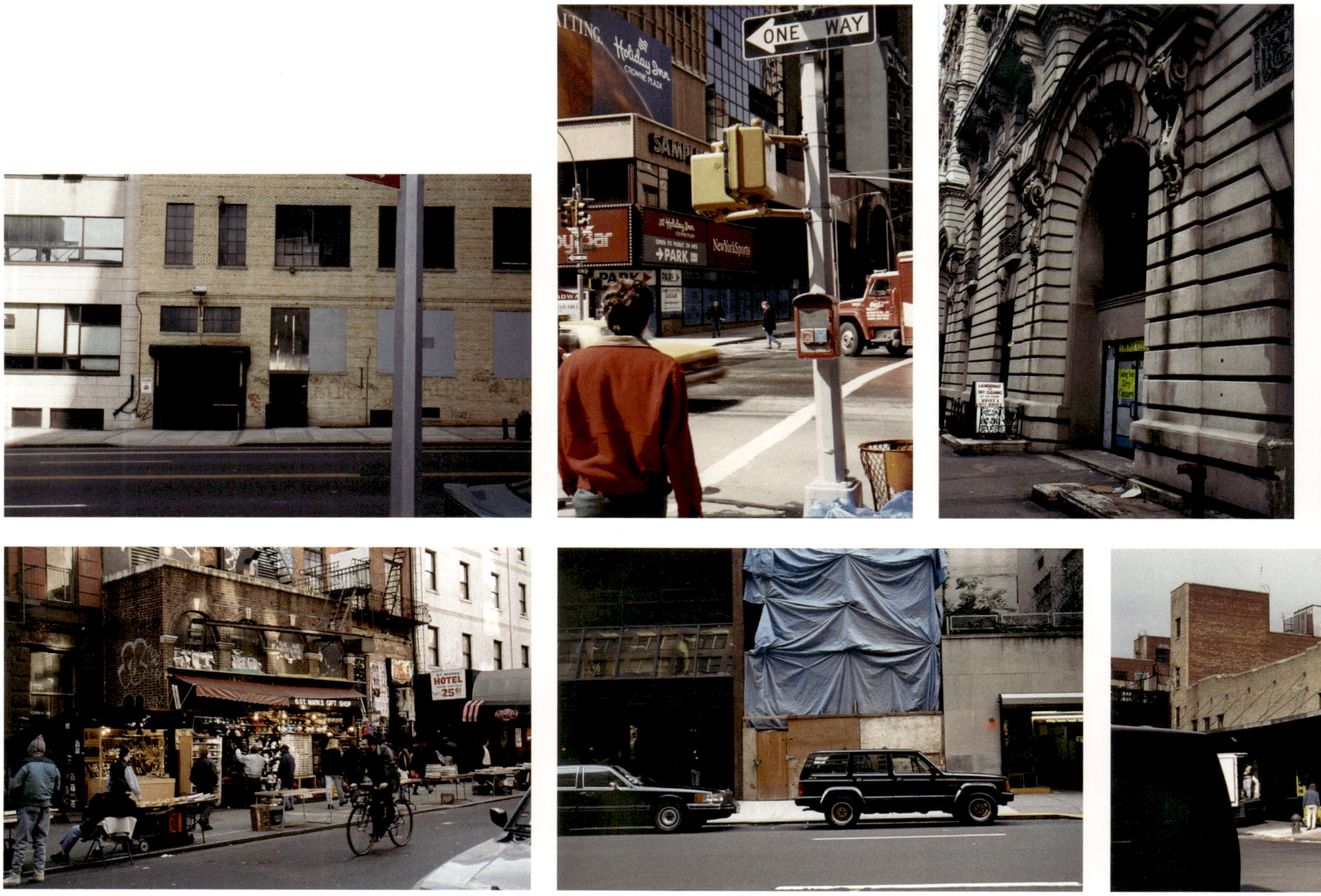

Plate 87 John Miller, *Clubs for America*, 1993

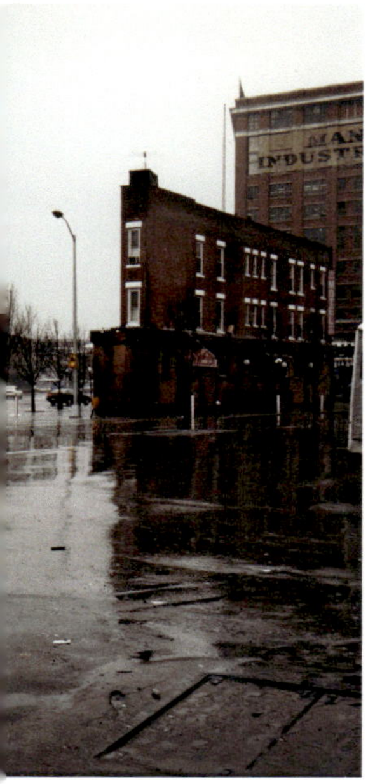

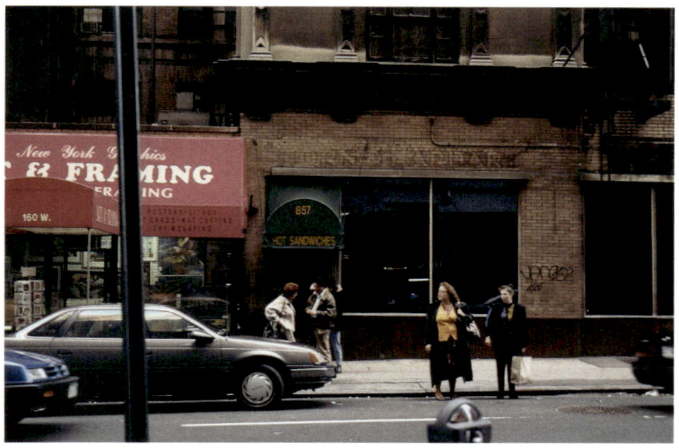
& FRAMING
160 W.
857
HOT SANDWICHES

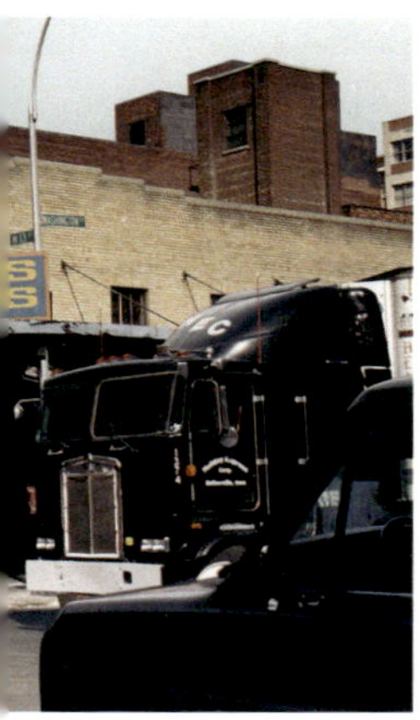

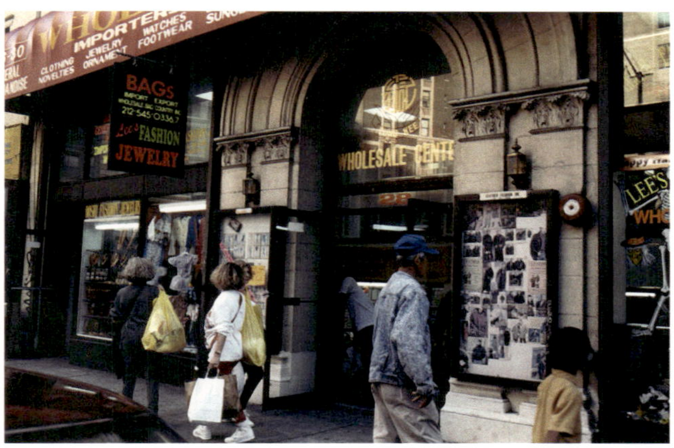
IMPORTERS
WATCHES
FOOTWEAR
CLOTHING
NOVELTIES
JEWELRY
BAGS
FASHION
JEWELRY

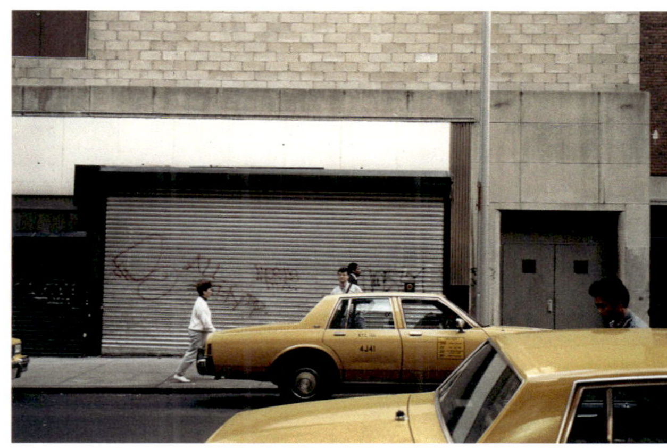

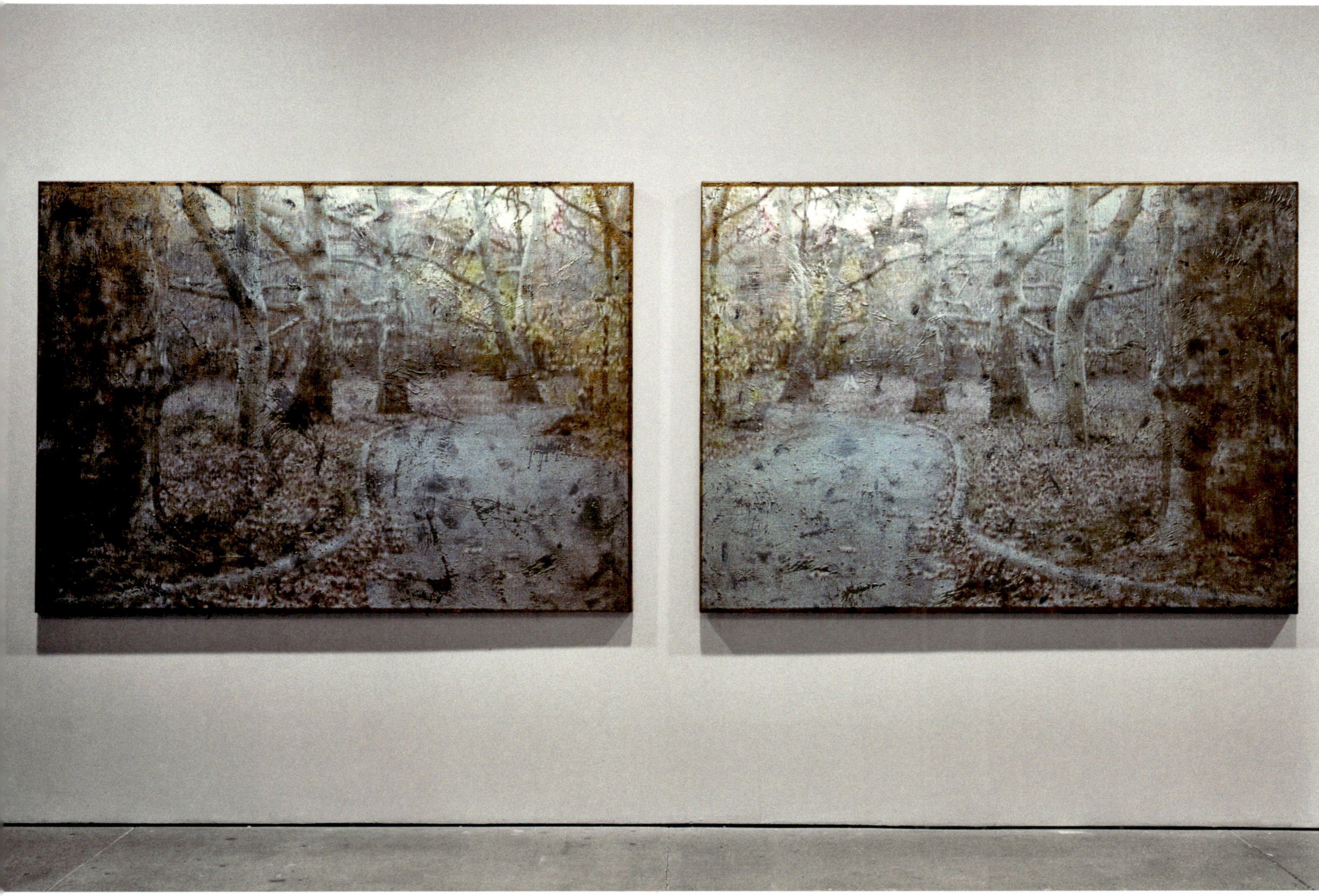

Plate 88 Donald Moffett, *Gold/Tupelo Plains*, 2003

affiliations—that one can, in other words, potentially define an "I" (however illusory) in relation to a "we" (however phantasmic).[9] If Sedgwick's compulsive look over her shoulder continued to remind her that New York—her old friend—had suddenly been rendered "unfamiliar," she nevertheless kept looking: an impulse shared by the artists I will discuss in this essay.

⋆

> *What I am suggesting is a model of the relations between bodies and cities that sees them, not as megalithic total entities, but as assemblages or collections of parts, capable of crossing the thresholds between substances to form linkages, machines, provisional and often temporary sub- or micro-groupings.... [T]heir interrelations involve a fundamentally disunified series of systems, a series of disparate flows, energies, events, or entities, bringing together or drawing apart their more or less temporary alignments.*
> —Elizabeth Grosz, "Bodies-Cities"

p. 124 Here is one view of Joan Jonas's 1972 performance *Delay Delay*: looking down and across a dirt- and debris-piled, nearly empty plot of urban terrain, over a narrow road on which two cars are moving, across another vacant lot on which one derelict building stands alone, we see, in the distance, the elevated West Side Highway and a hint of the Hudson River. But that is not all. About halfway into the field of vision offered by this photograph is a large sign stuck in the dirt and adorned with the big handwritten number "81." (The sign is one of many such markers, each indicating the number of paces it marks from the audience.) Beyond the cars, near the isolated building, are a few figures in a loose formation, clad in identical white jumpsuits and carrying various props. Filling the bottom third of the shot—and therefore closer than anything else in the foreground—is a woman's head and shoulders seen from behind, her hair swept up and pinned with a conch-shaped barrette, her gaze presumably directed to the exact place ours is.

This is not an image often reproduced. Over time, other photographic documentation of Jonas's *Delay Delay*—a work executed by thirteen nondancers in a ten-block area on the West Side of Manhattan a few blocks north of the World Trade Center (which was still under construction in 1972)—has been limited to a few canonical images. Perhaps the most famous is that of Jonas herself standing spread-eagled in a metal hoop, being rolled across an intersection by two other performers.[10] But for me, the lesser-known shot—taken by Carol Mersereau and accompanying a text written by Janelle Reiring for *The Drama Review* the year *Delay Delay* was performed—has come to represent a kind of primal scene. Indeed, it has taken me until now to fully realize how long-standing an impact the image has had on me. It was, for some reason, this very image, one that I'd encountered as I first learned about

Jonas's work, that invariably arose whenever I imagined Manhattan, even before my arrival on the East Coast, let alone in the city. What is stranger is that, having now lived in New York City for some thirteen years, it is *still* the image that stands in for the actual Manhattan that has come to be my home. What could it mean that even though the picture really shows a camera's anonymous gaze at (and beyond) the woman who occupies much of the frame, the vista registers as *her* view and, stranger still, as the view that has become my own? In *Delay Delay*, Jonas took over the hinterlands of an otherwise dense urban site in order to ritualize movement and spatialize time. Unmooring image and sound by plotting performers at varying distances in the field, Jonas elegantly literalized just how blurry the distinction is between direct experience and mediated image. Such a work sets the stage for younger artists who themselves play across space and time but whose "delays" may be accounted for differently.

Consider another category of layered view, this time of a New York pier as it stands today, or, rather, as it almost stands: the structure is a rambling jumble of thick pilings pushing up from the Hudson River, stubbornly approximating the foundation of a structure no longer there.[21] This is Pier 49, one of the "Christopher Street piers," a site of much history and few remains, somehow persistent, even obdurate, in its refusal to totally fade from view. It appears here in a photographic image created by Emily Roysdon as part of a public art proposal (as yet unrealized), giving a long, horizontal glance across the jagged, toothlike pilings. There is a memorial feel to this picture that I find inescapable, as though the pier's remains are more than an architectural ruin, a mapping of the constellation of a great many bodies and spirits. One is tempted to look across the broken pilings, as their stretch unfurls deeper into the river, and see a group of unnamed individuals rendered as pillars—even statues of sorts. This singular image shows just how little prodding one needs to impose one's content on an image; or, perhaps more positively, how impossibly full a place—even just a *name*—like Christopher Street can remain, despite its today so fully unresembling its former self. But if there is an intuitive precedent to identify with this defunct pier—a locus defined by the social and sexual encounters it no longer facilitates—Roysdon nonetheless interrupts this process. Skipping across the exposed stumps, in varying sizes that cause them to appear closer or farther away, are letters positioned gawkily, as though barely hovering in our field of vision. In capital letters (and using digital means to approximate real objects in space), Roysdon spells out the message "TALK IS TERRITORIAL." Always keen on wordplay, Roysdon—a founding member of LTTR (Lesbians to the Rescue)—routinely takes advantage of acronyms as sites of shifting condensation; "TALK IS TERRITORIAL," thus shortened, is "TIT." Yet for all its succinctness, the phrase is wildly ambiguous: Is this a warning or a celebration, a statement or a declaration?

Roysdon's return to the Christopher Street pier can be seen as playful, nostalgic, mournful, jealous, even accusatory. The piers have become icons of

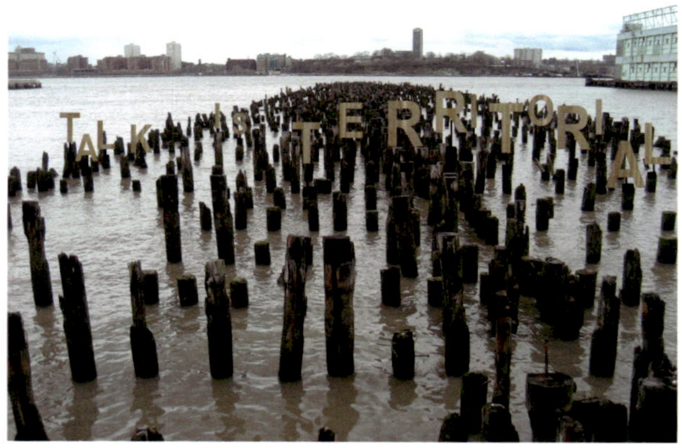

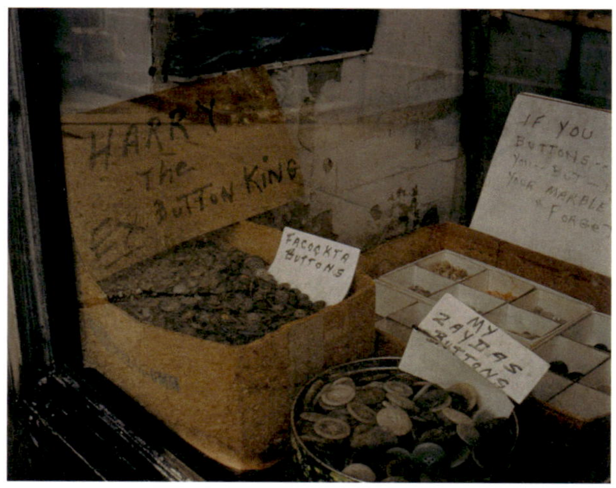

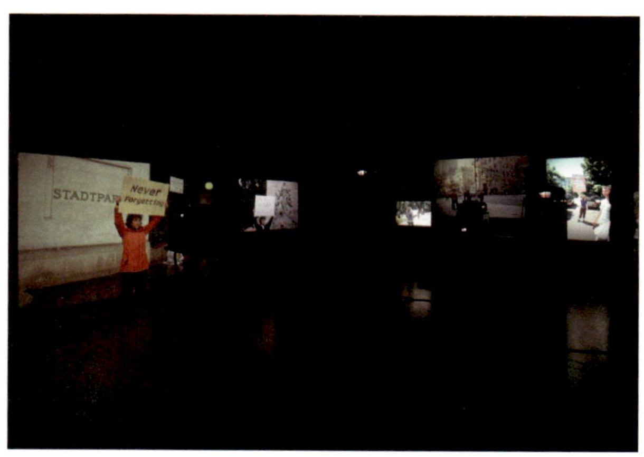

Emily Roysdon, *Talk Is Territorial*, 2007. Digital chromogenic print

Moyra Davey, *Harry the Ex-Button King*, 1994. Chromogenic print

Sharon Hayes, *In the Near Future,* 2005. Installation view, Kunstmuseum St. Gallen, Switzerland, September 19–November 22, 2009

anonymous gay sex of the 1970s; yet while the deterritorialized spaces of the nether reaches of the downtown West Side offered havens—though not always safe ones—for many variations of "non-normative" experience, these were recreations enjoyed almost exclusively by and between men.[12] Roysdon's *Talk Is Territorial* (2007) acts as a strategic p. 200 claiming of this history, and in this regard, resembles her *Untitled (David Wojnarowicz* pp. 172–75 *Project)*, made between 2001 and 2007. For this piece, a number of Roysdon's female friends took turns donning a Wojnarowicz mask and being photographed wearing it in various parts of Manhattan, effectively mimicking and thus resuscitating the earlier artist's *Arthur Rimbaud in New York* (1978–79). Commenting on this gesture, Roysdon pp. 165–70 expresses her interest in articulating a "queer relationship to history in the movement between time and space" or, as she calls it, "a mythical space."[13] Yet there is no clear or easy alignment between Wojnarowicz and Roysdon, nor is there a seamless evolution from gay liberation in the 70s to current feminist or queer politics; indeed, Roysdon is compelled to keep these elements apart. Asked in an interview how her lesbian identity squares with *Untitled*, Roysdon answered that it may not and that such identities should instead be held at bay, momentarily, or at the very least prodded to operate *otherwise*. Rather than modify her own politics so as to synchronize them with Wojnarowicz's history, or to assume too cleanly the mantle of genealogical heir, she succumbs to the urge to fully inhabit his space, to take him over: "I feel like him sometimes...and my desire is powerful."[14] If Wojnarowicz was looking for Rimbaud—imagining and *imaging* him in the present, creating and insisting on unlikely proximities—Roysdon compounds this already constricting and dilating multiplication of space and time by redoubling that impulse, literally keeping it alive.

In other words, Roysdon's desire to inhabit another time and/or another artist is layered, and it exceeds the subject it evokes: Roysdon *occupies* Wojnarowicz and is simultaneously *occupied by him*—not to mention *preoccupied with him*. The etymology of *occupy* is one worth pausing over so as to point to its ambiguity (one can equally well "occupy" space and time) and, perhaps more important, recall its employment beginning in the sixteenth century as a euphemism for sexual intercourse. For if the relay from Rimbaud to Wojnarowicz to Roysdon reveals an affinity for the seamy, it also occurs via a strangely sideways drift over many years but within a consistent place. To make this claim is to embrace an observation made by feminist philosopher Elizabeth Grosz in *Space, Time, and Perversion* that the city constitutes "a hinge between the population and the individual." Grosz goes on to speculate that the city is not only a place "for the regulation and administration of subjects but also... reinscribed by the particularities of its occupation and use."[15] In other words, Roysdon lingers on what Grosz calls "lateral or contingent connections," prioritizing them and pressing them into use. In very much the same fashion, Roysdon's own language emphasizes the fact that codes and conventions—however naturalized—are never neutral or conclusive. *Talk Is Territorial* underlines the fact that the body occupies the city and is occupied by it and that it is through this reciprocal exchange that both continue to be actively reformed.

Such "particularities" of "occupation and use"—and the possibility of spaces having more than one single, discrete dimension—have over the years become touchstones for contemporary artists who have insisted on filling aesthetic forms with intimate content. In the early to mid-90s, Tom Burr's allusions to promiscuous-pleasures-past resulted in his *42nd Street Structures* (1995), his lush and lonely return to 42nd Street's seedy theaters of a near-bygone era, and *Deep Purple* (2000), Burr's rendition of Richard Serra's *Tilted Arc* (1981). Burr's version of Serra's destroyed work is smaller than the original—wooden, movable, inappropriately plum-colored—and plays up the ever-debated concern that Serra's public works, with their bulk, act to shield illicit activities.[16] Highly charged and overtly subjective, Burr's works at once memorialize and clutch unbecomingly at what threatens to fade into the past. His palpable dismay, for instance, that certain sites for public sex—including the Ramble, Central Park's cruising zone, and New York City's public toilets—had become a kind of endangered pp. 192–93 species led him to evidence (in *In Loving Memory of: An American Garden [for Frank* p. 191 *O'Hara, "meet me in the park if you love me"]* [1993/2007] and *Unearthing the Public Restroom* [1994], respectively) something of their understated glory. In refusing to let them disappear, Burr developed perversely forensic, completely overdetermined renditions of them. This strategy of laying these sites bare by momentarily decoupling them from the bodies and activities that provide their meaning is also performed in related projects pp. 194–95 by John Miller and Donald Moffett. In Miller's 1993 *Clubs for America*, a series of seemingly banal photographs locates sites where sex clubs were once in business; a play on Dan Graham's 1966–67 *Homes for America*, Miller's work—picturing, for instance, a meat shop, a run-down hotel, a dry cleaners, and the obtuse surface of a dinged-up roll-down garage door without identification of any kind—emphasizes not seriality p. 197 and regulation but, rather, all that lies beneath. In Moffett's *Gold/Tupelo Plains* (2003), on the other hand, the artist homes in on the situatedness of sexual and other encounters by projecting film shot in the Ramble onto the gleaming gold surface of a painting that itself flickers into and out of abstraction. Offering a more or less impressionistic representation, Moffett would appear to locate the Ramble not so much on any map as in the imprints carried and held in a variety of minds and bodies.

Burr differs from these other artists, however, in how he highlights the persistent tension between things held together and things falling apart, using tactics that George Baker has described as "a continual interplay between reconstruction and re-architecture." This becomes clearer in recent work that accentuates the contingency of constructed meanings and constructed histories.[17] Using sculptural forms often on the verge of collapse and vitrines that often appear reminiscent of coffins, Burr collects (and connects) fragments of photographs, advertisements, and texts culled from public and private sources in order to produce and retain what he calls a "collaged moment."[18] Emphasizing the residual and the unconscious, these moments might be termed performances of adjacency; they insist that desire is more than an abstract force. If, as he puts it, his impulse is to move "like a rock skipping across the century,"[19] his work can then be seen to possess a certain logic in registering the persistent and resistant.

Zoe Leonard, too, is mindful of the periphery; her images verify that which is right before our eyes but nonetheless goes unseen. If her photographs are direct, straightforward, they at the same time carry the burden of an ambiguous history. Though she is often discussed as working with (and through) a "modernist" medium—analog photography and its attending idioms—it is perhaps just as important for her to be considered aligned with a group of "postmodernists" with whom she is rarely associated: Louise Lawler, Sherrie Levine, and Cindy Sherman among them. For Leonard's images do not proceed with any pretense of singularity, authenticity, or "pure documentation," but rather take into account the ways in which every picture redoubles its own effects. That is to say that while her images do continue to operate as indexes in the most literal fashion, they nonetheless also provide citations not only in terms of photographic genre but in terms of the subjects represented therein. Her pictures *reframe* things within their already cast borders, aesthetically but also culturally. Take, for instance, the series of photographs of bathroom and street graffiti she produced in the mid-90s, in which the "private" messages shown, while utterly generic, are at the same time deeply moving. These are images of space and language fully "public" yet also obscured. Ushering in the most prosaic evidence of fleeting occupations of space (of bathroom stalls, for instance) in the form of messages ("BLOW ME" and "NICOLE LOVES SUE"), Leonard's pictures call attention to the way subjects represent themselves and are understood by others, even when they are absent. They shore up what is *left*—left behind or cast off—but also what houses history, however mutely. In the late 90s and the first years of the millennium, Leonard took many pictures of the city devoid of its occupants—looking down to see timeless constellations of chewing gum spat and squished into sidewalks, looking up to find flocks of plastic bags caught in the bare branches of trees, looking sideways to find windows plastered over and painted into near invisibility. (One thinks here, too, of her powerful 1992–97 work titled *Strange Fruit*, an installation of empty, hand-sewn fruit skins produced by the artist as a way to grieve the loss of her friend Wojnarowicz, who died of AIDS in 1992). With Leonard's more recent project *Analogue* (1998–2007), our gaze is again *retrained*, refocused for us by the surety of Leonard's lens on the clothing, goods, and nearly closed stores selling obsolescent artifacts and remnants of all kinds as they circulate through the social and economic networks of New York and other cities. But as a whole, *Analogue* is a frame, a process of resignification put into practice.

That Leonard's work so often addresses the ways in which social space and conventions are framed by particular meanings compels me to return to

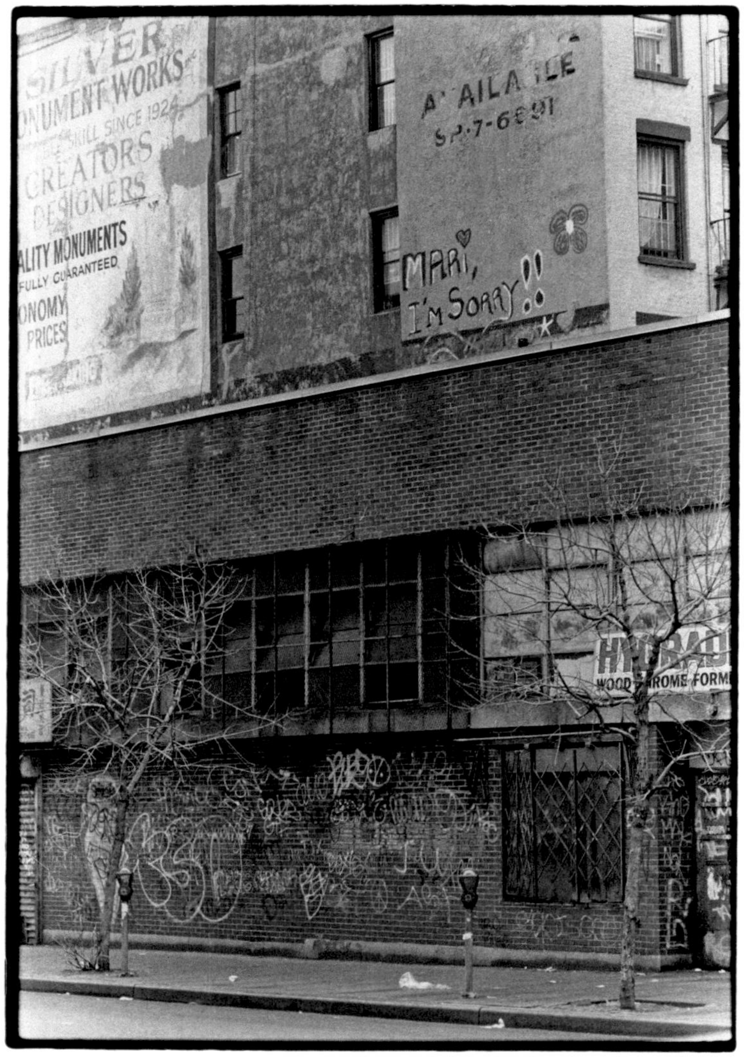

Plate 89 Zoe Leonard, *Mari, I'm Sorry (no. 2)*, 1995/1997

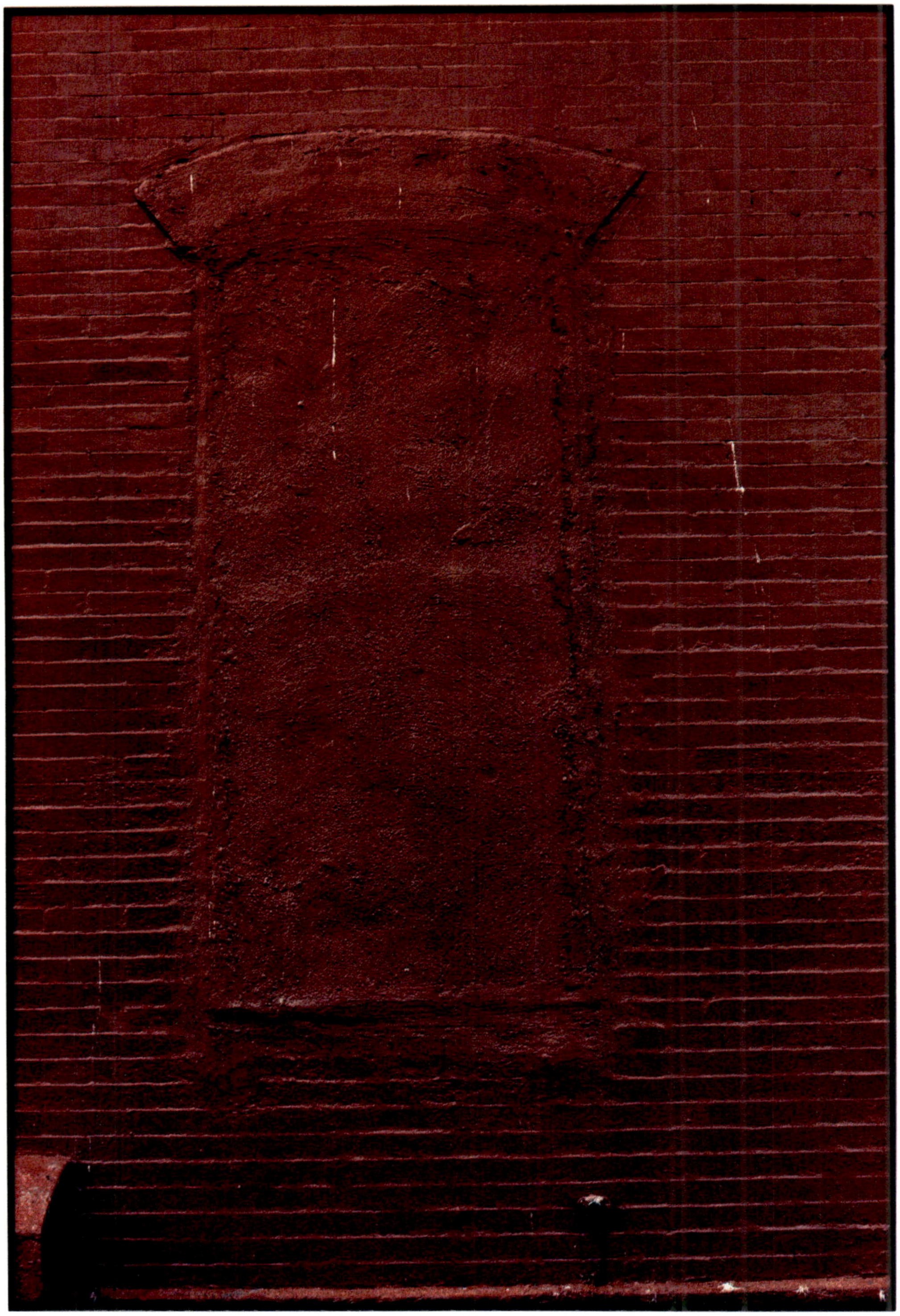

Plate 90 Zoe Leonard, *Red Wall*, 2001/2003

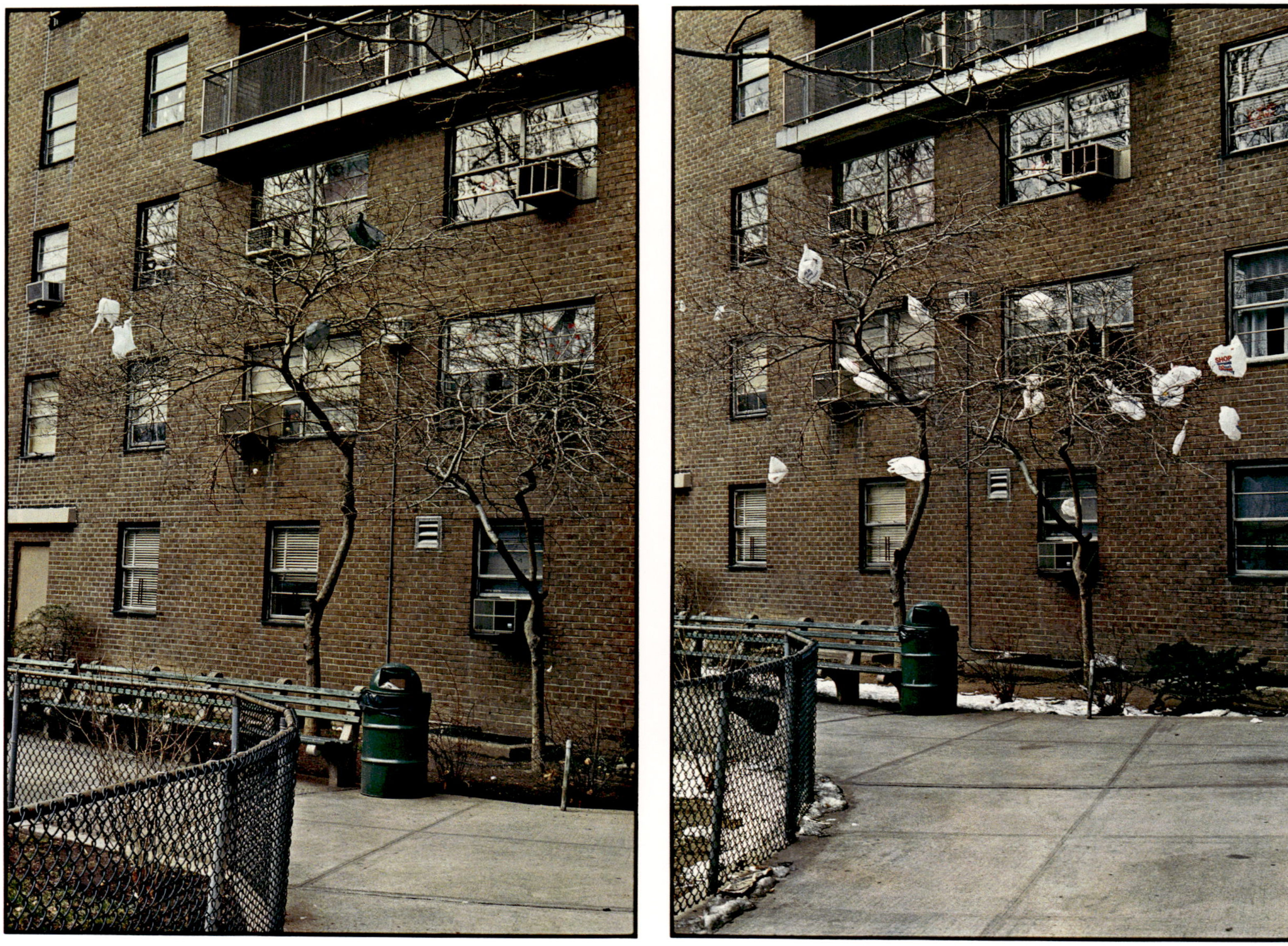

Plate 91 Zoe Leonard, *Untitled*, 2000

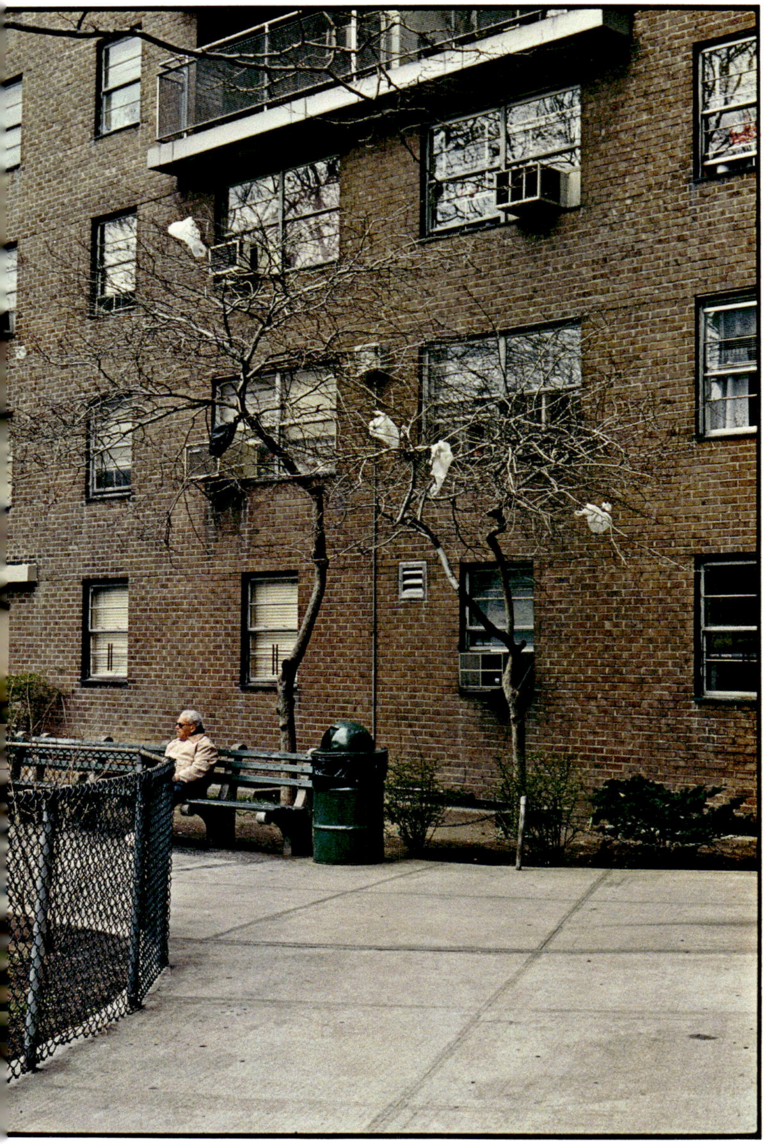

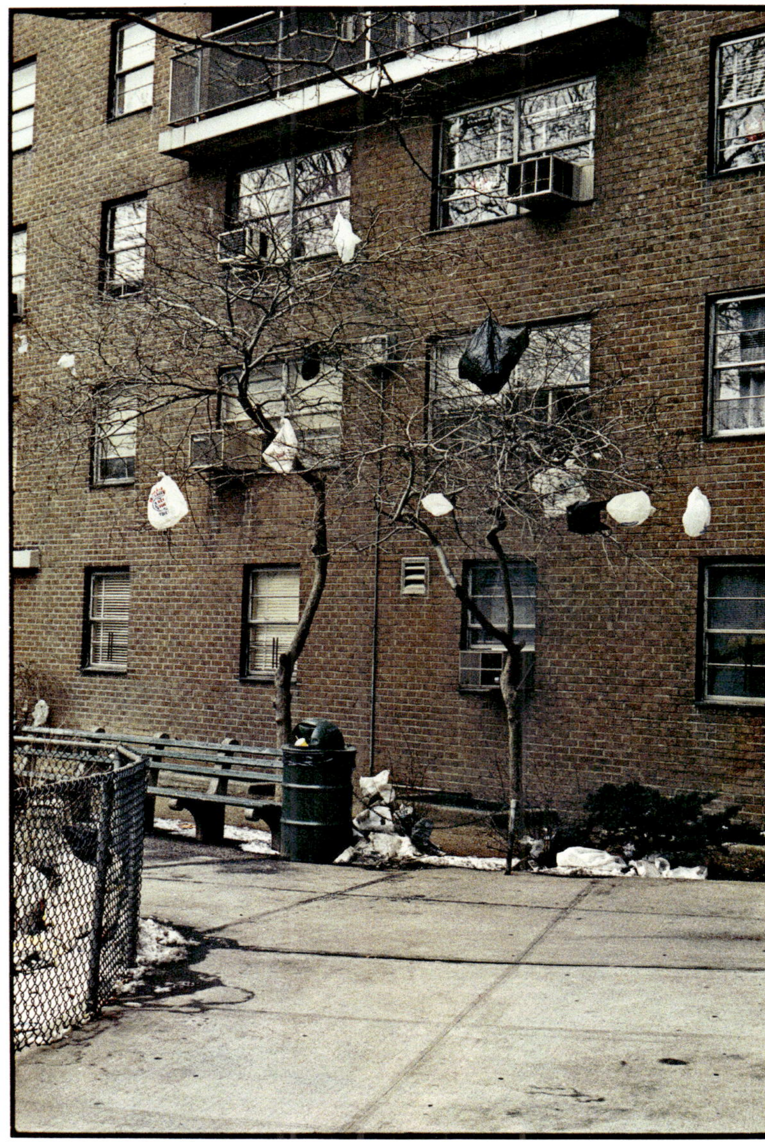

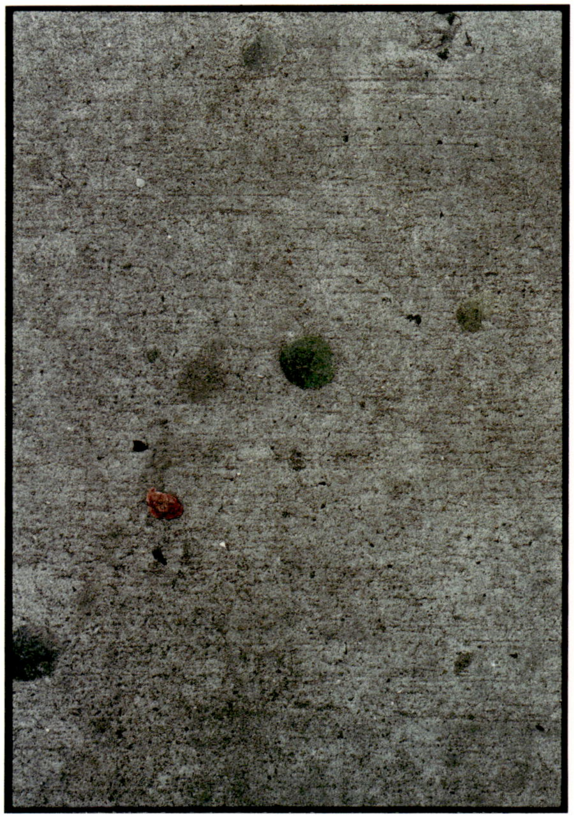

Plate 92 Zoe Leonard, *Bubblegum no. 1*, 2000/2003

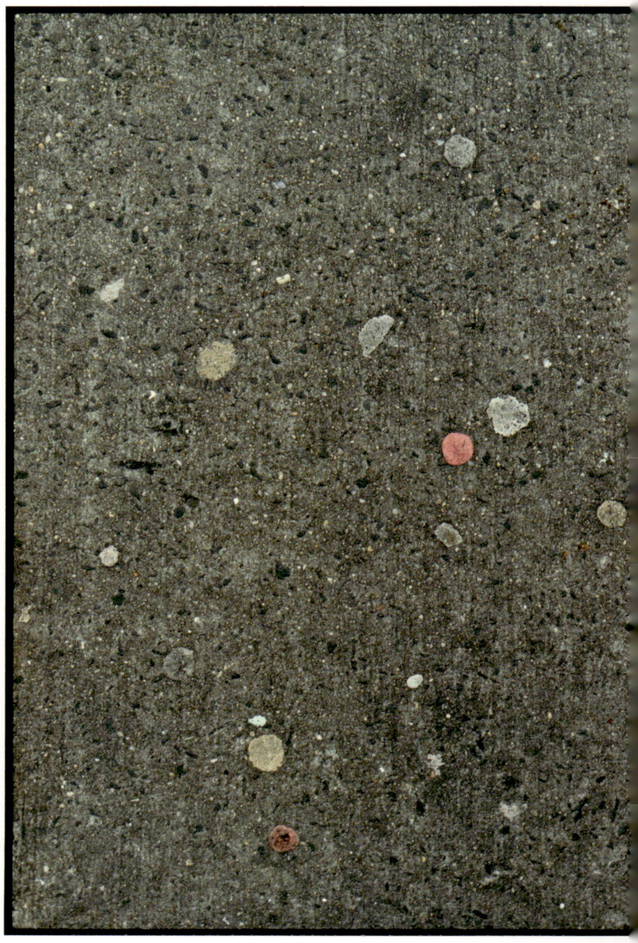

Plate 93 Zoe Leonard, *Bubblegum no. 2*, 2000/2003

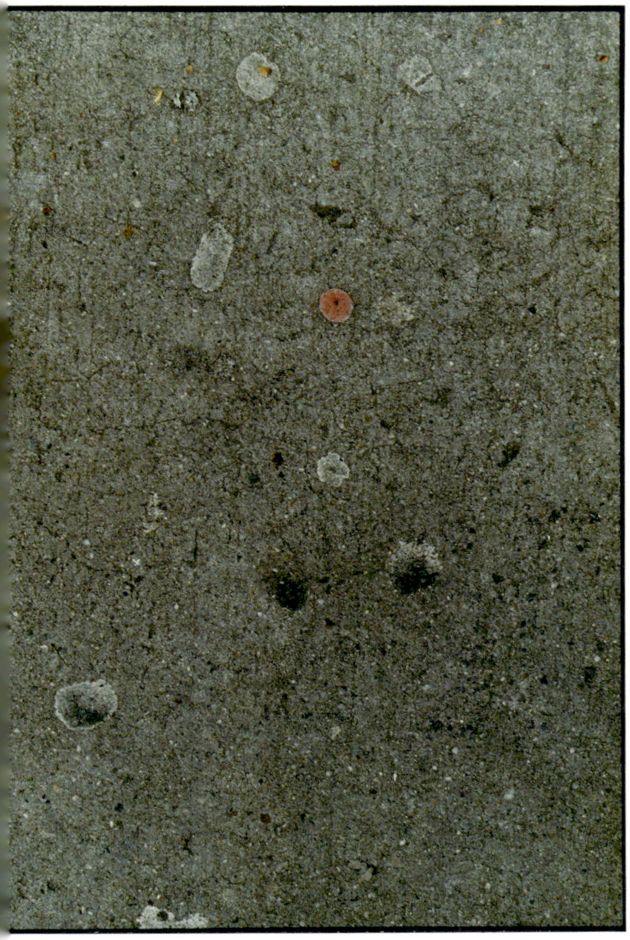

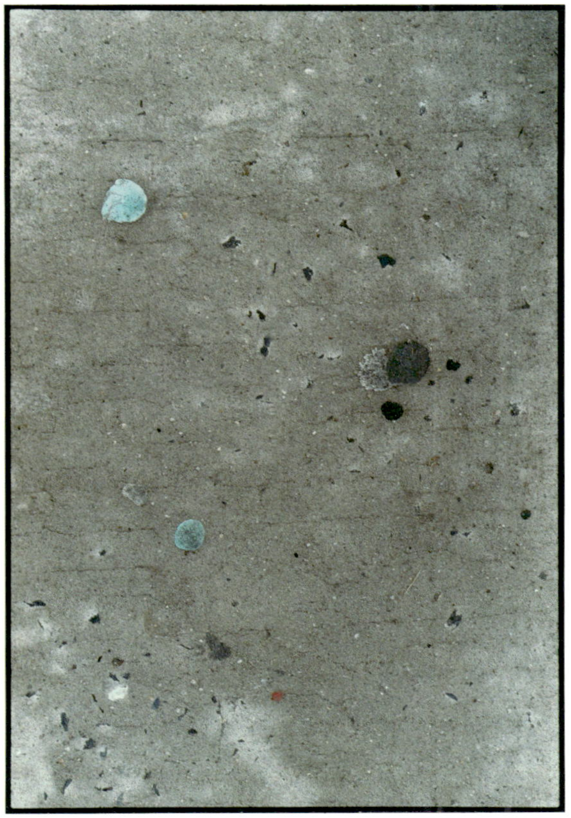

Plate 94 Zoe Leonard, *Bubblegum no. 5*, 2000/2003

Plate 95 Zoe Leonard, *Bubblegum no. 6*, 2000/2003

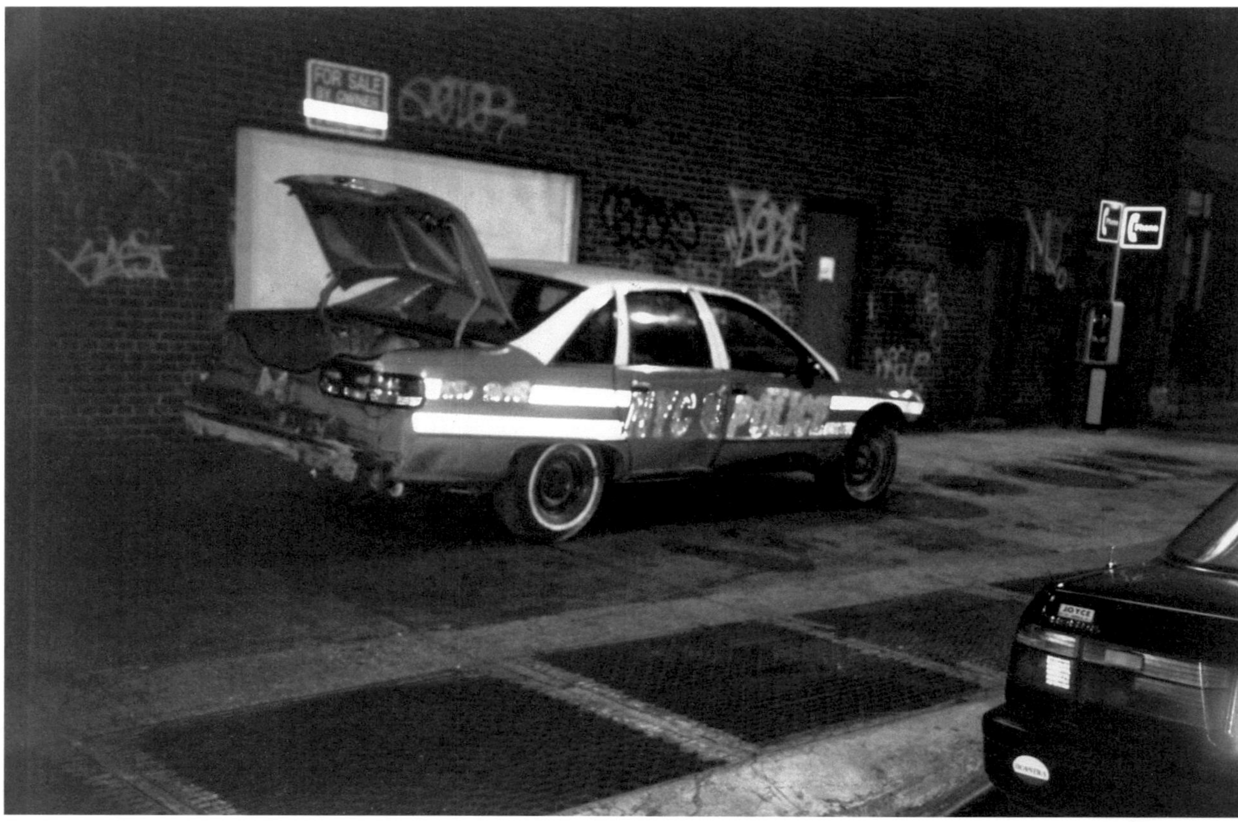

Plate 96 Christopher Wool, *East Broadway Breakdown*, 1994/2002

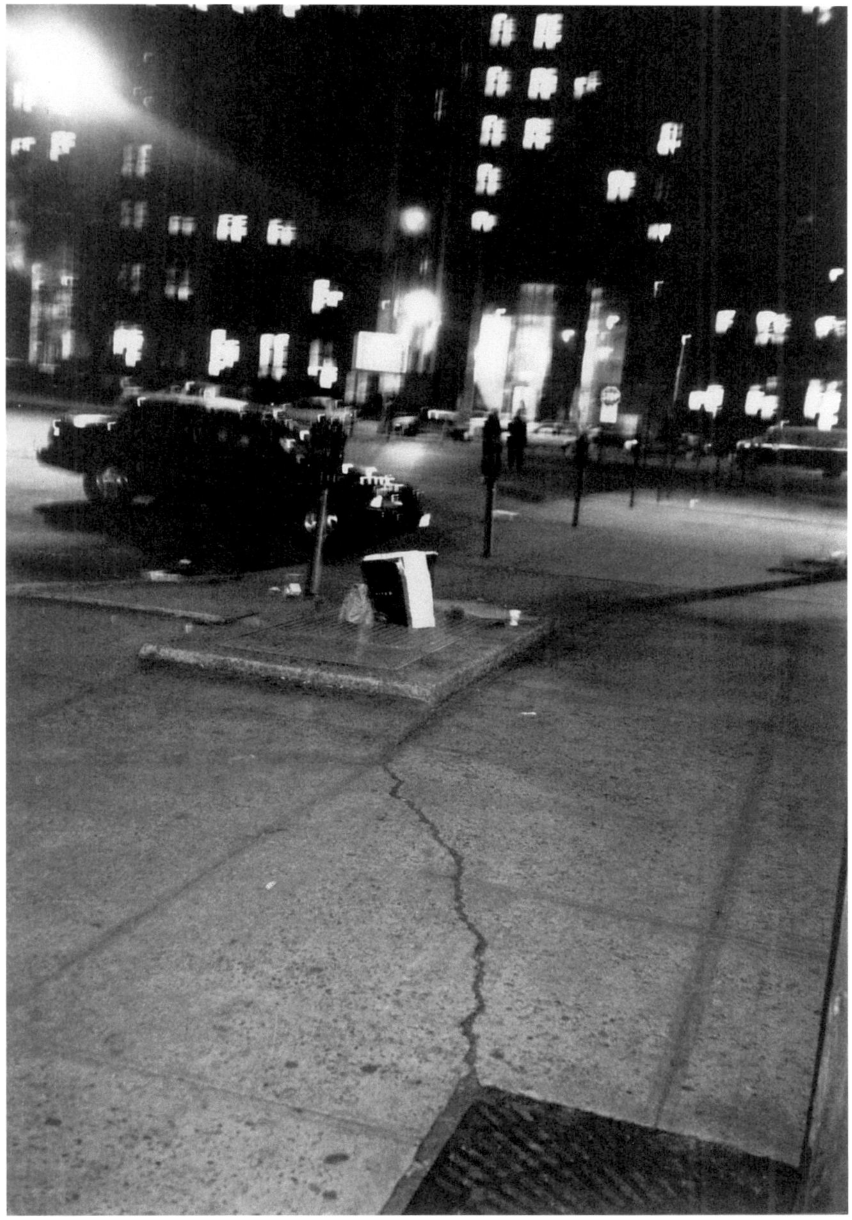

Plate 97 Christopher Wool, *East Broadway Breakdown*, 1994/2002

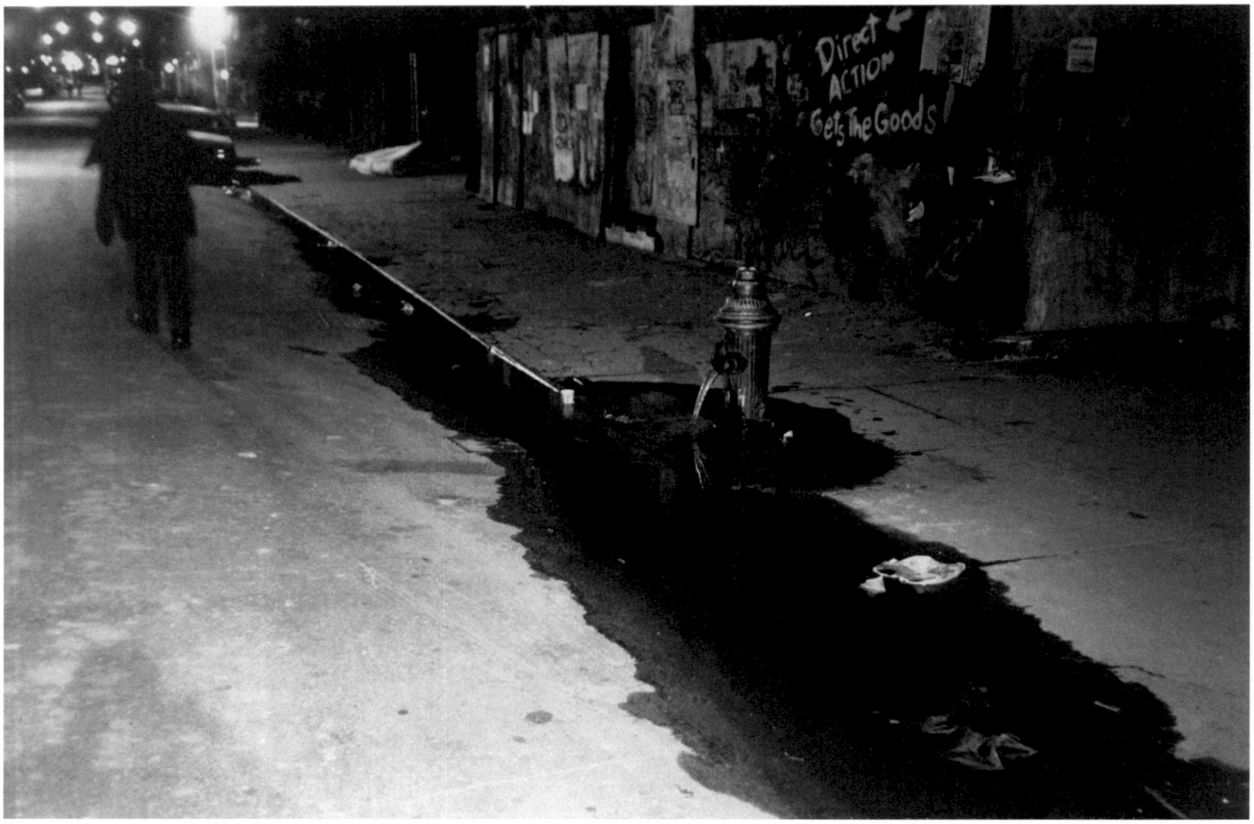

Plate 98 Christopher Wool, *East Broadway Breakdown*, 1994/2002

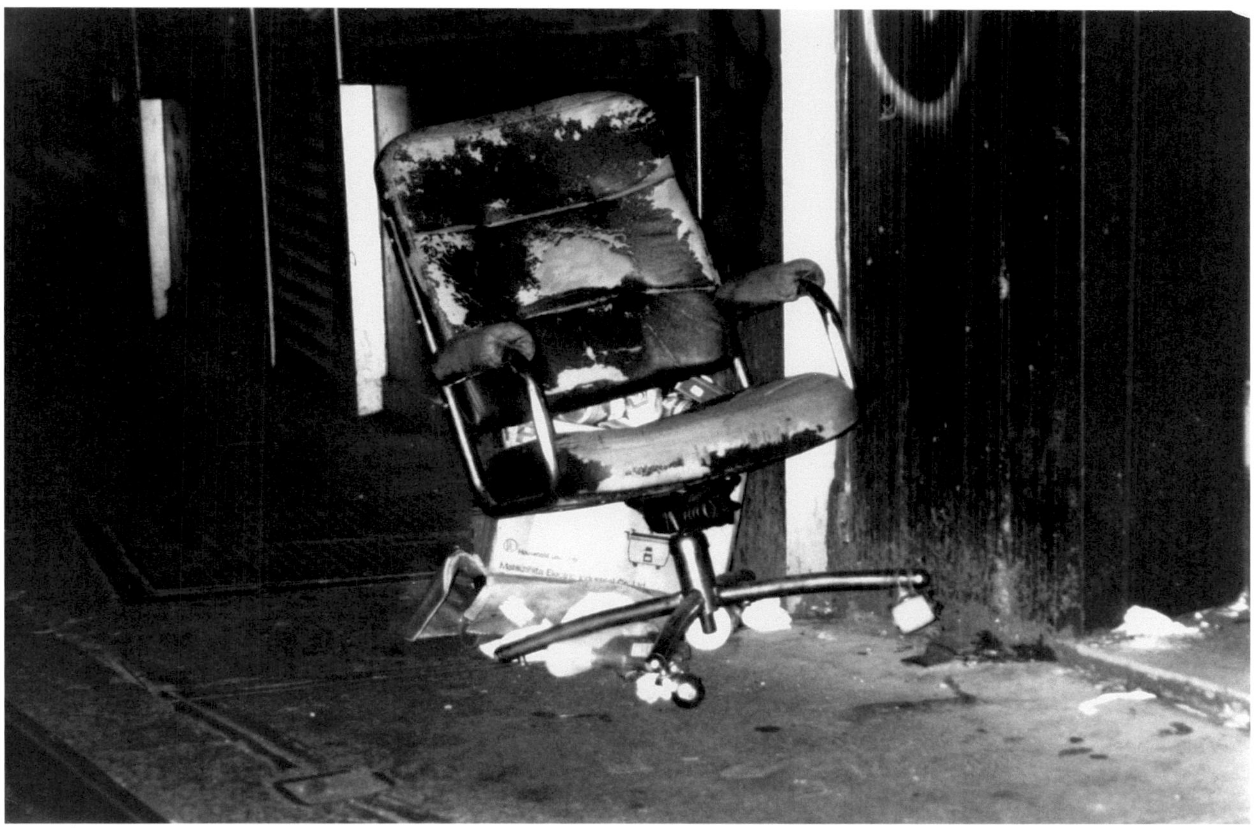

Plate 99 Christopher Wool, *East Broadway Breakdown*, 1994/2002

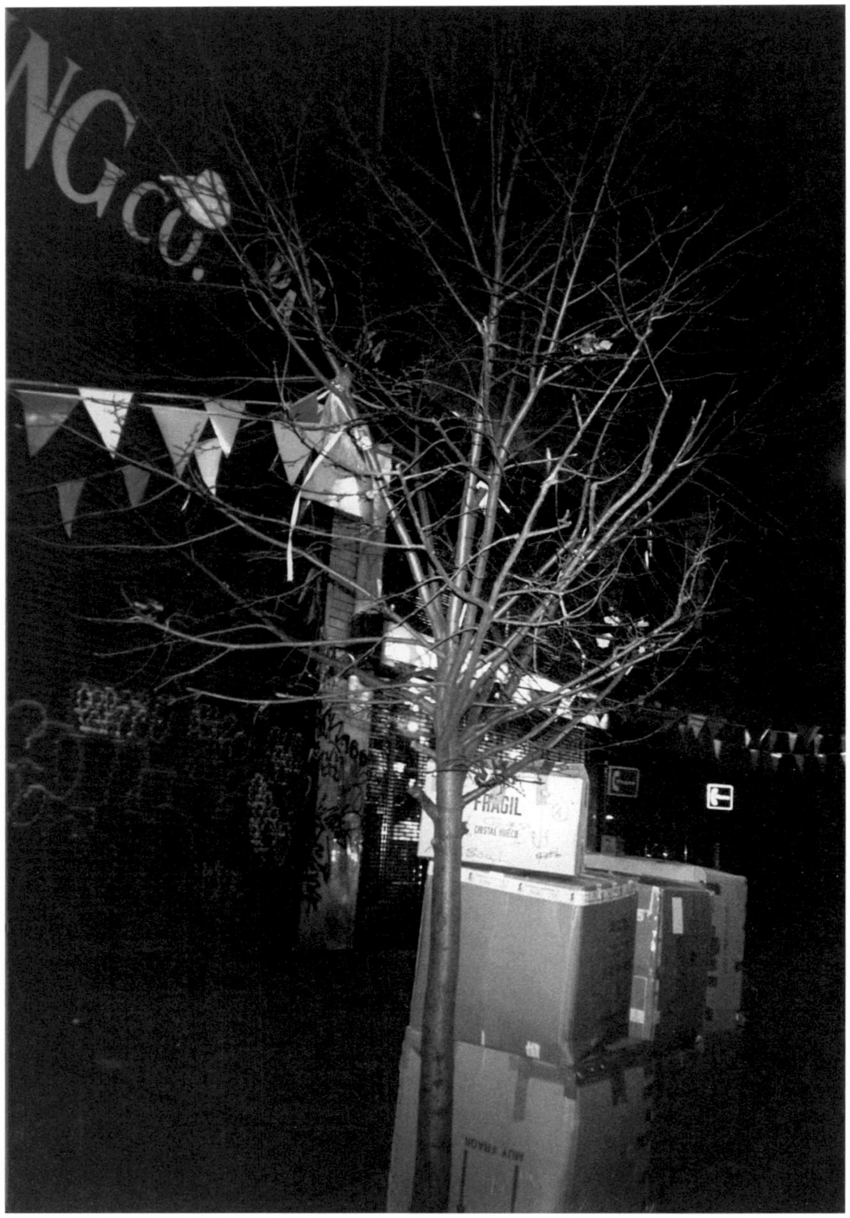

Plate 100 Christopher Wool, *East Broadway Breakdown*, 1994/2002

Rosalyn Deutsche's important discussion of "public" viewing as it pertains to artists—particularly feminist artists—not usually associated with "public art." In her essay "Agoraphobia," Deutsche discusses a little-known exhibition called *Public Vision*, which took place in 1982 at White Columns in New York, organized by Gretchen Bender, Nancy Dwyer, and Cindy Sherman.[20] Deutsche writes of the artists (all, incidentally, women) assembled there:

> They unsettled the modernist model of visual neutrality at its core by proposing that meaning arises only in an interactive space between viewer and image—but not between preexisting viewers or images. Rather, these artists explored the role played by vision in constituting the human subject and, moreover, in the continuous reproduction of this subject by social forms of visuality. They did not confine their analysis of the politics of the image to what appears inside the borders of a picture, within the visual field. Instead, they turned their attention to what is invisible there—the operations that generate the seemingly natural spaces of the image and the viewer. In so doing, these artists treated the image itself as a social relationship and the viewer as a subject constructed by the very object from which it formerly claimed detachment.[21]

Considering Leonard's work in Deutsche's terms—that the artist's images operate *as* social relations rather than just depicting them—allows for the possibility that these are not static "pictures," but that they act to *prompt*. In a 2008 essay called "Notes on Photography & Accident," Moyra Davey describes a lecture given by Leonard, her longtime friend, on December 4, 2006, at Dia Art Foundation in New York City on the art of Agnes Martin. Leonard decided not to show images of Martin's paintings (though she did screen excerpts from *Gabriel* [1976], the only film Martin ever made), because none of the many photographs Leonard had taken of them managed to capture their surface to her liking. Yet Davey left "the lecture with an incredibly vivid image of the absent, unseen photographs: classic, vintage, black-and-white Leonard, signature black frame line enclosing Martin's pale, gray, pencil-lined grids. Photographs of pencil marks.... But wait, did Agnes Martin even use pencil?"[22] Davey points to the way every image—particularly those constructed with discursive emphasis—exceeds itself, experienced at a particular moment in time but then perpetually revisited and revised in mnemonic recall (or the lack thereof). She also points to the way images begin to come undone (and begin to reconstitute themselves) the moment they are out of view. This reminds me of Davey's own metaphoric pictures of the city found in unexpected structures like bins and boxes of old buttons and in the images of the domestic interiors she has shared with her family. Davey refuses to abandon the anachronistic p. 200
(perhaps even romantic) notion of photography as "accident"; she refuses, that is, to abandon the idea that one cannot see what a photograph will yield until it is taken. Yet

pp. 253–55 in Davey's 1994 pictures of New York City newsstands, the kiosks intrigue not only in what they look like but also in the wares they exhibit. This is especially evident today, some fifteen years after they were taken, as newsstands are slowly disappearing from New York's streets; they are thus utterly specific while being neither *here* nor *there.*

★

> *The whole scheme of our culture knows very well what it is to be in or out, to be and to identify with something or to be totally exterior to it, to be homogenous or heterogeneous. But to Be-With... What is that?... It is proximity* without recovering one through the other.
>
> —Jean-Luc Nancy, "Love and Community"

pp. 220–23 In November 2005, Sharon Hayes performed the first iteration of *In the Near Future,* an action that took place over nine days and in nine locations around New York City. Holding signs bearing slogans borrowed from or invented in the spirit of past demonstrations ("Ratify ERA Now!" and "I Am a Man," in the first case; "Nothing Will Be as Before," in the second), Hayes occupied sites that were themselves highly coded, such as Saint Patrick's Cathedral, the site of a famous 1989 ACT UP protest.[23] Although *In the Near Future* can be characterized as a series of durational public performances, the time Hayes actually spends on the streets makes up only part of the piece. The other part comprises extensive photographic documentation of the event(s) produced by the artist's friends and colleagues. Thus, the work is situated both in and out of time and space. It offers anchors, but not firm ones, and asks that we question our identifications even as we embrace them.

Hayes has referred to some of her work's "quasi" nature. She has made quasi-documentaries, which is to say that she doesn't play by all of the rules, so to speak, of the documentary genre and has continually explored what it means to invoke modes of communication and address while testing the limits of decipherability. *In the Near Future* can be described as quasi-demonstrational, if we take *quasi* to mean that something is approaching something else but ultimately falling short.[24] *Quasi,* in other words, implies the calling up of a thing but without full identification; when something is "quasi" it fails—whether intentionally or not—to meet its own minimum requirements and, in so doing, comes up with an amended version of itself. This resulting adaptation may then reveal itself to be an entirely different, even opposite, impulse with different, even opposite, motivations.

It would seem that Hayes's demonstrations do indeed fail to meet the minimum requirements we expect from a demonstration. Her actions performed for *In the Near Future* involve only one demonstrator; they don't respond clearly to any visible or immediate event; they encounter little in the way of direct refutation from any institutional figure; and finally they fail to propose any consistent ideology (while Hayes doesn't carry signs bearing right-wing slogans and chooses sayings that express something of her own affinities, she nonetheless, over the course of a week, covers a broad range of potentially contradictory messages). Yet her works remain stubbornly readable as, and reminiscent of, willful, politically motivated demonstrations. After accounting for all of the ways in which her demonstrations don't act like demonstrations, one wonders, nonetheless, how they are so clearly recognizable as such.[25]

To better understand this contradiction, I turn to an unlikely source: John Searle. A student of the British philosopher J. L. Austin (famous for his designation of the "performative utterance"), Searle himself is best known for the hypothesis he laid out in his 1969 book *Speech Acts*. "Speaking a language," he asserts, "is engaging in a rule-governed form of behavior."[26] It is for this stricture-based account that most contemporary theorists of performativity discount Searle as far too positivist. Yet Searle is helpful here precisely for his rigid articulation of language's operations, particularly since his emphasis on systems is more complex than a simple description of rules of grammar or modes of general acculturation. Rules of speech, he argues, are acted out as conventions that we as human beings are made to grasp on such a deep level that sometimes we don't even know that we know them.[27] It is through the *deviation* from ordinary behavior that we can define the behavior itself, and not the other way around. It becomes a case of "I know it, but I don't know how." When something doesn't quite adhere to our conception of it, Searle argues, rather than feel puzzled one might feel reassured. Indeed, he writes, "We could not recognize borderline cases...as borderline cases if we did not grasp the concept to begin with. It is as much a test of man's mastery of the concept *green* that he has doubts about applying it to a glass of Chartreuse, as that he has no doubt at all about applying it to a healthy lawn or withholding it from fresh snow."[28]

Following Searle, then, our prior concept of what a demonstration *is* would seem to be secured, rather than placed into question, by Hayes's willingness to forego certain of its normative aspects. And this is, counterintuitively perhaps, where a critical aspect of Hayes's work resides. Asking us to revisit our conception of a "demonstration" or "political action," Hayes also asks us to subtly revise those conceptions. As Searle writes: "Two of the marks of rule-governed...behavior are that we generally recognize deviations from the pattern as somehow wrong or defective and that the rule...automatically covers new cases. Confronted with a case he has never seen before, the agent knows what to do."[29] But I would question, as does Hayes, where we are if the agent *doesn't* know precisely what to do. By invoking all of the rules and even the language of protest, Hayes leaves us in an interesting bind, whether we encounter her on the street or in the photo-documentation. While it may be the case that we come up against all of our previous expectations of what it means to be involved in a protest, we can't simply dismiss Hayes's as a deviation. We could argue

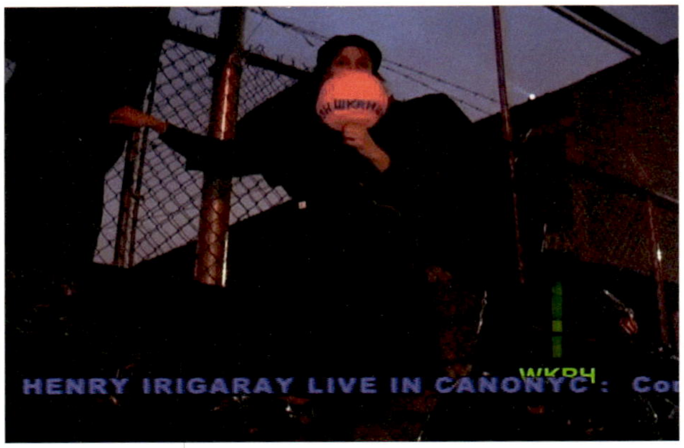

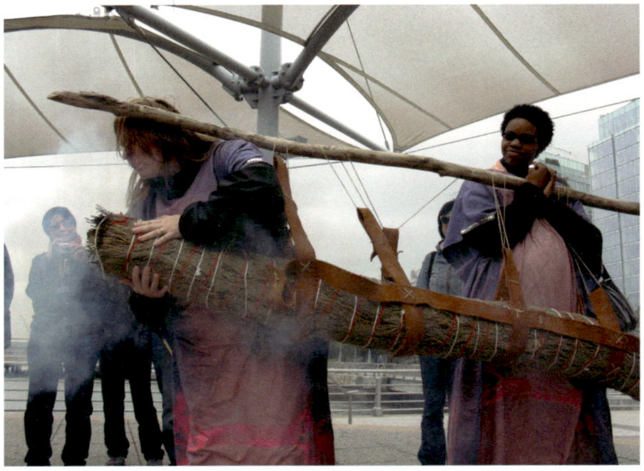

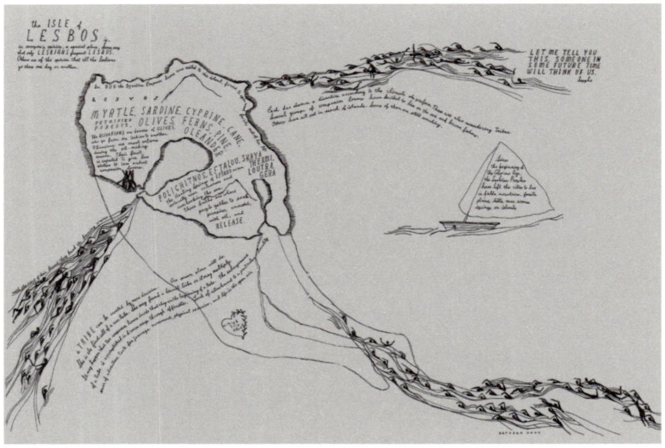

K8 Hardy and Wynne Greenwood, still from *New Report*, 2005. Video; color; sound; 12 min.

Jeanine Oleson, *The Greater New York Smudge Cleanse,* a series of public performances in fall 2008. West Village procession from Christopher Street pier to Stonewall Inn, New York, October 25, 2008. Photograph by Khaela Maricich

Ginger Brooks Takahashi and Dana Bishop-Root, *'A graphic of the island of lesbos with icons depicting different sites and tourist activities' for Ulrike Müller's collaborative drawing project 'Herstory Inventory,'* 2009. Ink on paper

that this is because her gestures are meant for consideration within the realm of "art" (a particular subset of borderline cases). And yet I see this explanation as the least expansive and least satisfying way to think through the inherent irresolution of *In the Near Future.*

I would like instead to return to a suggestion I made at the beginning of this essay as a way of concluding it. Given what we know of Sedgwick, Freud, and Flatley, might we view *In the Near Future* as a work occupied by more than a single "content"? Hayes has described her actions in the piece as a kind of "placeholder," a designation that implies occupation, or holding a position—in time, space, and thought. This occupation is about not only presence but also expectation. As a placeholder, moreover, Hayes is, obviously, a single person, but she actually assumes the place of any number of people or speculatively, potentially, holds open the place of *action.* Standing at particular sites, with particular signs, Hayes is also, in a more general sense, standing in for discourse and for dialogue. What makes these quasi-demonstrations particularly effective as political protests is their way of generating conversation, both in their immediate context and later—through critical texts, say, produced in their wake. In this way, it is possible to see how Hayes, as performer and as the first person, "I" simultaneously marks the space of the phantasmic "we."

This "we" is made even more materially present in the work Hayes created in 2008 at the Democratic and Republican national conventions in, respectively, Denver, Colorado, and Saint Paul, Minnesota. For this work, *Revolutionary Love: I Am Your Worst Fear, I Am Your Best Fantasy* (after a 1970 Christopher Street Liberation Day Parade placard), Hayes enlisted groups of self-identified queer people to come and read a text in unison that oscillated between love letter and political statement. Even when people stood reading with other people—temporarily summoned to participate—it was hard for them to be considered a community in any strict sense.

In a recent conversation, Hayes and I discussed the distinction Jean-Luc Nancy makes between *common being* and *being-in-common,* an idea Hayes has long considered in her work. Common being, Nancy argues, is based on a desire for a community that shares a common body: an organized whole or entity.[30] Nancy sees this desire as fruitless, dangerous, and largely impossible. On the other hand, a community with an absence of common being may still share among its individuals a feeling of being-in-common. Being-in-common has no fantasy of union to promote but rather operates on the idea that our commonality is experienced in the essential truth that we have nothing in common except our uncommonness. I close with Nancy's provocative idea as it relates to Hayes—who stands alone, but who also stands *in,* both during her performances and in the ensuing photographs—for it suggests that her practice straddles time, site, and self. Another term Nancy uses for *being-in-common* is *Being-With,* which he borrows from Heidegger. *With* suggests both proximity and distance, which appropriately defines "a quasi-empty category for all philosophy."[31]

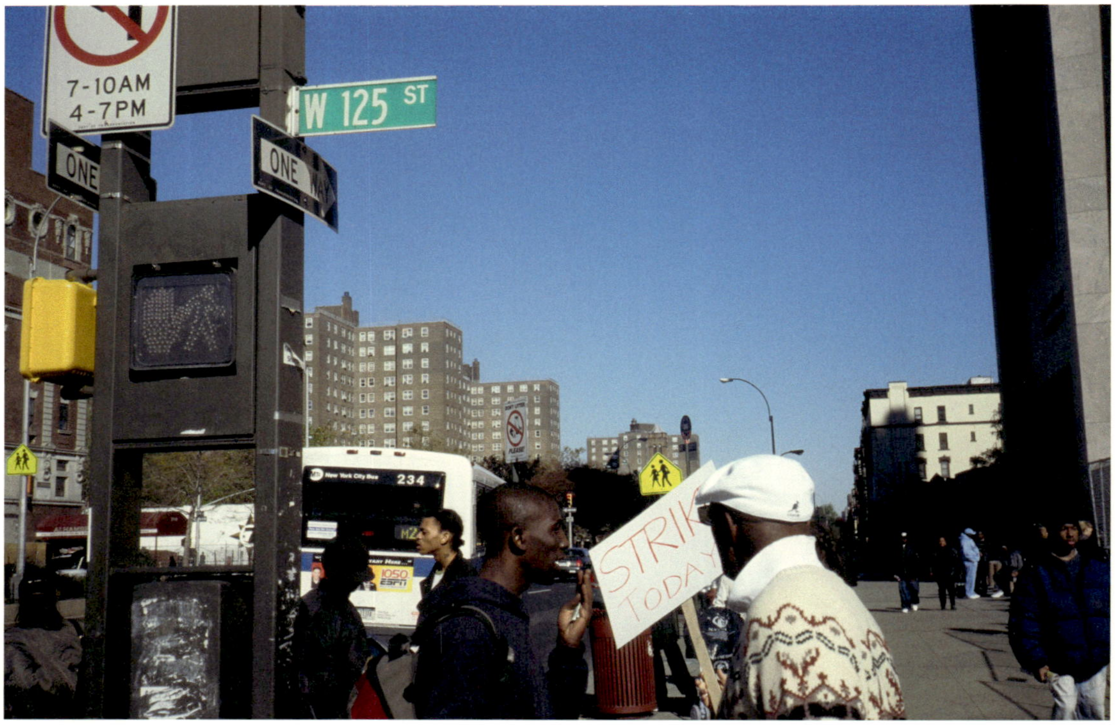

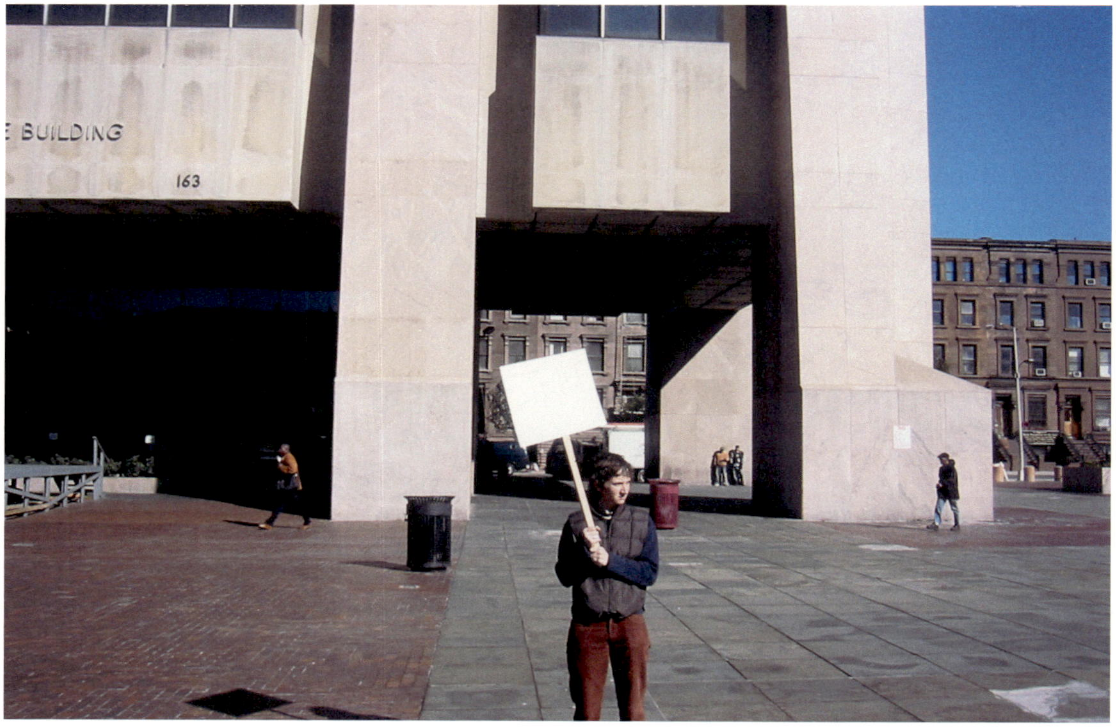

Plate 101 Sharon Hayes, *In the Near Future, New York*, 2005

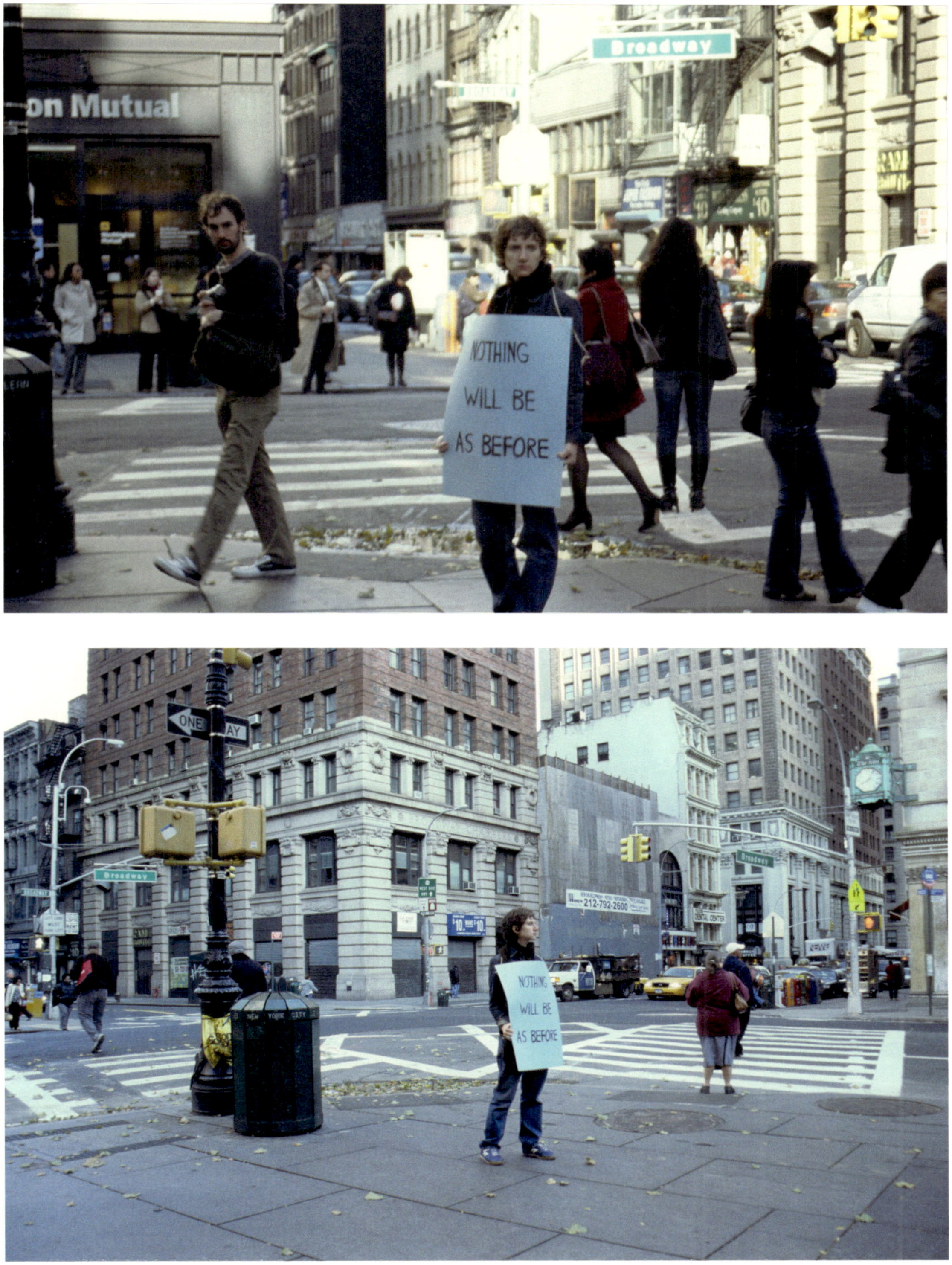

Plate 102 Sharon Hayes, *In the Near Future, New York*, 2005

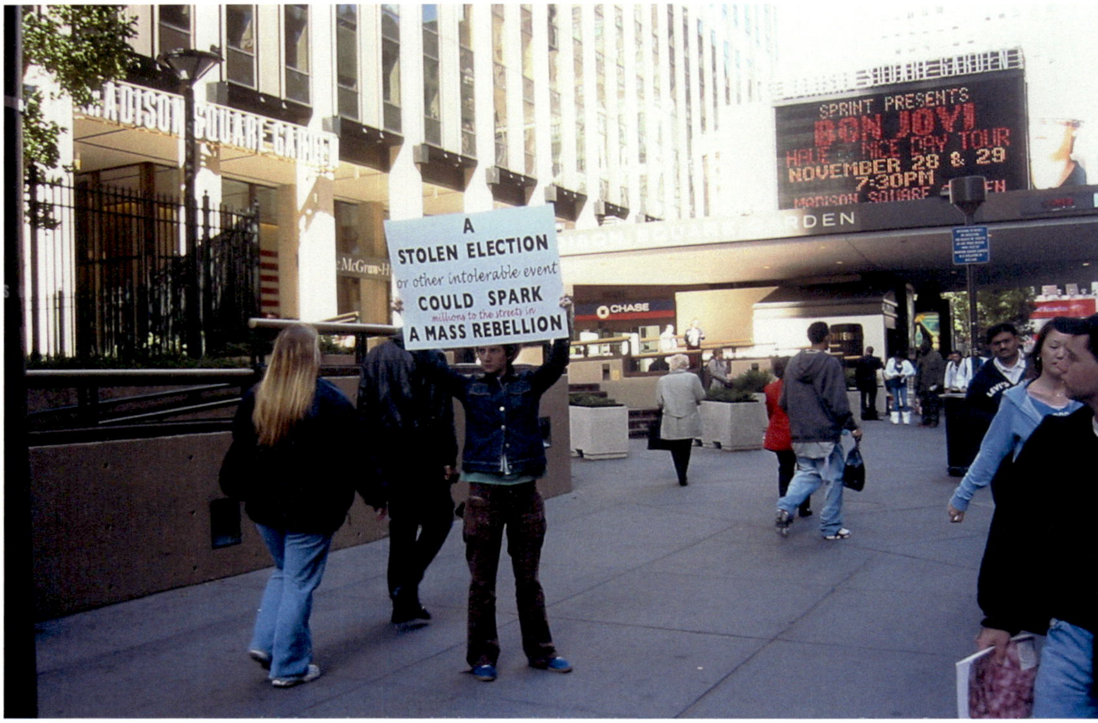

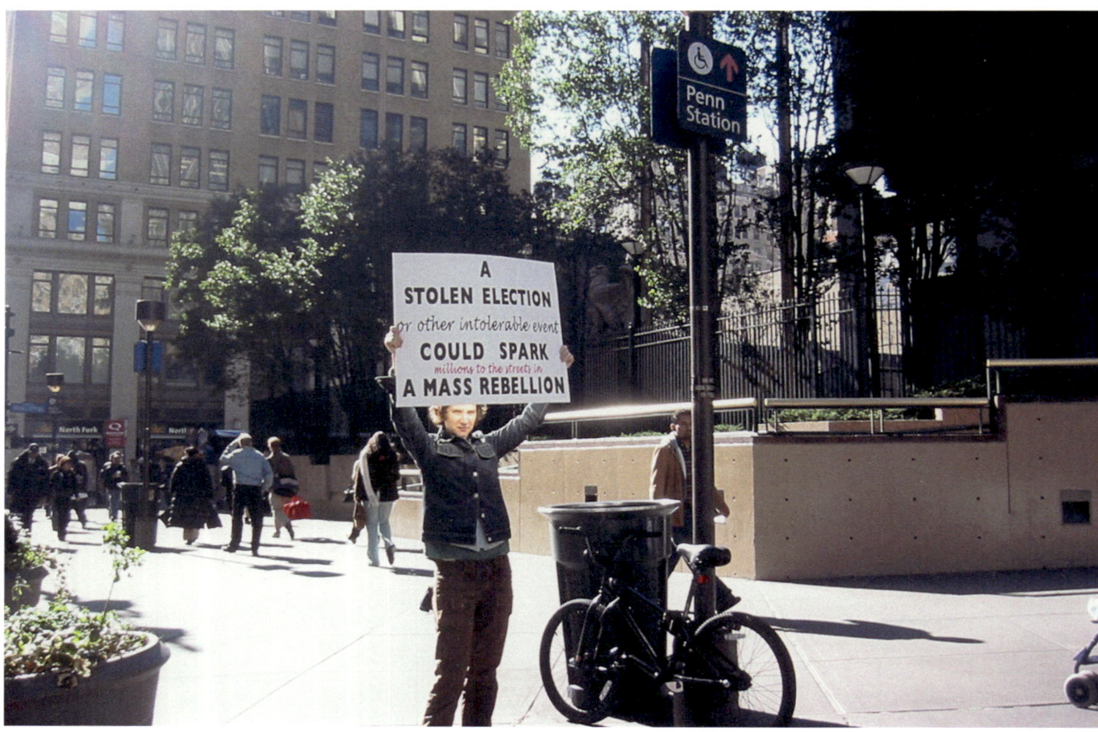

Plate 103 Sharon Hayes, *In the Near Future, New York*, 2005

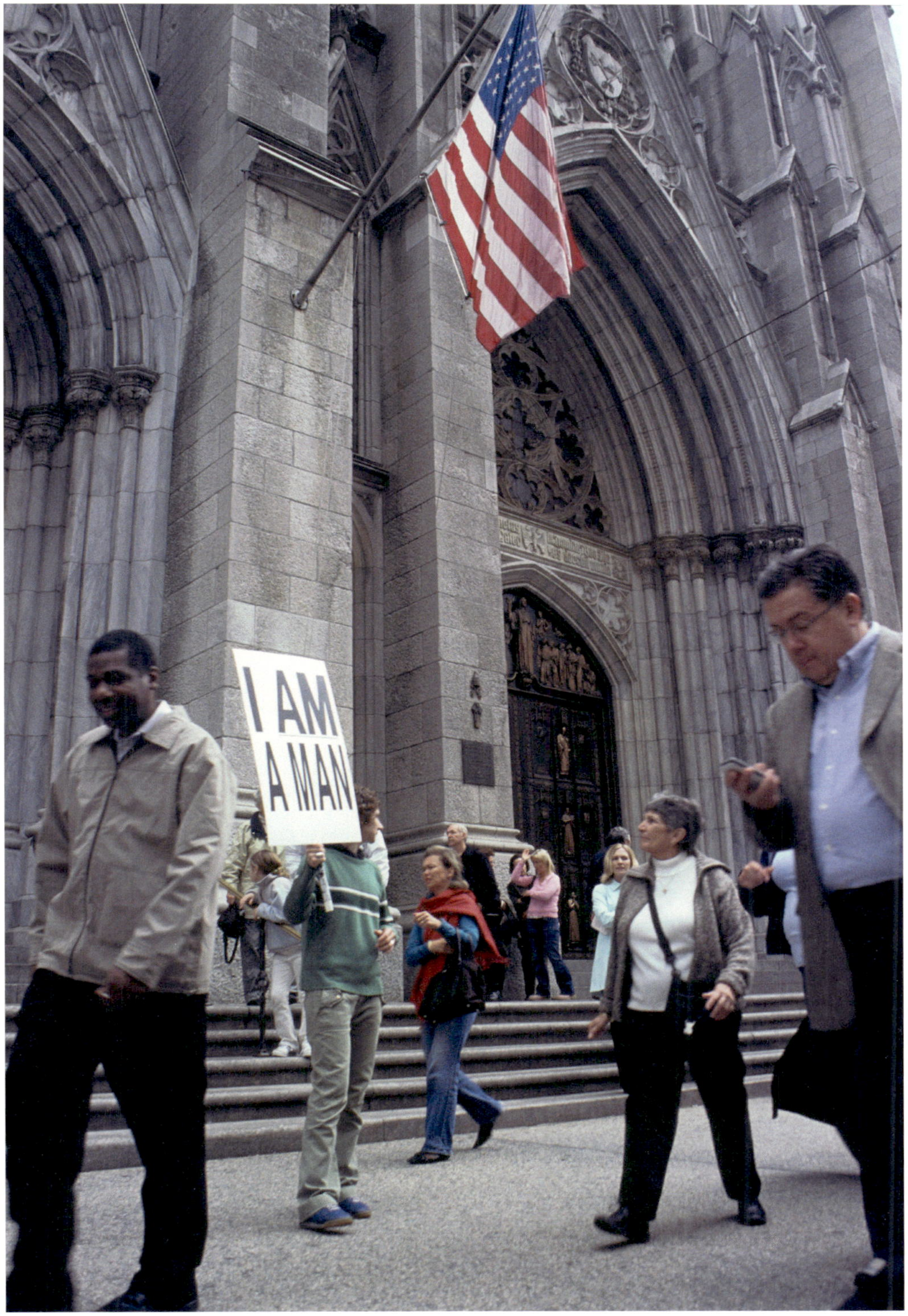

Plate 104 Sharon Hayes, *In the Near Future, New York*, 2005

But to further consider this phrase, *being with*, I would like to focus on just the word *with*—to ask that its emptiness be seen as representing a capacity for an impossible occupation of time and space. Though *being-in-common* admits breaches between subjects, it also constitutes spaces of relational possibility. Here, in addition to Hayes, I think of artists such as Andrea Geyer, whose *Interim* (2002) situates the body in a landscape that it produces at the same time that it narrates. An eighty-page newspaper, *Interim* follows a female protagonist—a "foreigner"—as she navigates New York City. The narrative—delivered in text and images—is shape-shifting and aimless, a meditation on the paradox of feeling a sense of isolation and sometimes even privacy while being in a public space. I think, as well, of Wynne Greenwood, who with Fawn Kreger produced *ROOM* (2005), an installation and performance that experimented with "nonhierarchical space" as it was articulated in feminist consciousness-raising groups in the 1970s. In another 2005 work, created with K8 Hardy, Greenwood made p. 218 *New Report*—a retro, forward-thinking, feminist rendition of how the news could be reported *otherwise*. Hitting the New York streets, the two interviewed women about their feelings, resuscitated the political gesture of bra burning, and vehemently disallowed all notions of "straight" reportage. There are other works that come to mind as well that deserve far more attention than these mere mentions. Ulrike Müller's current p. 218 project, for example, titled *Herstory Inventory*, presents "feminists, queer artists, and other interested people" with textual descriptions of archival material related to feminist movements of the 1970s and asks them to "re-draw" or "translate" this often-obscured p. 218 historical imagery; Jeanine Oleson's 2008 *The Greater New York Smudge Cleanse* employs an enormous burning sage bundle in order to "cleanse" various locations around New York of their "classism, heterosexism, imperialism, election anxiety, gentrification, eco-destruction, and greed." Both of these projects are overtly activist-inflected works that insist on pulling seemingly out-of-sync modes of communal production into the present and reflecting on how and why they continue to be useful and even oppositional.[32]

So, in addition to Nancy's *with*, which dismisses too readily perhaps the ramifications of *any* commonly shared foundation, I would include another term from Sedgwick, used in her work on affect to imagine non-normative modes of relationality: *beside*. In her somewhat messier formulation, Sedgwick attempts to articulate a shared, but not collapsed, mapping between bodies, between sites, through time. "*Beside*," she writes,

> is an interesting preposition...because there's nothing very dualistic about it; a number of elements may lie alongside one another, though not an infinity of them. *Beside* permits a spacious agnosticism about several of the linear logics that enforce dualistic thinking: noncontradiction or the law of the excluded middle, cause versus effect, subject versus object. Its interest does not, however, depend on a fantasy of metonymically egalitarian or even pacific relations, as

> any child knows who's shared a bed with siblings. *Beside* comprises a wide range of desiring, identifying, representing, repelling, paralleling, differentiating, rivaling, leaning, twisting, mimicking, withdrawing, attracting, aggressing, warping, and other relations.[33]

Picture a city as it is imagined and reimagined in relation to itself, its past lives placed alongside—in dialogue and tension with—its current and future possibilities. What I've described in this essay, then, with the help of artists who do just that: New York, beside itself.

Endnotes

1
Eve Kosofsky Sedgwick, *Touching Feeling: Affect, Pedagogy, Performativity* (Durham, NC: Duke University Press, 2003), p. 35. The chapter is a meditation on a triangulation of terms within a particular literary context; it is titled "Shame, Theatricality, and Queer Performativity: Henry James's *The Art of the Novel*" (in Sedgwick, *Touching Feeling,* pp. 35–65).

2
Ibid., p. 35. Internal quote is from Silvan Tomkins, *Shame and Its Sisters: A Silvan Tomkins Reader*, eds. Eve Kosofsky Sedgwick and Adam Frank (Durham, NC: Duke University Press, 1995), p. 135.

3
Sedgwick argues, "That's the double movement shame makes: toward painful individuation, toward uncontrollable relationality," and later goes on to grant it great productive potential in the realm of queer pleasure, identification, and play. Sedgwick, *Touching Feeling*, p. 37.

4
Sigmund Freud, *Civilization and Its Discontents*, vol. 21, *The Standard Edition of the Complete Psychological Works of Sigmund Freud*, ed. James Strachey (London: Hogarth Press, 1953–74), p. 69.

5
Freud continues with the example, adding, "This would mean that in Rome the palaces of the Caesars and the Septizonium of Septimius Severus would still be rising to their old height on the Palatine and that the castle of S. Angelo would still be carrying on its battlements and the beautiful statues which graced it until the siege by the Goths, and so on. But more than this. In the place occupied by the Palazzo Caffarelli would once more stand—without the Palazzo having to be removed—the Temple of Jupiter Capitolinus; and this not only in its latest shape, as the Romans of the Empire saw it, but also in its earliest one, when it still showed Etruscan forms and was ornamented with terra-cotta antefixes..." Ibid., p. 70.

6
Freud adds, as well, that the comparison between mind and city is unsuitable because his own theory of preservation relies on taking the brain up in a healthy state (and so not factoring in abnormalities or injuries), whereas in cities renewal is often enough the result of more violent kinds of "progress"—tearing down old buildings to put up new ones, for instance—and therefore proceeds quite oppositely. Ibid., pp. 70–71.

7
Of course, recent thinking about artists' use of the archive already puts pressure on the ways in which material can be brought forward from the past into the present. Hal Foster's "An Archival Impulse," for instance, posits a complex layering whereby the "archival" project "not only draws on informal archives but produces them as well, and does so in a way that underscores the nature of all archival materials as found yet constructed, factual yet fictive, public yet private." See Foster, "An Archival Impulse," *October* 110 (Fall 2004), pp. 3–22. More recently, Sharon Hayes and Julia Bryan-Wilson discussed the political possibilities of considering all archives—and thus, in effect, our relationship to "the past"—as inherently "queer" (a proposition borrowed by Bryan-Wilson from the art historian Christopher Reed). See Julia Bryan-Wilson, "We Have a Future: An Interview with Sharon Hayes," *Grey Room* 37 (Fall 2009), pp. 78–93. My approach here is indebted to these and other theorizations but differs in that I want to stress the deep tissue of *site*, to consider the psychic investments that, following Michel de Certeau, transform a "place" into a "space" and vice versa. For de Certeau, the former enables "a determination through objects that are ultimately reducible to the *being-there* of something dead, the law of a 'place'" while the latter produces "a determination through *operations* which... specify 'spaces' by the actions of historical *subjects* (a movement always seems to condition the production of a space and to associate it with a history)." Describing a necessarily dialectical function, de Certeau allows us to think of, say, Manhattan, as both the island it literally is *and* the myriad invested representations it has assumed over time. See Michel de Certeau, *The Practice of Everyday Life*, trans. Steven Rendall (Berkeley and Los Angeles: University of California Press, 1984), p. 118.

8
Jonathan Flatley, *Affective Mapping: Melancholia and the Politics of Modernism* (Cambridge, MA: Harvard University Press, 2008), p. 7.

9
Flatley writes, "I am concerned not with the creation of affective maps in general but with the ways an aesthetic practice might help with this process of affective mapping. My argument is that it does this not primarily through a realist representation of a social space in the world, but through a representation of the affective life of the reader herself or himself. Such a representation is accomplished by way of a self-estrangement that allows one to see oneself in relation to one's affective environment in its historicity, in relation to the relevant social-political anchors or landmarks in that environment, and to see the others who inhabit that landscape with me." *Affective Mapping,* p. 80. Flatley's case studies are not visual artists but writers—Henry James, W. E. B. Du Bois, and Andrei Platonov—but I think his argument applies interestingly to contemporary artistic practices such as those I discuss. I am thankful to Douglas Crimp for drawing my attention to Flatley's work. See Flatley, *Affective Mapping*, especially pp. 76–84.

10
The audience, though crucial to an understanding of the piece, is shown in some images, but from the perspective of the performers themselves. Gathered on the roof of 319 Greenwich Street, a five-story loft building, those watching *Delay Delay* are photographed from the west coordinate of an east-west axis, but because of their bird's-eye view, they appear more or less en masse and immobile. It should be noted that Jonas's 1973 film *Songdelay* uses material from the performance of *Delay Delay* but is not a document of that work; it, rather, pursues concerns inherent in the performance (perceptions of distance, representations of space, asymmetries between visual and auditory stimuli) as they operate filmically by, for instance, using different kinds of lenses and playing with cuts and pans. For descriptions of both *Delay Delay* and *Songdelay*, see *Joan Jonas: Scripts and Descriptions, 1968–1982*, ed. Douglas Crimp (Berkeley: University Art Museum, University of California, Berkeley; Eindhoven: Stedelijk Van Abbemuseum, 1983). See also the text written by Janelle Reiring, which very precisely details the work: "Joan Jonas' *Delay Delay*," *The Drama Review: TDR* 16 (September 1972), 142–50.

11
"Pile fields are a key element of the estuarine sanctuary. Instead of removing these wooden elements, which once functioned to support piers, the Hudson River Park Trust has committed to retaining the piles to provide habitat for various fish species. Many fish including juvenile Striped Bass take shelter in the piles, and sessile organisms—those that live in one spot for their entire lives—are particularly common." ("Life in the Pile Fields," http://www.hudsonriverpark.org/estuary/river_piles.asp [accessed March 1, 2010].)

12
This is a point addressed by Douglas Crimp in his essay published here and in his introduction to Alvin Baltrop's work for *Artforum*, where he points to the heavy traffic by gay men and male artists on the West Side piers in the 1970s and discusses Louise Lawler's *Birdcalls* (1972/1981) as a response to being excluded from the (all-male) shows there that she was employed to help create. See "On Alvin Baltrop," *Artforum* 46 (February 2008), p. 269.

13
In Jean Carlomusto, "Radiant Spaces: An Introduction to Emily Roysdon's Photograph Series *Untitled*," *GLQ* 10, no. 4 (2004), p. 674.

14
Ibid., p. 673.

15
Elizabeth Grosz, "Bodies-Cities," in *Space, Time, and Perversion* (New York: Routledge, 1995), p. 109. First published in *Sexuality & Space* (Princeton Papers on Architecture), ed. Beatriz Colomina (Princeton, NJ: Princeton Architectural Press, 1992). Grosz writes that one of the general effects induced by the cityscape is to "orient and organize familial, sexual, and social relations insofar as the city, as much as the state, divides cultural life into public and private domains, geographically dividing and defining the particular social position individuals and groups occupy. Lateral or contingent connections between individuals and social groups are established, constituting domestic and generational distinctions. These are the roles and means by which bodies are individuated to become subjects." Grosz, "Bodies-Cities," p. 109.
16
In a recent explication of the trajectory of his work, Burr—who has moved from looking at specific architectural histories to more seemingly sculpture-specific experiments with a kind of "figurative" Minimalist/Postminimalist vocabulary—said something that might be applied to all of his work compellingly: "Beyond distinctions between private and public realms, there is a moment in which things are, one might say, put on display and exposed, and privacy becomes part of a public arena and public discourse. It became more compelling, and riskier, for me to think about these conditions through a more antiquated notion: identities. Or, more specifically, identity as a condition that slips away at the moment of an intense public display." Tom Burr, with introduction by Joshua Decter, "Tom Burr Talks about 'Addict-Love,' 2008," *Artforum* 46 (February 2008), p. 260.
17
See George Baker, "The Other Side of the Wall," *October* 120 (Spring 2007), pp. 106–37.
18
Burr, "'Addict-Love,'" p. 261.
19
Ibid., p. 260.
20
The show included work by Gretchen Bender, Jennifer Bolande, Diane Buckler, Ellen Carey, Nancy Dwyer, Barbara Kruger, Louise Lawler, Sherrie Levine, Diane Shea, Cindy Sherman, Laurie Simmons, and Peggy Yunque.
21
Rosalyn Deutsche, "Agoraphobia," in *Evictions: Art and Spatial Politics* (Cambridge, MA: MIT Press, 1996), p. 296.
22
Moyra Davey, "Notes on Photography & Accident," in *Long Life Cool White: Photographs & Essays by Moyra Davey* (New Haven, CT: Yale University Press; Cambridge, MA: Harvard University Art Museums, 2008), p. 116. This book accompanies the exhibition *Long Life Cool White: Photographs by Moyra Davey*, curated by Helen Molesworth and on view at the Fogg Museum, Harvard University Art Museums, Cambridge, MA, February 28–June 20, 2008.
23
The work, which debuted in New York in 2005, has subsequently had iterations in Vienna, Warsaw, London, Paris, and Brussels. According to the artist, the piece is now completed. It is important to note that *In the Near Future*, for all its site-specificity, then, draws attention not only to individual places but also to places in general.
24
Hayes's use of "demonstration" is, in fact, less aligned with out-and-out activism and more with Bertolt Brecht's concept, one that posits the participant in epic theater as a "demonstrator," who—by distancing herself from her role visibly—plays a "practical purpose, intervenes socially." See Brecht, "The Street Scene: A Basic Model for an Epic Theatre," in *Brecht on Theatre: The Development of an Aesthetic*, ed. John Willett (New York: Hill and Wang, 1964), pp. 121–29.
25
I was fortunate to have participated in "Wieder und Wider: Performance Appropriated" at MUMOK in Vienna, during which time Hayes presented an iteration of *In the Near Future* and I gave a public response. The conference and events, organized by Barbara Clausen and Achim Hochdörfer, occurred from November 8 to 18, 2006. My comments on Hayes here are indebted to that week's exchange and to Hayes herself, who has been an invaluable and generous interlocutor over the years.
26
John R. Searle, *Speech Acts: An Essay in the Philosophy of Language* (Cambridge: Cambridge University Press, 1969), p. 41.
27
It is an argument that could be played out very interestingly in terms of normative behavior as well. One thinks here of Erich Fromm's argument that concepts of mental health are based less on real pathologies than on shared assumptions of what those might be, "consensual validation" of concepts, as he puts it. In Fromm, "The Psychology of Normalcy," *Dissent* 1 (Spring 1954), pp. 139–43.
28
Searle, *Speech Acts*, p. 8.
29
Ibid., p. 42.
30
See "Love and Community: A round-table discussion with Jean-Luc Nancy, Avital Ronell and Wolfgang Schirmacher," August 2001, the European Graduate School, http://www.egs.edu/faculty/nancy/nancy-roundtable-discussion2001.html (accessed November 1, 2006).
31
Ibid.
32
For a discussion of Geyer's work with regard to questions of subjectivity and national identity, see Nanna Debois's 2006 interview with the artist, http://www.andreageyer.info/Texts/Telling_a_Story.pdf (accessed December 15, 2009). I write about Greenwood's projects—as well as her band—in my "Girl, Interrupted: Tracy + the Plastics," *Artforum* 43 (Summer 2005), pp. 107, 110. Ulrike Müller's edited volume, *Work the Room: A Handbook of Performance Strategies* (Berlin: oe & b_books, 2006), gives a good sense of Müller's dedication to working collaboratively and poses intriguing questions about the politics of emotion. For more information on Oleson's *Smudge* project, see http://www.nycsmudge.com (accessed March 1, 2010). Also see Emily Roysdon's brochure (including contributions by Oleson and a number of other artists discussed in my own essay) for her curated project *Ecstatic Resistance* at Grand Arts in Kansas City (November 13, 2009–January 16, 2010) and X-Initiative in New York (November 21, 2009– February 6, 2010). Available online at http://www.emilyroysdon.com/index.php?/projects/ecstatic-resistance/ (accessed March 1, 2010).
33
Sedgwick, *Touching Feeling,* p. 8.

The Powers of Removal: Interventions in the Name of the City

Lytle Shaw

> "Here, *there used to be a bakery.*" "That's *where old lady Dupuis used to live.*" *It is striking...that the places people live in are like the presences of diverse absences. What can be seen designates what is no longer there:* "you see, *here there used to be...,*" *but it can no longer be seen. Demonstratives indicate the invisible identities of the visible: it is the very definition of a place, in fact, that it is composed by these series of displacements and effects among the fragmented strata that form it and that it plays on these moving layers.*
>
> —Michel de Certeau

> *Silence occludes the ordinary, the implied, the everyday, the unexceptional—all that is not considered important enough to be mentioned. Yet the significance of past events appears in these ordinary moments and people. That's why the quotidian is the limit of understanding, and the limit for speaking of the past.*
>
> —Matthew Buckingham

In 1904, after twenty-one years abroad, Henry James returned to Manhattan, the city of his childhood. His account of rapid and ruthless transformation is, in one sense, a classic aristocratic lament about the horrors of modernization. James recoils in terror at Ellis Island's ceaseless "ingurgitation" of foreigners (a process he compares to "sword-swallowing").[1] He is annoyed by the "flash of innumerable windows" that offer viewers immediate visual access to buildings' previously screened interior spaces,[2] revolted by the slapdash quality of so many of the new buildings, which "never begin to speak to you...with the authority of things of permanence," and outraged especially about the disappearance of his childhood house.[3] As he approached the site, James's imagination had already erected a commemorative tablet memorializing his accomplishments as a writer. Once at the site he was disappointed to discover that there was no place to hang it, since "the very wall that should have borne this inscription had been smashed as for demonstration that tablets, in New York, are unthinkable."[4] The upshot, then, is that New York offers no choice about whether or not to erect plaques, since any surface one might wish to saddle as support will soon disappear. And this leads to James's key, and perhaps surprising, insight about New York. Looking at several Lower Manhattan churches and noticing that, as taller buildings rise up around them, their traditional symbolic position is eclipsed, James ruminates:

> Afterwards, outside, again and again, the powers of removal struck me as looming awfully, in the newest mass of multiplied floors and windows visible at this point. *They*, ranged in this terrible erection, were going to bring in money—and was not money the only thing a self-respecting structure could be thought of as bringing in?[5]

James's horror of tall buildings, then, is not only that they dwarf churches and smaller structures that previously occupied their sites. It is also that this unarrestable process in turn acted to destabilize *all* buildings; thus, while contemplating any individual looming skyscraper, he was only able to imagine the even *more* monstrous tower that would eventually replace *it* in an infinite potlatch of hasty erections and violent removals.[6] Unlike Marx and Engels's famous claim that in capitalism "all that is solid melts into air," and unlike de Certeau's account of urban places as structured, by necessity, around impossible instances of deixis, James evokes not a onetime loss or a failed gesture of pointing but a sequence of abrupt meltings and just-as-sudden solidifications.[7]

By the mid-1970s much of the modern industrial infrastructure had succumbed to the powers James observed, rendering Lower Manhattan (outside of Wall Street proper) a thinly populated facade.[8] This is the city we see in Harry Shunk and János Kender's photographs from this period that show a decayed shell of once-glamorous, seemingly abandoned skyscrapers hemmed in by the dilapidated piers that previously sustained the world's largest harbor and pumped economic life into this downtown.[9] And this is the view we see through the window in the Danny Lyon photograph of an abandoned room overlooking Lower Manhattan skyscrapers. From these ruins we see, in Shunk-Kender's photographs, the World Trade Center rising, blatant embodiment of the transition from goods to services, from production and distribution to financial management.

But what precisely has been removed from Lower Manhattan? Is it our grounding in and familiarity with specific buildings destined to meet the wrecking ball? Or the wide array of "uses" (what Jane Jacobsites characterize as "healthy urbanism": the integration of goods and services, of labor and leisure, no longer possible in an increasingly parceled city) that steadily disappear, disaggregated to the outer boroughs? Or is it the loss of our belief in the idealism of a midcentury modernism—a modernism that replaced much of the fin-de-siècle urban infrastructure before giving way to a cynical barrage of heritage industry malls (as the geographer David Harvey would have it). Where should art with such concerns direct its energies? And what resources does this art have to figure these processes of removal, preserve modes of experience likely to otherwise vanish, and reflect on the general forces at play in urban transformation?

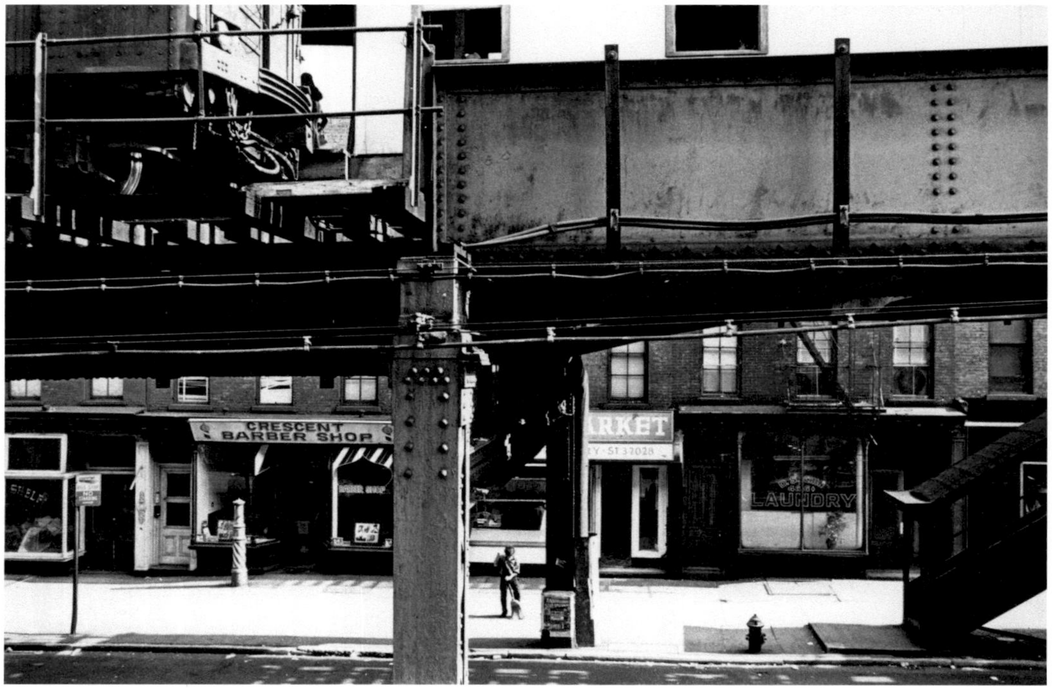

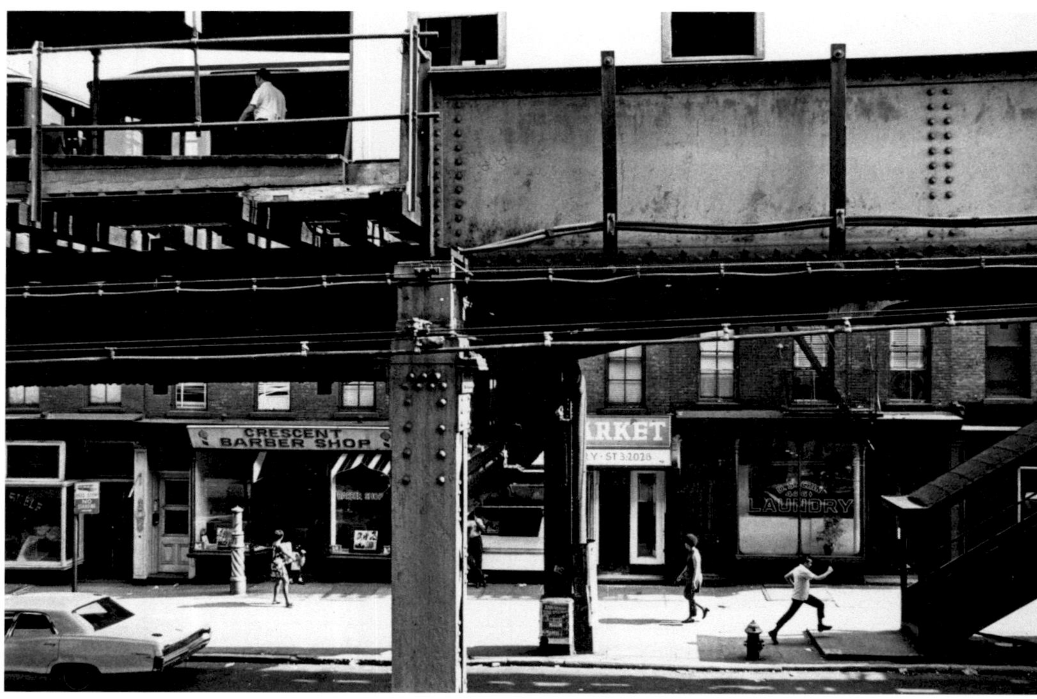

Plate 107–8 William Gedney, photographs of Myrtle Avenue view from Gedney's apartment window, c. 1969

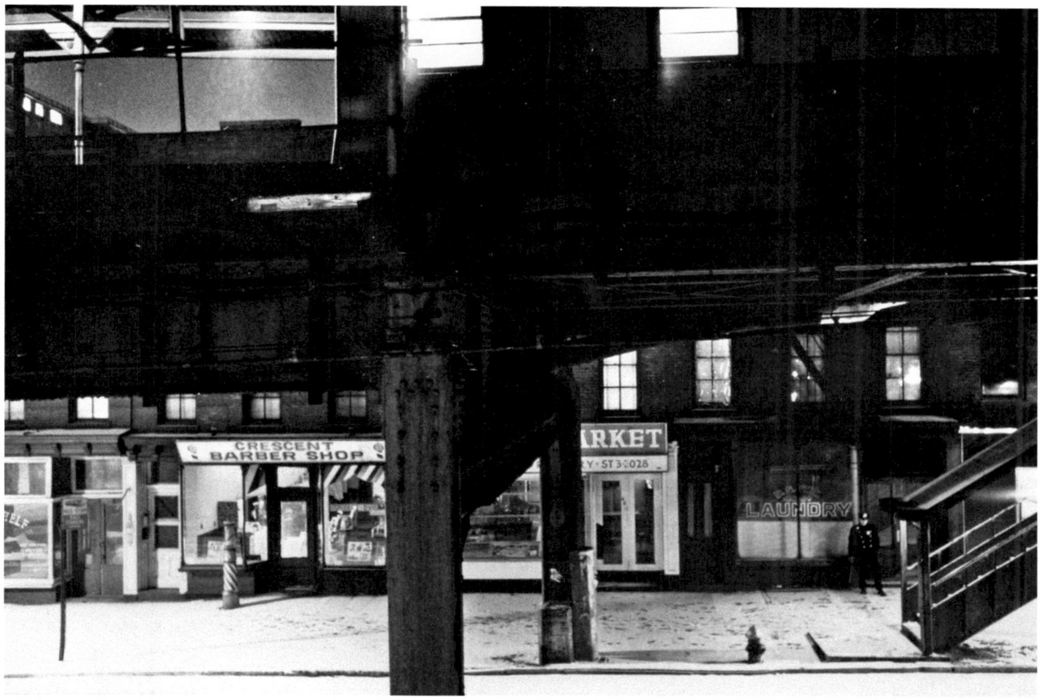

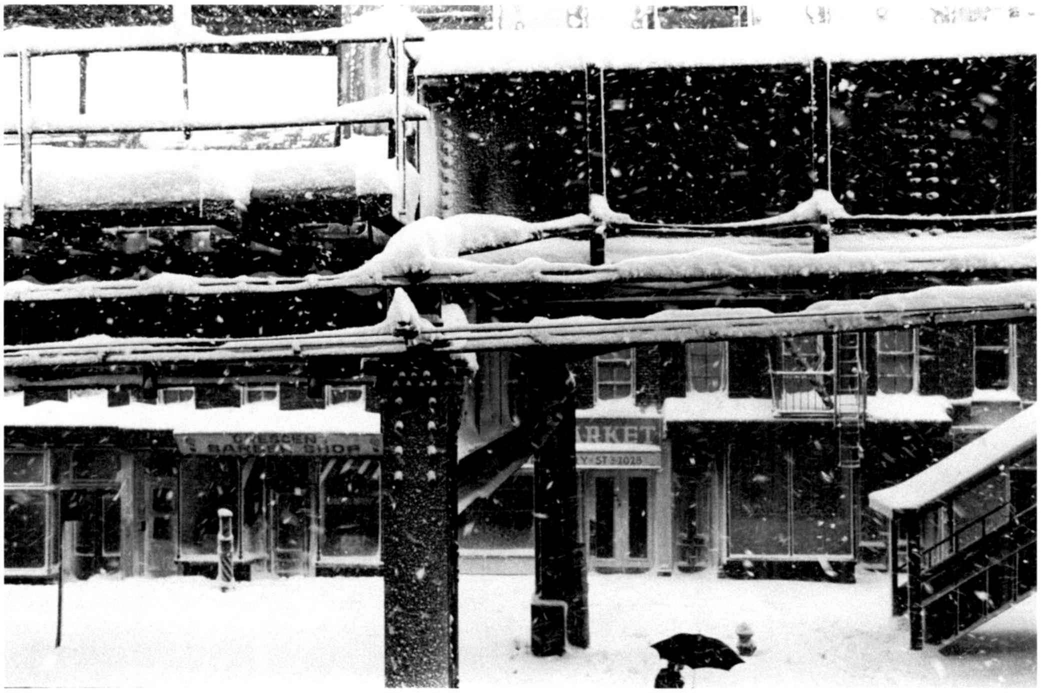

Plate 109–10 William Gedney, photographs of Myrtle Avenue view from Gedney's apartment window, 1967

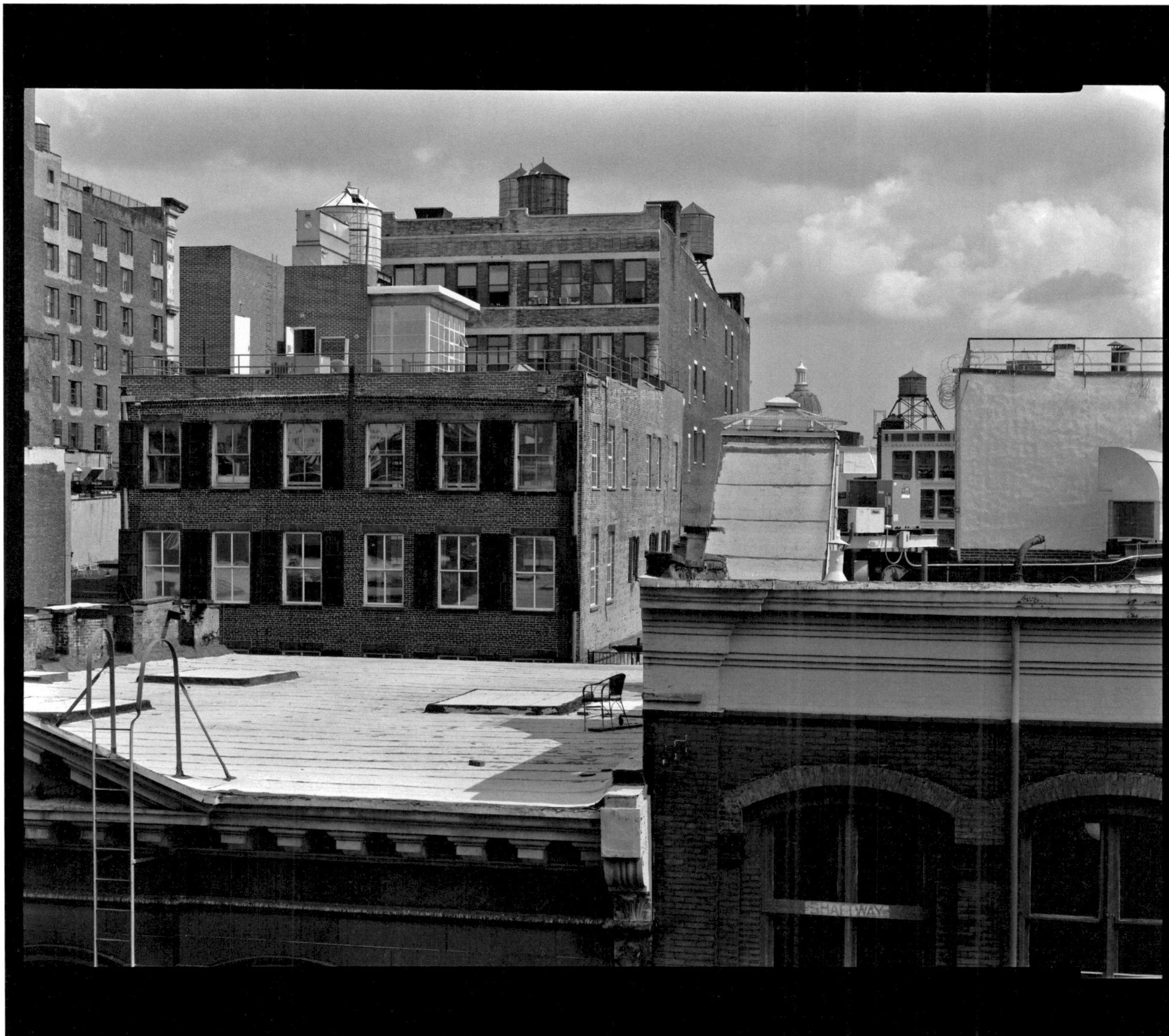

Plate 111 James Welling, *Eastern Window #1*, 1997–2000

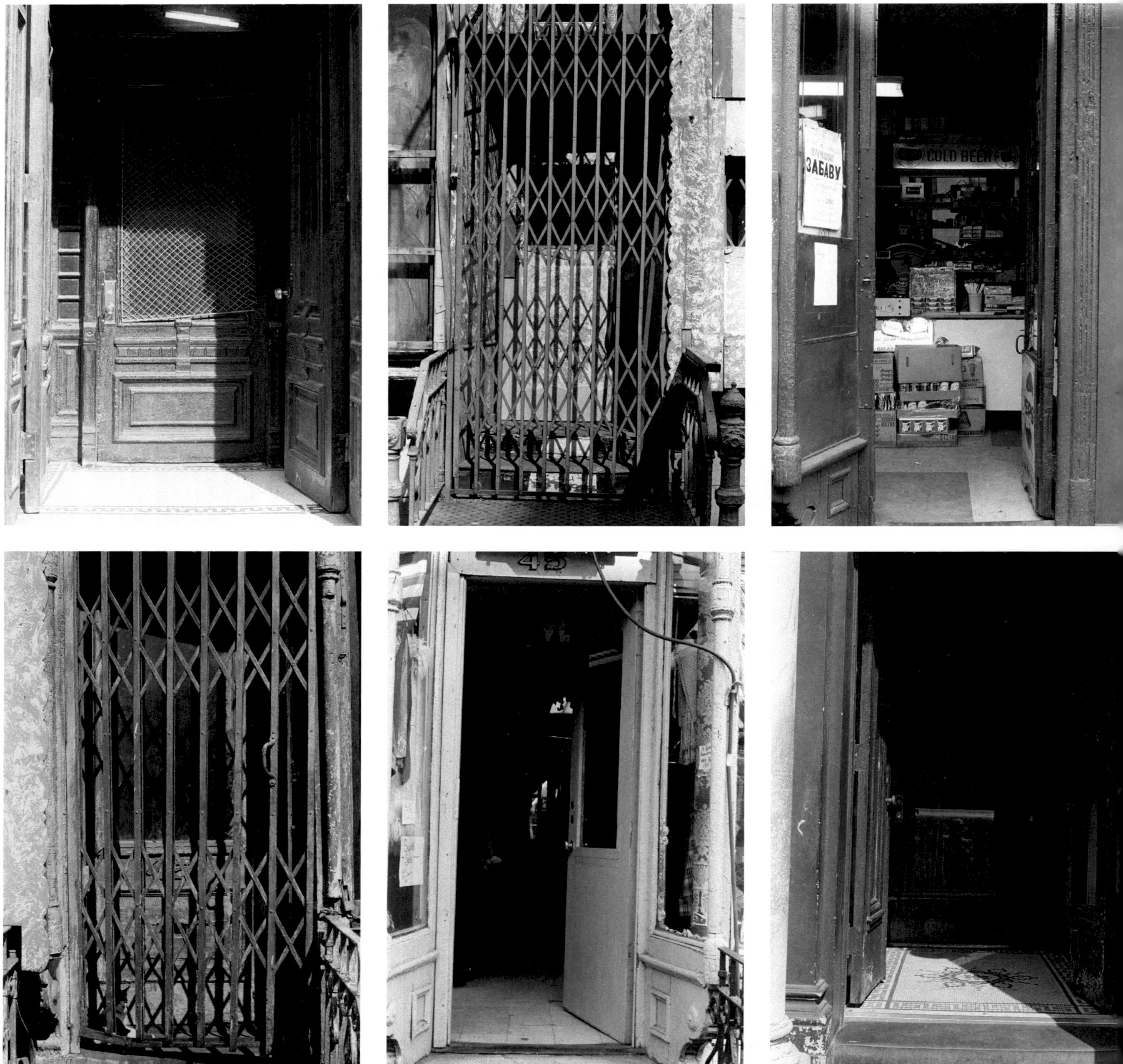

Plate 112 Roy Colmer, *Doors N.Y.C.: East 7th Street between 2nd Avenue and Cooper Square, Odd Numbers*, 1976

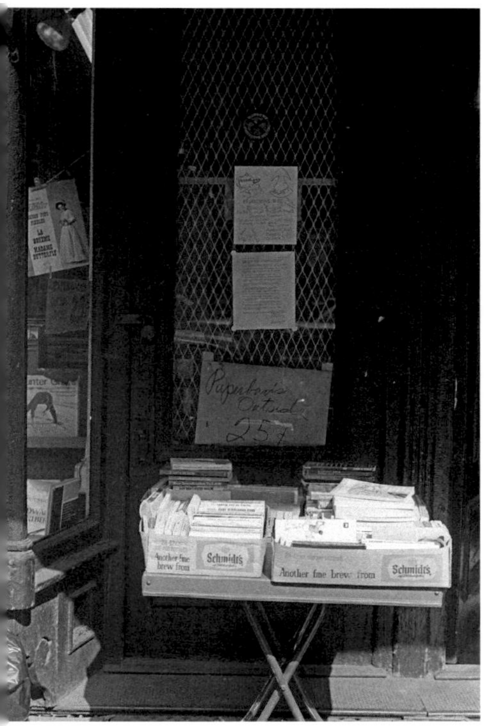
Schmidt's
Another fine brew from
Schmidt's

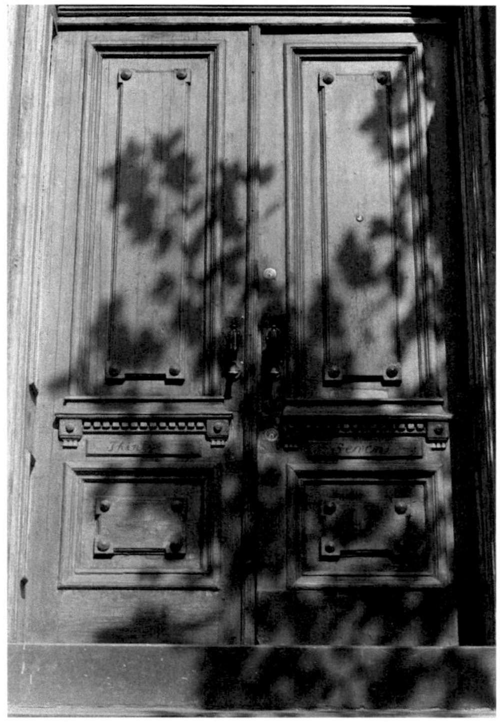

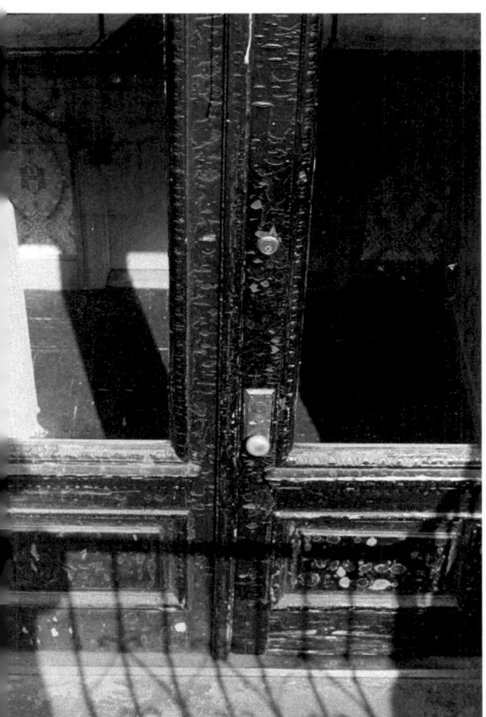

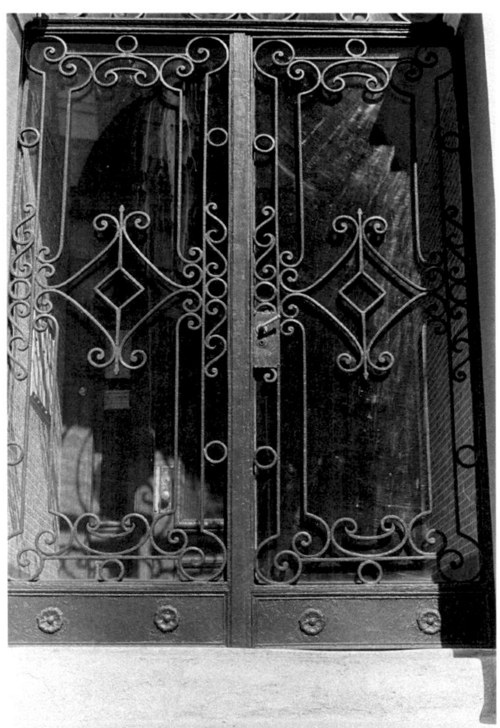

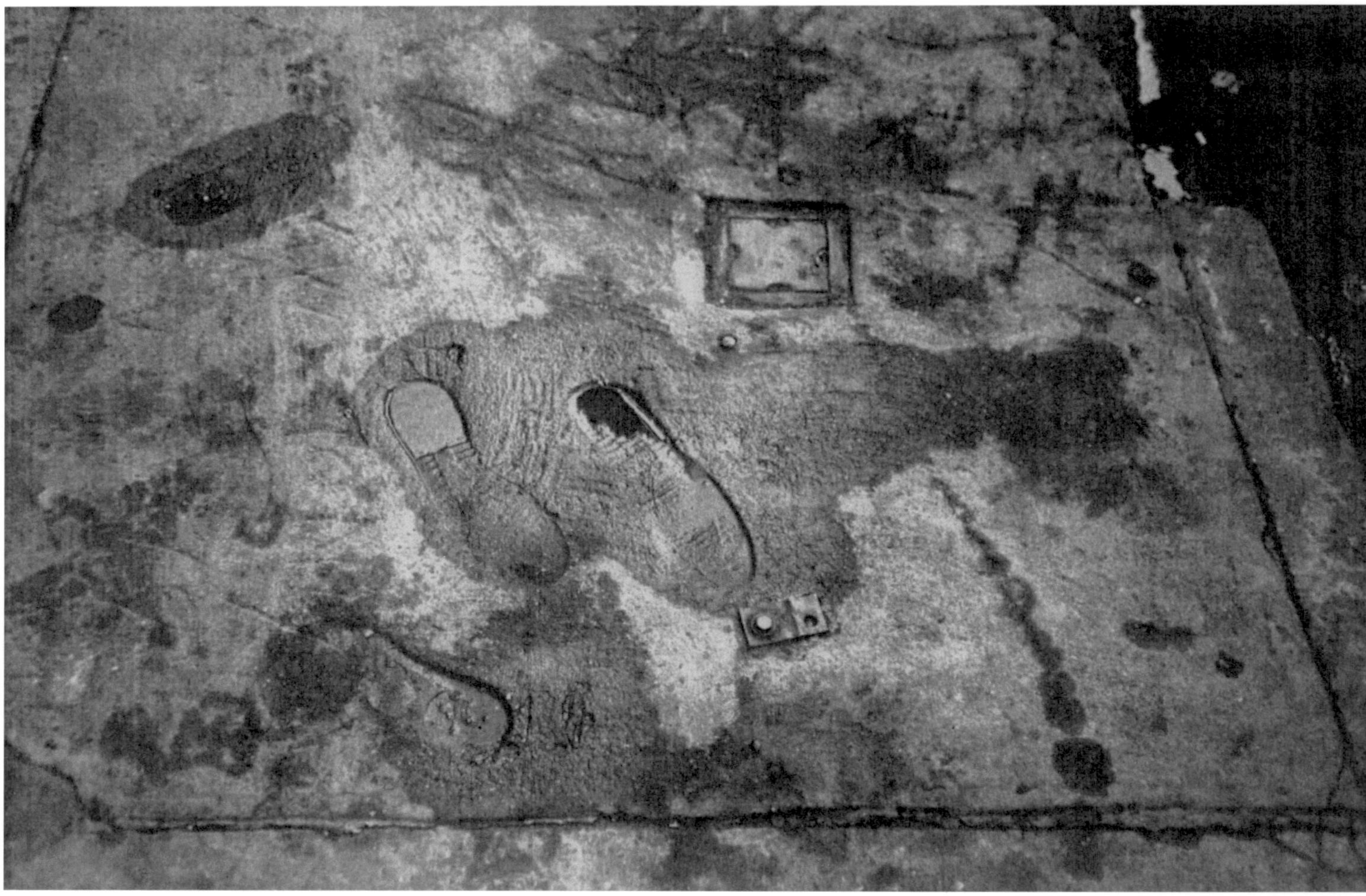

Plate 113 Stefan Brecht, double-page spread from *8th Avenue*, 1985

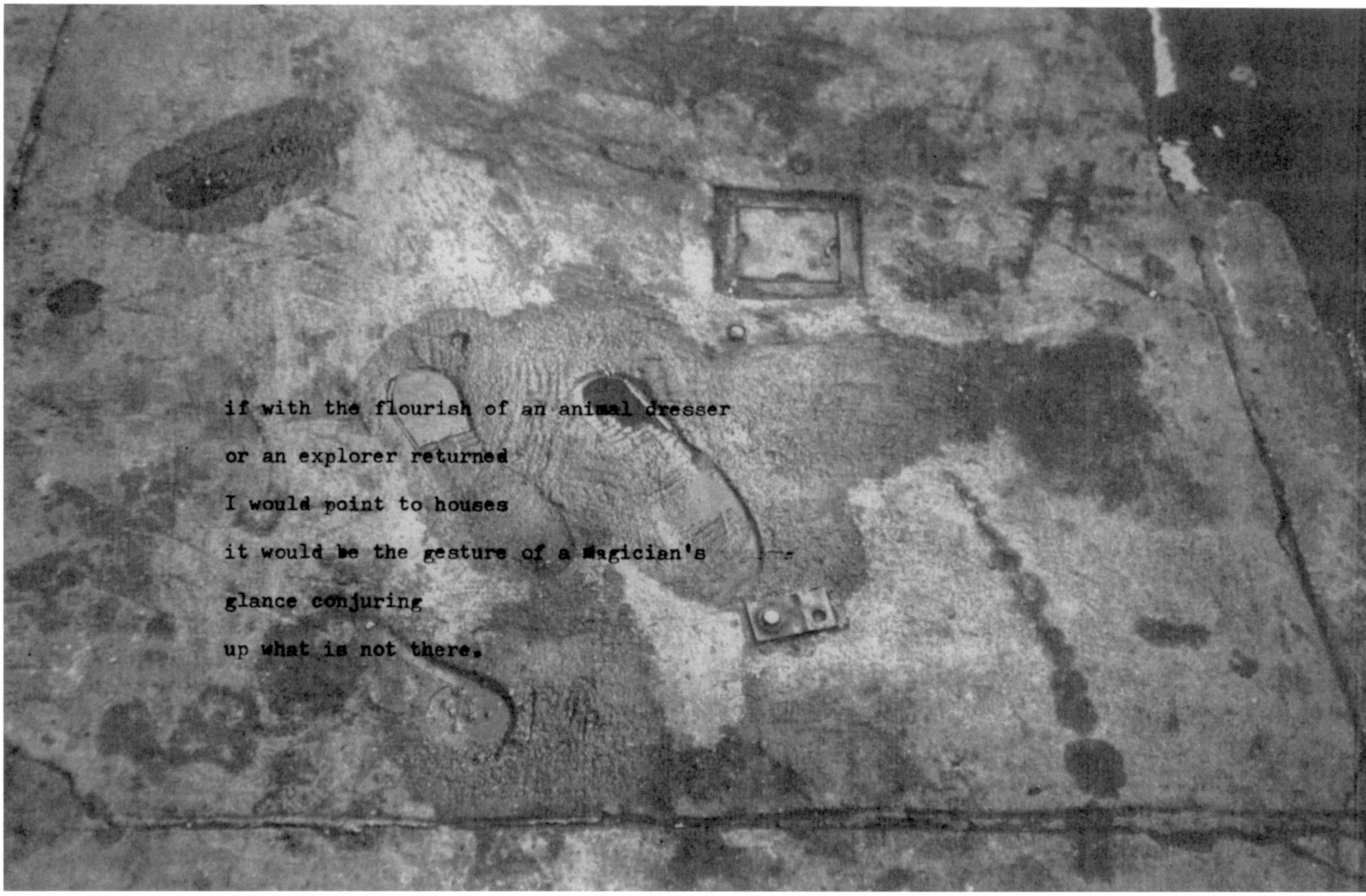
if with the flourish of an animal dresser
or an explorer returned
I would point to houses
it would be the gesture of a magician's
glance conjuring
up what is not there.

These questions, often identified with the term *public art*, have been the underlying focus of many artists since the mid-1970s. Yet debates over what constitutes public art have given rise not only to widely discrepant examples but to fundamentally opposing models and definitions of "publicness." Rosalyn Deutsche provides a sketch of two contrasting models:

> One is based on a strict division between an abstract, universalist public and a private arena of conflicting, partial interests. Champions of this concept treat public space as a realm of social plentitude that has declined—even vanished in a "postmodern" epoch of conflict, heterogeneity, and particularity. A contrasting position holds that a unitary public space is not "lost," but is, instead, what critic Bruce Robbins...calls a "phantom." In this view, the singular public space is a phantom because its claim to be fully inclusive is always an illusion. What is more, the very notion of an undivided social space is irremediably deceptive, constituted by disavowing plurality and conflict.[10]

Given the problems with the first model, Deutsche mounts a campaign to wrest the concept of public art away from such nostalgic and normative uses.[11] Though this is a project with which I am in sympathy, my own tack has been to cultivate terms at the other end of the spectrum, like *coterie*, that seem at first the self-evidently symptomatic opposite of the public or the community. Here the explicit partiality of coteries—social formations whose artistic or literary works eschew claims to universality and seem to address other members first—can allow for what I argue is paradoxically a robustly democratic politics.[12] Not succumbing to the myth of the once-great, now-fallen *public*, coterie writing or art can help anatomize the operations of the phantom public, can engage, that is, in an analogous attempt to critique the regressive and normative uses of the category of the public that Deutsche undertakes. Ultimately, though, I have doubts about whether it's possible to recode a familiar word like *public*, whose regressive meanings have become so ingrained. For this reason I'd like to consider the concept of the public only tangentially, under the slightly different heading *urbanism*—a term that, despite its problems, does not carry quite the same normative burden. By urbanism I do not mean the neutral or technocratic domain exhibited in much urban planning, but rather the diverse critical discourse produced by art critics, expatriate novelists, architects, social activists, historians, semioticians, geographers, and artists themselves.

Even if we frame the debate around urbanism, however, we are just as certain to encounter a fundamental division between symptomatic and critical modes of involvement with the city. David Harvey, for instance, sees Cindy Sherman's pp. 120–23 *Untitled Film Stills* (1977–80) as symptomatic of the regressive transformation of urban space brought on by neoliberalism.[13] Deutsche, by contrast, mounts a strong case that

Sherman's photographs are critical interventions; she claims they use the city as a stage in order to "appropriate and make visible the conventions that structure the cinematic images of femininity: lighting, gesture, pose, camera angle, focus, framing, address to the viewer."[14] In regards to this debate, one might traditionally imagine a spectrum with two poles: totality, on one side, and contingent identity (or positionality), on the other. The former is associated with a belief in the possibility of accurate and objective overviews (Harvey's position), and the latter with the claim that views will be inescapably tied to their viewers (Deutsche's). While Deutsche's argument strikes me as the more persuasive of the two, what fascinates me about many of the works in *Mixed Use, Manhattan* is how they can be understood to remap the terms of this debate.

In the midst of the urban and economic crisis of the 1970s, James Nares, an art student having just arrived from London, produced a film called *Pendulum* pp. 259–61 (1976). The film tracks what looks to be a concrete wrecking ball as it swings from a second-story walkway traversing Staple Street, in Tribeca, just where it opens onto Jay Street, which runs only two blocks, bookended by fin-de-siècle steel-frame masonry buildings (lofts and warehouses). These are the kinds of buildings that might have seemed scandalously new in James's time but that had already become antiquated and largely abandoned by the 1970s. The setting is deserted, as it would have had to be for the filming of such an extremely heavy concrete ball swinging precariously through public space.[15] But though we may periodically return to the dangers of the experiment and the social isolation required for it, *Pendulum* doesn't appear to have been intended as an audacious, confrontational public action. It rather asks us to study, even lose ourselves, in the wrecking ball's hypnotic motion. Over the course of the film's ample seventeen minutes and fifteen seconds, the angles and orientations change repeatedly. This denaturalizes any single perspective: from Jay Street (where the ball appears only at the end of its arc); from eye level; ground level; axially; from the perpendicular; the oblique, above (from the walkway), above even that (from the building *overlooking* the walkway); and finally from the orientation of the ball itself, as it glides through the air. Many of the sequences mesmerize: the ball rises toward us to fill the entire screen and then recedes, or cuts through shadows into visibility, seen against the backdrop of the sky above rooftops, stretching out at the far end of its arc against the downtown industrial architecture. Here we are immersed in a duration and movement not unlike motion-study sequences associated with Structuralist cinema. Even though Nares's film is not the record of a guerrilla event, it refuses to let the viewer forget that with any slight miscalculation or equipment failure the elegant pendulum could become a crushing, deadly menace.[16] And this leads us to the heart of the film, where we find ourselves, in effect, keeping time with what looks like a wrecking ball: the isolation required for the film's occurrence and the deindustrialization that turned this section of Lower Manhattan into a ghost town are the same conditions that will eventually

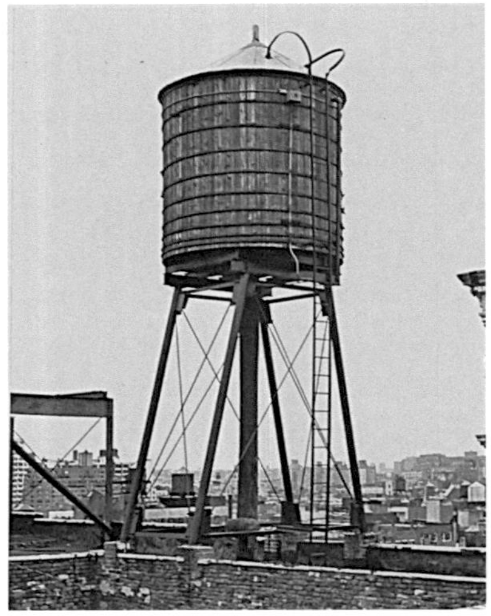
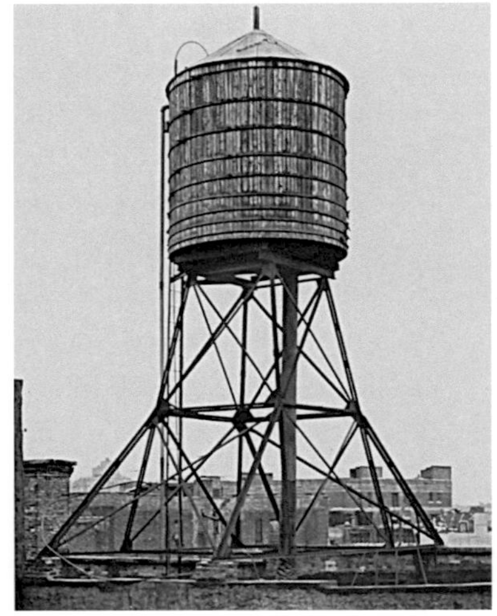
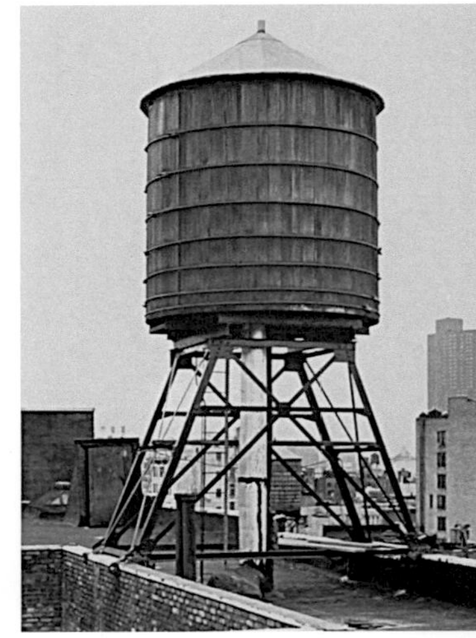
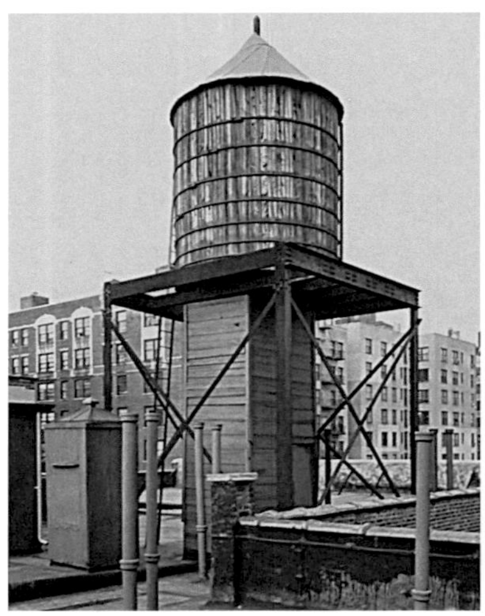
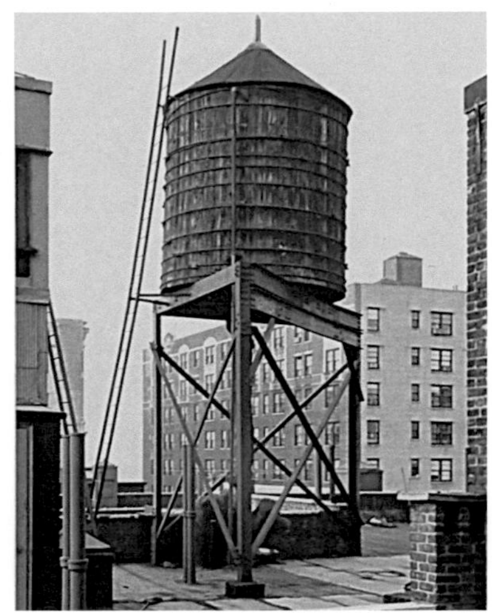
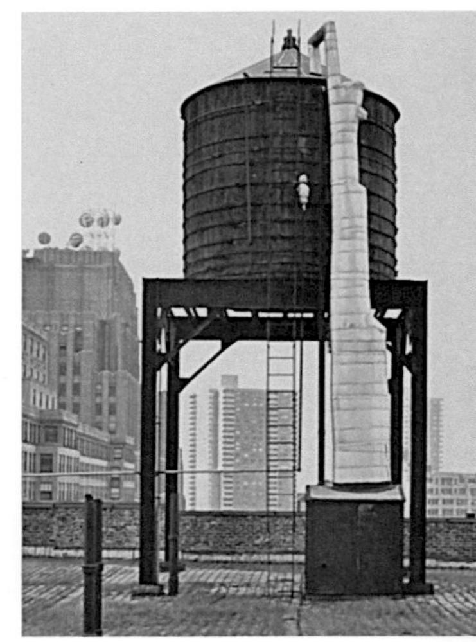
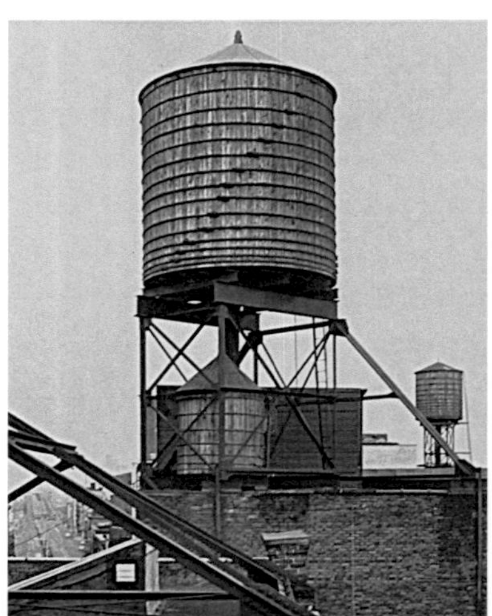
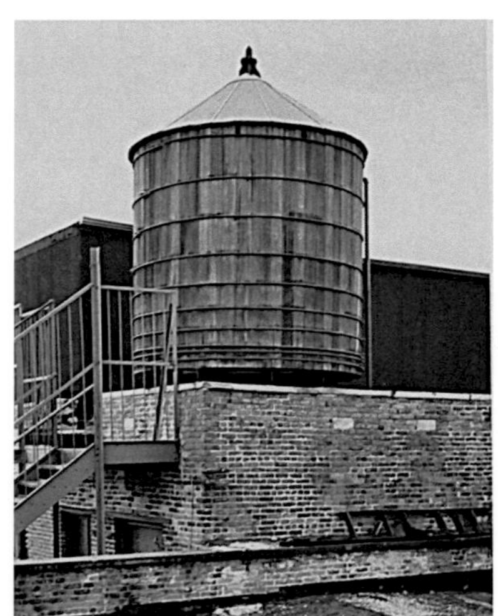
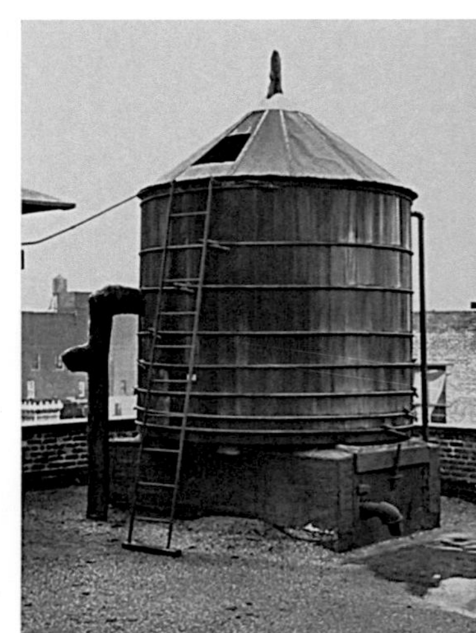

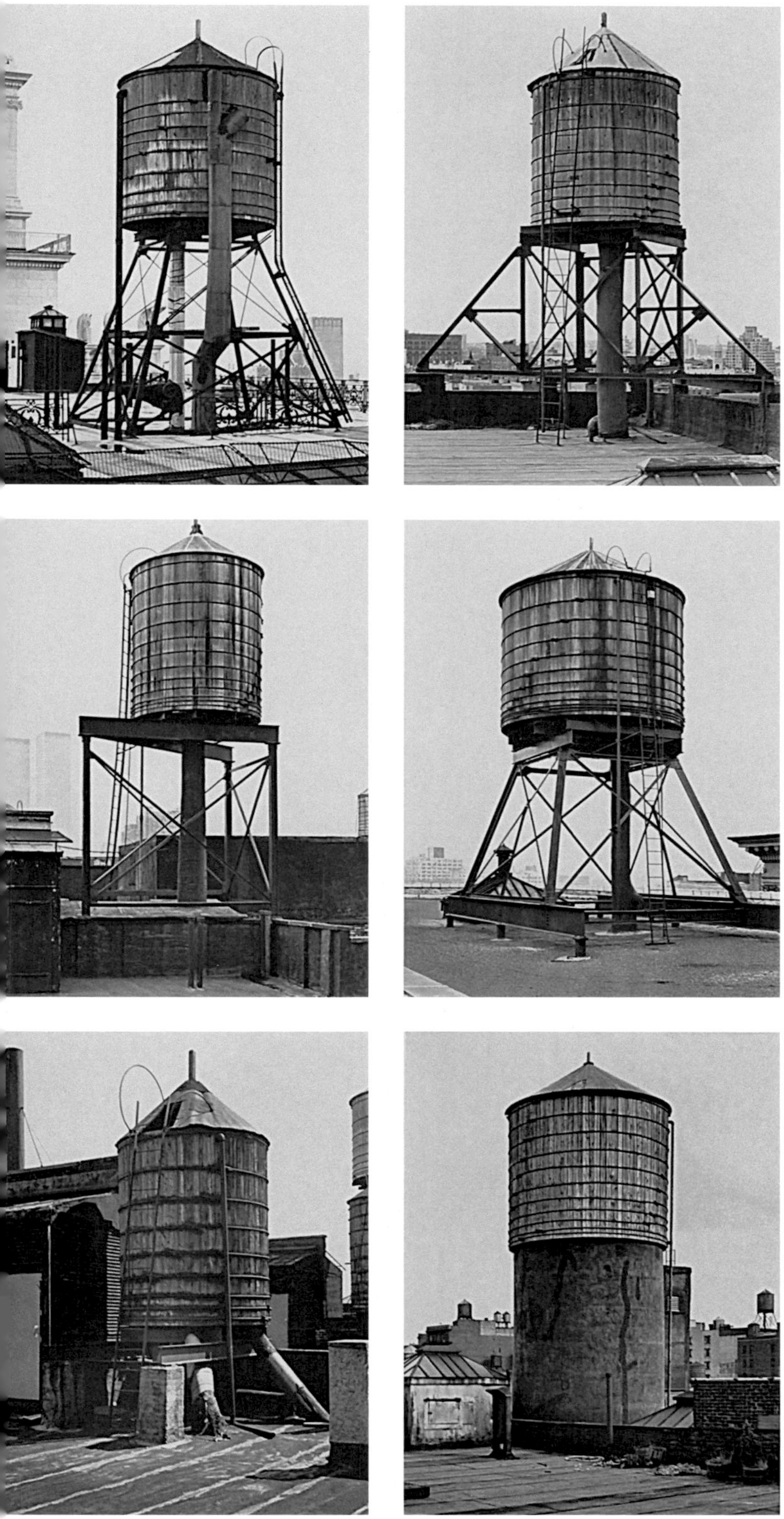

Plate 114 Bernd and Hilla Becher, *New York Water Towers*, 1988

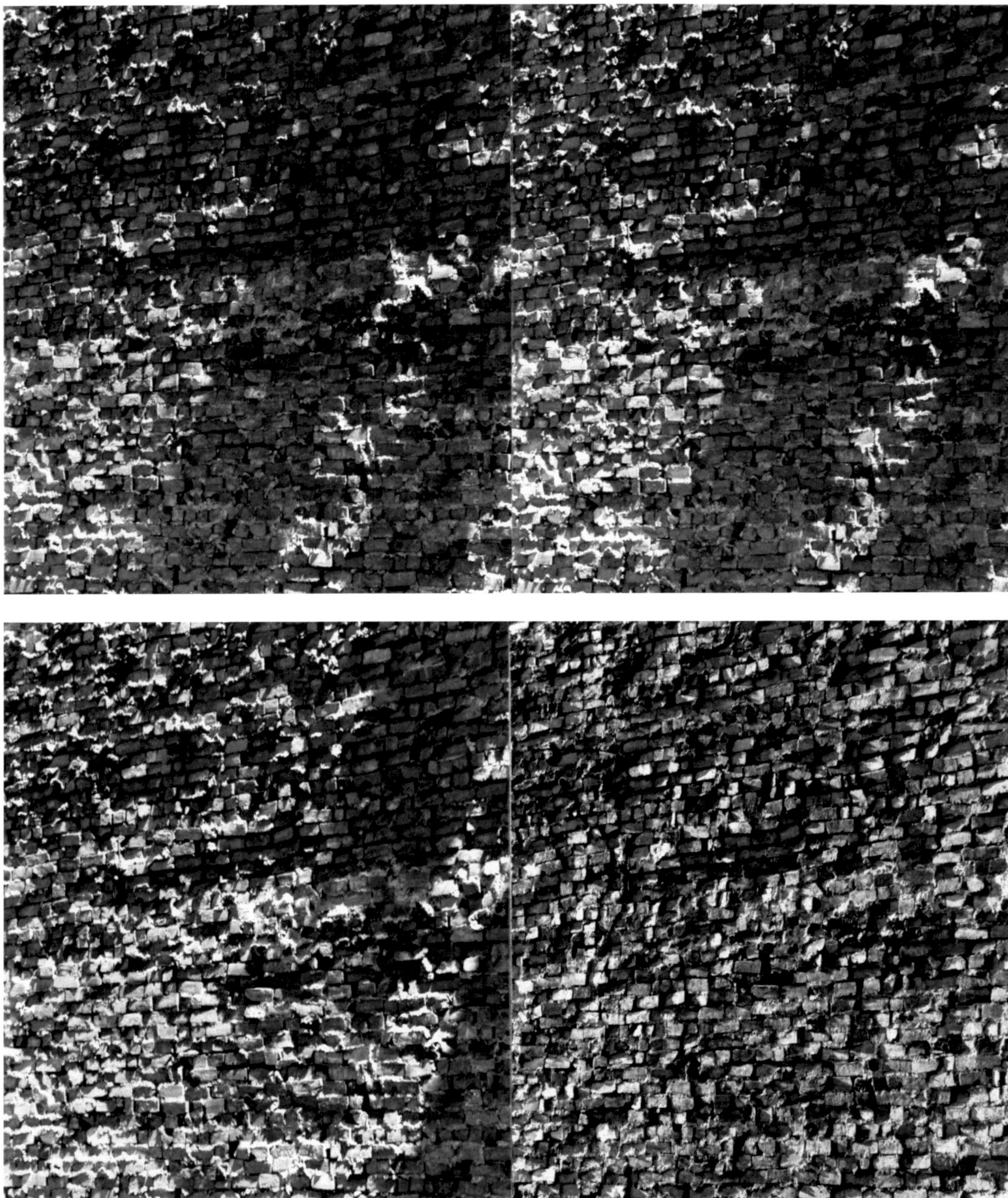

Plate 115 Sol LeWitt, *Brick Wall*, 1977

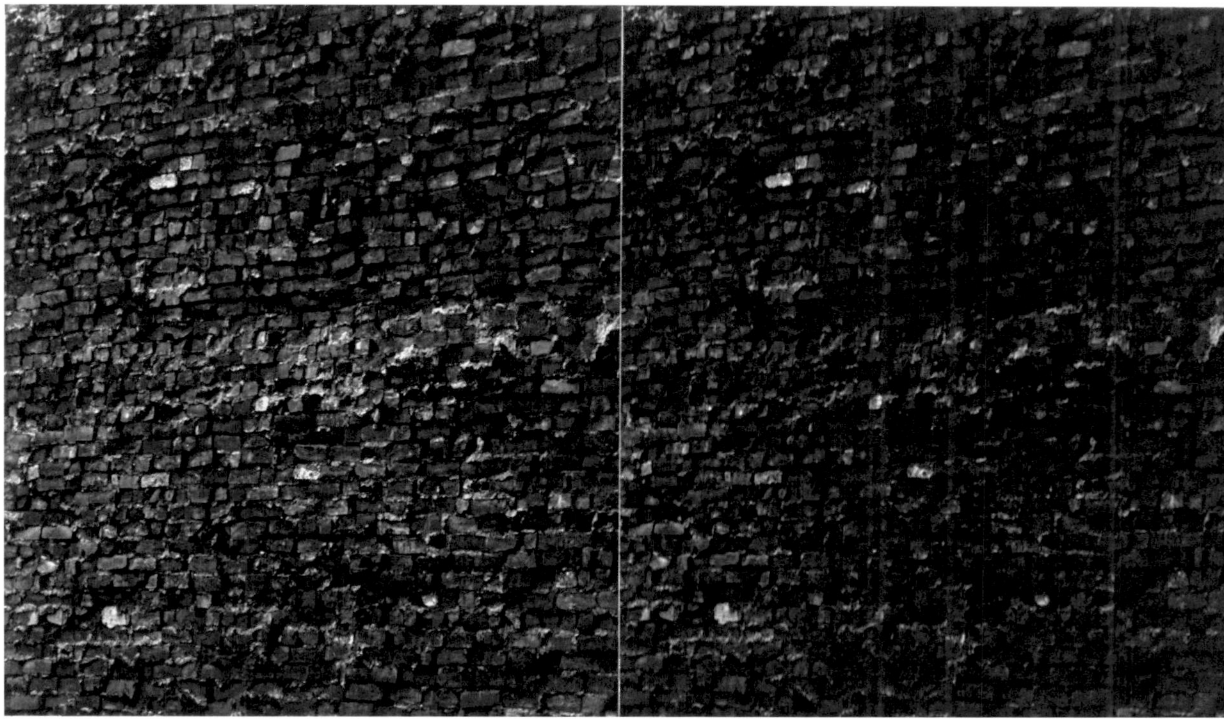

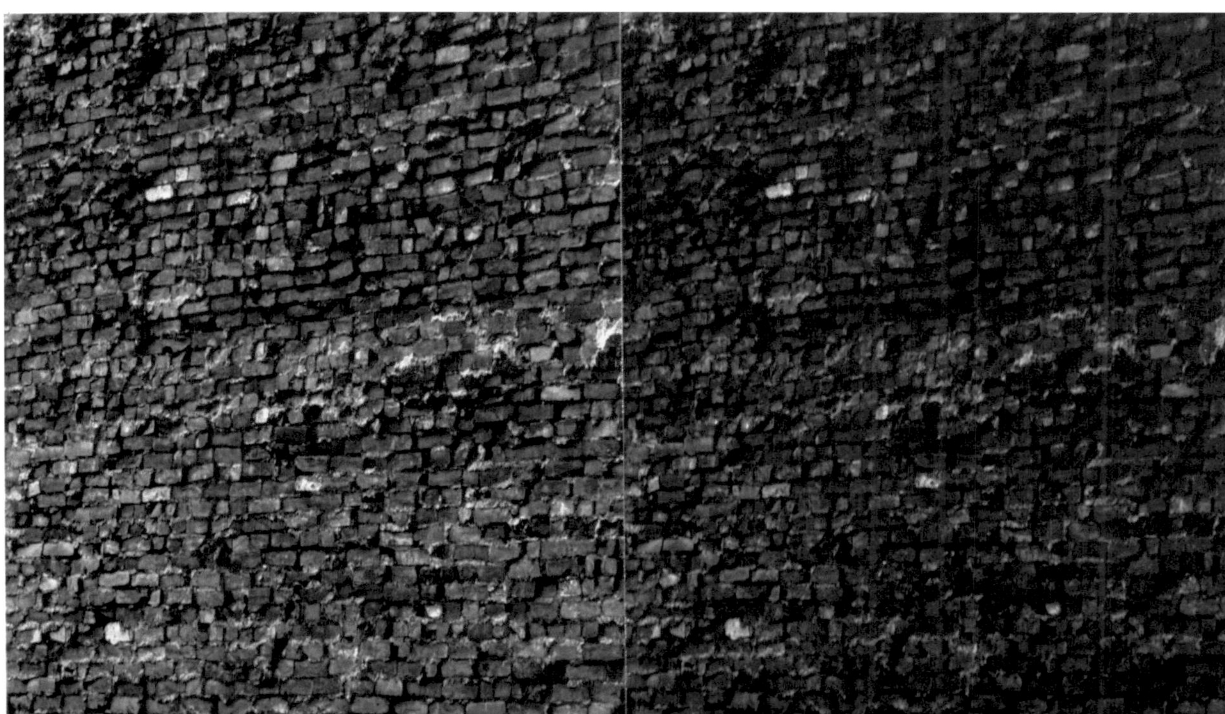

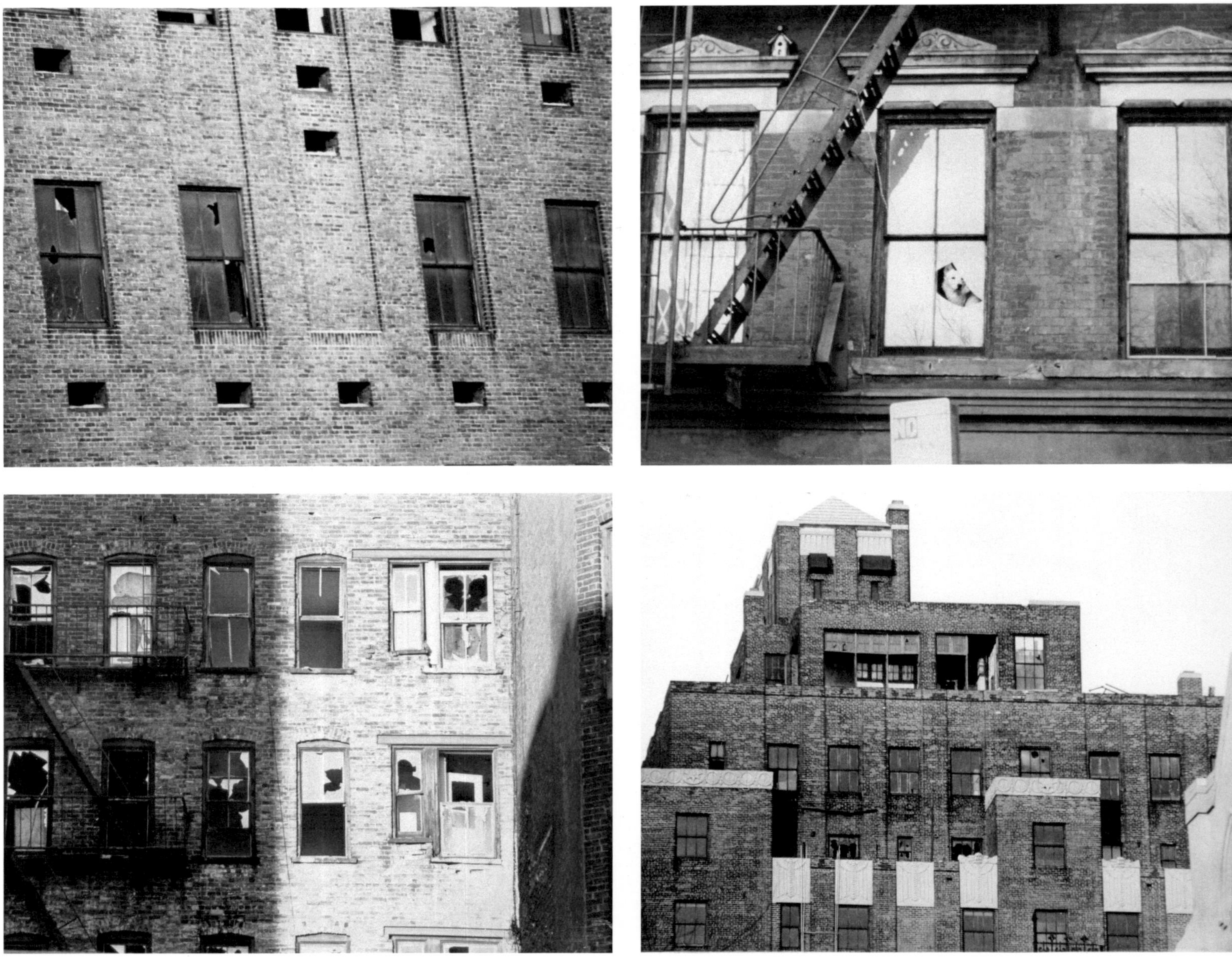

Plate 116 Gordon Matta-Clark, *Window Blow-Out*, 1973

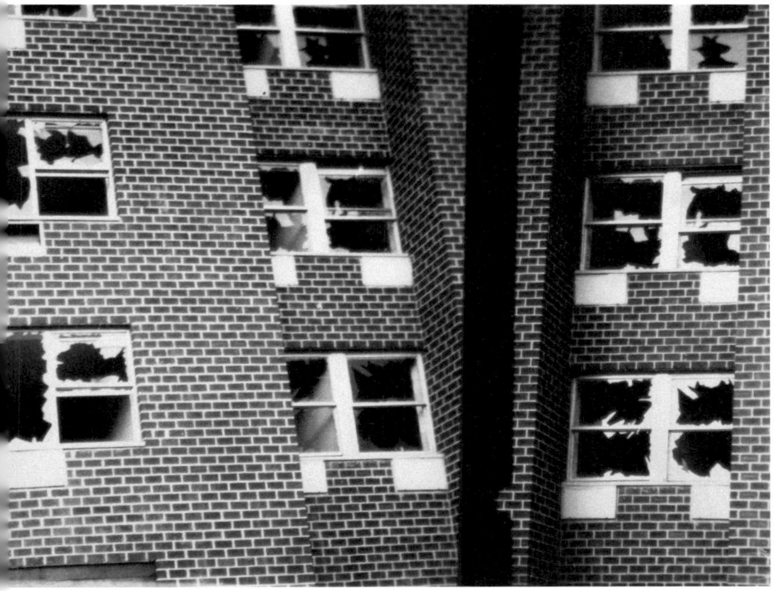

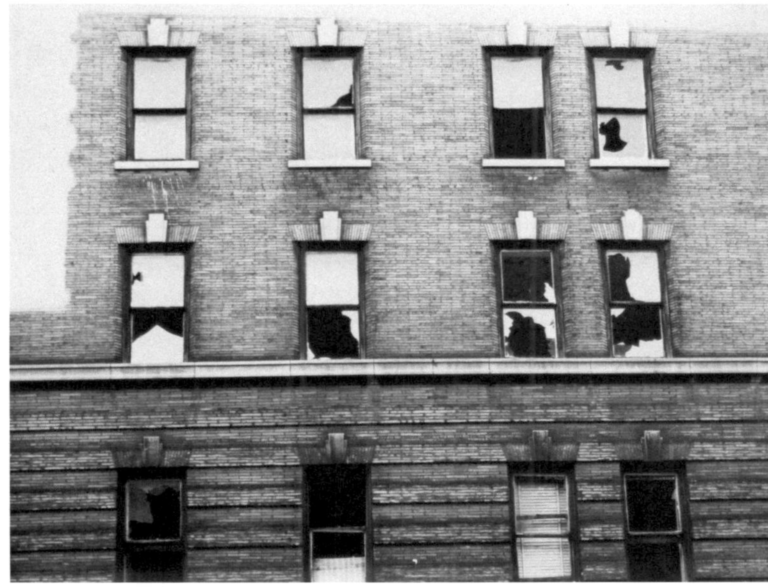

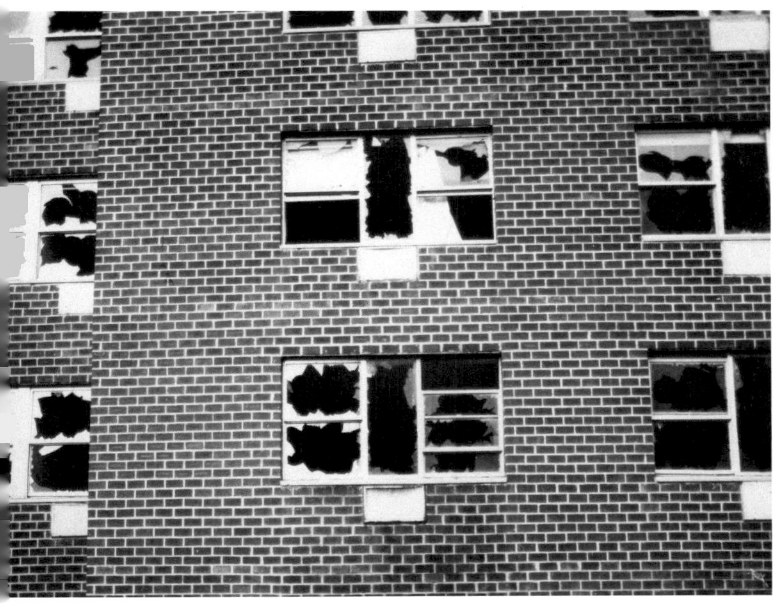

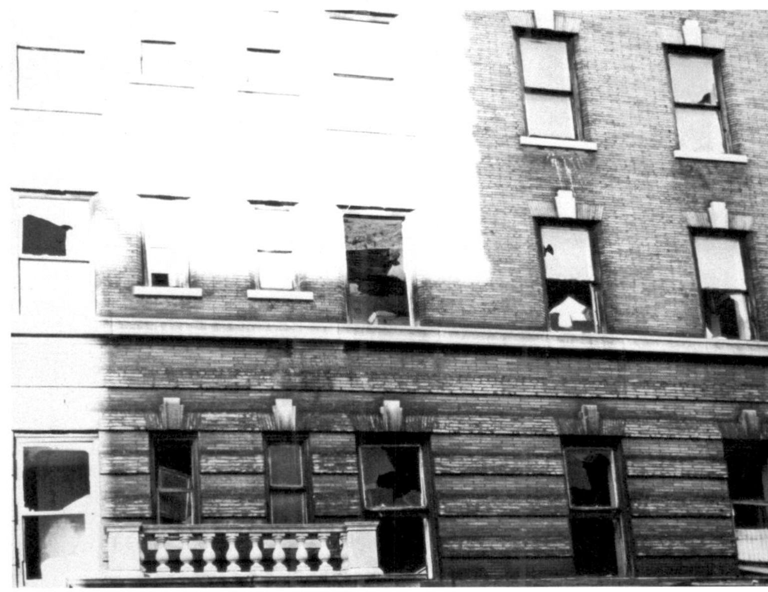

be addressed by the ball, itself an agent of historical destruction, and a keeper of time.[17] What is difficult to place about *Pendulum*, then, is its seamless integration of motion study and urban allegory, structuralist fascination with moving mass and activist attention to transformations in the built environment—the former seeming to influence the latter, as we lose ourselves in the film's mesmerizing force and gradually read this force in relation to its site.

Other sites that host, and seem to invite, both exploration and removal are evident in the work of Charles Simonds. These, by contrast, are less fully intact than those experienced in *Pendulum*. While some are literal ruins—heaps of bricks from recent demolitions in now-vacant lots—others are just unresolved "seams" between functional buildings: gaps, cracks, ambiguous interstructures. In overlapping areas such as these, Simonds sets himself up—clad in a puffy down parka, tweezers in hand, mounds of clay excavated on-site—and begins to model (in clay) one of the miniature temporary sculpture-cities he began constructing primarily on the Lower East Side,
p. 262 in the early 1970s. Simonds describes the project in the 1972 film *Dwellings*, a documentary on his work shot by David Troy, claiming that the structures are designed for "an imaginary group of little people who are migrating through the city...each dwelling tells part of the story of these people...including what they believe...some of the dwellings are ritual places...ruins...settlements."

p. 263 In a later film on Simonds made by Rudy Burckhardt, *Dwellings Winter* (1974), we see a jarring image of a burning car in the very lot where he is working. Eventually, firefighters arrive and put out the fire and restore disorder, while Simonds, unfazed, quietly tweezers-in tiny bricks to his emerging structure. Scenes like this—which typically end with a long pan of the completed artwork in its blighted context—suggest that Simonds ultimately winds up with his own *spatially manageable* ruin, contained within a sprawling, uncontainable, life-size ruin—the neighborhood itself. Periodically, groups of curious onlookers gather and ask questions. In the David Troy film, for instance, they (and therefore we) are told that Simonds's fictional little people are "dependent upon the flow of life around them and the kind of treatment they receive" and that "most people try to protect the little people." A few onlookers pause on the ethical implications of this injunction: "It's wrong to break them," one teenage boy announces for the camera, the tone of the question becomes that of the statement. The David Troy film, like most of Simonds's early critics, presents the art as redemptive. His work, in this regard, is viewed as exemplary: a creative intervention in a wasteland that incites initial curiosity in onlookers who were previously passive but have now been prompted into action and social responsibility. "These dreamlike miniature places are ephemeral and timeless," Lucy Lippard suggests, "but they also act as specific social metaphors, sparks for more permanent reconstructions of abandoned neighborhoods."[18]

Part of this impetus toward action stems from what critics take as clear references to the architecture of previous cultures. Here, again, is Lippard:

> Simonds's personal fantasies expand into political consciousness-raisers for his street audiences in part because by reinstating a sense of their pasts he allows them to identify with their own patches of the city and to consider molding their own futures. His tiny adobe houses and sensuous clay landscapes are a surprisingly universal image. In workers' neighborhoods in New York they recall Puerto Rico; in Paris, Tunisia; in Germany, Turkey.[19]

This reading mobilizes history into a seamless and universal source of identifications: each present viewer finding his cultural past is thus inspired and empowered to begin neighborhood-changing activities. But if Simonds's work does provide a "dreamlike peephole into other times and possibilities,"[20] what makes us assume that such times and places must be understood as purely empowering? The work in its context could also be read as an analogy between past and present ruins, between colonized or eradicated societies (like those of Native Americans in the Southwest) and current ones visibly undergoing crisis.[21] Simonds, thus, evokes a distant, anthropological future, a vantage from which one might "look back," paradoxically, onto the present—a kind of postapocalyptic temporality that invites us to imagine Manhattan itself as precisely the kind of ancient-day ruin it hosts within its crumbling infrastructure. This displacement casts each of Simonds's viewers as a future anthropologist, while each "intervention" emerges with a cool finality, the powers of removal figured not in generational, but in nearly geologic, terms.

Who, then, are the agents of removal? Are they knowable forces within the economy, familiar narratives of outsourcing and deindustrialization? Are they periodic reappraisals of the idea of the functional city? Or is removal's logic always alien, distant, mysterious? There is, in fact, a long history in the United States both of imagining narratives at the sites of mute anthropological ruins and projecting current conflicts onto those ruins. Perhaps the classic document of such reanimation and displacement is William Cullen Bryant's poem "The Prairies," begun on his 1832 trip to the wilds of Illinois, a state then just on the cusp of settlement by the westward movement of the seaboard population. Contemplating more thoroughgoing white settlement of this region and the consequent displacement of Native Americans, Bryant projects this drama onto a previous struggle between these Native Americans and the race of "mound-builders" they were initially thought to have displaced:[22] "The red man came— / The roaming hunter tribes, warlike and fierce, / And the mound-builders vanished from the earth."[23] What is most fascinating about this poem, though, is the distanced commentary Bryant uses to manage this transition:

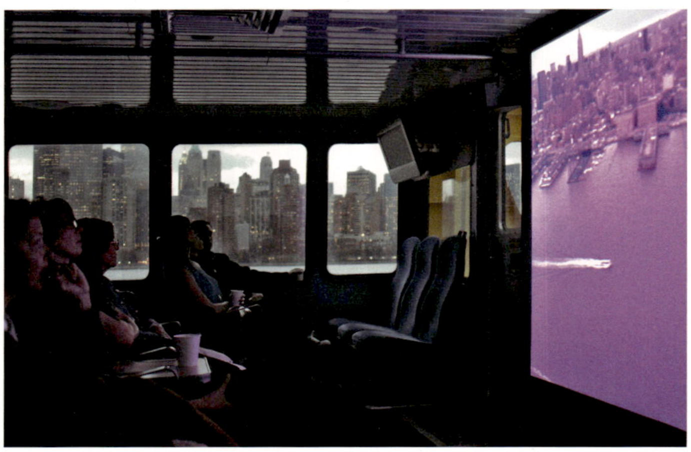

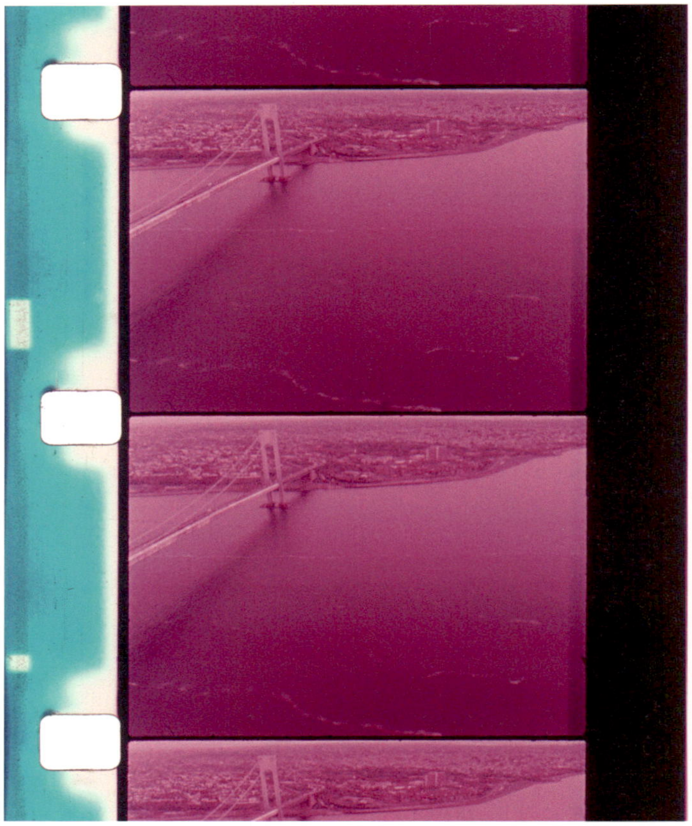

Muhheakantuck—Everything Has a Name screening on board a water taxi on the Hudson River, New York, March 2008. Photograph by Matthew Buckingham

Matthew Buckingham, stills from *Muhheakantuck—Everything Has a Name,* 2003. 16mm film; color; sound; 40 min.

> Thus change the forms of being. Thus arise
> Races of living things, glorious in strength,
> And perish, as the quickening breath of God
> Fills them, or is withdrawn.[24]

Abandoned mounds, like the crumbling bricks of Native American buildings, give us the occasion to contemplate the glories of this sequence of risings and perishings—regardless of whether or not we want to trace them back to a breathing God. What is unacceptable to a reader in 2010, of course, is the amazing passivity of Bryant's formulation—the implication that we are always somewhere off-screen when the violence of succession goes down.

Matthew Buckingham seeks to address both American historiography of this sort and its specific relation to Manhattan in his film *Muhheakantuck—Everything* p. 250 *Has a Name* (2003), which consists of a single view, shot from a helicopter as it flies from the Verrazano Narrows Bridge, up the Hudson River to a point near Ossining, New York, where it turns around and flies back.[25] The film is accompanied by a recording of Buckingham's own voice, as he meditates on historiography, violence, and language, among other topics, that seem to unfold with the landscape below.

In the context of urbanist artworks that seek to reframe our experience of the island and, in particular, to figure those looming "powers of removal" that lurk within built or crumbling architectural sites, Buckingham's film represents something of an end-move. The history I've sketched so far—James's lament about modernization at the turn of the century, Nares's and Simonds's various engagements with deindustrialization in the 1970s—implicitly accepts some version of built Manhattan (emerging or declining) as a given. Buckingham instead asks us to contemplate the *previous* removal of the Lenape tribe that made the settling of the city possible. In the film, we experience "Manhattan" only as a slowly passing and distant constellation of dully colored slabs (seen in grainy tint of magenta). The city is shown rising above a river, and while we recognize this river to be the Hudson, we are reminded by Buckingham that it was once called Muhheakantuck, the "River that Flows in Two Directions" (based on the fact that saltwater flows *up* the river about 150 miles).[26] As Michel de Certeau writes:

> [Names] detach themselves from the places they were supposed to define and serve as imaginary meeting-points on itineraries which, as metaphors, they determine for reasons that are foreign to their original value but may be recognized or not by passers-by. A strange toponymy that is detached from actual places and flies high over the city like a foggy geography of "meanings" held in suspension, directing the physical deambulations below.[27]

What de Certeau has in mind are the names of urban places (Parisian names, for example, like Saint-Pères, Concorde, and Place de L'Étoile) that are not up for contestation per se but have become uncoupled from any set or family of descriptive attributes, any definitive collection of associations—this because the experiences that might be associated with them are simply too broad to pin to any narrow collection of images.[28] If this is a problem associated with all proper names (and indeed all language), then ostensibly *urban* proper names stage it in a particularly vivid way: press just slightly on their promised concreteness and one arrives at an abyss of contingent association. Buckingham, however, aims to take this problem a step further, by imagining the deactivation of a name like "the Hudson," which has served as a gathering place for such associations for hundreds of years.[29]

But before he can do this, Buckingham must first address his own vantage point and claim to knowledge. Accordingly, the opening lines of his voice-over initiate the kind of masterful overview of the river and the city that the helicopter's aerial perspective seems to offer: "The dream of vertical ascent and hovering flight was first expressed in China in the form of a toy—a bamboo dragonfly that lifted straight up though the air when spun quickly." This dream, we are soon told, is one "of suspending time through distance, of cutting oneself off from the ordinary measures of time—surface time." In criticizing this fantasy, Buckingham situates his own journey not only up the Hudson but through the central harbors and canals of urbanist discourse, where the possibilities and limitations of suspended, vertical, even totalizing views of cities have generated some of the most important debates. Three of the texts I have already referenced seem especially relevant: first, de Certeau's previously quoted "Walking in the City," a semiotic account of urban walks as potentially subversive speech acts ("parole") within the "langue" of the city, which begins with a rumination on the view from the top of the World Trade Center. Next, David Harvey's appropriation (in *The Condition of Postmodernity*) of that same elevated view toward ends conspicuously different from de Certeau's—that is, toward a more singularly economic and totalizing picture of the city. And finally, Rosalyn Deutsche's *critique* of Harvey, which highlights the difference between de Certeau and Harvey's desired *uses* of de Certeau, as well as pointing out problems in Harvey's extension of his symptomatic and singularly economic account of postmodernity to the domain of art practice.

Buckingham's self-positioning in this debate is complex. Statements throughout the film suggest his identification with de Certeau's model of daily life. Buckingham has told us, echoing de Certeau, that "silence occludes the ordinary...the everyday," but that "the significance of past events appears in these ordinary moments and people." Therefore, for Buckingham, the quotidian becomes "the limit of understanding, and... speaking of the past." This implies that the film might be understood as a *corrective* to the dream of vertical ascent, with both its surface time and its totalizing or synoptic view: a newly calibrated temporal measure that might help us *unlearn* the overly familiar (surface) cultural image of Manhattan, great modern city on the river explored by Henry Hudson in 1609.[30] But Buckingham's recalibration of New York's

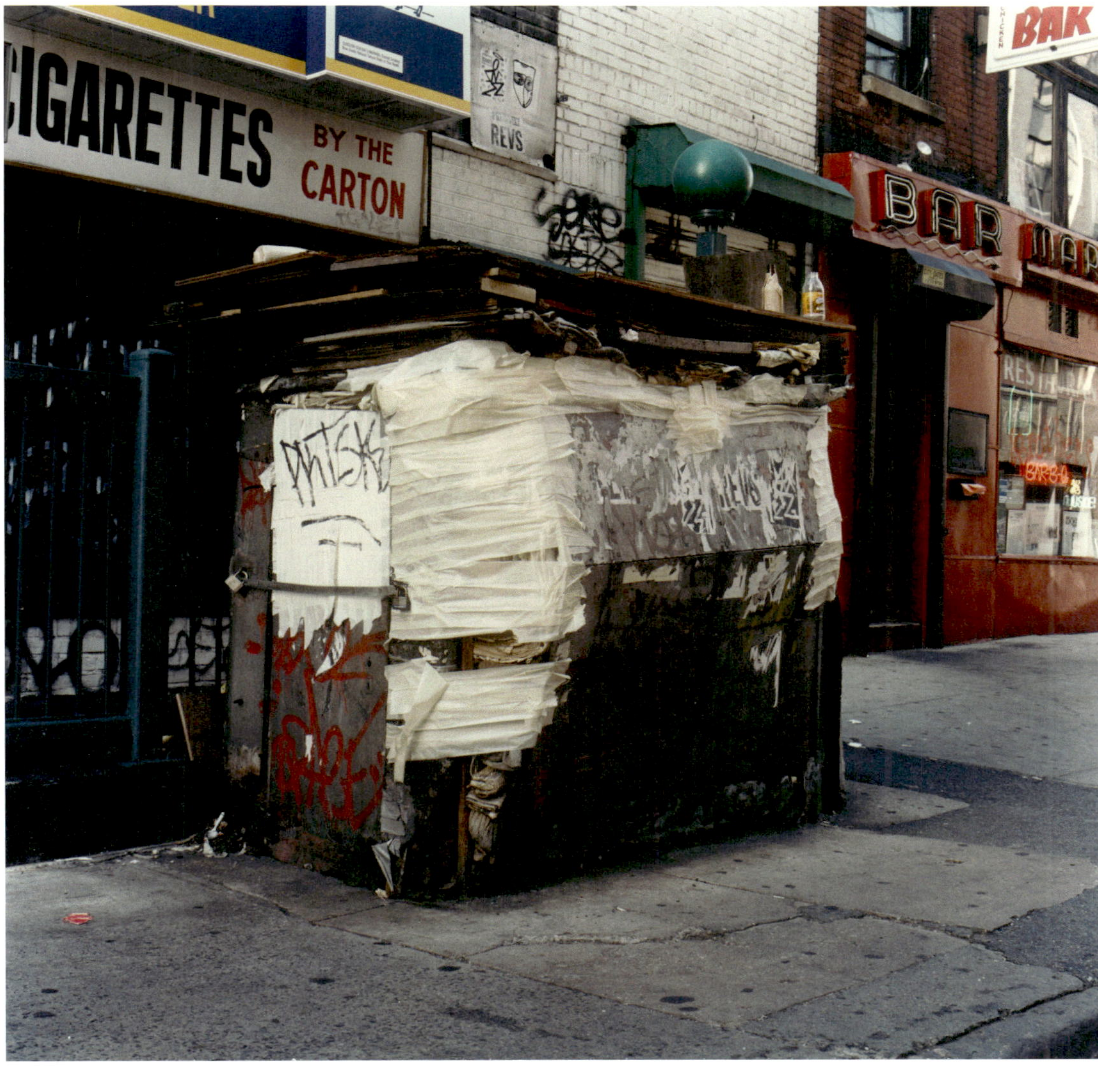

Plate 117 Moyra Davey, *Newsstand No. 1*, 1994

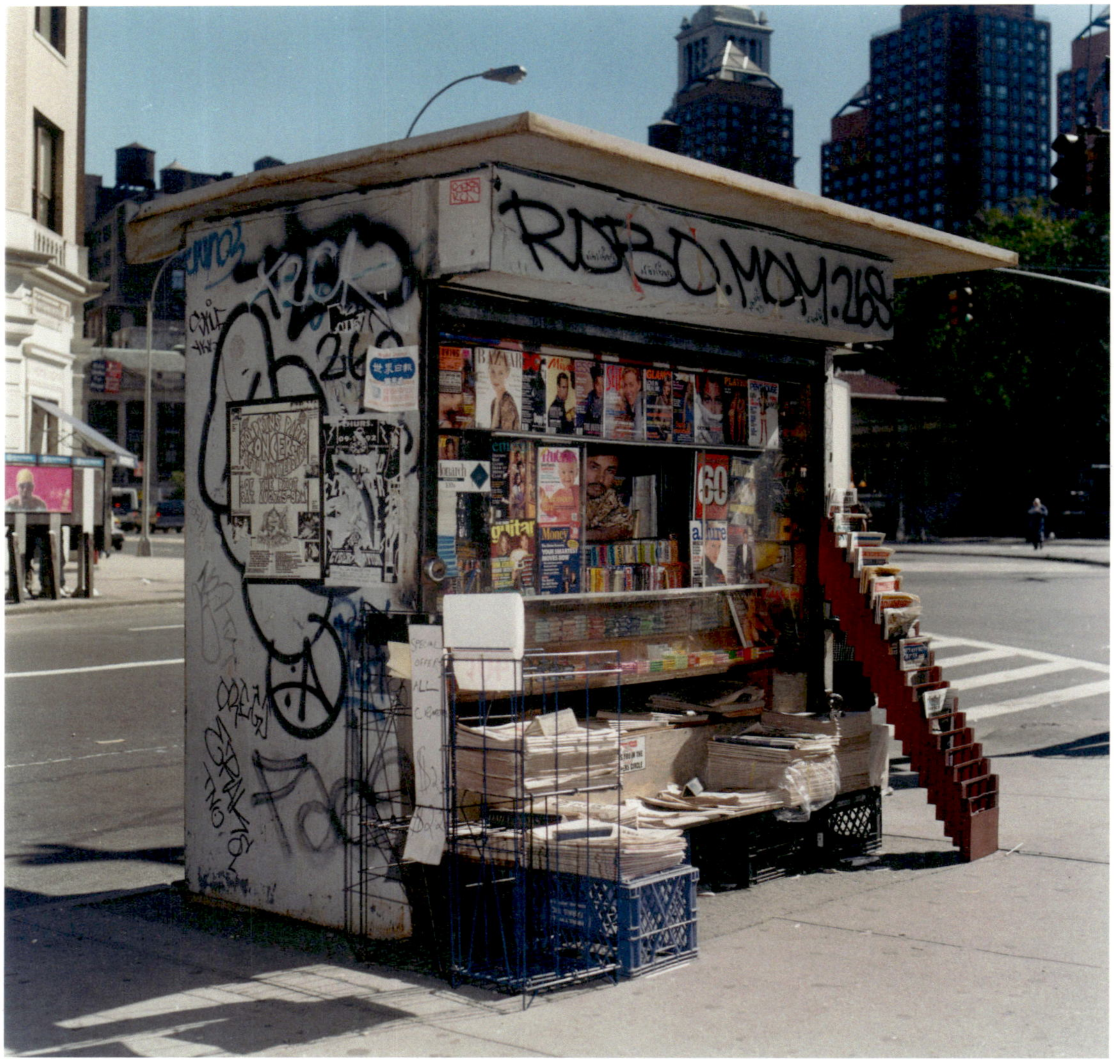

Plate 118 Moyra Davey, *Newsstand No. 19*, 1994

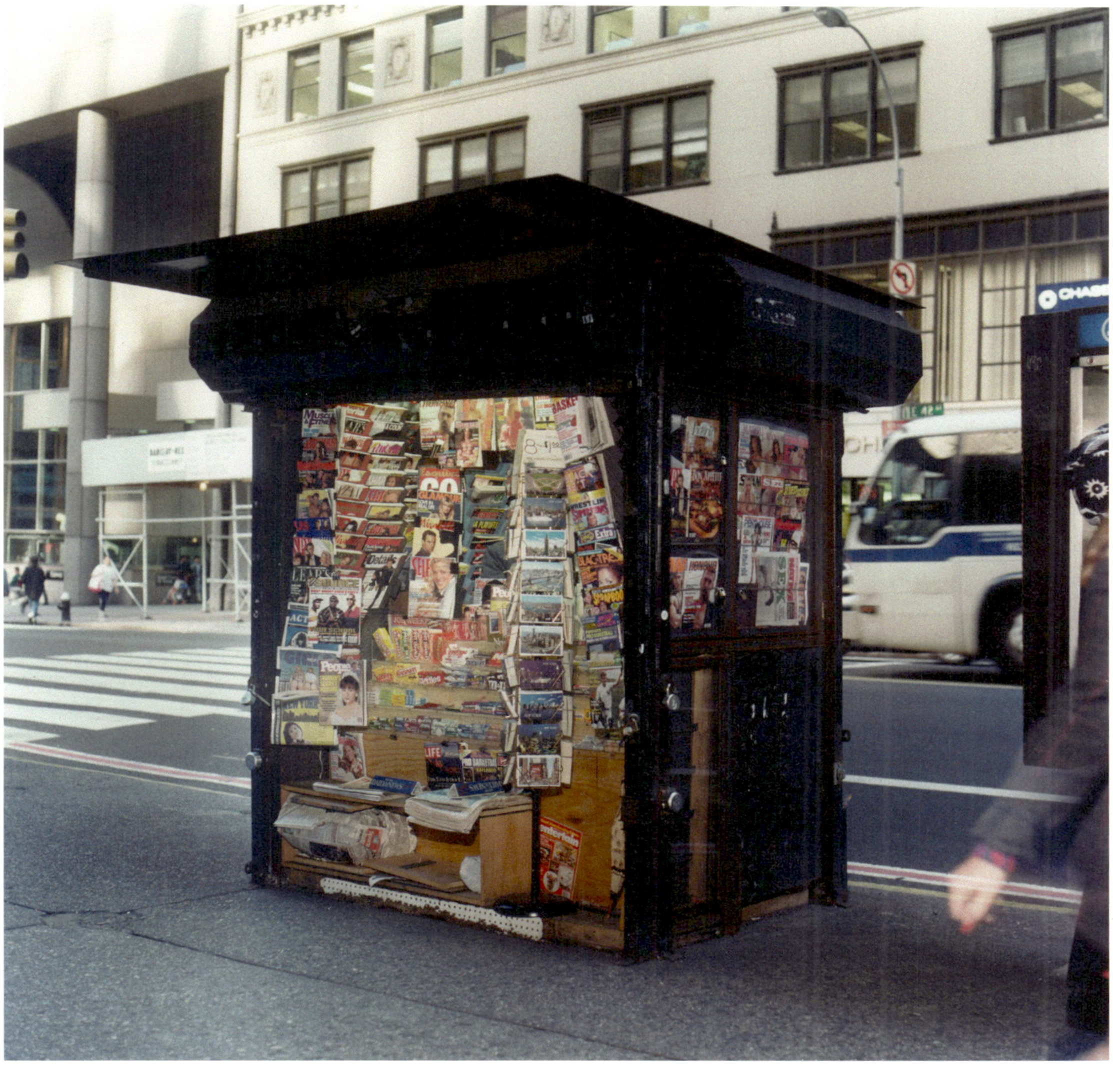

Plate 119 Moyra Davey, *Newsstand No. 21*, 1994

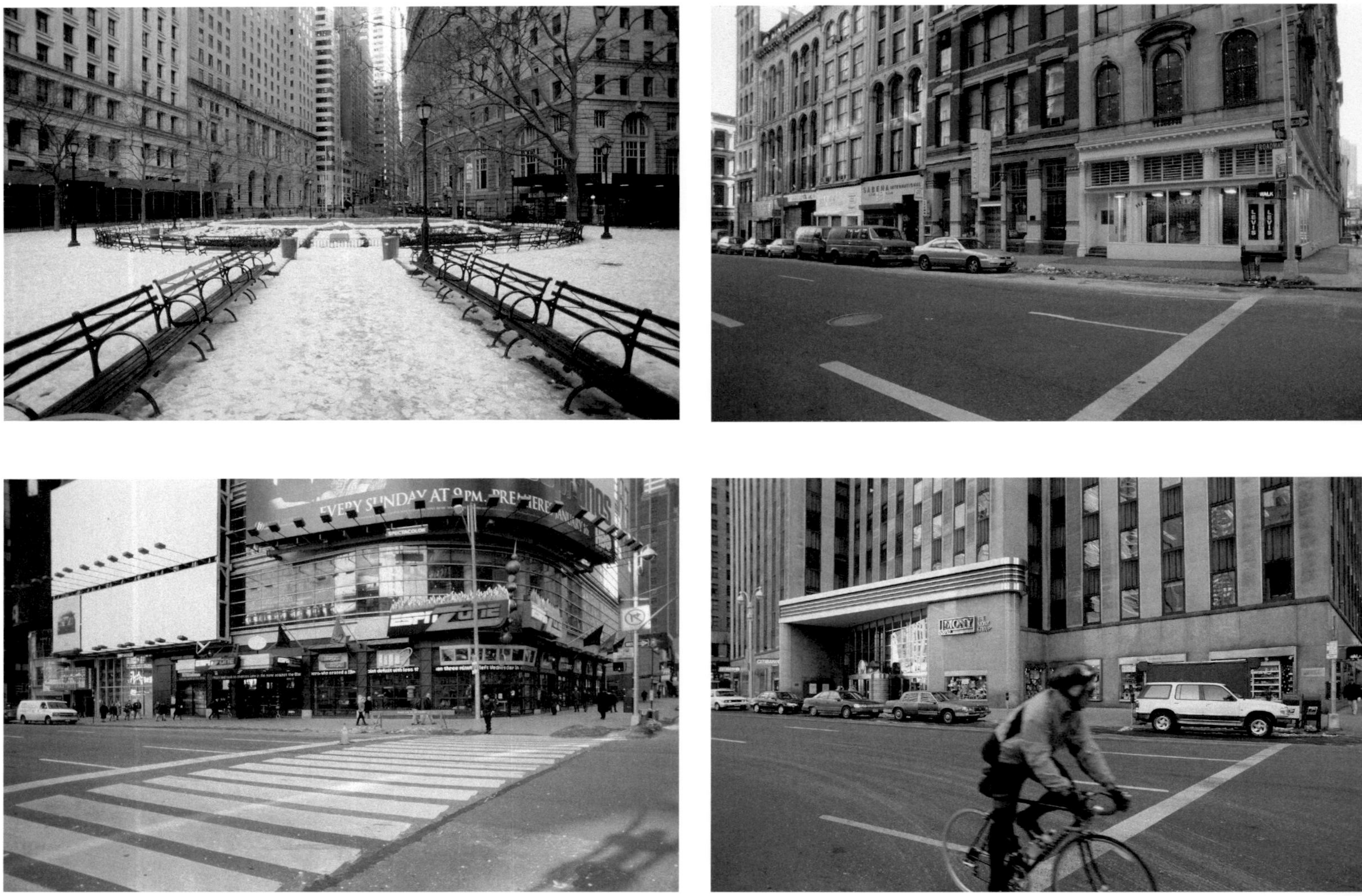

Plate 120 Matthew Buckingham, *One Side of Broadway*, 2005

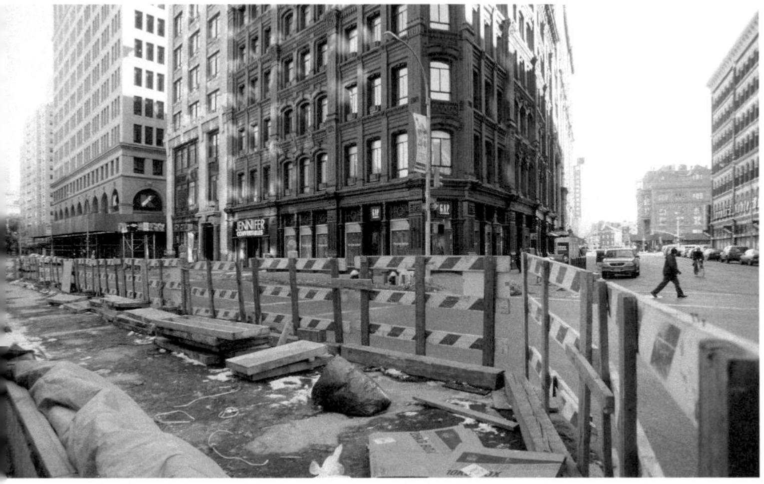

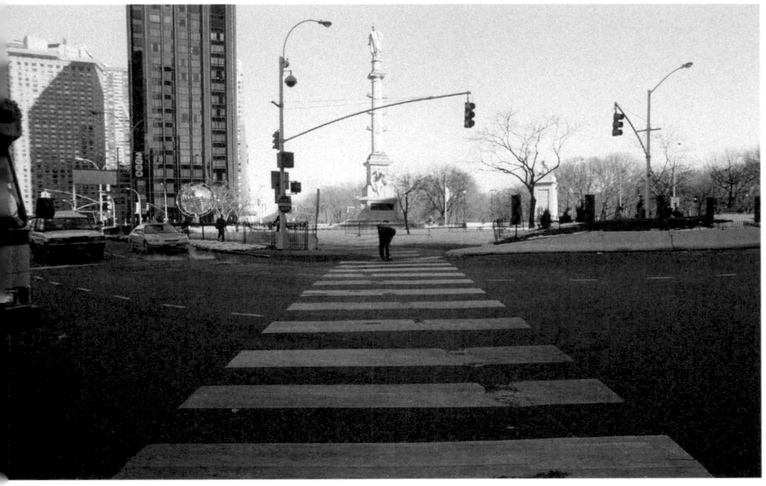

time and history will have to win out over just the sort of distanced and abstracted view he has brought in for questioning. Almost perversely, his entire film presents only a slowly moving overview of the city, its environs, and a substantial swath of territory north of it along the river.

Perhaps, then, we are to take the intervention of *Muhheakantuck* not as the literal view it offers (and implicitly critiques), but as the story it reframes. From this vantage, *Muhheakantuck* avoids the pitfalls of Russell Shorto's *The Island at the Center of the World*, in which New Amsterdam's nascent capitalism is seen as inherently aligned with progressive tolerance.[31] Buckingham's narrative instead provides an account of consistent European barbarism hitched to three main causal agents: the instrumentalizing machines of early capitalism like the Dutch East India Company; the larger culture of violence that produced the Thirty Years' War (1618–48), in which an estimated 7.5 million Germans alone died; and the ethnocentrism of the Dutch explorers that caused them to disregard native names and native languages more generally.[32] Meanwhile, the voice-over also develops a series of destabilizing metanarrative aphorisms that we are invited to read back into the film's own process of storytelling:[33] "Stories condense time the way that maps miniaturize space. But somehow, condensing time seems to distance the past from us rather than bringing it closer. What unfolds in a story, what really happens in a story, is language." In Buckingham's language, then, the clear division between corrective historical intervention and destabilizing metahistorical aphorism allows him to bring forward a new history of the river formerly known as the Hudson while at the same time casting doubt on "history" more generally.

Do these two seemingly opposite currents in *Muhheakantuck* ever meet or flow in unison? At one point, Buckingham ruminates precisely on this seam between the overview and the partial view: "In the dream of vertical ascent and hovering flight, we glimpse the cartographer's view, a fictional disembodied eye suspended high in the air. But as soon as we follow one line, or one river, and not another, a journey emerges, even if it is only a dream. And of course that journey unavoidably becomes a story." Given these terms, we might position Buckingham within the urbanist debates I've sketched by saying that while his journey (his historiographic task of reframing the river) could be accommodated within Harvey's model of main causes, solid words, and full-enough pictures, Buckingham's story—his reflection on what he himself has discovered in relation to what *one might* discover—is cast in the fluid semiotics and contingent social positions of de Certeau and Deutsche.

But inasmuch as de Certeau's concept of the everyday has been a claimed point of departure for Buckingham, one might certainly imagine another journey into this territory—perhaps we could call it *Supplement to Buckingham's Voyage*—in which surviving seventeenth-century objects themselves are used as the jumping-off spots for narrative: "the implied, the everyday, the unexceptional—everything not considered important enough to be mentioned." Certainly, attention to such everyday

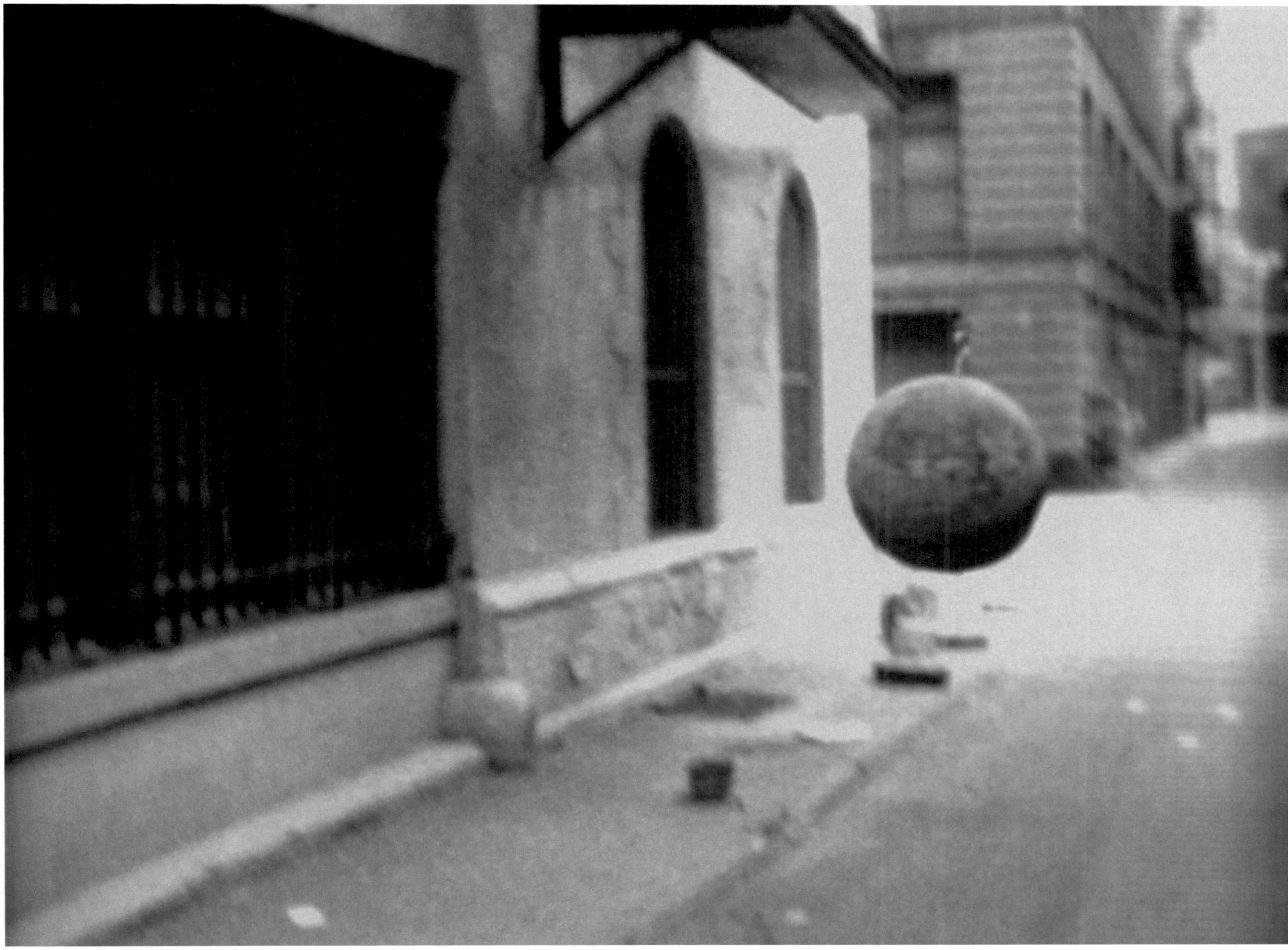

Plate 121 James Nares, still from *Pendulum*, 1976

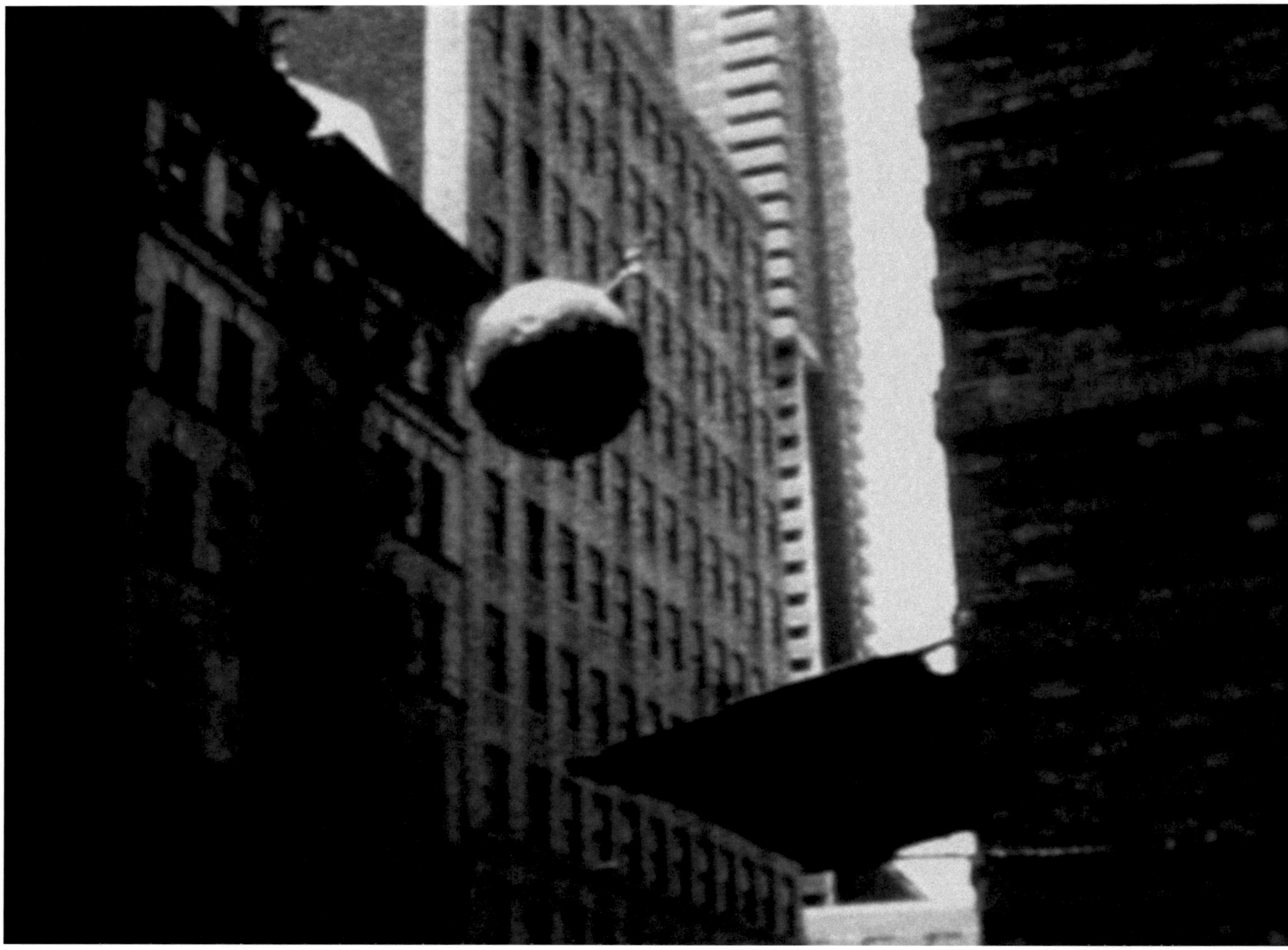

Plate 122 James Nares, still from *Pendulum*, 1976

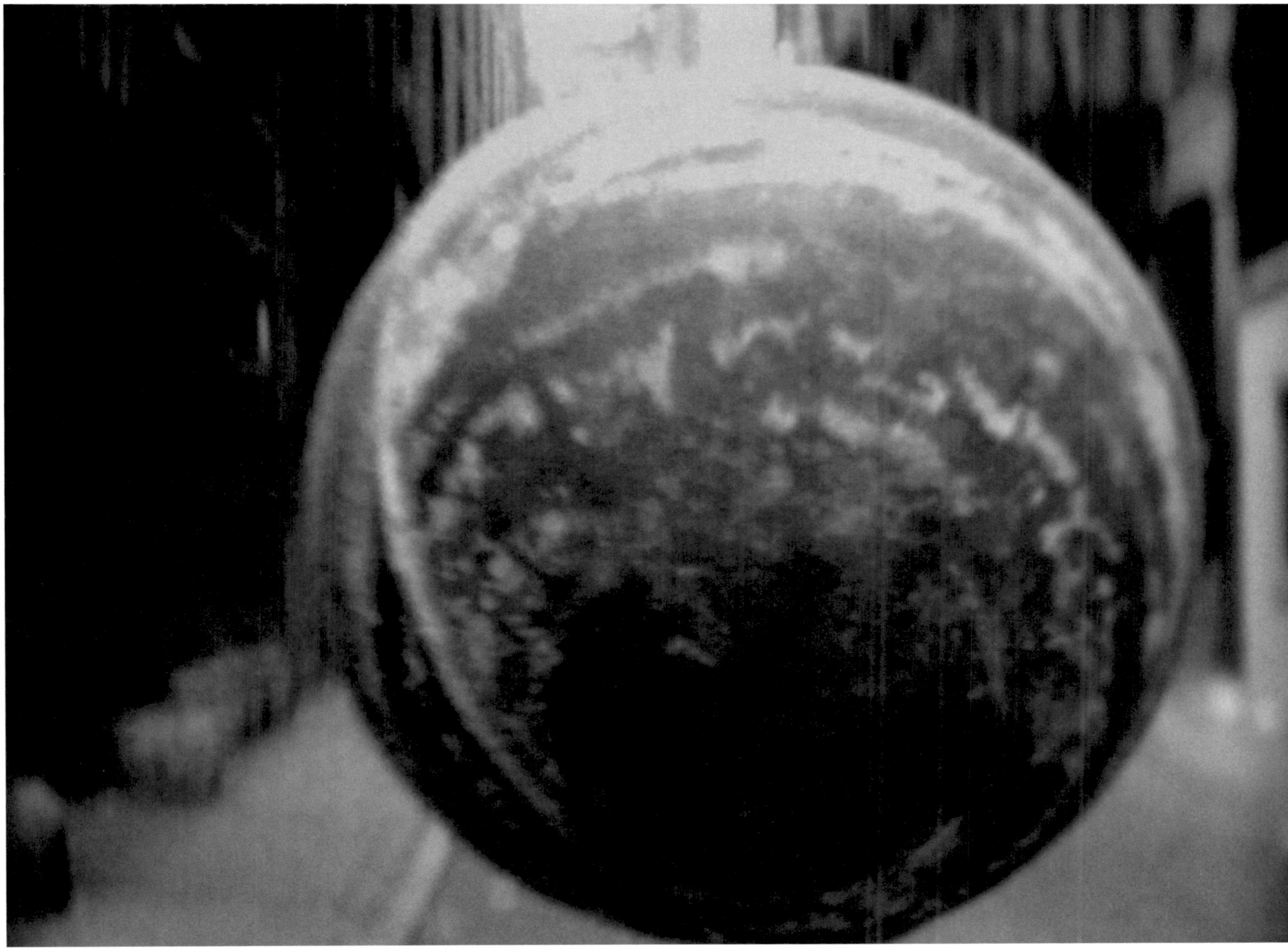

Plate 123 James Nares, still from *Pendulum*, 1976

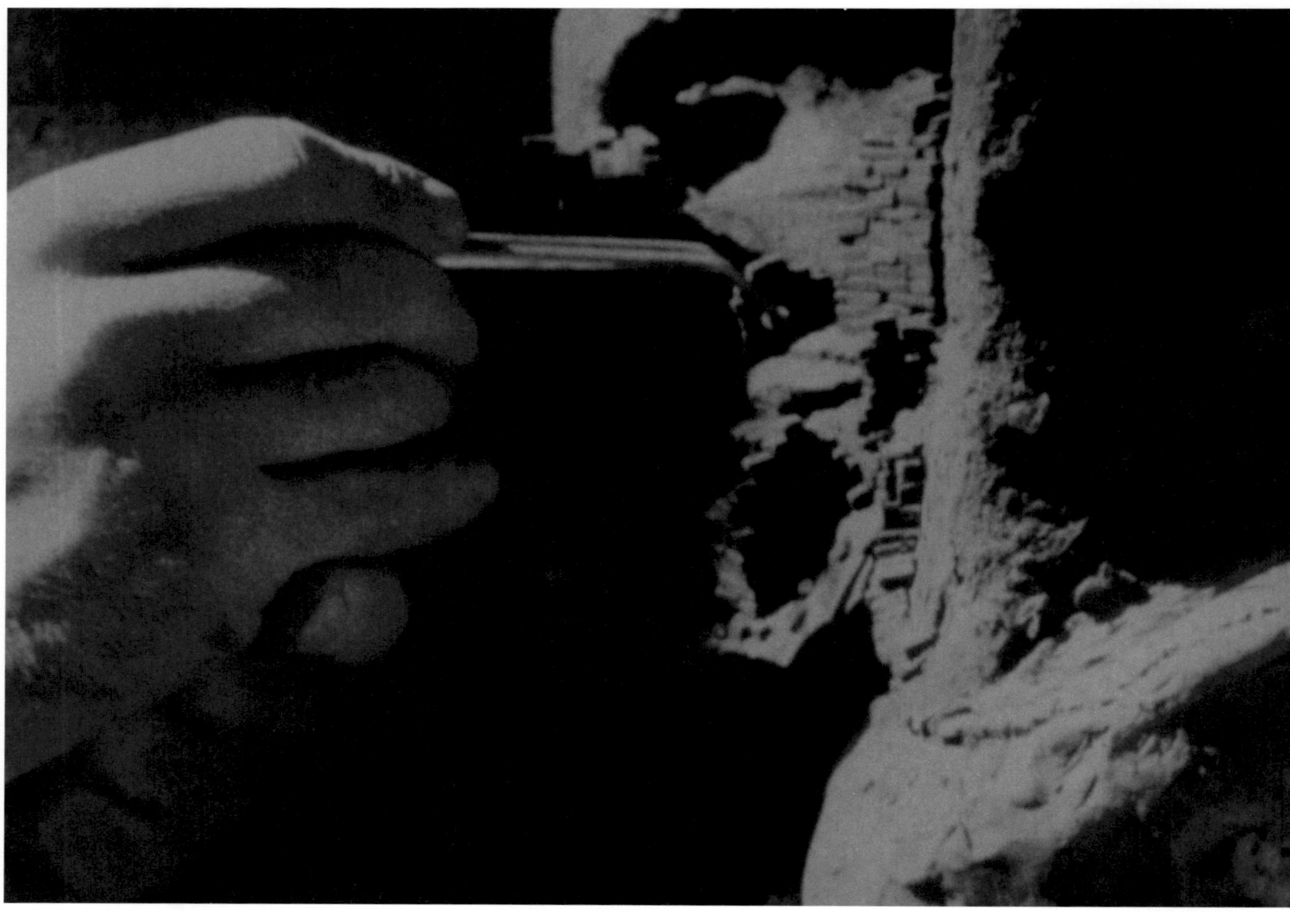

Plate 124 Charles Simonds, still from *Dwellings*, 1972

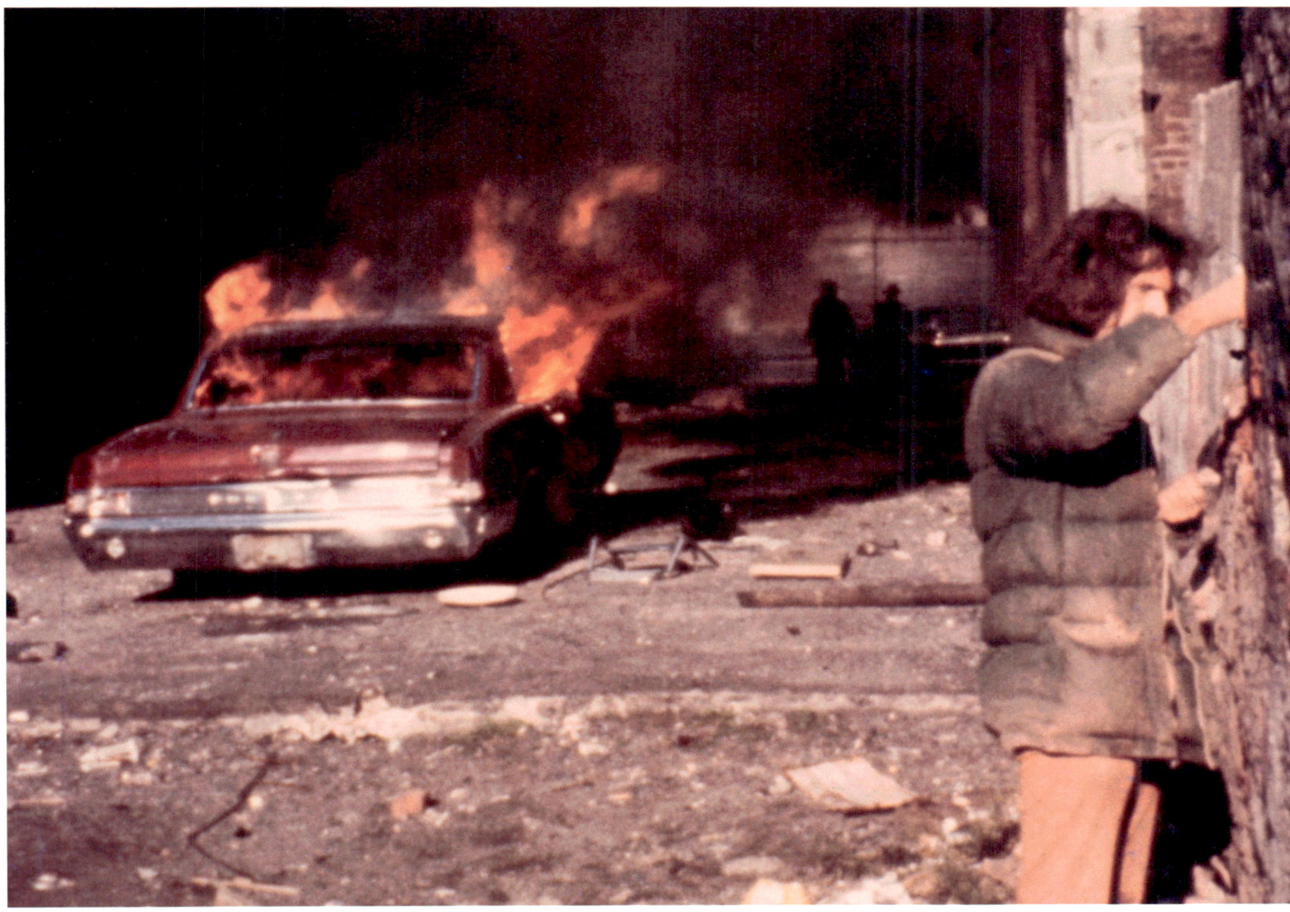

Plate 125 Charles Simonds, still from *Dwellings Winter*, 1974

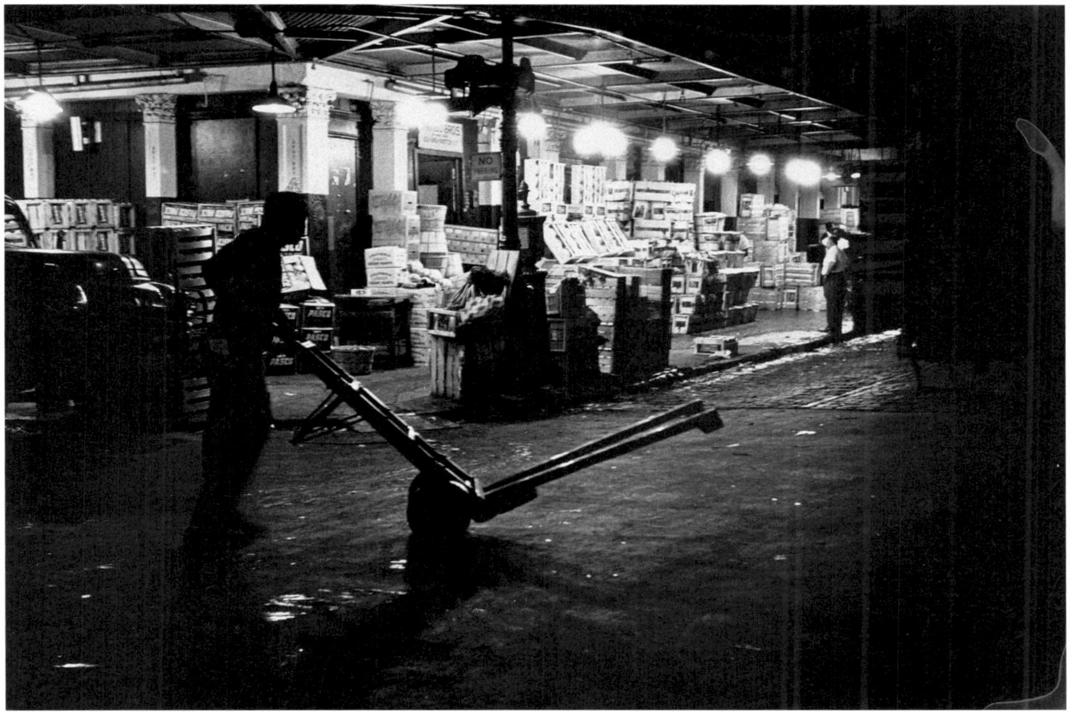

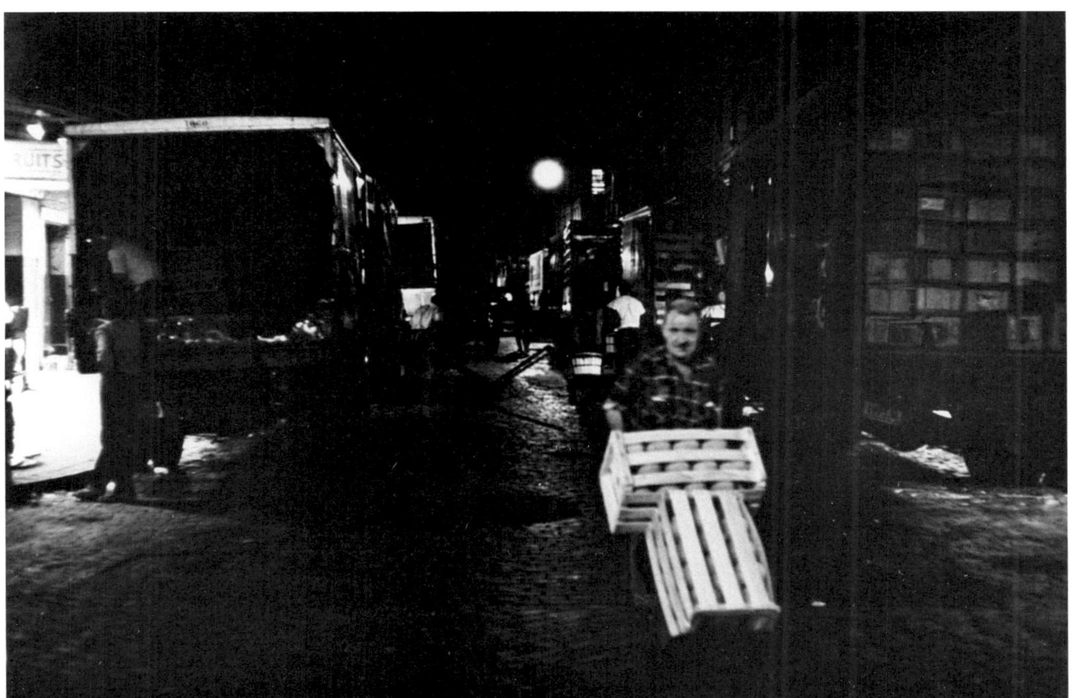

Plate 105–6 William Gedney, photographs of Washington Street Market, c. 1960

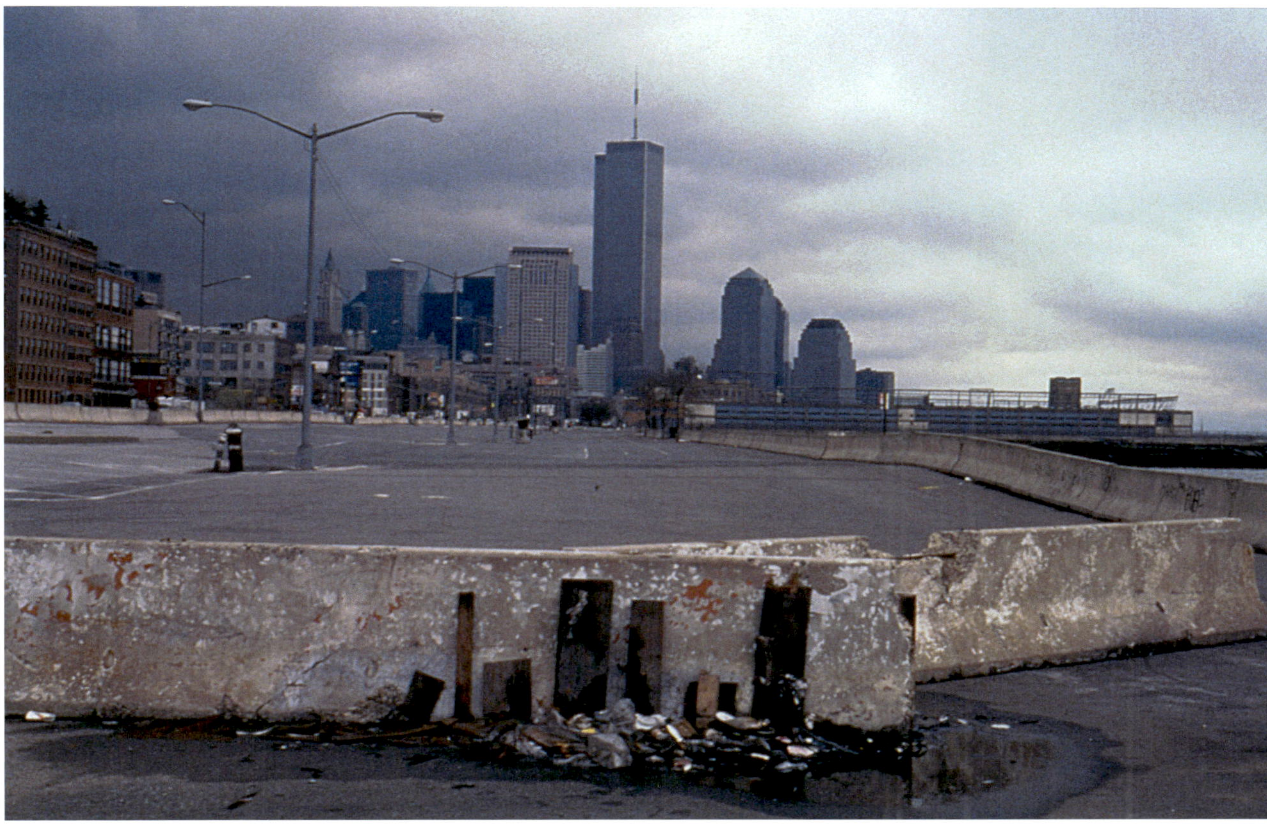

Plate 126 Gabriel Orozco, *Island within an Island* (*Isla en la Isla*), 1993

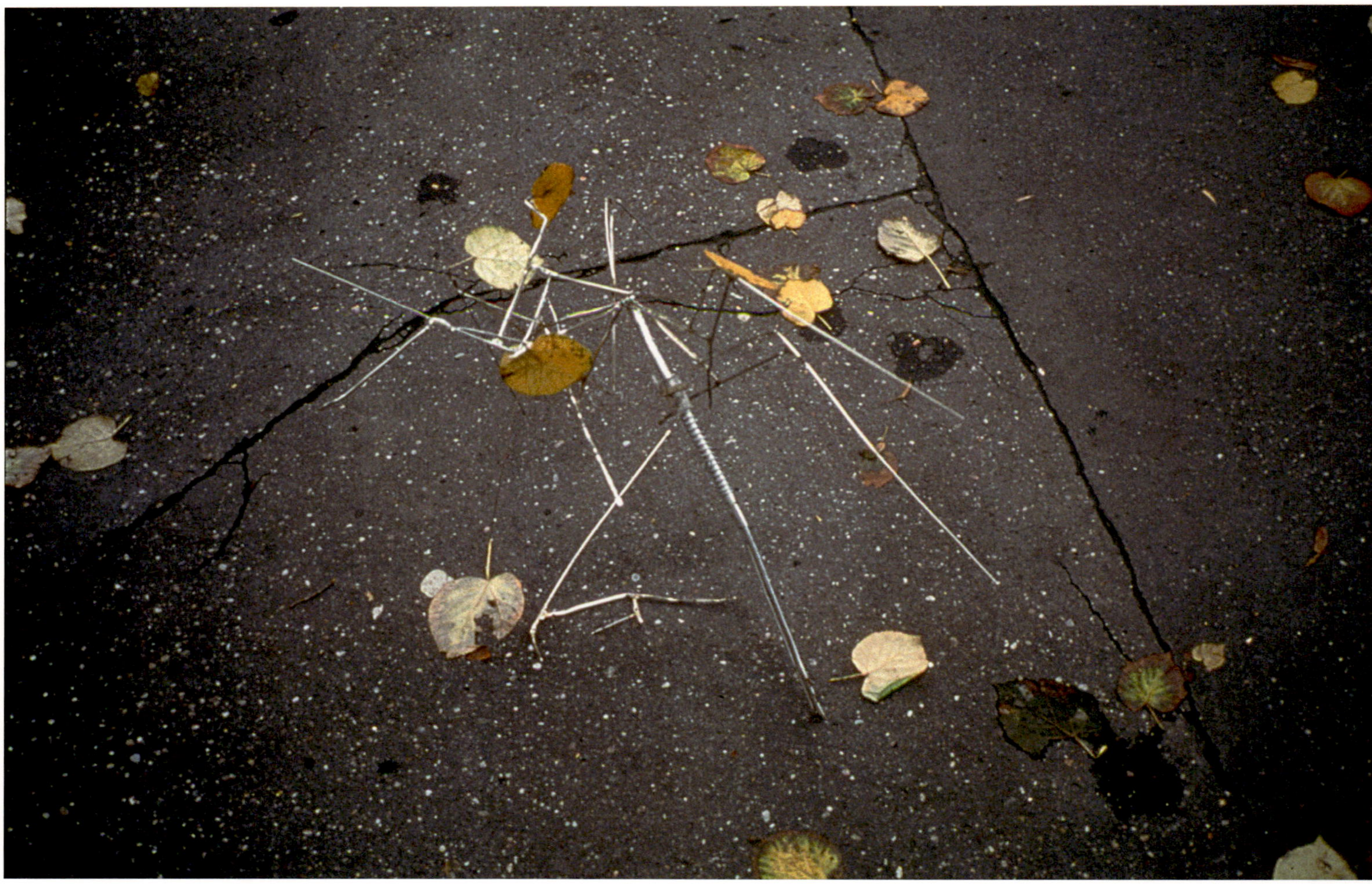

Plate 127 Gabriel Orozco, *Autumn Umbrella*, 1993

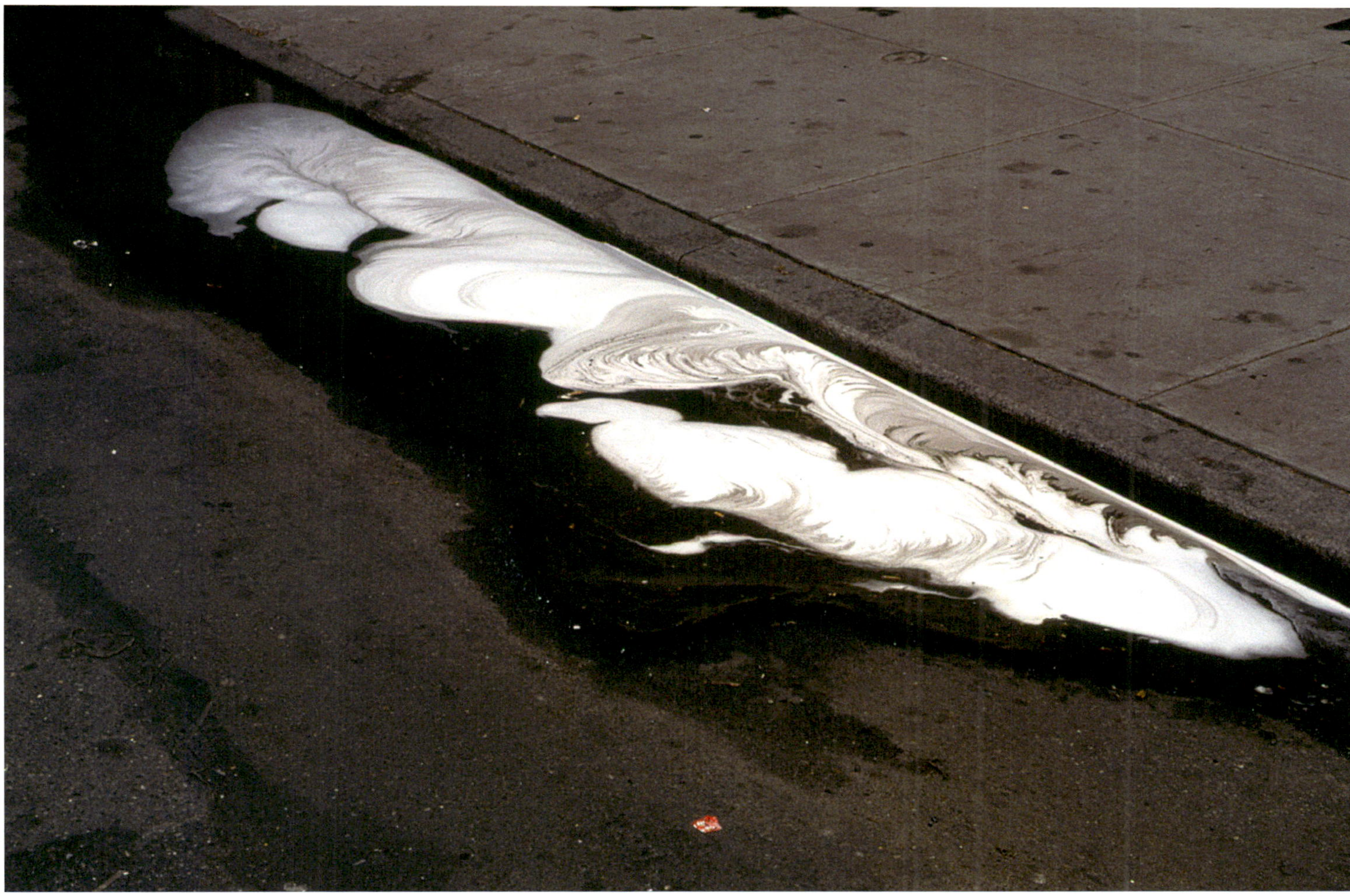

Plate 128 Gabriel Orozco, *Foam*, 1992

objects (albeit from the recent, not the distant, past) has been one of the guiding principles of another current of urbanist art, including some of Buckingham's own work.

Let me conclude, then, with a few projects turned in this direction—both within *Mixed Use, Manhattan* and without. If the easy criticism of such works is that they appear "slight," it's worth remembering, first, what I've implied above: that because of pervasive presuppositions about the nature of significant "content" it will always be an enormous *challenge* to turn attention to those elements in city life most likely to escape documentation, to remain implied, unstated, and therefore transient; and second, that most urbanist artwork involved with concepts of the quotidian proceeds through a serial logic in which an individual image is less important as mimetic proof of itself than as an element within a collection, to be understood comparatively. Here I'm thinking of a group of Manhattan-based photographic collections: Zoe Leonard's gum deposits, Gabriel Orozco's pools and leaf patterns, Christopher Wool's leaking fire hydrants and discarded furniture, Moyra Davey's newsstand typologies, Roy Colmer's doorways, and Stefan Brecht's irregular sidewalk patches along 8th Avenue. All these works gather detritus or the overlooked rather than focusing on the dramatic, conflictual elements of urban life.

pp. 208–9, 266–67
pp. 210–14, 253–55
pp. 236–37, 238–39

But if such work can be thought to "record" or "document," it does so not simply by preserving images, by arresting the ever-changing surface of the built world. For most of these works, all of the sensuous particularity of an individual image only comes into focus as such with the invention of the *category* of which this image will have been an instance. "Now we will notice sidewalk gum deposits," Leonard's photographs seem to say, and so they both alert us to these as a condition and produce an archive: a taxonomy of chewing-gum-based sidewalk stains. But such photographic speech acts always articulate something more. They seem to say: "If *this* can be a category, then imagine how many other categories are conceivable!" Therefore, one taxonomy invites you to invent another and to speculate on the contingencies of so many that already exist. When urbanism steps beyond assumptions about the economic as the master category, it can initiate indispensable discussion about its interpretive categories per se: this, rather than any specific version of materialist history, is what makes Walter Benjamin's *Arcades Project*, for instance, such an exemplary text; it invites reflection on the *production* of interpretive categories, on their juxtapositions, on the gathering and organizing of material.

Perhaps the richest work in this direction I have encountered is that of the group ENDCOMMERCIAL, for which the analysis of typical, recurrent, but unconceptualized (or unarticulated) phenomena in New York City gets organized by an enormous, playful taxonomy whose largest categories ("system," "order," and "identity") each branch off into three subcategories.[34] "System," for instance, covers "property phenomenon," "dysfunctional speech act," and "commerce." Under "dysfunctional speech act," then, we find enormous collections of images organized by "misspelling," "fading markets," and "empty signs." Each of these final categories might give rise to dozens of images of signs without messages, signs with almost illegible messages, or signs with garbled, overwritten, or simply misspelled messages. Emphasis, again, is not on the singularity of the image but on the articulation of a category. Others include taped-up car windows, welded tags on steel road plates, and spray-painted digging directions to pipe excavators. Each image is presented by juxtaposition with others within its grouping.

But rather than end with a paean to Benjaminian categories, let me instead conclude with a project that combines the quotidian mapping impulse of the above works with a more explicit performative dimension: Jimbo Blachly's *About 86 Springs* (2002), in which the artist, following the lead of a hundred-year-old guide to the springs and wells of New York by the classicist/hydrologist James Reuel Smith (1852–1935), revisits each of the now-blighted spring sites, documenting its current condition. The force of the project is not just the juxtaposed images of then and now (the sylvan glades become sloping sewage drains); nor is it a tale of ecological decline in the face of modernization. All of this is predictable. What is less so is what occurs when Blachly actually visits each of these sites, when he tries to *occupy* and *move within* this collection of overlooked, neglected, or abject spaces. The result is a remapping of the city through the medium of the walk—a remapping that combines the kind of urban taxonomy mentioned above with a more explicitly performative dimension. As de Certeau says: "The long poem of walking manipulates spatial organizations, no matter how panoptic they may be."[35] To occupy all of these seemingly unoccupiable locations is what is at issue in *About 86 Springs*: the backs of minivan lots and fast-food restaurants, the fenced-off interior courtyards of large housing complexes, damp concrete abutments below cantilevered office buildings. This is the map that emerges from Blachly's tour of the sealed portals of inspiration.

What is crucial, then, about James's "powers of removal" in the context of urbanist art is not the familiar articulation of loss, the claim that some previous experience of plentitude is now definitively over. James instead points to a seemingly endless chain of erasures and reconstitutions. But rather than understand this process as an inevitable cycle that would contain and neutralize any intervention he could imagine, he makes it his job to investigate the affects associated with each temporary crystallization of the urban world, the microenvironment that each version of the built world produces. The result is a plotless quotidian "history" of New York unlike anything else. If we extend James's concerns to the contexts of historiography, and in particular an urbanist historiography of daily life, we might suggest that here, too, removal is at issue not merely because discrete historical truths have been replaced by inaccuracies but because our dominant models of thinking historically *remain* limited by the symmetrical logic of traditional stories and their critical revisions.

Endnotes

1
Henry James, *The American Scene*, ed. Leon Edel. (Bloomington: Indiana University Press, 1968), p. 84.

2
Ibid., p. 76. This judgment translates a key problem for James's protagonists to the scale of the city. Consider, for instance, the first sentences of his short story "The Jolly Corner," about a New York–born writer who returns to the city after thirty years and spends his time fantasizing about how he would have turned out had he remained in the much crasser city: "'Everyone asks me what I "think" of everything,' said Spencer Brydon; 'and I make answer as I can—begging or dodging the question, putting them off with any nonsense. It wouldn't matter to any of them really,' he went on, 'for, even were it possible to meet in that stand-and-deliver way so silly a demand on so big a subject, my "thoughts" would still be almost altogether about something that concerns only myself.' He was talking to Miss Staverton, with whom for a couple of months now he had availed himself of every possible occasion to talk." *The Beast in the Jungle and Other Stories* (Mineola, NY: Dover, 1993), p. 73. For Brydon in the story, as for James in *The American Scene*, the demand that human subjects should operate as transparent conveyors of their impressions parallels the new and typically American architectural abomination of buildings purporting to inventory their interiors "transparently" via extensive windows. While the desire for such transparency in architecture is characterized as a mistake (and the belief in its possibility with humans seen as an illusion), James is obviously in control of the irony of Brydon's needing to stage this problem in relation to an interlocutor, Miss Staverton, who is simultaneously asked to listen and told that such listening will be fruitless.

3
James, *The American Scene*, p. 77. James is also irritated by the city's larger inability to make class distinctions legible on an urban level: "It was an extraordinary statement on the subject of New York that the space between Fourteenth Street and Washington Square *should* count for 'tone.'" Ibid., p. 88.

4
Ibid., p. 91. James's biographer Leon Edel tells us that the house was at 21 Washington Place, between Washington Square and Broadway. *Henry James: The Untried Years, 1843–1870* (New York: Avon, 1978), p. 40. Ultimately James compares the problem of sufficiently attending to his impressions to that of a "mob" trying to wedge its way into a streetcar: "the picture, as it comes back to me, is…so crowded with its features that I rejoice, I confess, in not having more of them to handle. No open apprehension, even if it be as open as a public vehicle plying for hire, can carry more than a certain amount of life, of a kind; and there was nothing at play in the outer air, at least, of the scene, during these glimpses, that didn't scramble for admission into mine very much as I had seen the mob seeking entrance to an up-town or a down-town electric car fight for life at one of the apertures." James, *The American Scene*, pp. 80–81.

5
Ibid., p. 94. James first notices this "fact at which no one, indeed, appears to be shocked" at Trinity Church and then elaborates on it at the "two most southward of the Fifth Avenue churches." Ibid., pp. 79, 92–93.

6
As Rem Koolhaas famously frames this process: "Its plot is: barbarism giving way to refinement. From these givens, its future can be extrapolated forever: since the exterminating principles never cease to act, it follows that what is refinement one moment will be barbarism the next. Therefore, the performance can never end or even progress in the conventional sense of dramatic plotting; it can only be the cyclic restatement of a single theme: creation and destruction irrevocably interlocked, endlessly reenacted." *Delirious New York: A Retroactive Manifesto for Manhattan* (New York: Monacelli Press, 1994), p. 15.

7
Karl Marx and Friedrich Engels, "Manifesto of the Communist Party," in *The Marx-Engels Reader*, ed. Robert C. Tucker (New York: Norton, 1978), p. 476.

8
The result was that the urban density James had noticed in southern Manhattan was now only a nine-to-five phenomenon, and limited to small areas within the financial market. Catherine Opie's more recent (2001) photographs of the Wall Street area on weekends and early mornings suggest something similar: a scene completely void of humans, a single-use Manhattan in frightening diagram form. These photographs, however, were taken after Lower Manhattan had grown more populated than it was in the 1970s.

9
And this is the view we see through the window in the Danny Lyon photograph of an abandoned, even ruinlike room—broken casements on the littered floor amid glass shards and wooden fragments—overlooking Lower Manhattan skyscrapers.

10
Rosalyn Deutsche, *Evictions: Art and Spatial Politics* (Cambridge, MA: MIT Press, 1996), p. xxiii.

11
Deutsche frames this project as follows: "Since the 1980s, art critics on the left have tried to reframe aesthetic debates about public space by abandoning normative evaluations of the word *public* in favor of functional analyses that examine its uses in particular historical circumstances." Ibid., p. 290.

12
I develop this argument in *Frank O'Hara: The Poetics of Coterie* (Iowa City: University of Iowa Press, 2006), which discusses the coterie as a potential critique of universality and the public not based on identity politics. This critical potential includes not just the coterie social formation itself but also how that formation operates within literary and social history. This is because coteries involve contingent models of social alliance rather than organic models of filiation: members select one another, just as they select their relevant precedents. This significantly contrasts coteries from families and nations—the two structures most commonly educed to explain social or aesthetic linkages.

13
Certainly one of the most influential economic interpreters of New York urbanism (and of postmodernity more generally), Harvey sees nascent neoliberalism not just as the new economic system that ruthlessly transformed Manhattan but also as the cultural engine that gave rise to early postmodern work like that of Cindy Sherman, which he understands essentially as a symptom. Thus, he sees Sherman's exploration of fluid feminine roles, instantly recognizable and endlessly transformable, as an ideological fiction the city tells about itself. He writes: "The photographs depict seemingly different women drawn from many walks of life. It takes a little while to realize, with a certain shock, that these are portraits of the same woman in different guises. Only the catalogue tells you that it is the artist herself who is that woman. The parallel with [Jonathan] Raban's insistence upon the plasticity of human personality through the malleability of appearances and surfaces is striking, as is the self-referential positioning of the authors to themselves as subjects. Cindy Sherman is considered a major figure in the postmodern movement." David Harvey, *The Condition of Postmodernity* (London: Blackwell, 1990), p. 7. In *Mixed Use, Manhattan*, for instance, one of Sherman's photographs presents a kind of vampish woman in a moment of pained introspection (licking wounds, plotting revenge?), the staginess of the pose brought out by the dilapidated Hudson piers and the Holland Tunnel ventilation tower in the background. Alienated, inward, gone to the city's margin's for some "fresh" air and time to think, this is an image of a recognizable subject position rather than a singular empirical subject; in another, we seem to capture a woman in the Civic Center, who, with her dark shades, raincoat, and hand over her face, is trying too hard to avoid being spotted. Our position downstairs and through a railing suggests that the photograph might be the work of a private detective or paparazzo. For Harvey, however, the very fluidity between these roles, and the fact that they all actually emerge from one human being (the photographer herself), suggest a mystified idea that cities specifically and postmodernism generally offer us an infinite realm of subject positions we can try on, and discard, an unlimited domain of situational selves. Cities, and the neoliberal economic regimes that have ruthlessly reshaped them, *want* us to think this, and Sherman has unwittingly produced their press release, while their "truth" (based on hard exclusions and immutable class divisions) is of course very different. Luckily, Sherman has been well defended by Rosalyn Deutsche and others.

14
Deutsche, *Evictions*, p. 233. Of Harvey's critique, Deutsche writes: "He sets up a single difference in social philosophy: an opposition between a preconstituted unity of relations that is the basis for political action versus pure difference that is the basis for political escapism" (Ibid., p. 217). Thus for Deutsche the "evictions" of her title are not merely those of people from cities but those of *discourses* like feminism from the dominant domain of what I'm calling urbanism.
15
Possibly Nares has friends watching from around the corners to be sure that people don't stumble into the deadly scene. But it's not clear. At one point, a car does drive by, but this is the only sign of other human beings than Nares himself and a woman with whom he works.
16
I learned only afterward that the ball is in fact a hollow copper sphere filled with water; whatever the reality of the prop, its evocation of a wrecking ball is both unmistakable and convincing.
17
At the very moment the film was made, just one block to the west, a huge three-block swath west of Hudson Street had been torn down, making way for "Independence Plaza North"—three forty-story high-rises looming over a public school, the Borough of Manhattan Community College, and a tiny constellation of relocated historical row houses.
18
Lucy Lippard, *Overlay: Contemporary Art and the Art of Prehistory* (New York: Pantheon, 1983), p. 57.
19
Ibid., p. 235.
20
Ibid.
21
John Hallmark Neff suggests that Simonds "evokes the presence of civilizations seemingly very remote from ours, cultures whose customs we reconstruct from the archaeological evidence of their dwelling sites, specifically those values embedded in their architecture. It is from the types of buildings, their detailed construction, apparent demise, and selective re-use that we are led to imagine the civic and religious priorities, the mind-set, the cosmology of these unseen builders whose very invisibility frees us to consider parallels with our own lives and futures." Neff also presents Simonds's pieces as temporal variants of the same site: "One can make the case that each of his pieces, whatever its size, in itself implies the entirety; that each part of the sequence (an open-ended, expanding class as opposed to the closed groups of a series) deals only with the same work in a different moment." John Hallmark Neff, "Charles Simonds's Engendered Places: Towards a Biology of Architecture," in *Charles Simonds* (Chicago: Museum of Contemporary Art Chicago, 1982), pp. 16, 13.
22
Archaeologists are now agreed that the mounds were in fact built by Native Americans, primarily during what is known at the Woodland period, roughly 1000 BCE–1000 CE. For an account of the debates in the United States that surrounded initial interest in the mounds (they had been noticed in the sixteenth century but were not closely examined until the 1770s), see Gordon M. Sayre, "The Mound Builders and the Imagination of American Antiquity in Jefferson, Bartram, and Chateaubriand," *Early American Literature* 33, no. 3 (1998), pp. 225–49.
23
William Cullen Bryant, *Poems* (Philadelphia: Henry Altemus, 1895), p. 52.
24
Ibid., p. 54.
25
As Buckingham describes it: "the film / flight turns around a little bit after the Tappan Zee Bridge near Ossining. There are two 20 minute rolls of 16mm (the longest continuous shot possible in that gauge) joined together to make up the film image. There was no deliberate significance to turning around at Ossining, this was the distance we were able to cover in that amount of time flying 160 miles per hour from a starting point below the Verrazano Bridge in New York Harbor.... At Ossining we lingered in the air for a few minutes while I changed magazines and then flew down-river just past the Statue of Liberty. We had strong headwinds from the south, so that trip was slower." E-mail to the author, March 8, 2010.
26
As Buckingham puts it in the voice-over: "What feels familiar is actually unknown because we think we already understand the things that are familiar to us."
27
Michel de Certeau, "Walking in the City," in *The Practice of Everyday Life*, trans. Steven Rendall (Berkeley and Los Angeles: University of California Press, 1984), p. 104.
28
In *Frank O'Hara: The Poetics of Coterie* I offer an account of how the problems that philosophers encounter with proper names (their reliance on, but inability to ensure, a secure set of associations) are precisely what recommend them to a poet like O'Hara—perhaps *the* twentieth-century American poet of the name.
29
Part of Buckingham's strategy for achieving this effect is emphasizing the many senses in which Hudson did not "discover" anything. For instance, in his voice-over, Buckingham says: "Far from being the first, Hudson's trip actually ended the period of visitation that preceded European colonization." Though Hudson was credited with the discovery immediately, his name did not actually become the main designation for the river until the nineteenth century.
30
One of the defamiliarizing gestures is to begin the narration proper (after the aphorisms on vantage points) with the lines "On September 11th, 1609, Henry Hudson and his crew sailed into the mouth of the river that would later bear his name." Certainly no viewer in 2003 could look at an image of Manhattan and hear the words "On September 11th" without thinking of 9/11. While Buckingham does not explicitly address the shared dates, the very form of his narrative asks us to step outside a framework in which 9/11 will be the ultimate point of pathos.
31
Russell Shorto, *The Island at the Center of the World: The Epic Story of Dutch Manhattan, the Forgotten Colony that Shaped America* (New York: Doubleday, 2004).
32
Though in the broad view Buckingham is not simply wrong, he does simplify the matter: we know that Adriaen van der Donck, for instance, paid extremely close attention to the language and culture of the Mohawks and Mahicans; see Shorto, *Island at the Center of the World*, p. 135, and also van der Donck's published writings, especially *A Description of the New Netherland* (Lincoln, Nebraska University Press, 2008), pp. 93 and ff.
33
For instance: "The fiction of history is to imagine the real. History makes reality desirable. It has the illusion of speaking itself, as if it simply happened." Another is: "The unknown is more than an occasion for possibility; it is a provocation that propels one on a journey, a route of unknowing, in which we experience many of the ways that we do not know something."
34
See Florian Bohm, Luca Pizzarone, and Wolfgang Scheppe, *ENDCOMMERCIAL/Reading the City* (Ostfildern-Ruit: Hatje Cantz, 2002).
35
De Certeau, *Practice of Everyday Life*, p. 101.

Housing in New York: A Brief History

Glenn Ligon

Forest Houses, 1000 Trinity Avenue, Bronx, 1960–1973

A public-housing project built in the mid-1950s. With 1,349 apartments in fifteen high-rise buildings surrounded by abundant green space, it was a Le Corbusier fantasy transplanted to the South Bronx. My mother claimed the projects were "beautiful" when we moved in. Given the decrepit tenements that surrounded us, I could see why she was grateful for our tiny, spartan apartment with its New York City Housing Authority–chosen paint scheme and blistering but reliable steam heat. In *The Flâneur,* Edmund White writes about a friend who defines a big city as a place where there are "blacks, tall buildings and you can stay up all night," but by the early 1970s the excitement of living in the "big city" that was the Forest Houses had worn off. Bad public policies and rising crime had caused the project and the neighborhood around it to deteriorate. Despite our eyewitness view of the birth of hip-hop ("Hoodlums," I was told. "Out there scratching up perfectly good records"), my mother decided that we needed to move to a safer area.

Baychester Houses, 1871 Schieffelin Place, Bronx, 1973–1982

In 1971 my mother got a job at Bronx Psychiatric Center, a large inpatient facility at the northeast edge of the borough. Facing an hour-long commute to work, she decided to apply to transfer to a project closer to her job. Moving between projects was not an easy thing. Under the guise of maintaining ethnic diversity (i.e., white tenants), it was nearly impossible for a black family to relocate to a project that wasn't already predominantly black, and the smaller, less chaotic housing projects in the northeast Bronx still had numerous white families living in them. Only letters from a social worker at my mother's job helped ensure our application was accepted. We moved to a six-story building on Schieffelin Place, named after the man who released sixty starlings in Central Park at the turn of the nineteenth century, the descendants of which now number over 200 million. The Baychester Houses were quiet, marginally integrated, and so far removed from the South Bronx that the subway station near our house had signs that indicated whether the arriving train was going "to the city" or coming "from the city."

168 Lafayette Avenue, Brooklyn, 1982–1983

When I graduated from college I decided to rent an apartment with a friend on the top floor of a brownstone in Fort Greene. In the early 1980s, Fort Greene was not the fashionable, pricey enclave it is now. When a friend asked a policeman about moving into the neighborhood, he replied, "Shake your head. I want to hear the wind rattle through it." While the apartment was fine, the owners of the building were notorious for their miserliness. During winter days there would be no heat in the building because "the heat is on when you are at home, not when you are at work." It didn't matter that I worked nights and that the boiler made no adjustments for weekends. When I complained to my friend Andrea about how "the Jews" were stingy with the heat and "the Jews" didn't keep the building up, she gave me a horrified look. "Glenn, I've never known you to be anti-Semitic," she said, her voice full of concern and reproach. "Anti-Semitic?" I responded, perplexed. "No, no, no. Not J-E-W. It's J-O-O. They're Korean."

380 Riverside Drive, Manhattan, 1983–1987

I sublet a co-op apartment with my boyfriend (whom I met when my toilet leaked into his apartment at 168 Lafayette Avenue). The owner bought it for her daughter to live in while she was in grad school at Columbia University, but it had sat empty for a couple of years. It was dark and needed a good paint job, but it was in a doorman building in a lively neighborhood. The sublet was illegal so I tried to keep a low profile in the building. I stayed there for four years, two years longer than the relationship lasted, and moved out only after a chance encounter with the owner of the apartment, whom I had only spoken with over the phone and who was clearly startled to find out that I was black. A week later her daughter called to say that her mother wanted me out.

Tech Place (formerly 100 Johnson Street), Brooklyn, 1987–1990

To support my nascent artistic career I took a freelance proofreading job at a law firm. When my sublet on Riverside Drive ended, one of my co-workers offered me space in a nineteenth-century wood-frame house he was renting on a two-block-long street in downtown Brooklyn. The apartment was an attic with sloping walls and a leaky roof, but it was big enough to use as a painting studio and had room leftover for a couch and a bed. Soon after I moved in, the owners of the building became embroiled in an eminent-domain dispute with the City, which wanted to expand the campus of the technical college across the street. Wary of a long fight over the house and tired of living with a roommate, I moved to a one-bedroom apartment in Washington Heights. The house was eventually condemned, and my former roommate used the small cash settlement he got from the City to resettle in Prague.

540 West 166th Street, Manhattan, 1990

A renovated apartment in a slowly gentrifying building in Washington Heights. It was across the street from Columbia Presbyterian Hospital and adjacent to the Audubon Ballroom, the spot where Malcolm X was assassinated. My neighbors, immigrants from the Dominican Republic who had moved into the building in the 1960s, were shocked at the rent I was paying, although I thought it was a bargain compared with other Manhattan neighborhoods. I lasted there six months, moving out after a flood caused my bathroom ceiling to collapse (with little response from the landlord) and I came home one day to find DEA helicopters circling the neighborhood and thirty policemen in riot gear escorting drug dealers out the front door.

195a Washington Park, Brooklyn, 1990–1995

A studio apartment in a brownstone facing Fort Greene Park. The neighborhood had changed since I lived there in the early 80s. Spike Lee's production company was a few blocks away, there were new restaurants and cafés opening, and the neighborhood delis had started to take down their floor-to-ceiling Plexiglas robbery shields. Older black residents were bewildered by the influx of people into overpriced rentals in what they still considered a marginal area. As far as they were concerned, we were all part of a conspiracy to run them out of their homes, and they made no distinction between young white gentrifiers and black ones. I stayed in the apartment for five years until I decided that I needed a bigger living space.

168 Prospect Place, Brooklyn, 1995–2002

A one-bedroom brownstone floor-through on a quiet, tree-lined street in Prospect Heights. My neighbor Herbie jokingly called the area "Dark Slope" because the complexion of its residents was dramatically different from that of those south of Flatbush Avenue in more affluent Park Slope. It was from the roof of this building that I watched the World Trade Center collapse in 2001 and on Flatbush Avenue that I directed traffic later that day, pressed into service by a cop who needed a break to use the bathroom.

535 Dean Street, Brooklyn, 2002–2007

A one-bedroom apartment in a converted factory building on the edge of the Long Island Rail Road train yard. The developers, gambling that soaring real estate prices in Park Slope would soon extend to Prospect Heights, created condos out of what was the long-empty *Daily News* printing plant. It was the first time I had owned real estate, buying the apartment from plans before construction had begun and waiting nearly a year and a half for the building to be finished. The apartment was on the fifth floor facing west and had an incredible view over the train yards of downtown Brooklyn and New Jersey. I realized this view would soon disappear when real estate developer Bruce Ratner announced plans for a Frank Gehry–designed basketball stadium and dozens of office and residential towers. If approved, it will be one of the largest developments ever built in the city and will dramatically change the character of the neighborhood. Facing ten years of construction and what was turning into a losing battle over eminent domain, overcrowding, and a lack of low-income housing, I decided to sell and move on.

395 Broadway, Manhattan, 2007–present

A condo building on the eastern edge of Tribeca. Converted in the early 1980s and adjacent to Chinatown, the building is full of Asian families who smartly favor low maintenance over doormen or an in-house gym. While most of my friends are moving to Brooklyn, seeking neighborhoodliness, more space, and lower costs, I decided that I liked living in this part of Manhattan, where nobody knows your name. Like any other neighborhood in New York, Tribeca is full of contradictions. Movie stars live around the corner from me, but at the base of my building is a shop called Western Spirit, which sells saddles, turquoise jewelry, and feathered headdresses to tourists, and from my roof I can see women sewing fake designer bags in garment factories that have been in continuous use since the nineteenth century.

My mother's dream was that she would end her days in a little yellow house in the country. She passed away, as I probably will, living in an apartment building with neighbors above and below. I was born here in New York, and like many other New Yorkers I lack imagination: the idea of living somewhere else has never occurred to me. Indeed, to live in New York is to have lived everywhere.

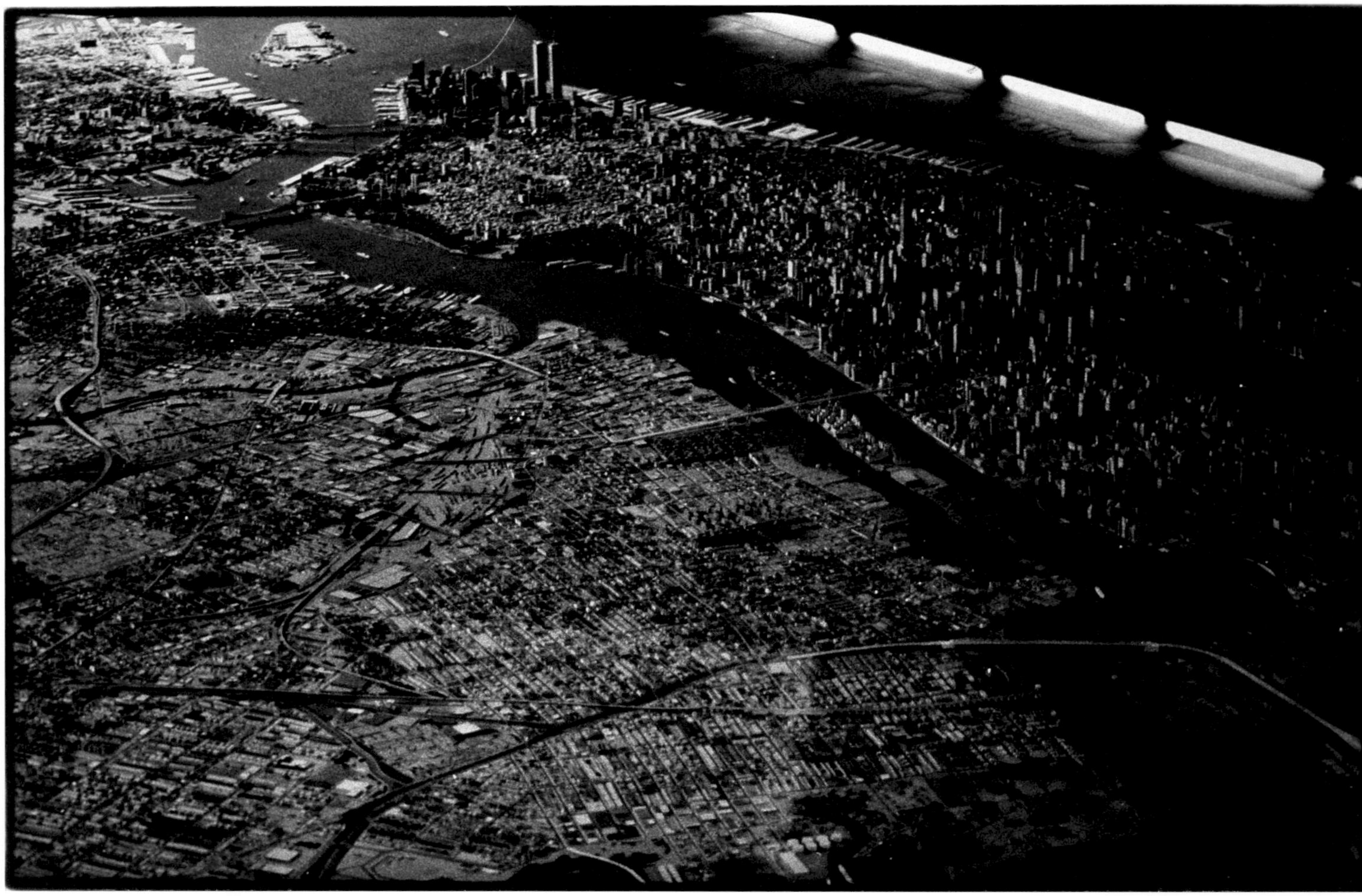

Plate 129 Zoe Leonard, *Model of New York no. 2*, 1989/1990

Timeline Lena Sze

1949

The American Housing Act is passed. It finances "slum clearance" and urban-renewal projects, as well as the construction of large-scale public housing in American cities.[1]

New York City subway fare is ten cents.

1950

The Port Authority Bus Terminal, the nation's largest and the world's busiest bus terminal, opens on Manhattan's West Side.

1954–1965

Mayoral administration of Robert Wagner (Democrat).

1954

The South Street Viaduct elevated portion of the Franklin D. Roosevelt Drive, blocking access to the waterfront, is completed on the Lower East Side.

1956

Containerization is introduced at Port Newark in New Jersey.[2]

1959

Groundbreaking for Lincoln Center. An African-American and Puerto Rican neighborhood called San Juan Hill is razed to make way for it.

Neighborhood activists including Jane Jacobs defeat Robert Moses's proposal to build a highway through the heart of Greenwich Village (Washington Square Park) and SoHo.

1961–1962

A coalition of residents, merchants, and activists block and eventually defeat the implementation of the Lower Manhattan Expressway proposal backed by Robert Moses, which would have destroyed parts of SoHo, Chinatown, and Little Italy.[3]

1961

Publication of Jane Jacobs's *The Death and Life of Great American Cities*.

1962

The Elizabeth–Port Authority Marine Terminal, the world's first all-container port facility, opens in New Jersey. By the end of the 1960s, the majority of regional shipping operations moves from New York City to New Jersey.

1963

Demolition of the old Penn Station begins. Galvanized by this event, activists and other urbanists advocate for "historic preservation" protections.

City commissions comprehensive plan for the New York waterfront from Battery Park to 72nd Street.

1964

The New York World's Fair opens in Flushing Meadows, Queens.

What may be the city's first gay rights demonstration is led by the Homosexual League of New York and the New York City League for Sexual Freedom.

The landmark federal Civil Rights Act is passed.

1965

World Trade Center construction begins.

Mayor Wagner signs the Landmarks Preservation Law.

Malcolm X is assassinated in the Audubon Ballroom in Washington Heights.

A blackout hits the Northeast. Very few reports of looting.

The landmark federal Immigration and Nationality Act, abolishing quotas based on national origin, is passed.

1966–1973

Mayoral administration of John V. Lindsay (Republican/Liberal/Democrat).

1966–1967

Commissioned by the New York State Council on the Arts, artist Danny Lyon takes photographs of nearly every building on sixty acres in Lower Manhattan south of Canal Street, which are in the process of being demolished for a series of developments, including the impending construction of the World Trade Center, the building of smaller residential and commercial buildings, the expansion of Pace University, the construction of the Brooklyn Bridge extension ramp, and the relocation of Washington Market. The area's remaking is the subject of Lyon's book of photographs and essays entitled *The Destruction of Lower Manhattan* (1969).

1966

Battery Park City is launched as an urban-renewal project. Landfill for the ninety-two-acre site will come from the World Trade Center excavation.

Andy Warhol opens a discotheque with multidisciplinary events dubbed the Exploding Plastic Inevitable at the Dom, formerly a Polish social club, located in the East Village.

City reaches an agreement with the Port Authority that the authority will make annual payments rather than pay taxes on privately leased portions of the World Trade Center.[4]

1967

An anti–Vietnam War demonstration in New York City brings out more than one hundred thousand protestors.

The New York City Council removes licensing requirements, which allows massage parlors in Times Square and elsewhere in the city to flourish. Prostitution and sex work are featured in many of these parlors.

Located in what is now Tribeca, Washington Market, the city's major produce center since the 1880s, moves to the Bronx.

1968

Built on top of the destroyed Penn Station, the new Madison Square Garden is completed.

A Students for a Democratic Society demonstration against Columbia University results in hundreds of arrests and dozens of injuries.

Robert Moses resigns from his final position as chairman of the Triborough Bridge and Tunnel Authority after forty-four years of working in various roles to construct public works.

The federal Fair Housing Act is passed.

1969–1977

New York City loses approximately five hundred thousand jobs in this period.[5]

1969

Black and Puerto Rican students protest at City College, resulting in a new open-admissions policy at the City University of New York (CUNY), which begins in 1970. This policy results in a dramatic increase in the enrollment of students of color in CUNY colleges.[6]

June 28. The Stonewall Riots occur after a late-night New York Police Department raid of the Stonewall Inn bar in Greenwich Village. This event is formative for the gay rights movement.

Puerto Rican students establish the New York chapter of the Young Lords Organization.[7]

New York City subway fare is twenty cents.

1970

Fifteen thousand people participate in the city's first gay pride march and rally on the first anniversary of the Stonewall Riots.

Co-op City, the largest cooperative housing development in the world with a capacity of approximately sixty thousand residents, is completed in the Bronx.

1971

The city adopts a zoning resolution allowing artists certified by the Department of Cultural Affairs to legally live in SoHo.

Founded in 1969, the Gay Activists Alliance moves into its headquarters: the firehouse at 99 Wooster Street in SoHo. It organizes protests and hosts events and parties at the space until arsonists burn it down in 1974.

1972

Still incomplete, the World Trade Center opens.

1973

The Green Guerrillas, an East Village–based grassroots group, obtains a rental lot from the city at Houston Street and Bowery and opens New York City's first community garden.[8]

April 4. Ribbon-cutting ceremony for the completion of the 110-story twin towers of the World Trade Center, designed by architect Minoru Yamasaki.

Portion of West Side Highway at Gansevoort Street collapses, leading to long-term closures and renovations on the West Side.

1974–1977

Mayoral administration of Abraham D. Beame (Democrat).

1974

Central Park designated a New York City landmark.

The federal government proposes Westway, a six-lane underground highway to replace the West Side Highway; first of many lawsuits to stop the development filed.

1975	October 30. *Daily News* headline: "Ford to City: Drop Dead," after President Gerald Ford rejects federal loan guarantees requested by a bankrupt New York City. New York's fiscal problems make it difficult for state-created agencies like the Battery Park Construction Authority to borrow money. Because of the fiscal crisis, CUNY trustees impose tuition charges. A long history of free tuition at CUNY colleges comes to an end.[9] Ellis Island becomes part of the Statue of Liberty National Monument. The city changes its J-51 tax-abatement law, allowing substantial benefits including abatements to property holders converting a commercial building into a residential one, accelerating the conversion of many loft and older office buildings in Manhattan into residential buildings.
1976	Zoning revision permits more buildings to legally house residents in SoHo. The NYC housing commissioner describes a "planned shrinkage" policy in which public services and institutions in poor neighborhoods like the South Bronx would be drastically cut as a fiscal austerity measure.
1977	July 13. Blackout. Widespread looting, arson, and violence ensue; approximately four thousand arrests. David Berkowitz admits to the 1976–77 "Son of Sam" serial killings in New York City. The New York City Landmarks Preservation Commission designates the South Street Seaport Historic District, leading to the area's designation as a historic district by the National Register of Historic Places in 1978. In 1979, the South Street development agreement allows for a shared lease between the Rouse Corporation, the South Street Seaport Museum, and the City and State of New York. This agreement is revised and approved by the NYC Board of Estimate in 1981.[10]
1978–1989	Mayoral administration of Edward I. Koch (Democrat).
1978	Construction begins on the Jacob K. Javits Convention Center in Midtown West. New York State passes the Canine Waste Law (Section 1310 of the Health Code), requiring dog owners to clean up their pets' fecal matter. New York City is the first major American city to have a "pooper scooper" law.
1980	The Central Park Conservancy is founded, on the heels of the fiscal crisis, by prominent civic activists and philanthropists. The Battery Park Construction Authority obtains mortgage insurance from the federal Department of Housing and Urban Development for first six buildings; construction begins on Battery Park City's residential development. The National Association for the Advancement of Colored People (NAACP) files a lawsuit alleging housing discrimination in the Starrett City housing complex in Brooklyn. The NAACP wins its case before the Supreme Court in 1988.
1981	Olympia and York Properties begins construction of the World Financial Center.
1982	The first residents move into Battery Park City when Gateway Plaza, Battery Park City's first phase of residential development, is completed. Loft law (or Article 7C of the Multiple Dwelling Law) legalizes studios in SoHo and Tribeca that artists had established in manufacturing lofts, offers protections for tenants against evictions from these lofts, and requires landlords to bring them up to code. Gay Men's Health Crisis (GMHC) is founded by a group of gay men meeting at the apartment of activist Larry Kramer.
1983	First shops in Fulton Market open at South Street Seaport.
1984	Construction begins on Rector Place, the second phase of residential development of Battery Park City.
1985	The World Financial Center opens. The federal government abandons Westway after several years of lawsuits and activism. New York City closes bathhouses and other sex clubs as a "public health" measure during the AIDS crisis.

1986	New York City subway fare goes from ninety cents to one dollar. The New York City Council passes a gay rights bill banning employment and housing discrimination based on sexual orientation.
1987	The final building of the World Trade Center complex opens. March 24. AIDS Coalition To Unleash Power (ACT UP) stages its first demonstration on Wall Street. October 19. Stock markets crash worldwide, causing "Black Monday."
1988	August 6–7. Riots between police and homeless, activists, and squatters occur in Tompkins Square Park in the East Village amid neighborhood concerns about gentrification and police brutality.
1989	Mandatory recycling takes effect in Manhattan.
1990–1993	Mayoral administration of David N. Dinkins (Democrat). Dinkins is the city's first and thus far only African-American mayor.
1990	A record 2,245 people are murdered in NYC during the year. After decades of white flight and the subsidized expansion of suburbs, the 1990 U.S. Census shows that non-Hispanic whites have become a minority in New York City.
1991–1992	Most of Tribeca designated a Historic District. Still a hot spot for homeless and activists, Tompkins Square Park in the East Village is closed by the city.
1991	Crown Heights Riots occur. Tensions run high in Brooklyn, especially among the African-American, Caribbean, Hasidic, and Orthodox Jewish communities. The excavation of a federal building at Broadway and Duane Street reveals a seventeenth- and eighteenth-century "African burial ground." The Times Square Business Improvement District (BID) is established.[11]
1992	Privately managed by the Bryant Park Restoration Corporation, the new Bryant Park opens. Tompkins Square Park reopens. Hudson River Park and Stuyvesant High School, at the northern boundary of Battery Park City, are completed; the complex now consists of eighteen luxury apartment buildings, four office towers, the Winter Garden shopping mall, and a 1.2-mile riverfront esplanade. The New York City Department of City Planning releases the "NYC Comprehensive Waterfront Plan: Reclaiming the City's Edge." Inspired by and allied with ACT UP, the Women's Action Coalition (WAC) is founded in New York.
1993	Terrorists bomb the World Trade Center.
1994–2001	Mayoral administration of Rudolph W. Giuliani (Republican).
1994	Mayor Giuliani begins his "quality of life" campaign, premised on the idea that tolerance of small criminal acts leads to a generally more lawless city. This policy includes aggressive policing of usually nonviolent offenses, such as subway fare-beating, marijuana possession, panhandling, and graffiti.[12]
1995	The New York City Council amends the Zoning Regulation of 1960, prohibiting adult-entertainment establishments from operating in residential and mixed-use zoned districts and requiring that they stand at least five hundred feet from schools, houses of worship, day-care centers, and one another. Once in effect, this amendment significantly decreases the number of adult-entertainment businesses in the city.
1996	The United States Coast Guard abandons Governor's Island after thirty years.
1997–2002	Community-garden activists clash with the city's policy of auctioning off or transferring community gardens to the Department of Housing Preservation and Development. Several dozen are destroyed or closed in this period.[13]

1998	The NYC Parks Department formally agrees to allow the Central Park Conservancy to manage Central Park. The New York State legislature passes the Hudson River Park Act, which formally designates the project area as a park and establishes the Hudson River Park Trust to continue the planning, construction, management, and operation of the park.
1999	CUNY ends its open-admissions policy for students. Unarmed African immigrant Amadou Diallo is shot to death in the Bronx by four New York Police Department officers, who are later acquitted on all charges. The Diallo case leads to large demonstrations.[14]
2001	September 11. Terrorists hijack passenger jets, which fly into the twin towers, causing the World Trade Center to collapse. Approximately three thousand victims die in New York City on that day.
2002–present	Mayoral administration of Michael R. Bloomberg (Republican).
2002–2008	Mayor Bloomberg, the Department of City Planning and the New York City Council rezone one-sixth of the city. Massive rezoning allows for the transformation of the cultural and economic character of much of the city. In some areas and blocks, extensive new development is now allowed, while other neighborhoods and blocks are protected from new residential and commercial development.
2002–2003	The federal government hands Governor's Island to New York State.
2002	The Lower Manhattan Development Corporation (LMDC) is created as a subsidiary of the Empire State Development Corporation. The LMDC is established by the State and City of New York after 9/11 with the goal of rebuilding Lower Manhattan. Renowned modernist architect Richard Meier designs two residential buildings on West Street at Perry Street, across from the Hudson River.[15]
2003	The Landmarks Preservation Commission designates the Gansevoort Market Historic District, encompassing the "Meatpacking District." Adjacent to the Hudson River on the far West Side of Manhattan, many of the meatpacking businesses (area public markets in operation since the 1880s), as well as the gay bars and sex clubs that operated in the neighborhood since at least the 1970s, have closed due to the area's recent gentrification.[16] Governor's Island, restricted by the government from residential development, opens up to visitors in the summer for a range of recreational, leisure, cultural, educational, and community uses.[17]
2004	The Metropolitan Transportation Authority discontinues use of tokens. The token is replaced by the Metrocard.
2005	The Fulton Fish Market moves from South Street on the Lower East Side to the Bronx. Its location in Lower Manhattan had been the site of public markets since 1822, making the fish market one of the largest and oldest continuing public markets in the United States.
2007	Public hearings are held about the redevelopment of the area known collectively as the Christopher Street Piers on the Lower West Side, known for its gay male cruising scene from the 1970s forward.[18]
2008	The New York City Council approves a controversial rezoning of historic 125th Street in Harlem.[19] The New York City Council approves a controversial rezoning of a large portion of the Lower East Side/East Village imposing height restrictions.[20] Prompted in part by a meltdown of the subprime-mortgage industry, stock markets plummet and initiate the global "Great Recession."
2009	The High Line, a much talked-about public park built on an abandoned elevated freight-train line, opens in the Meatpacking District and Chelsea.[21]
2010	The Gowanus Canal, a creek adjacent to the thriving industrial neighborhoods of nineteenth- and early twentieth-century South Brooklyn, is designated a Superfund cleanup site by the federal Environmental Protection Agency. The New York City Department of City Planning plans to release its new comprehensive waterfront plan, "Vision 2020." New York City subway fare is $2.25.

Endnotes

1
The American Housing Act helped reshape cities, while the Federal Housing Act of 1934, which established the Federal Housing Administration, was responsible for the rise of the postwar American suburb. This legislation made home mortgages easily available to families, though almost exclusively white ones. It helped establish a system of racial preferences and discriminatory industry-wide home mortgage, neighborhood-designation, and lending practices such as redlining and blockbusting. The federal housing legislation of the 1930s and 1940s dramatically reordered American urban and suburban geography and social life, leading to the fantastic growth of the midcentury middle-class suburb on the one hand and to the hollowing out of the inner city and downtown on the other.

2
Containerization is the process whereby cargo is shipped in large, intact container boxes in ships, requiring an automated system based around deep-water ports; it made global shipping much less expensive and revolutionized global commerce and trade. Prior to this technology, goods and objects were transported onto and off ships by manual labor and the sheer physical strength of individual workers, in a system known as "break-bulk." Several longtime maritime port cities, such as New York, were not able or did not adapt to the technology, which had severe effects on the economies and cultures of those cities and their often-famed waterfront neighborhoods.

3
Jane Jacobs became the chair of the Joint Committee to Stop the Lower Manhattan Expressway and, in a related protest, got arrested in 1968.

4
This agreement represented an early example of New York City's approach of providing tax breaks and subsidies to corporations, especially from the finance and real estate industries, from the 1960s forward. This approach intensified during the fiscal crisis of the 1970s, when the city tried to lure corporations into the high-end commercial and office space downtown in and around the World Trade Center. Mayor Giuliani vigorously pursued this economic-development strategy , as has Mayor Bloomberg in the wake of 9/11.

5
The majority of the jobs lost in this period were industrial. A number of these lost jobs also resulted when corporate headquarters began to move from New York City.

6
"Open admissions" ensured that all high school graduates, regardless of previous academic preparation, were guaranteed a slot in the CUNY system.

7
The Young Lords Organization was among that era's many political organizations, which also included the Black Panthers, I Wor Kuen, and the American Indian Movement. For supporters, they offered their long-neglected communities food and social services, self-defense training, political education and empowerment, and grassroots organizing. For detractors, some of these groups engaged in actions that, combining ethno-nationalist and Communist-inspired ideologies, could and did at times result in violence.

8
The Green Guerrillas, founded by Liz Christy, was an organization that engaged in "guerrilla" tactics such as throwing seed bombs into abandoned city lots and viewed gardening as a form of environmental politics and activism.

9
CUNY was long known as the "poor man's Harvard." In the early to mid-twentieth century when there were still quotas in place at many private institutions, CUNY educated many poor and working-class New Yorkers, including many Jewish New Yorkers, some of whom would become quite prominent.

10
Beginning in the 1960s and 70s, the Baltimore-based Rouse Company began to develop suburban shopping malls in the U.S. and to popularize a mode and aesthetic of commercial development known as the "festival marketplace," of which the current South Street Seaport in New York City is one of the most famous examples. Critics charge that this kind of mall environment is privatized, sanitized, and bereft of unique features that benefit local communities.

11
The Times Square BID and the Bryant Park Restoration Corporation (see 1992 entry) reflected a new era of public-private partnerships and neoliberal urban governance. These kinds of arrangements, increasingly popular and common, allow for "public" space that is maintained and controlled by the private sector. Opponents suggest that the erosion of the line between public and private allows for the state to shirk its traditional responsibilities.

12
Giuliani generated both fierce opposition and fierce support on the part of many New Yorkers. Critics charged that "quality of life" policing unfairly targeted poor and working-class people of color and immigrants, including street vendors, taxi drivers, "squeegee" men, the homeless, and young black and Latino males. Supporters claimed that Giuliani's often-gruff approach and style, as well his policies, helped turn New York City around economically and socially, particularly in the arena of street crime.

13
In 2003, a legal resolution allowed the gardens to be temporarily administered by the NYC Parks Department.

14
The Diallo death became a flash point for Giuliani's many critics, who pointed to a crime-fighting policy undergirded by police brutality and unfair treatment. Many were arrested in acts of civil disobedience.

15
Located in an area of historically industrial, waterfront, or other low-rise buildings, Meier's sixteen-story structures, which attracted several celebrity tenants, ushered in a dramatic change to the built environment of the far West Side.

16
In 2003, only 35 of what used to be 150 plus slaughterhouses and meatpacking plants remained. By 2005, the number dwindled to 20. Even fewer remain today due to the area's skyrocketing real estate prices and trendy cultural cachet (a number of fashion design houses have opened boutiques since the 1990s amid existing galleries and nightclubs).

17
Visitors took the short free ferry ride from the Battery Maritime Building in Lower Manhattan. This practice has continued every summer since.

18
Proposals for the redevelopment included a commercial entertainment complex, an educational space, or a services and drop-in center for young LGBT (lesbian, gay, bisexual, and transgendered) youth of color who had established a presence on Pier 40.

19
This rezoning allowed for more development in a taller commercial district. As with many recent rezoning battles in NYC, community residents and small businesses expressed concerns over gentrification, displacement, and out-of-scale development.

20
Residents of Chinatown and the Bowery expressed concerns that this rezoning meant that developers would instead intensify efforts to build up in their parts of the neighborhood rather than the whole of the Lower East Side.

21
Prompted by ten years of planning, the High Line was praised by some who pointed to it as an exemplar of twenty-first-century adaptive reuse and pedestrian-friendly open space. Critics charged that it facilitated the intensified gentrification and real estate development in the Meatpacking District and Chelsea.

Exhibition Checklist

Alvin Baltrop

Born 1948 Bronx, New York
Died 2004 New York
Lived and worked in New York

1
Untitled (from the series Pier Photographs), 1975–86
Gelatin silver print
4 ½ x 7 inches (11.4 x 17.7 cm)
The Alvin Baltrop Trust
Plate 45

2
Untitled (from the series Pier Photographs), 1975–86
Gelatin silver print
5 ¾ x 8 ½ inches (14.6 x 21.5 cm)
The Alvin Baltrop Trust
Plate 44

3
Untitled (from the series Pier Photographs), 1975–86
Gelatin silver print
6 ½ x 9 ¾ inches (16.5 x 24.7 cm)
The Alvin Baltrop Trust

4
Untitled (from the series Pier Photographs), 1975–86
Gelatin silver print
7 ¾ x 9 ¾ inches (19.6 x 24.7 cm)
The Alvin Baltrop Trust

5
Untitled (from the series Pier Photographs), 1975–86
Gelatin silver print
4 ½ x 6 ½ inches (11.4 x 16.5 cm)
The Alvin Baltrop Trust

6
Untitled (from the series Pier Photographs), 1975–86
Gelatin silver print
9 ½ x 6 ¼ inches (24.1 x 15.8 cm)
The Alvin Baltrop Trust

7
Untitled (from the series Pier Photographs), 1975–86
Gelatin silver print
6 ½ x 4 ½ inches (16.5 x 11.4 cm)
The Alvin Baltrop Trust

8
Untitled (from the series Pier Photographs), 1975–86
Gelatin silver print
9 ½ x 8 inches (24.7 x 20.3 cm)
The Alvin Baltrop Trust

9
Untitled (from the series Pier Photographs), 1975–86
Gelatin silver print
4 ¾ x 8 inches (12 x 20.3 cm)
The Alvin Baltrop Trust

10
Untitled (from the series Pier Photographs), 1975–86
Gelatin silver print
4 ½ x 7 inches (11.4 x 17.7 cm)
The Alvin Baltrop Trust

11
Untitled (from the series Pier Photographs), 1975–86
Gelatin silver print
7 ¼ x 9 ¼ inches (18.4 x 23.5 cm)
The Alvin Baltrop Trust

12
Untitled (from the series Pier Photographs), 1975–86
Gelatin silver print
7 ½ x 9 ½ inches (19 x 24.1 cm)
The Alvin Baltrop Trust

13
Untitled (from the series Pier Photographs), 1975–86
Gelatin silver print
4 ½ x 6 ¾ inches (11.4 x 17.1 cm)
The Alvin Baltrop Trust

14
Untitled (from the series Pier Photographs), 1975–86
Gelatin silver print
6 ½ x 4 ½ inches (16.5 x 11.4 cm)
The Alvin Baltrop Trust

15
Untitled (from the series Pier Photographs), 1975–86
Gelatin silver print
9 ¾ x 7 ¾ inches (24.7 x 19.6 cm)
The Alvin Baltrop Trust

16
Untitled (from the series Pier Photographs), 1975–86
Gelatin silver print
9 ¾ x 7 ¾ inches (24.7 x 19.6 cm)
The Alvin Baltrop Trust

17
Untitled (from the series Pier Photographs), 1975–86
Gelatin silver print
10 x 8 inches (25.4 x 20.3 cm)
The Alvin Baltrop Trust

18
Untitled (from the series Pier Photographs), 1975–86
Gelatin silver print
6 ½ x 4 ¼ inches (16.5 x 10.8 cm)
The Alvin Baltrop Trust

19
Untitled (from the series Pier Photographs), 1975–86
Gelatin silver print
6 ½ x 4 ½ inches (16.5 x 11.4 cm)
The Alvin Baltrop Trust
Plate 42

20
Untitled (from the series Pier Photographs), 1975–86
Gelatin silver print
4 ¼ x 6 ½ inches (10.8 x 16.5 cm)
The Alvin Baltrop Trust

21
Untitled (from the series Pier Photographs), 1975–86
Gelatin silver print
4 ½ x 6 ½ inches (11.4 x 16.5 cm)
The Alvin Baltrop Trust

22
Untitled (from the series Pier Photographs), 1975–86
Gelatin silver print
8 x 10 inches (20.3 x 25.4 cm)
The Alvin Baltrop Trust
Plate 41

23
Untitled (from the series Pier Photographs), 1975–86/2010
Gelatin silver print
6 x 9 inches (15.2 x 22.8 cm)
The Alvin Baltrop Trust

24
Untitled (from the series Pier Photographs), 1975–86/2010
Gelatin silver print
6 x 9 inches (15.2 x 22.8 cm)
The Alvin Baltrop Trust

25
Untitled (from the series Pier Photographs), 1975–86/2010
Gelatin silver print
6 x 9 inches (15.2 x 22.8 cm)
The Alvin Baltrop Trust

26
Untitled (from the series Pier Photographs), 1975–86/2010
Gelatin silver print
9 x 6 inches (22.8 x 15.2 cm)
The Alvin Baltrop Trust
Plate 43

27
Untitled (from the series Pier Photographs), 1975–86/2010
Gelatin silver print
6 x 9 inches (15.2 x 22.8 cm)
The Alvin Baltrop Trust

28
Untitled (from the series Pier Photographs), 1975–86/2010
Gelatin silver print
6 x 9 inches (15.2 x 22.8 cm)
The Alvin Baltrop Trust

29
Untitled (from the series Pier Photographs), 1975–86/2010
Gelatin silver print
6 x 9 inches (15.2 x 22.8 cm)
The Alvin Baltrop Trust

30
Untitled (from the series Pier Photographs), 1975–86/2010
Gelatin silver print
6 x 9 inches (15.2 x 22.8 cm)
The Alvin Baltrop Trust
31
Untitled (from the series Pier Photographs), 1975–86/2010
Gelatin silver print
9 x 6 inches (22.8 x 15.2 cm)
The Alvin Baltrop Trust
32
Untitled (from the series Pier Photographs), 1975–86/2010
Gelatin silver print
9 x 6 inches (22.8 x 15.2 cm)
The Alvin Baltrop Trust

Bernd and Hilla Becher

Bernd Becher
Born 1931 Siegen, Germany
Died 2007 Rostock, Germany
Lived and worked in Düsseldorf, Germany
Hilla Becher
Born 1934 Potsdam, Germany
Lives and works in Düsseldorf, Germany

33
New York Water Towers, 1988
Fifteen black-and-white photographs
15 ½ x 11 9/16 inches (39.3 x 29.2 cm), each
Private collection
Courtesy Sonnabend Gallery, New York
Plate 114

Dara Birnbaum

Born 1946 New York
Lives and works in New York

34
Liberty: A Dozen or So Views, 1976
Video transferred to DVD; black-and-white; sound; 11 min., 30 sec.
Courtesy Electronic Arts Intermix (EAI), New York
Plate 61

Jennifer Bolande

Born 1957 Cleveland, Ohio, USA
Lives and works in Joshua Tree and Los Angeles, California, USA

35
Globe Sightings: 65 Prince Street, NYC, 2000–2001
Digital chromogenic print
28 x 23 ½ inches (71.1 x 59.6 cm)
Collection the artist
36
Globe Sightings: 151 Spring Street, NYC, 2000–2001
Digital chromogenic print
28 x 23 ½ inches (71.1 x 59.6 cm)
Collection the artist
37
Globe Sightings: Avenue B & 7th Street, NYC, 2000–2001
Digital chromogenic print
23 ½ x 28 inches (59.6 x 71.1 cm)
Collection the artist
38
Globe Sightings: Avenue B, Day, NYC, 2000–2001
Digital chromogenic print
25 ½ x 23 ½ inches (65 x 59.6 cm)
Collection the artist
Plate 22
39
Globe Sightings: Avenue B, Twilight, NYC, 2000–2001
Digital chromogenic print
28 x 23 ½ inches (71.1 x 59.6 cm)
Collection the artist
40
Globe Sightings: East 4th Street, NYC, 2000–2001
Digital chromogenic print
26 ⅓ x 18 inches (66.8 x 45.5 cm)
Private collection
41
Globe Sightings: East 12th Street, NYC, 2000–2001
Digital chromogenic print
23 ½ x 28 inches (59.6 x 71.1 cm)
Collection the artist
42
Globe Sightings: East Broadway, NYC, 2000–2001
Digital chromogenic print
32 ½ x 38 ¾ inches (81.9 x 98.5 cm)
Collection the artist
43
Globe Sightings: Prince & Mulberry, NYC, 2000–2001
Digital chromogenic print
38 ½ x 27 ½ inches (98 x 70.1 cm)
Collection the artist
44
Globe Sightings: Rutherford Place, NYC, 2000–2001
Digital chromogenic print
32 ½ x 38 ½ inches (82.5 x 98 cm)
Collection the artist
Plate 23
45
Globe Sightings: St. Marks Place, NYC, 2000–2001
Digital chromogenic print
38 ½ x 32 ½ inches (98 x 82.5 cm)
Collection the artist
Plate 24
46
Globe Sightings: West 37th Street, NYC, 2000–2001
Digital chromogenic print
23 ½ x 28 inches (59.6 x 71.1 cm)
Collection the artist

Stefan Brecht

Born 1924 Berlin, Germany
Died 2009 New York
Lived and worked in New York

47
8th Avenue, 1985
Forty-eight unbound photocopied pages
8 ½ x 11 inches (21.5 x 27.9 cm)
Courtesy Rena Gill
Plate 113
48
8th Avenue
Soft cover book published 2006 by Onestar Press, Paris
5 ½ x 9 inches (14 x 22.8 cm)
49
8th Avenue Poems
Soft cover book published 2006 by Spuyten Duyvil, New York
8 ⅛ x 9 inches (20.6 x 22.8 cm)

Matthew Buckingham

Born 1963 Nevada, Iowa, USA
Lives and works in New York

50
One Side of Broadway, 2005
Continuous 35mm slide projection with eighty-one slides
Black-and-white; sound; 16 min.
Courtesy the artist and Murray Guy, New York
Plate 120

Tom Burr

Born 1963 New Haven, Connecticut, USA
Lives and works in New York

51
Unearthing the Public Restroom, 1994
Eight black-and-white photographs
14 x 17 1/10 inches (35.5 x 43.5 cm), each
Galerie Neu, Berlin
Plate 84
52
In Loving Memory of: An American Garden (for Frank O'Hara, "meet me in the park if you love me"), 1993/2007
Stained wood, Plexiglas, collaged paper and photographs, tacks
96 x 34 x 24 inches (243.8 x 86.4 x 61 cm)
Galerie Neu, Berlin
Plates 85–86

Roy Colmer

Born 1935 London, England
Lives and works in Los Angeles, California, USA

53
Doors N.Y.C.: 2nd Avenue between East 7th and East 8th Streets, Odd Numbers, 1976
Fifteen black-and-white photographs
5 x 3 ½ inches (12.7 x 8.8 cm)
Collection the artist
54
Doors N.Y.C.: East 7th Street between 2nd Avenue and Cooper Square, Odd Numbers, 1976
Thirty black-and-white photographs
5 x 3 ½ inches (12.7 x 8.8 cm)
Collection the artist
Plate 112
55
Doors N.Y.C.: Two Intersections, 1975–76
Photocopied book published 2001
3 ½ x 5 inches (8.8 x 12.7 cm)
Collection the artist

56
Movie Houses, N.Y.C., 1977–87
Photocopied book published 2003
5 x 3 ½ inches (12.7 x 8.8 cm)
Collection the artist
57
Trucks N.Y.C., 1977–88
Photocopied book published 2001
3 ½ x 5 inches (8.8 x 12.7 cm)
Private collection
58
W.T.C., 1993
Photocopied book published 2004
3 ½ x 5 inches (8.8 x 12.7 cm)
Private collection

Moyra Davey

Born 1958 Toronto, Ontario, Canada
Lives and works in New York

59
Newsstands, 1994
Eighteen chromogenic prints
20 x 20 inches (50.8 x 50.8 cm), each
Courtesy the artist and Murray Guy, New York
Plates 117–19

Terry Fox

Born 1943 Seattle, Washington, USA
Died 2008 Cologne, Germany
Lived and worked in Liege, Belgium

60
Lunar Rambles: Greenwich Street, 1976
Video transferred to DVD; color; sound; 32 min., 41 sec.
Museo Nacional Centro de Arte Reina Sofía, Madrid
61
Lunar Rambles: Brooklyn Bridge, 1976
Video transferred to DVD; color; sound; 33 min., 4 sec.
Museo Nacional Centro de Arte Reina Sofía, Madrid
Plate 65

William Gedney

Born 1932 Albany, New York, USA
Died 1989 New York
Lived and worked in New York

62
[Brooklyn Bridge wall with graffiti reading "Joe Black was here"], c. 1960
Black-and-white photograph
8 x 10 inches (20.3 x 25.4 cm)
William Gedney Collection, Archive of Documentary Arts, Duke University Libraries, Durham, North Carolina, USA
63
[Man on walkway of Brooklyn Bridge], c. 1960
Black-and-white photograph
14 x 20 inches (35.5 x 50.8 cm)
William Gedney Collection, Archive of Documentary Arts, Duke University Libraries, Durham, North Carolina, USA
64
[View from base of cable; tower, arches, and cables in the background], c. 1955
Black-and-white photograph
14 x 11 inches (35.5 x 27.9 cm)
William Gedney Collection, Archive of Documentary Arts, Duke University Libraries, Durham, North Carolina, USA
65
[Upward view very close to tower with arch on either side], c. 1955
Black-and-white photograph
14 x 11 inches (35.5 x 27.9 cm)
William Gedney Collection, Archive of Documentary Arts, Duke University Libraries, Durham, North Carolina, USA
66
[Bridge from street below at night], c. 1955
Black-and-white photograph
14 x 11 inches (35.5 x 27.9 cm)
William Gedney Collection, Archive of Documentary Arts, Duke University Libraries, Durham, North Carolina, USA
67
[Washington Street Market: Chambers Street corner, outside of the market], c. 1960
Black-and-white photograph
7 x 5 inches (17.7 x 12.7 cm)
William Gedney Collection, Archive of Documentary Arts, Duke University Libraries, Durham, North Carolina, USA
68
[Washington Street Market: street corner of market. Crates stacked and men talking under lights], c. 1960
Black-and-white photograph
7 x 5 inches (17.7 x 12.7 cm)
William Gedney Collection, Archive of Documentary Arts, Duke University Libraries, Durham, North Carolina, USA
69
[Washington Street Market: "Ben J. Koondel" sign with man walking under it], c. 1960
Black-and-white photograph
7 x 5 inches (17.7 x 12.7 cm)
William Gedney Collection, Archive of Documentary Arts, Duke University Libraries, Durham, North Carolina, USA
70
[Washington Street Market: man in shadow pulling crates on dolly], c. 1960
Black-and-white photograph
7 x 5 inches (17.7 x 12.7 cm)
William Gedney Collection, Archive of Documentary Arts, Duke University Libraries, Durham, North Carolina, USA
71
[Washington Street Market: street, daylight, truck being loaded], c. 1960
Black-and-white photograph
5 x 7 inches (12.7 x 17.7 cm)
William Gedney Collection, Archive of Documentary Arts, Duke University Libraries, Durham, North Carolina, USA
72
[Washington Street Market: African-American men loading a truck, daytime], c. 1960
Black-and-white photograph
5 x 7 inches (12.7 x 17.7 cm)
William Gedney Collection, Archive of Documentary Arts, Duke University Libraries, Durham, North Carolina, USA
73
[Washington Street Market: man rolling crates down street crowded with trucks at night], c. 1960
Black-and-white photograph
5 x 7 inches (12.7 x 17.7 cm)
William Gedney Collection, Archive of Documentary Arts, Duke University Libraries, Durham, North Carolina, USA
Plate 106
74
[Washington Street Market: outside market at night, a person pushing a cart down street], c. 1960
Black-and-white photograph
5 x 7 inches (12.7 x 17.7 cm)
William Gedney Collection, Archive of Documentary Arts, Duke University Libraries, Durham, North Carolina, USA
Plate 105
75
[Snow-covered street below tracks for elevated train during snowstorm; view from Gedney's apartment window], 1967
Black-and-white photograph
5 x 7 inches (12.7 x 17.7 cm)
William Gedney Collection, Archive of Documentary Arts, Duke University Libraries, Durham, North Carolina, USA
76
[Snow-covered street below tracks for elevated train during snowstorm; view from Gedney's apartment window], 1967
Black-and-white photograph
5 x 7 inches (12.7 x 17.7 cm)
William Gedney Collection, Archive of Documentary Arts, Duke University Libraries, Durham, North Carolina, USA
77
[Snow-covered street below tracks for elevated train, men and dog walking in opposite directions; view from Gedney's apartment window], 1967
Black-and-white photograph
5 x 7 inches (12.7 x 17.7 cm)
William Gedney Collection, Archive of Documentary Arts, Duke University Libraries, Durham, North Carolina, USA
78
[Snow-covered street below tracks for elevated train at night; view from Gedney's apartment window], 1967
Black-and-white photograph
5 x 7 inches (12.7 x 17.7 cm)
William Gedney Collection, Archive of Documentary Arts, Duke University Libraries, Durham, North Carolina, USA
Plate 110

79
[Snow-covered street below tracks for elevated train at night, policeman standing in front of laundry; view from Gedney's apartment window], 1967
Black-and-white photograph
5 x 7 inches (12.7 x 17.7 cm)
William Gedney Collection, Archive of Documentary Arts, Duke University Libraries, Durham, North Carolina, USA
Plate 109
80
[Truck on street below tracks for elevated train; view from Gedney's apartment window], 1967
Black-and-white photograph
5 x 7 inches (12.7 x 17.7 cm)
William Gedney Collection, Archive of Documentary Arts, Duke University Libraries, Durham, North Carolina, USA
81
[People walking along street underneath tracks for an elevated train; view from Gedney's apartment window], 1967
Black-and-white photograph
5 x 7 inches (12.7 x 17.7 cm)
William Gedney Collection, Archive of Documentary Arts, Duke University Libraries, Durham, North Carolina, USA
82
[Myrtle Avenue at night after heavy snowfall], c. 1969
Black-and-white photograph
5 x 7 inches (12.7 x 17.7 cm)
William Gedney Collection, Archive of Documentary Arts, Duke University Libraries, Durham, North Carolina, USA
83
[Myrtle Avenue with train and man sweeping], c. 1969
Black-and-white photograph
5 x 7 inches (12.7 x 17.7 cm)
William Gedney Collection, Archive of Documentary Arts, Duke University Libraries, Durham, North Carolina, USA
Plate 107
84
[Myrtle Avenue during the day], c. 1969
Black-and-white photograph
11 x 14 inches (27.9 x 35.5 cm)
William Gedney Collection, Archive of Documentary Arts, Duke University Libraries, Durham, North Carolina, USA
85
[Myrtle Avenue in snowstorm], c. 1969
Black-and-white photograph
11 x 14 inches (27.9 x 35.5 cm)
William Gedney Collection, Archive of Documentary Arts, Duke University Libraries, Durham, North Carolina, USA
86
[Myrtle Avenue from Gedney's apartment window; man running to stairs], c. 1969
Black-and-white photograph
5 x 7 inches (12.7 x 17.7 cm)
William Gedney Collection, Archive of Documentary Arts, Duke University Libraries, Durham, North Carolina, USA
Plate 108
87
[View of Myrtle Avenue from Gedney's apartment window], c. 1969
Black-and-white photograph
5 x 7 inches (12.7 x 17.7 cm)
William Gedney Collection, Archive of Documentary Arts, Duke University Libraries, Durham, North Carolina, USA

Bernard Guillot

Born 1950 Basel, Switzerland
Lives and works in Cairo, Egypt, and Paris, France

88
12th Avenue (dedicated to Orpheus and Eurydice), 1977
Thirty-two from a group of 184 gelatin silver prints
12 x 15 ½ inches (30.4 x 39.3 cm), each
Collection the artist
Plates 49–53

David Hammons

Born 1943 Springfield, Illinois, USA
Lives and works in New York

89
Phat Free, 1995
Video transferred to DVD; color; sound; 5 min., 4 sec.
Collection Eileen and Michael Cohen
Plate 66

Sharon Hayes

Born 1970 Baltimore, Maryland, USA
Lives and works in New York

90
In the Near Future, New York, 2005
Multiple-slide-projection installation, nine actions, nine projections; 223 original slides (729 in total)
Courtesy the artist and Tanya Leighton Gallery, Berlin
Plates 101–4

Peter Hujar

Born 1934 Trenton, New Jersey, USA
Died 1987 New York
Lived and worked in New York

91
Man on Pier, nd
Gelatin silver print
14 3/5 x 14 3/5 inches (37.1 x 37.1 cm)
The Peter Hujar Archive and Matthew Marks Gallery, New York
92
Hudson River (II), 1975
Gelatin silver print
14 3/5 x 14 3/5 inches (37.1 x 37.1 cm)
The Peter Hujar Archive and Matthew Marks Gallery, New York
93
Hudson River (IV), 1975
Gelatin silver print
14 3/5 x 14 3/5 inches (37.1 x 37.1 cm)
The Peter Hujar Archive and Matthew Marks Gallery, New York
Plate 40
94
City Hall at Night, 1976
Gelatin silver print
14 3/5 x 14 3/5 inches (37.1 x 37.1 cm)
The Peter Hujar Archive and Matthew Marks Gallery, New York
95
Foley Square, 1976
Gelatin silver print
14 3/5 x 14 3/5 inches (37.1 x 37.1 cm)
The Peter Hujar Archive and Matthew Marks Gallery, New York
96
Gas Station, 1976/2010
Pigmented ink print
14 3/5 x 14 3/5 inches (37.1 x 37.1 cm)
The Peter Hujar Archive and Matthew Marks Gallery, New York
97
Leroy Street, 1976
Gelatin silver print
14 3/5 x 14 3/5 inches (37.1 x 37.1 cm)
The Peter Hujar Archive and Matthew Marks Gallery, New York
98
Loading Dock at Night, 1976
Gelatin silver print
14 3/5 x 14 3/5 inches (37.1 x 37.1 cm)
The Peter Hujar Archive and Matthew Marks Gallery, New York
99
Lower Manhattan from the Harbor, 1976
Gelatin silver print
14 3/5 x 14 3/5 inches (37.1 x 37.1 cm)
The Peter Hujar Archive and Matthew Marks Gallery, New York
100
Nassau Street, 1976
Gelatin silver print
14 3/5 x 14 3/5 inches (37.1 x 37.1 cm)
The Peter Hujar Archive and Matthew Marks Gallery, New York
101
New Jersey—Night, 1976
Gelatin silver print
14 3/5 x 14 3/5 inches (37.1 x 37.1 cm)
The Peter Hujar Archive and Matthew Marks Gallery, New York
102
New York Downtown: Night, 1976
Gelatin silver print
14 3/5 x 14 3/5 inches (37.1 x 37.1 cm)
The Peter Hujar Archive and Matthew Marks Gallery, New York
103
Night, Downtown, 1976/2010
Pigmented ink print
14 3/5 x 14 3/5 inches (37.1 x 37.1 cm)
The Peter Hujar Archive and Matthew Marks Gallery, New York

104
Night Skyline and Parking Lots, 1976
Gelatin silver print
14 3/5 x 14 3/5 inches (37.1 x 37.1 cm)
The Peter Hujar Archive and Matthew Marks Gallery, New York
105
No Parking, 1976/2010
Pigmented ink print
14 3/5 x 14 3/5 inches (37.1 x 37.1 cm)
The Peter Hujar Archive and Matthew Marks Gallery, New York
106
Rock in Park, 1976
Gelatin silver print
14 3/5 x 14 3/5 inches (37.1 x 37.1 cm)
The Peter Hujar Archive and Matthew Marks Gallery, New York
107
San Gennaro Street Fair at Dawn (I), 1976
Gelatin silver print
14 3/5 x 14 3/5 inches (37.1 x 37.1 cm)
The Peter Hujar Archive and Matthew Marks Gallery, New York
108
San Gennaro Street Fair at Dawn (III), 1976
Gelatin silver print
14 3/5 x 14 3/5 inches (37.1 x 37.1 cm)
The Peter Hujar Archive and Matthew Marks Gallery, New York
109
Shrine at San Gennaro, 1976
Gelatin silver print
14 3/5 x 14 3/5 inches (37.1 x 37.1 cm)
The Peter Hujar Archive and Matthew Marks Gallery, New York
110
Stephen Varble, Soho, Franklin Street (III), 1976
Gelatin silver print
14 3/5 x 14 3/5 inches (37.1 x 37.1 cm)
The Peter Hujar Archive and Matthew Marks Gallery, New York
111
Triumph, 1976/2010
Pigmented ink print
14 3/5 x 14 3/5 inches (37.1 x 37.1 cm)
The Peter Hujar Archive and Matthew Marks Gallery, New York
112
Trucks, Night, 1976
Gelatin silver print
14 3/5 x 14 3/5 inches (37.1 x 37.1 cm)
The Peter Hujar Archive and Matthew Marks Gallery, New York
Plate 37
113
West Side Parking Lots, 1976/2010
Pigmented ink print
14 3/5 x 14 3/5 inches (37.1 x 37.1 cm)
The Peter Hujar Archive and Matthew Marks Gallery, New York
Plate 36
114
Woolworth Building, 1976
Gelatin silver print
14 3/5 x 14 3/5 inches (37.1 x 37.1 cm)
The Peter Hujar Archive and Matthew Marks Gallery, New York
115
World Trade Center at Twilight, 1976
Gelatin silver print
14 3/5 x 14 3/5 inches (37.1 x 37.1 cm)
The Peter Hujar Archive and Matthew Marks Gallery, New York
116
Man in Park, 1981
Gelatin silver print
14 3/5 x 14 3/5 inches (37.1 x 37.1 cm)
The Peter Hujar Archive and Matthew Marks Gallery, New York
117
Boy on Park Bench, 1981
Gelatin silver print
14 3/5 x 14 3/5 inches (37.1 x 37.1 cm)
The Peter Hujar Archive and Matthew Marks Gallery, New York
118
Gary in Park, 1981
Gelatin silver print
14 3/5 x 14 3/5 inches (37.1 x 37.1 cm)
The Peter Hujar Archive and Matthew Marks Gallery, New York
119
Pier-Five Doors, 1981
Gelatin silver print
14 3/5 x 14 3/5 inches (37.1 x 37.1 cm)
The Peter Hujar Archive and Matthew Marks Gallery, New York
120
Broken Chair—Pier, 1983
Gelatin silver print
14 3/5 x 14 3/5 inches (37.1 x 37.1 cm)
The Peter Hujar Archive and Matthew Marks Gallery, New York
121
Canal Street Piers: #2 Mural, 1983
Gelatin silver print
8 x 8 inches (20.2 x 20.2 cm)
The Peter Hujar Archive and Matthew Marks Gallery, New York
Plate 39
122
Canal Street Piers: Face and Writing on Wall, 1983
Gelatin silver print
8 x 8 inches (20.2 x 20.2 cm)
The Peter Hujar Archive and Matthew Marks Gallery, New York
123
Canal Street Piers: Fake Men on the Stairs, 1983
Gelatin silver print
8 x 8 inches (20.2 x 20.2 cm)
The Peter Hujar Archive and Matthew Marks Gallery, New York
124
Canal Street Piers: Man Painted on a Wall, 1983
Gelatin silver print
8 x 8 inches (20.2 x 20.2 cm)
The Peter Hujar Archive and Matthew Marks Gallery, New York
125
Canal Street Piers: Man Painting Figure Studies, 1983
Gelatin silver print
8 x 8 inches (20.2 x 20.2 cm)
The Peter Hujar Archive and Matthew Marks Gallery, New York
126
Canal Street Piers: Painting of Strongman in a Hallway, 1983
Gelatin silver print
8 x 8 inches (20.2 x 20.2 cm)
The Peter Hujar Archive and Matthew Marks Gallery, New York
127
Canal Street Piers: Window Paintings, 1983
Gelatin silver print
8 x 8 inches (20.2 x 20.2 cm)
The Peter Hujar Archive and Matthew Marks Gallery, New York
128
Hallway, Canal Street Pier, 1983
Gelatin silver print
14 3/5 x 14 3/5 inches (37.1 x 37.1 cm)
The Peter Hujar Archive and Matthew Marks Gallery, New York
129
Man at Pier 36, Canal Street, 1983
Gelatin silver print
14 3/5 x 14 3/5 inches (37.1 x 37.1 cm)
The Peter Hujar Archive and Matthew Marks Gallery, New York
130
Brooklyn Basketball Court (City Playground), 1985
Gelatin silver print
14 3/5 x 14 3/5 inches (37.1 x 37.1 cm)
The Peter Hujar Archive and Matthew Marks Gallery, New York
131
David Lighting Up, Manhattan—Night (I), 1985/2010
Pigmented ink print
14 3/5 x 14 3/5 inches (37.1 x 37.1 cm)
The Peter Hujar Archive and Matthew Marks Gallery, New York
Plate 38
132
David Wojnarowicz, Manhattan—Night (II), 1985
Gelatin silver print
14 3/5 x 14 3/5 inches (37.1 x 37.1 cm)
The Peter Hujar Archive and Matthew Marks Gallery, New York
133
David Wojnarowicz, Manhattan—Night (III), 1985
Gelatin silver print
14 3/5 x 14 3/5 inches (37.1 x 37.1 cm)
The Peter Hujar Archive and Matthew Marks Gallery, New York

134
Richie, 1985
Gelatin silver print
14 3/5 x 14 3/5 inches (37.1 x 37.1 cm)
The Peter Hujar Archive and Matthew Marks Gallery, New York

Joan Jonas

Born 1936 New York
Lives and works in New York

135
Songdelay, 1973
16mm film transferred to DVD; black-and-white; sound; 18 min., 35 sec.
Film: Robert Fiore
Museo Nacional Centro de Arte Reina Sofía, Madrid
Plate 46

Louise Lawler

Born 1947 Bronxville, New York, USA
Lives and works in New York

136
Birdcalls, 1972/1981
Audio recording; 7 min., 1 sec.
LeWitt Collection, Chester, Conneticut, USA
Plate 56
137
Volkswagen, 1978
Black-and-white postcard
5 1/2 x 3 1/2 inches (13.9 x 8.9 cm)
Collection Douglas Crimp
Plate 54
138
Truck, 1978
Black-and-white postcard
3 1/2 x 5 1/2 inches (8.9 x 13.9 cm)
Collection Douglas Crimp
Plate 55

Zoe Leonard

Born 1961 Liberty, New York, USA
Lives and works in New York

139
Model of New York no. 1, 1989/1990
Gelatin silver print
25 x 37 inches (63.5 x 94 cm)
Courtesy the artist and Galerie Gisela Capitain, Cologne
Frontispiece
140
Model of New York no. 2, 1989/1990
Gelatin silver print
25 1/2 x 40 inches (64.7 x 96.5 cm)
Courtesy the artist and Galerie Gisela Capitain, Cologne
Plate 129
141
Blow Me, 1994
Gelatin silver print
7 x 5 inches (17.8 x 12.7 cm)
Courtesy the artist and Galerie Gisela Capitain, Cologne
142
Gay + Proud + Dead, 1994
Gelatin silver print
6 3/4 x 8 1/2 inches (17.1 x 21.6 cm)
Courtesy the artist and Galerie Gisela Capitain, Cologne
143
I Love Pussy, 1994
Gelatin silver print
5 1/2 x 7 1/2 inches (14 x 19 cm)
Courtesy the artist and Galerie Gisela Capitain, Cologne
144
Lesbians, 1994
Gelatin silver print
5 3/8 x 7 5/8 inches (13.7 x 19.4 cm)
Courtesy the artist and Galerie Gisela Capitain, Cologne
145
Suck me, 1994/1997
Gelatin silver print
5 3/16 x 7 3/8 inches (13.2 x 18.7 cm)
Courtesy the artist and Galerie Gisela Capitain, Cologne
146
Nicole Loves Sue, 1995
Gelatin silver print
7 1/2 x 5 1/4 inches (19 x 13.3 cm)
Courtesy the artist and Galerie Gisela Capitain, Cologne
147
The Heart Is a Lonely Hunter, 1995
Gelatin silver print
7 1/2 x 5 1/4 inches (19 x 13.3 cm)
Courtesy the artist and Galerie Gisela Capitain, Cologne
148
Mari, I'm Sorry (no. 2), 1995/1997
Gelatin silver print
18 1/4 x 13 inches (46.4 x 33 cm)
Courtesy the artist and Galerie Gisela Capitain, Cologne
Plate 89
149
Flasher, 1997
Gelatin silver print
18 1/10 x 23 4/5 inches (46 cm x 60.5 cm)
Courtesy the artist and Galerie Gisela Capitain, Cologne
150
Tree + Fence, S. 3rd St., 1998/1999
Gelatin silver print
32 x 22 inches (81.3 x 55.9 cm)
Courtesy the artist and Galerie Gisela Capitain, Cologne
151
Untitled, 2000
Four dye transfer prints
30 x 20 1/2 inches (76.2 x 52.1 cm), each
Commission for the Centre National des Arts Plastiques, Paris
Courtesy the artist and Galerie Gisela Capitain, Cologne
Plate 91
152
Bubblegum no. 1, 2000/2003
Chromogenic print
16 1/8 x 11 1/8 inches (41 x 28.3 cm)
Courtesy the artist and Galerie Gisela Capitain, Cologne
Plate 92
153
Bubblegum no. 2, 2000/2003
Chromogenic print
18 1/4 x 12 1/2 inches (46.4 x 31.6 cm)
Courtesy the artist and Galerie Gisela Capitain, Cologne
Plate 93
154
Bubblegum no. 4, 2000/2003
Chromogenic print
16 1/4 x 11 1/4 inches (41.2 x 28.5 cm)
Courtesy the artist and Galerie Gisela Capitain, Cologne
155
Bubblegum no. 5, 2000/2003
Chromogenic print
18 1/2 x 12 5/8 inches (47 x 32.1 cm)
Courtesy the artist and Galerie Gisela Capitain, Cologne
Plate 94
156
Bubblegum no. 6, 2000/2003
Chromogenic print
15 7/8 x 11 inches (40.3 x 27.9 cm)
Courtesy the artist and Galerie Gisela Capitain, Cologne
Plate 95
157
Bubblegum no. 7, 2000/2003
Chromogenic print
19 x 13 inches (48.3 x 33 cm)
Courtesy the artist and Galerie Gisela Capitain, Cologne
158
Red Wall, 2001/2003
Dye transfer print
29 3/4 x 20 1/2 inches (75.6 x 52.1 cm)
Courtesy the artist and Galerie Gisela Capitain, Cologne
Plate 90
159
Wall, 2002
Gelatin silver print
41 3/4 x 29 3/4 inches (106 x 75.6 cm)
Courtesy the artist and Galerie Gisela Capitain, Cologne
160
Untitled (diptych), 2002/2003
Two chromogenic prints
14 5/8 x 20 inches (37.1 x 50.8 cm), each
Courtesy the artist and Galerie Gisela Capitain, Cologne

Sol LeWitt

Born 1928 Hartford, Connecticut, USA
Died 2007 New York
Lived and worked in New York and Chester, Connecticut, USA

161
Brick Wall, 1977
Thirty black-and-white photographs
14 ½ x 23 ¼ inches (36.8 x 59 cm), each
LeWitt Collection, Chester, Conneticut, USA
Plate 115

Glenn Ligon

Born 1960 Bronx, New York
Lives and works in New York

162
Housing in New York: A Brief History, 1960–2007, 2007
Silkscreen on wall
Ten parts: 35 ½ x 47 inches (90.1 x 119.3 cm), each
Courtesy the artist
See pp. 273–75

Robert Longo

Born 1953 Brooklyn, New York
Lives and works in New York

163
Untitled (Men in the Cities), 1979/2009
Three black-and-white photographs
20 x 16 inches (50.8 x 40.6 cm), each
Courtesy the artist and Metro Pictures, New York
Plate 21
164
Untitled (Men in the Cities), 1979/2009
Black-and-white photograph
20 x 16 inches (50.8 x 40.6 cm)
Courtesy the artist and Metro Pictures, New York
165
Untitled (Men in the Cities), 1979/2009
Black-and-white photograph
20 x 16 inches (50.8 x 40.6 cm)
Courtesy the artist and Metro Pictures, New York

Vera Lutter

Born 1960 Kaiserslautern, Germany
Lives and works in New York

166
North View, Old Slip, New York: October 10, 1994, 1994
Gelatin silver print
70 x 82 inches (177.8 x 208.2 cm)
Collection UniCredit Bank AG, Germany
Plate 14
167
South View, Old Slip, New York: October 8, 1994, 1994
Gelatin silver print
70 x 82 inches (177.8 x 208.2 cm)
Collection UniCredit Bank AG, Germany
Plate 13
168
West View, Old Slip, New York: November 11, 1994, 1994
Gelatin silver print
70 x 82 inches (177.8 x 208.2 cm)
Collection UniCredit Bank AG, Germany
Plate 15
169
East View, Old Slip, New York: April 29, 1995, 1995
Gelatin silver print
76 x 70 inches (193 x 177.8 cm)
Collection A. Selldorf
Plate 16

Danny Lyon

Born 1942 Brooklyn, New York
Lives and works in Maine and New Mexico, USA

From *The Destruction of Lower Manhattan*:

170
80 and 82 Beekman Street, 1967
Gelatin silver print
14 x 11 inches (35.5 x 27.9 cm)
Edwynn Houk Gallery, New York
171
100 Gold Street seen from the remains of the Tribune Building, 1967
Gelatin silver print
14 x 11 inches (35.5 x 27.9 cm)
Edwynn Houk Gallery, New York
172
185 West Street at Chambers, 1967
Gelatin silver print
11 x 14 inches (27.9 x 35.5 cm)
Edwynn Houk Gallery, New York
Plate 5
173
327, 329, and 331 Washington Street, between Jay and Harrison streets, 1967
Gelatin silver print
11 x 14 inches (27.9 x 35.5 cm)
Edwynn Houk Gallery, New York
Plate 4
174
A burner is lifted to cut the bolts in the cast-iron front of 82 Beekman Street, 1967
Gelatin silver print
14 x 11 inches (35.5 x 27.9 cm)
Edwynn Houk Gallery, New York
175
Lower Manhattan and the Brooklyn Bridge from above the East River, 1967
Gelatin silver print
14 x 11 inches (35.5 x 27.9 cm)
Edwynn Houk Gallery, New York
Plate 1
176
The north side of Jay Street at West and Caroline streets, 1967
Gelatin silver print
11 x 14 inches (27.9 x 35.5 cm)
Edwynn Houk Gallery, New York
177
The northwest corner of Washington and Chambers streets, 1967
Gelatin silver print
11 x 14 inches (27.9 x 35.5 cm)
Edwynn Houk Gallery, New York
178
The northwest corner of Washington at Harrison Street, 1967
Gelatin silver print
11 x 14 inches (27.9 x 35.5 cm)
Edwynn Houk Gallery, New York
179
View from a Gold Street rooftop looking east toward the rear of Fulton Street, 1967
Gelatin silver print
14 x 11 inches (35.5 x 27.9 cm)
Edwynn Houk Gallery, New York
180
View south on Cliff Street at its intersection with Beekman, 1967
Gelatin silver print
14 x 11 inches (35.5 x 27.9 cm)
Edwynn Houk Gallery, New York
Plate 3
181
View south from 88 Gold Street, 1967
Gelatin silver print
14 x 11 inches (35.5 x 27.9 cm)
Edwynn Houk Gallery, New York
Plate 7
182
View south from 100 Gold Street, 1967
Gelatin silver print
14 x 11 inches (35.5 x 27.9 cm)
Edwynn Houk Gallery, New York
183
View through the rear wall, 89 Beekman Street, 1967
Gelatin silver print
14 x 11 inches (35.5 x 27.9 cm)
Edwynn Houk Gallery, New York
Plate 6
184
View west from a Washington Street rooftop, 1967
Gelatin silver print
11 x 14 inches (27.9 x 35.5 cm)
Edwynn Houk Gallery, New York
Plate 2
185
Washington Street. View north from Chambers Street, 1967
Gelatin silver print
11 x 14 inches (27.9 x 35.5 cm)
Edwynn Houk Gallery, New York
186
West Street between Jay and Duane streets, 1967
Gelatin silver print
14 x 11 inches (35.5 x 27.9 cm)
Edwynn Houk Gallery, New York

Babette Mangolte

Born 1941 Montmorot (Jura), France
Lives and works in New York

187
Group Primary Accumulation (Trisha Brown, Central Park), 1972
Two black-and-white photographs
8 x 10 inches (20.3 x 25.4 cm), each
Courtesy Broadway 1602, New York
188
Light Touch (Robert Whitman), 1976
Eleven black-and-white photographs
8 x 10 inches (20.3 x 25.4 cm), each
Courtesy Broadway 1602, New York
Plate 47
189
Roof Piece (Trisha Brown), 1973
Contact sheet
20 x 16 inches (50.8 x 40.6 cm)
Courtesy Broadway 1602, New York
190
Roof Piece (Trisha Brown), 1973
Black-and-white photograph
16 x 20 inches (40.6 x 50.8 cm)
Courtesy Broadway 1602, New York
Plate 48
191
Woman Walking down a Ladder (Trisha Brown), 1973
Contact sheet
20 x 16 inches (50.8 x 40.6 cm)
Courtesy Broadway 1602, New York
192
Babette Mangolte and Lucinda Childs
Calico Mingling, 1973
16mm film transferred to DVD; black-and-white; sound; 9 min., 50 sec.
Plate 73

Gordon Matta-Clark

Born 1943 New York
Died 1978 New York
Lived and worked in New York

193
Window Blow-Out, 1973
Eight black-and-white photographs
11 x 14 inches (27.9 x 35.5 cm), each
Generali Foundation Collection, Vienna
Plate 116
194
City Slivers, 1976
16mm film transferred to video; color; silent; 15 min.
Museo Nacional Centro de Arte Reina Sofía, Madrid
Plate 67

Steve McQueen

Born 1969 London, England
Lives and works in Amsterdam, the Netherlands, and London, England

195
Static, 2009
35mm film transferred to DVD; color; sound; 7 min., 3 sec.
Courtesy Marian Goodman Gallery, New York
Plates 25–26 and p. 304

John Miller

Born 1954 Cleveland, Ohio, USA
Lives and works in New York and Berlin, Germany

196
Clubs for America, 1993
Ten color photographs
5 x 7 inches (12.7 x 17.7 cm), each
Courtesy the artist and Metro Pictures New York
Plate 87

Donald Moffett

Born 1955 Texas, USA
Lives and works in New York

197
Gold/Tunnel (from The Extravagant Vein), 2003
Video projection, oil and enamel on linen
54 x 96 inches (137.1 x 243.8 cm)
Courtesy Marianne Boesky Gallery, New York
198
Gold/Tupelo Plains, 2003
Video projection, oil and enamel on linen
Two panels: 60 x 80 inches (152.4 x 203.2 cm), each
Collection Alan Hergott and Curt Shepard
Plate 88

James Nares

Born 1953 London, England
Lives and works in New York

199
Pendulum, 1976
Super 8 transferred to DVD; black-and-white; sound; 17 min., 15 sec.
Courtesy the artist and Paul Kasmin Gallery, New York
Plates 121–23

Max Neuhaus

Born 1939 Beaumont, Texas, USA
Died 2009 Maratea, Italy
Lived and worked in New York and Capri, Italy

200
[Poster for *Public Supply I*, October 8, 1966, WBAI, New York], 1966
Black-and-white poster with text and diagram
17 x 11 inches (43.2 x 27.9 cm)
Dia Art Foundation, New York
Plate 17
201
[Poster for *American Can*], 1966
Black-and-white lithograph with text and photograph
7 3/4 x 9 5/8 inches (19.7 x 24.4 cm)
Dia Art Foundation, New York
202
[Program for *Listen*, March 27, 1966, Avenue D and East 14th Street, New York], 1966
Color stamp and typewritten text on paper
8 13/16 x 4 1/4 inches (22.4 x 10.8 cm)
Dia Art Foundation, New York
203
[Announcement "Max Neuhaus is Available in North America January through June 1967" with descriptions of *Listen*, *Public Supply I*, *American Can*, *Bi-Product*, and *Max-Feed*], c. 1966
Folded black-and-white announcement with photographs and text
33 x 14 inches (83.8 x 35.6 cm)
Dia Art Foundation, New York
204
[Announcement for *Listen*, May 20, 1967, 6th Avenue and West 9th Street, New York], 1967
Black-and-white card with text
3 5/16 x 5 5/8 inches (8.4 x 14.3 cm)
Dia Art Foundation, New York
205
[Poster for 3 Evenings of *Fan Music*, August 9–11, 1967, rooftops of 137–141 Bowery, New York], 1967
Black-and-white poster with text and hand-drawn graphic
17 1/4 x 11 inches (43.8 x 27.9 cm)
Dia Art Foundation, New York
206
[Poster for *Listen* with photograph of Brooklyn Bridge from South Street, New York], 1976
Published by the Institute for Art and Urban Resources, New York
Double-sided black-and-white mailer on newsprint
22 3/4 x 16 1/2 inches (57.8 x 41.9 cm)
Dia Art Foundation, New York
Plate 18
207
[Announcement for *Listen*, Jersey City, NJ], 1968
Black-and-white card with text
6 1/4 x 4 5/16 inches (15.9 x 11 cm)
Dia Art Foundation, New York
208
[Poster for *Listen*, July 21, 1968, Eighth International Artists' Seminar, Fairleigh Dickinson University, Madison, NJ], 1968
Black-and-white poster with text and hand-drawn graphic
11 x 8 13/16 inches (27.9 x 22.4 cm)
Dia Art Foundation, New York
209
[Announcement for *Water Whistle I*, May 7–8, 1971, Hayden Hall Swimming Pool, New York University, New York], 1971
Color poster with text and photograph by Peter Moore
8 1/4 x 13 3/8 inches (21 x 8.6 cm)
Dia Art Foundation, New York

210
[Postcard for *Water Whistle XV*, May 12, 1974, Carmine Street Pool, New York], 1974
Sponsored by Leo Castelli Gallery, New York
Black-and-white postcard with text and blue background on verso
3 ½ x 7 inches (8.9 x 17.8 cm)
Dia Art Foundation, New York
211
[Postcard for *Round*, November 19–21, 1976, U. S. Custom House, New York], 1976
Black-and-white postcard with photograph of interior of U.S. Custom House rotunda and text
5 ½ x 6 ½ inches (14 x 16.5 cm)
Dia Art Foundation, New York
212
[Poster for *Times Square*], 1977
Poster with text and color and black-and-white photographs
18 ½ x 24 ¼ inches (47 x 61.5 cm)
Dia Art Foundation, New York
213
[Postcard for *Max Neuhaus: A New Work (Underground)*, June–September, 1978, Abby Aldrich Rockefeller Sculpture Garden, Museum of Modern Art, New York], 1978
Black-and-white postcard with photograph and text
4 1/16 x 6 1/16 inches (10.3 x 15.4 cm)
Dia Art Foundation, New York

Catherine Opie

Born 1961 Sandusky, Ohio, USA
Lives and works in Los Angeles, California, USA

214
Untitled #2 (Wall Street), 2001
Iris print
16 x 40 inches (40.6 x 104.1 cm)
Courtesy Regen Projects, Los Angeles
Plate 11
215
Untitled #6 (Wall Street), 2001
Iris print
16 x 40 inches (40.6 x 104.1 cm)
Courtesy Regen Projects, Los Angeles
216
Untitled #8 (Wall Street), 2001
Iris print
16 x 40 inches (40.6 x 104.1 cm)
Courtesy Regen Projects, Los Angeles
217
Untitled #9 (Wall Street), 2001
Iris print
16 x 40 inches (40.6 x 104.1 cm)
Sender Collection, New York
218
Untitled #11 (Wall Street), 2001
Iris print
16 x 40 inches (40.6 x 104.1 cm)
Courtesy Regen Projects, Los Angeles
219
Untitled #14 (Wall Street), 2001
Iris print
16 x 40 inches (40.6 x 104.1 cm)
Courtesy Regen Projects, Los Angeles
Plate 12

Gabriel Orozco

Born 1962 Jalapa, Veracruz, Mexico
Lives and works in New York, Paris, France, and Mexico City, Mexico

220
Extension of a Reflection (*La extension del reflejo*), 1992
Chromogenic print
16 x 20 inches (40.6 x 50.8 cm)
Courtesy Marian Goodman Gallery, New York
221
Foam, 1992
Chromogenic print
16 x 20 inches (40.6 x 50.8 cm)
Courtesy Marian Goodman Gallery, New York
Plate 128
222
Leaves on a Car, 1992
Chromogenic print
16 x 20 inches (40.6 x 50.8 cm)
Courtesy Marian Goodman Gallery, New York
223
Autumn Umbrella, 1993
Chromogenic print
16 x 20 inches (40.6 x 50.8 cm)
Courtesy Marian Goodman Gallery, New York
Plate 127
224
Dog Urine in Snow (*Meada de perro*), 1993
Chromogenic print
16 x 20 inches (40.6 x 50.8 cm)
Courtesy Marian Goodman Gallery, New York
225
Island within an Island (*Isla en la Isla*), 1993
Chromogenic print
16 x 20 inches (40.6 x 50.8 cm)
Courtesy Marian Goodman Gallery, New York
Plate 126
226
Shadow of a Reflection (*La sombra del espejo*), 1999
Chromogenic print
16 x 20 inches (40.6 x 50.8 cm)
Courtesy Marian Goodman Gallery, New York

Barbara Probst

Born 1964 Munich, Germany
Lives and works in New York and Munich, Germany

227
Exposure #9: N.Y.C., Grand Central Station, 12.18.01, 1:21 p.m., 2001
Ultrachrome ink on cotton paper
Six parts: 34 x 51 inches (86 x 130 cm), each
Private collection, Germany
Courtesy Kuckei + Kuckei, Berlin, and Murray Guy, New York
Plate 19
228
Exposure #18: N.Y.C., 498 Seventh Avenue, 02.26.03, 1:29 p.m., 2003
Ultrachrome ink on cotton paper
Four parts: 44 x 29 ½ inches (112 x 75 cm), each
Private collection, Germany
Courtesy Kuckei + Kuckei, Berlin, and Murray Guy, New York
Plate 20

Emily Roysdon

Born 1977 Easton, Maryland, USA
Lives and works in New York and Stockholm, Sweden

229
Untitled (David Wojnarowicz Project), 2001–2007
Twelve gelatin silver prints, embroidery, and collage
11 x 14 inches (27.9 x 35.5 cm), each
Courtesy the artist
Plates 80–83
230
The Piers Untitled (#2), 2010
Gelatin silver print
29 ½ x 29 ½ inches (75 x 75 cm)
Courtesy the artist
231
The Piers Untitled (#5), 2010
Gelatin silver print
29 x 37 ¾ inches (74 x 96 cm)
Courtesy the artist

Cindy Sherman

Born 1954 Glen Ridge, New Jersey, USA
Lives and works in New York

232
Untitled Film Still #22, 1978
Gelatin silver print
29 x 36 ¼ inches (74 x 92 cm)
Courtesy the artist and Metro Pictures, New York
233
Untitled Film Still #25, 1978
Gelatin silver print
29 x 36 ¼ inches (74 x 92 cm)
Courtesy the artist and Metro Pictures, New York
234
Untitled Film Still #60, 1980
Gelatin silver print
34 ½ x 27 ⅜ inches (87 x 69.5 cm)
Courtesy the artist and Metro Pictures, New York
Plate 60
235
Untitled Film Still #63, 1980
Gelatin silver print
29 x 36 ¼ inches (74 x 92 cm)
Courtesy the artist and Metro Pictures, New York
Plate 59
236
Untitled Film Still #64, 1980
Gelatin silver print
26 2/11 x 36 ⅝ inches (66.5 x 93 cm)
Courtesy the artist and Metro Pictures, New York
Plate 57

237
Untitled Film Still #83, 1980
Gelatin silver print
26 2/11 x 36 1/4 inches (66.5 x 92 cm)
Courtesy the artist and Metro Pictures, New York

Shunk-Kender

Harry Shunk
Born 1924 Reudnitz, Germany
Died 2006 New York
János Kender
Born 1937 Baja, Hungary
Died unknown
The professional partnership named Shunk-Kender was formed in Paris in the late 1950s and dissolved in New York in 1973.

238
Projects: Pier 18, 1971
Curator: Willoughby Sharp
Photographs by Shunk-Kender and various artists
354 gelatin silver prints
Dimensions variable
Courtesy Löic Malle. A.A.S., Paris, and
The Roy Lichtenstein Foundation Collection
Plates 27–35

Charles Simonds

Born 1945 New York
Lives and works in New York

239
Dwellings, 1972
16mm film transferred to DVD; black-and-white; sound; 11 min.
Film: David Troy
Collection the artist
Plate 124
240
Dwellings Winter, 1974
16mm film transferred to DVD; color; sound; 13 min.
Film: Rudy Burckhardt
Collection the artist
Plate 125

Thomas Struth

Born 1954 Geldern, Germany
Lives and works in Düsseldorf, Germany

241
Water Street, New York/Wall Street, 1978
Black-and-white photograph
16 1/2 x 22 1/2 inches (41.3 x 57.3 cm)
Courtesy the artist
242
Broad Street, New York/Wall Street, 1978
Black-and-white photograph
15 1/10 x 21 inches (38.4 x 53.5 cm)
Courtesy the artist
243
Crosby Street, New York/SoHo, 1978
Black-and-white photograph
11 2/5 x 15 3/8 inches (29 x 39 cm)
Courtesy the artist
Plate 8
244
Lafayette Street (Grand Street), New York/SoHo, 1978
Black-and-white photograph
15 3/4 x 23 1/4 inches (40 x 59 cm)
Courtesy the artist
245
99th Street at 1st Avenue, New York/Harlem, 1978
Black-and-white photograph
15 3/4 x 22 inches (40 x 55.8 cm)
Courtesy the artist
246
115th Street at 2nd Avenue, New York/Harlem, 1978
Black-and-white photograph
14 1/2 x 20 1/2 inches (37 x 51.5 cm)
Courtesy the artist
Plate 9
247
West Broadway, New York/Tribeca, 1978
Black-and-white photograph
16 1/2 x 22 1/2 inches (41.3 x 57.3 cm)
Courtesy the artist
Plate 10
248
Washington Street, New York/Tribeca, 1978
Black-and-white photograph
15 3/4 x 21 7/8 inches (40 x 55.5 cm)
Courtesy the artist
249
Pine Street, New York, 1978
Black-and-white photograph
14 3/4 x 20 3/8 inches (37.5 x 51.7 cm)
Courtesy the artist

James Welling

Born 1951 Hartford, Connecticut, USA
Lives and works in Los Angeles, California, USA

250
Eastern Window, 1997–2000
Twenty gelatin silver prints
8 x 10 inches (20.3 x 25.4 cm), each
Courtesy Regen Projects, Los Angeles
Plate 111

David Wojnarowicz

Born 1954 Red Bank, New Jersey, USA
Died 1992 New York
Lived and worked in New York

251
Arthur Rimbaud in New York, 1978–79/2004
Forty-four gelatin silver prints
9 11/16 x 13 inches (24.6 x 32.8 cm), each
Museo Nacional Centro de Arte Reina Sofía, Madrid
Plates 74–79

Christopher Wool

Born 1955 Chicago, Illinois, USA
Lives and works in New York

252
East Broadway Breakdown, 1994/2002
160 black-and-white photographs
11 x 8 1/2 inches (27.9 x 21.6 cm), each
Courtesy the artist and Luhring Augustine, New York
Plates 96–100
253
Untitled, 2007
Enamel on linen
106 x 96 inches (269.2 x 243.8 cm)
Courtesy the artist and Luhring Augustine, New York
254
Untitled, 2008
Enamel on linen
106 x 96 inches (269.2 x 243.8 cm)
Courtesy the artist and Luhring Augustine, New York

Film Program
Douglas Crimp with Juan A. Suárez

New York City Fragments

James Nares
Ramp, 1976
Super 8 transferred to 16mm film; color; sound;
4 min., 45 sec.

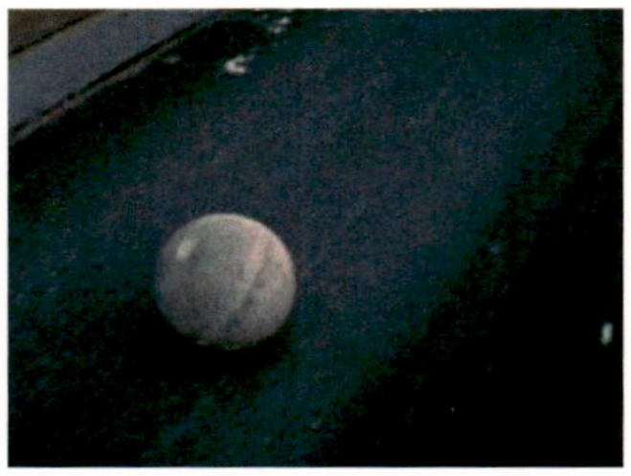

Twister, 1976
Super 8 transferred to 16mm film; black-and-white;
silent; 2 min.

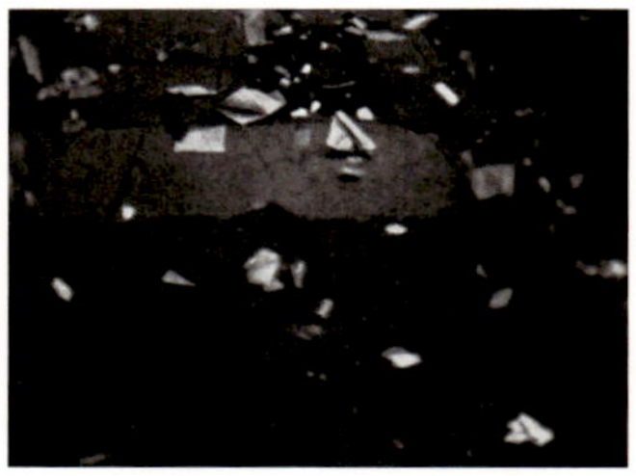

Gordon Matta-Clark
Day's End, 1975
Super 8 transferred to 16mm film; color; silent;
23 min., 10 sec.
Film: Betsy Sussler
Plate 68

Chantal Akerman
News from Home, 1976
16mm film; color; sound; 85 min.
Plate 64

New York City Portraits

Ken Jacobs
Window, 1964
16mm film; color; silent; 9 min., 34 sec.

Mel Bochner and Robert Moskowitz
New York Windows, 1966
16mm film; black-and-white; silent; 9 min.

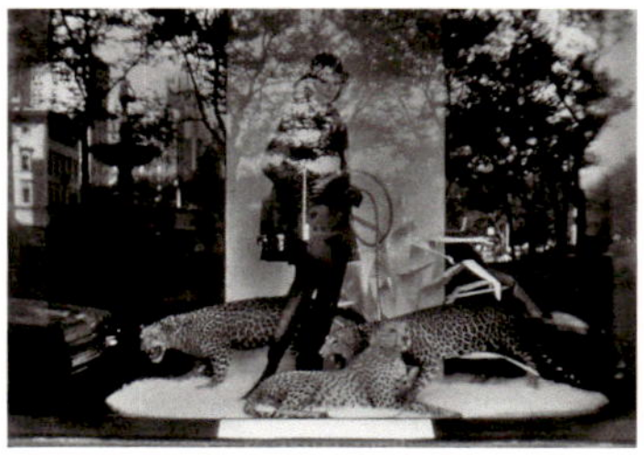

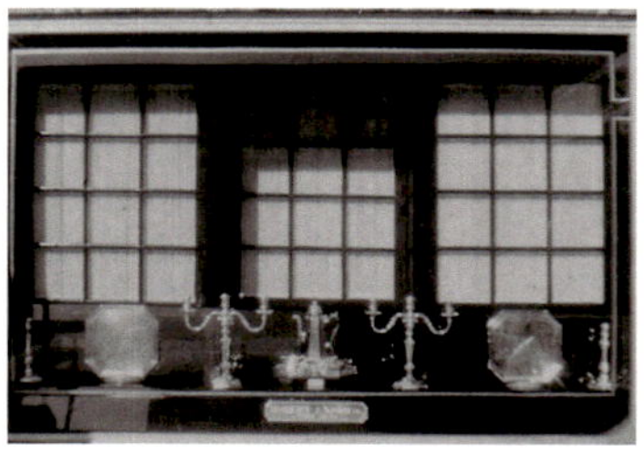

Rudy Burckhardt
Square Times, 1967
16mm film; color; sound; 6 min., 30 sec.

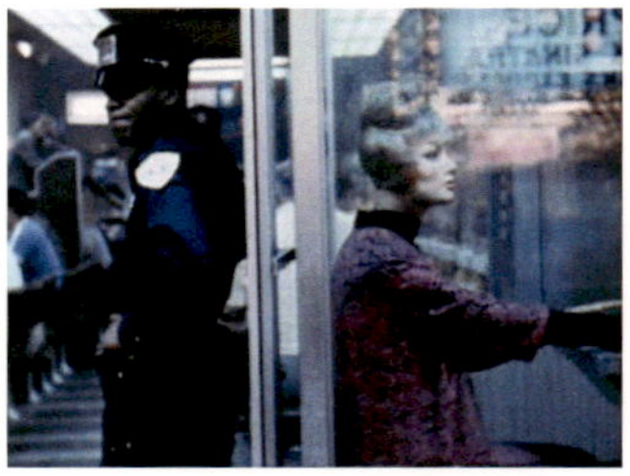

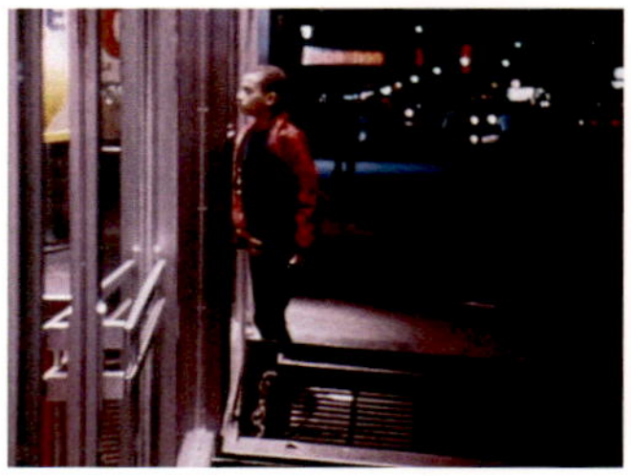

Sodom and Gomorrah, New York 10036, 1976
16mm film; color; sound; 6 min., 25 sec.

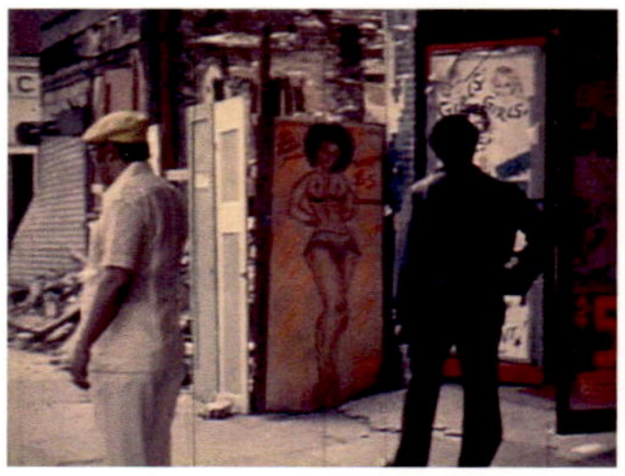

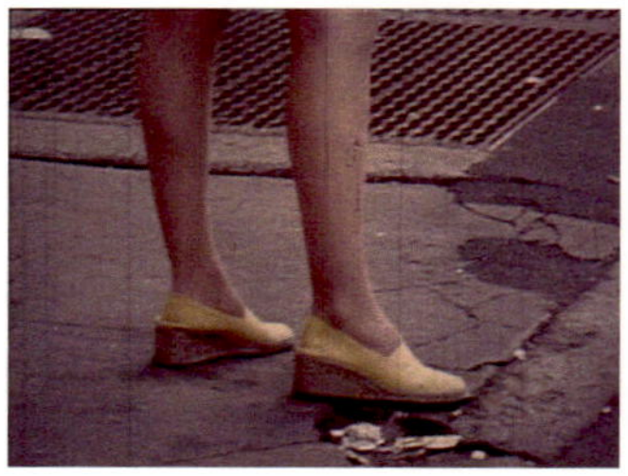

Default Averted, 1975
16mm film; black-and-white; sound; 19 min., 45 sec.

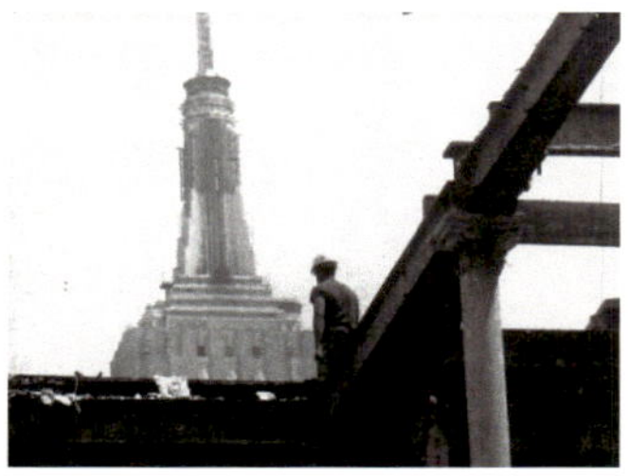

Peter Hutton
New York Portrait, Chapter I, 1978–79
16mm film; black-and-white; silent; 16 min.
Plate 69

New York Portrait, Chapter II, 1980–81
16mm film; black-and-white; silent; 16 min.
Plate 70

New York Portrait, Chapter III, 1990
16mm film; black-and-white; silent; 15 min.

Zoe Leonard and Nancy Brooks Brody
East River Park, 1991
16mm film; black-and-white; silent; 6 min., 53 sec.

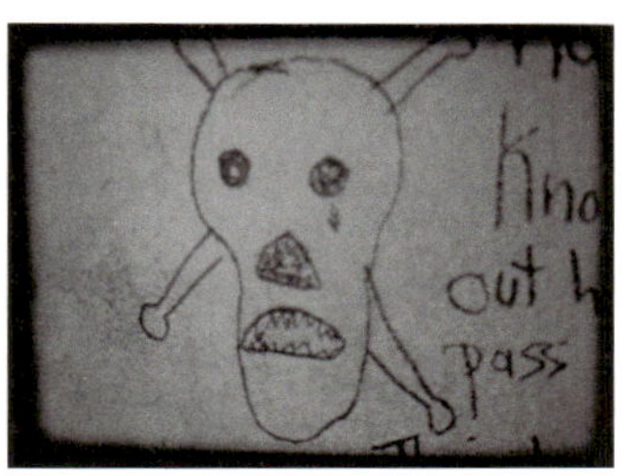

New York City Performances

Jack Smith
Scotch Tape, 1959–62
16mm film; color; sound; 3 min.
Plate 63

Ken Jacobs
The Whirled, 1956–63
Video; black-and-white and color; sound; 27 min.
Plate 62

Babette Mangolte and Lucinda Childs
Calico Mingling, 1973
16mm film; black-and-white; sound; 9 min., 50 sec.
Plate 73

Joan Jonas
Songdelay, 1973
16mm film transferred to DVD; black-and-white; sound; 18 min., 35 sec.
Plate 46

Gordon Matta-Clark
Clockshower, 1973
16mm film; color; silent; 13 min., 50 sec.

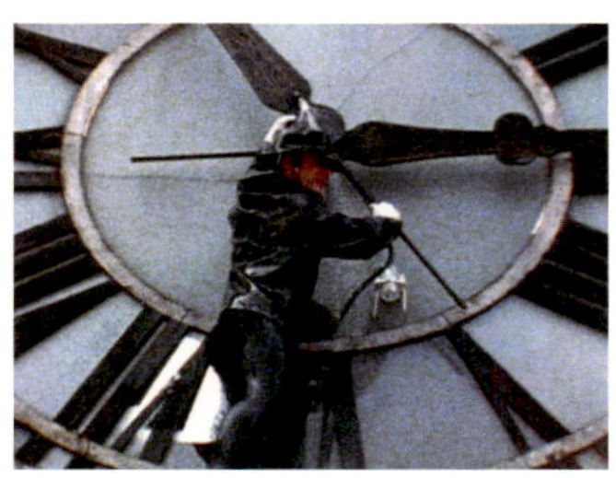

Vivienne Dick
She Had Her Gun All Ready, 1978
Super 8; color; sound; 26 min., 30 sec.

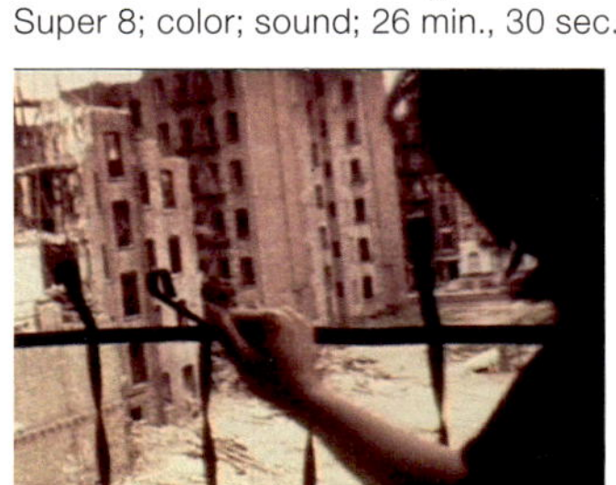

Abigail Child
Mutiny, 1983
16mm film; color; sound; 10 min.

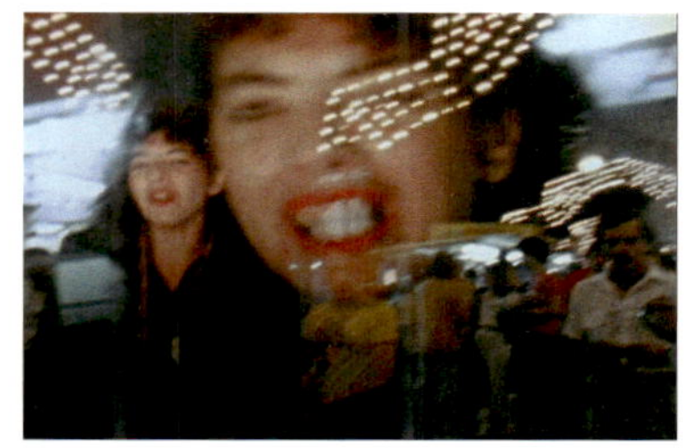

Charles Atlas
From an Island Summer, 1983–84
Video; color; sound; 13 min., 4 sec.

Rudy Burckhardt
Central Park in the Dark, 1985
16mm film; color; sound; 8 min.

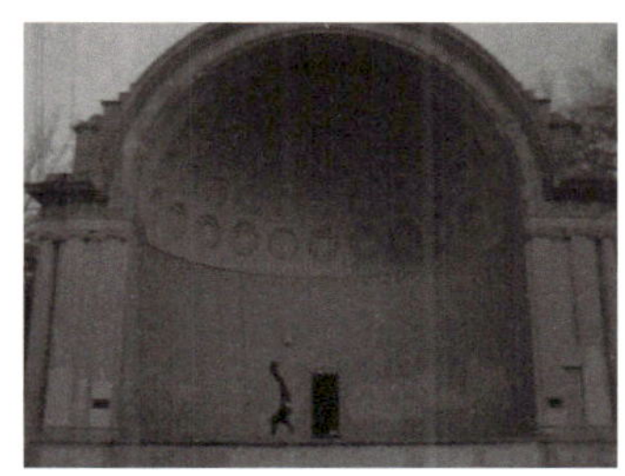

Nelson Sullivan
Drag Queens in Times Square, 1986
Video-8; color; sound; 7 min.
Plate 71

Charles Atlas
Mrs. Peanut Visits New York, 1999
Video; color; sound; 6 min., 5 sec.
Plate 72

Bibliography

Abu-Lughod, Janet. *From Urban Village to East Village: The Battle for New York's Lower East Side.* Oxford: Wiley-Blackwell, 1995.

Ault, Julie, ed. *Alternative Art New York, 1965–1985.* Minneapolis: University of Minnesota Press, 2002.

Block, René, Ursula Block, and Kurt Thöricht. *New York—Downtown Manhattan: Soho.* Berlin: Akademie der Künste, 1976.

Bohm, Florian, Luca Pizzarone, and Wolfgang Scheppe. *Endcommercial/Reading the City.* Ostfildern-Ruit: Hatje Cantz, 2002.

Bone, Kevin, ed. *The New York Waterfront: Evolution and Building Culture of the Port and Harbor.* New York: The Monicelli Press, 1997.

Brentano, Robyn, ed., with Mark Savitt, *112 Workshop, 112 Greene Street: History, Artists & Artworks.* New York: New York University Press, 1981.

Burrows, Edwin, and Mike Wallace. *Gotham: A History of New York City to 1898.* New York: Oxford University Press, 1999.

Buttenweiser, Ann. *Manhattan Water-Bound: Manhattan's Waterfront from the Seventeeth Century to the Present.* New York: New York University Press, 1987.

Caro, Robert A. *The Power Broker: Robert Moses and the Fall of New York.* New York: Random House, 1974.

De Certeau, Michel. *The Practice of Everyday Life.* Translated by Steven Rendall. Berkeley and Los Angeles: University of California Press, 1984.

Chisholm, Dianne. *Queer Constellations: Subcultural Space in the Wake of the City.* Minneapolis: University of Minnesota Press, 2005.

Crimp, Douglas, with Adam Rolston. *AIDS Demo Graphics.* Seattle: Bay Press, 1990.

Darton, Eric. *Divided We Stand: A Biography of New York's World Trade Center.* New York: Basic Books, 1999.

Delaney, Samuel. *Times Square Red, Times Square Blue.* New York and London: New York University Press, 1999.

Deutsche, Rosalyn. *Evictions: Art and Spatial Politics.* Cambridge, MA: MIT Press, 1996.

Fainstein, Susan. *The City Builders: Property Development in New York and London, 1980–2000.* Lawrence: University Press of Kansas, 2001.

Fitch, Robert. *The Assassination of New York.* Brooklyn, NY, and London: Verso, 1993.

Gandy, Matthew. *Concrete and Clay: Reworking Nature in New York City.* Cambridge, MA: MIT Press, 2003.

Gastil, Raymond. *Beyond the Edge: New York's New Waterfront.* Princeton, NJ: Princeton Architectural Press, 2002.

Ghent Urban Studies Team, ed. *Post Ex Sub Dis: Urban Fragmentations and Constructions.* Rotterdam: 010 Publishers, 2002.

Greenberg, Miriam. *Branding New York: How a City in Crisis Was Sold to the World.* New York: Routledge, 2008.

Jacobs, Jane. *The Death and Life of Great American Cities.* New York: Random House, 1961.

Koolhaas, Rem. *Delirious New York: A Retroactive Manifesto for Manhattan.* New York: Oxford University Press, 1978.

Kostelanetz, Richard. *SoHo: The Rise and Fall of an Artist's Colony.* New York and London: Routlege, 2003.

Laó-Montes, Agustín, and Arlene Dávila, eds. *Mambo Montage: The Latinization of New York* New York: Columbia University Press, 2001.

Lefebvre, Henri. *The Production of Space.* Translated by Donald Nicholson-Smith. Oxford: Blackwell Publishing, 1991.

Lopate, Phillip. *Waterfront: A Walk around Manhattan.* New York: Anchor Books, 2005.

McCorquodale, Duncan, ed. *Mapping New York.* London: Black Dog Publishing, 2009.

Mele, Christopher. *Selling the Lower East Side: Culture, Real Estate and Resistance in New York City.* Minneapolis: University of Minnesota Press, 2000.

Morris, James. *The Great Port: A Passage through New York.* New York: Harcourt, Brace & World, 1969.

Moscow, Henry. *The Street Book: An Encyclopedia of Manhattan's Street Names and Their Origins.* New York: Hagstrom, 1978.

Sanderson, Eric W. *Manahatta: A Natural History of New York City.* New York: Abrams, 2009.

Sante, Luc. *Low Life: Lures and Snares of Old New York.* New York: Farrar, Straus and Giroux, 1991.

Sassen, Saskia. *The Global City: New York, London, Tokyo.* Princeton, NJ: Princeton University Press, 2001.

Shorto, Russell. *The Island at the Center of the World: The Epic Story of Dutch Manhattan, the Forgotten Colony That Shaped America.* New York: Doubleday, 2004.

Smith, Neil. *The New Urban Frontier: Gentrification and the Revanchist City.* London: Routledge, 1996.

Sorkin, Michael. *Twenty Minutes in Manhattan.* London: Reaktion, 2009.

Sorkin, Michael, and Sharon Zukin, eds. *After the World Trade Center: Rethinking New York City.* New York: Routledge, 2002.

Taylor, Marvin J., ed. *The Downtown Book: The New York Art Scene 1974–1984.* Princeton, NJ: Princeton University Press; New York: Grey Art Gallery, New York University, 2006.

Van der Donck, Adriaen. *A Description of New Netherland.* Lincoln, Nebraska University Press, 2008.

Vergara, Camilo José. *Twin Towers Remembered.* New York: Princeton Architectural Press, 2001.

Wallis, Brian, ed. *If You Lived Here: The City in Art, Theory, and Social Activism: A Project by Martha Rosler.* Seattle: Bay Press, 1991.

Wojnarowicz, David. *The Waterfront Journals.* New York: Grove Press, 1996.

Zukin, Sharon. *Loft Living: Culture and Capital in Urban Change.* Piscataway, NJ: Rutgers University Press, 1989.

Contributors

Johanna Burton, a New York–based art historian and critic, was associate director and senior faculty member at the Whitney Independent Study Program in New York from 2008 to 2010 and was recently appointed director of the Graduate Program at the Center for Curatorial Studies, Bard College. She has written extensively on postwar and contemporary art for numerous publications, including *Artforum, October, Parkett,* and *Texte zur Kunst*; and she is the editor of *Cindy Sherman* (2006), a collection of critical essays on the artist for MIT Press's October Files series. Burton's other recent writings include texts on the women-only art magazine *Eau de Cologne* (published in *Witness to Her Art*, Center for Curatorial Studies, 2006) and Lee Lozano (Wexner Center, 2008); and she has written catalogue essays for recent career-survey exhibitions of Dara Birnbaum, Mel Bochner, and Mary Heilmann.

Lynne Cooke was appointed curator at Dia Art Foundation, New York in 1991 and in 2009 was named Dia's curator at large. In 2008, she became chief curator and deputy director at the Museo Nacional Centro de Arte Reina Sofía, Madrid. Co-curator of the 1991 Carnegie International and artistic director of the 1996 Sydney Biennale, she has also curated exhibitions in numerous venues in North America, Europe, and elsewhere. She has been on the faculty of the Center for Curatorial Studies at Bard College in addition to teaching as a visiting scholar in the graduate fine art departments of several universities including Yale and Columbia. In 2000 Cooke was awarded the Independent Curators International Agnes Gund Curatorial Award, and in 2006 she received the Award for Curatorial Excellence from the Center for Curatorial Studies at Bard College. Among her numerous publications are recent essays on the works of Rodney Graham, Jorge Pardo, Francis Alÿs, Richard Serra, Agnes Martin, and Zoe Leonard.

Douglas Crimp is Fanny Knapp Allen Professor of Art History at the University of Rochester. He began writing art criticism for *Art News* and *Art International* in the early 1970s and has published widely in such magazines as *Artforum* and *Art in America* as well as in scholarly journals. He is the author of *Melancholia and Moralism: Essays on AIDS and Queer Politics* (MIT Press, 2002) and *On the Museum's Ruins* (MIT Press, 1993). He was the curator of the *Pictures* exhibition at Artists Space, New York, in 1977, and an editor of *October* magazine from 1977 to 1990. He is currently working on a book about Andy Warhol's films and *Before Pictures,* a memoir of New York in the 1970s.

Glenn Ligon is a New York–based artist whose wide-ranging practice includes painting, photography, video, text, and online projects. His solo presentations include exhibitions at the Power Plant, Toronto, and touring (2005–2008), the Kunstverein Munich, Munich (2001), the Studio Museum in Harlem, New York (2001), and the Hirshhorn Museum and Sculpture Garden, Washington D.C. (1993). His work was also included in Documenta XI in 2002, the 1998 São Paulo Bienal, and the 1997 Venice Biennale. Among other awards, he has received the 2006 Skowhegan Medal for Painting, as well as a Guggenheim Fellowship and a Rockefeller Foundation residency.

Lytle Shaw teaches in the Department of English at New York University. His books of poetry include *Low Level Bureaucratic Structures: A Novel* (Shark, 1998), *Cable Factory 20* (Atelos, 1999), and *The Lobe Roof* (2002). He has also published a critical book, *Frank O'Hara: The Poetics of Coterie* (University of Iowa Press, 2006), and edited *Nineteen Lines: A Drawing Center Writing Anthology* (The Drawing Center/Roof, 2007). He is a regular contributor to *Cabinet* and has recently written essays on Gerard Byrne (Koenig Books, 2007), Robert Smithson (Dia Art Foundation, 2005), and Zoe Leonard (Dia Art Foundation, 2010), and on the Royal Art Lodge (The Drawing Center, 2003). His collaborative work with the artist Jimbo Blachly has been exhibited widely and is collected in *The Chadwick Family Papers: A Brief Public Glimpse.*

Juan A. Suárez teaches at the University of Murcia, Spain, and is the author of *Bike Boys, Drag Queens, and Superstars* (Indiana University Press, 1997), on the 1960s underground cinema; *Pop Modernism* (University of Illinois Press, 2007); and *Jim Jarmusch* (University of Illinois Press, 2007), and of essays on film, literature, and critical theory. Recent texts have appeared in the journals *Grey Room* and *ExitBook*, and in edited collections such as *Still Moving: Between Photography and Film*, eds. K. Beckman and J. Ma (Duke University Press, 2008) and *The Encyclopedia of Twentieth-Century American Fiction*, eds. D. Madden, P. O'Donnell, and J. Nieland (Wiley-Blackwell, 2010).

Lena Sze is a doctoral candidate in American studies at New York University. A poet and cultural worker, she has worked at the Asian Arts Initiative, the New York City Department of Cultural Affairs, and the Lower East Side Tenement Museum. She is the editor of *Chinatown Live(s): Oral Histories from Philadelphia's Chinatown* (New City Press, 2005), and her poems have been published in *A/P/A Journal* and *The Brooklyn Review*, among other publications.

David Wojnarowicz was an artist, filmmaker, writer, and activist. His books include *Close to the Knives* (Vintage Books, 1991), *The Waterfront Journals* (Grove Press, 1996), and *Memories That Smell Like Gasoline* (Artspace Books, 1992). Wojnarowicz, whose oeuvre includes paintings, photographs, performance, and films, had his first exhibitions in the early 1980s in galleries in New York's East Village and continued to show internationally. His work was the subject of a major retrospective organized by the New Museum, New York, in 1999. Wojnarowicz died in 1992 at the age of thirty-seven.

Acknowledgments

Realizing an exhibition in as short a time as it has taken to conceive and curate *Mixed Use, Manhattan* inevitably means that the organizers incur many debts and depend on the exceptional assistance and good will of numerous individuals. I am deeply grateful to my colleagues at the Reina Sofía Museum for their initial enthusiasm and their continuing support as this project grew in scale and ambition, in particular, Manuel J. Borja-Villel, Director, and Teresa Velázquez, head of exhibitions. The hard work of attending to myriad matters, both large and small, required to bring about an exhibition on this scale was expertly carried out by Rafael García Horrillo; to him and to my invaluable assistant, Beatriz Jordana, I am much indebted. Marcos Corrales's visual acumen and subtle intelligence contributed greatly to the exhibition design.

Special mention should also be made of colleagues who worked on this publication for their dedicated efforts: Kristin Poor, who expertly oversaw the demanding production of this book; Elisabeth Sherman and Analisa Bacall, who provided invaluable research; Mischa Leiner and his colleagues at CoDe, whose sensitive design brought elegant shape to this volume; and the scholars who contributed such substantial texts: Johanna Burton, Lytle Shaw, Juan A. Suárez, and Lena Sze. My deepest thanks go to Douglas Crimp, who has been the most perfect of collaborators: intellectually challenging, immensely knowledgeable, passionately engaged, and thoroughly involved in all facets of the show, the supporting film and seminar program, and this publication.

We are especially indebted to the artists participating in *Mixed Use, Manhattan*, who gave so generously of their works, their thoughts, their advice, and their encouragement:

Chantal Akerman, Charles Atlas, Hilla Becher, Dara Birnbaum, Mel Bochner, Jennifer Bolande, Matthew Buckingham, Tom Burr, Abigail Child, Roy Colmer, Moyra Davey, Vivienne Dick, Bernard Guillot, David Hammons, Sharon Hayes, Peter Hutton, Ken Jacobs, Joan Jonas, Louise Lawler, Zoe Leonard, Glenn Ligon, Robert Longo, Vera Lutter, Danny Lyon, Babette Mangolte, Steve McQueen, John Miller, Donald Moffett, Robert Moskowitz, James Nares, Catherine Opie, Gabriel Orozco, Barbara Probst, Emily Roysdon, Cindy Sherman, Charles Simonds, Thomas Struth, James Welling, and Christopher Wool

In addition, we are grateful to the following individuals:

Jacob Burckhardt, Kate Caldwell, Jesús Carrillo, Cat Celebrezze, Leah Churner, Barbara Clausen, Robert Coddington, Roger Conover, Jack Cowart, Lisa Darms, Jocelyn Davis, Rosalyn Deutsche, Wendy Dorsett, Aniko Erdosi, Regina Fiorito, Sam Frank, Stephanie Frontz, Karen Glynn, Janice Guy, Matthew Israel, Julia Jachs, Karen Kelly, Anke Kempkes, Josh Kline, Stephen Koch, Andrew Lampert, Shelley Lee, Vanessa Lopez, Rose Lord, Russell Lord, Lissa McClure, Ulrike Müller, Megan O'Connell, Teresa Ochoa de Zabalegui, Jeanine Oleson, Wendy Olsoff, Janet Passehl, John Passmore, Sheri Pasquarella, Jeffrey Peabody, Penny Pilkington, Stephen Pinson, Chris Rawson, Shaun Caley Regen, Ann Reynolds, Andrew Ross, Evan Ryer, Nelson Santos, Amy Sadao, Barbara Schröder, M. M. Serra, Jaime Shearn, Marc Siegel, Josh Siegel, Jeremy Sigler, Lola Sinreich, Antonio Sonnabend, Elisabeth Sussman, Gwenn Thomas, Randal Wilcox, Helene Winer, and Dave Yun

Lenders to the Exhibition

The Alvin Baltrop Trust

Marianne Boesky Gallery

Jennifer Bolande

Broadway 1602

Galerie Gisela Capitain

Eileen and Michael Cohen

Roy Colmer

Dia Art Foundation

Electronic Arts Intermix

Galerie Neu

William Gedney Collection, Archive of Documentary Arts, Duke University Libraries

Generali Foundation Collection

Rena Gill

Marian Goodman Gallery

Bernard Guillot

Alan Hergott and Curt Shepard

Edwynn Houk Gallery

The Peter Hujar Archive

Paul Kasmin Gallery

Kuckei + Kuckei

Tanya Leighton Gallery

Zoe Leonard

LeWitt Collection

The Roy Lichtenstein Foundation Collection

Glenn Ligon

Luhring Augustine

Loïc Malle, A.A.S.

Matthew Marks Gallery

Metro Pictures

Murray Guy

Museo Nacional Centro de Arte Reina Sofía

Regen Projects

Emily Roysdon

A. Selldorf

Sender Collection

Charles Simonds

Sonnabend Gallery

Specific Object / David Platzker

Thomas Struth

Collection UniCredit Bank AG

and the lenders who wish to remain anonymous

Photograph Credits

front cover, pp. 172–175 (plates 80–83), 200 (top): © Emily Roysdon

back cover, pp. 36, 67–81 (plates 27–35): Photography: Shunk-Kender © Roy Lichtenstein Foundation

pp. 4, 204–209 (plates 89–95), 276 (plate 129), 295 (bottom left): © Zoe Leonard. Courtesy Galerie Gisela Capitain, Cologne

pp. 12, 14–19 (plates 1–7): © Danny Lyon/Magnum Photos/Contacto

pp. 23–25 (plates 8–10): © Thomas Struth 2010

pp. 26–29 (plates 11–12): © Catherine Opie. Courtesy Gladstone Gallery, New York

pp. 30–33 (plates 13–16): © Vera Lutter. VEGAP, Madrid, 2010. Courtesy the artist

pp. 38–39 (plates 17–18) © Estate of Max Neuhaus

pp. 42–45 (plates 19–20): © Barbara Probst. VG Bild-Kunst, Bonn, and VEGAP, Madrid, 2010

pp. 46–47 (plate 21): Courtesy Robert Longo and Metro Pictures, New York

p. 49: © Jean-Louis Blondeau/Polaris Images

pp. 51–53 (plates 22–24): Courtesy Jennifer Bolande

pp. 54–57 (plates 25–26), 304: Courtesy Marian Goodman Gallery, New York

pp. 85–89 (plates 36–40): © The Peter Hujar Archive, 1987. Courtesy Matthew Marks Gallery, New York

pp. 90–95 (plates 41–45): © 2010 The Alvin Baltrop Trust

pp. 97 (top), 124 (bottom left): © Gwenn Thomas

pp. 97 (middle), 103 (plate 48), 160 (plate 73): © Babette Mangolte 1973. Courtesy Broadway 1602, New York

p. 97 (bottom): © Carol Mersereau

pp. 100–101 (plate 46): © Joan Jonas

p. 102 (plate 47): © Babette Mangolte 1976. Courtesy Broadway 1602, New York

pp. 109–113 (plates 49–53): © Bernard Guillot

pp. 118–119 (plates 54–56): Courtesy Louise Lawler and Metro Pictures, New York

pp. 120–123 (plates 57–60): Courtesy Cindy Sherman and Metro Pictures, New York

p. 124 (top left; right): © Gianfranco Gorgoni

p. 126 (plate 61): © Dara Birnbaum

p. 135 (plate 62): © Ken Jacobs

p. 136 (plate 63): © Estate of Jack Smith

p. 138 (plate 64): Courtesy Chantal Akerman and Galerie Marian Goodman, Paris

pp. 141 (plate 65), 159 (plate 72): Courtesy Electronic Arts Intermix (EAI), New York

p. 142 (plate 66): © David Hammons

pp. 145 (top; middle), 148 (plate 67), 149 (plate 68, bottom), 295 (top center): © Estate of Gordon Matta-Clark. VEGAP, Madrid, 2010. Courtesy Electronic Arts Intermix (EAI), New York

pp. 145 (bottom), 149 (plate 68, top): © Estate of Gordon Matta-Clark. VEGAP, Madrid, 2010. Courtesy David Zwirner Gallery, New York

pp. 151, 250, 256–257 (plate 120): Courtesy Matthew Buckingham and Murray Guy, New York

pp. 152–153 (plates 69–70): © Peter Hutton

p. 156 (plate 71): © 2010 Dick Richards

pp. 165–170 (plates 74–79): Collection Museo Nacional Centro de Arte Reina Sofía © Estate of David Wojnarowicz and PPOW Gallery, New York

pp. 191–193 (plates 84–86): © Tom Burr. Courtesy Galerie Neu, Berlin

pp. 194–195 (plate 87): Courtesy John Miller and Metro Pictures, New York

p. 197 (plate 88): Collection of Alan Hergott and Curt Shepard © Donald Moffett

pp. 200 (middle), 253–255 (plates 117–119): Courtesy Moyra Davey and Murray Guy, New York

p. 200 (bottom): Photograph by Stefan Rohner. Courtesy Sharon Hayes and Tanya Leighton Gallery, Berlin

pp. 210–214 (plates 96–100): © Christopher Wool. Courtesy the artist and Luhring Augustine, New York

p. 218 (top): © K8 Hardy and Wynne Greenwood

p. 218 (middle): © Jeanine Oleson

p. 218 (bottom): Courtesy Ulrike Müller and Ginger Brooks Takahashi

pp. 220–223 (plates 101–104): Courtesy Sharon Hayes and Tanya Leighton Gallery, Berlin

pp. 231–233 (plates 105–110): © 2010 Rare Book, Manuscript, and Special Collections Library at Duke University, Durham

p. 235 (plate 111): © James Welling. Courtesy Regen Projects, Los Angeles

pp. 236–237 (plate 112): © Roy Colmer 1976

pp. 238–239 (plate 113): © Estate of Stefan Brecht, Courtesy Rena Gill

pp. 242–243 (plate 114): © Hilla Becher. Courtesy Sonnabend Gallery, New York

pp. 244–245 (plate 115): © Estate of Sol LeWitt. VEGAP, Madrid, 2010

pp. 246–247 (plate 116): © Generali Foundation Collection. Photo: Werner Kaligofsky 1997. © Estate of Gordon Matta-Clark. VEGAP, Madrid, 2010

pp. 259–261 (plates 121–123), 294 (left): © James Nares. Courtesy the artist and Paul Kasmin Gallery, New York

pp. 262–263 (plates 124–125): © Charles Simonds. VEGAP, Madrid, 2010

pp. 265–267 (plates 126–128): © Gabriel Orozco. Courtesy Marian Goodman Gallery, New York

p. 294 (center): © Mel Bochner and Robert Moskowitz

pp. 294 (right), 295 (top left; bottom right): © Estate of Rudy Burckhardt. VEGAP, Madrid, 2010

p. 295 (bottom center): © Vivienne Dick

p. 295 (top right): © Abigail Child

Additional work illustrated

Cindy Sherman
Untitled Film Still #24, 1978
Gelatin silver print
26 2/11 x 36 5/8 inches (66.5 x 93 cm)
Plate 58

This book was published in conjunction with the exhibition *Mixed Use, Manhattan: Photography and Related Practices, 1970s to the Present*, Museo Nacional Centro de Arte Reina Sofía, June 10–September 27, 2010.

Exhibition

Curators
Lynne Cooke and Douglas Crimp

Coordination
Rafael García Horrillo

Research assistance
Elisabeth Sherman

Coordination assistance
Cristina Ojea Calahorra
Aurora Rabanal Torres
Cristina Guerras Manrique

Exhibition design
Marcos Corrales

Conservation
Juan Antonio Sáez Dégano
Eugenia Gimeno Pascual
Gema Álvaro Gómez
Clara Prieto de la Fuente

Registration
Iliana Naranjo Rodríguez
Clara Berástegui Pedro-Viejo
Patricia Alonso Pajuelo
R.O.A.

Management
Natalia Guaza
Ana Torres

Shipping
Manterola

Insurance
Poolsegur

Exhibition Assembly
Horche

Catalogue

Editors
Lynne Cooke and Douglas Crimp, with Kristin Poor

Editorial Activities Department Head MNCARS
María Luisa Blanco

Managing Editor
Kristin Poor

Coordination for MNCARS
Teresa Ochoa de Zabalegui

Copyeditor
Jeremy Sigler

Proofreader
Sam Frank

Research assistance
Analisa Bacall

Translation
Laura Suffield (pp. 8–10)

Design
Mischa Leiner, Jenny 8 del Corte Hirschfeld, CoDe. Communication and Design

Production
Julio López

Printed in Spain by
Artes Graficas Palermo, S.L.

Bound in Spain by Ramos

ISBN 978-0-262-01482-3
NIPO 553-10-01
Legal deposit M-30.035-2010
Library of Congress Cataloging-in-Publication Data

Mixed use, Manhattan : photography and related practices, 1970s to the present / edited by Lynne Cooke and Douglas Crimp; with Kristin Poor.
p. cm.
Catalog accompanying an exhibition opening at the Museo Nacional Centro de Arte Reina Sofía in Madrid in the summer of 2010.
Includes bibliographical references.
ISBN 978-0-262-01482-3 (hardcover : alk. paper)
1. Arts, American—New York (State)—New York—20th century. 2. Photography, Artistic—New York (State)—New York. 3. Manhattan (New York, N.Y.)—In art. 4. Manhattan (New York, N.Y.)—History—20th century—Pictorial works. 5. Arts and society—New York (State)—New York—History—20th century. 6. Artists—New York (State)—New York—Social conditions—20th century. 7. New York (N.Y.)—Social conditions—20th century. I. Cooke, Lynne. II. Crimp, Douglas. III. Poor, Kristin. IV. Museo Nacional Centro de Arte Reina Sofía. V. Title: Photography and related practices, 1970s to the present.
NX511.N4M59 2010
709.747'10744641—dc22
2010016514

Front cover: Emily Roysdon, *The Piers Untitled (#2)*, 2010 (detail)
Back cover: John Baldessari, *Hands Framing New York Harbor* (from *Projects: Pier 18*), 1971. Photograph by Shunk-Kender
p. 304: Steve McQueen, still from *Static*, 2009

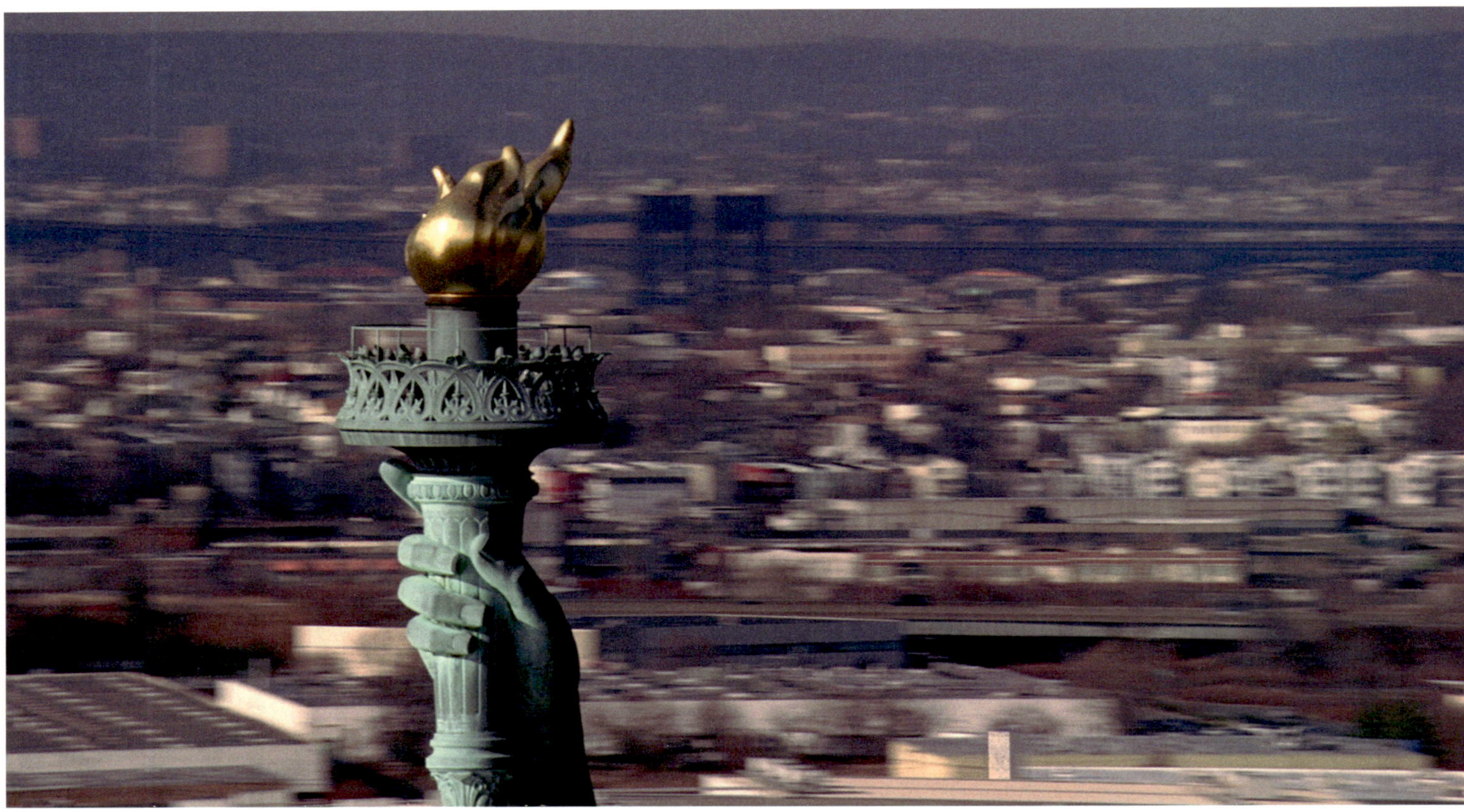